The Law of Evidence in Scotland

by

ALLAN GRIERSON WALKER, Q.C.,

Sheriff of Lanarkshire

and

NORMAN MACDONALD LOCKHART WALKER,

C.B.E., LL.D., ADVOCATE,

lately Sheriff-Substitute of Lanarkshire at Glasgow

WILLIAM HODGE & COMPANY LIMITED,
EDINBURGH AND GLASGOW,

First published 1964
Reprinted 1968
Reprinted 1980
Reprinted 1983
Reprinted 1986

Printed in Great Britain
by Bell & Bain Ltd, Glasgow

SBN 085279 120 8

PREFACE

When Sheriff Dobie died he left the manuscript of a book on Evidence, and we undertook "to see it through the press." As we proceeded, we came to be of opinion that the scheme and treatment could be improved, and we also received advice to that effect. Accordingly we have rewritten the book, a task which would have been very much more difficult without the material which Sheriff Dobie had collected.

For a time Professor D. M. Walker, Regius Professor of Law in the University of Glasgow, was associated with us, but he had to withdraw under pressure of other work. The writing of Chapter XVIII was undertaken by Mr. Peter G. B. McNeill, M.A., LL.B., Ph.D., Advocate. Mr. J. S. Forbes, Advocate, prepared the Table of Cases.

We have to acknowledge the help of Sheriff J. M. Cowan, Q.C., Sheriff C. D. L. Murray, Mr. Robert Macdonald, Procurator-Fiscal of the Lower Ward of Lanarkshire, Mr. J. C. Patterson, O.B.E., formerly Procurator-Fiscal at Hamilton, Mr. C. G. Hogg, Procurator-Fiscal at Cupar, and Mr. Joseph Mellick, Lecturer in Evidence and Procedure in the University of Glasgow, who either read and criticised portions of the manuscript or gave advice upon modern practice.

Dickson's great work was planned over a hundred years ago, and we have taken the bold step of planning *de novo*. We have tried to keep in view the practical situations in which questions of evidence arise, and to deal comprehensively in one place with each of these situations. A reconsideration of some of the rules of evidence is overdue, notably with regard to the need for writing in proof of certain obligations, but we have not attempted to suggest what form any restatement ought to take. Our aim has been to state what the law is. When this was impossible because it has never been decided, we have indicated the general principle which in our opinion most nearly applies. We think that we can safely say that we have cited no case which we have not read and fully considered.

A. G. W.

N. M. L. W.

Glasgow,
January, 1964.

CONTENTS

CONTENTS

CONTENTS

TABLE OF CASES

ix

TABLE OF CASES

TABLE OF CASES

xxv

B

TABLE OF STATUTES

TABLE OF STATUTES

CHAPTER I

ADMISSIBILITY AND RELEVANCY OF EVIDENCE—GENERAL

1. ADMISSIBILITY OF EVIDENCE

Admissible evidence is evidence which a court of law may both receive and consider for the purpose of deciding a particular case. To be admissible in this sense, evidence must satisfy two requirements—it must be relevant and it must conform to the peremptory rules of the law of evidence. Relevancy is defined more fully later in this chapter, and it is sufficient to say here that it depends upon the existence of some sort of logical relationship between the evidence and the subject matter of the case. Irrelevant evidence is never admissible, but even relevant evidence may be made inadmissible by one of the peremptory rules which the law prescribes. These rules, which are mainly negative in character, are imposed by the law for reasons of policy. They spring from the knowledge that the discovery of the truth by a human tribunal from what is said by human witnesses is a difficult task, and they attempt to limit the risk or the evil consequences of error by excluding certain kinds of evidence as being insufficiently reliable, or too remote, or as creating the possibility of unfairness or confusion. So, for example, a statement made by a person who is not a witness may be relevant, because it has a bearing on the subject matter of the case, but it may nevertheless be necessary to exclude it, because, as hearsay evidence,[1] a rule of law declares it to be inadmissible.

When objection to a line of evidence is taken during the course of an enquiry, it is sometimes impossible for the court to decide as to its admissibility until all the evidence has been heard. In these circumstances it is usual in civil proofs to allow the evidence to be received under reservation of its admissibility.[2] The advantage of this practice is that the evidence is recorded, and is thus available for consideration by the appeal court, even if the judge of first instance decides, after considering all the other evidence in the case, that it is inadmissible. It has also been commended as the normal and proper practice in summary criminal trials.[3] In a jury trial,

---

[1] See §§ 370 *et seq.*
[2] *McDonald* v. *Duncan*, 1933 S.C. 737, L. Anderson at p. 744.
[3] *Clark* v. *Stuart*, 1950 J.C. 8. See, however, *MacLeod* v. *Woodmuir Miners Welfare Society Social Club*, 1961 J.C. 5, at p. 8.

civil[2] or criminal,[4] the judge must accept responsibility for admitting or excluding evidence which is challenged as inadmissible, because a jury is more likely than a judge to be influenced by incompetent or irrelevant evidence. If evidence, later shown to be inadmissible, is in fact led, the judge must direct the jury to dismiss it from their minds,[5] and if he does so the jury are assumed to have followed the direction.[5]

2. ADMISSION OF EVIDENCE ILLEGALLY OBTAINED

(a) General. An example of evidence, which, although relevant, may be held to be inadmissible, is that which has been obtained illegally or irregularly. Such evidence may be real[6] or documentary,[7] or it may be oral evidence of confessions by an accused person,[8] and mention is made later of the legal and the illegal or irregular methods by which evidence may be obtained. When it has been established that a piece of evidence has been obtained illegally or irregularly, the question as to whether in a particular case it is admissible or inadmissible is frequently one of difficulty.

(b) Civil Causes. It has been held that in a divorce action a letter, written by the defender to the co-defender and stolen by the pursuer, is admissible evidence for the pursuer, the opinion being judicially expressed that the policy of the law is to admit almost all evidence which will throw light on disputed facts and enable justice to be done.[9] This decision was followed with some reluctance in a more recent case in the Outer House.[10] There has been no recent consideration of the general question by the Inner House. The Scottish decision at present ruling appears to be in conformity with the law of England.[11]

(c) Criminal Causes. It has been said that, from the standpoint of principle, "the law must strive to reconcile two highly important interests which are liable to come into conflict—(a) the interest of the citizen to be protected from illegal or irregular invasions of his liberties by the authorities, and (b) the interest of the State to secure that evidence bearing upon the commission of crime, and necessary to enable justice to be done, shall not

---

4 For the proper procedure when the admissibility of statements made by an accused person to the police is challenged, see *Chalmers* v. *H.M. Advocate*, 1954 J.C. 66, L. J.-G. Cooper at p. 80; *Manuel* v. *H.M. Advocate*, 1958 J.C. 41, at p. 49. It is briefly described in § 2, sub-para. (d).

5 *McEwan* v. *H.M. Advocate*, 1939 J.C. 26, at p. 31; *Parker and Barrie*, 1888, 16 R. (J.) 5, at p. 9. See also *Slater* y. *H.M. Advocate*, 1928 J.C. 94.

6 See § 2, sub-para. (c), §§ **417, 418.**

7 See § 2, sub-para. (c).

8 See §§ **39** *et seq.*

9 *Rattray* v. *Rattray*, 1897, 25 R. 315, L. Trayner at pp. 318-319.

10 *MacColl* v. *MacColl*, 1946 S.N. 80, S.L.T. 312.

11 *Kuruma* v. *Regina* [1955] A.C. 197. It was held by the Privy Council that, both in civil and criminal causes, the test of admissibility is relevancy, that if the evidence is relevant it is admissible, and that the court is not concerned with how it was obtained. *Cf. Rex* v. *Barker* [1941] 2 K.B. 381, where incriminating documents handed by the accused to an official of the Inland Revenue, after receiving an apparent offer of immunity from the prosecution, were held to be inadmissible in evidence.

2

be withheld from the courts of law on any merely formal or technical ground."[12]   When these interests conflict, the rule is that the evidence is inadmissible unless the illegality or irregularity associated with its procurement can be excused by the court.[13]   The decision as to whether it is excusable or not is discretionary, and, in making it, the court must take into consideration the gravity of the crime with which the accused is charged,[13] the seriousness or triviality of the irregularity,[14] the urgency of the investigation in the course of which the evidence was obtained,[15] the authority and good faith of those who obtained it,[14] and the question of fairness to the accused person.

In practice a distinction has been made between oral statements or admissions by an accused person, on the one hand, and real and documentary evidence, on the other.   In the case of oral statements or admissions irregularly obtained, there may be an uncertainty as to what was actually said, or as to the proper interpretation of it, which does not exist to the same extent with regard to real or documentary evidence.   Evidence of extrajudicial oral statements by an accused person, if irregularly obtained, is always in practice regarded as inadmissible, and the inadmissibility has been held also to apply to actings of an accused person, while in the company of police officers, arising from, and closely associated with, a statement irregularly obtained from him by them.[16]

Real or documentary evidence irregularly obtained, on the other hand, as far as the reported decisions disclose, was always in practice admitted prior to the Full Bench case of *Lawrie* v. *Muir*,[17] in which the earlier decisions are mentioned.   In that case, which concerned a relatively trivial statutory prosecution for selling milk in bottles belonging to other persons, the court, not without hesitation, disallowed the evidence, the balance being tilted in this direction by the fact that the milk bottles were obtained without proper warrant by Milk Marketing Board inspectors, who should have been aware that their powers were limited and that they did not have the common law discretionary powers of police officers.   Since that decision, applying the general rule which it laid down, the courts have disallowed such evidence in some cases, and allowed it in others.   Evidence *disallowed* has consisted (1) of scrapings from finger-nails taken from the accused by the police while he was in the police office, but before he was apprehended, the decision turning largely on the view that the police had no excuse for failing to legalise their action by the simple method of apprehending the accused before, rather than shortly after, the taking of the scrapings;[18] and (2) of

12 *Lawrie* v. *Muir*, 1950 J.C. 19, at p. 26.
13 *Ibid.*, at p.27.
14 *McGovern* v. *H.M. Advocate*, 1950 J.C. 33, at p. 37; *Fairley* v. *Fishmongers of London*, 1951 J.C. 14.
15 *McGovern* v. *H.M. Advocate* (*supra*); *H.M. Advocate* v. *Turnbull*, 1951 J.C. 96.
16 *Chalmers* v. *H.M. Advocate*, 1954 J.C. 66, at p. 76. See also *Mahler*, 1857, 2 Irv. 634 (confession to civilian witness, following upon earlier promise of immunity by police officer, held inadmissible).
17 *Lawrie* v. *Muir*, 1950 J.C. 19, at pp. 27-28. This matter is also discussed at § **417**, sub-para. (b).
18 *McGovern* v. *H.M. Advocate* (*supra*).

documents recovered in the accused's business premises relating to frauds other than the frauds referred to in the search warrant, there being no urgency to excuse the retention of the documents, since, while it could at once be seen that their retention was not justified by the warrant, it required an examination lasting for several months to discover in them the fraudulent matter which they were said to disclose.[19] Evidence *allowed* has been (1) salmon recovered without a warrant from a cold store by an inspector employed by private prosecutors, the ground of the decision being that the irregularity was trivial, and did not result from a deliberate intention of securing evidence unfairly;[20] and (2) a stolen attache case found by the police accidentally while searching the accused's house, with his permission, during their investigation of a crime other than the crime charged.[21] The ratio of the recent Scottish decisions has not been adopted in England.[11]

(d) Procedure in Criminal Jury Trial. When objection is taken to the admission of evidence alleged to have been irregularly obtained, the jury should be excluded, and the evidence bearing upon the attendant circumstances should be heard by the judge alone, including, if desired, the evidence of the accused himself. If the judge sustains the objection, the jury should be told nothing about the matter. If the objection is repelled, the case will proceed before the jury, and, if the Crown or the defence think it necessary, the evidence bearing upon the attendant circumstances can be the subject of examination and cross-examination a second time. It is then for the jury to decide as to the truth, weight and value of the evidence, in the light of the evidence as a whole, including, in the case of a statement or admission made by the accused person, a decision as to whether it was voluntarily and freely given.[21a]

3. RELEVANCY OF AVERMENTS

This must be distinguished from relevancy of evidence. Before a party to a civil action is allowed an enquiry, whether by proof or jury trial, he must in his written pleadings make averments of facts which are relevant in law to support his action or his defences. The averments are irrelevant when, even if they are proved, his case must necessarily fail.[22] If they are in this sense irrelevant the action will be dismissed or the defences repelled, without enquiry into the facts. In a criminal cause a charge, to be relevant, must meet the statutory requirements as to the specification of time and place, and must set forth facts sufficient to constitute a crime.[23] Relevancy

---

[19] *H.M. Advocate* v. *Turnbull (supra)*.

[20] *Fairley* v. *Fishmongers of London*, 1951 J.C. 14.

[21] *H.M. Advocate* v. *Hepper*, 1958 J.C. 39. See also *H.M. Advocate* v. *McKay*, 1961 J.C. 47.

[21a] *Chalmers* v. *H.M. Advocate*, 1954 J.C. 66, L. J-G. Cooper at p. 80, L. J-Cl. Thomson at p. 82; *Manuel* v. *H.M. Advocate*, 1958 J.C. 41, at p. 49.

[22] *Jamieson* v. *Jamieson*, 1952 S.C. (H.L.) 44, L. Normand at p. 50, L. Reid at p. 63. See also *Miller* v. *South of Scotland Electricity Board*, 1958 S.C. (H.L.) 20, commented on in *Blaikie* v. *British Transport Commission*, 1961 S.C. 44, at pp. 49-51.

[23] Renton and Brown, *Criminal Procedure* (3rd ed.) 56.

of averment, both in civil and in criminal causes, is governed by the substantive law applicable to the cause in question, and not by the law of evidence.

Although relevancy of averment is not part of the subject matter of the law of evidence, it has a bearing upon the question of evidence in several ways. If averments of fact are remitted to probation, without reservation as to their relevancy, evidence relevant to prove or disprove them is in general relevant evidence.[24] If the court restricts the method of proof by allowing a proof by writ, or by oath, or *habili modo* (by the kind of evidence appropriate to each part of the case), only the kind of evidence prescribed by the interlocutor is admissible. If the court reserves the question of the law and the relevancy of the averments until after evidence has been led, and allows a proof before answer, the reservation applies only to these two matters, and not to the admissibility of the evidence to be led. Inadmissible evidence is not thereby made admissible.[25]

4. RELEVANCY OF EVIDENCE—GENERAL

In very general terms relevant evidence may be said to be evidence which is logically connected with those matters in dispute between the parties, the *facta probanda*, which are under investigation by the court. These are sometimes called the matters, or the facts, in issue. To allow evidence to be led on other matters is of no assistance to the court, is a waste of time, and is unfair to the other party to the action, who could neither anticipate it nor be prepared to contradict it.[26] For the purposes of more detailed discussion, relevant evidence may be regarded as being either direct evidence of a fact in issue,[27] or evidence of a fact (*factum probationis*) bearing on the probability or improbability of a fact in issue,[28] or evidence of a fact which has a bearing only on the admissibility of other evidence, or on the credibility of a witness.[29]

5. DIRECT EVIDENCE OF FACTS IN ISSUE

Direct evidence is only available when the fact in issue is something appreciable by the senses or contained in a document. The evidence of witnesses who saw or heard the thing happen, or the evidence provided by the terms of the document itself, is clearly relevant, and the only question when such evidence is tendered, apart from any specialty as to the witnesses themselves, is whether the witnesses are truthful and reliable—whether, that is to say, they have accurately observed and remembered and truthfully related what occurred—or whether the document is genuine.[30]

[24] *Barr* v. *Bain*, 1896, 23 R. 1090; *Scott* v. *Cormack Heating Engineers*, 1942 S.C. 159, L.P. Normand at p. 162.
[25] *Robertson* v. *Murphy*, 1867, 6 M. 114; *Haldane* v. *Speirs*, 1872, 10 M. 537; Maclaren, *Court of Session Practice*, 552-553.
[26] Dickson, *Evidence* (3rd ed.) §1.
[27] See §5.
[28] See §6.
[29] See §7.
[30] Dickson, *Evidence* (3rd ed.) §63.

6. INDIRECT EVIDENCE OF FACTS IN ISSUE—GENERAL

Whether or not direct evidence of a fact in issue is available, evidence of any fact which renders probable or improbable the existence of the fact in issue is relevant. This includes any fact which is consistent or inconsistent with, or which gives rise to a logical inference regarding, the fact in issue. The whole circumstances surrounding the fact in issue are generally regarded as being in this category in so far as, with or without other evidence, they have a bearing or throw light upon it. So, for example, in a case which concerns the negligent driving of a motor vehicle, evidence of the behaviour of the vehicle shortly before and shortly after the collision is relevant;[31] where the case concerns the dangerous condition of a road and the road authority's knowledge of it, it may be relevant that accidents similar to that in question have occurred at the same place during the previous two months;[32] in a criminal trial for procuring abortion it is relevant to show how the pregnant woman was introduced to the accused person;[33] and it is relevant in a trial for housebreaking to show that the accused person was in the vicinity shortly before, and that he ran away from it immediately after, the time of its commission. In order to be relevant, however, evidence of surrounding circumstances must have a reasonably direct bearing on the subject under investigation, and must not be too remote from it either in time, place or character. What is, or is not, too remote for the purposes of relevancy, is a question of degree in each case.[34]

Evidence of facts from which the fact in issue can be inferred, especially when it is the whole evidence in the case, is commonly known as circumstantial evidence, and this is mentioned at greater length in the next chapter.[35] Occurrences which are contemporaneous, or roughly contemporaneous, with the main occurrence are part of the *res gestae*, and as such may be proved, even when evidence of them might in other circumstances be inadmissible. They are discussed in this connection later.[36]

7. FACTS AFFECTING ADMISSIBILITY OR CREDIBILITY OF OTHER EVIDENCE

(a) **Facts Affecting Admissibilty.** These facts are relevant,[37] not because they are directly associated with the fact in issue, but because they lay the foundation for evidence which is so associated. Proof of them may be prerequisite to a decision on the admissibility or inadmissibility of other evidence. The death of a person who would have been a witness, for example,

---

31 *Bark* v. *Scott*, 1954 S.C. 72, L. J-Cl. Cooper at p. 76.

32 *W. Alexander & Sons* v. *Dundee Corporation*, 1950 S.C. 123.

33 *Angus* v. *H.M. Advocate*, 1935 J.C. 1; *McEwan* v. *H.M. Advocate*, 1939 J.C. 26.

34 *Bark* v. *Scott* (*supra*), L. J-Cl. Cooper at pp. 75-76; *W. Alexander & Sons* v. *Dundee Corporation* (*supra*), L. J-Cl. Thomson at p. 131; *H.M. Advocate* v. *Kennedy*, 1907, 5 Adam 347, L. Salvesen at p. 349; *Gallagher* v. *Paton*, 1909 S.C. (J.) 50, L. McLaren at p. 55 (see the comment on this decision at § **28**, note 6); *H.M. Advocate* v. *Joseph*, 1929 J.C. 55, L. Murray at pp. 56-57.

35 See §§ **8** *et seq.*

36 See §§ **377, 378.**

37 They have also been characterised as irrelevant, but admissible. See Phipson, *Evidence* (9th ed.) 55.

or the destruction or irrecoverability of a relevant document, are facts which have no direct bearing on the subject matter of the cause, but they must be proved if the dead person's statement,[38] or a copy of the document,[39] is to be admissible in evidence. Similarly, the circumstances in which an accused person made a statement to the police may have nothing directly to do with the circumstances of the crime, but they must be proved before the admissibility of the statement itself is established.[40] There may also be mentioned under this heading the facts which form the basis of opinion evidence given by expert witnesses, which are sometimes relevant and admissible only because of the use which the expert witnesses make of them.[41]

(b) Facts Affecting Credibility. Evidence of such facts may be elicited from the witness himself in cross-examination, and examples of the questions which may be put to him for the purpose of testing credibility are given later.[42] Convictions of crimes inferring dishonesty are regarded as legitimate subjects of cross-examination for this purpose, but if the witness denies the convictions, his denial cannot be contradicted by parole evidence.[43] If a witness is examined as to the making of an earlier statement which is different from his evidence, and denies it, the examiner is authorised by statute to adduce evidence to prove the making of the earlier statement.[44] Apart from this statutory rule it is thought that evidence of facts affecting the credibility of a witness, apart from the evidence of the witness himself, is generally inadmissible unless the facts are also relevant to the questions at issue.[45] This is not because the facts are irrelevant, but because it is inexpedient to spend time on the investigation of collateral issues concerning persons who are not necessarily parties to the cause.[46] Thus it may be admissible to lead evidence that a witness was drunk at or about the time when he claims to have been assaulted,[47] or that he was not in a position to witness the commission of the crime which he describes in his evidence, because these facts are relevant to the decision of the case as well as to the credibility or reliability of the witness. On the other hand, even in a trial for rape, evidence that the alleged victim had acted immorally on specific occasions years before the commission of the crime, has been held to be inadmissible.[48]

---

[38] See § **371.**
[39] See §§ **229** *et seq.*
[40] See §§ **39** *et seq.*
[41] See § **413,** sub-para. (b).
[42] See § **342,** sub-para. (c).
[43] See § **345,** sub-para. (b).
[44] Evidence (Scotland) Act, 1852 (15 & 16 Vict. c. 27), s. 3. This subject is dealt with at § **343.**
[45] In *King* v. *King,* 1841, 4 D. 124, however, it was held competent not only to cross-examine a witness as to expressions of hostility to a party, but also to prove these by other evidence.
[46] *Kennedy,* 1896, 23 R. (J.) 28, L. J-Cl. Macdonald at p. 30; *Dickie,* 1897, 24 R. (J.) 82, at p. 83. As to the reasons for excluding collateral issues, see § **14.**
[47] *Falconer* v. *Brown,* 1893, 21 R. (J.) 1. It seems to be clearly implied that the evidence, if tendered, ought to have been admitted.
[48] *Reid,* 1861, 4 Irv. 124; *Dickie (supra).* As to evidence of character generally, see §§ **17, 20.**

CHAPTER II

CIRCUMSTANTIAL EVIDENCE

8. GENERAL

Circumstantial evidence is indirect evidence of a fact in issue. It consists of circumstances, admitted or proved, from which the existence of the fact in issue is inferred. Each circumstance by itself may be of little significance. It may be consistent both with the existence of the fact in issue and with some other possibility. But if, despite the other individual possibilities, all the circumstances agree in supporting the existence of the fact in issue, it may be proper to regard that fact as proved.[1] Examples are cited later, but here a simple illustration may be given. An unidentified man snatched a bag containing £50 in notes. Soon afterwards the accused was seen to run into a neighbouring back court carrying something, and to run from it carrying nothing. When arrested he had £50 in notes in his pocket, and the stolen bag was found in the back court. From each of these circumstances an innocent inference may be drawn. The accused may have been hurrying by a short cut to catch a train, a parcel may have been dropped unnoticed as he ran, he may have won £50 on a horse, while the bag may have been thrown away by another person. But each circumstance also yields an inference against the accused, and, in combination, point to him as the thief. The strength of the inference against him is increased if it is proved that the trains were not running because of a strike, that no parcel was found in the back court, that he had not won £50 on a horse, and that no other person entered the back court during the relevant period. Circumstantial evidence may be as good as if not better than direct testimony,[2] but since it, equally with direct evidence, is tainted by human fallibility,[3] failure to produce, without good reason, any direct evidence which is available may impair the

---

[1] A satisfactory definition is difficult. Wills, *Circumstantial Evidence* (7th ed.), in an ungrammatical sentence, appears to define it as the bearing on the fact to be proved of other and subsidiary facts (p. 6), and later as these subsidiary facts themselves (p. 18). Dickson, *Evidence* (3rd ed.) §68, seems to take the latter view.

[2] *Mackinnon* v. *Miller*, 1909 S.C. 373, L.P. Dunedin at p. 378; *Withers* v. *H.M. Advocate*, 1947 J.C. 109, L. J-G. Cooper at p. 115.

[3] *Mackinnon* v. *Miller*, *ut supra*.

[4] Dickson, *Evidence* (3rd ed.) §108 (7). In *Withers* v. *H.M. Advocate* (*supra*), the Crown produced positive evidence.

probative value of the circumstantial evidence.[4] The number of witnesses necessary to prove each circumstance is discussed later.[5]

9. PROBATIVE VALUE OF CIRCUMSTANTIAL EVIDENCE

(a) **Cable Analogy.** The probative force of circumstantial evidence has been thus described. "One circumstance may be of slight moment; another, tending to the same result, increases by its consistency with the first, the probability of the inference to be drawn from existence and co-existence; another is added, and another, all pointing in the same direction: giving added and increased strength to the cable of which it forms a component part. Men talk of a chain of facts. The comparison is inept.[6] The chain is weakened by the increasing number of its links . . . not so with circumstantial evidence. The cable gains increased strength by each added strand. The failure of proof as to one circumstance is but one strand from the cable."[7] If all the circumstances in combination—the strands in the cable— lead to a full and complete assurance of the fact in issue, an assurance or moral conviction which would induce a sound mind to act without doubt on the conclusions to which it naturally and reasonably leads,[8] the fact in issue may be regarded as proved. If, on the other hand, there is a single proved circumstance which is incompatible with the fact in issue, the proof of the fact in issue fails.[9] Even if the accused's finger prints are found in the premises which have been broken into, the jemmy used was his, and the stolen goods were found hidden in his bedroom, he must be acquitted of the theft if he was in prison when it occurred.

(b) **Chain Analogy.** As has been indicated above, the cable is usually regarded as the correct analogy with circumstantial evidence, and the view has been expressed that evidence consisting solely of a chain of independent facts, from which another fact inevitably follows, is not truly circumstantial evidence.[10] Such a chain of independent facts, however, has recently been described judicially as circumstantial evidence[11] in a prosecution where

5 See §§ **386, 387.**
6 The inaptness of the chain analogy is commented on in Wills, *Circumstantial Evidence* (7th ed.) 435. It is illustrated in *Forrester* v. *H.M. Advocate*, 1952 J.C. 31, where what broke was not a link in a chain, which would have been fatal to the conviction, but a strand in a cable, which left the appeal court free to consider whether the conviction might not be sustained.
7 Quoted by Dickson, *Evidence* (3rd ed.) § 95. For an example of the effect of the loss of one strand, see note 6 above.
8 Wills, *Circumstantial Evidence* (7th ed.) 10.
9 Dickson, *Evidence* (3rd ed.) §108 (5).
10 W. A. Wilson, *The Logic of Corroboration* (1960, 76 S.L.R. 101). The same opinion is implied in *Corroboration of Evidence in Scottish Criminal Law* (1958 S.L.T. (News) 137). Both these articles deal very fully with the principles underlying the acceptance of circumstantial evidence in Scotland.
11 *Gillespie* v. *Macmillan*, 1957 J.C. 31, L. J-G. Clyde at p. 36. The fact in issue was the speed of a motor car over a measured distance. This required for its proof (a) the exact distance, (b) the exact time of entry and (c) the exact time of departure. All three facts were necessary for the mathematical calculation of the speed of the vehicle, and none of the facts by itself gave rise to any significant inference.

proof of each of three facts was essential for conviction of the accused. If all three facts were proved, the inference, if inference it can be called, was certain and inevitable, and, in the case in question, consisted merely of a mathematical calculation. If any one of the three links in the chain was missing, the prosecution failed.[11] If facts of this kind can properly be described as circumstantial evidence, they constitute a very special kind of such evidence, having more in common with the independent facts which must all be proved before a person can be convicted of a compound crime,[12] than with circumstantial evidence as generally understood. A negative variant of this kind of evidence exists when proof of the fact in issue depends solely upon the exhaustive and complete exclusion and elimination of all the other possibilities.[13] In such a case also, if one of the links in the chain is missing, and one of the alternative possibilities has not been eliminated, proof of the fact in issue fails.[14]

10. POSSESSION OF INCRIMINATING ARTICLES

An accused person's possession, either before or after the commission of a crime, of a weapon or instrument used in connection with it, or his purchase or borrowing of, or attempt to purchase or borrow, such a weapon or instrument, is frequently relied upon. Purchase by Dr. Crippen[15] of hyoscene and by Dr. Pritchard[16] of unusually large quantities of tartar emetic, the poisons causing death in each case, was an item of the evidence on which each was convicted of murder. In the Mannings case, where the body of the murdered man was found embedded in lime, it was proved that about a fortnight before the murder the male accused ordered a quantity of lime of the kind "which would burn quickest."[17] The accused's jemmy may be associated with the commission of a housebreaking by showing that it exactly fits the marks made on a door which was forced, and the nature and characteristics of a wound may show that it was caused by a weapon similar to a weapon found in the accused's possession. Newspapers or periodicals in which articles have been wrapped, proved to have been distributed in a particular district on or about a particular date, may justify an inference which associates the article with an accused person, although it must be remembered in this connection that some periodicals are issued to the public in advance of the date which they bear. In the case of Dr. Ruxton portions of the victims' bodies, when found near Moffat, were wrapped in pages from an edition of the *Sunday Graphic* which was distributed only in the Lancaster area where Dr. Ruxton lived, and a copy of

[12] As to proof of compound crimes, see § **383**, sub-para. (b).
[13] *Withers* v. *H.M. Advocate*, 1947 J.C. 109, L. J-G. Cooper at p. 114.
[14] If an assault is proved to have been committed by one of a number of men, it may be brought home to the accused man by proving that none of the others in fact committed it. If exclusion alone is relied upon, each of the other possible assailants must be excluded before the accused may be convicted. See, for example, *Docherty* v. *H.M. Advocate*, 1945 J.C. 89.
[15] *Notable British Trials.*
[16] *Notable Scottish Trials; Notable British Trials.*
[17] Dickson, *Evidence* (3rd ed.) §103.

10

which had been delivered to his house.[18] When relying upon facts which show some association between a weapon or other article and an accused person, it is not sufficient merely to show that the accused person is the owner of the article. Articles are sometimes borrowed by the thief for use in connection with a crime, and it is common practice, when heavy and bulky articles are about to be stolen, to steal a lorry for the purpose of transporting them from the owner's premises. A murderer or a thief may use another person's weapon or instrument deliberately in order to direct suspicion towards the owner. In an old English case[19] concerned with the sending of threatening letters, a piece of paper used for the purpose was proved to have been torn from a larger sheet found in the accused's bureau, with the ragged edges of which it exactly fitted, and which shared the same water-mark. Insufficient attention was paid to the fact that the accused's son, together with other persons in the house, also had access to the bureau, which was kept unlocked. The accused was convicted, and it was thereupon discovered that his son was the writer of the letters. Possession of stolen property soon after the theft is frequently founded upon as a fact from which implication in the theft may be inferred.[20]

11. EVIDENCE LINKING ACCUSED WITH PREMISES, VEHICLE OR ARTICLE

Articles, such as an accused person's driving licence, found in premises broken into, or a button or piece of cloth apparently torn from a jacket by a sharp projection in a window, which are proved to be identical with the remaining buttons or material of the accused's coat, are examples of this kind of evidence. The possibility that another person was carrying the accused's driving licence, or wearing his coat, must not be forgotten. Bloodstains on the accused's clothing or person are relevant, though not in themselves conclusive evidence of association with murder or assault, and paint[21] or distemper stains, identical with, or similar to, paint or distemper on the walls of premises, are frequently founded upon. In a trial concerning safe-blowing the accused was convicted on three elements of circumstantial evidence:—(a) the possession soon after the theft of bank-notes stolen from the safe; (b) a cut on the accused's hand at the time of his arrest which corresponded with a tear on a rubber glove found near the scene of the crime; and (c) a small piece of pink material found in his coat pocket which corresponded with fibres said to be taken from a bedspread used in the safe-blowing. The conviction was quashed only because of a technical failure by the Crown to identify the fibres examined by the expert witnesses as fibres which had been taken from the pocket of the accused.[22] The advance in scientific and technical aids to the detection of crime, and the increased use of camera

---

[18] *Notable British Trials*; Wills, *Circumstantial Evidence* (7th ed.) 508. See also Professor John Glaister's notes on the Ruxton case in his *Medical Jurisprudence and Toxicology*.
[19] *Rex* v. *Looker* (1831), Dickson, *Evidence* (3rd ed.) §72.
[20] This subject is mentioned more fully at § **68.**
[21] See *Withers* v. *H.M. Advocate*, 1947 J.C. 109.
[22] *Forrester* v. *H.M. Advocate*, 1952 J.C. 28. For a comment on the reference in this case to a "chain" of circumstantial evidence, see § **9,** note 6.

and microscope to reveal evidence invisible to the naked eye, has greatly increased the scope of this kind of circumstantial evidence. A particular typewriter may be traced by a worn or defective letter, clothing by a laundry or manufacturer's mark, a bullet may be associated with a particular weapon by the rifling mark, the composition of dust or mud on an accused person's trousers, or of animal hairs on his coat, may associate him with a particular building or district. One of the most important examples of this kind of circumstantial evidence is that relating to finger-prints, which are mentioned in the next paragraph, and expert evidence with regard to handwriting is also mentioned later.[23]

12. FINGER-PRINT EVIDENCE

The police in Scotland are entitled, without a warrant, to take the finger-print impressions of a person apprehended on a criminal charge but not yet committed to prison.[24] These may be compared with finger-print impressions found at premises, or on articles, associated with the crime, in order to discover whether they were made by the same person. Evidence resulting from this comparison given by expert witnesses,[25] if accepted by the court or by the jury, is an important, and in many cases a conclusive, example of circumstantial evidence. The purpose of the comparison is to discover whether certain ridge characteristics, which make up the pattern in the finger-print, are identically arranged in both prints. When a sufficient number of these identical characteristics can be discovered, those skilled in finger-print identification can testify that the print found at the locus was in their opinion made by the finger of the accused. This evidence is given as a result of experience, in Great Britain and in many other countries, which shows that there is no known case of the prints of two individuals being identical.[26] In the leading case in Scotland[27] the facts were that a shop had been broken into, a safe blown open and money stolen. In the shop, after the crime had been committed, was found a wine bottle with certain prints. The bottle had been wrapped up in paper when the shop was closed. Police experts spoke to complete identity between sixteen characteristics of a print on the bottle with corresponding characteristics of one of the accused's prints, which was more than sufficient to justify the inference that the print on the bottle was the accused's. Apart from the fact that he lived in the neighbourhood, which was of no great importance, there was no other evidence against the accused. The jury convicted on that evidence, and it was held that they were entitled to do so. In a later case[28] similar evidence as to a palm print was held to be admissible and sufficient, if accepted by the jury, for the identification of the accused with the commission of the crime. Identification by finger-print is not regarded as infallible, but as providing

[23] See § 414, sub-para. (b).
[24] *Adair* v. *McGarry*, 1933 J.C. 72.
[25] As to expert witnesses generally, see § 414.
[26] The whole subject is more fully discussed in Wills, *Circumstantial Evidence* (7th ed.) 205 *et seq.*
[27] *Hamilton* v. *H.M. Advocate*, 1934 J.C. 1.
[28] *H.M. Advocate* v. *Rolley*, 1945 J.C. 155. A toe-print has since been accepted: *Gourlay*, *4th November*, 1952, 1953 S.L.T. (News) 45.

evidence of a degree of probability which is ample for judicial proof.[29] In Great Britain the experts are not prepared to commit themselves to the view that any two finger-prints have been made by the same person unless there are at least sixteen identical characteristics. There appears to be no reason, however, why a smaller number should not be deponed to, as part of the evidence in the case, if an imperfect or partial impression at the *locus* of the crime makes a complete comparison impossible, although, in such a case, the finger-print evidence alone might not be sufficient to justify a conviction. The correct inference to be drawn from a finger-print impression found in premises, or on an article, connected with the crime, may depend upon the accused person's normal association with the premises or the article. If the accused person is normally employed in the shop which is broken into, no inference of guilt arises, unless the impression is found in part of the shop from which he was normally excluded. If the accused person is not so employed, an inference of guilt may arise if his finger-print is found on the shop-keeper's side of the counter, but does not necessarily arise if it is found on the customers' side. An inference of guilt does not necessarily arise when the impression is found on the outside of a window, if it could reasonably have been made while the accused person was standing innocently upon the foot pavement. On the other hand, if the impression is found upon the inside of a window, or if impressions of both thumb and finger are found on opposite sides of a piece of glass broken from the window, the inference of guilt may be irresistible.

13. ANIMAL AND HUMAN CHARACTERISTICS AND CONDUCT

The normal behaviour and reactions of animals in given situations may find a place in circumstantial evidence. The curious incident of the dog which did not bark in the night-time, and Sherlock Holmes' inference therefrom,[30] were anticipated in a Scottish case[31] when a fierce watch-dog in charge of an empty shop was not heard by the neighbours to bark at the time when a theft was committed. It was part of the evidence on which the accused person was convicted that he had been a servant in the shop and was known to the dog. The actions of a police tracker dog were held to justify the conviction of a housebreaker. The dog, after it had been allowed to smell articles which had been disturbed by the housebreaker in the house broken into, was taken to the tenement where the accused resided. It led the police past the other flats in the tenement to the door of the accused's house on the top floor. Later, at a police office, it picked out shoes belonging to the accused from a number of shoes belonging to other persons.[32] Evidence regarding normal animal conduct is obviously important in the not infrequent proceedings, both civil and criminal, which are directly concerned with animals, such as actions of damages for breach of warranty or for injury to or by animals, and proceedings concerned with sheep stealing or sheep-worrying.

[29] See *Hamilton* v. *H.M. Advocate (supra)*; *H.M. Advocate* v. *Rolley (supra)*.
[30] Sir Arthur Conan Doyle, *Memoirs of Sherlock Holmes* (Penguin Edition) p. 32.
[31] *William Young*, 1828 (unreported), mentioned in Alison, I, 323.
[32] *Patterson* v. *Nixon*, 1960 J.C. 42.

The capability, training and skill of an accused person, or of the victim of a crime, may be elements in circumstantial evidence. An illiterate person, for example, is unlikely to have forged or fabricated a document. The mere strength of an accused person may be a factor of importance if the crime could have been committed only by a man of powerful physique.[33] In cases of assault, murder or culpable homicide the nature or direction of the wound may indicate the height and strength of the assailant, and whether he was right-handed or left-handed. An accused person's ability to travel in a given time, with the means of transport available, between one place and another, may indicate whether or not he had an opportunity of committing the crime.

The actions of an accused person before and after the commission of a crime frequently give rise to inferences which point towards his guilt. Attempts to fabricate evidence in order to indicate that no crime, or a crime of a different character, has been committed, are of this kind. So a window may be broken in order to suggest that a theft was committed by housebreaking instead of by a person living or working in the premises, and, if proved to have been done by the accused, may point to his guilt. It was the practice of Smith,[34] the "brides in the bath" murderer, to take the intended victim to a doctor with a history suggesting that she suffered from fits or seizures, and this formed part of the evidence at his trial. The attempted destruction or disposal of the body of a victim of murder is a further example, and is usually indicative of guilt, although an innocent person may sometimes destroy incriminating articles in order to avoid the risk of suspicion, arrest and trial.[35] Running away from the scene of the crime may be due to a guilty conscience, but may also arise from fear of wrongful arrest.[36] Motive, or apparent lack of motive, which may be an element of circumstantial evidence, is mentioned more fully later.[37] Previous threats of intention to harm the victim may be important, unless it is clear that they were uttered in mere bravado.[38] Even more important may be remarks made after a crime has been committed, if they are inconsistent with the innocence of the accused person.[39] Many a suspect has incriminated himself by too ready a denial of guilt of a crime which only the criminal could know to have been committed.

[33] See *Withers* v. *H.M. Advocate*, 1947 J.C. 109.
[34] *Rex* v. *Smith* (1915), 84 L.J. (K.B.) 2153; *Notable British Trials*.
[35] See *Ronald Light* (1920), *Life of Marshall Hall*, 396; *Green Bicycle Case* by H. R. Wakefield (1930). In this case the jury accepted the defence proposition that the green bicycle, and other incriminating articles belonging to the accused, who had been shell-shocked, were thrown by him into a canal because he was afraid of being wrongly suspected of the murder with which newspaper publicity had associated them.
[36] Dickson, *Evidence* (3rd ed.) §91.
[37] See § 27.
[38] More fully discussed in Best, *Evidence*, §458.
[39] Dickson, *Evidence* (3rd ed.) §92.

CHAPTER III

RELEVANCY OF EVIDENCE ON COLLATERAL ISSUES

14. GENERAL

Generally speaking evidence regarding an issue which is collateral to the main issue is inadmissible, either because the existence of a collateral fact does not render more probable the existence of the fact in issue, or simply because it is inexpedient to allow an enquiry to be confused and protracted by collateral enquiries into other matters. "Courts of law are not bound to admit the ascertainment of every disputed fact which may contribute, however slightly or indirectly, towards the solution of the issue to be tried. Regard must be had to the limitations which time and human liability to confusion impose upon the conduct of all trials. Experience shows that it is better to sacrifice the aid which might be got from the more or less uncertain solution of collateral issues, than to spend a great amount of time, and confuse the jury with what, in the end, even supposing it to be certain, has only an indirect bearing on the matter in hand."[1] The application in practice of this general proposition and the exceptions to it are considered in this chapter with reference to evidence of similar acts, evidence of character, and evidence of state of mind.

15. EVIDENCE OF SIMILAR ACTS—GENERAL RULE

When the question in issue is whether a person did a particular thing at a particular time, it is in general irrelevant to show that he did a similar thing on some other occasion. "The question being whether A said a certain thing to B," it is irrelevant "to show that A said something of the same sort upon another occasion to C."[2] In an action of damages for rape committed

---

1 *A.* v. *B.*, 1895, 22 R. 402, L.P. Robertson at p. 404. See also *H.* v. *P.*, 1905, 8 F. 232, L.P. Dunedin at p. 234; *Houston* v. *Aitken*, 1912 S.C. 1037, L. Skerrington (Ordinary) at p. 1038; *Swan* v. *Bowie*, 1948 S.C. 46, L.P. Cooper at p. 51.
2 *Oswald* v. *Fairs*, 1911 S.C. 257, L.P. Dunedin at p. 265.

on two specified days it was held irrelevant to prove that on other occasions the defender had attempted to ravish other women.[3] Where a pursuer sought to recover money alleged to have been paid as a result of misrepresentations, he was not allowed to prove that similar misrepresentations had been made by the same person to others.[4] Theft and attempted theft on two specified dates having been charged, it was said to be improper to lead evidence that the accused had been in the premises on earlier occasions when cash shortages had occurred.[5] Where the question in issue on a plea of *veritas* in an action of damages for slander was whether the pursuer, a married woman, had committed adultery with the defender, the latter was not allowed to prove that the pursuer had committed adultery with another man on another occasion.[6]

16. EVIDENCE OF SIMILAR ACTS—EXCEPTIONS TO GENERAL RULE

(a) General. In a case where a husband and wife claimed damages for a slander contained in anonymous letters sent to them by post, the pursuers were allowed to lead evidence about similar letters sent to other persons. This was not a true exception to the rule, since the evidence was allowed, not because it supported the probability of the pursuer's case, but because it was relevant to the only question really in issue, viz:—whether the letters received by the pursuers were in the defender's handwriting.[7] In an action of reduction of a trust disposition and settlement and two codicils, the instrumentary witnesses for each deed being the same two persons, Lord Justice-Clerk Inglis charged the jury that if they were satisfied regarding one of the deeds that the witnesses did not see the testator sign or hear him acknowledge his signature, that fact was relevant to their consideration of whether in the execution of the other deeds the same irregularity had occurred. The reason for this was said to be that if the testator, when executing one of the deeds, acted upon a mistaken belief as to the legal requirements for testing, it was not improbable that he acted in the same way with regard to the others.[8] Although this is an apparent exception to the general rule, it must be noted that the three deeds were closely related in date and in subject matter, were under reduction in the same action, and bore to be signed and witnessed by the same three persons, and its use as a precedent should perhaps be restricted to these circumstances.

(b) Consistorial Causes. To protect the matrimonial bond against

---

3 *A.* v. *B.*, 1895, 22 R. 402.

4 *Inglis* v. *National Bank of Scotland*, 1909 S.C. 1038; *Advertising Concessions (Parent) Co.* v. *Paterson, Sons & Co.* (O.H.) 1908, 16 S.L.T. 654. For cases where such evidence has been admitted as relevant only to proof of guilty knowledge or intention in a criminal charge, see § 28.

5 *Coventry* v. *Douglas*, 1944 J.C. 13, L. J-G. Normand at p. 19.

6 *H.* v. *P.*, 1905, 8 F. 232. See also *C.* v. *M.*, 1923 S.C. 1.

7 *Swan* v. *Bowie*, 1948 S.C. 46. This evidence was intended to form the basis for skilled evidence as to the handwriting: see § 414, sub-para. (b). See also *Knutzen* v. *Mauritzen* (O.H.) 1918, 1 S.L.T. 85.

8 *Morrison* v. *Maclean's Trs.*, 1862, 24 D. 625, at p. 630.

injury,[9] the general rule has been relaxed in actions of divorce for adultery, and the court has admitted evidence of attempted adultery or indecent conduct on the part of the defender with persons other than the co-defender, as supporting the probability of the acts of adultery founded upon.[10] The relaxation does not extend to the co-defender's misconduct with persons other than the defender, evidence of which is irrelevant and inadmissible.[11] Evidence of earlier adultery, which has been condoned, between the defender and the co-defender,[12] or between him and someone other than the co-defender,[13] or of adultery committed after the raising of the action,[14] although it cannot be founded upon as a ground of judgment, may be relevant as throwing light on the conduct founded on as proof of adultery, or on the nature of the association between the defender and the co-defender. The value of such evidence as corroboration is mentioned later.[15]

(c) **Affiliation and Aliment.**   In actions of affiliation and aliment evidence of acts of intercourse between the parties, other than those alleged to have caused the conception of the child, is admissible, and may be relevant as throwing light on the probable relationship between the parties at the date of the conception.   Evidence that the pursuer had intercourse with other men at or about the time of conception is also relevant, because it has a direct bearing upon the main question in issue, viz:—whether the defender is the father of the child.   A judicial suggestion that evidence of intercourse between the defender and other women is also relevant, has not been adopted in practice.   All these matters are mentioned more fully later.[16]

(d) **Criminal Causes.**   Another exception to the rule occurs when evidence of similar acts of an accused person in a criminal cause is admitted in order to establish motive[17] or guilty knowledge or intention,[18] and examples of such evidence are given later.

17. EVIDENCE OF CHARACTER—GENERAL

The good or bad character of a party to a cause is generally a matter which is collateral to the main issue, and evidence of it is accordingly in general inadmissible.[19]   With regard to the character of the defender in a

[9] *H.* v. *P.*, 1905, 8 F. 232, L.P. Dunedin at p. 234; *A.* v. *B.*, 1895, 22 R. 402, L.P. Robertson at p. 404.
[10] *Whyte* v. *Whyte*, 1884, 11 R. 710; *Wilson* v. *Wilson* (O.H.) 1955 S.L.T. (Notes) 81.
[11] *King* v. *King*, 1842, 4 D. 590; *Johnston* v. *Johnston*, 1903, 5 F. 659.
[12] *Collins* v. *Collins*, 1884, 11 R. (H.L.) 19, L. Blackburn at p. 29; *Robertson* v. *Robertson*, 1888, 15 R. 1001, L. Young at pp. 1003-1004.
[13] *Nicol* v. *Nicol* (O.H.) 1938 S.L.T. 98.
[14] *Ross* v. *Ross*, 1928 S.C. 600.
[15] See § **167.**
[16] See § **172.**
[17] See § **27.**
[18] See § **28.**
[19] Dickson, *Evidence* (3rd ed.) §6.

civil action there seem to be few exceptions to this rule.[20] So, in an action of damages for rape, evidence that the defender was a man of brutal and licentious disposition was held irrelevant,[21] and evidence regarding the defender's character has been held irrelevant in actions of damages for slander,[22] assault,[23] wrongous imprisonment,[24] and breach of contract,[25] and in an action for reduction of a testamentary deed on the ground of facility, circumvention and fraud.[26] The character of the pursuer, however, is sometimes a fact in issue, or has a direct bearing on such a fact, and evidence regarding it is then admissible. In an action of damages for assault against a police constable who had instructions to remove bad characters from a race-course, and who had forcibly ejected the pursuer, evidence of the pursuer's bad character was allowed in order to establish that the ejection was justifiable and did not constitute an assault.[27] And in other actions of damages the pursuer's character may be relevant to the question of *quantum*, the following being examples:—actions founded on slander, seduction and breach of promise of marriage;[28] an action by a widow for solatium in respect of her husband's death, when evidence of her immoral conduct may be relevant to establish that her life with her husband had not been normally happy;[29] an action of damages for bodily injury resulting in loss of business profits when evidence that the pursuer's losses were partly due to his intemperate habits was admitted.[30] Evidence of character in criminal causes is dealt with later in this chapter.[31] Even when general evidence as to character or reputation is held to be admissible, evidence of specific criminal or immoral acts may be disallowed on the practical ground of inexpediency.[32]

18. CHARACTER IN SLANDER ACTIONS

It has been said that in actions of damages for slander, the pursuer

[20] *Clark* v. *Spence*, 1825, 3 Mur. 450, at p. 474. There is an apparent exception in the admission of evidence of similar acts of adultery or fornication, which indirectly affects the defender's character, in divorce and affiliation actions. See § 16, sub-paras. (b) (c). *Cf.* also, L.P. Robertson in *A.* v. *B.*, 1895, 22 R. 402, at p. 404, who said that if the defender admitted in cross-examination that he had tried to ravish other women this might properly be regarded as making it more probable that he had ravished the pursuer.

[21] *A.* v. *B.* (*supra*).

[22] *Scott* v. *McGavin*, 1821, 2 Mur. 484, at p. 493; *Cooper* v. *Macintosh*, 1823, 3 Mur. 357, at p. 359.

[23] *Haddaway* v. *Goddard*, 1816, 1 Mur. 148, at p. 151.

[24] *Simpson* v. *Liddle*, 1821, 2 Mur. 579, at p. 580.

[25] *Kitchen* v. *Fisher*, 1821, 2 Mur. 584, at p. 591.

[26] *Clark* v. *Spence*, 1825, 3 Mur. 450.

[27] *Wallace* v. *Mooney*, 1885, 12 R. 710.

[28] See §§ 18, 19.

[29] *Donnelly* v. *Glasgow Corporation* (O.H.) 1949 S.L.T. 362.

[30] *Butchart* v. *Dundee & Arbroath Railway Co.*, 1859, 22 D. 184.

[31] See §§ 20-23.

[32] *C.* v. *M.*, 1923 S.C. 1 (slander). L.P. Clyde said that while substantive evidence might not be led about specific acts of adultery committed by the pursuer, they might have a bearing on character and credibility and could be put to her in cross-examination, if fair notice, not necessarily on record, was given. Cross-examination was similarly

necessarily puts his character in issue.[33] The pursuer is entitled to substantiate his claim for damages by proving that he is of good character, and the defender, in order to mitigate damages, is entitled to prove the contrary.[34] In this connection, however, it is more accurate to speak of "reputed character" than of "character," because it is loss of reputation rather than loss of character for which damages are claimed. When the defender seeks to mitigate damages, "the point of such a defence is not that [the pursuer] *is* a bad character, but that she *has* a bad character."[35] So, in a slander action, the defender in mitigation of damages was allowed to prove that the pursuer was well known as a person of loose and immoral character, but not that she had committed adultery on specific occasions.[36]

19. CHARACTER IN ACTIONS FOR SEDUCTION AND BREACH OF PROMISE OF MARRIAGE

In these actions also it has been said that the pursuer's character is necessarily put in issue.[37] In an action for seduction the pursuer is not bound to prove her own good character, but her character may be considered by the jury as supporting the probability or improbability of her consent having been obtained by dole.[38] In an action for breach of promise of marriage it is relevant to prove as a defence to the action that, unknown to the defender, the pursuer has had an illegitimate child, because on discovering the fact the defender may resile from the engagement.[39] In these actions, also, evidence as to the pursuer's character is relevant to the question of *quantum* of damages.

20. CHARACTER IN CRIMINAL CAUSES

(a) **Of Victim or Complainer.** The accused may, if notice has been given,[40] attack the character of the injured person in cases of murder or assault, and in cases of rape, attempted rape, or similar assaults on women. In cases of murder or assault he may prove that the injured person was of a violent or quarrelsome disposition,[41] but not the commission of specific acts of violence.[42] It has been held that the victim may be cross-examined,

permitted, but in relation only to credibility, in *A.* v. *B.*, 1895, 22 R. 402 (damages for rape) and *H.* v. *P.*, 1905, 8 F. 232 (slander), Lord Ordinary at p. 234.
[33] *Hyslop* v. *Miller*, 1816, 1 Mur. 43, at p. 49; *Bern's Exr.* v. *Montrose Asylum*, 1893, 20 R. 859, L. McLaren at p. 863; *C.* v. *M.*, 1923 S.C. 1, L.P. Clyde at p. 4.
[34] *McNeill* v. *Rorison*, 1847, 10 D. 15, L. J-Cl. Hope at p. 34, L. Moncreiff at pp. 26, 27. This is subject to the exception that the defender may not prove the truth of the slander complained of, even in mitigation of damages, without a plea and counter issue of *veritas*. On this point see also *Paul* v. *Jackson*, 1884, 11 R. 460; *Browne* v. *McFarlane*, 1889, 16 R. 368.
[35] *C.* v. *M.*, *(supra)*, L.P. Clyde at p. 4.
[36] *C.* v. *M.* *(supra)*. See also *McCulloch* v. *Litt*, 1851, 13 D. 960 (evidence of current rumour allowed).
[37] *Bern's Exr.* v. *Montrose Asylum*, 1893, 20 R. 859, L. McLaren at p. 863.
[38] *Walker* v. *McIsaac*, 1857, 19 D. 340; Dickson, *Evidence* (3rd ed.) §10.
[39] *Fletcher* v. *Grant*, 1878, 6 R. 59; *Brodie* v. *Macgregor*, 1900, 8 S.L.T. 86.
[40] *Dickie* v. *H.M. Advocate*, 1897, 24 R. (J.) 82, at pp. 83, 87; Alison, II, 533; *Brown*, 1836, 1 Swin. 293.
[41] *Blair*, 1836, Bell's Notes, 294; *Irving*, 1838, 2 Swin. 109; *Fletcher*, 1846, Ark. 171.
[42] *Irving (supra)*; *Fletcher (supra)*.

apparently without notice, as to his insobriety at the time of the assault, and that evidence may be led for the defence regarding it.[43] The prosecutor is entitled to ask a witness whether the victim was quarrelsome or inoffensive.[44] In cases of rape or of similar assaults upon women, the accused may attack the woman's character for chastity, and may lead evidence that at the time she was reputedly of bad moral character,[45] that she associated with prostitutes, but not that her friends were otherwise of bad character,[46] and that she had previously had intercourse with the accused.[45] He may not lead evidence to prove specific acts of intercourse with other men, unless, possibly, these are so closely connected with the alleged rape as to form part of the *res gestæ*.[45] Evidence of unchastity after the date of the crime is generally inadmissible.[47] The Crown may lead evidence that the victim was of good character.[48]

(b) Of Persons not Present at Trial. In certain circumstances evidence has been admitted as to the character of persons who were neither the victim nor the accused, and who were not witnesses at the trial. In reset cases, in order to establish guilty knowledge, the Crown has been allowed to prove that the persons frequenting the accused's shop were thieves or dealers in stolen property,[49] and that the man from whom the accused, in his declaration, admitted obtaining the stolen watch, was a dealer in stolen watches.[50] On a charge of brothel keeping the prosecutor may lead evidence that women seen by witnesses to enter the premises are known by them to be prostitutes.[51] In a case of rape or of a similar assault upon a woman, the accused, on giving notice of an attack on the woman's chastity, may lead evidence that her associates are common prostitutes, but not that they are otherwise of bad character.[52]

21. CHARACTER OF ACCUSED PERSON—GENERAL

The accused's good character may always be proved for the defence.[53] An attack by the Crown, on the other hand, on the accused's character is generally inadmissible,[54] although evidence, otherwise relevant, which

---

[43] *Falconer* v. *Brown*, 1893, 21 R. (J.) 1. It would seem that the evidence was regarded as the possible basis of a defence related to assault or provocation by the complainer (see L. McLaren at p. 3), but this is by no means clear.

[44] *Porteous*, 1841, Bell's Notes, 293.

[45] *Dickie* v. *H.M. Advocate*, 1897, 24 R. (J.) 82.

[46] *Webster*, 1847, Ark. 269.

[47] *Leitch*, 1838, 2 Swin. 112.

[48] *McMillan*, 1846, Ark. 209; Dickson, *Evidence* (3rd ed.) §7.

[49] *Burns* v. *Hart and Young*, 1856, 2 Irv. 571.

[50] *Gracie* v. *Stuart*, 1884, 11 R. (J.) 22.

[51] *Macpherson* v. *Crisp*, 1919 J.C. 1. See also *McLaren* v. *Macleod*, 1913 S.C. (J.) 61.

[52] *Webster*, 1847, Ark. 269.

[53] Dickson, *Evidence* (3rd ed.) §15. See also *Slater* v. *H.M. Advocate*, 1928 J.C. 94, at p. 105.

[54] e.g. *Burns* v. *Hart and Young*, 1856, 2 Irv. 571 (a reset charge, where the allowance of evidence that the accused was habit and repute a resetter was held fatal to the conviction). See also Dickson, *Evidence* (3rd ed.) §15. For circumstances in which the accused's bad character may be mentioned in evidence, see §§ **22, 358.**

indicates that the accused is of bad character, will not on that account be excluded. If a man is charged with the murder of his mistress, the immoral relationship between them must necessarily be disclosed. A voluntary statement by the accused, which is admissible in evidence, is not excluded merely because it incidentally betrays his previous bad character.[55] In the case of Oscar Slater,[56] who was charged with the murder of an old lady, it was proved that a box in her house had been broken open and that a valuable brooch was missing. Evidence was led for the Crown to show that the accused, who pretended to be a dentist, in fact made money by gambling and dealing in jewels, and it also came out in evidence that he was living on the earnings of prostitution. It was held on appeal that the first item of evidence was relevant as showing a motive for the taking of jewellery, but that the evidence regarding the earnings of prostitution, while it could not have been excluded owing to the nature of the defence, was wholly irrelevant to the issue, and that the jury should have been instructed to ignore it. Where a writing, which is held to be relevant and admissible as a piece of documentary evidence, contains irrelevant matter which is prejudicial to the accused, the judge must warn the jury against allowing their verdict to be affected by the irrelevant matter.[57] It has been held proper to bring out from a reluctant witness for the Crown that an attempt at intimidation was made on her by someone representing the accused, but the jury should be directed that this evidence is relevant only to explain the witness's demeanour, and is not evidence against the accused.[58]

22. CRIMINAL RECORD OF ACCUSED PERSON

Apart from questions of character in general, express statutory provision is made for excluding the accused's previous convictions from the knowledge of the court, prior to a conviction or a plea of guilty. In solemn procedure previous convictions may not be referred to in presence of the jury before the verdict is returned, nor laid before the presiding judge until the prosecutor moves for sentence, save where it is competent to lead evidence regarding them *in causa* in support of a substantive charge.[59] In summary procedure a similar provision is in force.[60] Certain statutes expressly provide that previous convictions may be proved *in causa*. So, for the purpose of proving guilty knowledge in a reset case, the prosecutor, if he gives seven days' notice to the accused in writing, may prove previous convictions of offences

[55] *H.M. Advocate* v. *McFadyen*, 1926 J.C. 93. See also *Turner* v. *Underwood* [1948] 2 K.B. 284.
[56] *Slater* v. *H.M. Advocate* (*supra*).
[57] *McEwan* v. *H.M. Advocate*, 1939 J.C. 26 (a letter). This must be distinguished from a report by an expert witness, read by him in the witness box for convenience as part of his parole evidence. In such a case a conviction will be quashed if the expert is allowed to read any part of his report which is inadmissible and prejudicial to the accused. *Grant* v. *H.M. Advocate*, 1938 J.C. 7 (report of a medical witness); *McEwan* v. *H.M. Advocate* (*supra*), at pp. 32, 33-34.
[58] *Manson* v. *H.M. Advocate*, 1951 J.C. 49.
[59] Criminal Procedure (Scotland) Act, 1887 (50 & 51 Vict. c. 35), s. 67; Criminal Justice (Scotland) Act, 1949 (12, 13 & 14 Geo. VI. c. 94), s. 39.
[60] Summary Jurisdiction (Scotland) Act, 1954 (2 & 3 Eliz. II. c. 48), s. 31.

inferring fraud or dishonesty obtained during the preceding five years, provided that he has first led evidence to establish that the accused was in possession of stolen property.[61] And previous convictions may be proved to support a charge that the accused is a known or reputed thief found in possession of articles for which he cannot satisfactorily account.[62] It has been held that accidental or incidental reference by a witness to a previous conviction may not necessarily be fatal to a conviction,[63] and evidence that a witness examined a photograph of the accused in an album in the police station is not regarded as a disclosure of the accused's criminal record.[64]

23. CROSS-EXAMINATION OF ACCUSED AS TO CHARACTER

This subject is dealt with later in connection with specialties of witnesses.[65]

24. EVIDENCE OF STATE OF MIND—GENERAL

A party's state of mind at a particular time cannot be proved by direct evidence. When such a state of mind is one of the facts in issue, or is relevant to a fact in issue, it can be proved only by inferences drawn from other facts, and the collateral issues associated with these other facts are in these circumstances relevant and admissible in evidence.[66]

25. STATE OF MIND IN CIVIL CAUSES

When in reparation actions the defender's knowledge of the existence of a danger is one of the matters in issue, evidence is admissible of earlier accidents or injuries arising from the same danger from which his knowledge at the relevant time may be inferred. The collateral facts which it is intended to prove must be averred in the pleadings. Evidence was admitted that a person other than the pursuer had previously fallen down a stairway in public-house premises;[67] that the absence of a side-guard between the wheels of tramcars had caused similar earlier injuries to pedestrians;[68] and, in an action against a road authority, that four earlier skidding accidents had occurred on the street, the dangerous condition of which was blamed for the accident to the pursuers' omnibus.[69] On the same principle, in an action of damages against the owner of a dog by a person whom it has bitten, evidence that it has bitten other persons is admissible to establish

---

61 Prevention of Crimes Act, 1871 (34 & 35 Vict. c. 112), s. 19; *Watson* v. *H.M. Advocate*, 1894, 21 R. (J.) 26.
62 Burgh Police (Scotland) Act, 1892 (55 & 56 Vict. c. 55), s. 409; *Moir* v. *Mitchell*, 1939 J.C. 81. See also *McGregor* v. *Macdonald*, 1952 J.C. 4 (Glasgow Police (Further Powers) Act, 1892, s. 25).
63 *Kepple* v. *H.M. Advocate*, 1936 J.C. 76. See also *Haslam* v. *H.M. Advocate*, 1936 J.C. 82, L. J-Cl. Aitchison at p. 85; *Clark* v. *Connell*, 1952 J.C. 119.
64 *Corcoran* v. *H.M. Advocate*, 1932 J.C. 42.
65 See § **358.**
66 Dickson, *Evidence* (3rd ed.) §19.
67 *Cairns* v. *Boyd*, 1879, 6 R. 1004.
68 *Gibb* v. *Edinburgh & District Tramways Co.*, 1912 S.C. 580.
69 *W. Alexander & Sons* v. *Dundee Corporation*, 1950 S.C. 123.

the owner's knowledge of its vicious disposition.[70] When the defender's malice is one of the facts in issue, and is not presumed, but must be proved independently,[71] as in some reparation actions based on intentional injury, evidence of collateral facts from which malice may be inferred is admissible. In this case also the facts must be averred. The following are examples of such facts:—in a case of judicial slander the defender's knowledge that the defamatory averments were untrue, and the facts from which that knowledge could be inferred;[72] in other cases of slander uttered on privileged occasions, the defender's failure to make reasonable enquiry into the truth of the defamatory statements,[73] needless publicity given to the slander,[74] antecedent indications of ill-will,[75] and the fact that the language used was unnecessarily violent, persistent and intemperate.[76]

26. STATE OF MIND IN CRIMINAL CAUSES

(a) **General.** Evidence of collateral facts may be admissible in criminal causes in order to establish motive[77] or guilty knowledge and intention,[78] and these subjects are dealt with in the following paragraphs. The rules regarding the proximity of the collateral fact to the crime charged, and the necessity for notice being given of the collateral issue to be raised, are common to the whole of this subject, and are mentioned below in this paragraph.

(b) **Proximity of Collateral Fact to Crime Charged.** The general test regarding the relevancy of indirect evidence applies. In order to be relevant the collateral fact which it is desired to prove must not be too remote from the crime charged in time, place or character, what is or is not too remote for this purpose being a question of degree in each case.[79]

(c) **Notice of the Collateral Issue.** Evidence of the commission of a crime other than the crime principally libelled, although it may be relevant, is inadmissible unless the indictment or complaint gives notice of it, either by libelling the other crime as a substantive charge,[80] or by averring the

---

[70] *Cowan* v. *Dalziel*, 1877, 5 R. 241; *Gordon* v. *Mackenzie*, 1913 S.C. 109. See also *McIntyre* v. *Carmichael*, 1870, 8 M. 570 (damages for sheep killing based on common law fault).

[71] For the substantive law on this subject, see Glegg, *Reparation* (4th ed.) 14-17, 154 *et seq.*, 160, 185 *et seq.*, 195 *et seq.* See also p. 119 (relevance of malice in assessment of damages).

[72] *Mitchell* v. *Smith*, 1919 S.C. 664.

[73] *Dinnie* v. *Hengler*, 1910 S.C. 4.

[74] *Ingram* v. *Russell*, 1893, 20 R. 771.

[75] *Suzor* v. *McLachlan*, 1914 S.C. 306.

[76] *Gall* v. *Slessor*, 1907 S.C. 708; *Riddell* v. *Glasgow Corporation*, 1910 S.C. 693 (revd. on another point, 1911 S.C. (H.L.) 35).

[77] See § 27.

[78] See § 28.

[79] For judicial dicta on this point, see § 6, note 34.

[80] *H.M. Advocate* v. *Pritchard*, 1865, 5 Irv. 88; *H.M. Advocate* v. *Wishart*, 1870, 1 Couper, 463; *H.M. Advocate* v. *Monson*, 1893, 21 R. (J.) 5; *Robertson* v. *Watson*, 1949 J.C. 73.

facts relating to it which the evidence is intended to establish.[81] This rule applies even when the collateral evidence relates only to a statutory offence.[82] When the collateral fact is the forgery of a document by the accused, some difficulty has arisen in the application of this rule. It has been held that, when the crime libelled is the uttering of a forged document, evidence that the accused himself committed the forgery is admissible without notice,[83] because forgery by itself is not a crime, although the better practice may be to give notice.[84] When, however, it is desired to prove the forgery and uttering of a document as collateral to the commission of another kind of crime, such as murder,[85] theft[86] or fraud,[87] notice is needed to make the evidence admissible because uttering is a crime. The old rule, mentioned by Dickson,[88] which, in murder cases, required notice of an intention to prove acts inferring malice only if they occurred more than a fortnight before the crime, no longer applies.[89] The present practice requires an express allegation of antecedent malice as a matter of fair notice,[90] unless the acts to be proved form part of the *res gestæ*, probably on the view that the acts usually relied upon are threats or physical assaults which are themselves crimes. Collateral evidence, other than that relating to a crime not charged, is usually[91] admissible without notice, in accordance with the general rule that a party need not disclose in advance the evidence by which he hopes to prove his case.[92]

27. MOTIVE IN CRIMINAL CAUSES

The Crown need not prove a motive for the commission of a crime,[93] and, indeed, it may be impossible to discover a rational motive for some crimes which are clearly proved to have been committed. A. A. Rouse, merely to avoid the claims of his many paramours, killed an unknown man and left him in a burning car, so that he himself might be thought to be dead.[94]

---

81 *H.M. Advocate* v. *Joseph*, 1929 J.C. 55; *H.M. Advocate* v. *Tully*, 1935 J.C. 8; *Griffen* v. *H.M. Advocate*, 1940 J.C. 1. An exception to this rule seems to have been sanctioned in *Gallagher* v. *Paton*, 1909 S.C. (J.) 50. See § **28**, note 6.

82 *H.M. Advocate* v. *Tully* (*supra*); *Robertson* v. *Watson* (*supra*).

83 *Barr* v. *H.M. Advocate*, 1927 J.C. 51.

84 *Ibid.*, L. J-Cl. Alness at p. 56.

85 *H.M. Advocate* v. *Monson*, 1893, 21 R. (J.) 5. Although L. J-Cl. Macdonald speaks only of forgery, it seems clear that the collateral evidence must necessarily also have included uttering. See on this point L. J-Cl. Alness in *Barr* v. *H.M. Advocate* (*supra*) at p. 55.

86 *Cameron* v. *Waugh*, 1937 J.C. 5. Here, also, the accused must have uttered the documents if they were to assist him in committing the theft charged.

87 *Griffen* v. *H.M. Advocate*, 1940 J.C. 1.

88 See Dickson, *Evidence* (3rd ed.) §20.

89 See *H.M. Advocate* v. *Kennedy*, 1907, 5 Adam, 347.

90 Macdonald, *Criminal Law* (5th ed.) 306; *H.M. Advocate* v. *Flanders*, 1961 S.L.T. 425.

91 For a statutory exception regarding reset, see § **22**.

92 *Ritchie and Morren*, 1841, 2 Swin., 581 (see § **28**, note 7); *H.M. Advocate* v. *Rae*, 1888, 15 R. (J.) 80, at pp. 81-82; *H.M. Advocate* v. *Monson*, 1893, 21 R. (J.) 5, L. J-Cl. Macdonald at p. 7; *Barr* v. *H.M. Advocate*, 1927 J.C. 51, L. J-Cl. Alness at p. 56.

93 Hume, I, 254; Macdonald, *Criminal Law* (5th ed.) 1.

94 *Notable British Trials.*

Apparent absence of motive, however, may be an important element in favour of the defence,[95] and evidence of motive in support of the case for the Crown is always admissible. In the case of Madeleine Smith[96] (1857), the motive alleged for the murder of an importunate lover was the wish to be free to marry another man. In the case of Dr. Pritchard,[97] evidence was admitted of familiarities with a maidservant, causing jealousy to the wife, as relevant to a possible motive for the murder of the latter. In the case of Donald Merrett[94] (1927), evidence that his mother must inevitably discover that he had uttered cheques bearing her forged signature, was relied on as showing a motive for her murder. In other murder cases evidence of earlier assaults and threats of violence has been allowed as relevant to the motive of hatred or revenge.[98] Evidence that Oscar Slater[99] was a dealer in jewels was held relevant to a possible motive for the murder of a woman from whom a valuable brooch had been stolen. In all crimes associated with dishonesty the impecuniosity of the accused is relevant to the question of motive, and evidence that the accused had previously pawned some of his own property was admitted for this purpose in a case of wilful fire-raising.[1]

28. GUILTY KNOWLEDGE AND INTENTION

Dole, or corrupt and evil intent (*mens rea*), is a necessary element in crimes,[2] as distinct from statutory offences.[3] It is inferred, however, from proof of the crime itself, and does not need to be separately established. The Crown may nevertheless lead evidence of collateral facts from which guilty intention or guilty knowledge may be inferred, and such evidence is both admissible and necessary when the act itself is neutral in quality, and is susceptible either of a guilty or of an innocent interpretation such as accident, self defence or unintentional injury or deceit. So, in a charge of wilful fire-raising evidence was admitted that shortly before the fire the accused removed some of his own goods from the building,[4] and, in a case of murder of an illegitimate child by its parents, the Crown, in order to show knowledge and premeditation, was allowed to prove that both accused discussed the question of the mother's pregnancy with a doctor five months

---

95 Dickson, *Evidence* (3rd ed.) §83.
96 *Notable Scottish Trials.*
97 *H.M. Advocate* v. *Pritchard*, 1865, 5 Irv. 88, at p. 100 (also reported in *Notable Scottish Trials*).
98 *H.M. Advocate* v. *Kennedy*, 1907, 5 Adam, 347; *Millar*, 1837, 1 Swin. 483, at 486; *Salt*, 1860, 3 Irv. 549. In *Stewart*, 1855, 2 Irv. 166, expressions indicative of violence shortly after the murder were admitted as part of the *res gestæ.*
99 *Slater* v. *H.M. Advocate*, 1928 J.C. 94.
1 *Rosenberg*, 1842, 1 *Broun*, 266.
2 Hume, I, 21, 22; Macdonald, *Criminal Law* (5th ed.) 1.
3 Some statutory offences may be committed without *mens rea*. See *Gordon* v. *Shaw*, 1908 S.C. (J.) 17; *Anderson* v. *Rose*, 1919 J.C. 20; *Beattie* v. *Waugh*, 1920 J.C. 64; *Howman* v. *Russell*, 1923 J.C. 32; *Mitchell* v. *Morrison*, 1938 J.C. 64. *Cf. Nimmo* v. *Lanarkshire Tramways Co.*, 1912 S.C. (J.) 23; *Galbraith's Stores* v. *McIntyre*, 1912 S.C. (J.) 66; *Masterton & Collier* v. *Soutar*, 1912 S.C. (J.) 74.
4 *McCreadie*, 1862, 4 Irv. 214. See also *H.M. Advocate* v. *Smillie*, 1883, 10 R. (J.) 70 at p. 71.

C

before the child's birth.[5] In charges relating to fraudulent pretences, and the uttering of forged documents, the Crown must establish knowledge that the representations or the documents were false, and for this purpose evidence of the accused's earlier or later actings may be admissible. So, where the accused was charged with defrauding a shop assistant of the cost of an advertisement in a directory, on the pretence that her employer made this payment annually, evidence of other shopkeepers and shop assistants in the same town was admitted to show that similar false representations were made to them on the same day.[6] In that case Lord McLaren said: "A false statement made to one person may be explained away, but when a system of false statements is proved, the probability is very great that the statements were designedly made."[6] When the charge was that of uttering a base shilling, evidence that on the same night the accused had offered coins to other persons, who had rejected them as bad, was admitted to show his knowledge of their falsity at the time of the act charged.[7] When an accused was charged, as part of a fraudulent scheme, with uttering a forged draft and pretending that it was genuine, evidence was admitted that in the following month he pretended in Belgium that a similar forged draft was genuine.[8] This evidence was allowed, not because the commission of a similar crime made it probable that the accused committed the crime charged, which would have been an irrelevant consideration, but as relevant to show that the act charged was done of design and not by accident. One means of proving guilty knowledge in a case of uttering is to establish that the accused himself forged the document uttered, and evidence to this effect is admissible for that purpose.[9] In order to prove guilt in a charge of reset the Crown must lead evidence from which the accused's knowledge that the articles were stolen can be inferred, the time, place and circumstances of the accused's possession being sometimes sufficient for this purpose.[10]

[5] *H.M. Advocate* v. *Wishart*, 1870, 1 Couper, 463.
[6] *Gallagher* v. *Paton*, 1909 S.C. (J.) 50, at p. 55. The judicial opinions contain no comment on the fact that the evidence of the collateral false representations was allowed without notice. The decision seems to be an exception to the rule mentioned in § 26, sub-para. (c).
[7] *Ritchie and Morren*, 1841, 2 Swin. 581. This evidence was allowed without notice, which, if the earlier attempts are to be regarded as criminal, is in conflict with the rule mentioned in § 26, sub-para. (c). The court may have thought that they could not be established as criminal without proof of guilty knowledge at the times when they were committed.
[8] *H.M. Advocate* v. *Joseph*, 1929 J.C. 55.
[9] *Barr* v. *H.M. Advocate*, 1927 J.C. 51. See also the trial of Donald Merrett, *Notable British Trials*.
[10] Macdonald, *Criminal Law* (5th ed.) 67. See also the reference to reset in § 22.

CHAPTER IV

ADMISSIBILITY OF EVIDENCE OF EXTRAJUDICIAL ADMISSIONS AND CONFESSIONS

29. GENERAL

An extrajudicial admission or confession made by a party must be distinguished from a judicial admission. The latter, which is conclusive against and binding upon the party making it for the purpose of the cause in which it is made, is mentioned later.[1] In this chapter "admission" is used as meaning a statement against interest in relation to a civil cause, and "confession" as meaning a statement against interest in relation to a criminal cause. The general rule is that evidence of a statement against interest, whether oral[2] or written,[3] made extrajudicially by a party to a cause, is admissible against him.[4] Such statements, if proved, are not by themselves

---

1 See §§ **48, 49.**
2 *Foggo* v. *Hill*, 1840, 2 D. 1322 (statement by party that partial payment made by other party); *Fraser* v. *Wilson*, 1842, 4 D. 1171 (statement by party to solicitor precognoscing him regarding another action); *Gordon* v. *Stewart*, 1842, 5 D. 8 (admission by defender that he committed assault sued for); *Greig* v. *Morice*, 1838, 16 S. 338 (declaration before kirk session by pursuer in affiliation and aliment action that father of child was a man other than defender); *Morrison* v. *Burrell*, 1947 J.C. 43 (confession of fraud by accused sub-postmaster to Post Office investigators).
3 *Dowling* v. *Henderson & Son*, 1890, 17 R. 921 (correspondence); *Anderson* v. *Anderson*, 1848, 11 D. 118 (newspaper advertisement); *Thom* v. *North British Banking Co.*, 1850, 13 D. 134; *British Linen Co.* v. *Thomson*, 1853, 15 D. 314; *Muir* v. *Goldie's Trs.* (O.H.) 1898, 6 S.L.T. 188; *Palestine Transport and Shipping Co.* v. *Greenock Dockyard Co.* (O.H.) 1947 S.N. 162 (entry in ship's log). When the admission is contained in a letter, the contents of the letter to which it was a reply may also be proved for the purpose of identifying the subject matter of the admission: *MacBain* v. *MacBain*, 1930 S.C. (H.L.) 72, L. Hailsham, L. Dunedin at p. 75.

conclusive against the party making them as in the case of judicial admissions. Evidence of them is relevant either because it may throw light on the party's credibility as a witness,[5] or as an adminicle of evidence in the cause, which may be important or unimportant, and which must be considered along with all the other evidence led. The fact that a statement is made against interest is supposed to indicate that it is more likely to be true than false.[4] When the statement has been made in the course of a precognition taken for the purposes of other proceedings, it would appear that evidence of it is inadmissible, in so far at least as directed against the accused in a criminal cause.[6] In a civil cause evidence of such a statement has been held admissible,[7] but the decisions on this point may have to be read along with more recent decisions regarding previous statements made by witnesses, which are mentioned later.[8] The rules applicable to the use of a qualified extrajudicial admission are the same as those applying to qualified judicial admissions.[9] Admissions made by a party in the course of abortive negotiations for a settlement of the dispute are not admissible in evidence, since these matters usually proceed upon mutual concessions.[10] It appears that an oral admission, which was interrupted before completion, may be proved for what it is worth, but the fact of the interruption must be considered in assessing its value, because it may have prevented the party from adding a qualification or explanation materially altering its meaning.[11]

30. PROOF AND PROBATIVE EFFECT OF EXTRAJUDICIAL ADMISSIONS AND CONFESSIONS

The nature and quantity of the evidence needed to prove the terms of an admission or confession, and the fact that it was made by the party concerned, are governed by the general rules as to sufficiency of evidence.[12] The testimony of a single witness to the making of a confession is an item of evidence which may be considered along with other facts, independently proved, to form a sufficiency of circumstantial proof.[13] An extrajudicial admission, when proved, does not preclude the party making it from stating a case which contradicts it. Its probative effect depends upon its terms and its importance in relation to the facts in issue in the cause, and to some extent on whether the cause is civil or criminal. In a civil cause the

---

4 Dickson, *Evidence* (3rd ed.) §297.
5 See § 7, sub-para. (b).
6 *Cook* v. *McNeill*, 1906, 8 F. (J.) 57.
7 *Fraser* v. *Wilson*, 1842, 4 D. 1171, at p. 1173; *Morrison* v. *Somerville*, 1860, 23 D. 232, L. J-Cl. Inglis at p. 238.
8 See § 343, sub-para. (b).
9 See § 48, sub-para. (a).
10 Dickson, *Evidence* (3rd ed.) §305; *Fyfe* v. *Miller*, 1835, 13 S. 809; *Williamson* v. *Taylor*, 1845, 7 D. 842. The English rule appears to be that offers of compromise, made expressly or impliedly "without prejudice," are inadmissible in evidence as admissions, provided they relate to the dispute depending between the same parties: Phipson, *Evidence* (9th ed.) 233-234.
11 Dickson, *Evidence* (3rd ed.) §309.
12 See §§ 380 *et seq.*
13 See § 386.

party who made the admission is entitled to establish that it was made for some secondary reason and was not true, and the whole circumstances in which it was made are relevant to qualify or explain its terms. If it was made in the course of proceedings with a third party, as a result of a mistaken view of the law, its importance in the subsequent action will be negligible,[14] and it is thought that an admission shown to have been made under a mistaken view of the facts may be of little importance, if the true facts are established. If, for example, a man admits paternity in the belief that the child will be born in June, his admission may be of little value if the birth in fact occurs in December. If, however, a party is unable to qualify or explain away an extrajudicial admission which he is proved to have made, and which concedes the whole foundation of his opponent's case, it is thought that little, if any, further evidence, apart from proof of the surrounding or background circumstances, is necessary to establish the case against him. This is a matter, however, on which it is difficult to generalise, since in each case the probative weight to be attached to such an admission must depend upon the circumstances of the particular case. In criminal causes the accused cannot be convicted upon proof of his extrajudicial confession alone, even if the commission of the crime is independently proved.[15] To justify a conviction there must in addition be other evidence which associates the accused with the commission of the crime, and this evidence may be direct or circumstantial.[16] Another confession made by the accused, even if in different terms and made to other persons, is not sufficient, it is thought, for this purpose, since both confessions may have been falsely made for the same ulterior reason.[17] Proof of an accused person's incriminating actions, however, at or after the commission of the crime,[18] and even after apprehension,[19] have been held sufficient to support a confession, particularly when these were associated with real evidence connected with the commission of the crime, such as the murdered body or clothing of the victim, pointed out to the police by the accused.[19] The accused is entitled to show that the confession was made in circumstances, or for reasons, which nullify or reduce its apparently incriminating character.[20]

31. PRISONERS' DECLARATIONS

Although it may not be entirely accurate to describe these as extrajudicial, their effect as evidence is similar to that of extrajudicial confessions, and they are accordingly included briefly in this chapter. Judicial examina-

---

[14] *Beattie and Muir* v. *Brown*, 1883, 11 R. 250.

[15] *Connolly* v. *H.M. Advocate*, 1958 S.L.T. 79; Dickson, *Evidence* (3rd ed.) §352; Hume, II, 333.

[16] For circumstantial evidence, see §§ **8** *et seq.*

[17] Question mentioned but not decided in *Banaghan*, 1888, 15 R. (J.) 39.

[18] *Costello* v. *Macpherson*, 1922 J.C. 9; *Chalmers* v. *H.M. Advocate*, 1954 J.C. 66, L. J-G. Cooper at p. 76.

[19] *Manuel* v. *H.M. Advocate*, 1958 J.C. 41; Alison, II, 580. See also *Connolly* v. *H.M. Advocate* (*supra*). *Cf. Chalmers* v. *H.M. Advocate* (*supra*), where the incriminating actings of the accused, after his detention by the police, were held to be indistinguishable from, and to add nothing to, a confession previously made.

[20] For examples of false confessions, see Dickson, *Evidence* (3rd ed.) §§380-383.

tion of prisoners is a relic of the days when the accused person was not a competent witness. A declaration is not now taken from a prisoner, when brought before the sheriff for examination, if he or his solicitor intimates that he does not desire to emit one,[21] and the taking of a declaration is in modern practice a very rare event.[22] The prosecutor alone is entitled to put the declaration in evidence,[23] but if the accused wishes the declaration to be read in court, the prosecutor usually consents. The declaration does not need to be proved in order to be admissible as evidence against the accused.[24] It becomes evidence if it is entered in the list of productions annexed to the indictment,[25] tendered as evidence by the prosecutor, and read to the jury by the clerk of court. Before the declaration is read, however, the accused may attempt to impugn it, and for that purpose may lead the evidence of the persons present when it was taken, even if these are not included in his or the prosecutor's list of witnesses, the prosecutor being entitled to lead similar evidence in rebuttal.[24] The declaration can never by itself be sufficient evidence of the accused's guilt, as if it were the equivalent of a plea of guilty, and, even if it includes a virtual admission of guilt, it must be corroborated by other evidence before a conviction is justified.[26] A declaration is not admissible as evidence against a co-accused,[23] and it is doubtful whether it can be founded upon in his favour.[27] A declaration emitted by an accused in respect of one charge may be used as evidence against him on a subsequent charge involving the same *species facti*, provided the later charge is less serious in character than the earlier.[28] So a declaration taken on a charge of assault, mobbing and rioting was held admissible in a subsequent trial for breach of the peace.[28] At one time a declaration was regarded as admissible in evidence against the party who emitted it in a subsequent civil cause to which he was a party.[29] It was later held,[30] however, that such a use of a declaration is inadmissible on the ground *inter alia* that a judicial examination is held in private. It is thought that this objection could not be held to apply if the declaration had been used as evidence in a criminal trial.

21 Summary Jurisdiction (Scotland) Act, 1908 (8 Edw. VII. c. 65), s. 77 (1) (not repealed: Summary Jurisdiction (Scotland) Act. 1954 (2 & 3 Eliz. II. c. 48), s. 78, Sch. 4).
22 For the procedure to be followed in the taking of a declaration, see Renton and Brown, *Criminal Procedure* (3rd ed.) pp. 41-42, 456-457.
23 Dickson, *Evidence* (3rd ed.) §337; Macdonald, *Criminal Law* (5th ed.) 329.
24 Criminal Procedure (Scotland) Act, 1887 (50 & 51 Vict. c. 35), s. 69; Macdonald, *Criminal Law* (5th ed.) 328.
25 Criminal Procedure (Scotland) Act, 1887 (50 & 51 Vict. c. 35), s. 19.
26 Dickson, *Evidence* (3rd ed.) §339.
27 Dickson, *Evidence* (3rd ed.) §338.
28 *Macdougall* v. *Maclullich*, 1887, 14 R. (J.) 17; Macdonald, *Criminal Law* (5th ed.) 328. See also *Willis* v. *H.M. Advocate*, 1941 J.C. 1.
29 For a reference to the earlier cases, see Dickson, *Evidence* (3rd ed.) §289.
30 *Little* v. *Smith*, 1847, 9 D. 737. See the comments on this case in Dickson, *Evidence* (3rd ed.) §290.
31 *Cairns* v. *Marianski*, 1850, 12 D. 1286; 1852, 1 Macq. 212, L. Truro at p. 226; *Aitchison* v. *Aitchison*, 1877, 4 R. 899, L. Ormidale at p. 921; *McGhie* v. *McKirdy*, 1850, 12 D. 442, at p. 444; Dickson, *Evidence* (3rd ed.) §§293, 295. See also *Morrison* v. *Somerville*, 1860, 23 D. 232, L. J-Cl. Inglis at p. 238.

32. JUDICIAL ADMISSIONS IN ANOTHER CAUSE

Despite some earlier doubts[31] it now seems to be accepted that a judicial admission[32] made by a party in a civil cause may be proved against him as an extrajudicial admission in a subsequent civil cause in which he is also a party.[33] Even in the earlier decisions this general statement received some judicial approval.[34] As with any other extrajudicial admission it is not conclusive against the party making it,[35] and the question as to whether it was authorised by the party,[36] any qualifications attached to it,[33] and the circumstances in which it was made,[36] are all relevant to its importance or unimportance as a piece of evidence. On the same principle a judicial confession of guilt in a criminal cause, i.e. a plea of guilty, as distinct from the verdict in that cause, is admissible in evidence against the person making it in a subsequent civil cause to which he is a party.[37] So a plea of guilty to a charge of assault may be proved in evidence against the person making it in a subsequent action against him for divorce or separation on the ground of cruelty, whereas the fact that he was convicted after a plea of not guilty may not. The decree or verdict in an earlier cause, whether civil or criminal, as distinct from a judicial admission in that cause, is not admissible in evidence in another cause[38] except for the following limited purposes:— when it is the foundation of a plea of *res judicata*,[39] when it is a decree *in rem* or declaratory of status,[39] when it is an essential preliminary to the later action (as, for example, a decree constituting a debt which must precede an action of furthcoming), when its use in evidence in the later cause is authorised by statute,[40] and when the fact of its pronouncement, as distinct from its merits, is part of the relevant background of the later cause.

33. ADMISSIONS AND CONFESSIONS MADE AS A WITNESS IN ANOTHER CAUSE

Statements made by a party when giving evidence on oath in another cause, whether he was a party to the other cause or not,[41] are in general admissible in evidence against him as extrajudicial admissions or confessions.[42] A statement by a witness in a civil proof that he, and not the defender, was the writer of a threatening letter, was held admissible in evidence against him at his subsequent trial on a criminal charge of sending

---

[32] See § **48**.

[33] *Jackson* v. *Glasgow Corporation*, 1956 S.C. 354, L.P. Clyde at p. 359, L. Russell at p. 362, L. Sorn at p. 365.

[34] *Cairns* v. *Marianski*, 1850, 12 D., L. Medwyn at p. 1292, L. J-Cl. Hope at p. 1296; *Mollison's Trs.* v. *Crawfurd*, 1851, 13 D. 1075.

[35] Dickson, *Evidence* (3rd ed.) §293.

[36] *Aitchison* v. *Aitchison*, 1877, 4 R. 899, L. J-Cl. Moncreiff at p. 914. See also *Morrison* v. *Somerville*, 1860, 23 D. 232, at p. 238.

[37] *Mackay* v. *Bolton*, 1897, 4 S.L.T. 321; Dickson, *Evidence* (3rd ed.) §389.

[38] *Devlin* v. *Earl*, 1895, 3 S.L.T. 166; Dickson, *Evidence* (3rd ed.) §§386, 387; Alison, II, 67; *cf.* Bell, *Principles*, §2216. Three judicial departures from this rule, in actions of divorce for adultery, are discussed at § **164**.

[39] See §§ **50, 51**.

[40] e.g. Divorce (Scotland) Act, 1938 (1 & 2 Geo. VI. c. 50), s. 4 (2). See § **164**.

the threatening letter.[41] Evidence of a confession made by an accused in exculpation of another person, charged at an earlier date with the same crime, was held admissible against him,[43] although a deposition made by an accused in another person's sequestration was excluded when he was charged with embezzlement of the fund referred to in it.[44] In a civil action an oath on reference in an earlier action was held admissible against the trustees of the person making it,[45] and a statement made on oath in a party's earlier deposition as a haver,[46] in so far as it was in answer to questions proper to be put to a haver,[47] was allowed to be used against him on the merits of the action. The making of the admission will normally be proved by the evidence of the shorthand writer and the production of his notes, with such other corroborative evidence as may be available,[41] but even when shorthand notes were taken, proof by purely oral evidence has been said to be sufficient.[48]

34. IMPLIED ADMISSIONS AND CONFESSIONS

Since an admission or confession may in some cases be inferred from a party's silence or inaction in response to a statement made to him orally or in writing, evidence of such statements is relevant and admissible for this purpose.[49] Whether or not the party's silence or inaction gives rise to such an inference or implication is a question of fact in each case. The general rule is that when the statement made to the party is such that he would normally repudiate it if untrue, failure to repudiate will infer an admission of its truth.[50] The inference will be made more readily, at least in a civil cause, if the statement made to him is to his prejudice, and his failure to repudiate it may lead another person to believe in its truth.[51] When a merchant's account has been rendered, an implied admission of its accuracy will generally arise if no objection is made within a reasonable time[52] or if a partial payment has been made,[53] and, if certain items only are challenged, this will generally be regarded as an implied admission that the other items are accurate.[54] Failure to repudiate statements in a letter, however, relating

---

41 *Banaghan*, 1888, 15 R. (J.) 39.
42 Dickson, *Evidence* (3rd ed.) §288.
43 *Edmison*, 1866, 1 S.L.R. 107.
44 *Fleming*, 1885, 5 Couper, 552, at p. 581.
45 *Hunter* v. *Nicolson*, 1836, 15 S. 159.
46 *Boyd* v. *Anderson*, 1823, 2 S. 323; *Thomson* v. *Thomson*, 1829, 8 S. 156; *Home* v. *Hardy*, 1842, 4 D. 1184.
47 See *Dye* v. *Reid*, 1831, 9 S. 342.
48 *McGiveran* v. *Auld*, 1894, 21 R. (J.) 69, at p. 72.
49 Dickson, *Evidence* (3rd ed.) §368. For implied judicial admissions, see § **48**, sub-para. (d).
50 *Dowling* v. *Henderson & Son*, 1890, 17 R. 921.
51 Dickson, *Evidence* (3rd ed.) §367.
52 Dickson, *Evidence* (3rd ed.) §367; Phipson, *Evidence* (9th ed.) 260; *Smith* v. *Maxwell*, 1833, 11 S. 323, L. Cringletie at p. 324.
53 *George* v. *Scott*, 1832, 10 S. 443, at p. 445.
54 Dickson, *Evidence* (3rd ed.) §370; Phipson, *Evidence* (9th ed.) 260. The position may be different where there is a general objection to the account as a whole coupled with a specification of particular items: Dickson, *ibid.*

to a matter with which the recipient is not concerned, does not imply an admission of the truth of these statements.[55]

In a criminal cause no admission of guilt may legitimately be inferred from the fact that the accused, when charged with the crime, either says nothing or says that he has nothing to say, since he is entitled to reserve his defence.[56] A statement made in the hearing of the accused by a co-accused to the police officer who was apprehending both of them was held to be relevant to support an inference that, by remaining silent, the accused impliedly admitted the statement, and evidence of the statement was held admissible *quantum valeat* for that purpose.[57] Here also it is a question of fact in each case as to whether such an inference may legitimately be drawn, and the implied admission can only arise if the accused was reasonably called upon to repudiate the statement.[58]

35. ADMISSIONS AND CONFESSIONS CONTAINED IN WRITINGS

The same general principles[60] apply to written as to oral admissions and confessions. Thus a statement in a deed or other document, even if it concerns a transaction with a person who is not a party to the action, is admissible as an adminicle of evidence against the party who made it.[61] It is thought that an earlier doubt on this point[62] is the result of confusion between the admissibility as evidence of a statement against interest, with which this chapter is primarily concerned, and the sufficiency of such evidence as supporting a plea of personal bar.[63] The view that an admission contained in a document which had not been uttered,[64] such as a letter not dispatched[65] or a pleading not lodged in court,[66] is not admissible in evidence, is thought not to be valid as a general statement.[67] In an action of divorce for adultery,

---

[55] *British Linen Co.* v. *Cowan*, 1906, 8 F. 704, L. Ardwall at p. 708, L. J-Cl. Macdonald at p. 710, L. Stormonth-Darling at p. 713. For circumstances in which it was held that a letter, which did not repudiate a debt mentioned in the letter to which it was a reply, was not a written admission of the debt, see *MacBain* v. *MacBain*, 1930 S.C. (H.L.) 72.

[56] *Robertson* v. *Maxwell*, 1951 J.C. 11 at p. 14. *Cf.* Dickson, *Evidence* (3rd ed.) §370; Alison, II, 518.

[57] *Lewis* v. *Blair*, 1858, 3 Irv. 16.

[58] Dickson, *Evidence* (3rd ed.) §§370-371; Phipson, *Evidence* (9th ed.) 258.

[60] See §§ **29, 30.**

[61] See *Macfie* v. *Callender and Oban Railway Co.*, 1897, 24 R. 1156; 1898, 25 R. (H.L.) 19, an action of declarator that land belonging to the defenders was superfluous to their requirements, where evidence of writings and minutes concerning earlier negotiations by the defenders with other persons, for the sale or lease of the land, was considered by the court as relevant to the contention that the land was superfluous.

[62] Dickson, *Evidence* (3rd ed.) §299.

[63] See *Macfie* v. *Callender and Oban Railway Co.* (*supra*), 24 R. at pp. 1168 *et seq*; 25 R. (H.L.), L.C. Halsbury at p. 20.

[64] Dickson, *Evidence* (3rd ed.) 303.

[65] *Livingston* v. *Murray*, 1831, 9 S. 757.

[66] *Gavin* v. *Montgomerie*, 1830, 9 S. 213.

[67] See *Watson* v. *Watson*, 1934 S.C. 374, where *Livingston* v. *Murray* (*supra*) and *Gavin* v. *Montgomerie* (*supra*) were discussed. Since the document has not been uttered, it is not evidence of concluded intention, but it may be evidence of the writer's knowledge or state of mind, or it may bear on some disputed collateral issue.

a diary in the defender's handwriting,[68] and a draft letter written by the defender and found torn up in a bureau,[69] containing statements from which the commission of adultery could be inferred, were held admissible as evidence against her.

36. ADMISSIONS MADE VICARIOUSLY

An admission made by his predecessor in title may be proved against a party, if the predecessor, at the time when it was made, had the interest in the subject matter which the party subsequently acquired, and the admission relates to that interest. Thus in an action for recovery of a debt by an assignee[70] or by the executor of the original creditor,[71] evidence of an admission by the cedent made before the granting of the assignation, or by the deceased creditor, is admissible against the assignee or the executor, as the case may be, and evidence of an admission by a bankrupt before sequestration, if made without collusion, is admissible against the general body of creditors.[72] In the same way admissions made by a trustee in a sequestration may be admissible in evidence against the creditors.[73] An admission by an agent, made with the express authority of a party, is admissible in evidence against the party.[74] An admission made by an agent with his implied authority is similarly admissible, and it will usually be so regarded if it related to a matter in respect of which the agent was employed by the party, and if the agent was still so employed when it was made.[75] An admission, the making of which was outside the scope of the agent's authority, or an admission made after the agency has ceased as to matters which occurred during the agency, is not admissible in evidence against the principal.[76] Applying a similar principle, a partner's admission concerning

---

[68] *Creasey* v. *Creasey*, 1931 S.C. 9. But see § **391**.

[69] *Watson* v. *Watson* (*supra*).

[70] Dickson, *Evidence* (3rd ed.) §356. For the rules obtaining in England, where the matter has been more fully developed, see Phipson, *Evidence* (9th ed.) 239 *et seq*.

[71] *Ibid*. It is thought that the same rule would apply in an action for damages for physical injury, pursued by the executor of the person who was injured and subsequently died, in respect of a statement against interest made by the deceased. *Cf. Traynor's Executrix* v. *Bairds and Scottish Steel*, (O.H.) 1957 S.C. 311, where the executrix sought to use *in her favour* a statement made in precognition.

[72] Dickson, *Evidence* (3rd ed.) §357.

[73] *Buchanan* v. *Magistrates of Dunfermline*, 1828, 7 S. 35; *cf. Ellis* v. *White*, 1849, 11 D. 1347.

[74] Dickson, *Evidence* (3rd ed.) §358. See also § **304**, sub-para. (b), and *Dryburgh* v. *Macpherson* (O.H.) 1944 S.L.T. 116; *Fisher* v. *Fisher*, 1952 S.C. 347, L.P. Cooper at p. 351. These cases vouch the proposition that a letter written by a solicitor with the authority of his client may be regarded as the client's writ. *A fortiori*, it is thought, an admission in such a letter may be proved as an adminicle of evidence against the client. *Cf. Smith* v. *Smith*, 1869, 8 M. 239, where the solicitor's letters were not proved to have been authorised by the client.

[75] Bowstead, *Agency* (11th ed.) 230; Dickson, *Evidence* (3rd ed.) §359; *McLean and Hope* v. *Fleming*, 1871, 9 M. (H.L.) 38, at pp. 41, 44 (bill of lading signed by shipmaster); *Mitchell* v. *Berwick*, 1845, 7 D. 382, at p. 384 (admission by factor as to rent paid by tenant); *Aitchison* v. *Robertson*, 1846, 9 D. 15 (purchasing agent).

[76] Dickson, *Evidence* (3rd ed.) §359. The same general principle applies to admissions by

partnership affairs and in the ordinary course of its business is admissible in evidence against the firm.[77]   When a defender is sued in respect of the negligence of his servant, an extrajudicial admission by the servant regarding his alleged act of negligence is not admissible in evidence against the defender, since the servant had no implied authority to make it.[78]   A statement or admission by a servant, on the other hand, which it was part of the normal duties of his employment to make, such as a receipt contemporaneously issued for goods or money received on his employer's behalf, is admissible in evidence against the employer.[79]   An admission by one of a body of trustees may be proved *quantum valeat* against the estate which he represents, unless he has an interest adverse to the estate.[80]   Mere possession of a common interest, however, does not make an admission by one person so interested admissible in evidence against the others, so that an admission made by a part owner,[81] an acceptor of a bill of exchange[81] or a defender in an action,[82] as such, is not admissible in evidence against a co-proprietor, another acceptor or a co-defender.   If a party to an action has referred his opponent for information regarding some transaction to another person, a statement regarding the transaction by that person is admissible in evidence against the party.[83]   The admission of a spouse, as such, is not admissible in evidence against the other spouse, so that an extrajudicial admission of negligence by a husband is not admissible in evidence against his wife in an action in which, as pursuer, she seeks to establish negligence against the other driver.[84]   Either spouse, however, may have express or implied authority as the other's agent to make admissions which will be admissible against the other in accordance with the general principles mentioned above, the wife's *præpositura* being an obvious example.[85]

37. CONFESSIONS MADE VICARIOUSLY

When concert between two or more accused is proved, anything said or written by one of them in relation to the preparation, execution or completion of their common criminal enterprise is admissible in evidence against all of them.[86]   Apart from this, however, a confession of, or inferring,

directors and officials of limited companies, corporations and public bodies.   See Phipson, *Evidence* (9th ed.) 250.

[77] Partnership Act, 1890 (53 & 54 Vict. c. 39), s. 15.   The common law rule was the same: Dickson, *Evidence* (3rd ed.) §353; *Nisbet's Trs.* v. *Morrison's Trs.*, 1829, 7 S. 307, L. Glenlee at p. 310.
[78] *Livingstone* v. *Strachan Crerar and Jones*, 1923 S.C. 794; *Scott* v. *Cormack Heating Engineers*, 1942 S.C. 159.   See also Phipson, *Evidence* (9th ed.) 251.
[79] See Phipson, *Evidence* (9th ed.) 251.
[80] Dickson, *Evidence* (3rd ed.) §354.
[81] Dickson, *Evidence* (3rd ed.) §355.
[82] *Creasey* v. *Creasey*, 1931 S.C. 9; Dickson, *Evidence* (3rd ed.) §355.
[83] Phipson, *Evidence* (9th ed.) 255; Dickson, *Evidence* (3rd ed.) §358.   The principle applied in *Cooper* v. *Hamilton*, 1824, 2 S. 609 (affd. on expenses 1826, 2 W. & S. 59) was similar to this.   See also *Mackay* v. *Ure*, 1847, 10 D. 179.
[84] *Jackson* v. *Glasgow Corporation*, 1956 S.C. 354.
[85] Walton, *Husband and Wife* (3rd ed.) 201 *et seq.*
[86] Dickson, *Evidence* (3rd ed.) §363; Macdonald *Criminal Law* (5th ed.) 315-316.   See also *Cameron*, 1911 S.C. (J.) 110; *Tobin* v. *H.M. Advocate*, 1934 J.C. 60.

guilt by one accused is not admissible as evidence against another.[87] If evidence of a confession by one accused is led as admissible against him, and its terms implicate another accused, the jury must be directed to disregard it as evidence against the other accused.[88]

38. ADMISSIONS IMPROPERLY OBTAINED

The admissibility of evidence in civil causes which has been improperly obtained was mentioned in general terms in an earlier chapter,[89] where it was noted that a letter written by the defender and stolen by the pursuer has been held to be admissible in evidence against the defender.[89] There appears to be no case in which the Scottish courts have had to consider the admissibility of admissions obtained in some other improper way, as, for example, by threats or compulsion, or by trickery or deceit. It is probable that admissions made in response to a threatened use of legal diligence, even if that includes imprisonment, would be held to be admissible in evidence.[90] It is possible that an admission obtained by threats which were illegal and unwarrantable, or by deceit or trickery, might also be held to be admissible *quantum valeat*, the whole circumstances in which it was obtained being relevant to the question of whether the admission was true or false.[91]

39. CONFESSIONS IMPROPERLY OBTAINED—GENERAL

The admissibility of evidence in criminal causes which has been improperly obtained was mentioned in general terms in an earlier chapter,[92] where the admissibility of real and documentary evidence so obtained was dealt with in some detail. The following paragraphs in this chapter deal, from the point of view of admissibility in evidence, with the distinction between confessions which are regarded as properly, and those which are regarded as improperly, obtained. In modern practice extrajudicial confessions improperly obtained are held to be inadmissible in evidence against the accused person. It may be said in general terms that, whatever the circumstances in which it was made, a confession which is truly voluntary, may be proved against the accused in relation even to the gravest crimes,[93] although a voluntary statement by a foreigner, after he had been cautioned and charged, was held to be inadmissible because an interpreter was not present.[94] What is or is not voluntary

---

[87] *Milroy*, 1839, Bell's Notes, 291; *Kemp*, 1891, 3 White, 17; Dickson, *Evidence* (3rd ed.) §363. The silence of an accused person after a statement made by another person in his presence may be founded on as an implied admission, and evidence of the other person's statement may be admissible for that purpose. See § 34.

[88] *Monson*, 1893, 21 R. (J.) 5, at p. 9; *Stark and Smith* v. *H.M. Advocate*, 1938 J.C. 170, at p. 174; Dickson, *Evidence* (3rd ed.) §366.

[89] See § 2, sub-para. (b).

[90] See Dickson, *Evidence* (3rd ed.) §308; Gloag, *Contract* (2nd ed.) 489-490. This appears to be the English rule: Phipson, *Evidence* (9th ed.) 234.

[91] See Dickson, *Evidence* (3rd ed.) §307.

[92] See § 2, sub-para. (c).

[93] *Manuel* v. *H.M. Advocate*, 1958 J.C. 41, at p. 48; *Smith* v. *Lamb*, 1888, 15 R. (J.) 54; Hume, II, 333; Dickson, *Evidence* (3rd ed.) §§343, 344.

[94] *H.M. Advocate* v. *Ollson*, 1941 J.C. 63.

in this connection is mentioned in the following paragraphs. Conversations between fellow prisoners have been allowed to be proved,[95] even when obtained by eavesdropping,[96] but in a more recent case proof was refused of what several prisoners shouted to each other when in the cells.[97] A statement by an accused, otherwise admissible, will not be excluded merely because it discloses his previous bad character.[98]

40. CONFESSIONS MADE TO UNOFFICIAL PERSONS

It seems clear that confessions made to persons not associated with the judiciary or the prosecutor or the police are not regarded as improperly obtained merely because they are emitted in response to questions. Thus statements made by a sub-postmaster to Post Office investigators,[99] and by a railway employee to a stationmaster,[1] in answer to questions, were admitted in evidence against the accused. The view has been expressed that confessions are equally admissible in evidence, even if made as a result of threats, undue influence or inducements by persons not associated with the judiciary, prosecutor or police.[2] The decisions, however, do not uniformly support this view.[3] It is thought that fundamentally the matter is one of fairness to the accused[4] and the likelihood or otherwise that the inducement or threat resulted in the making of a false confession.[5] Letters written by prisoners to unofficial persons outside the prison, intercepted by the prison authorities, have been held to be admissible in evidence against them,[6] but in a more recent case only for the limited purpose of proving the accused's handwriting.[7] A statement made by the accused, while in prison on a charge of murder, to his brother, was admitted in evidence against him.[8] A statement made by the accused to a police surgeon, who visited his house in order to examine the body of the murdered person, was held to be admissible.[9]

95 *Brown*, 1833, Bell's Notes, 244; *Miller*, 1837, Bell's Notes, 244.
96 *Johnston*, 1845, 2 Broun, 401.
97 *H.M. Advocate* v. *Keen*, 1926 J.C. 1. The reason for the rejection is not stated.
98 See § **21**, note 55.
99 *Morrison* v. *Burrell*, 1947 J.C. 43.
1 *Waddell* v. *Kinnaird*, 1922 J.C. 40. It is thought that the presence of two police constables during the interrogation would now be regarded as making the evidence inadmissible, and that the dissenting opinion of Lord Ormidale would be followed.
2 Alison, II, 581; Dickson, *Evidence* (3rd ed.) §345.
3 See *Robertson*, 1853, 1 Irv. 219; *Turner*, 1853, 1 Irv. 285; *Graham*, 1876, 3 Couper 217; *cf. Honeyman* v. *Smith*, 1815, Hume, II, 335, note, where the confession, despite an earlier promise of immunity, was made in a declaration properly taken before the sheriff. See also *Simpson*, 1889, 2 White, 298.
4 *H.M. Advocate* v. *Aitken*, 1926 J.C. 83; *H.M. Advocate* v. *Rigg*, 1946 J.C. 1.
5 Dickson, *Evidence* (3rd ed.) §344 (first sentence).
6 *Fawcett*, 1869, 1 Couper, 183.
7 *H.M. Advocate* v. *Walsh*, 1922 J.C. 82. The Lord Justice-Clerk (Scott Dickson) found it unnecessary to decide whether the letter would have been admissible as a confession.
8 *H.M. Advocate* v. *Parker*, 1944 J.C. 49.
9 *Duff*, 1910, 6 Adam, 248. It may be noted, however, that in *Reid* v. *Nixon*, 1948 J.C. 68 (L. J-Cl. Cooper at p. 72) it was a matter of concession (although not of decision) that a police surgeon, when examining a person charged with a breach of s. 6 of the

41. THREATS OR INDUCEMENTS BY OFFICIAL PERSONS

A confession made as a result of threats, promises or undue influence by a sheriff, presiding magistrate or any other person officially connected with the judicial proceedings, or by the prosecutor or anyone on his behalf,[10] or by the police,[11] is improperly obtained and inadmissible in evidence against the person making it. Confessions made to prison officers are regarded as in the same category as confessions made to the police.[12] A statement obtained from the accused as a result of misrepresentation by the police has been held to be inadmissible.[13]

42. STATEMENTS MADE TO POLICE—GENERAL

It is difficult to deduce general rules on this topic,[14] because each decision depends upon its own facts.[15] A good deal, however, turns upon the stage of the police investigation[16] at which the statement is made. It has been said that there are three relevant stages—(1) before police suspicion has focussed on the accused, (2) while he is detained on suspicion, and (3) after he has been charged.[17] In none of the decisions,[18] however, has any distinction been explained between statements made during the second stage and those made during the third, and it is thought that only two stages require consideration, the stage before, and the stage after, suspicion has focussed upon the accused.

43. STATEMENTS TO POLICE—BEFORE SUSPICION FOCUSSED ON ACCUSED

This category includes any statement made by an accused person to the police during the early stages of their enquiry into the circumstances of a

Road Traffic Act, 1960, is acting as the hand of the police, and not as an independent medical referee. See also *Forrester* v. *H.M. Advocate*, 1952 J.C. 28.

[10] Alison, II, 581; Dickson, *Evidence* (3rd ed.) §344.
[11] Dickson, *Evidence* (3rd ed.) §344; *Watt*, 1834, Bell's Notes, 244; *Mahler*, 1857, 2 Irv. 634; *Millar*, 1859, 3 Irv. 406.
[12] *Proudfoot*, 1882, 9 R. (J.) 19.
[13] *Kerr* v. *Mackay*, 1853, 1 Irv. 213.
[14] It is sometimes said to be a question of admissibility of evidence, sometimes of judicial discretion. See *Waddell* v. *Kinnaird*, 1922 J.C. 40, at p. 49. The point is academic, and the two views were combined by Lord Ormidale (at p. 54), who, after citing Lord Young's opinion that it was not a question of competency, used the phrase "inadmissible in the sense that it should not have been admitted."
[15] *Chalmers* v. *H.M. Advocate*, 1954 J.C. 66, L. J-G. Cooper at pp. 77-78.
[16] Strictly speaking the court has nothing to do with how the police conduct their investigation: *Chalmers* v. *H.M. Advocate* (*supra*) at p. 77. The only question for the court is whether evidence of a statement ought to be admitted. Although as in *Stark & Smith* v. *H.M. Advocate*, 1938 J.C. 170, the opinions may dwell upon the improper conduct of the police, the ground of judgment is not that the police behaved wrongly, but that evidence wrongly obtained has been admitted. The police are concerned to discover who committed a crime, and it is the advocate depute or the procurator fiscal who decides what evidence shall be tendered at the trial.
[17] *Bell* v. *H.M. Advocate*, 1945 J.C. 61.
[18] *Bell* v. *H.M. Advocate* (*supra*); *Chalmers* v. *H.M. Advocate* (*supra*), at pp. 78, 82; *H.M. Advocate* v. *Rigg*, 1946 J.C. 1.

crime, at a time when they do not suspect him to be the perpetrator,[19] or when their suspicion is directed towards him only in the sense that he is one of a number of persons whose movements at the relevant times must be investigated in the course of the enquiry.[20] A statement which falls into this category is admissible in evidence against the accused in spite of the fact that it was made in response to questions by the police, and was not preceded by the usual caution.[21] When a member of the crew of a vessel had been identified as one of two persons who had committed a crime, and the police suspected that his accomplice might be one of the other members of the crew, they went on board and asked the accused, who was the ship's cook, to account for his movements on the night in question. In the course of the questions and answers which followed, the accused made an admission which implicated him as the accomplice. No caution had been given before the admission was made, but evidence of the statement was admitted.[20] The position might be the same when an accused is questioned merely because he lives in a house in which a crime has been committed.

44. STATEMENTS TO POLICE—AFTER SUSPICION FOCUSSED ON ACCUSED

This category includes any statement made at, or after, the time when the suspicions of the police have focussed upon the accused, and when he is under serious consideration by them as the perpetrator of the crime.[22] To decide when a particular statement falls into this, rather than into the first, category is sometimes difficult. It is not essential for its inclusion in the second category that the statement should be made while the accused is being detained by the police,[23] but, if it is so made, it is thought that it will usually be regarded as falling into this category. Detention, for this purpose, includes what has been called "detaining on suspicion," and cases where, although technically the accused has accompanied the police voluntarily in response to a request, he is not for practical purposes a free agent.[24] The rule governing the admissibility as evidence of statements falling into this category is discussed in the following paragraphs.

45. FAILURE TO GIVE USUAL CAUTION—ABSENCE OF SOLICITOR

In determining whether a statement in the second category is, or is not, admissible in evidence, it is usually relevant to consider whether the usual caution[25] was given by the police before the statement was made. It is proper practice that, when a person is charged with a crime, the caution

---

19 *Chalmers* v. *H.M. Advocate*, 1954 J.C. 66, L. J-G. Cooper at p. 78, L. J-Cl. Thomson at p. 81.
20 *Bell* v. *H.M. Advocate*, 1945 J.C. 61.
21 For the terms of the usual caution, see § **45**, note 25.
22 *H.M. Advocate* v. *Aitken*, 1926 J.C. 83; *Chalmers* v. *H.M. Advocate*, 1954 J.C. 66, L. J-G. Cooper at p. 78, L. J-Cl. Thomson at pp. 81-82.
23 *Chalmers* v. *H.M. Advocate* (*supra*), L. J-Cl. Thomson at p. 82.
24 *H.M. Advocate* v. *Rigg*, 1946 J.C. 1; *Chalmers* v. *H.M. Advocate* (*supra*), at pp. 75, 78.
25 The usual caution is that no reply need be made, but that if a reply is made, it will be written down and may be used in evidence.

should be given, since, without it, the reading of the charge may be interpreted by the accused as a question, or as an invitation to reply, in which case any statement then made is not spontaneous and voluntary. If, for some reason, it is necessary to delay the charging of the suspected person, it is probably desirable that a caution should be given as soon as the police enquiry has reached the point at which any statement subsequently made would fall into the second, rather than into the first, category. In what was probably a border-line case, the fact that a caution had been given half an hour before the statement was made seems to have weighed the balance in favour of its admissibility.[26] The omission of a caution at this point, however, does not necessarily make a subsequent statement inadmissible. So a statement in this category, made before the accused was cautioned and charged, was nevertheless admitted as being truly spontaneous and voluntary.[27] The mere giving of a caution will not render admissible statements which are improperly obtained.[28] A voluntary statement has not hitherto been rejected solely because the accused did not exercise his right[29] to send for his solicitor,[30] or because the police did not remind him of his right.[31]

46. DEFINITION OF VOLUNTARY STATEMENT—ANSWERS TO CHARGE—INTERROGATION BY POLICE

The general rule regarding the admissibility of all statements made to the police after their suspicions have focussed upon the accused can be stated both positively and negatively. A statement is admissible if it was truly spontaneous and voluntary, whether it was made before[32] or after[33] the accused was charged. It has been said that a voluntary statement is one which is given freely, not in response to pressure or inducement, and not elicited by cross-examination, apart from such questions as are necessary to elucidate the meaning of what has been said.[34] Negatively it may be said that a statement in this category is not regarded as voluntary, and is not admissible, if it was made in answer to questions as to the accused's association with the crime for which he is tried.[35] The ultimate test is that of fair-

---

[26] *Mills* v. *H.M. Advocate*, 1935 J.C. 77, at p. 81.

[27] *Hodgson* v. *Macpherson*, 1913 S.C. (J.) 68; *Costello* v. *Macpherson*, 1922 J.C. 9.

[28] *Chalmers* v. *H.M. Advocate*, 1954 J.C. 66, at p. 79.

[29] Criminal Procedure (Scotland) Act, 1887 (50 & 51 Vict. c. 35), s. 17.

[30] *H.M. Advocate* v. *Cunningham*, 1939 J.C. 61.

[31] *H.M. Advocate* v. *Fox*, 1947 J.C. 30.

[32] *Hodgson* v. *Macpherson*, 1913 S.C. (J.) 68; *Costello* v. *Macpherson*, 1922 J.C. 9, L. J-Cl. Scott Dickson at p. 12; *Mills* v. *H.M. Advocate*, 1935 J.C. 77, L. J-Cl. Aitchison at p. 81; *Chalmers* v. *H.M. Advocate*, 1954 J.C. 66, L. J-Cl. Thomson at pp. 81-82.

[33] *H.M. Advocate* v. *Laing*, 1871, 2 Couper 23; *H.M. Advocate* v. *Aitken*, 1926 J.C. 83, L. Anderson at p. 86; *H.M. Advocate* v. *McFadyen*, 1926 J.C. 93; *Wade* v. *Robertson*, 1948 J.C. 117, L. J-Cl. Thomson at p. 120.

[34] *Chalmers* v. *H.M. Advocate* (*supra*), L. J-Cl. Thomson at p. 82; *Manuel* v. *H.M. Advocate*, 1958 J.C. 41, at p. 48.

[35] *Hay*, 1858, 3 Irv. 181; *Stark & Smith* v. *H.M. Advocate*, 1938 J.C. 170; *Wade* v. *Robertson* (*supra*), at p. 120; *H.M. Advocate* v. *Rigg*, 1946 J.C. 1. See also the cases cited in notes 32, 33 above.

ness to the accused.[36] The youth of the person making the statement,[37] his mental or physical distress at the time it was made,[37] the gravity of the crime,[37] and the refusal to admit his solicitor to the police station[38] are factors which have influenced the court in holding that the statement was not voluntary, or, more generally, that its admission would be unfair. It is in - accordance with the general rule that any reply made to the charge, if the accused was cautioned,[39] is normally admissible in evidence,[33] but the reply may be regarded as inadmissible if it is in substance a repetition of an admission elicited earlier in response to improper cross-examination by the police,[40] or if its terms indicate that the accused misunderstood the nature of the crime with which he had been charged.[41] As already indicated,[42] no inference adverse to the accused arises from the fact that, when charged, he does not reply. A reply to a charge of murder was admitted in evidence although the subsequent trial was for culpable homicide.[43] In a converse case, when the charge at the trial was one of capital murder, evidence of a statement made in reply to an earlier charge of assault was disallowed,[44] but this decision is not to be regarded as establishing a general rule on this point which is still open.[45] Apart from the special case of capital murder, a reply may be admitted, even if the charge at the trial is more serious than that to which the reply was made, if both the crimes are in the same category, if both, for example, are crimes inferring dishonesty or crimes relating to personal violence, and if both crimes substantially cover the same *species facti*.[46] While it may sometimes be difficult to decide as to the effect upon admissibility of interrogation by the police before a charge is made, there can be no doubt that, once a charge has been made, any statements made in answer to questions put by the police are inadmissible.[47] Even an answer, made by the accused in a police office after he had been charged, to a question put, not to him but to another police officer, was disallowed on the ground that he might mistakenly have thought that the question was addressed to him.[48]

36 *H.M. Advocate* v. *Aitken (supra)*, at p. 86; *H.M. Advocate* v. *Rigg (supra)*, at p. 5.
37 *H.M. Advocate* v. *Aitken (supra)*; *H.M. Advocate* v. *Rigg (supra)*; *Chalmers* v. *H.M. Advocate (supra)*.
38 *H.M. Advocate* v. *Aitken*, 1926 J.C. 83.
39 See § **45**.
40 *Chalmers* v. *H.M. Advocate*, 1954 J.C. 66, at pp. 69-70, 77.
41 *H.M. Advocate* v. *McSwiggan*, 1937 J.C. 50.
42 See § **34**.
43 *Willis* v. *H.M. Advocate*, 1941 J.C. 1.
44 *H.M. Advocate* v. *Graham*, 1958 S.L.T. 167.
45 *McAdam* v. *H.M. Advocate*, 1960 J.C. 1; *H.M. Advocate* v. *Taylor*, 1963 S.L.T. 53.
46 *McAdam* v. *H.M. Advocate (supra)*; *H.M. Advocate* v. *Cunningham*, 1939 J.C. 61.
47 *H.M. Advocate* v. *Aitken*, 1926 J.C. 83, at p. 86; *Stark & Smith* v. *H.M. Advocate*, 1938 J.C. 170; *Wade* v. *Robertson*, 1948 J.C. 117. Earlier suggestions in such cases as *Paterson*, 1842, 1 Broun 388, *Wylie*, 1858, 3 Irv. 218 and *Gracie* v. *Stuart*, 1884, 11 R. (J.) 22, that questions may be put at the time when the charge is made, would not now, it is thought, be acceptable.
48 *H.M. Advocate* v. *Lieser*, 1926 J.C. 88.

CHAPTER V.

PROOF—JUDICIAL ADMISSIONS—RES JUDICATA—
JUDICIAL KNOWLEDGE

47. PROOF—GENERAL

Evidence, although the most important, is not the only method of establishing facts. In civil causes, subject to some exceptions in consistorial actions,[1] evidence is unnecessary and may be inadmissible if the fact to be proved has been judicially admitted by the other party, has already been adjudicated upon by a competent court (*res judicata*), or is within judicial knowledge. Judicial admissions, *res judicata* and judicial knowledge, in civil and criminal causes, are dealt with in this chapter. Presumptions, which may render evidence inadmissible[2] or unnecessary,[3] or which affect the burden of proof, are dealt with in the next chapter.

48. JUDICIAL ADMISSIONS—CIVIL CAUSES

(a) **General.** In civil actions, other than consistorial,[4] judicial admissions are in themselves, and without anything more, conclusive against the party making them, for the purposes of the action in which they are made.[5] In order to be the equivalent of proof and to make evidence of the fact to be proved unnecessary, they must be clear and unequivocal, and must be read along with any qualifications and explanations which accompany them.[6] A qualified admission may be founded upon as the equivalent of proof by the party in whose favour it is made only if he is able to disprove the qualification, and this is true whether the qualification is intrinsic or extrinsic.[7] If the proof

---

1 See § **161.**
2 See § **55.**
3 See §§ **56** *et seq.*
4 See § **161.**
5 Stair, iv, 45, 5; Erskine, iv, 2, 33; *Scottish Marine Insurance Co.* v. *Turner*, 1853, 1 Macq. 334, at p. 340.
6 *Lee* v. *National Coal Board*, 1955 S.C. 151, at pp. 158-159; *Darnley* v. *Kirkwood*, 1845, 7 D. 595; *Chrystal* v. *Chrystal*, 1900, 2 F. 373; *Baikie* v. *Glasgow Corporation*, 1922 S.C. (H.L.) 144; *London & Edinburgh Steam Shipping Co.* v. *The Admiralty*, 1920 S.C. 309.
7 *Picken* v. *Arundale Co.*, 1872, 10 M. 987; *Chrystal* v. *Chrystal (supra)*, at pp. 375-376, 377-378; Dickson, *Evidence* (3rd ed.) §§312, 313; Bell, *Principles*, §2218.

allowed to a party who wishes to found upon a qualified admission is restricted to writ or oath, it is not sufficient for him to disprove the qualification by parole evidence.[8] When writing is essential to the constitution, as distinct from the proof, of a contract, a judicial admission that agreement was arrived at does not take the place of a writing.[9] Judicial admissions may be made in the following ways.

(b) Minute of Admissions. A minute lodged in process by a party, or by the parties jointly, is a competent method of recording admissions, and is the appropriate method of bringing them to the notice of a jury, who are denied access to the written pleadings.[10] A joint minute does not exclude consideration of admissions made in the closed record or of the terms of documents admitted in the closed record to be genuine,[11] but, unless the contrary appears, it excludes all other or additional evidence on the matters admitted.[12]

(c) Oral Admissions made at the Bar. In practice admissions are frequently made orally by counsel or solicitors at the bar, and are acted upon by the parties and by the court. The admission or consent is usually noted in the interlocutor following upon it, or, if made in the course of a proof, in the notes of evidence. If an interlocutor incorrectly records an admission thought to have been made by counsel, the party may nevertheless be bound by it unless the mistake is challenged at once.[13]

(d) Admissions in Closed Record. It is unnecessary to lead evidence to prove matters which have been admitted by the other party.[14] This is true only, however, of admissions, and is not true of unadmitted averments, even if made by the other party. The latter must be proved in the ordinary way by the party who wishes to found on them.[15] Subsidiary pleas and averments, made on the assumption that the party's principal contention may be overruled, are not construed as admissions fatal to the main conten-

---

8 See § **118**, note 16.
9 See § **92**, sub-para. (c).
10 Rules of Court, II, 142; *Lee* v. *National Coal Board* (*supra*), at pp. 159, 161. In the Court of Session either party may call on the other to admit any facts or documents: Rules of Court, II, 125.
11 *Nisbet* v. *Cairns*, 1864, 2 M. 863.
12 *London & Edinburgh Steam Shipping Co.* v. *The Admiralty*, 1920 S.C. 309.
13 *Lauder* v. *National Bank of Scotland*, 1918, 1 S.L.T. 43. See also *Whyte* v. *Whyte*, 1895, 23 R. 320 (consent by solicitor in sheriff court).
14 Admissions deleted from the pleadings before the record is closed are not binding on the party, but may be the subject of cross-examination and comment by his opponent. Dickson, *Evidence* (3rd ed.) §282; *Lennox* v. *National Coal Board* (O.H.) 1955 S.C. 438. Statements made in a Preliminary Act have the effect of formal admissions of fact: Rules of Court, III, 160 (g).
15 *Lee* v. *National Coal Board*, 1955 S.C. 151, L. Russell at pp. 158-159, L. Sorn at p. 160; *Stewart* v. *Glasgow Corporation*, 1958 S.C. 28, L.P. Clyde at p. 39, L. Russell at p. 45; *Wilson* v. *Clyde Rigging and Boiler Scaling Co. Ltd.*, 1959 S.C. 328 ("believed and averred"). *Cf.* Dickson, *Evidence* (3rd ed.) 417; Bell, *Principles*, §2218.

tion, if they are clearly stated as alternatives.[16] Admissions may be implied. Both in the Court of Session[17] and in the sheriff court[18] an averment made by one party of a fact within the knowledge of the other party is held by implication to be admitted if it is not denied by the other party. The words "not admitted" are not the equivalent of a denial for this purpose.[19] The different rule which applies when, as a result of prescription, the party wishing to found upon such an implied admission must prove his case by writ or oath, is mentioned later.[20] A reference by a party to a document for its terms is not an implied admission that the document exists, unless its existence is a fact within his knowledge.[21]

(e) **Special Case.** This is a statutory process[22] whereby the agreed statement of facts, presented to the court for its opinion upon the law, is binding upon all the parties to it, and renders evidence both unnecessary and inadmissible.

49. JUDICIAL ADMISSIONS—CRIMINAL CAUSES

A plea of guilty to a charge or to part of a charge, which is accepted by the prosecutor, and which is not later withdrawn with the leave of the court,[23] is a judicial admission which is conclusive against the accused. It enables the prosecutor to move for, and the court to pronounce, sentence, without evidence having been led. It is tendered in open court, in solemn procedure orally by the accused or his counsel or solicitor, and in summary procedure orally or by letter.[24] In solemn procedure, when the plea of guilty is recorded by the clerk of court, the accused, if not a company,[25] signs it, and the judge appends his signature.[26] In summary procedure the plea, when recorded, is signed by the judge or by the clerk of court.[27] If a plea of guilty is not accepted by the prosecutor, and he insists on his right[28] to lead evidence in

[16] Dickson, *Evidence* (3rd ed.) §277, and cases cited; *Miller* v. *Miller*, 1898, 25 R. 995.
[17] A. S. 11th July, 1828, s. 105; Maclaren, *Court of Session Practice*, 375; *Pegler* v. *Northern Agricultural Implement Co.*, 1877, 4 R. 435, at p. 438; *Central Motor Engineering Co.* v. *Galbraith*, 1918 S.C. 755, at pp. 765, 770; *Gilmour* v. *Scottish Clan Motorways* (O.H.) 1928 S.N. 19.
[18] Sheriff Court (Scotland) Act, 1907 (7 Edw. VII. c. 51) (as amended), Rule 44.
[19] *Ellis* v. *Fraser*, 1840, 3 D. 264, at p. 271. See also *Stephen* v. *Pirie*, 1832, 10 S. 279.
[20] See § 132, sub-para. (b).
[21] *Pringle* v. *Bremner & Stirling*, 1867, 5 M. (H.L.) 55.
[22] Court of Session Act, 1868 (31 & 32 Vict. c. 100), s. 63.
[23] The High Court of Justiciary has a statutory power in certain circumstances to allow a plea of guilty to be withdrawn: Criminal Procedure (Scotland) Act, 1887 (50 & 51 Vict. c. 35), s. 41. It is thought that it may be allowed by other courts in exceptional circumstances. See *Williams* v. *Linton*, 1878, 6 R. (J.) 12; *Spowart* v. *Burr*, 1895, 22 R. (J.) 30, at p. 33; *Nicol* v. *Brown*, 1951 J.C. 87.
[24] Summary Jurisdiction (Scotland) Act, 1954 (2 & 3 Eliz. II. c. 48), s. 26 (3). In solemn procedure, acceptance of a partial plea of guilty ought to be signed by the prosecutor.
[25] Criminal Justice (Scotland) Act, 1949 (12, 13 & 14 Geo. VI. c. 49), s. 40 (6).
[26] Criminal Procedure (Scotland) Act, 1887 (50 & 51 Vict. c. 35), s. 28.
[27] Summary Jurisdiction (Scotland) Act, 1954 (2 & 3 Eliz. II. c. 48), s. 28.
[28] *Strathern* v. *Sloan*, 1937 J.C. 76. The proper method of recording the plea in such circumstances is indicated in the opinions.

support of the charge, or if the court allows the plea to be withdrawn,[23] the fact that it has been tendered must not be used against the accused or disclosed to the jury, the accused must not be questioned about it even if he gives evidence inconsistent with it,[28] and he may be acquitted in spite of it.

Apart from the judicial admission contained in a plea of guilty, the only[29] method in a criminal cause whereby a fact may in certain circumstances be established without evidence is regulated by statute. In summary procedure[30] a minute of admissions may be accepted in lieu of evidence as proof of any fact admitted by the opposite party. (Agreed documents or copies may be the subject of a similar minute.) In solemn procedure[31] such a minute may be similarly accepted, but with reference only to a document (or its copy), the person by whom it was written, executed or received, and the time and place of its writing, execution or receipt. Both in solemn and in summary procedure such a minute is admissible only when the accused has legal assistance in his defence.

A special defence, such as that of self-defence, may suggest an implied admission by the accused that he did the act complained of, albeit justifiably, but it is thought that nothing in such a special defence can have the effect of relieving the Crown of the burden of proving the commission of the act, or of preventing the accused from contending that its commission has not been proved.[32]

50. RES JUDICATA—GENERAL

When a matter has been the subject of judicial determination by a competent tribunal, the determination excludes any subsequent litigation in regard to the same matter between the same parties on the same grounds.[33] In the case of some determinations (decrees *in rem*), which are mentioned in the next paragraph, the exclusion applies even when the parties are not the same. The plea of *res judicata*, so described, is a plea in bar of subsequent litigation, and in Scotland it is generally so regarded. In England it appears that a similar result is attained by regarding the earlier determination as conclusive evidence or conclusive proof in any subsequent litigation of the matters determined.[34] On either statement the result of a successful plea of *res judicata* is that evidence is neither necessary nor admissible with regard to the issues previously determined. Since the subject is not truly part of the law of evidence, it is dealt with only briefly[35] in this and the next

---

29 *Tullis* v. *Millar*, 1899, 1 F. (J.) 75; *Brown* v. *Macpherson*, 1918 J.C. 3, at p. 8.

30 Summary Jurisdiction (Scotland) Act, 1954 (2 & 3 Eliz. II. c. 48), s. 36.

31 Administration of Justice Act, 1933 (23 & 24 Geo. V. c. 41), s. 20, as amended by Criminal Procedure (Scotland) Act, 1938 (1 & 2 Geo. VI. c. 48), s. 12.

32 This was conceded by the Crown in *H.M. Advocate* v. *McGlone*, 1955 J.C. 14. See also *Owens* v. *H.M. Advocate*, 1946 J.C. 119, L. J-G. Normand at p. 124; Dickson, *Evidence* (3rd ed.) §374.

33 Dickson, *Evidence* (3rd ed.) §385.

34 Phipson, *Evidence* (9th ed.), 424-436.

35 For a fuller statement of this branch of law, see *Encyclopædia of the Laws of Scotland*, Vol. 12, pp. 550 *et seq.*, Vol. 9, pp. 395 *et seq.*

paragraph with reference both to civil and criminal causes and the relationship between them.

51. RES JUDICATA—CIVIL AND CRIMINAL CAUSES

(a) **Civil Causes.** The following elements are essential for a successful plea of *res judicata:*—(i) The earlier determination must be made by a competent court, which may be a foreign[36] or an inferior[37] court. (ii) The earlier determination must be pronounced *in foro contentioso*,[38] without fraud or collusion.[38] A decree by default[39] will support the plea, but a decree in absence[40] and a decree of dismissal,[41] will not. As to a decree resulting from a compromise, conflicting views have been expressed.[42] (iii) The subject matter of the two litigations must be the same.[43] (iv) The *media concludendi*, or points in controversy between the parties, in the two litigations must be the same.[44] Negligence arising from breach of common law duty and negligence arising from breach of statutory duty constitute one and the same *medium concludendi* for this purpose.[45] (v) Except where the earlier decree is a decree *in rem*, both litigations must be between the same parties or between their authors, successors, representatives, cedents or assignees.[46] When the earlier judgment is a judgment *in rem*, which includes for this purpose a judgment affecting status, a plea of *res judicata*

[36] Special provision is also made for the reciprocal enforcement of decrees between the different parts of Great Britain and Ireland: Judgments Extension Act, 1868 (31 & 32 Vict. c. 54); Inferior Courts Judgments Extension Act, 1882 (45 & 46 Vict. c. 31); between the British Dominions: Administration of Justice Act, 1920 (10 & 11 Geo. V. c. 81) Pt. II; and between United Kingdom and foreign countries: Foreign Judgments (Reciprocal Enforcement) Act, 1933 (23 & 24 Geo. V. c. 13).

[37] Stair, iv, 40, 16: *cf.* Erskine, iv, 3, 7. A decree of judicial separation pronounced by a competent inferior court in England has been held not to bar a later action for divorce for desertion in the Court of Session, which was the court of the domicile: *Murray* v. *Murray* (O.H.) 1957 S.L.T. 41.

[38] *Lockyer* v. *Ferryman*, 1876, 3 R. 882, L. Gifford at p. 911. In a sheriff court action defences must have been lodged: *Esso Petroleum Co.* v. *Law*, 1956 S.C. 33.

[39] *Forrest* v. *Dunlop*, 1875, 3 R. 15.

[40] Erskine, iv, 3, 6; *Mackintosh* v. *Smith and Lowe*, 1864, 2 M. 1261: 1865, 3 M. (H.L.) 6; *Fulton* v. *Earl of Eglinton*, 1895, 22 R. 823, L.P. Robertson at p. 824. A decree in an undefended consistorial action is a decree in absence although pronounced after proof: *Paterson* v. *Paterson*, 1958 S.C. 141.

[41] *Duke of Sutherland* v. *Reed*, 1890, 18 R. 252; *Menzies* v. *Menzies*, 1893, 20 R. (H.L.) 108, L. Watson at p. 111. *Cf. Malcolm Muir Ltd.* v. *Jamieson*, 1947 S.C. 314, L. Mackay at p. 321. See also *Paterson* v. *Paterson (supra)*.

[42] Maclaren, *Court of Session Practice*, 396, founding upon *White* v. *Lord Morton's Trs.*, 1866, 4 M. (H.L.) 53; *Jenkins* v. *Robertson*, 1867, 5 M. (H.L.) 27 (decree following a compromise will not support the plea). *Cf. Young* v. *Young's Trs.* (O.H.) 1957 S.C. 318, following *Glasgow and South Western Railway Co.* v. *Boyd & Forrest*, 1918 S.C. (H.L.) 14.

[43] *Leith Dock Commrs.* v. *Miles*, 1866, 4 M. (H.L.) 14, L. Chelmsford at p. 19.

[44] *North British Railway Co.* v. *Lanarkshire & Dunbartonshire Railway Co.*, 1897, 24 R. 564, L. Kinnear at p. 572; *Edinburgh & District Water Trs.* v. *Clippens Oil Co.*, 1899, 1 F. 899, L.P. Robertson at p. 907, L. Kinnear at p. 909; *Malcolm Muir Ltd.* v. *Jamieson (supra)*.

[45] *Matuszczyk* v. *National Coal Board* (O.H.) 1955 S.C. 418.

[46] Stair, iv, 40, 16; Erskine, iv, 3, 3; *Allen* v. *McCombie's Trs.*, 1909 S.C. 710, L.P. Dunedin at p. 715 (beneficiary); *Ryan* v. *McBurnie*, 1940 S.C. 173 (assignee).

will be upheld not only against the original parties, but against any other person who desires to litigate with regard to the same matter.[47]

(b) Criminal Causes. A conviction or an acquittal in a criminal court, even where the former proceeds upon a plea of guilty and without trial,[48] is *res judicata* in relation to any subsequent criminal proceedings upon the same charge.[49] A charge of assault and a subsequent charge of murder, as a result of death ensuing from the same assault, are regarded as different charges for this purpose.[50] The English practice, when pronouncing sentence in respect of the crime charged, of taking into account other crimes with which the accused is not yet formally charged, does not support a plea of *res judicata* when the accused is later charged in a Scottish court with one of these other crimes.[51]

(c) Civil and Criminal Causes Inter Se. Apart from the rare exceptions aftermentioned, the same matter may properly be adjudicated upon both in the criminal and in the civil court without justifying a plea of *res judicata* in either.[52] The exceptions to this rule have arisen where the proceedings in the criminal court were of a quasi-civil character and the parties in both proceedings were the same.[53]

52. JUDICIAL KNOWLEDGE—GENERAL

It is unnecessary, and sometimes incompetent, to lead evidence regarding matters which fall within judicial knowledge.[54] The judge will himself take notice of these matters, either because he is bound by statute to do so, or because it is customary for judges to do so. In general they are matters which can be immediately ascertained from sources of indisputable accuracy, or which are so notorious as to be indisputable. If a matter is one which is judicially noticed, a judge may refresh his memory or supplement his knowledge regarding it by consulting recognised works of reference, such as dictionaries[55] or text-books.[56] While it is unnecessary to prove matters

47 *Administrator of Austrian Property* v. *Von Lorang*, 1926 S.C. 598, L. Sands at pp. 620, 622, 627; 1927 S.C. (H.L.) 80. See also *Murray* v. *Murray* (O.H.) 1957 S.L.T. 41.
48 *Hilson* v. *Easson*, 1914 S.C. (J.) 99, L. Anderson at p. 107.
49 Macdonald, *Criminal Law* (5th ed.) 272, and cases there cited.
50 *Stewart*, 1866, 5 Irv. 310; *O'Connor*, 1882, 10 R. (J.) 40.
51 *Hilson* v. *Easson* (*supra*).
52 Hume, II, 71, 479; Dickson, *Evidence* (3rd ed.) §385; *Wood* v. *North British Railway Co.*, 1899, 1 F. 562; *Faculty of Procurators of Glasgow* v. *Colquhoun*, 1900, 2 F. 1192; *Wilson* v. *Bennett*, 1904, 6 F. 269; *Wilson* v. *Murphy* (O.H.) 1936 S.L.T. 564.
53 Dickson, *Evidence* (3rd ed.) §385; *Young* v. *Mitchell*, 1874, 1 R. 1011, L.P. Inglis at p. 1013; *Kennedy* v. *Wise*, 1890, 17 R. 1036.
54 This subject has been developed more fully in the English text-books. See Phipson, *Evidence* (9th ed.), 19-27.
55 e.g. *Edinburgh Corporation* v. *Lord Advocate*, 1923 S.C. 112; *Rutherford & Son* v. *Miln & Co.*, 1941 S.C. 125; *Inland Revenue* v. *Russell*, 1955 S.C. 237.
56 e.g. *Williamson* v. *McClelland*, 1913 S.C. 678; *G's Trs.* v. *G.*, 1936 S.C. 837, at pp. 847-848; *Henderson* v. *Somers*, 1876, 3 R. 997, at p. 998; *Whyte* v. *Whyte*, 1884, 11 R. 710, at p. 712. In considering the possible period of gestation, the court may adopt a wider latitude in this respect in affiliation cases than in cases concerning divorce and legitimacy,

within judicial knowledge, evidence may sometimes be necessary regarding their applicability or inapplicability to the particular case.[57] Apart from the matters which are recognised as being within judicial knowledge, it is improper for a judge to proceed upon his personal knowledge of the facts in issue,[58] or upon his own examination of passages in text-books.[59] Thus he may not use his own observations of a locus[60] or of documents,[61] made after the conclusion of a proof, to contradict or supplement the evidence of the witnesses.

53. MATTERS WITHIN JUDICIAL KNOWLEDGE

The following matters have been judicially noticed in the Scottish courts:—

(a) **Acts of Parliament and Statutory Orders.** With certain exceptions, these must, by statute, be judicially noticed, and evidence regarding them would be excluded. They are dealt with more fully later.[62] Acts of Sederunt and Acts of Adjournal are also mentioned later.[62] It is the duty of counsel and of solicitors to draw the attention of the court to the existence of any relevant statute, whether it appears to assist the party concerned or not.[63]

(b) **Law and Judicial Procedure.** Scots law, including Scottish judicial decisions in the House of Lords and the lower courts, and the practice and procedure of the Scottish courts, are within judicial knowledge, and evidence regarding these matters is excluded. Failure on the part of counsel or solicitors to draw the attention of the court to a relevant authority may be reflected in the award of expenses.[64] Judicial notice is also taken, as having a persuasive effect, of decisions of the Judicial Committee of the Privy Council, of the House of Lords in English cases,[65] and of the English courts, having reference to a branch of law assimilated to Scots Law, or to the interpretation of a statute which applies also to Scotland. The necessity for proof of English law and foreign law in general is dealt with later.[66]

where the proof must be beyond reasonable doubt: *Preston-Jones* v. *Preston-Jones* [1951] A.C. 391, L. Normand at p. 407.
[57] See generally *Gibb* v. *Edinburgh and District Tramways Co.*, 1912 S.C. 580; *Dyer* v. *Wilsons & Clyde Coal Co.*, 1915 S.C. 199.
[58] *Morrison* v. *Monro*, 1854, 1 Irv. 599.
[59] *Davie* v. *Magistrates of Edinburgh*, 1953 S.C. 34, at p. 41.
[60] *Hattie* v. *Leitch*, 1889, 16 R. 1128. With regard to inspections by jurors, see *Sutherland* v. *Prestongrange Coal Co.*, 1888, 15 R. 494; *Hope* v. *Gemmell*, 1898, 1 F. 74. Cf. *Sime* v. *Linton*, 1897, 24 R. (J.) 70.
[61] *McCann* v. *Adair*, 1951 J.C. 127. See also § **414**, sub-para. (c).
[62] See §§ **193** et seq.
[63] *Glebe Sugar Refining Co.* v. *Greenock Harbour Trs.*, 1921 S.C. (H.L.) 72.
[64] *Glebe Sugar Refining Co.* v. *Greenock Harbour Trs.* (supra); *Mitchell* v. *Mackersy*, 1905, 8 F. 198; *Baker* v. *Glasgow Corporation*, 1916 S.C. 199.
[65] As to the effect of a House of Lords decision in an English case, see *Orr Ewing* v. *Orr Ewing's Trs.*, 1884, 11 R. 600; 1885, 13 R. (H.L.) 1; *Glasgow Corporation* v. *Central Land Board*, 1956 S.C. (H.L.) 1. In *McMillan* v. *B.P. Refinery (Grangemouth) Ltd.*, 1961 S.L.T. (Notes) 79, it appears to have been accepted without comment by the Second Division that a decision of the Court of Session was over-ruled by a later House of Lords decision in an English case.
[66] See § **415**.

(c) Facts of History and Public National Events. Examples of these are the history of the unions and divisions of the Christian churches,[67] and the oath taken by the Sovereign on accession to the throne regarding the rights of the Church of Scotland.[68]

(d) Facts of General Economic and Social Custom and Behaviour. Examples include the facts of the calendar,[69] general economic conditions,[70] changes in the value of money,[71] the general practices of business men and bankers,[72] the normal scope and effect of recognised classes of contracts,[73] the conditions of the local labour market and the average wages of different classes of workmen,[74] the differences between the habits and equipment of legitimate anglers and salmon poachers,[75] and the accepted conventions of society.[76]

(e) Facts of Nature. Examples include the normal period of human gestation,[77] fertility,[78] and survivance,[79] the mischievous habits of children,[80] the vicious propensities of animals,[81] (but not the effect of hand-stripping in the milking of cows)[82] and the elementary principles of dynamics.[83]

---

[67] *Renouf's Trs.* v. *Haining*, 1919 S.C. 497.

[68] *McCormick* v. *Lord Advocate*, 1953 S.C. 396, at p. 410.

[69] *Goodwin*, 1837, 1 Swin. 431.

[70] *Naismith* v. *Assessor for Renfrewshire*, 1921 S.C. 615.

[71] *Sands* v. *Devan*, 1945 S.C. 380; *Kelly* v. *Glasgow Corporation*, 1949 S.C. 496: 1951 S.C. (H.L.) 15.

[72] *Crerar* v. *Bank of Scotland*, 1921 S.C. 736; 1922 S.C. (H.L.) 137.

[73] *Muirhead & Turnbull* v. *Dickson*, 1905, 7 F. 686; *Taylor* v. *Wylie & Lochhead*, 1912 S.C. 978.

[74] *Keane* v. *Mount Vernon Colliery Co.*, 1933 S.C. (H.L.) 1, L. Buckmaster at p. 6; *Moore* v. *Harland & Wolff*, 1937 S.C. 707.

[75] *Oliver* v. *Hislop*, 1946 J.C. 20; *Cruickshank* v. *Smith*, 1949 J.C. 134.

[76] *Bennet Clark* v. *Bennet Clark*, 1909 S.C. 591; *Ross* v. *Ross*, 1930 S.C. (H.L.) 1.

[77] See § **169.**

[78] *G.'s Trs.* v. *G.*, 1936 S.C. 837. The court was primarily concerned to declare, as applicable in all but a certain class of future cases, a rebuttable *presumptio juris* that fertility ends at fifty-three years. The facts regarding normal capacity for child-bearing, however, on which this presumption was founded, were regarded as being within judicial knowledge.

[79] The presumption in favour of survivance (see § **69**) has been recognised as terminating at a hundred years from the date of birth (see, e.g., *Bruce* v. *Smith*, 1871, 10 M. 130). This recognition was based on judicial knowledge of the ages normally attained by human beings.

[80] *Taylor* v. *Glasgow Corporation*, 1922 S.C. (H.L.) 1.

[81] *Hennigan* v. *McVey*, 1882, 9 R. 411; *Harper* v. *Great North of Scotland Railway Co.*, 1886, 13 R. 1139.

[82] *Dickie* v. *Corbett*, 1954 J.C. 57, L. Sorn at p. 65, L. J-G. Cooper at pp. 62-63.

[83] *Ballard* v. *North British Railway Co.*, 1923 S.C. (H.L.) 43; *Carruthers* v. *Macgregor*, 1927 S.C. 816, at pp. 819-820.

CHAPTER VI

PROOF—PRESUMPTIONS

54. PRESUMPTIONS—GENERAL

A presumption has been said to be an inference as to the existence of one fact from a knowledge of the existence of another fact, drawn solely by virtue of previous experience of the ordinary connection between the known and inferred facts, and independent of any process of reasoning in the particular case. It has been said to differ from an inference from circumstantial evidence in that the latter is the result of reason exercised upon the facts of the particular case, or of reason and experience combined.[1] Various classifications of presumptions have been attempted, but none is entirely satisfactory or particularly useful. It is proposed to mention only the threefold classification of presumptions *juris et de jure, juris tantum,* and *hominis vel judicis.* Presumptions *juris et de jure* are irrebuttable, and, as rules of one or other of the branches of substantive law, do not fall within the scope of the law of evidence except in the sense that they exclude evidence. Presumptions *juris tantum* and *hominis vel judicis* may to a greater or less degree take the place of evidence and affect the burden of proof,[2] one of their principal uses being to establish facts which, by their nature, are incapable of proof by direct evidence.

55. IRREBUTTABLE PRESUMPTIONS JURIS ET DE JURE

These cannot be contradicted by evidence to the contrary, however

[1] Dickson, *Evidence* (3rd ed.) §§64, 109.
[2] Dickson, *Evidence* (3rd ed.) §§27, 115.

strong.[3] In most cases they are rules of the branches of the substantive law to which they relate rather than of the law of evidence. In some cases they resemble fictions of law,[4] and they arise both from statute and from the common law. They are sometimes based on a reasonable inference from the established facts, but frequently arise only from considerations of public policy.[5] The following are a few examples: (*a*) that a right is satisfied or abandoned if the creditor has abstained from its enforcement for twenty years (long negative prescription):[6] (*b*) that if there has been possession of heritage for twenty years on a habile title, the earlier title is in order (long positive prescription):[7] (*c*) that a pupil is incapable of giving proper consent to a contract,[8] a child under eight years of age of committing a crime or offence,[9] a girl under sixteen years of age of consenting to sexual intercourse,[10] a person under sixteen years of age of consenting to marriage:[11] (*d*) that a woman who conceals her pregnancy throughout its whole period, and fails to call for or make use of help, is criminally indifferent to the fate of her child;[12] (*e*) in virtue of the Companies Act,[13] that a certificate of incorporation indicates compliance with the initial formalities regarding registration of the company; that, unless a poll is demanded, a chairman's declaration that an extraordinary or special resolution is carried, indicates that the requisite majority voted in its favour.[14]

56. REBUTTABLE PRESUMPTIONS—JURIS TANTUM AND HOMINIS VEL JUDICIS

A presumption *juris* differs[15] from a presumption *hominis vel judicis* in that it has been recognised as such by statute, custom or judicial decision.[16]

---

3 Stair, iv, 45, 14; Erskine, iv, 2, 35.

4 For the distinction between them, see Erskine, iv. 2, 38.

5 Dickson, *Evidence* (3rd ed.) §111. If a statute provides that A "shall be deemed to be" B, the court may not hold that A is not in fact B, but is bound by the statutory presumption: *Ferguson* v. *Macmillan*, 1954 J.C. 38, L. J-G. Cooper at p. 44.

6 Act, 1617, c. 12; Conveyancing (Scotland) Act, 1924 (14 & 15 Geo. V. c. 27), s. 17; Bell, *Principles*, §606.

7 Act, 1617, c. 12; Conveyancing (Scotland) Act, 1924 (14 & 15 Geo. V. c. 27), s. 16; Bell, *Principles*, §606.

8 Stair, i, 10, 13; Erskine, iii, 1, 16.

9 Children and Young Persons (Scotland) Act, 1937 (1 Edw. VIII and 1 Geo. VI. c. 37), s. 55. The common law rule is that no child under seven years of age may be punished for crime. Hume I. 35; Alison, I, 666. A boy of under fourteen years of age has been convicted of rape. *Lord Advocate* v. *Fulton*, 1841, 2 Swin. 564.

10 Criminal Law Amendment Act, 1885 (48 & 49 Vict. c. 69), ss. 4, 5; Criminal Law, Amendment Act, 1922 (12 & 13 Geo. V. c. 56), s. 1.

11 Age of Marriage Act, 1929 (19 & 20 Geo. V. c. 36), s. 1.

12 Hume, I, 293; Alison, I, 153; Concealment of Birth (Scotland) Act, 1809 (49 Geo. III c. 14), s, 2.

13 1948 (11 & 12 Geo. VI. c. 38).

14 *Ibid.* s. 15 (1); s. 141 (3).

15 For a discussion of the difference, see *Millar* v. *Mitchell, Cadell & Co.*, 1860, 22 D. 833, at pp. 844-845.

16 Erskine, iv, 2, 37. For an example of the creation of such a presumption by judicial decision, see *G.'s Trs.* v. *G.*, 1936 S.C. 837 (Court of Seven Judges).

Until it has been so recognised it is a presumption of fact only.[17] In general the fact or facts which bring it into existence are well-defined, easily ascertainable and of general occurrence. Presumptions *hominis vel judicis*, sometimes called presumptions of fact, on the other hand, emerge, if they emerge at all, only after consideration of the particular circumstances of each case,[18] and are frequently difficult to distinguish from the inference drawn from circumstantial evidence.[19] Judicial recognition of such a presumption in one case is a precedent for its subsequent recognition in another case only where the circumstances are identical or closely analogous. An example of this distinction between the two types of presumption may be seen by comparing the presumption that (subject to certain exceptions) a woman of fifty-three years of age is incapable of child-bearing,[20] which is a *presumptio juris*, with the presumption (*hominis vel judicis*) of unseaworthiness when a ship breaks down or sinks soon after commencing its voyage.[21] The presumption regarding child-bearing inevitably arises as soon as the age of the woman has been proved or admitted. The presumption of unseaworthiness emerges only if it is justified by the whole circumstances, proved or admitted, of the particular case.

57. EFFECT OF REBUTTABLE PRESUMPTIONS ON EVIDENCE AND PROOF

Rebuttable presumptions of both classes vary in strength, but all are conclusive in the absence of contradiction.[22] It follows from this that the onus of rebutting such a presumption is on the party who wishes to contradict it, and this he may generally do either by disproving the existence of the presumed fact or by proving facts from which a stronger contrary presumption arises.[23] The strength or weakness of a presumption is important only if there is such contrary evidence or contrary presumption. A *presumptio juris* is not necessarily stronger than a *presumptio hominis vel judicis*. The presumption of innocence, for example, which is a *presumptio juris*, is displaced in the courts, as a matter of every day occurrence, by presumptions *hominis vel judicis* and by circumstantial evidence.[24] A general presumption, however, is weaker than, and will be displaced by, a special presumption arising from the facts of the particular case.[25] So the general presumption in

---

[17] *Millar* v. *Mitchell, Cadell & Co. (supra)*, at pp. 844, 845.

[18] Erskine, iv, 2, 36, 37.

[19] *Millar* v. *Mitchell, Cadell & Co. (supra)*, at p. 844. An inference which is not sufficiently strong to place upon the party adversely affected by it the burden of displacing it, ought not to be regarded as a presumption but merely as an item of circumstantial evidence. As to circumstantial evidence, see §§ **8** *et seq.*

[20] *G.'s Trs.* v. *G. (supra)*.

[21] For examples of the many facts which may have to be considered before the presumption arises, see Lord Shaw in *Klein* v. *Lindsay*, 1911 S.C. (H.L.) 9, at pp. 14-15.

[22] Erskine, iv, 2, 36, 37; Dickson, *Evidence* (3rd ed.) §112.

[23] The onus may also be discharged by referring to the opponent's oath: see §§ **308** *et seq.* The circumstances in which proof is restricted to writ or oath are referred to later: see §§ **117** *et seq.*, **131** *et seq.*

[24] Dickson, *Evidence* (3rd ed.) §112; *Campbell* v. *Campbell*, 1866, 4 M. 867, L. Ardmillan at p. 988.

[25] *Millar* v. *Mitchell, Cadell & Co.*, 1860, 22 D. 833, L. Neaves at p. 847. It is thought

favour of seaworthiness[26] may be displaced by a special presumption of unseaworthiness arising from the fact that the ship in question foundered at the commencement of the voyage, the general presumption in favour of sanity by the special presumption arising from the appointment on the ground of insanity of a *curator bonis* to the estate of the person concerned,[27] and the general presumption of innocence by the special presumption of guilt arising from the accused's possession of recently stolen property in criminative circumstances.[28] The standard of proof required for the rebuttal of presumptions is mentioned later.[29]

58. EXAMPLES OF REBUTTABLE PRESUMPTIONS

Each branch of substantive law has associated with it its own group of presumptions, and the text-books on these subjects should be referred to for a more detailed study. To provide a complete list of presumptions in a book on the law of evidence is neither possible nor particularly helpful. An attempt, however, has been made in the following paragraphs of this chapter to indicate some of the main groups of rebuttable presumptions, with examples in each group of the leading presumptions, and of the contrary presumptions where they exist. Reference may also be made to the examples[30] given in the next chapter of inferences of fact which have been held to have the same effect as presumptions in discharging or shifting the burden of proof.

59. PRESUMPTIONS AS TO PHYSICAL AND MENTAL POWERS OF A HUMAN BEING

(a) General. There is a general presumption that the ordinary course of nature has run, and that human beings possess ordinary powers and faculties both physical and mental.[31]

(b) Duration of Life. This is mentioned later in connection with the continuance of existing conditions.[32]

(c) Child-Begetting and Child-Bearing. Men are presumed to be capable of begetting children within the usual ages.[31] With regard to child-bearing, where interests other than those of possible unborn children are affected, the law still appears to be that there is no age at which a woman is presumed incapable of giving birth to a child.[33] Where no such interests are affected,

that this rule will solve in practice most questions arising from the relative strengths of presumptions. It does not assist in the rare case where a conflict between two general presumptions arises from the pleadings on the question of who must lead in the proof. See, for example, § **73**, note 2.

26 *Klein* v. *Lindsay*, 1911 S.C. (H.L.) 9, L. Shaw at pp. 14-15.
27 See § **59**, sub-para. (d).
28 See § **68**.
29 See §§ **82, 83** (criminal causes), §§ **85, 86** (civil causes).
30 See §§ **78, 81** (civil causes), § **83** (criminal causes).
31 Dickson, *Evidence* (3rd ed.) §114 (1).
32 See § **69**.
33 *G.'s Trs.* v. *G.*, 1936 S.C. 837 (Seven Judges), L.P. Normand at p. 844, L. J-Cl. Aitchison at p. 849; *Rackstraw* v. *Douglas*, 1917 S.C. 284; *Inland Revenue* v. *Bone*, 1927 S.C. 698.

however, there is a presumption *juris tantum* that a woman who has ~ttained 53 years of age is incapable of bearing children.[34]

(d) Sanity. A person is presumed to be sane.[35] The contrary presumption is that a person who has been cognosced,[36] or to whom, in accordance with modern practice, a tutor-at-law[37] or *curator bonis* has been appointed in respect of unsoundness of mind, is insane.[38]

60. PRESUMPTIONS SUPPORTING REGULARITY AND VALIDITY

(a) General. The general presumption is *omnia rite et solenniter acta præsumuntur.*[39] This presumption applies with especial force when it is sought to disturb an earlier transaction after a long period of time. When this occurs "every intendment should be made in favour of what has been done as being lawfully and properly done."[40]

(b) Judicial and Official Actings. There is a presumption that a person purporting to act in a public capacity has authority to do so. This presumption has been applied to an interim sheriff-substitute,[41] a procurator-fiscal[42] and other officials.[43] In connection with revenue officials there are statutory presumptions to the same effect.[44]

(c) Acts of Administrative and Public Bodies. There is a presumption, when a course of procedure has followed upon the public act of an administrative body, that the act, and the formalities associated with it, were legally and regularly performed.[45] On the other hand there is no presumption that the weight of a motor-lorry, as recorded on a railway weigh-bridge, is accurate.[46]

(d) Feuing Restrictions. There is a presumption that a building which has existed for a long time was originally constructed in conformity with the titles.[47]

[34] *G.'s Trs.* v. *G.* (*supra*).
[35] Bell, *Principles*, §2103; Dickson, *Evidence* (3rd ed.) §§27, 114 (1); *H.M. Advocate* v. *Mitchell*, 1951 J.C. 53. See also *H.M. Advocate* v. *Braithwaite*, 1945 J.C. 55, at p. 58.
[36] Dickson, *Evidence* (3rd ed.) §114 (1); Erskine, i, 7, 49; Bell, *Principles*, §2103.
[37] *Dick* v. *Douglas*, 1924 S.C. 787, provides an example of such an appointment.
[38] As to the presumption that the insanity continues, see § **69.**
[39] Dickson, *Evidence* (3rd ed.) §114 (4).
[40] *Bain* v. *Assets Co.*, 1905, 7 F. (H.L.) 104, L.C. Halsbury at p. 106.
[41] *Marr* v. *Procurator Fiscal of Midlothian*, 1881, 8 R. (J.) 21.
[42] *Hill* v. *Finlayson*, 1883, 10 R. (J.) 66.
[43] *McAlpine* v. *Campbell*, 1840, 2 D. 481 (schoolmaster); *McLeod*, 1858, 3 Irv. 79 (postmaster); *Smith and Milne*, 1859, 3 Irv. 506 (water bailiff); *Borthwick* v. *Lord Advocate*, 1862, 1 M. 94 (revenue officer).
[44] Inland Revenue Regulation Act, 1890 (53 & 54 Vict. c. 21), s. 24 (3); Income Tax Act, 1952 (15 & 16 Geo. VI. c. 10), s. 521.
[45] *Presbytery of Stirling* v. *Heritors of Larbert and Dunipace*, 1902, 4 F. 1048 (statutory commissioners); *Scott* v. *Mags. of Dunoon*, 1909 S.C. 1093 (local authority); *Hamilton* v. *Fyfe*, 1907 S.C. (J.) 79 (statutory order by local authority).
[46] *Grierson* v. *Clark*, 1958 J.C. 22.
[47] *Sutherland* v. *Barbour*, 1887, 15 R. 62.

(e) Judicial Records and Other Documents. It is presumed that the decrees or other acts recorded in old judicial records were validly and properly pronounced or performed.[48] When a deed appears to have been executed in accordance with the statutory solemnities, it is presumed that these solemnities have been complied with, and that it has been subscribed by the apparent granter of it.[49] This presumption does not apply to the untested signature of the drawer of a bill of exchange.[50] If the terms of a lost deed are proved by secondary evidence, the original deed is presumed to have been duly stamped,[51] and when a deed bears traces of having been stamped there appears to be a presumption that the stamp was for the correct amount.[51] The following documents are presumed to have been executed on the dates which they bear: holograph testamentary writings,[52] bills of exchange and acceptances or endorsements thereon,[53] and, at least for ordinary commercial purposes, other mercantile documents.[54]

(f) Business Books and Office Administration. Business books, if they appear to have been regularly kept, are presumed to be accurate.[55] When the regular practice of a business house with regard to the dispatching of letters has been proved, it is presumed that a particular letter was dispatched in the usual way.[56]

(g) Regular Marriages. The general presumption is thought to apply to the validity of a regular marriage, which is proved to have been duly solemnised and registered. This subject is mentioned later.[57]

61. PRESUMPTIONS REGARDING DONATION

There is a strong presumption against donation, the brocard *donatio non presumitur* being an understatement of the position.[58] When moveable property has passed from one person to another the onus placed by the presumption upon the person alleging donation is to prove it by evidence

---

[48] *Duke of Athole* v. *Lord Advocate*, 1880, 7 R. 583, at p. 589. See also *Heritors of Old Machar* v. *The Ministers*, 1870, 8 M. 168, at p. 169.

[49] *Brown* v. *Duncan*, 1888, 15 R. 511; *Ferrie* v. *Ferrie's Trs.*, 1863, 1 M. 291, at p. 298; *Baird's Trs.* v. *Murray*, 1883, 11 R. 153, at pp. 161-162, 164; *Young* v. *Paton*, 1910 S.C. 63. This is dealt with more fully at § **178**, sub-para. (b).

[50] *McIntyre* v. *National Bank of Scotland*, 1910 S.C. 150.

[51] See § **237**.

[52] Conveyancing (Scotland) Act, 1874 (37 & 38 Vict. c. 94), s. 40.

[53] Bills of Exchange Act, 1882 (45 & 46 Vict. c. 61), s. 13 (1).

[54] See § **107**.

[55] Erskine, iv, 2, 4; Dickson, *Evidence* (3rd ed.) §114 (2). See also *McLaren* v. *Liddell's Trs.*, 1862, 24 D. 577.

[56] Dickson, *Evidence* (3rd ed.) §§28, 114 (2), 304; *Robertson* v. *Gamack*, 1835, 14 S. 139; *Stock* v. *Aitken*, 1846, 9 D. 75; *Mackenzie* v. *Dott*, 1861, 23 D. 1310; *Guthrie* v. *Stewart*, 1926 S.C. 743.

[57] See § **155**.

[58] Stair, i, 8, 2; iv, 45, 17 (14); Erskine, iii, 3, 92; Dickson, *Evidence* (3rd ed.) §158; *Sharp* v. *Paton*, 1883, 10 R. 1000, L.P. Inglis at p. 1006; *Dawson* v. *McKenzie*, 1891, 19 R. 261, L.P. Robertson at p. 271; *Brownlee's Executrix* v. *Brownlee*, 1908 S.C. 232, L.P. Dunedin at p. 242.

which is reasonably convincing, and which is so clear as to displace all other explanations put forward in evidence as being reasonable in the known circumstances of the case.[59] If the transfer can on the evidence be ascribed to a purpose other than donation, the onus has not been discharged.[60] The presumption applies with more than its usual strength when the transfer is by a debtor to his creditor, the brocard (*debitor non presumitur donare*) being once again an understatement.[61] The general presumption applies to accumulated savings made by a wife from payments received from her husband for household maintenance, even if the husband is absent from the home, unless the separation is due to voluntary agreement, judicial decree or wilful misconduct of either spouse.[62] It applies also when services are rendered or money is lent by one person to another, the presumption being that payment for the services was intended[63] and that interest is payable on the loan.[64] When the person to whom services are rendered,[65] or a loan is made,[66] is a near relative, the onus of proving that the services were gratuitous or that the loan was free of interest is more easily discharged. When payments are made by a parent or by a person *in loco parentis* there may be a presumption, contrary to the general presumption, that the payments are gifts made *ex pietate*, in which event the onus is upon the person seeking repayment to prove the contrary.[67] Whether or not such a presumption arises must depend upon the exact relationship of the parties and the whole surrounding circumstances. There is a further reference to donation in the next paragraph, and the mode of proof of donation is dealt with in a later chapter.[68]

62. PRESUMPTION FROM ACKNOWLEDGMENT OF RECEIPT OF MONEY

An unqualified[69] written[70] acknowledgment of the receipt of money,

[59] *Grant's Trs.* v. *McDonald*, 1939 S.C. 448, L. Carmont at p. 471. The position is different when the subject is heritage and the disponee is infeft, and the Act, 1696, c. 25 applies, in which case the disponer or truster must prove trust by writ or oath of the disponee: see §§ **122, 123.**

[60] *Grant's Trs.* v. *McDonald* (*supra*), L.P. Normand at pp. 460-461. See also *British Linen Co.* v. *Martin*, 1849, 11 D. 1004, L. Fullerton at p. 1008, L. Jeffrey at p. 1011.

[61] Stair, i, 8, 2; Erskine, iii, 3, 93; Dickson, *Evidence* (3rd ed.) §165; *Johnstone* v. *Haviland*, 1896, 23 R. (H.L.) 6, L. Herschell at p. 9.

[62] *Preston* v. *Preston*, 1950 S.C. 253. See also *Smith* v. *Smith*, 1933 S.C. 701; *Logan* v. *Logan*, 1920 S.C. 537.

[63] *Landless* v. *Wilson*, 1880, 8 R. 289. See also *Taylor* v. *Forbes*, 1853, 24 D. 19. For the old authorities regarding the provision of board and lodging, see Dickson, *Evidence* (3rd ed.) §163.

[64] *Smellie's Executrix* v. *Smellie*, 1933 S.C. 725. Interest on an I.O.U. is presumed to be payable from the date of the demand for repayment of the principal sum: *Winestone* v. *Wolifson*, 1954 S.C. 77.

[65] *Anderson* v. *Halley*, 1847, 9 D. 1222; *Thomson* v. *Thomson's Tr.*, 1889, 16 R. 333; *Miller* v. *Miller*, 1898, 25 R. 995; *Urquhart* v. *Urquhart's Tr.*, 1905, 8 F. 42; *Russel* v. *McClymont*, 1906, 8 F. 821. For a modern case as to the provision of board and lodging, see *Turnbull* v. *Brien*, 1908 S.C. 313.

[66] *Smellie's Executrix* v. *Smellie* (*supra*).

[67] Dickson, *Evidence* (3rd ed.) §159; *Malcolm* v. *Campbell*, 1889, 17 R. 255, at pp. 257, 259; *Macalister's Trs.* v. *Macalister*, 1827, 5 S. 204.

signed by the granter, raises a presumption that the money was received on loan, or on some other footing inferring an obligation to repay, and places upon the recipient the onus of proving that it was not so received.[71] An I.O.U. is an acknowledgment producing this result,[72] the payee's endorsement upon a cheque in his favour is not.[73] It is not easy to reconcile the judicial dicta, but it would appear that the presumption arises not from the mere admission or proof that money has been paid, which has been said by itself to raise no presumption of any kind,[74] but because the written acknowledgment has been granted as a document of debt and is in the grantee's possession as such when repayment is demanded.[75] A judicial admission of the receipt of money does, however, raise a presumption of loan, or of an obligation to repay, if, but only if, the defender avers that the money was received as a gift,[76] unless the relationship between the parties is such as to raise a contrary presumption of the kind referred to in the last paragraph.[77]

63. PRESUMPTION THAT PAYMENT IS BY PROPER DEBTOR

When a debt has been paid, the presumption is that it has been paid by the debtor,[78] and when the payment has in fact been made by another it will *in dubio* be presumed to have been made with the debtor's funds.[79] The

[68] See §§ 149-151.

[69] For examples of *qualified* acknowledgments which were held not to give rise to the presumption, see *Duncan's Trs.* v. *Shand*, 1873, 11 M. 254, L. J-Cl. Moncreiff at p. 257 (qualification that sum received in payment of debt of honour); *Patrick* v. *Patrick's Trs.*, 1904, 6 F. 836 (qualification that sum received on loan bequeathed by borrower to lender in his will).

[70] As to proof of loan, see §§ 118-121.

[71] *Martin* v. *Crawford*, 1850, 12 D. 960; *Thomson* v. *Geekie*, 1861, 23 D. 693, L. Wood at p. 698, L. Cowan at p. 699, L. J-Cl. Inglis at p. 701; *Gill* v. *Gill*, 1907 S.C. 532, L. Low at p. 537. When the defender avers repayment, he must usually prove this by his opponent's writ or oath: see §§ 125, 127; and the same may be true if it is averred that the money belonged to the defender: see *Gill* v. *Gill* (*supra*).

[72] See § 119, sub-para. (c).

[73] See § 120.

[74] *Penney* v. *Aitken*, 1927 S.C. 673, L. Ormidale at p. 680, L. Anderson at p. 682; *Gill* v. *Gill* (*supra*), L. Low at p. 537; *Haldane* v. *Speirs*, 1872, 10 M. 537, L.P. Inglis at p. 541; *Duncan's Trs.* v. *Shand*, 1873, 11 M. 254, L. Neaves at p. 259. *Cf. Fraser* v. *Bruce*, 1857, 20 D. 115, at pp. 118-119, and Lord Murray's opinion in *Clark's Executrix* v. *Brown*, 1935 S.C. 110, at p. 118, that an unqualified judicial admission of the receipt of money gives rise to the presumption.

[75] *Wink* v. *Speirs*, 1868, 6 M. 657, L. Neaves at p. 658; *Haldane* v. *Speirs* (*supra*), L.P. Inglis at p. 541; *Duncan's Trs.* v. *Shand* (*supra*), L. Neaves at p. 259; *Nimmo* v. *Nimmo*, 1873, 11 M. 446, L. Neaves at p. 449, L. Cowan at pp. 449-450; *Dunn's Tr.* v. *Hardy*, 1896, 23 R. 621, L. Kinnear at p. 633; *Clark's Executrix* v. *Brown* (*supra*), L. J-Cl. Aitchison at pp. 120-121.

[76] *Penney* v. *Aitken* (*supra*), at pp. 681, 683; *Penman* v. *White* (O.H.) 1957 S.C. 338; *McVea* v. *Reid*, 1958 S.L.T. (Sh. Ct.) 60. *Cf. Malcolm* v. *Campbell*, 1889, 17 R. 255, L. Lee at p. 257, L. Kyllachy at p. 258, L. J-Cl. Macdonald at p. 259, where, contrary to what is stated in *Penman* v. *White*, the onus of proof was regarded as resting upon the pursuer. For a further comment on *Penman* v. *White*, see § 73, note 2.

[77] See § 61, note 67.

[78] Dickson, *Evidence* (3rd ed.) §189; Bell, *Principles*, §559.

[79] Erskine, iii, 4, 6.

D

presumption, though it may be weakened, is not displaced, if the payment has been made by the debtor's father.[80]

64. PRESUMPTION FROM APOCHA TRIUM ANNORUM

In the case of obligations prestable by termly payments, such as rents, feuduties or interest, the production of receipts for three consecutive termly payments raises a presumption that all prior instalments have been paid.[81] The presumption is dependent on the reiteration of written discharges without reservation or qualification regarding the earlier period,[82] and a single discharge, though covering three or more consecutive instalments, will not raise it.[83] Receipts for payments to account are not enough, though several of these, discharging in aggregate the amount due at a particular term, would be accepted as a receipt for that term,[83] and the presumption was held to apply where receipts for the balance of rent for five consecutive years were produced.[83] The three terms must be consecutive and the intervention of an unvouched term elides the presumption. Receipts for payments in driblets not appropriated to any term, but amounting in aggregate to payment for three years, would probably not raise the presumption.[84] Where one or more of the later discharges are by an heir the position seems doubtful,[85] but it is immaterial that one or more of the discharges were to the original debtor, and the rest to his representative or successor.[86] Discharges by a singular successor in lands, or an assignee of a bond, raise no presumption that earlier payments to the original landlord or creditor have been settled.[87] Receipts by a factor with a general power of management will probably suffice, but not by one who merely acts *ad hoc* in receiving rents.[88] Receipts by successive factors will not raise the presumption.[89] More recent opinion seems to support the view that the presumption may be rebutted by parole evidence,[90] the earlier view being that proof is limited to the writ or oath of the debtor.[91]

[80] *Welsh* v. *Welsh's Trs.*, 1878, 5 R. 542.
[81] Stair, i, 18, 2; Erskine, iii, 4, 10; Bell, *Principles*, §567; Dickson, *Evidence* (3rd ed.) §§177-184. The institutional writers deal with yearly or half-yearly payments. Dickson concedes quarterly instalments, but there is no authority in regard to payments at more frequent intervals save Rankine (*Leases* (3rd ed.) 321), who would extend the rule to even shorter periods.
[82] Stair, i, 18, 2; Dickson, *Evidence* (3rd ed.) §184.
[83] Dickson, *Evidence* (3rd ed.) §177; *Hunter* v. *Kinnaird's Trs.*, 1829, 7 S. 548.
[84] Rankine, *Leases* (3rd ed.) 321.
[85] Gloag, *Contract* (2nd ed.) 719, note 1.
[86] Dickson, *Evidence* (3rd ed.) §179; Rankine, *Leases* (3rd ed.) 321.
[87] Gloag, *Contract* (2nd ed.) 718.
[88] Stair, i, 18, 2; Dickson, *Evidence* (3rd ed.) §180. In Rankine's view it is enough if the granter of the receipts held the landlord's order to receive the rents (*Leases* (3rd ed.) 820).
[89] Dickson, *Evidence* (3rd ed.) §180.
[90] *Cameron* v. *Panton's Trs.*, 1891, 18 R. 728, L. Kincairney at p. 729; *Stenhouse* v. *Stenhouse's Trs.*, 1899, 36 S.L.R. 637. See also Bell, *Principles*, §567. *Hunter* v. *Kinnaird's Trs.*, 1829, 7 S. 548, where proof was limited to writ or oath, seems to have proceeded on the specialty that the receipts bore to be for the balance of the rent.
[91] Stair, i, 18, 2; Erskine, iii, 4, 10; Dickson, *Evidence* (3rd ed.) §184. See also Rankine, *Leases* (3rd ed.) 321.

65. PRESUMPTION AS TO PAYMENT OF HOTEL BILLS

There is a presumption that a hotel bill has been paid before the guest is allowed to leave the hotel, which places upon the hotelkeeper the onus of proving *prout de jure* not only the constitution but the subsistence of the alleged debt.[92]

66. PRESUMPTIONS FROM POSSESSION OR DESTRUCTION OF DOCUMENTS

There is a strong presumption that a deed found in the grantee's possession has been duly delivered.[93] The presumption may be rebutted by proof that possession was obtained by fraud, or for some purpose, such as for safe custody, which was not intended to place it outwith the granter's control.[94] Proof in rebuttal may be *prout de jure*,[94] unless the grantee is said to hold in trust for the granter, when proof must be by writ or oath.[95] When a will, which is known to have been made and to have been in the testator's custody, is not discovered on his death, he is presumed to have destroyed it *animo revocandi*,[96] and there is a similar presumption when an undelivered deed is found mutilated in the granter's possession.[97]

When a written obligation or document of debt is found in the hands of the debtor or cautioner[98] or of one of the obligants, it is presumed that payment has been made or that the obligation has been implemented or extinguished[99] (*chirographum apud debitorem repertum presumitur solutum*), but the presumption does not apply to bilateral deeds,[1] and is not easily applied to a heritable right which is not normally extinguished without a formal deed.[1] When the presumption applies and the creditor offers to rebut it by proving that he surrendered the document for some special temporary purpose without abandoning his right to it, it was at one time held that proof must be by the debtor's writ or oath, the creditor's averment being regarded as an averment of trust.[2] In more recent cases, however, proof *prout de jure* has been allowed, the question for decision being whether or not the document was truly delivered as a surrendered document of debt by the creditor to the debtor.[3] As always when fraud is averred,[4] an averment

---

[92] *Barnet* v. *Colvill*, 1840, 2 D. 337; Bell, *Principles*, §568; Dickson, *Evidence* (3rd ed.) §114 (2).

[93] Stair, i, 7, 14; iv, 42, 8; Erskine, iii, 2, 43; Dickson, *Evidence* (3rd ed.) §§114 (2), 936.

[94] Dickson, *Evidence* (3rd ed.) §938; Gloag, *Contract* (2nd ed.) 71; *McAslan* v. *Glen*, 1859, 21 D. 511; *Semple* v. *Kyle*, 1902, 4 F. 421.

[95] As to declarator of trust, see §§ **122, 123.**

[96] Dickson, *Evidence* (3rd ed.) §114 (2); *Bonthrone* v. *Ireland*, 1883, 10 R. 779, L. Young at p. 790. For facts regarded as insufficient to rebut the presumption, see *Clyde* v. *Clyde* (O.H.) 1958 S.C. 343.

[97] Dickson, *Evidence* (3rd ed.) §114 (2).

[98] Stair, i, 7, 14; Erskine, iii, 4, 5.

[99] Stair, i, 7, 14, iv, 45, 24; Erskine, iii, 4, 5; Dickson, *Evidence* (3rd ed.) §173.

[1] Dickson, *Evidence* (3rd ed.) §173.

[2] Dickson, *Evidence* (3rd ed.) §933, and three seventeenth-century decisions there cited.

[3] *Knox* v. *Crawford*, 1862, 24 D. 1088, referred to and followed in *Henry* v. *Miller*, 1884, 11 R. 713, L.P. Inglis at pp. 716-717. See also *Ferguson, Davidson & Co.* v. *Jolly's Tr.*, 1880, 7 R. 500, L. Mure at p. 504.

[4] See § **152.** As to the standard of proof of fraud required in a civil action, see § **85.**

that the document was obtained by fraud may be proved *prout de jure*.[5]

When a creditor in a written obligation cannot produce his document of debt, it is presumed that the document was returned to the debtor as cancelled on payment of the debt, or that it was destroyed or cancelled by the creditor in order to extinguish the debt.[6] The presumption applies mainly, however, to writings which are usually cancelled or destroyed when their purpose has been served, such as bills of exchange, promissory notes and personal bonds. With regard to a deed which is not normally revoked in this way, such, for example, as a bond and disposition in security, the presumption, if it applies at all, is more easily rebutted.[7]

67. PRESUMPTIONS FROM POSSESSION OF HERITABLE AND MOVEABLE PROPERTY

The underlying maxim is *in pari causa melior est conditio possidentis*.[8] Long continued possession of heritable property raises a presumption that it has a legal origin, if such an origin is possible,[9] and it is this presumption which underlies the positive prescriptions relating to an estate in land,[10] a right of servitude[11] or a public right of way,[11] and the law relating to possessory judgments.[12] There is a particular application of the general presumption with reference to thirteen years' possession by a minister of any heritable subject as part of his benefice.[13] The possessor of corporeal moveables is presumed to be the owner, and the onus of establishing his own title rests upon anyone who asserts the contrary.[14] In order to discharge this onus it is not enough to prove that the goods were once the property of the person claiming them. He must show that he lost possession by theft, or by granting possession to a liferenter or under a contract of loan, hiring, hire-purchase, deposit or pledge or in other similar circumstances which made it impossible for the present possessor to be the owner.[14] The position of a creditor who seeks to attach by diligence the goods of a third party in the possession of the debtor, in reliance upon the doctrine of reputed ownership, is special and is not dealt with here.[15]

---

5 Dickson, *Evidence* (3rd ed.) §934.
6 *Walker* v. *Nisbet*, 1915 S.C. 639; Dickson, *Evidence* (3rd ed.) §175; Gloag, *Contract* (2nd ed.) 717.
7 See the distinction made in *Winchester* v. *Smith*, 1863, 1 M. 685, L.P. McNeill, L. Curriehill, L. Ardmillan at p. 689; *Clyde* v. *Clyde* (*supra*), at p. 345. Bonds and dispositions in security, however, may be proved to have been discharged *rebus et factis*. See § **126**, sub-para. (d), note 38. See also § **234**.
8 Erskine, ii, 1, 24; Bell, *Principles*, §1313.
9 *Clippens Oil Co.* v. *Edinburgh and District Water Trs.*, 1903, 6 F. (H.L.) 7, L.C. Halsbury at p. 8. See also note 11 below.
10 Conveyancing (Scotland) Act, 1924 (14 & 15 Geo. V. c. 27), s. 16 (1).
11 Conveyancing (Scotland) Act, 1924 (14 & 15 Geo. V. c. 27), s. 16 (2). In *Magistrates of Edinburgh* v. *North British Railway Co.*, 1904, 6 F. 620, at pp. 636-637, the establishment of a public right of way was held to be legally impossible.
12 Stair, iv, 26, 3; Erskine, iv, 1, 50. See also *Galloway* v. *Cowden*, 1885, 12 R. 578; *Calder* v. *Adam*, 1870, 8 M. 645; *McKerron* v. *Gordon*, 1876, 3 R. 429.
13 Stair, ii, 8, 29; Erskine, iii, 7, 33; Connell, *Parishes*, 439 *et seq.*
14 Stair, ii, 1, 42; Erskine, ii, 1, 24; Dickson, *Evidence* (3rd ed.) §§149-151; Bell, *Principles*, §§1313, 1314.

68. PRESUMPTION FROM POSSESSION OF STOLEN PROPERTY

Possession of stolen property by itself may be no more than a piece of circumstantial evidence.[16] In certain circumstances, however, it may give rise to a presumption that the possessor was the thief,[17] so as to throw upon him the onus of providing an explanation of his possession which is consistent with his innocence, and which the court or the jury is prepared to accept as true, or at least as raising a reasonable doubt in his favour.[18] Proof of possession depends upon the circumstances of each case. A servant acting in the ordinary course of his duties is not a possessor for this purpose.[19] The occupier of premises upon which the stolen property is found is normally the possessor,[20] but this is not necessarily so when other persons also have access thereto.[21] When a number of persons are associated together in dealing with the stolen property, all may be regarded as its possessors, whether physically in possession of it or not.[22] Before the presumption can arise it must be proved that the interval between the crime and the accused's possession of the stolen goods was short, and that there were criminative circumstances associated therewith.[23] What is regarded as a short interval depends upon the nature of the stolen goods,[24] a longer interval being usually regarded as sufficient to raise the presumption when the goods are cumbersome than when they are small and easily negotiable.[16] The criminative circumstances must be such as to suggest that the possession was not innocent, as, for example, that the goods were of a kind or quantity which would not normally be in the accused's possession at the hour and place at which they were found, or that they were of a kind not normally dealt with by the accused in the course of his business,[25] or that the accused's actions at or about the time of his possession were in some other way indicative of guilt. The fact that the accused said nothing when cautioned by the police and charged with the crime is not a criminative circumstance for this purpose.[26]

---

[15] For a recent discussion of the subject, see *George Hopkinson Ltd.* v. *Napier & Son*, 1953 S.C. 139, L.P. Cooper at pp. 145-149. See also *Scott* v. *Price*, 1837, 15 S. 916 (liferent); *Marston* v. *Kerr's Tr.*, 1879, 6 R. 898 (hiring); *Murdoch & Co.* v. *Greig*, 1889, 16 R. 396 (hire-purchase); *Robertson* v. *McIntyre*, 1882, 9 R. 772 (lease).

[16] Dickson, *Evidence* (3rd ed.) §157.

[17] The presumption of guilt covers any form of theft including theft by housebreaking: *Christie* v. *H.M. Advocate*, 1939 J.C. 72: but probably not a crime involving the use of violence: L. Fleming at p. 75.

[18] Hume, I, 3; Alison, I, 320; Dickson, *Evidence* (3rd ed.) §157. The evidence of the accused alone, if believed, is enough for this purpose.

[19] *Simpson* v. *H.M. Advocate*, 1952 J.C. 1.

[20] See *Brannan* v. *H.M. Advocate*, 1954 J.C. 87.

[21] *Cryans* v. *Nixon*, 1955 J.C. 1.

[22] *H.M. Advocate* v. *Browne*, 1903, 6 F. (J.) 24. See also *McAtee*, 1903, 5 F. (J.) 67, at p. 69.

[23] *Fox* v. *Patterson*, 1948 J.C. 104; *Brannan* v. *H.M. Advocate*, 1954 J.C. 87.

[24] *Hannah and Higgins*, 1836, 1 Swin. 289 (clothes—two months too long); *H.M. Advocate* v. *Browne* (*supra*), (bank notes of large denominations—three weeks not too long).

[25] *Cf. Fox* v. *Patterson* (*supra*).

[26] *Collins* v. *H.M. Advocate*, 1959 S.L.T. (Notes) 27.

69. PRESUMPTIONS SUPPORTING CONTINUANCE OF EXISTING CONDITIONS

Conditions proved to have existed are presumed to continue in existence.[27] One application of this general presumption is the presumption that human life extends for a period of between eighty and one hundred years.[28] Statutory provision is made for restricting the effect of this presumption by petition to the court in connection with the succession to the estate[29] or the dissolution of the marriage[30] of a person who has disappeared for seven years. When two persons die as a result of a common calamity there is no presumption as to the survivorship of either of them.[31] Other particular applications of the general presumption are as follows: a person's domicile of origin is presumed to continue until he has acquired another domicile by actual residence, with the intention of abandoning the domicile of origin, the burden of proving the change (*animo et facto*) being upon the party asserting it;[32] insanity, when established in an appropriate process, is presumed to continue;[33] a general mandate is presumed to continue until discharged;[34] the relationship of debtor and creditor is presumed to continue until it is proved to have been terminated;[35] when a husband is proved to have left his wife with the intention to desert her, this intention is presumed to continue until the contrary is proved;[36] when a husband is proved to have been a habitual drunkard at the date of his wife's separation from him, there is a presumption that the habit of drunkenness has continued until the date of the proof;[37] a servant in the general employment of a party is presumed to continue in that employment, and the onus of proving that

---

[27] Dickson, *Evidence* (3rd ed.) §114 (5).

[28] *Secretary of State for Scotland* v. *Sutherland,* 1944 S.C. 79, L.P. Normand at p. 84, L. Moncrieff at p. 85; Dickson, *Evidence* (3rd ed.) §116. For circumstances sufficient to rebut the presumption, see *Greig* v. *Merchant Company of Edinburgh*, 1921 S.C. 76; *X.* v. *Society of Solicitors in Supreme Courts of Scotland* (O.H.) 1937 S.L.T. 87, and authorities cited in Dickson.

[29] Presumption of Life Limitation (Scotland) Act, 1891 (54 & 55 Vict. c. 29). The court is the Court of Session, or, when the value of the estate does not exceed £500, the sheriff court. See *Jones* (O.H.) 1923 S.L.T. 31; *Murray* v. *Chalmers* (O.H.) 1913, 1 S.L.T. 223; *Barr* v. *Campbell*, 1925 S.C. 317; *Shepherd's Trs.* v. *Brown* (O.H.) 1902, 9 S.L.T. 487; *Andrews* (O.H.) 1901, 9 S.L.T. 117; *Dear* v. *Lumgair* (O.H.) 1906, 13 S.L.T. 850.

[30] Divorce (Scotland) Act, 1938 (1 & 2 Geo. VI. c. 50), s. 5. The court is the Court of Session. See *Lench* v. *Lench*, 1945 S.C. 295; *Labacianskas* v. *Labacianskas*, 1949 S.C. 280; *Secretary of State* v. *Sutherland*, 1944 S.C. 79; *Gilchrist*, 1950 S.L.T. (Notes) 6.

[31] *Drummond's J.F.* v. *H.M. Advocate*, 1944 S.C. 298; *Mitchell's Executrix* v. *Gordon's Factor*, 1953 S.C. 176; *Ross's J.F.* v. *Martin*, 1955 S.C. (H.L.) 56. The statutory presumption (Law of Property Act, 1925 (15 & 16 Geo. V. c. 20), s. 184), that the elder of two persons dies before the younger, applies only to England.

[32] Dickson, *Evidence* (3rd ed.) §27; *Aikman* v. *Aikman*, 1861, 3 Macq. 854, L. Wensleydale at p. 877. See also *Liverpool Royal Infirmary* v. *Ramsay*, 1930 S.C. (H.L.) 83; *McLelland* v. *McLelland*, 1942 S.C. 502; *Labacianskas* v. *Labacianskas*, 1949 S.C. 280.

[33] Bell, *Principles*, §2103; Dickson, *Evidence* (3rd ed.) §35. For the presumptions regarding sanity and insanity, see **§ 59**, sub-para. (d).

[34] Bell, *Commentaries*, I, 488; Dickson, *Evidence* (3rd ed.) §114 (5).

[35] Dickson, *Evidence* (3rd ed.) §114 (5).

[36] *Parker* v. *Parker*, 1926 S.C. 574; *Anderson* v. *Anderson* (O.H.) 1955 S.C. 428. *Cf. Mudie* v. *Mudie*, 1956 S.C. 318, at pp. 330, 334 (supervening insanity).

[37] *Cox* v. *Cox*, 1942 S.C. 352.

pro hac vice he became the servant of another, rests upon the party who makes the assertion.[38]

70. PRESUMPTIONS SUPPORTING INNOCENCE, MORALITY AND PROPRIETY

The maxim applicable to these presumptions is *odiosa et inhonesta non sunt in lege præsumenda*.[39] There are presumptions favouring innocence of crime[40] and innocence of adultery.[41] It has been said that there is a presumption of legitimacy,[42] but it is thought that this arises only where the person concerned has been accorded the status of legitimacy during his life-time,[43] or where one of the presumptions associated with an undisputed marriage applies. The presumption based on recognised status has arisen in the past when the parents were married irregularly, and particularly when the marriage was sought to be proved by cohabitation with habit and repute,[44] a form of marriage which by its nature is not immediately verifiable. With the increased accuracy of the marriage registers and the invalidity since 1940[45] of two of the three forms of irregular marriage,[45] this presumption may perhaps be of diminishing importance in the future. Of the presumptions associated with an undisputed marriage, one is that a man who marries a woman in the knowledge that she is pregnant, when there has been courtship and opportunity of access, is the father of the unborn child.[46] The other is *pater est quem nuptiæ demonstrant*, the presumption that all children conceived during lawful wedlock are legitimate, the husband of the mother at the time of conception being the father.[47] It has been said, but not decided, that this presumption arises only from a regular marriage.[48] The standard

---

[38] *Malley* v. *London, Midland & Scottish Railway Co.*, 1944 S.C. 129, at pp. 137, 149, 152.

[39] Dickson, *Evidence* (3rd ed.) §114 (6). Once again the brocard is an understatement.

[40] Macdonald, *Criminal Law of Scotland* (5th ed.) 339; *Slater* v. *H.M. Advocate*, 1928 J.C. 94, at p. 105.

[41] *Currie* v. *Currie* (O.H.) 1950 S.C. 10, at p. 15. As to proof of adultery, see § **160**.

[42] Dickson, *Evidence* (3rd ed.) §27; *Mackay* v. *Mackay*, 1855, 17 D. 494, at p. 500.

[43] *Campbell* v. *Campbell*, 1866, 4 M. 867, at pp. 886, 929, 931, 932, 939, 951, 987: 1867, 5 M. (H.L.) 115, at p. 124; Fraser, *Parent and Child* (3rd ed.) 22. See also *Deans's J.F.* v. *Deans*, 1912 S.C. 441, L.P. Dunedin at p. 450; *Lapsley* v. *Grierson*, 1845, 8 D. 34, L. J-Cl. Hope at p. 46. *Cf. Gardner* v. *Gardner*, 1876, 3 R., L. Neaves at p. 714.

[44] See *Campbell* v. *Campbell* (*supra*).

[45] Marriage (Scotland) Act, 1939 (2 & 3 Geo. VI. c. 34), s. 5; Marriage (Scotland) Act, 1939, (Commencement) Order, 1940. Marriage by declaration *de presenti* and by promise *subsequente copula*, contracted after July 1st, 1940, are invalid. For an example of a marriage by cohabitation with habit and repute constituted after that date, see *A.B.* v. *C.D.* (O.H.) 1957 S.C. 415. As to proof of irregular marriages, see §§ **156, 157**.

[46] *Imre* v. *Mitchell*, 1958 S.C. 439; *Gardner* v. *Gardner*, 1876, 3 R. 695; 1877, 4 R. (H.L.) 56. The opinion has been expressed that the presumption also applies when the child is born prematurely before the marriage can be effected: L.P. Clyde in *Imre* v. *Mitchell* (*supra*), at p. 463, L. Sorn at pp. 472-473. For opinions as to the presumptions arising when a man marries a woman with an illegitimate child, and when he marries his mistress who has an illegitimate child, see L. Sorn and L. Carmont in *Imre* v. *Mitchell* (*supra*).

[47] Stair, iii, 3, 42; Erskine, i, 6, 49; Fraser, *Parent and Child* (3rd ed.) 1. See also *Imre* v. *Mitchell* (*supra*).

[48] *Swinton* v. *Swinton*, 1862, 24 D. 833, L. Deas at p. 838. *Cf.* Stair, iii, 3, 42; iv, 45, 20.

of proof required to rebut this presumption is the same as that which is needed to rebut the presumption against illegitimacy.[49]

There is in civil causes a general presumption against delict, such as fraud,[50] and quasi-delict, such as negligence or breach of duty.[51] With regard to fraud, a contrary presumption may arise from the nature and appearance of articles sold,[52] from the fact that the vendors of two second-hand cash registers, which the purchasers believed to be new, held themselves out as manufacturers and vendors of such registers,[53] and from the fact that the person in whose favour a deed or obligation was granted was a person having, through relationship or official or professional position, a power to influence the granter in his favour.[54] With regard to negligence, the contrary presumptions or inferences are mentioned later.[55]

71. PRESUMPTIONS REGARDING INSOLVENCY

As a result of judicial construction of the Act, 1621 c. 18, there is a *presumptio juris* in all challenges after insolvency of deeds granted to conjunct and confident persons (*a*) that the insolvency existed at the date of the deed, and (*b*) that the deed was granted without value.[56]

---

[49] See § **86.**

[50] See, for example, *Gibson* v. *National Cash Register*, 1925 S.C. 500; *Cullen's Tr.* v. *Johnston*, 1865, 3 M. 935, L.P. McNeill at p. 937; *Campbell* v. *Aberdeen Insurance Co.*, 1841, 3 D. 1010. For the standard of proof required to rebut the presumption against fraud in a civil cause, see § **85.**

[51] See, for example, *McLure, Naismith, Brodie & Macfarlane* v. *Stewart*, 1887, 15 R. (H.L.) 1; *Alexander* v. *Phillip*, 1899, 1 F. 985. For the standard of proof required to rebut the presumption, see § **85.**

[52] *Patterson* v. *Landsberg & Son*, 1905, 7 F. 675, L. Kyllachy at p. 681 (inference of fraud from fact that alleged antiques, not in fact old, had the appearance of age).

[53] *Gibson* v. *National Cash Register Co.*, 1925 S.C. 500.

[54] *Grieve* v. *Cunningham*, 1869, 8 M. 317 (solicitor); *Gray* v. *Binny*, 1879, 7 R. 332 (parent and child). For a general discussion of the position of solicitor, clergyman, doctor and parent, see *Forbes* v. *Forbes's Trs.* (O.H.) 1957 S.C. 325; *Munro* v. *Strain*, 1874, 1 R. 522, at p. 525; *McKechnie* v. *McKechnie's Trs.*, 1908 S.C. 93, at pp. 97-98.

[55] See §§ **79, 80, 81.**

[56] Bell, *Commentaries*, II, 172, 179; Goudy, *Bankruptcy* (4th ed.) 43, 55.

CHAPTER VII

BURDEN OF PROOF IN CIVIL AND CRIMINAL CAUSES

72. CIVIL CAUSES—GENERAL

With regard to each disputed issue of fact arising in the course of a litigation, the burden of proof (*onus probandi*) rests upon either one party or the other. This means, in very general terms, that if on any issue of fact no evidence is led, or the evidence leaves the matter in doubt, the party upon whom the burden of proof rests has not discharged it, and accordingly fails on that issue. It makes no difference to his failure that his opponent may not have proved his own averments. The question as to where the burden of proof rests may have to be considered by the court before the enquiry commences in order to determine which party must first lead evidence, or at the end of the enquiry in order properly to consider the effect of the evidence led upon the decision of the case as a whole. An assessment of the court's probable answer to the question may also have to be made by the parties' counsel or solicitors during the course of the enquiry, with a view to deciding whether, or to what extent, to lead evidence.

73. WHO MUST LEAD IN THE PROOF

It is thought that this is less important in Scotland than it is in England,[1] where a number of procedural consequences, unknown in Scotland, appear to follow from a decision of the question. In Scotland the question is usually unimportant, apart from the supposed tactical advantage, either of making an initial good impression upon the court in favour of the party who leads, or, in the case of the party who follows, of knowing the strength or weakness of his opponent's case before his own evidence need be led. Some difficulty and importance, however, may attach to the decision when the burden resting upon one party may be discharged only by the writ or oath

---

[1] Phipson, *Evidence* (9th ed.) 42-43.

of the opponent, whereas the burden resting upon the other may be discharged by proof *prout de jure*. In such a case the decision as to which party must lead in the proof may be of fundamental importance in the final decision of the cause.[2] No difficulty arises in the normal case where the initial burden of proof rests upon the pursuer, and where he leads in the proof. There is equally no difficulty in the less usual case where the pursuer's averments, if relevant and sufficient to support his conclusions, are admitted by the defender, in which event the initial burden of proving his defence, whatever it may be, rests upon the latter, and he leads in the proof. But where each party, as disclosed by his own averments, must rebut a presumption in order to succeed, the question may be more difficult, and must depend, failing agreement, upon a comparison of the strengths of the two presumptions.[2] So, for example, the party who must rebut a special as compared with a general presumption may be ordered to lead.[3] The question of who shall lead, however, is usually decided by the court as a matter of convenience upon a *prima facie* view of the incidence of the burden of proof, and without arriving at a concluded view upon it.[4] If nothing to the contrary is said in an interlocutor issued before the proof, the pursuer must lead.[5]

74. BURDEN OF PROOF AS AFFECTING FINAL JUDGMENT

Counsel or solicitors for the parties may have to make their own assessment of the incidence of the burden of proof as the proof progresses.[6] The court, on the other hand, apart from the question of who must lead,[7] is concerned with the question of burden of proof only when all the evidence on both sides has been led,[8] and, even then, only if it is unable to come to a definite conclusion on the evidence, or some part of it, and must then decide which party has to suffer as a result.[9] When the truth is clear, that is to say, the question of who had the duty of making it clear becomes unimportant. When it is not clear, either because there was no evidence, or because the

---

2 As an example of such a case, see *Penman* v. *White* (O.H.) 1957 S.C. 338, where the pursuer averred that he gave money on loan, and the defender averred that he received the money as a gift. If the pursuer had been ordained to lead in the proof he would presumably have been restricted to proof by writ or oath of the defender, and might have failed because of this restriction. But the presumption against loan was relatively weak and that against donation was strong. (See L. Ormidale, at p. 679, in *Penney* v. *Aitken*, 1927 S.C. 673.) The initial burden of proof was, therefore, held to rest upon the defender, who was ordained to lead, the pursuer being allowed a conjunct probation *prout de jure*. It therefore became possible, it would appear, for the pursuer to obtain repayment of the sum sued for without having proved the loan by writ or oath. As to this decision, see also § 62, note 76.

3 *Millar* v. *Mitchell*, 1860, 22 D. 833, at p. 836. See L. Neaves at p. 847. See also § 57 as to the relative strengths of presumptions.

4 See, for example, *Gibson* v. *Adams*, 1875, 3 R. 144.

5 Maclaren, *Court of Session Practice*, 554; Dobie, *Sheriff Court Practice*, 182. The defender, of course, may agree to lead.

6 See § 72.

7 See § 73.

8 *Ballingall* v. *Glasgow Corporation*, 1948 S.C. 160, L. Mackay at p. 164.

9 *Thomas* v. *Thomas*, 1947 S.C. (H.L.) 45, L. Thankerton at p. 54; *Milne* v. *Townsend*, 1892, 19 R. 830, L. Adam at p. 836, L. McLaren at p. 837.

evidence was insufficient in quantity or quality for the purpose, the question of where the burden lies must usually be decided before judgment can be given. The burdens of proof resting upon the parties initially, and the order in which they must be discharged, are determined by the averments and admissions in the written pleadings, and from any presumptions or inferences of fact which clearly arise therefrom. They may shift from time to time during the leading of evidence, as a result of presumptions or inferences of fact to which, in the opinion of the court, the evidence gives rise. These matters are considered in more detail in the following paragraphs.

75. GENERAL RULES AS TO INCIDENCE OF BURDEN OF PROOF

The burden of proof may be placed by statute upon one or other of the parties. So, for example, in a pension claim for death or disablement due to war service the onus is upon the Minister of Pensions to prove that the claimant is not entitled to a pension,[10] and there are statutory provisions regarding bills of exchange and promissory notes.[11] Apart from such statutory provisions the following are suggested as general rules, one or more of which may indicate where the burden of proof lies, either initially upon the pleadings or at any subsequent stage of the enquiry. They are not mutually exclusive and may be regarded as different statements or facets of one general rule.

(*a*) The burden of proof lies on the party who will fail if no evidence at all is led.[12] This means that in the normal case the burden, initially at least, rests upon the pursuer, since, in accordance with the maxim *melior est conditio possidentis vel defendentis*, the pursuer cannot, by merely raising an action, require his opponent to disprove his allegations as a condition of escaping liability. It also means that if, at any stage of the case, the judicial admissions or the evidence give rise to a presumption or inference of fact, which, if not rebutted, entitles one of the parties to success, the burden of rebutting the presumption or inference of fact rests upon his opponent.

(*b*) The burden of proof rests on the party who alleges the affirmative. The maxim is *ei qui affirmat, non ei qui negat, incumbit probatio*.[13] So, if liability for negligence[14] or breach of contract[15] is admitted, but the defender avers that the pursuer's injury or damage is partly attributable to his own subsequent negligence or failure to minimise his loss, the onus of proving these averments rests upon the defender, and it is not for the pursuer to justify his actions. In applying this rule the substance and not the grammar of the allegation is considered, so that an allegation of negligence, for example, is regarded as affirmative, whether it charges the other party with

---

10 Royal Warrant, December, 1943 (Cdm. 6489), Art. 4; *Irving* v. *Minister of Pensions*, 1945 S.C. 21; *Mitchell* v. *Minister of Pensions*, 1945 S.C. 131; *Brown* v. *Minister of Pensions*, 1946 S.C. 471.

11 Bills of Exchange Act, 1882 (45 & 46 Vict. c. 61), ss. 13, 21 (2) (3), 30, 32 (5), 63 (3), 65 (4)

12 Dickson, *Evidence* (3rd ed.) §25.

13 Dickson, *Evidence* (3rd ed.) §26. See also *Clyde Navigation Trs.* v. *Barclay Curle & Co.*, 1876, 3 R (H.L.) 44; *Alexander* v. *Philip*, 1899, 1 F. 985.

14 *S.S. "Baron Vernon"* v. *S.S. "Metagama,"* 1928 S.C. (H.L.) 21.

15 *Connal, Cotton & Co.* v. *Fisher, Renwick & Co.*, 1882, 10 R. 824.

doing something he ought not to have done, or with not doing something he ought to have done.[16] Similarly the onus of proving that he has not received a document may rest upon the party making the assertion, if the proved facts raise an inference that he received it in the ordinary course of delivery or posting.[17]

(c) When a fact is peculiarly within the knowledge of one of the parties, very slight evidence will suffice to shift the burden of proof from his opponent, and to lay upon him the burden of proving his own averment, whether affirmative or negative, about the fact in question.[18] When, for example, it is proved by the pursuer that his property has been destroyed or damaged while in the possession of the defender as a borrower,[19] hirer,[20] stabler,[21] depositary,[22] hotel keeper,[23] or under some similar contract or arrangement,[24] the burden of proving that it was destroyed or damaged without fault on his part rests upon the defender. The same rule applies to carriage by land[25] or sea,[26] and has been said to apply to the proper maintenance by omnibus proprietors of a tyre which burst and caused injury to a passenger.[27]

(d) When a statute provides that an order shall be pronounced or refused if it appears to the court,[28] or if the court is satisfied,[29] that something has or has not occurred, the party who will fail if there is no appearance or satisfaction has the burden of making it appear, or of satisfying the court, as the case may be. When a right is given by statute subject to a qualification or to an exception, the question arises as to whether the onus of showing that the qualification or exception does not apply rests upon the party seeking the right, or whether his opponent must prove that it is applicable. No clear principle of construction is provided by the reported decisions

[16] See *McClure, Naismith, Brodie & Macfarlane* v. *Stewart*, 1887, 15 R. (H.L.) 1, L. Herschell at p. 12, and Dickson, *Evidence* (3rd ed.) §34.

[17] *Guthrie* v. *Stewart*, 1926 S.C. 743, L. J-Cl. Alness and L. Ormidale at p. 747, and cases in Dickson, *Evidence* (3rd ed.) §28, notes (d) (e).

[18] *McClure, Naismith, Brodie & Macfarlane* v. *Stewart* (*supra*), L.C. Halsbury at pp. 2-3; *Cruickshank* v. *Smith*, 1949 J.C. 134, L. Jamieson at pp. 151-152. See also *Lockhart* v. *Barr*, 1941 S.C. 578, at p. 585; 1943 S.C. (H.L.) 1.

[19] *Bain* v. *Strang*, 1888, 16 R. 186.

[20] *Wilson* v. *Orr*, 1879, 7 R. 266.

[21] *Mustard* v. *Paterson*, 1923 S.C. 142.

[22] *Taylor* v. *Nisbet*, 1901, 4 F. 79; *cf. Sutherland* v. *Hutton*, 1896, 23 R. 718 (questioned in *Mustard* v. *Paterson* (*supra*), at p. 149).

[23] *Burns* v. *Royal Hotel* (*St. Andrews*) *Ltd.*, 1958 S.C. 354 (motor car in hotel garage).

[24] *Sinclair* v. *Juner*, 1952 S.C. 35 (motor car in repairer's garage); *Copland* v. *Brogan*, 1916 S.C. 277 (gratuitous mandatary). See also the general observations on the earlier decisions in *Burns* v. *Royal Hotel* (*St. Andrews*), *Ltd.* (*supra*).

[25] *Anderson* v. *North British Railway Co.*, 1875, 2 R. 443.

[26] *Williams* v. *Dobbie*, 1884, 11 R. 982; *Bishop* v. *Mersey & Clyde Navigation Steam Co.*, 1830, 8 S. 558; *Langland & Sons* v. *McMaster & Co.*, 1907 S.C. 1090. See also bills of lading cases:—*Horsley* v. *J. & A. D. Grimond*, 1894, 21 R. 410; *Smith & Co.* v. *Bedouin Steam Navigation Co.*, 1895, 23 R. (H.L.) 1; *cf. Craig Line Steamship Co.* v. *North British Storage & Transit Co.*, 1921 S.C. 114. The Carriage of Goods by Sea Act, 1924 (14 & 15 Geo. V. c. 22), may now affect statements in a bill of lading.

[27] *Elliott* v. *Young's Bus Service*, 1945 S.C. 445, L. Mackay at p. 459.

[28] *McLaughlin* v. *Caledonia Stevedoring Co.*, 1938 S.C. (H.L.) 31; *Moore* v. *Harland & Wolff*, 1937 S.C. 707.

which leave the position in some doubt,[30] but the judicial pronouncements on the analogous problem in criminal causes may provide some guide.[31]

(*e*) The burden of proof lies upon the party against whom on the pleadings, or at any later stage in the enquiry, a presumption operates, or, if there are presumptions operating against both parties, upon the party who must overcome the stronger presumption.[32]

76. BURDEN OF PROOF AS DISCLOSED BY THE PLEADINGS

When both parties make substantive averments, each must normally bear the burden of proving his own, but the burdens do not arise contemporaneously. The initial burden rests upon one of them, and the burden upon the other arises only when that initial burden has been discharged.[33] The initial burden normally rests upon the pursuer. If a pursuer avers negligence, and the defender avers contributory negligence, the burden resting upon the defender of proving contributory negligence need never be discharged if the pursuer fails first to discharge the initial burden resting upon him. Similarly, if a pursuer sues for payment for work done or for the price of goods sold, he must prove that the work was instructed and performed or that the goods were ordered and delivered before the defender need discharge the onus resting upon him of proving that the work was defective or the goods disconform to contract. The initial burden of proof, however, may rest upon the defender if in his pleadings he has admitted some or all of the pursuer's averments. This occurs when the averments so admitted are held to give rise to a presumption or inference of fact which, if not rebutted, must result in the pursuer's success, and in such a case the initial burden of proof rests upon the defender. If in an action of damages in respect of the negligent driving of a tramcar the defenders were to admit in their pleadings that the pursuer, while a passenger, was thrown from his seat and injured as a result of the violent application of the brake, the initial burden of disproving the negligence of the tramcar driver would rest upon the defenders.[34] Similarly, if a defender admits in his pleadings that the pursuer performed work on his instructions, or sold and delivered goods to him on his order, the initial burden of proving that he is not liable to pay for the work or for the goods rests upon him.[35] Even when the pursuer's averments disclose that he must rebut a presumption in order to succeed, the initial burden of proof may nevertheless rest upon the defender if his own admissions and averments disclose the existence of a stronger presumption operating against him, as where a pursuer avers that he gave money on loan and the defender avers

[29] *Kerrigan* v. *Nelson*, 1946 S.C. 388; *McCallum* v. *Arthur*, 1955 S.C. 188, at pp. 197, 198.
[30] *Coul* v. *Ayr County Council*, 1909 S.C. 422, L.P. Dunedin at p. 424; *cf. Brydon* v. *Railway Executive*, 1957 S.C. 282, L. Patrick at pp. 290-291.
[31] See § **83**, sub-para. (d), note 8.
[32] See § **57**.
[33] This is not necessarily true when there is a counter-claim in which the defender, who is truly the pursuer, may insist, whether the pursuer in the action succeeds or fails.
[34] See § **81**.
[35] *Carruthers* v. *Macgregor*, 1927 S.C. 816, L. Murray at p. 822; *cf. McIntyre* v. *Clow*, 1875, 2 R. 278 (where the building collapsed before it was completed and handed over).

that he received it as a gift.[36] Presumptions as affecting the burden of proof generally were mentioned in the last chapter,[37] and those associated with negligence are mentioned later in this chapter.[38]

77. SHIFTING OF BURDEN OF PROOF—GENERAL

The party upon whom the initial burden of proof rests may discharge that burden by leading evidence which either proves conclusively the fact necessary for his success or gives rise to a presumption that it exists. In the latter case, if the presumption is rebuttable, the burden of proof shifts to the other party, who must either lead evidence to rebut the presumption against him or fail in the action or issue of fact in question. If in the examples suggested in the last paragraph regarding the violent braking of a tramcar, the performance of work and the sale of goods, the defender does not admit the facts which give rise to the presumption in the pursuer's favour, the initial burden of proof rests upon the pursuer. The burden shifts to the defender, however, if the pursuer leads evidence and proves the facts which give rise to such a presumption. When this occurs in the case of the injury to the passenger in the tramcar, the defenders, in order to escape liability, must prove that, despite the violent braking of the vehicle, the tramcar driver was not negligent, and, in the cases of the performance of work and the sale of goods, the defender must prove that for some good reason he is not bound to pay for the work which was performed on his instructions, or for the goods which were sold and delivered to him.[39] One method by which a party may shift the burden of proof from his own shoulders to those of his opponent is by leading sufficient evidence to bring into operation a presumption in his favour which is stronger than the presumption initially operating against him. A party who, in order to succeed, must establish that a woman is beyond the age of child-bearing will rebut the general presumption that there is no such age,[40] and shift the onus of proof to his opponent, if (no interests being affected other than those of unborn children) he proves that the woman is at least 53 years of age. A special and stronger presumption[40a] then operates in his favour, and it is for his opponent to prove, if he can, that the woman is in fact capable of child-bearing. If a party's case depends upon proving a person's present insanity he may overcome the general presumption in favour of sanity[40] by proving that at an earlier date a *curator bonis* was appointed to that person on the ground of his unsoundness of mind.[40] This raises a particular and stronger presumption of insanity,[40a] which, coupled with the presumption that the insanity thus established has continued,[41] shifts to the opponent the burden of proving that the person

---

[36] See § **73**, note 2.

[37] See §§ **56** *et seq.*

[38] See §§ **79-81.**

[39] For another example, see *Reilly* v. *Beardmore & Co.*, 1947 S.C. 275, L.P. Cooper at p. 278, L. Carmont at p. 280 (injury caused by parting of the cable of a crane—breach of Factories Act, 1937 (1 Ed. VIII & 1 Geo. VI. c. 67), s. 23).

[40] See § **59**, sub-paras. (c) (d).

[40a] See § **57.**

[41] See § **69.**

concerned is in fact sane. The burden of proof may shift more than once in the course of a proof.[42]

78. EXAMPLES OF SHIFTING OF BURDEN OF PROOF—CONTRACT

Two examples were suggested in the last paragraph. Two others, both relating to contract, are given in greater detail here. A pursuer sued a garage proprietor for damages for the loss of his motor car which had been left for repair, and which had been destroyed by fire while in the defender's possession. It was held that the pursuer discharged the initial onus resting upon him by proving (first) that the contract with the defender included an element of *locatio custodiæ* and (secondly) that the defender, as its custodier, had failed to return the motor car to him. The onus then shifted to the defender to establish by evidence at least a *prima facie*[43] case that the fire which destroyed the motor car was accidental, in the sense that he was not to blame for it. Had the defender been able to do this the onus would have shifted again to the pursuer to prove, if he could, that the fire had in fact been caused by the defender's negligence.[43] If an owner of cargo proves that it was shipped in good condition and, when delivered, was damaged by sea water, the onus of proof shifts to the ship-owner to prove that the damage occurred without fault on the part of the ship. He may discharge this by proving that the ship met with weather of such severity as to open her seams, thus causing the damage to the cargo, whereupon the onus shifts back to the owner of the cargo to prove that, despite the weather, the damage both to ship and cargo was caused by fault on the part of those in charge of the ship, as, for example, by failing to supply sufficient dunnage.[44]

79. SHIFTING OF BURDEN OF PROOF—NEGLIGENCE

In actions of damages for loss and injury caused by negligence certain presumptions or inferences of fact have been accepted by the courts from time to time as shifting the onus of proof from the pursuer to the defender. It may be said in general terms that in such cases the onus shifts to the defender when an inference of negligence on his part arises from the circumstances, proved or admitted, in which the accident or injury occurred. Examples of such presumptions or inferences are given later.[45] The relation-

---

[42] Dickson, *Evidence* (3rd ed.) §35; *Gibson* v. *National Cash Register Co.*, 1925 S.C. 500, L. J-Cl. Alness at p. 504; *Clyde Navigation Trs.* v. *Barclay Curle & Co.*, 1876, 3 R. (H.L.) 44, L. Selborne at p. 51. In *Mactavish's J.F.* v. *Michael's Trs.* 1912 S.C. 425 (action against endorser for balance of sum due under a bill of exchange), the burden of proof was held to have shifted twice in the course of the proof.

[43] *Sinclair* v. *Juner*, 1952 S.C. 35, L. Keith at pp. 46-47, 48. This case, however, must be read along with *Burns* v. *Royal Hotel (St. Andrews) Ltd.*, 1958 S.C. 354, L.P. Clyde at pp. 362-363, L. Sorn at p. 366. It was there held that a *prima facie* case is not enough if it means no more than proof that the defender took all reasonable care. He must either prove conclusively that the loss occurred for some reason other than his own negligence, or he must prove facts from which an inference to the same effect clearly arises. See also *Macrae* v. *K. & I. Ltd.*, (O.H.) 1962 S.L.T. (Notes) 90.

[44] *Williams* v. *Dobbie*, 1884, 11 R. 982.

[45] See § 81.

ship of *res ipsa loquitur* to the above general statement is discussed in the next paragraph. When the onus shifts to the defender he must normally establish the cause of the accident before he can dissociate it from his own negligence.[46] When the exact cause of the accident is not established it is difficult but not necessarily impossible[47] for the defender to discharge the onus. He does not necessarily do so, at least where the cause of the occurrence is left in doubt, by proving merely that he took all the usual precautions.[48]

80. RES IPSA LOQUITUR

Confusion has been caused by regarding this maxim as if it were an exception to the general statement suggested in the last paragraph instead of a somewhat incomplete Latin rendering of it. It has sometimes been construed as meaning that the mere occurrence of an accident infers negligence and places the onus of disproving negligence upon the defender. The mere occurrence of an accident, however, cannot by itself give rise to such an inference,[49] whereas the circumstances of and surrounding its occurrence may do so. The maxim is not a legal principle,[50] but merely a presumption of fact depending upon the circumstances of each case.[51] Whether it applies or not depends upon whether in the circumstances of the particular case the mere fact of the occurrence is relevant to infer negligence.[52] So described, the maxim seems to be indistinguishable from the general statement, but, because it has sometimes been regarded as an exception to it, the courts have from time to time thought it necessary to limit its application to certain classes of case. It has been said to apply "where the thing is shown to be under the management of the defendant or his servants, and the accident is such as in the ordinary course of things does not happen if those who have the management use proper care,"[53] but to be limited to cases in which a state of apparent stability has been disturbed without the intervention of personal activities which can be spoken to by witnesses,[54] or where the thing which causes the injury is outside human control at the moment of the accident.[55] It is thought that for practical purposes these limitations are now unhelpful,

---

[46] *The Merchant Prince* [1892] P. 179; *Burns* v. *Royal Hotel* (*St. Andrews*) *Ltd.*, 1958 S.C. 354; *Marshall* v. *Russian Oil Products Ltd.*, 1938 S.C. 773.

[47] *Marshall* v. *Russian Oil Products Ltd.* (*supra*), L. J-Cl. Aitchison at p. 791; *Burns* v. *Royal Hotel* (*St. Andrews*) *Ltd.* (*supra*), L.P. Clyde at p. 362, L. Sorn at p. 366.

[48] *Burns* v. *Royal Hotel* (*St. Andrews*) *Ltd.* (*supra*), L.P. Clyde at p. 362.

[49] *O'Hara* v. *Central S.M.T. Co.*, 1941 S.C. 363, L. Carmont at p. 391; *Alexander* v. *Phillip*, 1899, 1 F. 985.

[50] *Ballard* v. *North British Railway Co.*, 1923 S.C. (H.L.) 43, L. Shaw at p. 56.

[51] *O'Hara* v. *Central S.M.T. Co.* (*supra*), L.P. Normand at p. 377. See also L. Carmont at p. 391.

[52] *Ballard* v. *North British Railway Co.* (*supra*), L. Dunedin at p. 53.

[53] Erle C.J. in *Scott* v. *London & St. Katherine's Dock Co.*, 1865, 3 H. & C. 596, at p. 601, quoted with approval in *Ballard* v. *North British Railway Co.* (*supra*), at pp. 48, 55, 56, and *Milliken* v. *Glasgow Corporation*, 1918 S.C. 857, L. Salvesen at p. 867.

[54] *O'Hara* v. *Central S.M.T. Co.*, 1941 S.C. 363, L. Moncrieff at p. 388, L.P. Normand at p. 377.

[55] *Inglis* v. *London, Midland and Scottish Railway Co.*, 1941 S.C. 551, L.P. Normand at p. 559.

since the presumptions of negligence arising from the circumstances to which they refer have the same effect upon onus of proof as the similar presumptions arising from the many other circumstances covered by the general statement. It is true that Lord Dunedin, in *Ballard* v. *North British Railway Co.*,[56] seemed to suggest that the onus of proof resting upon the defender when the maxim applies, might be different from that resting upon him as a result of a presumption from surrounding circumstances generally, since in the former case the defender might not always need to disprove negligence. He suggested that in certain circumstances it might be enough for the defender to put forward, apparently without proof, an explanation of the accident other than his own negligence, and then "the cogency of the fact of the accident by itself disappears and the pursuer is left as he began, namely, that he has to show negligence."[56] It is suggested, however, that if the facts relied upon by the pursuer are equally susceptible of two explanations, one being the negligence of the defender and the other something else, such as the skidding of a vehicle[57] or the bursting of a tyre,[58] the evidence is neutral on the question of negligence and the onus never shifts to the defender.[58a] That this is the true position seems to be implicit in the words of Lord Dunedin quoted above.[59] It is sufficient, however, to note that Lord Dunedin's view that the defender may be able to discharge without proof the onus resting upon him was not shared by the majority in that case,[60] and that it has been rejected in more recent decisions.[61] This seems to remove any shred of reason for regarding the maxim as limited to certain classes of case. It is thought, accordingly, either that the maxim should cease to be used because, if construed literally, it tends to mislead, or that it should be applied to all cases where an inference of fault arises from the circumstances surrounding an accident. On either view, the cases in which the maxim has been held to apply may be added to the examples of the application of the general statement which are given in the next paragraph.

81. EXAMPLES OF SHIFTING OF BURDEN OF PROOF—NEGLIGENCE

In actions arising out of collisions at sea the onus of disproving fault is upon an overtaking vessel,[62] or a vessel which collides during daylight with

---

[56] *Ballard* v. *North British Railway Co.*, 1923 S.C. (H.L.) 43, at p. 54.

[57] *Laurie* v. *Raglan Building Co., Ltd.* [1942] 1 K.B. 152.

[58] *Elliot* v. *Young's Bus Service*, 1945 S.C. 445, L. J-Cl. Cooper at p. 455, L. Mackay at p. 458, *cf.* L. Jamieson at pp. 464-465; *Barkway* v. *South Wales Transport Co.* [1948] 2 All E.R. 460. See also *Henderson* v. *Mair*, 1928 S.C. 1, and § **81**, notes 75, 76.

[58a] In *Brown* v. *Rolls Royce Ltd.*, 1960 S.C. (H.L.) 22, the evidence seems to have been regarded as neutral in this sense. See L. Denning at p. 28.

[59] See L. Carmont in *O'Hara* v. *Central S.M.T. Co.*, 1940 S.C. 363, at p. 393, and Evershed, M. R., in *Moore* v. *R. Fox & Sons* [1956] 1 Q.B. 596, at p. 614.

[60] *Ballard* v. *North British Railway Co.* (*supra*), L. Haldane at pp. 49-51, L. Finlay at p. 52, L. Shaw at p. 56. See L. Carmont's note on this point in *O'Hara* v. *Central S.M.T. Co.* (*supra*), at p. 393, and his opinion on the whole question at pp. 390-394. See also L. Moncrieff in *Mars* v. *Glasgow Corporation*, 1940 S.C. 202, at p. 209, and L. Wark in *Marshall* v. *Russian Oil Products Ltd.*, 1938 S.C. 773, at pp. 810, 811.

[61] *O'Hara* v. *Central S.M.T. Co.* (*supra*); *Moore* v. *R. Fox & Sons* (*supra*), Evershed M. R., at p. 608.

a vessel moored or at anchor.[63] A pursuer whose son was killed when he fell from the off-side doorway of the railway compartment in which he was travelling, proved that the door was not interfered with by the passengers during the journey from the last station and that it was improbable that it had been interfered with by passengers or strangers while at the station. An inference of negligence on the part of the railway company's servants was thereupon held to arise, and the onus of disproving their negligence shifted to the defenders.[64] When a pursuer's property was damaged by flooding from a burst water pipe in property owned and occupied by the defender, it was held that a presumption of negligence on the part of the latter arose from the fact that the pipe was thirty years old and had needed repairs on six occasions during the year preceding the burst.[65] When a barrel of petrol exploded and set fire to a pursuer's bakery premises while it was being delivered there on behalf of the defenders, the barrel being the property of and under their control, and there being no evidence that the leakage was caused by negligence in unloading,[66] an inference that the defenders were negligent in failing to provide a suitable barrel was held to arise, the onus of rebutting which fell upon them.[67] Following a collision on a single line of railway between a power-driven trolley and a runaway bogie, as a result of which a man on the trolley was killed, it was proved that the defenders' servants, who had been loading the bogie on a gradient of 1 in 50, removed a scotch from beneath its wheel, that thereafter it was prevented, if prevented at all, from running down the incline only by a brake, and that immediately after the removal of the scotch it moved off and gathered speed. It was held that the onus then shifted to the defenders to absolve their employees from the inference of negligence which arose.[68] It has been held that when a horse is either left unattended or otherwise uncontrolled and bolts, and a pedestrian is injured, there is a presumption of fault against the driver, the onus of rebutting which rests upon him,[69] but this has been thought to need reconsideration,[70] and the whole circumstances surrounding the bolting must probably be looked at before the question of onus can be decided.[71] When a pedestrian in broad daylight is walking steadily along[72]

[62] Owners of the "Hilda" v. Owners of the "Australia," 1884, 12 R. 76. See Article 24 of the Regulations for Preventing Collisions at Sea, made under the Merchant Shipping Act, 1894 (57 & 58 Vict. c. 60), s. 418.
[63] Marsden, Collisions at Sea (10th ed.) 37.
[64] Inglis v. London, Midland and Scottish Railway Co., 1941 S.C. 551, L.P. Normand at p. 559, L. Moncrieff at pp. 562-563. See also Burns v. North British Railway Co., 1914 S.C. 754.
[65] Moffat & Co. v. Park, 1877, 5 R. 13, L. Ormidale at p. 15, L. Gifford at p. 17.
[66] Marshall & Son v. Russian Oil Products Ltd., 1938 S.C. 773, L. Wark at p. 810.
[67] Marshall & Son v. Russian Oil Products Ltd. (supra), following Erle, C. J., in Scott v. London & St. Katherine's Dock Co. (1865) 3 H. & C. 596, at p. 601, and Ballard v. North British Railway Co., 1923 S.C. (H.L.) 43, at p. 45.
[68] Gunn v. McAdam & Son, 1949 S.C. 31, at pp. 38, 40.
[69] Snee v. Durkie, 1903, 6 F. 42.
[70] Ballantyne v. Hamilton, 1938 S.N. 57; 1938 S.L.T. 468, L. Moncrieff at p. 471.
[71] Hendry v. McDougall, 1923 S.C. 378, L. J-Cl. Alness at p. 382, L. Anderson at p. 387; cf. L. Ormidale at p. 383, L. Hunter at p. 386. As to damage caused by an unattended and driverless motor vehicle, see McCusker v. Armstrong, 1946 S.N. 113.
[72] Anderson v. Blackwood, 1886, 13 R. 443.

or across[73] a road and is knocked down by a vehicle, in circumstances which would have enabled the driver by slowing down or stopping to avoid the collision, the onus is upon the driver to prove that he was not at fault.[74] If an omnibus swerves on to the pavement and collides with an object there and a passenger is injured, there is *prima facie* evidence of negligent driving which the owners of the omnibus, as defenders, must rebut.[75] They do not do so merely by proving that the swerve was caused by the bursting of a tyre,[75] because that fact is neutral on the question of negligence. They must go further and prove that the bursting of the tyre was not the result of a faulty system of tyre maintenance or otherwise due to their negligence.[76] When a public service vehicle is so driven that the safety of a passenger is imperilled, the peril so created raises an inference of negligent driving which the driver's employers must rebut in order to escape liability,[77] and this general statement has been applied to the sudden application of the magnetic brake of a tramcar which threw a standing passenger[78] and seated passengers[79] to the floor, the sudden swerving to the right of an omnibus moving gradually to the left, which threw a passenger from the platform on to the road,[80] and the collision of an omnibus with a road-side fence.[81] It is thought that in order that the inference of negligence may arise when the injury is caused merely by braking or swerving, the passenger must have been taking normal precautions for his own safety.[82]

---

[73] *Clerk* v. *Petrie*, 1879, 6 R. 1076.
[74] *Craig* v. *Glasgow Corporation*, 1919 S.C. (H.L.) 1, L. Dunedin at p. 11 (visibility 100 yards during hours of darkness).
[75] *Elliot* v. *Young's Bus Service*, 1945 S.C. 445, L. J-Cl. Cooper at p. 455; *Barkway* v. *South Wales Transport Co.* [1948] 2 All E.R. 460, Asquith, L. J., at p. 471 (reversed on another point [1950] A.C. 185, the House of Lords insisting upon a more stringent proof of a proper system of tyre maintenance than had been required by the Court of Appeal: see [1950] 1 All E.R. 392).
[76] *Elliot* v. *Young's Bus Service (supra); Barkway* v. *South Wales Transport Co. (supra).* In *Elliot* v. *Young's Bus Service* differing reasons are given for placing the onus of proof upon the defenders: (1) an inference of negligent driving arose because the omnibus mounted the pavement (L. J-Cl. Cooper at p. 455): (2) the facts regarding the maintenance of their tyres being peculiarly within the knowledge of the defenders (see § 75 (c)), the onus of proof was on them (L. Mackay at p. 459): (3) an inference of negligence arose from the fact that the tyre burst (L. Jamieson at pp. 464-465).
[77] *O'Hara* v. *Central S.M.T. Co.*, 1941 S.C. 363, L. Normand at p. 375; *Sutherland* v. *Glasgow Corporation*, 1951 S.C. (H.L.) 1, L. Normand at p. 7. *Cf. Ballingall* v. *Glasgow Corporation*, 1948 S.C. 160, L. Jamieson at pp. 168-169.
[78] *Sutherland* v. *Glasgow Corporation (supra).*
[79] *Mars* v. *Glasgow Corporation*, 1940 S.C. 202.
[80] *O'Hara* v. *Central S.M.T. Co. (supra).*
[81] *Doonan* v. *S.M.T. Co.*, 1950 S.C. 136.
[82] *O'Hara* v. *Central S.M.T. Co.*, 1941 S.C. 363, L. Fleming at p. 384 ("a passenger who was taking due care of her own safety"). It was clearly proved that the pursuer was holding on tightly to the handrail (p. 366). In *Sutherland* v. *Glasgow Corporation (supra)*, although the pursuer was standing, it was found in fact (p. 2) that the driver knew or ought to have known that she had not had time to take her seat. In *Mars* v. *Glasgow Corporation (supra)*, the pursuer was seated. *Cf.*, however, *Allam* v. *Western S.M.T. Co.*, 1943 S.N. 69, where the Lord Chancellor (Viscount Simon) said that, at least in crowded wartime conditions, the driver owed a duty of care to standing passengers who are not "holding on."

82. CRIMINAL CAUSES—ONUS ON PROSECUTOR—STANDARD OF PROOF

Because of the presumption of innocence,[83] the burden of proof of a criminal charge rests upon the Crown throughout the trial.[84] It is for the Crown to prove the accused's guilt beyond reasonable doubt, and it is not for the accused to prove his own innocence.[85] The doubt must be reasonable in that it must not be a strained or fanciful acceptance of remote possibilities.[86] If at the conclusion of the evidence for both parties a reasonable doubt exists in the mind of the jury as to the accused's guilt, he must be acquitted. Even in a case where the onus of proof has shifted for some purpose to the defence,[87] with regard, for example, to a special defence of alibi[88] or self defence,[89] a reasonable doubt of the accused's guilt may arise from the uncorroborated evidence, if believed, of the accused or of some other witness for the defence, in which case there must be an acquittal although the special defence has not been proved.[90]

83. ONUS ON ACCUSED—STANDARD OF PROOF

(a) **General.** Although the burden of proving guilt beyond reasonable doubt rests upon the Crown throughout the trial,[91] there are occasions when on certain issues or for certain purposes a burden of proof is placed upon the defence. When this occurs the onus may be discharged by satisfying the jury on a balance of probabilities of the fact or facts which the accused desires to establish, the higher standard of proof beyond reasonable doubt being unnecessary.[92] As already stated,[91] the accused may fail to discharge the onus, perhaps because his own evidence or the evidence of some other defence witness is uncorroborated, but this evidence, if believed, may nevertheless be sufficient to raise in the minds of the jury a reasonable doubt as to his guilt.[93] The occasions when, subject to what has been said above, the

---

[83] *Slater* v. *H.M. Advocate*, 1928 J.C. 94, at p. 105.

[84] *Lennie* v. *H.M. Advocate*, 1946 J.C. 79, at p. 80; *Owens* v. *H.M. Advocate*, 1946 J.C. 119, at p. 124.

[85] Renton and Brown, *Criminal Procedure* (3rd ed.) 402. Recent attempts in England to find a satisfactory alternative to the expression "reasonable doubt" (*Rex* v. *Summers* [1952] W.N. 185) have not been particularly successful. (*Rex* v. *Hepworth and Fearnley* [1955] 2 Q.B. 600.) In Scotland the traditional expression is still used. See *Shaw* v. *H.M. Advocate*, 1953 J.C. 51, L. J-Cl. Thomson at p. 54.

[86] *Irving* v. *Minister of Pensions*, 1945 S.C. 21, L. J-Cl. Cooper at p. 29.

[87] See § 83.

[88] *Lennie* v. *H.M. Advocate* (*supra*), at p. 81. See also *Dickson* v. *H.M. Advocate*, 1950 J.C. 1.

[89] *Hillan* v. *H.M. Advocate*, 1937 J.C. 53, at p. 59; *Owens* v. *H.M. Advocate*, 1946 J.C. 119, at p. 124; *H.M.Advocate* v. *Docherty*, 1954 J.C. 1, at p. 6.

[90] This is not true of the special defence of insanity at the time of the crime. See § 83, note 93.

[91] See § 82.

[92] *Robertson* v. *Watson*, 1949 J.C. 73, L. J-G. Cooper at p. 88; *H.M. Advocate* v. *Mitchell*, 1951 J.C. 53, at pp. 53-54.

[93] This is not true, it is thought, of the special defence of insanity at the time of the crime, when, in order to obtain an acquittal on the ground of insanity alone, the accused's insanity at the time of the crime must be proved on a balance of probabilities: *H.M. Advocate* v. *Kidd*, 1960 J.C. 61, at pp. 68-69; *H.M. Advocate* v. *Braithwaite*, 1945 J.C. 55.

onus of proof is placed upon the accused are mentioned in the following sub-paragraphs.

(b) Special Defences. When a special defence is stated by the accused, the onus of proving it is upon him. The most usual examples are insanity at the time of the crime charged,[94] alibi[95] and self defence.[95] Akin to these is the plea, restricted to charges of murder, of diminished responsibility due to intoxication[96] or some other form of mental impairment,[97] which may have the effect of reducing the crime from murder to culpable homicide.

(c) Presumption of Guilt from Proved Facts. When the facts proved by the Crown raise a presumption of the guilt of the accused person, unless other facts or another explanation of the facts are put forward, the onus of establishing these other matters rests upon the accused.[98] This is especially the case where the facts are peculiarly within the accused's own knowledge.[99] When a man was seen in the early morning near a coal bunker carrying a parcel which was found to contain coal, and when he gave the police an explanation of the source of the coal which he later contradicted, these facts, when proved, were held to justify a conviction of theft unless the accused gave evidence justifying his possession of the coal, which he did not do.[1] The onus placed upon the accused as a result of his possession of recently stolen property has been mentioned earlier.[2] In a charge of concealment of pregnancy, when the pregnancy has been proved, the onus passes to the accused to prove that she disclosed her pregnant state to some person.[3] When it was proved, in a charge of fishing for salmon without permission from the proprietors, that the accused were on the water at 4.50 a.m. in the possession of gear suitable only for illegal salmon fishing, it was held that an inference arose that the accused had no permission from the proprietors, and that, since the accused had led no evidence to rebut this inference, they ought to have been convicted.[4] When an accused was charged as the person registered in terms of the Burgh Police (Scotland) Acts for keeping certain premises as a place of public refreshment, and the prosecutor produced the relative register containing her name and a form of application for registration bearing to be signed by her, it was held that, failing evidence led by the

---

94 *H.M. Advocate* v. *Mitchell* (*supra*). See note 93 above.

95 See § **82**, notes 88, 89. For other examples, see Renton and Brown, *Criminal Procedure* (3rd ed.) 75.

96 It is thought that intoxication produces this result only if it renders the accused incapable of forming at the time the intention of killing or doing serious injury. See *H.M. Advocate* v. *Campbell*, 1921 J.C. 1, L. J-Cl. Scott Dickson at pp. 2, 3, 4; *H.M. Advocate* v. *Savage*, 1923 J.C. 49, L. J-Cl. Alness at p. 51; *Kennedy* v. *H.M. Advocate*, 1944 J.C. 171; *Carraher* v. *H.M. Advocate*, 1946 J.C. 108.

97 *H.M.Advocate* v. *Braithwaite*, 1945 J.C. 55, at p. 58; *H.M.Advocate* v. *Savage* (*supra*).

98 *H.M. Advocate* v. *Hardy*, 1938 J.C. 144.

99 Dickson, *Evidence* (3rd ed.) §32; *H.M. Advocate* v. *Hardy* (*supra*), at p. 147; *Cruickshank* v. *Smith*, 1949 J.C. 134, L. Jamieson at pp. 151 *et seq*.

1 *Costello* v. *Macpherson*, 1922 J.C. 9. See also *Dewar* v. *H.M. Advocate*, 1945 J.C. 5.

2 See § **68.**

3 Dickson, *Evidence* (3rd ed.) §§29, 32.

4 *Cruickshank* v. *Smith*, 1949 J.C. 134.

accused repudiating her signature, the proof of registration was adequate.[5] It is thought that, on a charge of failing to report a road traffic accident to the police within twenty-four hours, it is sufficient for the prosecutor to prove that no reports have been received at local police stations, and that thereupon the onus shifts to the accused to prove that he reported at another police station.[6]

(d) Onus Placed on Accused by Statute. Two general statutory provisions[7] have the effect of placing a limited onus of proof upon the accused in certain cases. They are as follows: any exception, exemption, proviso, excuse or qualification, whether it does or does not accompany in the same section the description of the offence in the statute or order creating the offence, may be proved by the accused, but need not be specified or negatived in the complaint, and no proof in relation to such exception, exemption, proviso, excuse or qualification is required on behalf of the prosecution;[8] where an offence is alleged to be committed in any special capacity, as by the holder of a licence, master of a vessel, occupier of a house or the like, the fact that the accused possesses the qualification necessary to the commission of the offence, unless challenged by preliminary objection before his plea is recorded, is held as admitted.[9] In addition to these general provisions many statutes and statutory instruments create presumptions against the accused, the onus of rebutting which rests upon him, or provide that the accused may prove specific defences in answer to the case proved against him by the prosecution.[10]

[5] *Frame* v. *Fyfe*, 1948 J.C. 140, L. Mackay at p. 149.
[6] Road Traffic Act, 1960 (8 & 9 Eliz. II. c. 16), s. 77 (2). See *Wood* v. *MacLean*, 1947 J.C. 18.
[7] *Solemn Procedure.* Summary Jurisdiction (Scotland) Act, 1908 (8 Edw. VII. c. 65), ss. 19 (3) (5), 77 (4); Criminal Justice (Scotland) Act, 1949 (12, 13 & 14 Geo. VI. c. 94), s. 34; Summary Jurisdiction (Scotland) Act, 1954 (2 & 3 Eliz. II. c. 48), Sch. 4. *Summary Procedure.* Summary Jurisdiction (Scotland) Act, 1954 (2 & 3 Eliz. II. c. 48), s. 16 (d) (f).
[8] This provision has been discussed in *Archibald* v. *Plean Colliery Co.*, 1924 J.C. 77; *Chalmers* v. *Speedwell Wire Co.*, 1942 J.C. 42; *Din* v. *Adair*, 1947 J.C. 145; *Muir* v. *Grant & Co.*, 1948 J.C. 42; *Cruickshank* v. *Smith*, 1949 J.C. 134; *British Transport Commission* v. *Dalgleish*, 1955 J.C. 80.
[9] This provision has been discussed in *Archibald* v. *Plean Colliery Co.* (*supra*); *Shiach* v. *Farquhar*, 1929 J.C. 88; *Smith* v. *Grant*, 1932 J.C. 36; *Smith* v. *Ross*, 1937 J.C. 65; *Wilson* v. *Brown*, 1947 J.C. 81; *Frame* v. *Fyfe* (*supra*).
[10] Recent examples are: Bankruptcy (Scotland) Act, 1913 (3 & 4 Geo. V. c. 20), s. 178 (A); Customs and Excise Act, 1952 (15 & 16 Geo. VI. and 1 Eliz. II. c. 44), s. 290 (2); Prevention of Crime Act, 1953 (1 & 2 Eliz. II. c. 14), s. 1 (1); Road Traffic Act, 1956 (4 & 5 Eliz. II. c. 67), s. 9 (1).

CHAPTER VIII

STANDARD OF PROOF—DIFFERENCES BETWEEN AVERMENT AND PROOF

84. STANDARD OF PROOF—CRIMINAL CAUSES

The standard of proof needed to discharge an onus or to rebut a presumption or inference of fact in criminal causes was described in the last chapter.[1]

85. STANDARD OF PROOF—CIVIL CAUSES—GENERAL RULE

Apart from the exceptions mentioned in the next paragraph, the standard of proof needed to discharge an onus or to rebut a presumption in a civil cause is not so high or so exacting as that required of a prosecutor in a criminal cause. It does not need to be proof beyond reasonable doubt.[2] When the evidence is circumstantial and the proved facts give rise to a number of conflicting inferences, the inference which is the more probable will prevail.[3] If all are equally consistent with the proved facts and none is more probable than the others, nothing has been proved, and he on whom lies the onus of proof fails.[3] If, however, the evidence satisfies the jury or the court of the probability of that which must be established, the onus of proof is discharged.[4] The decision has been said to turn upon a balance[5] or preponderance[6] of probabilities. When negligence is in issue the standard of probability applies not only to the proof of negligence, whether that consist in common law fault or breach of statutory duty, but also to the proof that the injury resulted therefrom.[7] Independently proved facts and circumstances corroborate the evidence of a single eye-witness if they show that his

---

1 See §§ **82, 83.**
2 *Hendry* v. *Clan Line Steamers, Ltd.,* 1949 S.C. 320.
3 *Hendry* v. *Clan Line Steamers, Ltd. (supra),* L. Jamieson at p. 328.
4 *Robertson* v. *Watson,* 1949 J.C. 73, L. J-G. Cooper at p. 88, quoted as applying also to civil causes by L. J-Cl. Thomson in *Hendry* v. *Clan Line Steamers, Ltd. (supra),* at pp. 323-324.
5 *Simpson* v. *London, Midland & Scottish Railway Co.,* 1931 S.C. (H.L.) 15, L. Dunedin at p. 20.
6 *Rex* v. *Carr-Briant* [1943], K.B. 607, at p. 611.
7 *Wardlaw* v. *Bonnington Castings,* 1956 S.C. (H.L.) 26, L. Reid at p. 31, L. Tucker at p. 34; *Kenyon* v. *Bell* (O.H.) 1953 S.C. 125, L. Guthrie at p. 128.

narrative is the most probable account of what occurred.[8] Consideration by
the jury or by the court of the probability of a party's averments being true
must, however, proceed upon evidence supporting these averments, and not
upon conjecture as to what would probably have been established if such
evidence had been led. Thus a party cannot discharge the onus of proving
his case by leading only the evidence of the opponent and his employees
which contradicts it, and by arguing that, since the evidence was manifestly
false, the opposite of it must be true.[9] The evidence necessary to discharge
the somewhat heavy onus of proving donation has been mentioned earlier.[10]
The question as to whether in a civil cause the commission of a crime, such
as fraud, must be proved by the standard of proof appropriate to criminal
proceedings, or whether proof on a balance of probabilities is sufficient, has
not received much consideration in Scotland,[11] although it has been said
that the criminal standard applies.[12] The most recent decision in England
supports the view that proof on a balance of probabilities is enough.[13]
If a party to a contract founds upon an oral warranty, he must prove by
satisfactory evidence the very words spoken.[14]

86. EXCEPTIONS TO THE GENERAL RULE

Adultery in an action of divorce or of separation and aliment must be
proved beyond reasonable doubt, and guilt of sodomy or bestiality in an
action of divorce, when an extract of a conviction is not produced, must
also, it is thought, be proved in the same way.[15] The presumption against
illegitimacy, when it arises,[16] may be redargued only by proof beyond reasonable doubt.[17] The same standard of proof is required before the Minister of
Pensions may discharge the onus resting upon him under the Royal Warrant.[18]

87. DIFFERENCES BETWEEN AVERMENT AND PROOF—CIVIL CAUSES

The Scottish system of written pleadings is designed to give notice of the

---

[8] O'Hara v. Central S.M.T. Co., 1941 S.C. 363, L.P. Normand at p. 379.
[9] Cameron v. Yeats, 1899, 1 F. 456.
[10] See § 61.
[11] In Gibson v. National Cash Register Co., 1925 S.C. 500 (damages for fraud) the matter is not discussed.
[12] Arnott v. Burt, 1872, 11 M. 62, L. Neaves at p. 74. It has also been said that it must be proved by very clear evidence: Wink v. Speirs, 1867, 6 M. 77, L. J-Cl. Patton at p. 80; Cullen's Tr. v. Johnston, 1865, 3 M. 935, L.P. McNeill at p. 937.
[13] Hornal v. Neuberger Products, Ltd. [1957] 1 Q.B. 247. For a discussion of the English decisions, see Cross, Evidence (1958) 123-124.
[14] Robeson v. Waugh, 1874, 2 R. 63; Mackie v. Riddell, 1874, 2 R. 115.
[15] See § 160.
[16] As to this, see § 70.
[17] Preston-Jones v. Preston-Jones [1951] A.C. 391, at pp. 400, 412, 417; Dickson, Evidence (3rd ed.) §143; Mackay v. Mackay, 1855, 17 D. 494, L.P. McNeill at p. 500. The husband's impotency or impossibility of access, however (see Stair, iii, 3, 42; Erskine, i, 6, 50), need not now be proved. There may be other evidence which will satisfy the court that the husband de facto is not the father of the child. See Mackay v. Mackay (supra); Brodie v. Dyce, 1872, 11 M. 142; Gardner v. Gardner, 1877, 4 R. (H.L.) 56,

facts and of the pleas-in-law which are to be relied upon by each party, and to prevent either from proving other facts or founding upon other legal pleas to the detriment of an opponent who has had no opportunity of bringing evidence with regard to them. If for any reason evidence of such facts has been received, or argument in support of a plea-in-law not stated has been allowed, judgment ought not to be pronounced until the party concerned has amended his pleadings,[19] and his opponent has had an opportunity of answering, and of leading further proof, if he so desires.[20] When, however, the opponent has had ample notice of the case made against him, it may not matter that the facts proved, if they justify the remedy sought, are not entirely in line in matters of detail with what has been averred.[21] As a general rule it is sufficient if a party proves the substance of what he avers.[22] So, in an action of damages for negligent driving of a motor vehicle, when it was averred that a child was struck while both his feet were on the pavement and the evidence showed that one or both were in the gutter, it was held that the discrepancy was not material to the general case of negligent driving which had been averred, and on which evidence had been led, and that the case ought not to have been withdrawn from the jury.[23] On the other hand exact conformity between the proof and the averment has been held essential in a case of oral slander, as to the precise words of the alleged slanderous statement,[24] and as to the identity of a person in whose presence it was uttered.[25] What is or is not a material divergence is a question of degree in each case.[26] A party need not necessarily prove all his averments. It is sufficient if he establishes facts consistent with and within the ambit of his averments, which entitle him in law to the remedy which he seeks.[21] In an action of damages for negligent driving the pursuer usually avers that the defender has failed in a number of duties, such as the duty to drive at a safe speed, to keep the vehicle under proper control and not to change direction without giving adequate warning of his intention. He will succeed if he establishes that the accident was caused by negligence in respect of any one of these faults, although he may fail to prove the commission of the others. And when, in an action of reduction, fraud and undue influence are averred

---

L. Gordon at p. 74; *Montgomery* v. *Montgomery*, 1881, 8 R. 403; *Steedman* v. *Steedman*, 1887, 14 R. 1066; *Coles* v. *Homer*, 1893, 22 R. 716.

[18] See § **75**, note 10.

[19] *Black* v. *John Williams & Co. (Wishaw)*, 1924 S.C. (H.L.) 22; *"Vitruvia" S.S. Co.* v. *Ropner Shipping Co.*, 1924 S.C. (H.L.) 31. For the court's powers to allow amendment, see Rules of Court, 1948, Rule 117 (a) (i)-(vii) (Court of Session); Sheriff Courts (Scotland) Act, 1907 (7 Edw. VII c. 51), Rule 79 (Sheriff Court).

[20] *Oswald* v. *Fairs*, 1911 S.C. 257.

[21] *Gunn* v. *McAdam & Son*, 1949 S.C. 31. But *cf. Lawrence* v. *Sir William Arrol & Co.*, 1958 S.C. 348.

[22] Dickson, *Evidence* (3rd ed.) §41.

[23] *McDonald* v. *Duncan*, 1933 S.C. 737. It must be noted that the evidence referred to was admitted without challenge on the part of the defender. See also *Livingstone* v. *Strachan, Crerar & Jones*, 1923 S.C. 794; *Brown* v. *Ross*, 1935 S.N. 9. *Cf. Littlejohn* v. *Brown & Co.*, 1909 S.C. 169.

[24] *Martin* v. *McLean*, 1844, 6 D. 981.

[25] *Broomfield* v. *Greig*, 1868, 6 M. 992. See also *Walker* v. *Cumming*, 1868, 6 M. 318.

[26] *McDonald* v. *Duncan* (*supra*), L. Murray at p. 745, L. Wark at p. 746.

and pleaded, decree may be pronounced on the ground of undue influence although fraud is negatived.[27] The same rule does not necessarily apply to a cause remitted to a jury, where the pursuer will fail if he does not obtain a favourable verdict on the issue, even if the issue includes more than is necessary for his success.[28]

88. DIFFERENCES BETWEEN LIBEL AND PROOF—CRIMINAL CAUSES

Any discrepancy between the libel and the evidence led was at one time fatal to the prosecutor's success, but this strictness is considerably mitigated by the wide power of amendment now given by statute.[29] Briefly put, the charge may, subject to the discretion of the court, be amended so as to cure any error or defect therein or any discrepancy or variance between it and the evidence, provided that the character of the crime or offence is not changed and that an adjournment is allowed if the accused would, without it, be prejudiced in conducting his defence. Specifications of time, place and quantity, moreover, are read as if subject to a latitude implied by statute,[30] such as "in or near," "or thereby" and the like, unless proof of the exact time, place or quantity libelled. is essential to the proof of the crime or offence. Thus, on a charge of theft or reset of a specified number of articles, proof of the theft or reset of only some of them justifies a verdict of guilty as libelled,[31] since the words "or part thereof" are by implication read into all such statements of quantities,[30] but when it is essential to the proof of a statutory offence that, of the articles making up a consignment, those over a certain size shall exceed a specified proportion of the whole, proof that a part of the consignment contained an excessive proportion of over-size articles does not justify a conviction.[32]

The following statutory provisions also have a bearing on this subject: under a charge of robbery, or of theft, or of breach of trust and embezzlement, or of falsehood, fraud and wilful imposition the accused may be convicted of reset; under a charge of robbery, or of breach of trust and embezzlement, or of falsehood, fraud and wilful imposition the accused may be convicted of theft; and under a charge of theft the accused may be convicted of

---

27 *Gray* v. *Binny*, 1879, 7 R. 332. See also *Petrie* v. *Forsyth*, 1874, 2 R. 214; *Forbes* v. *Forbes Trs.*, 1957 S.C. 325, L. Guthrie at p. 330.

28 *Balmer* v. *Hogarth*, 1830, 8 S. 715. As to adjustment of the issue, see *Black* v. *Duncan*, 1924 S.C. 738.

29 *Solemn Procedure.* Summary Jurisdiction (Scotland) Act, 1908 (8 Edw. VII. c. 65), ss. 30, 77 (4); Criminal Procedure (Scotland) Act, 1887 (50 & 51 Vict. c. 35), s. 70. *Summary Procedure.* Summary Jurisdiction (Scotland) Act, 1954 (2 & 3 Eliz. II. c. 48), s. 27. For a full discussion and citation of authority on the subject matter of this paragraph, see Renton and Brown, *Criminal Procedure* (3rd ed.) 56 *et seq.*, 63 *et seq.*, 106, 125 *et seq.*, 208, 250 *et seq.*

30 Criminal Procedure (Scotland) Act, 1887 (50 & 51 Vict. c. 35), ss. 10, 11; Summary Jurisdiction (Scotland) Act, 1954 (2 & 3 Eliz. II. c. 48), s. 2, Sch. I.

31 *Gold* v. *Neilson*, 1908 S.C. (J.) 5; *Myers* v. *H.M. Advocate*, 1936 J.C. 1.

32 *Pattullo, Barr & Co.* v. *McLean*, 1947 J.C. 50. See also *Heatlie* v. *Reid*, 1961 J.C. 70 (sale of milk); *Macdonald* v. *Patterson*, 1894, 21 R. (J.) 38 (sale of exciseable liquor on Sunday); *Sharpe* v. *Donald*, 1935 J.C. 37; *cf. Bain* v. *Agnew*, 1952 J.C. 108 (sale of liquor after permitted hours in private room not part of certificated premises).

breach of trust and embezzlement or of falsehood, fraud and wilful imposition, or may be convicted of theft although the circumstances proved may in law amount to robbery;[33] where a completed crime is charged it is competent to convict only of an attempt to commit the crime, and, if the attempt alone is charged, the accused may be convicted of the attempt though the evidence be sufficient to prove completion of the crime;[34] where a crime is charged as having been committed with a particular intent or with particular circumstances of aggravation it is competent to convict of the crime without the intent or aggravation;[35] where a statutory offence is also criminal at common law, or where the facts proved in a case do not amount to a contravention of the statute, but do amount to a crime at common law, it is lawful to convict of the common law crime.[36] It is not, however, competent to lead evidence not relevant to the statutory offence charged in order to establish a common law crime,[37] and the statutory relaxations generally cannot be extended by analogy to other circumstances which the statutory provisions do not in terms cover. Thus on a statutory charge under the Defence Regulations of theft of a controlled article, a conviction of the distinct statutory offence of reset of a controlled article was held incompetent.[38]

As has been indicated above, it is not necessary in order to justify a conviction that the prosecutor must prove all the averments contained in a charge. It is enough that he proves facts consistent with and within the ambit of his averments from which the essential elements of the crime or offence may be inferred.[39] Proof of any part of what is charged, if it is itself a crime or offence, justifies a conviction of that crime or offence,[35] and a superfluous statement[40] in the charge, or, provided evidence is led which proves the identity, particulars given about any person, corporation, company, place or thing,[41] need not be proved.

---

[33] Criminal Procedure (Scotland) Act, 1887 (50 & 51 Vict. c. 35), s. 59; Summary Jurisdiction (Scotland) Act, 1954 (2 & 3 Eliz. II. c. 48), s. 2, Sch. I.

[34] Criminal Procedure (Scotland) Act, 1887 (50 & 51 Vict. c. 35), s. 61; Summary Jurisdiction (Scotland) Act, 1954 (2 & 3 Eliz. II. c. 48), s. 2, Sch. I.

[35] Criminal Procedure (Scotland) Act, 1887 (50 & 51 Vict. c. 35), s. 60; Summary Jurisdiction (Scotland) Act, 1954 (2 & 3 Eliz. II. c. 48), s. 2, Sch. I.

[36] Criminal Procedure (Scotland) Act, 1887 (50 & 51 Vict. c. 35), s. 62; Summary Jurisdiction (Scotland) Act, 1954 (2 & 3 Eliz. II. c. 48), s. 2, Sch. I.

[37] *Markland* v. *H.M. Advocate*, 1891, 18 R. (J.) 50.

[38] *Mitchell* v. *Adair*, 1949 J.C. 114.

[39] Evidence of murder by poisoning on a libel of murder by stabbing would not justify a verdict of guilty as libelled. Macdonald, *Criminal Law* (5th ed.) 341.

[40] Macdonald, *Criminal Law* (5th ed.) 336; *Henderson* v. *Callender*, 1878, 6 R. (J.) 1.

[41] Criminal Procedure (Scotland) Act, 1887 (50 & 51 Vict. c. 35), s. 68; Summary Jurisdiction (Scotland) Act, 1954 (2 & 3 Eliz. II. c. 48), s. 2, Sch. I.

CHAPTER IX

MATTERS REQUIRING SOLEMN OR HOLOGRAPH WRITING

89. THE SCOPE OF THE CHAPTER

The law which requires writing for the constitution or proof of certain obligations is so uncertain and unsatisfactory that it is almost impossible to state a principle which is of general application. In attempting to state the law as it is, it is difficult not to adopt the course, so often adopted by the courts, of dealing with each kind of obligation as if it were contained in a water-tight compartment, and without regard to the anomalies arising from the application of different rules to other analogous obligations. An attempt to deal with the subject as a whole was last made in the Whole Court case of *Paterson* v. *Paterson*.[1] This case has recently been criticised as misrepresenting the earlier law,[2] but until the law is re-stated by the House of Lords or the Whole Court or by statute, the decision, if not perhaps all its *obiter dicta*, must be regarded as authoritative, in spite of any anomalies to which it may give rise. Briefly put, the proposition accepted by the majority in *Paterson* v. *Paterson* was that the solemnities prescribed by the authentication statutes[3] applied only to obligations which require writing for their constitution (*obligationes literis*), and did not apply to obligations which require writing, not for their constitution, but only for their proof (*in modum probationis*). For the latter, informal writings were held to be sufficient. The other points of distinction between these two kinds of obligation are mentioned in a later paragraph.[4]

An attempt has been made in this and the following chapters to apply

---

[1] 1897, 25 R. 144.
[2] See J. J. Gow, *Constitution and Proof of Voluntary Obligations*, Part II, Juridical Review, 1961, 119 *et seq.*
[3] See § 90.
[4] See § 92.

the distinction mentioned above between *obligationes literis* and obligations which must be proved by writing. The former class, with which this chapter deals, must clearly include obligations relating to heritage and contracts of service for more than a year. Contracts which the parties have committed to writing and submissions and decrees-arbitral have been included in this chapter with considerable hesitation, in view of the uncertainty attaching to them. Testamentary settlements, by which the rights and obligations arising on the testator's death are constituted, are also dealt with in this chapter.

Cautionary obligations, contracts of insurance and transfers of incorporeal rights in moveables, cannot be placed with any certainty in either of the two classes mentioned above, and they are mentioned in the next chapter, together with writings *in re mercatoria*, which form an exception to the rule requiring solemn or holograph writing for the constitution of *obligationes literis*. Obligations which require writing only *in modum probationis*, and which may therefore be proved by writ or oath or judicial admission, are dealt with in Chapters XI and XII.

90. THE AUTHENTICATION STATUTES

A series of statutes enacted in the sixteenth and seventeenth centuries,[5] sometimes called the authentication statutes, prescribed certain solemnities[6] for the execution of the deeds to which they applied. Any such deed which lacked the prescribed solemnities was declared to be null and void or to "make no faith in judgment or outwith."[7] The deeds enumerated in the statutes, the language of which varies in this matter, cover a wide range, but may be summarised as including contracts, obligations and bonds of great importance,[8] and writings importing heritable title. The application of the statutes to deeds constituting or transmitting heritable title has always been fairly clear, but until 1897 there was uncertainty and conflict of judicial opinion as to their further scope and application. The distinction made in that year by the Whole Court decision of *Paterson* v. *Paterson*[9] between *obligationes literis*, to which the statutes apply, and obligations which require writing only *in modum probationis*, to which they do not apply, was mentioned in the previous paragraph.[10]

91. HOLOGRAPH WRITING AS EQUIVALENT OF SOLEMN WRITING

Holograph writs were not mentioned at all in the authentication statutes,[11] and were accordingly not expressly authorised by the statutes as adequate alternatives to deeds solemnly executed.[12] It would appear nevertheless

---

5 1540, c. 117; 1555, c. 29; 1579, c. 80; 1593, c. 179; 1681, c. 5; 1696, c. 15.
6 For the nature of these solemnities as amended and still applicable, see §§ **176** *et seq.*
7 This is subject, however, to the effect of holograph writing (see § **91**), and of *rei interventus* and homologation (see §§ **94, 280**).
8 i.e. those concerning a sum exceeding £100 Scots: Erskine, iii, 2, 10.
9 1897, 25 R. 144.
10 See § **89.**
11 See § **90.**
12 *Paterson* v. *Paterson*, 1897, 25 R. 144, L. Trayner at p. 163.

that, although not probative,[13] they are as valid for their purposes in point of form as deeds which are executed in accordance with the statutory solemnities.[14] The requisites of a valid holograph writing are mentioned in a later chapter.[15]

92. POINTS OF DISTINCTION BETWEEN OBLIGATIONES LITERIS AND OBLIGATIONS REQUIRING WRITING FOR THEIR PROOF

(a) General. The main point of distinction, namely that the authentication statutes apply only to *obligationes literis*, was authoritatively settled by the Whole Court decision of *Paterson* v. *Paterson*.[16] The following further points of distinction either flow from this, or were stated in the majority opinions in that case to be corollaries of it.

(b) Proof of the Obligation in a Litigation. The constitution of *obligationes literis* can be established only by production of the obligatory or constitutive writing, which must be solemnly executed[17] or holograph.[18] This is subject to the exceptions that writs *in re mercatoria*,[19] unless relating to heritage or contracts of service, may be informal, and that, when homologation or *rei interventus* has followed upon oral agreements proved by writ or oath, or upon informal writings, these may be founded upon in a litigation.[20] Obligations requiring writing only for their proof, on the other hand, which may have been constituted orally, may be proved by writings which need not be obligatory in their terms, and which need not be solemnly executed or holograph.[21] As is mentioned in the next sub-paragraph, their constitution may alternatively be referred to the opponent's oath, or established by judicial admission.

(c) Judicial Admissions and Reference to Oath. The mere judicial admission[22] of an *obligatio literis* does not enable it to be founded upon in a litigation, since the admission does not take the place of the essential

---

[13] They are not probative because their authenticity, if not admitted by the opponent, must be proved by the person founding upon them, unlike solemnly executed documents which prove themselves. See § 189. One practical result of this is that a purchaser of heritage would be justified in refusing to accept from the seller a holograph non-tested disposition, the authenticity of which he and his successors in title might be quite unable to prove.

[14] Stair, iv, 42, 6; Erskine, iii, 2, 22; Dickson, *Evidence* (3rd ed.) §§754 *et seq.* See also *Harper* v. *Green*, 1938 S.C. 198; *Cranston*, 1890, 17 R, 410, L. McLaren at p. 415; *Anderson* v. *Gill*, 1858, 20 D. 1326: (H.L.) 7; 3 Macqu. 180. L. McLaren's opinion was that the authentication statutes related only to deeds written by a person other than the granter, with the result that holograph writings, which were effective for all purposes prior to the statutes, continued, and still continue, to be so effective. See McLaren, *Wills and Succession* (3rd ed.) I, 276-7, and his dissenting opinion in *Macdonald* v. *Cuthbertson*, 1890, 18 R. 101, at p. 107.

[15] See §§ 190 *et seq.*

[16] 1897, 25 R. 144. This is referred to in §§ 89, 90.

[17] See §§ 90, 176 *et seq.*

[18] See §§ 91, 190 *et seq.*

[19] See §§ 105 *et seq.*

[20] See § 94.

[21] For the requirements of proof by writ, see §§ 302 *et seq.*

writing.[23] It may be described as an admission of a legal nonentity, or, alternatively, as an admission merely of an obligation from which the party has the right to withdraw.[24] This rule applies whether the action is for implement of the contract or for damages for its breach.[25] For similar reasons a reference to oath of such a contract is incompetent.[26] Dicta in certain cases,[27] which appear to indicate that an *obligatio literis* may be referred to oath, must be read as partial statements of the law, and as being made on the assumption that *rei interventus* was, or could have been averred, in which case proof of the contract by writ or oath would have been permissible.[20] On the other hand, obligations which require writing only for their proof are held to be proved if they are judicially admitted,[22] or if they are referred to oath and the oath is affirmative of the reference.[28]

93. CONTRACTS RELATING TO HERITAGE

These contracts are *obligationes literis*,[29] and can therefore be constituted only by writing which is either executed in accordance with the statutory solemnities,[30] or is holograph[31] of, or adopted[32] as holograph by, the party or parties.[33] Before such a contract may be founded upon in an action, whether for its implement or for damages for its breach,[34] a writing of the kind described above must be produced. A mere judicial admission that such a contract was agreed is useless, and a reference of it to oath is incompetent.[34] The contracts to which the general rule applies include all

---

[22] As to judicial admissions generally, see § **48**.

[23] *Jamieson* v. *Edinburgh Mutual Investment Building Society*, 1913, 2 S.L.T. 52.

[24] Gloag, *Contract* (2nd ed.) 162.

[25] *Allan* v. *Gilchrist*, 1875, 2 R. 587.

[26] *Perdikou* v. *Pattison*, 1958 S.L.T. 153 (lease), L. J-Cl. Thomson at p. 157, L. Patrick at p. 158, L. Mackintosh and L. Blades at p. 159; *Dickson* v. *Blair*, 1871, 10 M. 41; Stair, iv, 44, 5; Erskine, iii, 2, 2; iv, 2, 9.

[27] Such, for example, as *Paterson* v. *Earl of Fife*, 1865, 3 M. 423; *Allan* v. *Gilchrist* (*supra*); *Govan New Bowling-Green Club* v. *Geddes*, 1898, 25 R. 485.

[28] As to reference to oath generally, see §§ **308** *et seq.*

[29] See §§ **89, 90.**

[30] See §§ **90, 176** *et seq.*

[31] See §§ **91, 190** *et seq.* In practice a holograph deed transmitting heritable title *inter vivos*, which is not solemnly executed, would be unacceptable to the disponee, since it is not probative: see § **91**, note 13.

[32] *Maitland's Trs.* v. *Maitland*, 1871, 10 M. 79, L.P. Inglis at p. 88. A typewritten acceptance of an offer to purchase, enclosed with a holograph covering letter which made reference to it, was held sufficiently adopted as holograph for this purpose: *McGinn* v. *Shearer*, 1947 S.C. 334.

[33] When the contract consists of an offer and acceptance, each, if not solemnly executed, must be signed by, and holograph of, or adopted as holograph by, its granter: Erskine, iii, 2, 2; More's Notes to Stair, lxv; Dickson, *Evidence* (3rd ed.) §549; *Goldston* v. *Young*, 1868, 7 M. 188; *Scottish Lands and Building Co.* v. *Shaw*, 1880, 7 R. 756. If one of the writings is solemnly executed or holograph, but the other is not, neither party is bound; *Malcolm* v. *Campbell*, 1891, 19 R. 278. A unilateral promise or letter of obligation, on the other hand, not requiring acceptance, is by itself valid and binding, if it is solemnly executed, holograph or adopted as holograph: Bell, *Principles*, §889; Erskine, iii, 3, 88; Gloag, *Contract*, (2nd ed.) 166; *Sichi* v. *Biagi*, 1946 S.N. 66.

[34] See § **92**, sub-para. (c).

forms of purchase or sale of heritable subjects, a sale by public roup being no exception,[35] and all contracts regarding subordinate rights in heritable property, such as heritable securities.[36] Positive servitudes may be constituted by prescription,[37] implied grant or reservation[38] or acquiescence,[39] as well as by express grant, but with regard to negative servitudes it has been said that the general rule is absolute.[40] The general rule also applies to all leases, with the exception of leases for not more than a year, which may be proved by parole evidence.[41]

94. EXCEPTIONS RELATING TO HERITAGE

When homologation or *rei interventus* has followed upon an oral agreement proved by writ or oath, or upon an informal writing, the contract may be enforced.[42] The exception regarding leases for not more than a year was mentioned in the previous paragraph. Exceptions to the general rule were also allowed in the following instances, when oral evidence or informal writing was held to be admissible:—an agreement to take over from a tenant his responsibilities in respect of the last eighteen months of his lease and to pay him £15 for the fittings;[43] a claim by a builder for the cost of alterations to a house, which he was in the process of building, made at the suggestion of the defender, who had an option to purchase the house which she later decided not to exercise;[44] a contract that neither party should buy certain heritage without allowing the other to join in the purchase;[45] an arrangement between the brothers and sisters of a heritable proprietrix that they would build a tenement on her land, on the understanding that they would share in the subjects in proportion to their contributions;[46] the purchase of the stock, crop, buildings and implements on a small holding of which the heritable element (a shed and some raspberry bushes) represented less than one quarter of the total

[35] *Shiell* v. *Guthrie's Trs.*, 1874, 1 R. 1083.
[36] Gloag, *Contract* (2nd ed.) 163.
[37] Stair, ii, 7, 2; Erskine, ii, 9, 3.
[38] *Ewart* v. *Cochrane*, 1861, 4 Macqu. 117; *Menzies* v. *Marquis of Breadalbane*, 1901, 4 F. 59.
[39] *Macgregor* v. *Balfour*, 1899, 2 F. 345, L. P. Balfour at p. 351.
[40] Gloag, *Contract* (2nd ed.) 163; *Dundas* v. *Blair*, 1886, 13 R. 759; *Inglis* v. *Clark*, 1901, 4 F. 288; *Metcalfe* v. *Purdon*, 1902, 4 F. 507. *Cf. Heron* v. *Gray*, 1880, 8 R. 155; Bell, *Principles* (10th ed.) §994, note (g).
[41] Stair, ii, 9, 4; Erskine, iii, 2, 2. Bell (*Principles*, §1187) indicates that the matter may be referred to the granter's oath, but it is thought that this only applies when *rei interventus* is founded upon. See *Perdikou* v. *Pattison*, 1958 S.L.T. 153 and § **92**, sub-para. (c).
[42] *Allan* v. *Gilchrist*, 1875, 2 R. 587; *Gibson* v. *Adams*, 1875, 3 R. 144; *Dickson* v. *Blair*, 1871, 10 M. 41, at p. 45; *Walker* v. *Flint*, 1863, 1 M. 417; *Stewart* v. *Ferguson*, 1841, 3 D. 668, L. Ivory (Ordinary) at p. 674; *Bathie* v. *Lord Wharncliffe*, 1873, 11 M. 490 (draft lease). See also §§ **280** *et seq.*
[43] *Kinninmont* v. *Paxton*, 1892, 20 R. 128. See also *Moncrieff* v. *Seivwright*, 1896, 33 S.L.R. 456; *Rigg* v. *Mather* (O.H.) 1902, 10 S.L.T. 426.
[44] *Hamilton* v. *Lochrane*, 1899, 1 F. 478. See also *Woddrop* v. *Speirs* (O.H.) 1906, 44 S.L.R. 22.
[45] *Mungall* v. *Bowhill Coal Co.*, 1904, 12 S.L.T. 80, 262.
[46] *Mackay* v. *Rodger* (O.H.) 1907, 15 S.L.T. 42. See also *Bell* v. *Bell*, 1841, 3 D. 1201.

value;[47] a compromise of a litigation although its terms concerned heritable property.[48] The common feature in these exceptional cases appears to be that the contract relates only incidentally, or to a minor extent, to heritage.

95. CONTRACTS OF SERVICE

Contracts of service for not more than one year may be constituted orally, and proved *prout de jure* or by reference to the opponent's oath.[49] Apart from these, such contracts are *obligationes literis*[50] and can therefore be constituted only by writing which is either executed by both parties in accordance with the statutory solemnities,[51] or is holograph[52] of, or adopted as holograph by, both of them.[49] Before a contract for a term of years may be founded upon in an action, either for its implement[53] or for damages for its breach,[54] a writing of the kind described above must be produced. A mere judicial admission of the existence of such a contract is useless, and a reference of it to oath is incompetent.[55] The general rule probably does not apply to a contract of undefined duration to do a particular piece of work,[56] and was held not to apply to an engagement for five years at an annual salary and a commission on goods sold.[57] It is no exception to the general rule that, when services have in fact been rendered from year to year for a period of years, without remuneration having been received, the servant claiming arrears of wages may prove *prout de jure* the facts from which a right to remuneration may be inferred.[58] The mitigation of the general rule arising from *rei interventus*, homologation and adoption is mentioned later.[59]

47 *Allan* v. *Millar*, 1932 S.C. 620.
48 *Anderson* v. *Dick*, 1901, 4 F. 68; *Torbat* v. *Torbat's Trs.* (O.H.) 1906, 14 S.L.T. 830. But see *Cook* v. *Grubb*, 1963 S.L.T. 78.
49 Bell, *Principles*, §173; Dickson, *Evidence* (3rd ed.) §567; Gloag, *Contract* (2nd ed.) 179; *Cook* v. *Grubb* (*supra*), at pp. 81, 84, 86, 88; *Murray* v. *Roussel Laboratories Ltd.* (O.H.) 1960 S.L.T. (Notes) 31; *Nisbet* v. *Percy*, 1951 S.C. 350, L.P. Cooper at p. 355; *Stewart* v. *McCall*, 1869, 7 M. 544.
50 See §§ **89, 90.**
51 See §§ **90, 176** *et seq.*
52 See §§ **91, 190** *et seq.*
53 *Stewart* v. *McCall* (*supra*).
54 *Nisbet* v. *Percy* (*supra*).
55 See § **92**, sub-para. (c), and Bell, *Principles*, §173; Dickson, *Evidence* (3rd ed.) §§567, 569. In *Dumbarton Glass Co.* v. *Coatsworth*, 1847, 9 D. 732, L. Jeffrey, at p. 736, speaks of the possibility of the contract being admitted and of its being proveable *scripto*, which implied that a reference to oath might have been competent. This, however, was before the decision of *Paterson* v. *Paterson*. See § **89.**
56 Gloag, *Contract* (2nd ed.) 180.
57 *Pickin* v. *Hawkes*, 1878, 5 R. 676. See the comments in Gloag, *Contract* (2nd ed.) 180, on this not very illuminating case.
58 *Thomson* v. *Thomson's Tr.*, 1889, 16 R. 333; *Anderson* v. *Halley*, 1847, 9 D. 1222; *Smellie* v. *Gillespie*, 1833, 12 S. 125. See also *Davies* v. *City of Glasgow Friendly Society*, 1935 S.C. 224.
59 See §§ **280** *et seq.* for the general principles. For the decisions on the application of *rei interventus* to contracts of service, see Gloag, *Contract* (2nd ed.) 179. See also *Cook* v. *Grubb* (*supra*).

E

96. CONTRACTS WHICH PARTIES HAVE COMMITTED TO WRITING —GENERAL

This and the following paragraphs relate to contracts which, apart from the agreement of the parties, do not require writing for their constitution. The title of the paragraph is ambiguous and requires elucidation, and the same ambiguity is present in some of the other expressions which have been used to describe this class of contract, such as "where a formal writing is stipulated for,"[60] "where the obligation is expressed in writing,"[61] and "when the parties agree that their arrangements are to be embodied in a formal written contract."[62] The parties to a contract may reduce it to writing for one or other of two purposes. They may intend the writing to constitute the agreement, so that, without the writing, there is no agreement, or at least there is *locus poenitentiæ*. On the other hand, they may intend the writing to be merely a record or formal confirmation of a binding contract, which has already been constituted orally or by informal writing. It is only the first of these alternatives, it is thought, which gives rise to *obligationes literis*.[63] The two kinds of contracts, and the mode of distinguishing between them, are dealt with separately in the following paragraphs. The position of bonds and similar unilateral written obligations is also mentioned separately.

In *Paterson* v. *Paterson*[64] there are dicta which might be read as suggesting that the category into which the contract is to be placed depends, not upon the intention of the parties, but upon the terms of the writing. The distinction is made between writings which contain express words of obligation and those which merely record facts from which obligations may be inferred, and there are suggestions that the former relate to *obligationes literis*,[65] while the latter do not.[66] "Obligatory writing" is spoken of as providing the test.[67] It is thought that this distinction is intended to relate rather to the authentication of the writing, and the use which is made of it, than to the nature of the obligations themselves. Thus a party to an obligatory writing may found upon it as the sole basis of his action[68] only if it is

---

[60] *Rederi Aktiebolaget Nordstjernan* v. *Salvesen & Co.*, 1903, 6 F. 64, L. Moncreiff at p. 75 (rev. on another point 1905, 7 F. (H.L.) 101).

[61] *Paterson* v. *Paterson*, 1897, 25 R. 144, L. Kyllachy at p. 174.

[62] *Van Laun & Co.* v. *Neilson Reid & Co.*, 1904, 6 F. 644, L. Kinnear at p. 652.

[63] See §§ **89, 90, 92.**

[64] 1897, 25 R. 144.

[65] *Ibid.*, L. Kyllachy at pp. 172, 173, 177.

[66] "The distinction . . . depends . . . on the character of the writing": *ibid.*, L. Kyllachy at p. 174. See also the approval by L. Trayner (p. 163), L. Kyllachy (p. 173), L. Kincairney (p. 181), of L. Benholme's dictum in *Thoms* v. *Thoms*, 1867, 6 M. 174, at p. 176:— "The scope of the statutes is confined to those writings by which a person becomes directly bound, and which form the substantive *vincula* upon which action may be raised." L. Kincairney (p. 181) remarks upon the shadowy and technical nature of the distinction.

[67] *Ibid.*, L. Pearson at p. 183.

[68] Prior to the enactment of the Rules of Court it was necessary to libel a liquid document of debt in the conclusions of the summons. Maclaren, *Court of Session Practice*, 295. Although this is no longer necessary, it ought to be made clear in the condescendence whether or not the document is being founded upon as the substantive cause of action.

solemnly executed or holograph or one of the exceptions applies, and this is true even if he might alternatively have sued upon an antecedent binding oral agreement, in support of which the writing, whether properly authenticated or not, might have been used as evidence. But whether or not the obligations of the parties are to be regarded as *obligationes literis* must depend, it is thought, upon their agreement, and not solely upon the terms of the writing.[69] Only if this is the test can it be truly said that "by . . . agreement of the parties obligations or rights require writing for their constitution,"[70] or that "the parties have mutually selected the writing as the proof and measure of their contract, its existence and terms (being) *partes contractus.*"[71]

97. CONTRACTS WHICH ARE OBLIGATIONES LITERIS

When the parties to a contract, which may be constituted orally, agree expressly or by implication that they will not be bound until a written contract has been executed, the resulting obligations are to be regarded as *obligationes literis,*[72] with all the consequences flowing therefrom.[73] The authentication statutes apply to the writing unless it is holograph,[74] the contract can be founded upon in a litigation only if the writing is produced, and a judicial admission or reference to oath cannot take the place of its production.[73] As with other *obligationes literis,* however, if homologation or *rei interventus* follows upon an oral or informal written agreement, that agreement may be proved by writ or referred to oath.[75] It would appear that a contract of this kind may be constituted in an informal writing, even

---

See *Encyclopædia of Scottish Legal Styles*, I, 59. The distinction between the alternative methods of stating the pursuer's claim is mentioned by L. P. Dunedin in *Hope* v. *Derwent Rolling Mills*, 1905, 7 F. 837, at p. 844.

[69] In *Van Laun & Co.* v. *Neilson, Reid & Co.*, 1904, 6 F. 644, L. Kinnear, at p. 652, said that when parties agree that their arrangements are to be embodied in a formal written contract, there is *locus pœnitentiæ* until the written contract is executed. This statement of the law has been criticised as too wide: Gloag, *Contract* (2nd ed.) 43. It is thought to be valid only if the whole circumstances warrant an inference that the parties so intended.

[70] *Paterson* v. *Paterson (supra)*, L. Moncreiff at p. 168.

[71] Dickson, *Evidence* (3rd ed.) §206.

[72] See §§ **89, 90.**

[73] See § **92.**

[74] In *Hutchinson* v. *Ferrier*, 1851, 13 D. 837: 1852, 1 Macqu. 196, which is difficult to understand, a lease from year to year, which could have been constituted orally, was confirmed annually by missive letters, which were presumably holograph. In the Court of Session it was held that the letters were rightly rejected, when tendered in evidence, because they were unstamped. The opinion was also expressed that the lease could be proved in no other way, presumably on the footing that the contract was of the kind to which this paragraph refers. It seems likely, however, that Lord Fullerton's dissenting opinion states the true position.

[75] In *Clark* v. *Clark's Trs.*, 1860, 23 D. 74, where *rei interventus* had followed upon a written contract of co-partnery which was defective in form, it was held that the partnership could be established only by production of the writing. It is thought that, had the other party to the contract not been dead, reference to his oath would have been a permissible alternative. As to homologation and *rei interventus* generally, see §§ **280** *et seq.*

without homologation or *rei interventus*, if it is *in re mercatoria*,[76] and in this respect it differs from contracts relating to heritage and contracts of service for a term of years, which cannot be so constituted.[77] In connection with the kind of contract dealt with in this paragraph no question of using the writing as evidence of an earlier oral bargain can arise, because, *ex hypothesi*, no bargain ever existed.

98. CONTRACTS WHICH ARE NOT OBLIGATIONES LITERIS

When an agreement has been constituted orally or by informal writings, and the parties decide to execute a formal written contract which they intend to be merely a record or formal confirmation of the earlier binding agreement, the resulting obligations are *not* to be regarded as *obligationes literis*, with the consequences previously mentioned.[78] They may be proved *prout de jure* unless they are obligations proveable only by writing,[79] in which case they may be proved by writ or referred to oath. In neither case is production of a formal written contract essential. These considerations cease to be of practical importance if both parties to such an agreement in fact execute a formal and effective written contract with the intention that it should take the place of the earlier agreement. In that event, the formal contract becomes the measure of the rights and obligations of the parties, and it is then incompetent for either party to attempt to contradict, modify or explain the formal contract by reference to the earlier agreement.[80] Before the formal contract may be founded upon by either party in a litigation as a liquid document of debt or as the sole foundation of his case,[81] it must be solemnly executed or holograph, unless it is *in re mercatoria*.[82]

99. ASCERTAINMENT OF INTENTION OF PARTIES

When an oral or informal agreement has been negotiated, which the parties agree shall be embodied in a formal written contract, the question as to whether *locus pœnitentiœ* exists until the formal writing is executed, in which case their obligations are *obligationes literis*, or whether, on the other hand, the obligations, orally or informally constituted, are instantly binding, and are not *obligationes literis*,[83] must be answered in the light of the whole circumstances in each case.[84] "It is perfectly possible for the

[76] See, for example, *Buttery & Co.* v. *Inglis*, 1877, 5 R. 58; 1878, 5 R. (H.L.) 87. The deed embodying the contract was informally executed, but was agreed to be *in re mercatoria*. See 5 R. (H.L.) at p. 87 (note). It was held by the House of Lords that only the written contract could be looked at.

[77] See § **105.**

[78] See § **97.**

[79] For the matters which may be proved only by writ, see §§ **117** *et seq.*

[80] See § **246.**

[81] See note 68 above.

[82] *Thoms* v. *Thoms*, 1867, 6 M. 174, L. Benholme at p. 176; *Paterson* v. *Paterson*, 1897, 25 R. 144, L. Trayner at p. 163, L. Kyllachy at p. 173, L. Kincairney at p. 181.

[83] See §§ **97, 98.** See also § **92.**

[84] *Stobo Ltd.* v. *Morrisons (Gowns) Ltd.*, 1949 S.C. 184; *Rederi Aktiebolaget Nordstjernan* v. *Salvesen & Co.*, 1903, 6 F. 64, L. Moncreiff at p. 75 (revd. on another point 1905,

parties to an apparent contract to provide that there shall be *locus pœnitentiæ* until the terms of their agreement have been reduced to a formal contract; but the bare fact that the parties to a completed agreement stipulate that it shall be embodied in a formal contract does not necessarily import that they are still in the stage of negotiation. In each instance it is a matter of the construction of the correspondence in the light of the facts, proved or averred, on which side of the border line the case lies."[85]

Locus pœnitentiæ was held to exist, and the contract was therefore *obligatio literis*, in the following circumstances. The defenders agreed, "subject to contract," that if they bought two shops from the owners, they would sell one of them to the pursuers. The decision was based *inter alia* upon the unlikelihood that the parties intended to be conclusively bound before the conditions of purchase from the original proprietors, particularly with regard to servitudes and rights in common with neighbouring properties, were adjusted.[85] The pursuers sued for commission said to be due under an oral contract, in which was incorporated an unsigned memorandum setting forth its terms, the opening words of which were:—"The undersigned firms agree that they will enter into a proper legal contract, when prepared, with [the pursuers]." The decision in this instance turned mainly upon a construction of the words quoted above.[86]

Locus pœnitentiæ was held *not* to exist, and the contract was therefore not *obligatio literis*, in the following circumstances. The pursuer made to the defenders, who were Police Commissioners, an offer to compromise a claim, one of the conditions being "that a formal deed of agreement embodying the stipulations . . . above written and other necessary formal clauses shall be prepared by the Commissioners' agent and revised by the agent of [the pursuer], and shall be executed by the Commissioners and [the pursuer] within fourteen days." The Commissioners accepted the offer, with one alteration, which, in turn, was accepted by the pursuer. It was held that the purpose of the proposed deed was merely to put the concluded agreement into formal terms.[87] A similar decision, it is thought, would follow if, in an oral or informal contract for the transfer of shares in a company or in a ship, where statute requires that the transfer itself must be in formal writing,[88] there were included the words "subject to transfer (or bill of sale) drawn out in due form."[89] The inclusion of these words in the acceptance of an offer cannot infer *locus pœnitentiæ* until the transfers or bills of sale are executed, "merely because the acceptor puts into words what the law would imply as the method in which an agreement, *ex hypothesi* complete, would be carried into legal effect."[90]

---

7 F. (H.L.) 101); Bell, *Principles*, §25. For a comment on L. Kinnear's statement in *Van Laun & Co.* v. *Neilson Reid & Co.*, 1904, 6 F. 644, at p. 652, see § **96**, note 69.

85 *Stobo Ltd.* v. *Morrisons (Gowns) Ltd. (supra)*, L. P. Cooper at p. 192.

86 *Van Laun & Co.* v. *Neilson Reid & Co. (supra)*.

87 *Smeaton* v. *St. Andrews Police Commissioners*, 1871, 9 M. (H.L.) 24.

88 See § **116**.

89 This is on the analogy of *Erskine* v. *Glendinning*, 1871, 9 M. 656, L.P. Inglis at p. 659. That case is itself not in point as an example, since it related to a lease of heritage, and was therefore necessarily concerned with *obligationes literis*.

90 *Stobo Ltd.* v. *Morrisons (Gowns) Ltd.*, 1949 S.C. 184, L. P. Cooper at pp. 191-192.

100. UNILATERAL WRITTEN OBLIGATIONS

It is thought that ·a unilateral obligation, which may be constituted orally, becomes an *obligatio literis* only in the comparatively rare event of its being constituted for the first time in a bond or similar obligatory document. If, for example, without prior communings between them, one person executes, and sends to another person, a bond in which he obliges himself to pay money or to perform some act in the future, the obligation thereby undertaken is an *obligatio literis*,[91] with all the consequences flowing therefrom.[92] The authentication statutes apply to the bond unless it is holograph or *in re mercatoria*,[93] and the obligation may be founded upon in a litigation only if the bond is produced.[92] Since *ex hypothesi* no oral promise exists which may be judicially admitted or proved by writ or referred to oath, these modes of proof cannot arise.[92] If the bond, however, is defective in form, it may probably, as with other *obligationes literis*, be founded upon by the creditor when it is followed by homologation or *rei interventus*.[94]

Most bonds, however, are granted as liquid documents of debt in order to facilitate the recovery or enforcement of obligations already incurred. In these circumstances it is thought to be wrong to suggest that the mere granting of a bond by the debtor can convert his existing obligation into an *obligatio literis*, and can thereby compel the creditor to found upon the bond as the only method of constituting his right. If A borrows a sum of money from B, he thereby comes under obligation to repay, which may be proved by writ or oath.[95] When A grants a bond in respect of the loan, it cannot be the presumed intention of the parties that if B loses the bond, or it is in some way defective in form, A need not repay the money. If a debtor under a joint and several obligation pays the whole debt, or a cautioner pays the principal debtor's debt, the law implies an immediate right of relief.[96] He can hardly be presumed to have abandoned his right because he accepts an express undertaking upon which, for some reason, he may not be able to found. In such circumstances, if the bond is solemnly executed or holograph,[97] the creditor may found upon it, if he wishes, as a liquid document of debt.[98] But the granting of an obligatory document does not necessarily extinguish the original obligation,[99] and if the obligatory document is defective, or for some reason the creditor chooses not to found upon it,

---

[91] See §§ **89, 90.**

[92] See § **92.**

[93] As an example of such a bond which was held to be *in re mercatoria*, see *Beardmore & Co.* v. *Barry*, 1928 S.C. 101; (H.L.) 47.

[94] As to homologation and *rei interventus* generally, see §§ **280** *et seq.*

[95] As to proof of loan, see § **118.**

[96] Stair, i, 8, 9; Erskine, iii, 3, 74.

[97] *Thoms* v. *Thoms*, 1867, 6 M. 174, L. Benholme at p. 176; *Paterson* v. *Paterson*, 1897, 25 R. 144, L. Trayner at p. 163, L. Kyllachy at p. 173, L. Kincairney at p. 181.

[98] As to the distinction between the alternative methods of stating the pursuer's claim, see § **96**, note 68. See also L. Pearson's reference in *Paterson* v. *Paterson*, at pp. 183-184, to the way in which a bond, although unnecessary for the constitution of loan, may be used to found an action for its repayment.

[99] *Thom* v. *North British Banking Co.*, 1850, 13 D. 134, L. Fullerton at p. 143; Gloag, *Contract* (2nd ed.) 187.

he may prove the antecedent obligation by evidence, which, depending upon the rule of evidence relating to the obligation, may be oral or may be restricted to writ or oath.[1]   Although there have been judicial doubts on the point,[2] there seems to be no reason why the bond, whether defective in form or not, should not be used as part of that evidence, if it contains admissions of the antecedent obligation.[3]   This view avoids the anomaly, inherent in the contrary view, that if a debtor signs a typed note "I have received on loan from John Smith £100," the creditor can use the note as proof by writ, but if the further words "and I promise to repay it" are included, he cannot.[4]   When, however, a bond has been accepted by the creditor as taking the place of the original obligation, or is founded upon by him in a litigation as a liquid document of debt, it then becomes the sole measure of the rights and obligations of the parties, and it is thereafter incompetent to contradict, modify or explain it by reference to the earlier transaction.

101. ARBITRATION

(a) **General.**   The many conflicting decisions as to what is required to constitute or prove submissions and decrees-arbitral (awards) make it difficult to deduce general principles.[5]   The subject is included in this chapter only because submissions regarding heritage, apart from certain exceptions, are *obligationes literis*, and it is thought that submissions regarding moveables, to which one or other of the numerous exceptions does not apply, are to be similarly regarded.   Submissions relating to heritage and those relating to moveables are mentioned separately in the next two paragraphs. It is thought that the following may be stated as general rules which apply to both categories.

(b) **Agricultural Leases.**   In arbitrations regarding agricultural leases, whether they relate to heritage such as buildings and fences,[6] or to the valuation of moveables such as crops, manure, and implements,[7] the submission and the decree-arbitral, though they must be in writing and signed by the granters, need not be solemnly executed or holograph.[8]

1   *Hope* v. *Derwent Rolling Mills*, 1905, 7 F. 837; *Duncan's Trs.* v. *Shand*, 1872, 10 M. 984.
2   *Paterson* v. *Paterson*, 1897, 25 R. 144, L. Kyllachy at p. 174, L. Kincairney at p. 181, L. Pearson at p. 187.
3   *Paterson* v. *Paterson* (*supra*), L. Kyllachy at pp. 177-178.
4   The anomaly is mentioned by L. Young in *Paterson* v. *Paterson* (*supra*), at p. 151.
5   This becomes obvious from a perusal of Bell, *Arbitration* (2nd ed.) §§61, 62, 67, 81, 86-88, 91, 93, 94; Dickson, *Evidence* (3rd ed.) §§553, 562, 789, 792; Irons and Melville, *Arbitration*, 51, 52; Guild, *Arbitration*, 18-22, 77, 82.
6   *McGregor* v. *Stevenson*, 1847, 9 D. 1056.
7   *Cameron* v. *Nicol*, 1930 S.C. 1, L. Sands at p. 15 (award not tested); *Gibson* v. *Fotheringham*, 1914 S.C. 987, L. Hunter at pp. 993-994, L. J-Cl. Macdonald at p. 996; *Davidson* v. *Logan*, 1908 S.C. 350, L. Low at pp. 366-367, L. Stormonth-Darling at p. 368; *Nivison* v. *Howat*, 1883, 11 R. 182, L. Craighill at p. 191 (both submission and award informal).
8   *McLaren* v. *Aikman*, 1939 S.C. 222, L. J-Cl. Aitchison at pp. 227, 228, L. Wark at pp. 229-230, L. Carmont at p. 231.   It is thought that most arbitrations of this kind are now conducted under the Agricultural Holdings (Scotland) Act, 1949 (12 & 13 Geo. VI

(c) Submissions in re mercatoria. The same rule applies to a submission and a decree-arbitral *in re mercatoria*, which may be contained in informal documents.[9] If the genuineness of the documents is disputed, it may be proved *prout de jure*.[10]

(d) Authentication of Decree Arbitral (Award). When the submission in any arbitration is solemnly executed by, or is holograph of, the parties, then, unless it relates to an agricultural lease or a mercantile transaction, the decree-arbitral, in order to be binding, must be in writing similarly authenticated, and such writing is the only evidence by which it may be proved.[11]

(e) Rei Interventus. In any case in which the submission and decree-arbitral ought to be solemnly executed or holograph, informal documents will bind the parties if they are followed by *rei interventus*,[12] homologation[13] or adoption.[14] In such a case the acts constituting *rei interventus*, homologation or adoption may be proved by parole evidence, but the terms of the submission must be proved by writ or oath.[15]

(f) Remit to Man of Skill. Except in arbitrations arising out of agricultural leases,[16] the submission and decree-arbitral in a remit for valuation to a man of skill must be as formal as in any other arbitration.[17]

c. 75), ss. 75, 76, 99, Sch. 6, para. 23, the statutory forms being provided by the Agricultural Holdings (Specification of Forms) (Scotland) Instrument, 1960 (S.I. No. 1337). The award must be signed before witnesses or be holograph: *ibid.*, Sch. 1; Connell, *Agricultural Holdings (Scotland) Acts* (5th ed.), 75. It is not clear whether a joint appointment of an arbiter by the parties, which takes the place of a submission, need necessarily be holograph or tested. See Connell, 62-63, 276.

9 *McLaren* v. *Aikman* (*supra*), L. J-Cl. Aitchison at pp. 227-228; *Dykes* v. *Roy*, 1869, 7 M. 357, L. Neaves at p. 360; *Hope* v. *Crookston Bros*, 1890, 17 R. 868. As to writings *in re mercatoria* generally, see §§ 105 *et seq.*
10 Dickson, *Evidence* (3rd ed.) §793.
11 *McLaren* v. *Aikman* (*supra*), L. J-Cl. Aitchison at p. 227, L. Wark at p. 229; *Dykes* v. *Roy* (*supra*), L. Neaves at p. 360; *Lang* v. *Brown*, 1852, 15 D. 38, L. Fullerton at p. 44; affd. 1855, 2 Macqu. 93; *Earl of Hopetoun* v. *Scots Mines Co.*, 1856, 18 D. 739, L. Curriehill at p. 748, L. Benholme at p. 757.
12 Bell, *Arbitration* (2nd ed.) §62; *Otto* v. *Weir*, 1871, 9 M. 660, L. J-Cl. Moncreiff at p. 661 (heritage).
13 Bell, *Arbitration* (2nd ed.) §62; *Robertson* v. *Boyd and Winans*, 1885, 12 R. 419 (heritage); *Dykes* v. *Roy*, 1869, 7 M. 357, at pp. 359, 360 (moveables). In connection with a disputed claim to pasturage, two of the three parties signed a submission to a named arbiter, who issued a decree-arbitral. One of the signatories claimed the right to resile because the third party had not signed the submission. It was held that, although the submission was invalid, all were bound by it because it had been homologated by the third party in respect of his appearing and leading evidence before the arbiter. *Brown* v. *Gardner*, 1739, M. 5659, 8474.
14 *Dykes* v. *Roy* (*supra*), at pp. 359, 360. For *rei interventus*, homologation and adoption generally, see §§ 280 *et seq.*
15 *Procurator Fiscal of Roxburgh* v. *Ker*, 1672, M. 12410; Dickson, *Evidence* (3rd ed.) §832.
16 *Cameron* v. *Nicol*, 1930 S.C. 1, L. Sands at p. 15; *Davidson* v. *Logan*, 1908 S.C. 350, L. Low at pp. 366-367; *Nivison* v. *Howat*, 1883, 11 R. 182.
17 *McLaren* v. *Aikman*, 1939 S.C. 222, L. J-Cl. Aitchison at p. 228, L. Wark at p. 229; *Stewart* v. *Williamson*, 1909 S.C. 1254, L. P. Dunedin at p. 1258, L. Kinnear at p. 1258; 1910 S.C. (H.L.) 47.

(g) Joint Memorial for Opinion of Counsel. An opinion of counsel on a joint memorial, which states that the parties have agreed to be bound by the opinion, is as binding as a decree-arbitral, and it is sufficient both for constitution and for proof of the submission and the award, that the memorial and the opinion are signed without witnesses in accordance with normal practice.[18]

(h) Judicial Reference. A judicial reference, which is signed without witnesses by the parties or their counsel or solicitors,[19] becomes irrevocable when the court has interponed authority to it,[20] and the referee's report or award following thereon, which may also be signed by him without witnesses,[21] is sufficient foundation, if not challenged on some matter of substance, for the pronouncement of a decree in conformity therewith.[21]

102. ARBITRATIONS REGARDING HERITAGE

The contract of submission in an arbitration relating to heritage must be constituted by writing which is executed by the parties in accordance with the statutory solemnities, or is holograph of or adopted as holograph by them.[22] It follows from this that the decree-arbitral must be contained in a similar writing,[23] and, since the solemnity is necessary for the constitution of the contract, that it is incompetent to refer the question of the submission to the oath of the opponent.[24] It also follows that the production of such writing is the only means by which a submission or decree-arbitral may be founded upon in a litigation. The mitigation of the strictness of this rule in connection with agricultural leases, and when *rei interventus*, homologation or adoption has followed informal writings, was mentioned in the last paragraph. A practice, now obsolete,[25] whereby in a question of disputed marches, after an oral reference, the arbiter, with the consent of the parties, placed the march stones in position, was an exception to the rule, consent to the placing of the stones being regarded as completion of the contract by adoption or homologation.[26]

103. ARBITRATIONS REGARDING MOVEABLES

Arbitrations associated with agricultural leases or mercantile transactions,

---

[18] Bell, *Arbitration* (2nd ed.) §69; Dickson, *Evidence* (3rd ed.) §792; *Dykes* v. *Roy*, 1869, 7 M. 357, L. Cowan at p. 360; *Fraser* v. *Lord Lovat*, 1850, 7 Bell App. 171.
[19] Bell, *Arbitration* (2nd ed.) §513.
[20] Bell, *Arbitration* (2nd ed.) §519; Dickson, *Evidence* (3rd ed.) §563; *Reid* v. *Henderson*, 1841, 3 D. 1102; *Walker & Co.* v. *Stewart*, 1855, 2 Macqu. 424.
[21] Bell, *Arbitration* (2nd ed.) §§533, 535; Dickson, *Evidence* (3rd ed.) §792.
[22] Bell, *Arbitration* (2nd ed.) §§93, 94; Dickson, *Evidence* (3rd ed.) §553; *Robertson* v. *Boyd and Winans*, 1885, 12 R. 419, L. Rutherfurd Clark at p. 427; *McLaren* v. *Aikman*, 1939 S.C. 222. As to contracts relating to heritage generally, see §§ **93, 94.**
[23] See § **101,** sub-para. (d), and authorities in note 22 above.
[24] See § **92,** sub-para. (c).
[25] Guild, *Arbitration*, 21.
[26] *Livingston* v. *Feuars of Falhouse*, 1662 M. 2200; *Procurator Fiscal of Roxburgh* v. *Ker*, 1672 M. 12410; Irons and Melville, *Arbitration*, 52. A somewhat similar practice was approved in *Otto* v. *Weir*, 1871, 9 M. 660, where the subsequent building of a march fence would apparently have been regarded as *rei interventus*.

in which the submissions and the decrees-arbitral may be proved by informal writings, were mentioned earlier,[27] as were informal submissions followed by *rei interventus*, homologation or adoption. Any submission which does not fall into one or other of these categories is thought, apart from one exception, to require solemnly executed or holograph writing for its constitution,[28] and it follows that the decree-arbitral must be incorporated in a similar writing.[29] If, however, this is too wide a statement of the rule, it may, it is thought, at least be safely said that submissions which are in fact reduced by the parties to writing must usually be regarded as *obligationes literis* for all purposes.[30] The exception relates to matters of small importance (probably £100 Scots or less) in which the submission may be constituted orally and proved by the writ or oath of the opponent, or even by parole evidence.[31]

104. TESTAMENTARY SETTLEMENTS

With one unimportant exception, rights and obligations arising under testamentary settlements made in Scotland, must be constituted in writings which are either executed in accordance with the statutory solemnities,[32] or are holograph[33] of, or adopted[33] as holograph by, the testator, and subscribed[34] by him.[35] The admissibility of parole evidence in connection

[27] See § **101**, sub-paras. (b) (c) (e).
[28] Bell, *Arbitration* (2nd ed.) §§61, 62, 67; Guild, *Arbitration*, 20; Gloag, *Contract* (2nd ed.) 185; Erskine, iii, 2, 6; *Paterson* v. *Paterson*, 1897, 25 R. 144, L. Pearson at p. 183. See also *Fraser* v. *Williamson*, 1773, M. 8476 (debt of £93), where parole evidence of the submission was held inadmissible, and *Ferrie* v. *Mitchell*, 1824, 3 S. 75 (promissory note for £414), where a reference of an oral submission to the oath of the opponent was held incompetent. *Cf.*, however, Bell, *Arbitration* (2nd ed.) §§93, 94; Guild *Arbitration*, 21, and see note 31 below.
[29] See § **101**, sub-para. (d).
[30] See § **97**.
[31] Bell, *Arbitration* (2nd ed.) §§81-88, 91; Guild, *Arbitration*, 19, 21. The exception appears to be founded on *A.* v. *B.*, 1746 M. 8475, the entire report of which consists of the following sentence:—"Verbal submissions and decrees-arbitral *inter rusticos*, for matters of small importance, are probable by witnesses." *Cf.* Dickson, *Evidence* (3rd ed.) §562, who states generally that all oral submissions regarding moveables may be proved by writ or oath, or, if unimportant, by parole. In view, however, of the decision in *Ferrie* v. *Mitchell* (*supra*) (promissory note for £414), where even a reference to oath of the submission was held incompetent, it would seem that, apart from agricultural leases, mercantile matters, and *rei interventus*, homologation or adoption, oral submissions should now be regarded as enforceable only when they relate to £100 Scots or less.
[32] As to the statutory solemnities generally, see §§ **90, 176** *et seq.*
[33] As to holograph writings generally, see §§ **91, 190** *et seq.*
[34] *Robbie* v. *Carr*, 1959 S.L.T. (Notes) 16; *McLay* v. *Farrell*, 1950 S.C. 149; *Stenhouse* v. *Stenhouse*, 1922 S.C. 370; *Taylor's Executrices* v. *Thom*, 1914 S.C. 79; *Foley* v. *Costello*, 1904, 6 F. 365; *Goldie* v. *Shedden*, 1885, 13 R. 138; *Skinner* v. *Forbes*, 1883, 11 R. 88; *Dunlop* v. *Dunlop*, 1839, 1 D. 912. *Cf. Fraser's Executrix* v. *Fraser's C.B.*, 1931 S.C. 536.
[35] McLaren, *Wills and Succession* (3rd ed.) I, 273 *et seq.* Any writing of a testamentary character on which confirmation of executors-nominate was issued prior to July 1, 1938, is deemed to be probative: Conveyancing Amendment (Scotland) Act, 1938 (1 & 2 Geo. VI. c. 24), s. 11.

with the interpretation of such writings is mentioned later.[36] The exception is a bequest of moveables of a value not exceeding £8 6s. 8d., which may be nuncupative (expressed orally), and proved by parole evidence.[37] A nuncupative bequest of more than £8 6s. 8d. is valid to the extent only of that sum,[37] but a person may make a number of nuncupative bequests, each of which is valid to the extent of £8 6s. 8d.[38] An oral direction to a residuary or universal legatee to pay a legacy of any amount is effective as a trust, and, as such, may be proved, not by parole evidence, but only by the writ or oath of the alleged trustee,[39] but this does not apply to a direction given to an executor-nominate or testamentary trustee who has himself no beneficial interest in the estate.[40] It is doubtful whether the relaxation in formality of execution allowed by Roman Law for a soldier's will (*testamentum militare*), which has been incorporated by statute[41] into English law, has ever formed part of the law of Scotland.[42] The rules regarding a testamentary settlement made outside Scotland are dealt with later.[43]

[36] On this matter, see §§ **267** *et seq.*
[37] Stair, iii, 8, 36; Erskine, iii, 9, 7; Bell, *Principles*, §1869; McLaren, *Wills and Succession* (3rd ed.) I, 573; *Kelly* v. *Kelly*, 1861, 23 D. 703.
[38] Bell, *Principles*, §1874; McLaren, *Wills and Succession* (3rd ed.) I, 573.
[39] Erskine, iii, 9, 7; Bell, *Principles*, §1869; McLaren, *Wills and Succession* (3rd ed.) I, 573. As to proof of trust generally, see §§ **122, 123.**
[40] Bell, *Principles*, §1869; McLaren, *Wills and Succession* (3rd ed.) I, 573; *Forsyth's Trs.* v. *McLean*, 1854, 16 D. 343. Such a direction may, of course, be proved to be effective as a nuncupative legacy to the extent of £8 6s. 8d.
[41] Wills Act, 1837 (7 Will. IV & 1 Vict., c. 26), s. 11; Wills (Soldiers and Sailors) Act, 1918 (7 & 8 Geo. V. c. 58).
[42] *Stuart* v. *Stuart,* 1942 S.C. 510.
[43] See § **423,** sub-para. (b).

CHAPTER X

WRITINGS IN RE MERCATORIA AND MISCELLANEOUS MATTERS REQUIRING WRITING

105. WRITINGS IN RE MERCATORIA

The exception attaching to these writings has no significance apart from the application of the authentication statutes.[1] A writing which is *in re mercatoria* may be informally executed in circumstances where, were it not *in re mercatoria*, it must be solemnly executed or holograph in order to comply with the authentication statutes.[2] The essential requirements of the informal writing are mentioned later.[3] The exception relating to writings *in re mercatoria*, however, does not apply to contracts relating to heritage[4] or contracts of service for more than a year,[5] which because of their subject matter are *obligationes literis*,[6] even if they are in some way associated with a mercantile transaction. It would appear, accordingly, that, whatever may have been the original importance of writings *in re mercatoria*, their practical application is now very limited. They are thought now to be relevant only to an obligation which, although it could have been constituted orally, is agreed by the parties to be binding only when a formal written contract has been executed in respect of it,[7] or which is constituted for the first time in a unilateral written obligation such as a bond.[8] In such a case the writing

---

[1] See § **90**.
[2] Erskine, iii, 2, 24; Bell, *Commentaries*, I, 342; Bell, *Principles*, §21; Dickson, *Evidence* (3rd ed.) §793; Gloag, *Contract* (2nd ed.) 185; *McLaren* v. *Aikman*, 1939 S.C. 222, L. J-Cl. Aitchison at p. 228.
[3] See § **107**.
[4] Gloag, *Contract* (2nd ed.) 185. In *Danish Dairy Co.* v. *Gillespie*, 1922 S.C. 656 (lease of business premises for a term of years), it was not argued that the writing was *in re mercatoria*. As to contracts relating to heritage generally, see §§ **93, 94**.
[5] Gloag, *Contract* (2nd ed.) 185; *Stewart* v. *McCall*, 1869, 7 M.544. As to contracts of service generally, see § **95**.
[6] As to these, see § **89**.
[7] See § **97**.
[8] See § **100**.

must be solemnly executed or holograph unless it is *in re mercatoria*, when it may be informally executed. The position of cautionary obligations,[9] and of the writings referred to in the statutes dealing with hire-purchase and credit-sale agreements[10] is so obscure, that it cannot be said with certainty whether or not the exception for writings *in re mercatoria* is relevant to them. There have been judicial indications of an opinion that an obligation, which *ex facie* is *res mercatoria*, may lose its normal privilege, and may need solemn or holograph writing for its constitution, if it is shown to be granted for some ulterior purpose, in order, for example, to provide security for a loan.[11]

106. DEFINITION OF RES MERCATORIA

The expression must be given a wide interpretation.[12] It relates to "what are properly mercantile dealings," and has been defined in general as including "all the variety of engagements or mandates or acknowledgments which the infinite occasions of trade may require."[13] Such obligations include[13] bills of exchange,[14] promissory notes[14] and bank cheques,[14] orders for goods, mandates[15] and procurations, guarantees,[16] offers to sell or buy merchandise or to transport it from place to place,[17] and acceptances thereof. In particular, the following have been held to be writings *in re mercatoria:*—an obligation in favour of a company of which the obligant was a director, undertaken as part of a compromise of an earlier transaction to subscribe at any time on request for 48,000 of the company's shares;[18] accession by a creditor to a composition settlement of an insolvent's affairs;[19] an obligation to purchase an engine and certain fittings in heritable premises, and at the same time to relieve the other party of his obligations as tenant under a lease of the premises;[20] an agreement to pay for advertising space on the walls of Post Offices;[21] a submission and decree-arbitral in a dispute as to whether seed supplied under a contract of sale was conform to sample;[22]

---

9 See § **113.**
10 See § **114.**
11 See *Commercial Bank* v. *Kennard*, 1859, 21 D. 864, L. P. McNeill at p. 870; *McAdie* v. *McAdie's Executrix*, 1883, 10 R. 741, L. J-Cl. Moncreiff at p. 744. Lord Rutherfurd Clark dissented in the last mentioned case, which Gloag ((2nd ed.) 186) considered to be of doubtful authority.
12 *Beardmore & Co.* v. *Barry*, 1928 S.C. 101, L. J-Cl. Alness at p. 110; 1928 S.C. (H.L.) 47; Gloag, *Contract*, (2nd ed.) 185.
13 The definition and these examples are from Bell, *Commentaries*, I, 342.
14 As to bills of exchange, bank cheques and promissory notes, see §§ **109** *et seq.* A letter acknowledging that one of the obligants under a promissory note, granted of even date therewith, was truly a cautioner, was itself held to be a writing *in re mercatoria: Thoms* v. *Thoms*, 1867, 6 M. 174.
15 As to mandates generally, see § **148.**
16 As to cautionary obligations, see § **113.**
17 See also § **145.**
18 *Beardmore & Co.* v. *Barry* (*supra*).
19 Bell, *Commentaries*, II, 398-9; *Henry* v. *Strachan & Spence*, 1897, 24 R. 1045.
20 *Kinninmont* v. *Paxton*, 1892, 20 R. 128.
21 *United Kingdom Advertising Co.* v. *Glasgow Bag-Wash Laundry*, 1926 S.C. 303.
22 *Dykes* v. *Roy*, 1869, 7 M. 357.

a warrant by a firm of ironfounders undertaking to deliver iron to the order of a named person;[23] a guarantee of payment for goods supplied and to be supplied;[24] and a letter by a bank acknowledging that certain bonds, originally held for a third party, were held on account of the pursuer's cedents.[25] The question as to whether a loan of money can give rise to an obligation *in re mercatoria*[26] is now irrelevant.[27]

107. AUTHENTICATION, MODE OF PROOF AND DATE OF THE INFORMAL WRITING

A writing *in re mercatoria* is sufficiently authenticated if it is subscribed[28] by the parties, or initialled[29] by them. The genuineness of the subscription or of the initials, if disputed, must be proved, and the proof may be by parole evidence.[30] The subject matter of this paragraph has much in common with the nature and mode of proof of the writing required to satisfy proof by writ of party, which is dealt with in a later chapter.[31]

The date of an informal writing *in re mercatoria*, which is admitted or proved to be subscribed or initialled by the obligant, does not need to be independently proved,[32] at least for the mercantile purpose for which the writing was granted.[33] When the date is of importance for some other purpose, as in a question with a trustee in bankruptcy, for example, independent evidence of its accuracy may be necessary.[33]

108. DOCQUETS ON ACCOUNTS

Docquets of approval, adjustment, acknowledgment or discharge, written upon business books or mercantile accounts, and subscribed by the person interested, are admissible in the same way as documents solemnly

---

23 This is thought to be implied by *Commercial Bank* v. *Kennard*, 1859, 21 D. 864, as between the original parties to the writing. (See Gloag, *Contract* (2nd ed.) 186). The decision turned upon a plea of no title to sue, which was upheld against the holders of the writing, who were not parties to it.

24 *Paterson* v. *Wright*, Jan. 31, 1810 F.C.; 1814, 6 Paton 38. As to whether writings *in re mercatoria* are now relevant to cautionary obligations, see § **113.**

25 *Stuart* v. *Potter, Choate & Prentice*, 1911, 1 S.L.T. 377.

26 Discussed in *Hamilton's Exrs.* v. *Struthers*, 1858, 21 D. 51, L. Mackenzie at p. 53, L. Curriehill at pp. 60-61; *Purvis* v. *Dowie*, 1869, 7 M. 764.

27 See *Paterson* v. *Paterson*, 1897, 25 R. 144 and §§ **118-121.**

28 Bell, *Commentaries*, I, 342; Dickson, *Evidence* (3rd ed.) §793.

29 Bell, *Commentaries*, I, 343; Dickson, *Evidence* (3rd ed.) §793. Authentication by cross or mark may also be sufficient (Dickson, *Evidence* (3rd ed.) §§672, 793), at least when it is proved to be the party's accustomed mode of transacting business (Bell, *Commentaries*, I, 343; *Rose* v. *Johnston*, 1878, 5 R. 600, L. Ormidale at p. 604), but perhaps only if the writing was read over to, and orally adopted by the party before he made the cross or mark (*Rose* v. *Johnston* (*supra*), L. J-Cl. Moncreiff at pp. 603-4). As to authentication by cross or mark, see also *Morton* v. *French*, 1908 S.C. 171; *Forbes' Exrs.* v. *Western Bank*, 1856, 16 D. 242, 807; *Craig* v. *Scobie*, 1832, 10 S. 510.

30 Erskine, iii, 2, 24; Bell, *Commentaries*, I, 342; Bell, *Principles*, §21; Dickson, *Evidence* (3rd ed.) §793.

31 See § **303.**

32 Bell, *Commentaries*, I, 343.

33 Dickson, *Evidence* (3rd ed.) §794. See also *Purvis* v. *Dowie*, 1869, 7 M. 764.

executed or holograph,[34] and are in the same position with regard to authentication and proof as other mercantile writings.[35] Although it has been said that the ordinary solemnities are necessary in connection with docquets on accounts which are not truly mercantile,[36] accounts of a character similar to mercantile accounts, although not necessarily between merchants, have in practice been regarded by the courts for this purpose as if they were mercantile accounts. So, for example, an acknowledgment by a farmer, subscribed by him, and written upon an account for deliveries of farm stock and advances of money made to him by his uncle, who was also a farmer, during the period of a year, was regarded as being "of the nature of a mercantile transaction."[37] Although the question of lack of authentication was not judicially mentioned, effect has been given to docquets, which were merely subscribed, on accounts between a solicitor and client,[38] a banker and customer in connection with a cash credit,[39] a man and his brother, rendered annually for many years, in respect of advances of money,[40] and an inspector of poor and a parochial board, rendered annually for thirteen years.[41] The court has refused, on the other hand, to regard as if it were a mercantile account, a statement of a number of loans, which mentioned merely the dates and sums, not vouched by or relative to any business book or document, and bearing an acknowledgment signed by the alleged debtor on the eve of his bankruptcy in favour of the alleged creditor, who was his brother-in-law.[42] The effect given to a docquet must depend upon its terms and the whole surrounding circumstances. The docquet may be reduced on the ground that its signature was induced by fraud or misrepresentation or on some other competent ground. If it is not reduced, the court will usually allow any error which appears on the face of the account, such as an arithmetical error[43] or an error of accounting,[44] to be corrected, but will not allow an enquiry into matters extrinsic to the account, which may be alleged to affect its accuracy.[45] The party challenging a

---

[34] *McLaren* v. *Liddell's Trs.*, 1860, 22 D. 373, L. Cowan at p. 378; Dickson, *Evidence* (3rd ed.) §797.

[35] See §106. There is also authority for the view that such docquets, if holograph, are effective although not subscribed: Stair, iv, 42, 6; Dickson, *Evidence* (3rd ed.) §799.

[36] Erskine, iii, 2, 24; Dickson, *Evidence* (3rd ed.) §798.

[37] *Stephen* v. *Pirie*, 1832, 10 S. 279, L. Balgray at p. 281. The other judges, although not regarding the transaction as being *in re mercatoria*, concurred in regarding the acknowledgment as effective.

[38] *Elder* v. *Smith*, 1829, 7 S. 656.

[39] *Walker* v. *Drummond*, 1836, 14 S. 780.

[40] *Boswell* v. *Montgomerie*, 1836, 14 S. 554.

[41] *Laing* v. *Laing*, 1862, 24 D. 1362.

[42] *Laidlaw* v. *Wilson*, 1844, 6 D. 530. See also *McAdie* v. *McAdie's Executrix*, 1883, 10 R. 741.

[43] *McLaren* v. *Liddell's Trs.*, 1862, 24 D. 577, L. J-Cl. Inglis at p. 584.

[44] *Ibid.*, L. Benholme at p. 585.

[45] *Walker* v. *Drummond*, 1836, 14 S. 780. The only error alleged in the docquetted accounts did not appear *ex facie* of the accounts or of the ledger from which they were compiled, but was said to be discoverable from an examination of certain private books of the bank. See the Lord Ordinary's findings at p. 784. The bank's claim, based upon a correction of the accounts, was refused without enquiry.

docquetted account must aver specific objections to it, and, if proof of the objections is allowed, has the onus of proving them.[46] There is no onus upon the other party, at least at the outset, to prove that the account is accurate.[46]

109. BILLS OF EXCHANGE, BANK CHEQUES AND PROMISSORY NOTES—GENERAL

A bill of exchange is an unconditional order in writing, addressed by one person to another, signed by the person giving it, requiring the person to whom it is addressed to pay on demand, or at a fixed or determinable future time, a sum certain in money to, or to the order of, a specified person, or to bearer.[47] A cheque is a bill of exchange drawn on a banker payable on demand.[48] A promissory note is an unconditional promise in writing made by one person to another signed by the maker, engaging to pay, on demand or at a fixed or determinable future time, a sum certain in money, to, or to the order of, a specified person or to bearer.[49] The rules regarding the interpretation and negotiation of these documents, and the respective liabilities of the parties to them, are prescribed in the Bills of Exchange Act, 1882,[47] and are not dealt with here. The following paragraphs mention only the specialties of constitution of the obligations arising under these documents, and proof of the facts relevant to them. Prescription of bills of exchange is mentioned in a later chapter.[50] In the following paragraphs references to bills of exchange are intended to include references to bank cheques and promissory notes.

110. BILLS OF EXCHANGE AS WRITINGS IN RE MERCATORIA

At common law bills of exchange are recognised as writings *in re mercatoria*,[51] and they may accordingly be authenticated in the same way as other writings *in re mercatoria*.[52] Cheques[53] and promissory notes[53] are similarly privileged. As in the case of other mercantile documents, if the signature on a bill of exchange is disputed, the onus of proving that it is genuine rests upon the party founding upon it.[54] The earlier rule that a bill of exchange is sufficiently signed by the drawer if the document is in

---

[46] *Laing* v. *Laing*, 1862, 24 D. 1362, L. J-Cl. Inglis at p. 1366, L. Cowan at p. 1367; *Struthers* v. *Smith*, 1913 S.C. 1116, L.P. Dunedin at pp. 1119-1120.

[47] Bills of Exchange Act, 1882 (45 & 46 Vict. c. 61), s. 3.

[48] *Ibid*. s. 73.

[49] *Ibid*. s. 83 (1). See also s. 89. An alleged promissory note payable "to A or B or their order," was held to be uncertain as to the payee, and not to be a mercantile document, so that it had to be either solemnly executed or holograph in order to be effective: *Thomson* v. *Philp*, 1867, 5 M. 679. See in this connection the Bills of Exchange Act, 1882, s. 7 (2).

[50] See §§ 131 *et seq.*

[51] Dickson, *Evidence* (3rd ed.) §801. For a definition of bill of exchange, see § 109.

[52] See § 107. See also Bills of Exchange Act, 1882 (45 & 46 Vict. c. 61) ss. 3 (1), 17 (2), 32 (1). As to authentication of a bill of exchange by initials and by mark, see Dickson, *Evidence* (3rd ed.) §802.

[53] For definitions, see § 109.

[54] *McIntyre* v. *National Bank of Scotland*, 1910 S.C. 150.

his own handwriting and his name is in the body of it,[55] would probably not now be followed,[56] and the validity of a bill of exchange signed by the executor of the drawer after the latter's death,[57] has been doubted.[58] The completion of blanks in bills is dealt with later.[59]

The following are statutory specialties with regard to the signature of bills of exchange:—when a bill is wanting in any material particular, the person in possession of it has a *prima facie* authority to fill up the omission in any way he thinks fit;[60] a person whose signature to a bill is required need not sign by his own hand, and it is sufficient if his signature is written thereon by some other person by or under his authority;[61] when a bill must be signed by a corporation it is sufficient if it is sealed with the corporate seal,[62] but this is not essential, and the company's signature may be effected by another person adhibiting his own signature for or on behalf of the company;[63] signature of a bill by procuration operates as a notice that the agent has only a limited authority to sign, and the principal is only bound by such signature if the agent in so signing was acting within the actual limits of his authority;[64] a person signing a bill who adds to his signature words indicating that he signs for or on behalf of a principal, or in a representative character, is not personally liable thereon,[65] but, if a signatory intends to bind a third party and not himself, the obligation must unambiguously bear that meaning,[66] the onus of proving that the alleged principal only is bound being on those who assert it,[67] and the mere addition to the signature of words describing the signatory as agent, or as filling a representative character, does not exempt him from personal liability;[65] when a person signs a bill in a trade name, or an assumed name, he is liable thereon as if he had signed it in his own name, and the signature of the name of a firm is equivalent to the signature by the person signing of the names of all persons liable as partners in that firm.[68]

55 Bell, *Principles*, §311; Dickson, *Evidence* (3rd ed.) §805.
56 A bill of exchange must be signed: Bills of Exchange Act, 1882 (45 & 46 Vict. c. 61), s. 3. "Signed" is now interpreted as meaning "subscribed": see *Waterson's Trs.* v. *St. Giles Boys' Club*, 1943 S.C. 369, L. J-Cl. Cooper at p. 374.
57 Bell, *Commentaries*, I, 416; Dickson, *Evidence* (3rd ed.) §805.
58 *Lawson's Exrs.* v. *Watson*, 1907 S.C. 1353, L. McLaren at p. 1357, L. Pearson at p. 1358.
59 See § **184**, sub-para. (a).
60 Bills of Exchange Act, 1882 (45 & 46 Vict. c. 61), s. 20 (1). It has been held that the drawer may sign even after the acceptor and payee are dead, and at any time before the bill is produced in judgment: *Shaw* v. *Farquhar*, 1761 M. 1444; *Cathcart* v. *Dick's Reps.*, 1748 M. 1439; Bell, *Commentaries*, I, 421; Bell, *Principles*, §311.
61 *Ibid.* s. 91 (1).
62 *Ibid.* s. 91 (2).
63 *Ibid.*, ss. 25, 26. See also the Companies Act, 1948 (11 & 12 Geo. VI. c. 38), s. 33 and *Brebner* v. *Henderson*, 1925 S.C. 643.
64 *Ibid.* s. 25.
65 *Ibid.* s. 26 (1). The question of whether words added to the signature are merely descriptive of the signatory or, on the other hand, have the effect of relieving the signatory of liability, is one which must be answered by interpretation of the document as a whole: *Brebner* v. *Henderson* (*supra*).
66 *Brebner* v. *Henderson* (*supra*), L.P. Clyde at p. 647.
67 *Brebner* v. *Henderson*, 1925 S.C. 643, L. Sands at p. 648.
68 Bills of Exchange Act, 1882 (45 & 46 Vict. c. 61), s. 23 (1) (2).

The law with regard to the date of a bill of exchange is similar in principle to that relating to documents *in re mercatoria* generally,[69] with certain statutory additions. When a bill, or an acceptance or indorsement thereon, is dated, the date is deemed to be the true date unless the contrary is proved.[70] A bill is not invalid because it is undated,[71] or ante-dated or post-dated,[72] and when a bill payable at a fixed period after date is issued undated, any holder may insert the true date, and the bill is payable accordingly.[73] If a wrong date is inserted and the bill subsequently comes into the hands of a holder in due course, the bill operates and is payable as if the date so inserted was the true date.[73]

111. SUMMARY DILIGENCE ON BILLS OF EXCHANGE

The Scottish law and practice with regard to summary diligence upon a bill of exchange was not in any way altered or affected by the Bills of Exchange Act, 1882, or by any repeal affected thereby.[74] In order that summary diligence may be competent, the bill must be complete, and in particular must be dated,[75] and subscribed[76] by the drawer. Authentication by initials[77] or by mark[78] are not sufficient for this purpose, but a signature per procuration would appear to be unobjectionable.[79] If the bill is complete at the time when it is sought to do summary diligence upon it, it is immaterial that it was originally signed on a blank stamped paper, or was otherwise incomplete when originally delivered, and that it was subsequently completed as authorised by statute.[80]

112. PAROLE EVIDENCE AS TO LIABILITY ON BILLS OF EXCHANGE

Section 100 of the Bills of Exchange Act, 1882,[81] provides that, in any judicial proceeding in Scotland, any fact relating to a bill of exchange, bank cheque or promissory note, which is relevant to any question of liability thereon, may be proved by parole evidence. This section was received without enthusiasm by the Scottish courts and examples of circumstances

---

[69] See § 107.
[70] Bills of Exchange Act, 1882 (45 & 46 Vict. c. 61), s. 13 (1).
[71] *Ibid.* s. 3 (4) (a).
[72] *Ibid.* s. 13 (2).
[73] *Ibid.* s. 12.
[74] Bills of Exchange Act, 1882 (45 & 46 Vict. c. 61) s. 98.
[75] Dickson, *Evidence* (3rd ed.) §802; *Cameron* v. *Morrison*, 1869, 7 M. 382. The Mercantile Law Amendment (Scotland) Act, 1856 (19 & 20 Vict. c. 60), s. 10, which made this explicit, and to which the opinions in *Cameron* v. *Morrison* (*supra*) referred, was repealed by the Bills of Exchange Act, 1882, but it is thought that, in terms of s. 98 of that Act, the existing law on this point remained unchanged.
[76] Bell, *Principles*, §311; Dickson, *Evidence* (3rd ed.) §§802, 807. See also *Lawson's Exrs.* v. *Watson*, 1907 S.C. 1353, and § 110, note 56.
[77] Dickson, *Evidence* (3rd ed.) §§671, 802.
[78] Dickson, *Evidence* (3rd ed.) §§673, 802.
[79] *Summers* v. *Marianski*, 1843, 6 D. 286; *Turnbull* v. *McKie*, 1822, 1 S. 331.
[80] *Cameron* v. *Morrison*, 1869, 7 M. 382. Authority for completion of an inchoate or incomplete bill is given by the Bills of Exchange Act, 1882, s. 20.
[81] 45 & 46 Vict. c. 61.

in which it has been judicially held to apply are few. The general common law rule, which provides that performance,[82] discharge[82] or variation[83] of an obligation constituted by writing may not be proved by parole evidence, is mentioned later. It has been authoritatively decided that this general rule, in spite of the apparently clear terms of the section mentioned above, continues to apply to bills of exchange, and that their payment,[84] discharge or variation[85] may not be proved by parole evidence. Parole evidence was also held to be inadmissible to prove an oral undertaking that payment on a promissory note or bill would not be demanded until the debtor was in a position to pay without detriment to his business, so long as he continued to pay interest,[86] or until sufficient working capital had been raised by the business concerned.[87] Decisions, moreover, which allowed the acceptor of a bill of exchange to prove by parole evidence an oral agreement to renew the bill from time to time when it became due during the currency of a lease,[88] or an oral agreement by the indorsee that if the bill was in his hands at maturity he would not call upon the acceptor to retire it,[89] have been disapproved.[90]

The section, however, has been said to apply, but only as between the drawer and acceptor,[91] in order to allow proof by parole evidence that the bill was granted for the accommodation of the drawer, and that, although the apparent creditor, he is in truth the debtor.[92] Parole evidence, moreover, has been held to be admissible to prove either that the bill of exchange, although bearing to be granted for an onerous consideration, was not in fact so granted,[93] or that a contractual undertaking, which represented the onerous consideration for the bill, was not, or could not be, implemented. A person, *ex facie* liable under a bill of exchange, was allowed to prove by parole evidence, and so to escape liability, that the bill was granted in terms of a contract under which goods were to be delivered when the bill became payable, and that the goods were not tendered when payment was demanded,[93] or were properly rejected as disconform to contract.[94] Similarly parole evidence was regarded as admissible to prove that a bill was

---

[82] See § **125.**

[83] See §§ **240, 247, 279.**

[84] *Nicol's Trs.* v. *Sutherland,* 1951 S.C. (H.L.) 21; *Robertson* v. *Thomson,* 1900, 3 F. 5.

[85] *National Bank of Australasia* v. *Turnbull & Co.,* 1891, 18 R. 629, L.P. Inglis at p. 634, L. McLaren at p. 638; *Gibson's Trs.* v. *Galloway,* 1896, 23 R. 414, L. McLaren at p. 416; *Stagg & Robson Ltd.* v. *Stirling,* 1908 S.C. 675. These decisions were approved in *Nicol's Trs.* v. *Sutherland* (*supra*), L. Simonds at pp. 26-27, L. Normand at p. 32, L. Reid at pp. 43-44.

[86] *Gibson's Trs.* v. *Galloway,* 1896, 23 R. 414.

[87] *Manchester & Liverpool District Banking Co.* v. *Ferguson & Co.,* 1905, 7 F. 865.

[88] *Drybrough & Co., Ltd.* v. *Roy,* 1903, 5 F. 665.

[89] *Viani & Co.* v. *Gunn & Co.,* 1904, 6 F. 989.

[90] *Nicol's Trs.* v. *Sutherland,* 1951 S.C. (H.L.) 21, L. Normand at p. 31 (with regard only to *Drybrough*; for his reference to *Viani & Co.,* see p. 29), and L. Reid at p. 43.

[91] *National Bank of Australasia* v. *Turnbull & Co.,* 1891, 18 R. 629, L.P. Inglis at p. 635.

[92] *Nicol's Trs.* v. *Sutherland* (*supra*), L. Simonds at p. 27; *Stagg & Robson Ltd.* v. *Stirling,* 1908 S.C. 675, L. P. Dunedin at p. 679.

[93] *Marr & Sons* v. *Lindsay,* 1881, 18 S.L.R. 721, L. P. Inglis at p. 723.

[94] *Wallace & Brown* v. *Robinson, Fleming & Co.,* 1885, 22 S.L.R. 830.

granted as part of a partnership agreement from which the debtor under the bill resiled, with the result that, implement of a partnership agreement being in law unenforceable, payment of the bill could not be insisted in.[95]

Apart altogether from section 100 of the Bills of Exchange Act, a bill of exchange is incomplete and revocable until it is delivered,[96] and it has been said that not only the fact of delivery, but also the purpose for which it is made, may be proved by parole evidence.[91]

113. CAUTIONARY OBLIGATIONS

All cautionary obligations must be in writing and subscribed by the person undertaking the obligation, and otherwise they have no effect.[97] The obligations affected by this statutory provision include all guarantees, securities or cautionary obligations made or granted by any person for any other person, and all representations and assurances as to the character, conduct, credit, ability,[98] trade or dealings of any person, made or granted to the effect or for the purpose of enabling such person to obtain credit, money, goods, or postponement of payment of any debt, or of any other obligation demandable from him.[97]

The terms of the statutory provision seem to indicate fairly clearly that writing is necessary for the constitution of the obligation, and not merely for its proof. "Shall have no effect"[97] seems to produce the same result as "shall be null and void and make no faith"—the expression used in the authentication statutes, which have been held to deal with the constitution of obligations.[99] But contrary views have been expressed,[1] and the question, like most questions related to this topic, must be regarded as undecided. The writing is necessary whether the obligation is relied upon as a cause of action or as the basis of a defence,[2] and even when the obligation is alleged to have been undertaken fraudulently.[3]

---

[95] *Pert* v. *Bruce* 1937, S.L.T. 475.

[96] Bills of Exchange Act, 1882 (45 & 46 Vict. c. 61), s. 21. The giving of notice of acceptance may be the equivalent of delivery.

[97] Mercantile Law Amendment (Scotland) Act, 1856 (19 & 20 Vict. c. 60), s. 6. The application of the Act to the customary recourse agreement between a finance company and a dealer, in connection with hire-purchase transactions, is discussed in Gow, *The Law of Hire-Purchase*, 167.

[98] This has been construed as meaning ability to pay. *Irving* v. *Burns*, 1915 S.C. 260.

[99] See §§ **89, 90.**

[1] Bell, *Principles*, §249 A; *Walker's Trs.* v. *McKinlay*, 1880, 7 R. (H.L.) 85, L. Blackburn at p. 88; *Wallace* v. *Gibson*, 1895, 22 R. (H.L.) 56, L. Wellwood (Ordinary) at p. 59. It was conceded that the terms of the statute indicated that the writing was necessary for constitution, but it was argued that, since the purpose of the statute was to assimilate the law of Scotland to that of England, and in England the writing was needed only as evidence of the obligation, the opposite construction ought to be placed upon it. As to the Scottish law on the point prior to the passing of the 1856 Act, opinions have differed, but the weight of authority favoured the view that writing was required as evidence, but not for constitution: Erskine, iv, 2, 20; Bell, *Principles*, §18; Dickson, *Evidence* (3rd ed.) §600; Gloag and Irvine, *Rights in Security*, 684 *et seq. Cf. Church of England Life Assurance Co.* v. *Hodges*, 1857, 19 D. 414, L. J-Cl. Hope at pp. 421-2, L. Cowan at p. 425.

[2] *Union Bank of Scotland* v. *Taylor*, 1925 S.C. 835.

[3] *Clydesdale Bank* v. *Paton*, 1896, 23 R. (H.L.) 22.

A more important question, which must also be regarded as undecided,[4] relates to the authentication of the writing. If the authentication statutes[5] are regarded as applying, then, in order that it may be founded upon, the writing in which the obligation is expressed must be solemnly executed[6] or holograph,[7] and there is authority for the view that such authentication is required.[8] If this view be correct, it is mitigated in the usual way when the writing is *in re mercatoria*,[9] or when *rei interventus* has occurred, as, for example, by the making of advances on the faith of the obligation,[10] in both of which cases a writing subscribed by the granter without witnesses is sufficient on either view of the law.

The state of the law before 1856 is so doubtful,[1] that it seems impossible to state with certainty what changes the Mercantile Law Amendment (Scotland) Act[97] effected or was intended to effect. Only one of the possible views as to the present state of the law regarding cautionary obligations will enable them to be fitted into the framework created by *Paterson* v. *Paterson*,[11] the view, namely, that a cautionary obligation requires for its constitution a writing which, with the usual exceptions, is either solemnly executed or holograph. It is thought, however, that this view fails to give effect to the terms of the statute, which provide that a writing subscribed by the granter is the only essential requirement. The special rule created by the statute, therefore, is thought to be that a cautionary obligation, in order that it may be founded upon, must be embodied in a writing which is subscribed by the granter, and which need not be tested, and that the writing must be produced.

114. HIRE-PURCHASE AND CREDIT-SALE AGREEMENTS

A statutory rule[12] applies to any hire-purchase contract, as defined,[13] in respect of an article not exceeding £300[14] in value. No such contract, and no contract of cautionry for, or guarantee of, the performance of any

---

4 See Gloag and Irvine, *Rights in Security*, 684 *et seq.*, 721 *et seq.*; Gloag, *Contract* (2nd ed.), 184; Encyclopedia of the Laws of Scotland, III, para. 373; Gloag and Henderson, *Introduction to the Law of Scotland* (6th ed.) 206.
5 See § **90.**
6 See §§ **90, 176** *et seq.*
7 See §§ **91, 188** *et seq.*
8 Bell, *Principles*, §§248, 249 A; Dickson, *Evidence*, (3rd ed.) §603.
9 *Johnston* v. *Grant*, 1844, 6 D. 875; *National Bank of Scotland* v. *Campbell*, 1892, 19 R. 885. In both these cases the writing was held to have been validated *rei interventu*, but it was assumed that, if the writing had been *in re mercatoria*, it would have been valid on that ground also. See also Bell, *Principles*, §249 A; Dickson, *Evidence* (3rd ed.) §604; Gloag, *Contract* (2nd ed.) 184. As to writings *in re mercatoria* generally, see §§ **105** *et seq.*
10 *Johnston* v. *Grant* (*supra*); *National Bank of Scotland* v. *Campbell* (*supra*); *Snaddon* v. *London, Edinburgh and Glasgow Assurance Co.*, 1902, 5 F. 182, L. Trayner at p. 186. As to *rei interventus* generally, see §§ **280** *et seq.*
11 1897, 25 R. 144.
12 Hire Purchase and Small Debt (Scotland) Act, 1932 (22 & 23 Geo. V. c. 38).
13 *Ibid.*, s. 1.
14 As amended by the Hire-Purchase Act, 1954 (2 & 3 Eliz. II. c. 51), s. 4 (1).

obligation under such a contract, is binding on any person as hirer, purchaser, cautioner or guarantor, unless the contract is signed by such person.[15] A similar rule applies to a credit-sale agreement, for a total purchase price not exceeding £1,000 in the case of livestock and £300 in the case of other goods, under which the purchase price is payable by five or more instalments.[16] The seller under such an agreement, if the total purchase price exceeds £5, cannot enforce it, or any guarantee associated with it, against the buyer or guarantor, unless a note or memorandum of the agreement is made and signed by the buyer and by or on behalf of all the other parties.[17]

The constitution or proof of these obligations gives rise to questions similar to those arising from the Mercantile Law Amendment (Scotland) Act, 1856,[18] in relation to cautionary obligations. In the only reported case which has so far raised the point, it was held that, in view of the statutory provision, it is unnecessary that the purchaser's subscription should be witnessed by two witnesses.[19] The purchaser's subscription of a printed form in which the essential details, later completed by the vendors, were blank, was held not to be a subscription of the contract within the meaning of the statute.[19]

It is thought that, as in the case of cautionary obligations, these obligations cannot be fitted into the framework created by *Paterson* v. *Paterson*, and that they must be regarded as being subject to a special statutory rule. Before an obligation by the hirer or purchaser may be founded upon, it must be embodied in a writing, which is subscribed by the hirer in a hire-purchase contract and by all the parties in a credit-sale agreement, which need not be tested, and which must be produced.[20]

115. CONTRACTS OF INSURANCE

(a) **Marine Insurance.** By statute[21] a contract of marine insurance is not admissible in evidence unless it is embodied in a marine policy containing certain statutory requirements,[22] but the contract is deemed to have been concluded when the proposal of the assured was accepted by the insurer,[23] and, if a duly stamped policy has been issued, reference may be made to

---

[15] *Ibid.*, s. 2.

[16] Hire-Purchase Act, 1938 (1 & 2 Geo. VI. c. 53), ss. 1, 21; Hire-Purchase Act, 1954 (2 & 3 Eliz. II. c. 51; applied to Scotland by Credit-Sale Agreements (Scotland) Act, 1961 (9 & 10 Eliz. II. c. 56).

[17] *Ibid.*, s. 3.

[18] 19 & 20 Vict. c. 60, s. 6. See § 113.

[19] *United Dominions Trust (Commercial) Ltd.* v. *Lindsay*, 1959 S.L.T. (Sh.Ct.) 58. It was also doubted by the sheriff-substitute whether *rei interventus* (or homologation) could cure the defect arising from the absence of the purchaser's subscription. *English* v. *Donnelly*, 1959 S.L.T. 2 decided that the provisions are mandatory, but was not otherwise concerned with this question.

[20] The matter is discussed at length in Gow, *The Law of Hire-Purchase*, 38 *et seq.*, and Gow, *Constitution and Proof of Voluntary Obligations*, Part I, Juridical Review, 1961, 7 *et seq.*

[21] *Marine Insurance Act*, 1906 (6 Edw. VII. c. 41).

[22] *Ibid.*, s. 22. As to a form of policy and the statutory meaning of customary terms and expressions, see s. 31, Sch. 1.

[23] *Ibid.*, s. 21.

the slip or covering note[24] for the purpose *inter alia* of discovering the date when the contract was concluded.[23]

(b) General. At common law the position with regard to the contract of insurance generally is uncertain. It has been stated that a contract of insurance can only be made in writing, and that the only admissible evidence of such a contract is a policy or an informal writing followed by *rei interventus*, as, for example, acceptance of a premium.[25] When that statement was made, however, the attention of the court was not called to an early case[26] where opinions were expressed that an oral contract of insurance can be proved by parole evidence, and in a more recent case in the Outer House[27] it was accepted by the defenders and by the court that a contract of insurance can be constituted orally and proved by parole evidence. A cover note embodied in a letter, which provided *inter alia* that a policy should be applied for before the ship sailed, was held to be an offer to insure which could be accepted by an oral application for a policy, and the making of such an application having been proved by parole evidence, the defendants were ordained to issue a formal policy in terms of the cover note.[28] If a contract of fidelity insurance includes a cautionary obligation, it is thought that the rule with regard to cautionary obligations applies, and that the obligation may be constituted and proved only by a writing subscribed by the person undertaking it.[29]

116. TRANSFERS OF INCORPOREAL RIGHTS IN MOVEABLES

A distinction must be made between an actual assignation or transfer of an incorporeal right in moveables and a contract which merely creates an obligation to assign or transfer. It is thought that, as a general rule, an actual transfer of such rights,[30] at least when the rights themselves are constituted in writing,[31] may be constituted only in writing which is solemnly executed[32] or holograph,[33] or in an informal writing followed by *rei interventus* or homologation.[34] Special statutory provisions apply to certain

---

24 *Ibid.*, s. 89.
25 *McElroy* v. *London Assurance Corporation*, 1897, 24 R. 287, L. McLaren at pp. 290-291. In Gloag, *Contract* (2nd ed.) 181, this is preferred as a correct statement of the law. Erskine (iii, 3, 17) mentions the matter only incidentally in relation to the consensual contract of affreightment, and refers to an obligation in writing styled a policy of insurance. Bell (*Principles*, §§465, 467) describes the contract as consensual, but says that it is invariably embodied in a policy.
26 *Christie* v. *North British Insurance Co.*, 1825, 3 S. 360, at p. 362.
27 *Parker & Co. (Sandbank) Ltd.* v. *Western Assurance Co.* (O.H.) 1925 S.L.T. 131.
28 *Bhugwandass* v. *Netherlands Insurance Co.*, 1888, 14 App. Cas. 83.
29 Mercantile Law Amendment (Scotland) Act, 1856 (19 & 20 Vict. c. 60), s. 6. See § 113.
30 Dickson, *Evidence* (3rd ed.) §560.
31 *McMurrich's Trs.* v. *McMurrich's Trs.*, 1903, 6 F. 121, L. McLaren at p. 126; Bell, *Commentaries*, I, 345. The cases cited in Gloag, *Contract* (2nd ed.) 180, in support of the opinion that writing is required only for proof and not for constitution, seem to refer, not to an actual transfer or assignation, but to an agreement to transfer or assign.
32 See §§ 90, 176 *et seq.*
33 See §§ 91, 188 *et seq.*
34 *Jeffreys* v. *Kyle*, 1856, 18 D. 906, L. Curriehill at p. 912: 1859, 3 Macqu. 611.

kinds of transfers, such as transfers of shares,[35] assignations of patents[36] and copyrights,[37] and bills of sale of shares in a British ship.[38]

The suggested rule applies only to the actual assignation or transfer of the right. A contract which merely creates an obligation to assign or transfer may be concluded orally or by informal writings, and may be proved by parole evidence. It is thought that this distinction is general,[39] and it has been held to apply to contractual obligations to allot or transfer company shares or debentures,[40] and shares in a ship,[41] and to assign the goodwill of a business.[42]

[35] Companies Act, 1948 (11 & 12 Geo. VI. c. 38), ss. 73, 75. The form is regulated by the company's Articles of Association.

[36] Patents Act, 1949 (12, 13 & 14 Geo. VI. c. 87), s. 74.

[37] Copyright Act, 1956 (4 & 5 Eliz. II. c. 74), s. 36 (3). The assignment must be in writing and signed by or on behalf of the assignor. In *Jeffreys* v. *Kyle* (*supra*), on a construction of the statutes then in force, it was held that an untested receipt might constitute a valid assignation of a copyright.

[38] Merchant Shipping Act, 1894 (57 & 58 Vict. c. 60), s. 24, Sch. 1. One witness is sufficient.

[39] *Nelson Mitchell* v. *City of Glasgow Bank*, 1878, 6 R. 420, L. Shand at p. 435 (affd. 6 R. (H.L.) 66).

[40] *Goldie* v. *Torrance*, 1882, 10 R. 174; *Devlin* v. *McKelvie*, 1915 S.C. 180; *Wilson* v. *Dunlop Bremner & Co. Ltd.*, 1921, 1 S.L.T. 35, 354. See also *Beardmore & Co.* v. *Barry*, 1928 S.C. 101; (H.L.) 47, where the defender was held bound to accept an allotment of shares in implement of an informal written obligation, not, however, because the contract dealt with an allotment of shares, but because, on the assumption that the obligation was a bond (see § **100**) to which the authentication statutes would normally have applied, it was *in re mercatoria* and in any event *rei interventus* had followed upon it. There is a statutory exception in the case of contracts entered into for the sale or transfer of shares or stock of any joint stock banking company in the United Kingdom, other than the Banks of England and Ireland, which are null and void unless they are in writing and contain certain prescribed information: The Banking Companies (Shares) Act, 1867 (30 & 31 Vict. c. 29), s. 1; *Nelson Mitchell* v. *City of Glasgow Bank* (*supra*).

[41] *McConnachie* v. *Geddes*, 1918 S.C. 391.

[42] *Moncrieff* v. *Seivwright*, 1896, 33 S.L.R. 456.

CHAPTER XI

MATTERS REQUIRING PROOF BY WRIT OR OATH

117. GENERAL

This and the succeeding chapter are concerned with matters which, as a general rule, may be constituted orally, but which may be proved only by the writ of the other party. These are distinguishable, on the one hand, from *obligationes literis*, which require solemn or holograph writing for their constitution,[1] and, on the other hand, from matters, such as the consensual contracts, which may be both constituted orally and proved by parole evidence.[2] Since either party to a litigation may refer to the oath of his opponent the whole cause or any disputed question of fact,[3] except an *obligatio literis*[4] or a consistorial cause,[5] it follows that reference to oath is always an alternative to proof by the opponent's writ. Without the above explanation the expression "proof by writ or oath," although customary and useful as a short description, may be misleading.[6] It is true that the statutes which limit the mode of proof of certain obligations after the termination of a prescriptive period,[7] use the expression "writ or oath," and that in some of the decisions with regard to them the judges proceed upon the precise words of the statute.[8] This does not, it is thought, alter the fact that the sole requirement of the law regarding the matters referred to in this and the succeeding chapter is proof by writ, reference to oath

---

[1] As to these, see §§ **89** *et seq.*
[2] For examples of this group, see §§ **144** *et seq.*
[3] See §§ **308** *et seq.*
[4] See § **92,** sub-para. (c).
[5] See §§ **156,** sub-paras. (b) (c), **317.**
[6] Lord Young in *Paterson* v. *Paterson*, 1897, 25 R. 144, at p. 152, remarks on the true relationship between proof by writ and reference to oath. This relationship is demonstrated in the interlocutors pronounced in the sheriff court in *Hamilton* v. *Hamilton's Executrix*, 1950 S.C. 39, at pp. 39, 40.
[7] See §§ **131** *et seq.*
[8] e.g. *Bertram & Co.* v. *Stewart's Trs.*, 1874, 2 R. 255.

being a right which may always be exercised by the party, subject to the overriding discretion of the court.[3]

When a defender wishes to found upon one of the prescriptions which limit the mode of proof to writ or oath, he must state a plea to that effect in his defences, and the court must normally either sustain or repel this plea before proof is allowed, upon a consideration of the pursuer's averments and of the terms of the account or other document sued upon.[9] If, through a failure to state such a plea, a proof *prout de jure* is allowed and acquiesced in, the court must then decide the case on the evidence led.[9] It seems probable that if a similar situation arose in connection with any of the other matters which ought to be proved by writ or oath, as, for example, in an action for repayment of a loan, the same rule would be applied.

When the receipt of money on loan is judicially admitted without qualification, the admission may be founded upon, and further proof of the loan by writ or oath is unnecessary.[10] The same rule applies to an admission of trust,[11] and is thought to be applicable to all obligations which may be proved by writ of party.[12]

The nature and requirements of proof by writ of party[13] and of reference to oath,[14] are dealt with later.

118. LOAN OF MONEY

The receipt on loan of money exceeding £8 6s. 8d.,[15] which is not judicially admitted without qualification,[16] may be proved only by the writ of the alleged borrower or by reference to his oath.[17] When the judicial admission,[16] or written acknowledgment[18] or admission on oath,[19] upon which the

---

9   See § **131**.
10 See § **118**.
11 See § **122**.
12 Judicial admissions in relation to prescriptions are mentioned at § **132**, sub-para. (b).
13 See §§ **302** *et seq.*
14 See §§ **308** *et seq.*
15 A loan not exceeding £8 6s. 8d. may be proved *prout de jure*: Erskine, iv, 2, 20; *Annand's Trs.* v. *Annand*, 1869, 7 M. 526.   Even for such a loan, the stricter proof may sometimes be required: L. Deas in *Annand's Trs.* v. *Annand* (*supra*), at p. 529.   Proof by writ or oath is required if the original loan exceeded £8 6s. 8d., even if the balance sued for is less: *Clark* v. *Glen*, 1836, 14 S. 966.
16 When the judicial admission is qualified, the qualification must be disproved by the writ or oath of the defender before the pursuer may found upon the admission: *Walker* v. *Garlick* (O.H.), 1940 S.L.T. 208 (averment that loan repaid); *Kerr's Trs.* v. *Ker*, 1883, 11 R. 108, L.P. Inglis at p. 116 (averment that claim abandoned); *McKie* v. *Wilson*, 1951 S.C. 15 (averment that money received for services rendered).   A judicial admission of the mere receipt of money, as distinct from a judicial admission of loan, does not usually raise a presumption of loan so as to relieve the pursuer of the burden of proving loan by writ or oath, unless the admission is coupled with an averment that the money was received as a gift.   As to this, see § **62**.
17 Stair, iv, 43, 4; Erskine, iv, 2, 20; Bell, *Principles*, §2257; Gloag, *Contract* (2nd ed.) 192; *Haldane* v. *Speirs*, 1872, 10 M. 537.   The rule does not apply to a loan of corporeal moveables, which may be proved *prout de jure*: *Scot* v. *Fletcher*, 1665, M. 11, 616; *Geddes* v. *Geddes*, 1678 M. 12, 730.
18 See L. Trayner's illustration in *Patrick* v. *Patrick's Trs.*, 1904, 6 F. 836, at p. 839.
19 *Newlands* v. *McKinlay*, 1885, 13 R. 353.   This decision seems to be contrary to principle. The matter is discussed further at § **311**, sub-para. (b).

pursuer relies as proof of loan, is qualified by an assertion of repayment, the proof of loan fails. When, however, a loan of money has been proved in one or other of the ways mentioned, the burden of proving repayment by the lender's writ or oath rests upon the borrower.[20]

The rule has not been applied in the following circumstances. A current account extending over several years between a solicitor and a client, which, in addition to credit entries, included on the debit side a large number of advances made by the solicitor to the client, was vouched, as to five of these advances, only by cheques in the client's favour indorsed by him. It was held that, while the indorsation on a cheque is not a writing sufficient for the proof of loan,[21] the indorsed cheques were sufficient vouchers, not of loans, but of the credit items in an account current between an agent and his principal.[22] In an action by the trustee in a sequestration, against the son of the bankrupt, for a decree ordaining him to convey to the pursuer heritable property which had been taken in the defender's name by the bankrupt, the defender averred that he held the property as security for loans made by him to the bankrupt. It was held that the alleged loans need not necessarily be proved by the bankrupt's writ, and a proof *habili modo* was allowed, the question before the court being, not a question of constituting a loan, but a question of the terms upon which a man who has got heritable property in his own name should be asked to reconvey that property to the person from whom he got it.[23] In an action for payment of a sum of money representing a few individual loans of £5 each, and some relatively large sums said to have been expended by the pursuer on the defender's behalf, a proof *habili modo* was allowed on the footing that if the pursuer was able to prove that the larger payments were made by him as the defender's agent, the proof need not be restricted to writ or oath.[24] The mere fact, however, that the loan to be proved is one of a series of similar loans between the parties, does not prevent the application of the general rule.[25]

119. WRITINGS FROM WHICH LOAN INFERRED

(a) **General.** Proof by writ of party[26] and reference to oath of party[27]

---

[20] *Thiem's Trs.* v. *Collie*, 1899, 1 F. 764; *Fraser* v. *Bruce*, 1857, 20 D. 115. As to proof of discharge or payment, see §§ **125, 127.**

[21] See § **120.**

[22] *Robb* v. *Robb's Trs.*, 1884, 11 R. 881, L. Young at p. 886, L. Craighill at p. 887.

[23] *Smith's Tr.* v. *Smith*, 1911 S.C. 653. The *ratio decidendi* in this case was thus described by L.P. Cooper in *McKie* v. *Wilson*, 1951 S.C. 15, at p. 20.

[24] *Boyd* v. *Millar*, 1933 S.N. 106, 1934 S.N. 7. *Cf. Grant's Executrix* v. *Grant* (O.H.) 1922 S.L.T. 156, where an executrix sued a son for the balance of an account kept by a father in respect of his intromissions as factor with his son's properties and of payments made on the son's behalf. No accounts were rendered during the father's lifetime, and no acknowledgment of debt was made by the son, who was forisfamiliated, the only record of the transactions being the entries in the father's business books, which were carefully kept. It was held that the father's business books did not afford sufficient "natural proof" that the father intended to create the relationship of debtor and creditor between his son and himself.

[25] *McKie* v. *Wilson*, 1951 S.C. 15. See also *Smith's Tr.* v. *Smith*, 1911 S.C. 653, L.P. Dunedin at p. 659.

[26] See §§ **302** *et seq.*

115

are dealt with generally later. If a proof of loan by writ of party is allowed, a writing granted by the alleged debtor, which expressly acknowledges the loan as such, will normally discharge the onus of proof resting upon the party who alleges loan, and this may be true even if the writing is signed, not by the borrower, but by another person on his behalf, who is proved to have signed on his instructions.[28] Difficulties occur, however, when the writing founded upon does not expressly refer to loan, and the question then to be decided is whether a sufficient presumption or inference arises, from the terms of the writing founded upon, to discharge or shift the burden of proof. An unqualified written acknowledgment of the receipt of money, signed by the granter and delivered to the grantee, raises a presumption that the money was received on loan, or on some other footing inferring an obligation to repay, and places upon the recipient the onus of proving that it was not so received. This presumption, and the authorities relating to it, have already been discussed.[29]

(b) Bill of Exchange as Writ of Borrower. A bill of exchange or promissory note may be granted as additional security to the creditor in respect of a loan. In these circumstances questions may arise as to whether the bill of exchange, if for any reason it is inoperative as such, may be used as written evidence of the loan in the course of a proof by writ. In a case which was not concerned with loan, but with an accounting between a farmer and a horse proprietor, it was held that a bill of exchange which had been signed by the horse proprietor as acceptor, but which was useless as a bill of exchange because it had not been signed by the farmer as drawer, was nevertheless a written acknowledgment of indebtedness by the horse proprietor, or a written proof of his indebtedness, which placed upon him the onus of proving payment by the writ or oath of the farmer.[30] There seems no reason, therefore, why a bill of exchange or promissory note, whether it be complete or incomplete, if it is signed by the debtor, and can be construed as referring to a loan obtained from the creditor, should not be founded upon, if the creditor so elects, in a proof of the loan by writ. The position is more doubtful, however, if the bill or promissory note has prescribed.[31] In a case in which proof of a loan by writ was allowed, it was said: "I do not think it was intended (by the Act creating sexennial prescription) wholly to exclude the bill itself as an adminicle of evidence. It would hardly be possible in many cases to lead proof by writ about the constitution of a . . . loan without some reference to the bill. The bill, along with the other writs of the debtor, may be an adminicle of evidence going to prove that a loan was truly made."[32] In another case, where the loan was held to be sufficiently proved by other writs of the debtor, it was said:—"Although,

[27] See §§ **308** *et seq.*
[28] *Bryan* v. *Butters Bros. & Co.*, 1892, 19 R. 490. See also notes 42-44 below.
[29] See § **62.**
[30] *Lawson's Executors* v. *Watson*, 1907 S.C. 1353.
[31] As to sexennial prescription of bills of exchange, see §§ **134, 135.**
[32] *MacBain* v. *MacBain*, 1929 S.C. 213 (affd. 1930 S.C. (H.L.) 72), L.P. Clyde at p. 216. See also L. Morison at p. 219.

the (promissory) note being prescribed, the creditor cannot now found upon it as a document of debt, I am of opinion that he may do so by way of evidence to prove the constitution of the debt."[33] If the prescribed bill, however, may be regarded as a written acknowledgment of debt in support of the proof of loan, it is difficult to understand what other or better proof is needed. But, in the two cases above referred to,[34] the prescribed bill was not regarded as conclusive of the matter, and in other cases[35] the prescribed bill was either not founded upon or was expressly repudiated as part of the proof, although, if it could have been founded upon, it would probably have been conclusive. Although the matter is not free from doubt, it is thought that a prescribed bill may be used in a proof by writ of loan for the same purpose as in a proof by writ of the debt which it itself contains, namely to explain or elucidate the other writs upon which the creditor founds. Thus if the creditor proves by writ *aliunde* the constitution of a loan associated with a bill, he may refer to the prescribed bill to prove the amount of the loan.[36]

(c) **Examples.** The following are examples of writings which have been held sufficient to raise a presumption that money was received by the alleged debtor from the alleged creditor, by way of loan or under an obligation to repay:—a receipt dated, and signed by the debtor, in the following terms "Received from (the creditor) the sum of £30 sterling as per agreement";[37] a receipt, signed by the debtor, "Received the sum of £48 11s.," written upon an order to a Savings Bank, signed by the creditor, instructing the Savings Bank to pay £47 10s. to the bearer on production of the creditor's deposit book;[38] a document, dated, signed by the debtor and addressed to the creditor, in the following terms: "IOU the sum of £235 sterling, interest to be at 4% per annum from date"[39] and a document ,signed and dated, in the following terms "IOU Mary A. Black £150";[40] an unqualified[29] acknowledgment of the receipt of money contained in a letter or letters addressed by the debtor,[41] or by his solicitor[42] or agent[43] with his authority,[44] to the creditor, the correspondence of which the letters form part being relevant to

---

[33] *Nisbet* v. *Neil's Tr.*, 1869, 7 M. 1097, L.P. Inglis at p. 1099.

[34] *MacBain* v. *MacBain* (*supra*); *Nisbet* v. *Neil's Tr.* (*supra*).

[35] *Hunter* v. *Thomson*, 1843, 5 D. 1285 (proof *prout de jure*—price of horse); *Blake* v. *Turner*, 1860, 23 D. 15 (proof by writ—loan).

[36] *MacBain* v. *MacBain* (*supra*), L. Sands at pp. 217-218. As to the similar rule suggested for proof of the debt in a prescribed bill, see § **135**, sub-para. (a).

[37] *Thomson* v. *Geekie*, 1861, 23 D. 693.

[38] *Gill* v. *Gill*, 1907 S.C. 532.

[39] *Thiem's Trs.* v. *Collie*, 1899, 1 F. 764.

[40] *Black* v. *Gibb*, 1940 S.C. 24. If the transaction with which it is associated is real and not fictitious, an IOU is an acknowledgment of debt which imports an obligation to repay, and it is immaterial that no money passes at the time when the IOU is granted: L.P. Normand, at pp. 26-27, L. Moncrieff at pp. 28-29. See also *Thiem's Trs.* v. *Collie* (*supra*), L. J-Cl. Macdonald at p. 767; *Paterson* v. *Wilson*, 1883, 21 S.L.R. 272. *Cf. Bishop* v. *Bryce*, 1910 S.C. 426; *Dinesmann & Co.* v. *John Mair & Co.* (O.H.) 1912, 1 S.L.T. 217.

[41] *McKeen* v. *Adair*, 1864, 2 M. 392. The letter need not be contemporaneous with the constitution of the debt: *Carmichael's Tr.* v. *Carmichael*, 1929 S.C. 265, L.P. Clyde at p. 268; but is valueless if granted after the debtor's sequestration.

the interpretation of the acknowledgment in question.[45] The effect of entries in a debtor's books is mentioned in a later paragraph.[46]

120. WRITINGS FROM WHICH LOAN NOT INFERRED

The following are examples of writings which have been held *not* to raise a presumption that money was received by the alleged debtor from the alleged creditor by way of loan:—the debtor's endorsement upon a cheque in his favour for the amount of the sum sued for,[47] or upon a deposit receipt for that amount;[48] a letter written by the debtor to the creditor referring to a debt owed by him or to a payment received by him, without reference to any particular loan or sum of money,[49] or such a letter which refers only to a loan received in the past without admitting indebtedness at the date of the letter;[50] a letter by the debtor, written in answer to a letter by the creditor requesting repayment of a loan, in which the debt was neither expressly admitted nor repudiated;[51] and a letter by the debtor, addressed not to the creditor, but to a third party, which acknowledged only the receipt of money.[52] The effect of entries in the debtor's books is mentioned in the next paragraph.

121. ENTRIES IN DEBTOR'S BOOKS

The effect of entries in the debtor's books is uncertain. A jotting

---

[42] *Dryburgh* v. *Macpherson*, 1944 S.L.T. 116; *Fisher* v. *Fisher*, 1952 S.C. 347, L.P. Cooper at p. 351. In *Laidlaw* v. *Shaw*, 1886, 13 R. 724, a letter addressed by the debtor's solicitor, not to the creditor, but to his own client, in which the sum in question was expressly referred to as having been borrowed from the creditor, was held to be a sufficient writing for the purposes of establishing the loan.

[43] *Clark's Executrix* v. *Brown*, 1935 S.C. 110, L. Hunter at p. 116, L. Murray at p. 118; *McGregor* v. *McGregor*, 1860, 22 D. 1264 (letters by debtor's bank-agent to creditor, referring to the loan).

[44] In *Smith* v. *Smith*, 1869, 8 M. 239, an admission of the receipt of money contained in a letter by the debtor's solicitor was held not to be the constructive writ of the debtor because it was not proved to have been written with his authority. For general dicta as to writings which may be proved to be constructively the writs of the debtor, see *McGregor* v. *McGregor* (*supra*), L.P. McNeill at p. 1268, L. Deas at p. 1271; *Paterson* v. *Paterson*, 1897, 25 R. 144, L. Trayner at p. 164, L. Pearson at p. 184; *Clark's Executrix* v. *Brown* (*supra*), L. Hunter at p. 116, L. J-Cl. Aitchison at p. 122.

[45] *McKeen* v. *Adair*, 1864, 2 M. 392; *Duncan's Trs.* v. *Shand*, 1873, 11 M. 254, L. Cowan at p. 258; *MacBain* v. *MacBain*, 1930 S.C. (H.L.) 72, L. Hailsham at p. 75, L. Dunedin at p. 75; *Dryburgh* v. *Macpherson*, 1944 S.L.T. 116.

[46] See § 121.

[47] *Haldane* v. *Speirs*, 1872, 10 M. 537; *Dunn's Tr.* v. *Hardy*, 1896, 23 R. 621; *Scotland* v. *Scotland*, 1909 S.C. 505. Such an endorsement is proof only of the passing of money and raises no presumption as to the purpose of the payment.

[48] *Nimmo* v. *Nimmo*, 1873, 11 M. 446, L. Neaves at p. 449, L. Cowan at p. 450.

[49] *Rutherford's Exrs.* v. *Marshall*, 1861, 23 D. 1276; *Morison's Trs.* v. *Mitchell*, (O.H.) 1925 S.L.T. 231.

[50] *Patrick* v. *Patrick's Trs.*, 1904, 6 F. 836.

[51] *MacBain* v. *MacBain*, 1929 S.C. 213; 1930 S.C. (H.L.) 72. See the reference to this case at § 119, sub-para. (b).

[52] *Wink* v. *Speirs*, 1868, 6 M. 657, L. Neaves at p. 658; *Haldane* v. *Speirs* (*supra*), L.P. Inglis at p. 541; *Dunn's Tr.* v. *Hardy* (*supra*). Cf. *Wilson* v. *Scott* (O.H.) 1908, 15 S.L.T. 948 (triennial prescription). For the position when the letter to the third party acknowledges the debt, see *Emslie* v. *Duff*, 1865, 3 M. 854, and § 305.

"Borrowed from Rob £215," written in pencil in the debtor's pocket-book, was held not sufficient to prove loan.[53] It has been said that entries in regularly kept business books might raise an inference of loan,[54] and such entries coupled with other writings have in fact been held sufficient to prove loan,[55] but there seems to be no decided case in which such entries by themselves have been held sufficient for that purpose. As was suggested earlier, the presumption of loan arises, not from the mere receipt of money, but because a written acknowledgment has been granted as a document of debt and is in the creditor's possession when payment is demanded, and a mere entry in the debtor's business books is not the equivalent of the granting of such an acknowledgment.[56] An entry in a solicitor's business books is not to be regarded as constructively the writ of his client.[57] An entry made by the cashier or book-keeper of a firm in the firm's business books, coupled with his written acknowledgment to the creditor of the loan, may be sufficient to establish loan in an action against the firm and its partners,[58] and the position with regard to a company is similar.[59]

122. DECLARATOR OF TRUST—THE RULE

When a deed declares in absolute terms that a right of property, whether heritable[60] or moveable,[60] exists in one person, and the right is claimed by another person in an appropriate action, the trust may be proved only by the writ or oath of the alleged trustee.[61] The rule and its application result from judicial interpretation of the Act, 1696, c. 25, which provides: "that no action of declarator of trust shall be sustained as to any deed of trust made for hereafter except upon a declaration or back-bond of trust lawfully subscribed by the person alleged to be the trustee, and against

---

[53] *Wink* v. *Speirs*, 1868, 6 M. 657.
[54] *Wink* v. *Speirs* (*supra*), L. Neaves at p. 658. In *McRae* v. *Williamson Bros.*, 1877, 14 S.L.R. 562, where entries in the business books of the defending firm were held to relate only to payments received for the personal benefit of one of the partners, it seems to have been implied that if the entries had related to the receipt of money by and for the firm, otherwise than in payment of debts due to the firm, a loan of money to the firm would have been sufficiently proved.
[55] *Muir* v. *Goldie's Trs.*, 1898, 6 S.L.T. 188 (endorsements, some in debtor's handwriting and some in creditor's, upon the back of a prescribed bill for the same debt, noting payments of interest on the debt, coupled with entries in debtor's books relating to similar payments); *Hope* v. *Derwent Rolling Mills Co. Ltd.*, 1905, 7 F. 837 (a cheque, which vouched the passing of a sum of money, coupled with a post entry in pencil in the debtor's cash book crediting the pursuer with that sum, and a similar entry in the account kept with the pursuer in the debtor's books: the defence, being very technical, was treated critically by the court (L.P. Dunedin at p. 842), and the decision should probably not be regarded as of general application); *Kenney* v. *Walker*, 1836, 14 S. 803 (letter to creditor by firm's cashier acknowledging loan, coupled with entry, expressly referring to loan, made by him in firm's business books).
[56] See § **62.**
[57] *Fisher* v. *Fisher*, 1952, S.C. 347.
[58] *Kenney* v. *Walker* (*supra*); *Bryan* v. *Butters Bros. & Co.*, 1892, 19 R. 490.
[59] *Field* v. *R. H. Thomson & Co.* (O.H.) 1902, 10 S.L.T. 261. See also *Hope* v. *Derwent Rolling Mills Co. Ltd.*, 1905, 7 F. 837.
[60] Dickson, *Evidence* (3rd ed.) §579.
[61] *Laird & Co.* v. *Laird and Rutherfurd*, 1884, 12 R. 294, L.P. Inglis at p. 297.

whom, or his heirs or assignees, the declarator shall be intended, or unless the same be referred to the oath of party *simpliciter*; declaring that this Act shall not extend to the indorsation of bills of exchange or the notes of any trading company." In spite of the terms of the statute, unsigned writings have in certain circumstances been regarded as the writ of the alleged trustee.[62] Thus unsigned entries in the business books of the firm of which the alleged trustee was a partner, which he admitted were either made by him personally or on his instructions, were held to be his writ for the purpose of establishing trust,[63] as were unsigned holograph entries in the books of a deceased trustee showing the receipt of money, coupled with letters from the pursuer found in the deceased's repositories explaining why the money had passed.[64] The general requirements of proof by writ are thought to apply, and these, and reference to oath of party, are dealt with later.[65] Proof by writ or oath is unnecessary if the existence of the trust is judicially admitted.[66] If the existence of a trust is proved by writ or oath or is judicially admitted, its terms may be proved *prout de jure*.[67] Whether there is a deed of trust which brings a case within the operation of the statute depends primarily upon the pursuer's averments, and the statute applies when the pursuer alleges that property vested in the defender by a written title truly belongs to the pursuer, whether the word "trust" is used in his pleadings or not.[68] The rule now applies to transactions between spouses as it does to other persons,[69] and, if the rule is otherwise applicable, it is immaterial that the defender avers that he obtained his title by way of donation.[70]

123. LIMITATIONS OF THE RULE

The rule is applied subject to certain limitations,[71] and when the circumstances are such as to exclude the application of the rule the pursuer may prove his case *prout de jure*. The limitations are mentioned in the following sub-paragraphs:—

[62] *Thomson* v. *Lindsay*, 1873, 1 R. 65; *Seth* v. *Hain*, 1855, 17 D. 1117, L. J-Cl. Hope at p. 1124, L. Wood at p. 1125; *Knox* v. *Martin*, 1850, 12 D. 719. See McLaren, *Wills and Succession* (3rd ed.) II, 1066. *Cf. Walker* v. *Buchanan, Kennedy & Co.*, 1857, 20 D. 259, L. Deas at p. 269.

[63] *Knox* v. *Martin* (*supra*).

[64] *Thomson* v. *Lindsay* (*supra*).

[65] See §§ **302** *et seq.* (proof by writ); §§ **308** *et seq.* (reference to oath).

[66] *Seth* v. *Hain* (*supra*).

[67] *Livingstone* v. *Allan*, 1900, 3 F. 233, L.P. Balfour at p. 237; *National Bank of Scotland* v. *Mackie's Trs.* (O.H.) 1905, 13 S.L.T. 383; Dickson, *Evidence* (3rd ed.) §587. See also *Cairns* v. *Davidson*, 1913 S.C. 1054, L. Skerrington (Ordinary) at p. 1055, L. Guthrie at pp. 1058-9; *Grant* v. *Grant* (O.H.), 1898, 6 S.L.T. 203.

[68] *McNairn's Executrix* v. *Litster*, 1939 S.C. 72, L. Fleming at p. 77.

[69] *Inglis* v. *Smyth's Executrix* (O.H.), 1959 S.L.T. (Notes) 78; *Weissenbruch* v. *Weissenbruch* (O.H.), 1961 S.C. 340. *Cf. Anderson* v. *Anderson's Tr.* (O.H.), 1898, 6 S.L.T. 204; *Galloway* v. *Galloway*, 1929 S.C. 160, L. J-Cl. Alness at p. 166, L. Hunter at p. 170, L. Anderson at p. 171, L. Ormidale (*contra*) at p. 169.

[70] *Chalmers* v. *Chalmers*, 1845, 7 D. 865; *Newton* v. *Newton*, 1923 S.C. 15, L. Hunter at p. 22, L. Anderson at pp. 23-24; *Robertson* v. *Robertson* (O.H.), 1929 S.L.T. 510. As to proof of donation generally, see §§ **61, 62, 149-151.**

[71] For a general judicial reference to the limitations, see *Marshall* v. *Lyell*, 1859, 21 D. 514, L.P. Inglis at p. 521.

(a) The rule is not applied unless the defender holds the property under a deed or document of title.[72]

(b) The rule is not applied unless the document under which the defender holds the property is a conveyance or transfer or assignation of title to ownership, as distinct from a document which entitles him merely to obtain payment of money or to possess.[73] So, for example, the rule has been regarded as applicable when the deed consisted of a conveyance of heritage recorded in the Register of Sasines,[74] a grant of letters patent registered in the Register of Patents,[75] a transfer of shares registered in the register of members of the company[76] and an assignation of an extract decree obtained against a third person.[77] On the other hand, the rule was not applied when the deed consisted of a deposit receipt in name of the defender,[78] or a recorded transfer of War Loan to the defender,[79] on the ground that these documents indicated only the person to whom the bank must pay, and were not conclusive of the ownership of the fund in question.[80] It has been said not to apply to a bearer bond on the ground that it is transmitted by mere delivery and without the need for a written transfer or assignation.[81] In a strong dissenting opinion,[82] which has received subsequent judicial support,[73] the distinction was also made between a conveyance, transfer or assignation, on the one hand, and a mere contract to convey, transfer or assign, of which missives of sale constitute an example, on the other, and it was said that only a document in the first of these categories can be a "deed of trust" within the meaning of the statute. The decision of the court, however, was otherwise, and the rule was applied to missives of sale largely on the ground that the alleged trustee, who had purchased under missives with the pursuer's authority, was not acting as a professional agent, being neither

---

72 See the reference to "deed of trust" in the statute. In *Gardiner* v. *Cowie*, 1897, 4 S.L.T. 256, proof *prout de jure* was allowed because it was not apparent from the pursuer's averments that the defender held under a deed.

73 Bell, *Principles* §1995 (1), note (*l*); Mackenzie Stuart, *Trusts*, 14, 15; *Dunn* v. *Pratt*, 1898, 25 R. 461, L. Kinnear (dissenting) at p. 469; *Anderson* v. *Yorston* (O.H.) 1906, 14 S.L.T. 54; *Cairns* v. *Davidson*, 1913 S.C. 1054, L. Salvesen at pp. 1057-1058; *McConnachie* v. *Geddes*, 1918 S.C. 391, L. Salvesen at pp. 399-400; *Newton* v. *Newton*, 1923 S.C. 15, L. Sands at p. 25; *Beveridge* v. *Beveridge* (O.H.), 1925 S.L.T. 234.

74 *Marshall* v. *Lyell* (*supra*); *Newton* v. *Newton* (*supra*); *Robertson* v. *Robertson* (O.H.) 1929 S.L.T. 510.

75 *Laird & Co.* v. *Laird & Rutherfurd*, 1884, 12 R. 294.

76 *Anderson* v. *Yorston* (*supra*). See also *Newton* v. *Newton* (*supra*), L. Sands at p. 25.

77 *Purnell* v. *Shannon*, 1894, 22 R. 74.

78 *Cairns* v. *Davidson*, 1913 S.C. 1054; *Newton* v. *Newton*, 1923 S.C. 15, L. Sands at p. 25; *Weissenbruch* v. *Weissenbruch* (O.H.), 1961 S.C. 340. See also *Anderson* v. *North of Scotland Bank*, 1901, 4 F. 49. Cf. *National Bank of Scotland* v. *Mackie's Trs.* (O.H.), 1905, 13 S.L.T. 383.

79 *Beveridge* v. *Beveridge* (O.H.) 1925 S.L.T. 234; *Kennedy* v. *Macrae*, 1946 S.C. 118, L. Keith at p. 121. For another decision about War Stock, see *McNair's Executrix* v. *Litster*, 1939 S.C. 72.

80 See *Anderson* v. *North of Scotland Bank*, 1901, 4 F. 49, L. McLaren at p. 54.

81 *Newton* v. *Newton* (*supra*), L. Sands at p. 25.

82 *Dunn* v. *Pratt*, 1898, 25 R. 461, L. Kinnear at p. 469.

F

a solicitor nor a land agent.[83] With regard to moveables, it has been said that even if the defender's title is contained in missives, the rule does not apply unless writing is legally necessary for the constitution of the title.[84]

(c) The rule has been held not to apply unless the alleged trustee has, *ex facie* of the title, the whole rights of *dominium* and the full *jus disponendi* in the subjects. Although certain War Stock was registered in name of the defender, she was held not to have the full *dominium* and *jus disponendi* in it, because the truster had retained in his own possession the relative certificates without which the defender could not effectively have sold the stock, and proof *prout de jure* was allowed.[85]

(d) The rule is not applied unless the alleged trustee's title to the property was obtained with the consent of the alleged truster.[86] So the pursuer may prove *prout de jure* that in taking the title in his own name the defender acted in breach of his instructions as the pursuer's agent or mandatory,[86] or that the pursuer's consent was obtained by fraud[87] or misrepresentation.[88] But averments of fraud which relate only to the refusal of the alleged trustee to acknowledge or implement the trust purposes do not prevent the rule from being applied, and it is only fraud affecting the constitution of the trustee's title which has this result.[87] When the trust arises from the intervention of the trustee as *negotiorum gestor* the rule does not apply, since the truster has not consented to the trustee's title.[89] If the title is taken in the trustee's name with the truster's consent, the fact that it is obtained from a third party does not prevent the application of the rule.[90] When a person purchases heritage with his own money and gives an undertaking to a third person that he will dispone the property to him on payment of the

---

83 See *Dunn* v. *Pratt* (*supra*), L.P. Robertson at p. 466, L. McLaren at p. 468. Lord McLaren said that when one person is employed to buy for another in his own name and the transaction can be referred to any known category of agency, the statute is excluded, and proof is not limited to writ or oath. See sub. para. **(f)** below.

84 *McConnachie* v. *Geddes*, 1918 S.C. 391, L. Dundas at pp. 396-7, L. Salvesen at p. 398 (missives for purchase of shares in a ship).

85 *McNair's Executrix* v. *Litster*, 1939 S.C. 72, L.P. Normand at p. 77, L. Fleming at p. 78. *Beveridge* v. *Beveridge* (see note 79 above), although mentioned in argument, was not referred to in the opinions.

86 *Mackay* v. *Ambrose*, 1829, 7 S. 699, L. Glenlee at p. 702; *Horne* v. *Morrison*, 1877, 4 R. 977; *Pant Mawr Quarry Co.* v. *Fleming*, 1883, 10 R. 457; *Dunn* v. *Pratt* (*supra*), L. Adam at p. 468; *Anderson* v. *Yorston* (*supra*), at pp. 55-56; *McConnachie* v. *Geddes* (*supra*), L. Dundas at p. 396.

87 *Marshall* v. *Lyell*, 1859, 21 D. 514, L. J-Cl. Inglis at p. 521; *Wink* v. *Speirs*, 1867, 6 M. 77; *Tennent* v. *Tennent's Trs.*, 1868, 6 M. 840, L. Ardmillan at p. 874: *cf.* L. Barcaple at p. 846, L. Deas at p. 859; *Galloway* v. *Galloway*, 1929 S.C. 160, L. Ormidale at p. 169. As to proof of fraud generally, see § **152**.

88 *Galloway* v. *Galloway* (*supra*), L. J-Cl. Alness at p. 167, L. Ormidale at p. 169.

89 *Marshall* v. *Lyell* (*supra*), L.P. Inglis at pp. 521-523, where *Spreul* v. *Crawford*, 1741, M. 16, 201 is commented on.

90 *Marshall* v. *Lyell* (*supra*), L.P. Inglis at p. 521; *Laird & Co.* v. *Laird & Rutherfurd*, 1884, 12 R. 294, L. Shand at pp. 297-298; *Anderson* v. *Yorston* (O.H.) 1906, 14 S.L.T. 54; *Newton* v. *Newton*, 1923 S.C. 15, L. Hunter at p. 23.

original price, the purchaser does not hold in trust, because the third person had no title to consent to the purchase, and the rule does not apply.[91]

(e) The rule applies only when the pursuer in the action is the truster or his successor in title. If the action is at the instance of a person who was not a party to the constitution of the trust, but has an interest to prove its existence in order to substantiate a claim against the truster or the trustee, he may prove it *prout de jure*.[92] Equally, if the pursuer is the person who holds property on an *ex facie* absolute title, he may prove *prout de jure* that he is in fact a trustee.[93]

(f) It has been said that when one person is employed to buy for another in his own name, and the transaction can be referred to any known category of agency, it is outside the statute.[94] If this is to be regarded as of general application, there must be uncertainty in many cases as to whether the transaction is properly to be regarded as a trust, or as agency or mandate, because, as was said in the same case,[95] every case of trust is, in a sense, a case of mandate. In two cases it was held that the rule did not apply when a partner, on behalf of his firm, held money[96] or an insurance policy on his own life,[97] but in a later case,[98] where partnership was also involved, and where the rule was applied, the earlier cases were distinguished because no "deed of trust" was present in them. As mentioned above,[99] when an agent entered into missives for the purchase of heritage, the missives were held to be a "deed of trust" largely because the purchasing agent was not professional, with the implication that if he had been a solicitor or a land agent the rule might not have been applied. It is thought that the application of the rule in such cases must continue to be a matter of uncertainty and difficulty unless the clear-cut distinction made in Lord Kinnear's dissenting opinion[99] is adopted as the test of what is, and what is not, a "deed of trust" within the meaning of the statute.

124. OBLIGATIONS OF RELIEF

(a) **Express Obligations.** These may be proved only by the writ of the

[91] *Govan New Bowling-Green Club* v. *Geddes*, 1898, 25 R. 485.

[92] See § **265.**

[93] *Murdoch* v. *Wyllie*, 1832, 10 S. 445; Dickson, *Evidence* (3rd ed.) §582.

[94] *Dunn* v. *Pratt*, 1898, 25 R. 461, L. McLaren at p. 468. See also *Beveridge* v. *Beveridge*, (O.H.) 1925 S.L.T. 234. Lord McLaren's reference to agency must be distinguished from a breach of the contract of agency or mandate in taking a title in the agent's or mandatory's name contrary to his principal's instructions, for which see sub-para. **(d)** above.

[95] *Dunn* v. *Pratt* (*supra*), L.P. Robertson at p. 466.

[96] *Baptist Churches* v. *Taylor*, 1841, 3 D. 1030.

[97] *Forrester* v. *Robson's Trs.*, 1875, 2 R. 755. See also *Munro* v. *Stein* (O.H.), 1961 S.C. 362 (heritage).

[98] *Laird & Co.* v. *Laird & Rutherfurd*, 1884, 12 R. 294, L.P. Inglis at p. 297. In *Horne* v. *Morrison*, 1877, 4 R. 977, where partnership was also alleged, the rule was held not to apply, solely on the ground that the pursuer had not agreed to the title being taken in the defender's name: see sub-para. **(d)** above.

[99] See sub-para. **(b)** above.

party said to have undertaken the obligation, or by reference to his oath.[1] Proof by writ of party[2] and reference to oath of party[3] are dealt with generally later.

(b) Implied Obligations. When an obligation of relief arises by force of law, there can be no question of proof of the obligation. Nothing can or need be proved other than the facts from which the obligation emerges, and these may be proved *prout de jure*.[4] So, for example, it may be proved by parole evidence that the pursuer, although bound as a principal to the creditor, is in fact a cautioner in relation to his co-debtor, the defender, and that he has paid the debt, and, if he proves these facts, the defender's obligation to relieve him arises by force of law.[5] There is also authority for the proposition that when, as between co-cautioners, the normal rights of relief have been varied by agreement, the true relationship between the co-obligants may be proved by parole evidence.[6]

(c) Relief as Part of Another Contract. It has been said that an obligation of relief may be proved by parole evidence "when it forms part of a transaction which may be established by that means."[7] No authority was cited for the passage quoted, which was based upon the analogy of a similar rule of the common law with regard to cautionary obligations. The passage, however, has been accepted without criticism, except as to its width, but was held to apply only to cases where the obligation of relief is an integral part of a contract regarding moveables.[8]

125. PERFORMANCE AND DISCHARGE OF OBLIGATIONS CONSTITUTED OR VOUCHED BY WRITING—THE RULE

When an obligation is constituted in writing,[9] or is vouched by a document of debt,[10] its discharge or performance may be proved only by the writ of the other party or by reference to his oath. The rule has been said to be

---

1 *Devlin* v. *McKelvie*, 1915 S.C. 180; Gloag, *Contract* (2nd ed.) 195; Erskine, iv, 2, 20. The rule was assumed in *Clark* v. *Callender*, 9 Mar., 1819, F.C., 1819, 6 Paton, 422; *Maconochie* v. *Stirling*, 1864 2 M. 1104; *Thoms* v. *Thoms*, 1867, 6 M. 174; *Woddrop* v. *Speirs* (O.H.) 1906, 14 S.L.T. 319.

2 See §§ **302** *et seq.*

3 See §§ **308** *et seq.*

4 Gloag, *Contract* (2nd ed.) 195.

5 Bell, *Principles*, §267; *Lindsay* v. *Barmcotte*, 1851, 13 D. 718, L. Cuninghame at p. 725; *Thow's Tr.* v. *Young*, 1910 S.C. 588, L. Skerrington at p. 593, L.P. Dunedin at p. 595.

6 *Hamilton & Co.* v. *Freeth*, 1889, 16 R. 1022; *Crosbie* v. *Brown*, 1900, 3 F. 83. For the principle applicable, see **§261.**

7 Dickson, *Evidence* (3rd ed.) §606.

8 *Devlin* v. *McKelvie*, 1915 S.C. 180, L. Salvesen at p. 187, L. Guthrie at p. 189.

9 Stair, iv, 43, 4; Erskine, iv, 2, 21; Dickson, *Evidence* (3rd ed.) §610; *Keanie* v. *Keanie*, 1940 S.C. 549; *Nicol's Trs.* v. *Sutherland*, 1951 S.C. (H.L.) 21 (approving *Robertson* v. *Thomson*, 1900 3 F. 5).

10 *Thiem's Trs.* v. *Collie*, 1899, 1 F. 764, L. Trayner at pp. 774, 778, L. Moncreiff at p. 780; Gloag, *Contract* (2nd ed.) 715. For the different rule when the written acknowledgment is qualified by an assertion that the debt has been paid or satisfied, or when a judicial admission founded upon is similarly qualified, see § **62**, note 69, § **118**, note 16.

in accordance with the maxim *unumquodque eodem modo dissolvitur quo colligatur*.[11] If the maxim is truly the basis of the rule, one would have expected that the discharge ought to be embodied in a writing having the same solemnities as that which constituted the original obligation, with the usual exception where there is *rei interventus* or homologation, and that, apart from this exception, reference of an oral discharge to oath would be regarded as incompetent.[12] The rule, however, appears to be firmly established. So, for example, if a creditor sues upon a bill of exchange[13] or an IOU[10] or for payment of a debt vouched by an incomplete bill of exchange,[14] and is met by a defence of payment, the defender must prove payment by the pursuer's writ or oath, and if a person, holding shares under a back-letter of trust granted by himself, seeks a declarator that the shares were subsequently given to him by the truster, he must prove this by the truster's writ or oath.[15] The rule applies even if the payments alleged to have been made are each less than £8 6s. 8d.[16] Some of the examples given above are also subject to the rule which provides that payment of money under an antecedent obligation requires proof by the creditor's writ or oath.[17] Proof by writ of party[18] and reference to oath of party[19] are dealt with later. When the creditor under a written obligation denies the validity of the obligation and the debtor seeks to prove that he has made payments in respect of it, not for the purpose of discharging it, but for some other purpose, as, for example, to establish *rei interventus*, the opinion has been expressed that the rule does not apply, and that the fact of payment may be proved *prout de jure*.[20] Other exceptions to the rule are mentioned in the next paragraph.

126. EXCEPTIONS TO THE RULE

(a) Obligations Ad Factum Præstandum. The performance of such obligations by supplying goods, erecting buildings, building ships, completing a voyage, performing services, delivery by a tenant of produce in terms of his lease, or the like, may be proved *prout de jure*.[21]

[11] See, for example, *Nicol's Trs.* v. *Sutherland (supra)*, L. Simonds at p. 26, L. Normand at p. 29.
[12] As to written obligations, see §§ **89** *et seq.* As to reference to oath in this connection, see § **92**, sub-para. (c). For a discussion of a similar question regarding an agreement to rescind a written obligation, see Gloag, *Contract* (2nd ed.) 392-393.
[13] *Nicol's Trs.* v. *Sutherland (supra); Robertson* v. *Thomson*, 1900, 3 F. 5; *Patrick* v. *Watt*, 1859, 21 D. 637. The rule applies in spite of the Bills of Exchange Act, 1882, s. 100. See § **112.**
[14] *Lawson's Exrs.* v. *Watson*, 1907 S.C. 1353, the sheriff at p. 1357, approved by the Inner House.
[15] *Keanie* v. *Keanie*, 1940 S.C. 549.
[16] *Robertson* v. *Thomson (supra)*; Dickson, *Evidence* (3rd ed.) §610.
[17] See § **127.**
[18] See §§ **302** *et seq.*
[19] See §§ **308** *et seq.*
[20] *Foggo* v. *Hill*, 1840, 2 D. 1322, L. Fullerton at p. 1334; Dickson, *Evidence* (3rd ed.) §614. Proof by the creditor of payments made by the debtor is mentioned at § **126,** sub-para. (c).
[21] Stair, iv, 43, 4; Erskine, iv, 2, 21; Gloag, *Contract* (2nd ed.) 720. As to a tenant delivering produce in terms of the lease, see Rankine, *Leases* (3rd ed.) 319, 320.

(b) Payments Obtained by Fraud. It is thought that the general rule, which allows averments of fraud[22] to be proved by parole evidence, applies, and that if, for example, the debtor under a written obligation is fraudulently induced to make payment on the representation that a receipt will be granted, and the creditor refuses to deliver the receipt, the payment may be proved by parole evidence.[23]

(c) Proof by Creditor of Payment made by Debtor. On occasions it is the creditor and not the debtor who desires to prove that payment has been made under a written obligation, as, for example, when it is hoped to prove possession of heritage as an inference from the receiving of rent,[24] or when homologation[25] or *rei interventus*[26] is in issue. Since in such circumstances it is usually difficult for the creditor to prove the debtor's payment by the debtor's writ, proof *prout de jure* is allowed. This exception, however, does not apply in favour of a creditor under a prescribed debt or bill of exchange, when, if the creditor wishes to establish resting owing by proving payments, he must do so by the debtor's writ or oath.[27]

(d) Payment, Performance and Discharge Inferred from Facts and Circumstances. Facts and circumstances which give rise to an inevitable inference that a written obligation has been satisfied or discharged,[28] or which are inconsistent with its continued subsistence[29] or with its remaining in the hands of the holder as a living document of debt,[30] may be proved *prout de jure*. Such circumstantial proof of payment, performance or discharge will be sustained only if it is beyond reasonable doubt.[31] Circumstances which have been suggested as giving rise to such an inference, when the obligation is of long standing, are the failure of the creditor to take interest when he had an opportunity to do so, the failure of the creditor while intromitting with the debtor's estate to retain the sum due under the obligation, the failure of the creditor to claim payment under the obligation

---

[22] As to this see § **152.**
[23] See Erskine, iv, ii, 21. The converse is also true. When a receipt was sent to the debtor merely as a reminder that payment was due and was retained and founded on by him as a true receipt, proof *prout de jure* of the circumstances in which the receipt came into the debtor's hands was allowed: *Henry* v. *Miller*, 1884, 11 R. 713. See also *Kirkwood* v. *Bryce*, 1871, 8 S.L.R. 435.
[24] *Chalmers* v. *Lord Craigievar*, 1628 M. 12, 368; *Ross* v. *Elliot*, 1630 M. 12, 369.
[25] Erskine, iii, 3, 50.
[26] *Foggo* v. *Hill*, 1840, 2 D. 1322, L. Fullerton at p. 1334.
[27] See § **132**, sub-para. (c).
[28] *A. & A. Campbell* v. *Campbell's Exrs.*, 1910, 2 S.L.T. 240, L. Skerrington at p. 241; *Mackintosh* v. *Mackintosh*, 1928 S.C. 83, L. Constable at p. 88.
[29] *Chrystal* v. *Chrystal*, 1900 2 F. 373, L. McLaren at p. 379.
[30] *Bishop* v. *Bryce*, 1910 S.C. 426, L. Johnston at pp. 435-436. See also L.P. Dunedin at p. 430. The dicta referred to in this and the two preceding notes were quoted with approval in *McKenzie's Executrix* v. *Morrison's Trs.*, 1930 S.C. 830, L. J-Cl. Alness at p. 834.
[31] *Thiem's Trs.* v. *Collie*, 1899. 1 F. 764, L. Moncreiff at p. 780; approved in *Chrystal* v. *Chrystal (supra)*, L. McLaren at p. 379: *McKenzie's Executrix* v. *Morrison's Trs. (supra)*, L. J-Cl. Alness at pp. 834, 836.

if he were indigent and the debtor opulent, and the taking of a subsequent obligation for a greater sum and the claiming of interest on the later and not on the earlier obligation, without mention of the earlier obligation.[32] Parole proof of facts and circumstances has been allowed, and the defence has been sustained in the following cases. The creditor under a written acknowledgment of loan, signed by his brother, made no claim for payment or for interest for nearly twenty years and until the debtor had been dead for five years. The debtor was in good financial circumstances throughout, while the creditor was frequently short of money. The creditor kept the debtor's business books for six years, including his own account with the debtor which concluded with a debit balance against him, but there was no entry relative to the loan sued for, and no demand for payment of capital or interest was made during the debtor's life. The debt was held to have been satisfied long before the debtor's death.[33] The creditor in an IOU made no claim against the debtor, who was his partner, and with whom he was on unfriendly terms, during the lives of either of them, and it was made by his executrix, who had found the document among worthless papers, thirty years after it was granted. Twenty years before the raising of the action, as the result of an arbitration following the dissolution of the partnership, a very much larger sum than the sum mentioned in the IOU was paid by the debtor to the creditor. The creditor was in embarrassed financial circumstances. The discharge of the debt due under the IOU was held to have been proved beyond reasonable doubt.[34] The creditor under an IOU for £300 made no claim against the debtor until twelve years after it was granted. Three months after the IOU was granted shares of a nominal value of £300 in a company controlled by the debtor were issued to the creditor, upon which he was subsequently paid dividends, and there was neither averment nor evidence that he made any payment for these shares apart from the indebtedness represented by the IOU. The creditor was himself a director of the company, and for some time acted as its secretary. It was held that, since the creditor had received the value of the sum mentioned in the IOU in the shape of shares, the IOU, which should have been redelivered to the debtor when the shares were issued, was no longer a living document of debt in the creditor's hands.[35] No claim was made under a probative acknowledgment of debt during the lives of the parties, and an action for payment was not raised until almost forty years after the granting of the document. The document was held to have been impliedly discharged, or not to be conclusive evidence of the subsistence of the debt, in view of the delay and the fact that there had been a subsequent settlement of business transactions between the parties, who were father and son, in consequence of which the creditor had received payments under the debtor's trust disposition and

---

[32] Stair, iv, 45, 23.

[33] *Ryrie* v. *Ryrie*, 1840, 2 D. 1210.

[34] *McKenzie's Executrix* v. *Morrison's Trs. (supra)*. See also *Spence* v. *Paterson's Trs.*, 1873, 1 R. 46; *Robson* v. *Bywater*, 1870, 8 M. 757.

[35] *Bishop* v. *Bryce*, 1910 S.C. 426. It has been held that the granter of an I.O.U. cannot be allowed to prove that no debt ever existed: *McCreadie's Trs.* v. *McCreadie* (O.H.) 1897, 5 S.L.T. 153, approved in *Black* v. *Gibb*, 1940 S.C. 24, L. Moncrieff at p. 28.

settlement in excess of the sum mentioned in the acknowledgment of debt.[36] It was suggested in the last-mentioned case that the decision might have been different if the document in question had been a bond or obligatory instrument, such as a promissory note, instead of a mere acknowledgment of indebtedness which was in the same class as an IOU.[37] Formal bonds and dispositions in security, however, have in fact been held to be ineffectual, without formal discharge, after an enquiry into facts and circumstances similar to those referred to in the foregoing examples.[38] When the receiving of a loan was judicially admitted by the defender, he was assoilzied after proof that the IOU which he had granted in respect of it had been handed to him by the creditor to be destroyed, since she wished to make him a gift of the money.[39] The fact that a creditor has accepted payment of, and discharged, more recent debts,[40] or has accepted later obligations from the debtor for the same or larger amounts,[41] or has himself made payments or granted obligations to the debtor at a later date,[42] supports the inference that the obligation has been discharged in the course of a subsequent transaction, but by itself is not necessarily conclusive.[43]

127. PAYMENT OF MONEY UNDER ANTECEDENT OBLIGATIONS

(a) The Rule. The payment of a sum of money in implement of an antecedent obligation, even if the obligation is not expressed in writing, may as a general rule be proved only by the writ of the creditor or by reference to his oath,[44] unless the sum is £8 6s. 8d. or less.[45] Proof by writ of party[46] and reference to oath of party[47] are dealt with elsewhere. The rule applies to payment of the price of goods sold on credit:[48] payment of rent under an oral lease:[49] payment by a solicitor to his client of money in his hands

---

[36] *Neilson's Trs.* v. *Neilson's Trs.*, 1883, 11 R. 119.

[37] *Neilson's Trs.* v. *Neilson's Trs. (supra)*, L. Young at pp. 123-124. See *Bishop* v. *Bryce (supra)*, L. Johnston at p. 435.

[38] *Thomson's Trs.* v. *Monteith's Tr.*, 1834, 12 S. 842; *Mackie* v. *Watson*, 1837, 16 S. 73. See also *Graham* v. *Veitch*, 1823, 2 S. 509, where it was held that the discharge of an old bond might be established *rebus et factis*, but that although the case was one of extreme hardship, there being strong circumstantial evidence indicating payment, the facts were not utterly irreconcileable with the idea that the bond was still due, and that effect must be given to it.

[39] *Anderson's Trs.* v. *Webster*, 1883, 11 R. 35.

[40] *McKenzie's Executrix* v. *Morrison's Trs.*, 1930 S.C. 830; *Neilson's Trs.* v. *Neilson's Trs. (supra)*; *Patrick* v. *Watt*, 1859, 21 D. 637; *Norkat* v. *Hume*, 1624 M. 12, 701; *Cameron* v. *Panton's Trs.*, 1891, 18 R. 728.

[41] *Norkat* v. *Hume (supra)*; *Lady Ardblair* v. *Her Husband*, 1678 M. 11, 384.

[42] *Hallyburton* v. *Blair*, 1837, 15 S. 750; *Veatch* v. *Paterson*, 1664 M. 11, 383; *Somerville* v. *Muirhead's Exrs.*, 1675 M. 11, 384.

[43] *Carnowa* v. *Stewart*, 1611 M. 11, 382; *Somerville* v. *Muirhead's Exrs. (supra)*; *Lady Ardblair* v. *Her Husband (supra)*; *Hallyburton* v. *Blair (supra)*; *Patrick* v. *Watt (supra)*; *Cameron* v. *Panton's Trs. (supra)*.

[44] *Burt* v. *Laing*, 1925 S.C. 181, L.P. Clyde at pp. 183-184, L. Sands at p. 185; Dickson, *Evidence* (3rd ed.) §615. See also Bell, *Principles*, §2257.

[45] Erskine, iv, 2, 21; Dickson, *Evidence* (3rd ed.) §615.

[46] See §§ 302 *et seq.*

[47] See §§ 308 *et seq.*

belonging to the client:[50] payment of the sum due under a prescribed bill of exchange which was proved by writ to be due and resting owing at the date of the debtor's death:[51] repayment of a loan of money:[52] and payment by a builder to a sub-contractor of sums to account of the contract price, which, in terms of the contract, ought to have been paid weekly as the work progressed.[53] There seems to be some doubt as to whether the rule always applies to the payment of weekly wages,[54] at least in the case of domestic servants whose wages are usually paid without receipts being taken.[55] But the rule is not applicable unless the obligation is antecedent. So it does not apply when the payment is alleged to have been an integral part of an obligation constituted orally,[56] and to have been made at the same time as the creation of the obligation and *unico contextu* with it,[57] because in such circumstances writing is not expected on either side.[58] It does not apply, therefore, to the price of goods sold for ready money when payment is alleged to have been made at the time of the purchase or of the delivery of the goods,[59] and is the immediate counterpart of delivery.[60] It has also been held not to apply to the payment by a mandant to a mandatory of a sum of money at the same time as the giving of the instructions for its investment which constituted the mandate.[61] In such cases the payment,

[48] *Shaw* v. *Wright*, 1877, 5 R. 245; *Young* v. *Thomson*, 1909 S.C. 529, L. Dundas at p. 536; *Tod* v. *Flockhart*, 1799, Hume 498. As to the competency of proving the terms of a receipt or similar document, which has been lost or destroyed, as part of the defence to an action for payment, see *Young* v. *Thomson (supra)*; *James Scott & Co. (Electrical Engineers) Ltd.* v. *McIntosh*, 1960 S.L.T. (Sh. Ct.) 15.

[49] Rankine, *Leases* (3rd ed.) 320; *Earl of Lauderdale* v. *Tenants*, 1662 M. 12, 362.

[50] *Mackenzie* v. *Brodie*, 1859, 21 D. 1048, at p. 1052. See also *Cairns* v. *Garroch's Crs.*, 1747 M. 11, 389 (factor). The position is different when the person who must prove payment is merely the "hand" of the owner of the money. See *Tosh* v. *Ogilvy*, 1873, 1 R. 254 (proof by parole allowed but held insufficient), and cases cited in sub-para. (b).

[51] *Jackson* v. *Ogilvie's Exr.*, 1935 S.C. 154.

[52] *Thiem's Trs.* v. *Collie*, 1899, 1 F. 764, L. Trayner at p. 778; *Jackson* v. *Ogilvie's Exr. (supra)*, L. Moncrieff (Ordinary) at p. 160. In practice repayment of a loan of money is usually subject to the rule which requires discharge of an obligation vouched by writing to be proved by writ or oath. See § 118.

[53] *Hope Brothers* v. *Morrison* (O.H.) 1960 S.C. 1.

[54] *Brown* v. *Mason*, 1856, 19 D. 137. Proof *prout de jure* was allowed because the payments alleged to have been made were each under £8 6s. 8d. Lord Deas, however (at p. 138) reserved his opinion as to whether, even apart from this, payment of weekly wages must always be proved by writ or oath.

[55] *Annand's Trs.* v. *Annand*, 1869, 7 M. 526. This decision was concerned with proof of loan, but Lord Deas (at p. 530) said that it was known that servants' wages (in this case grieve, cook and housemaid) are generally paid without taking receipts.

[56] Bell, *Principles*, §565. See also Dickson, *Evidence* (3rd ed.) §616; Gloag, *Contract* (2nd ed.) 717.

[57] *Burt* v. *Laing*, 1925 S.C. 181, L. Sands at p. 185.

[58] Dickson, *Evidence* (3rd ed.) §616.

[59] Dickson, *Evidence* (3rd ed.) §616; Gloag, *Contract* (2nd ed,), 717; *Stewart* v. *Gordon*, 1831, 9 S. 466. In *Macdonald* v. *Callender*, 1786 M. 12, 366, parole proof of payment a few days after delivery was allowed, but this decision was regarded as doubtful by Baron Hume (*sub voce Tod* v. *Flockhart, supra*, at p. 499), Dickson, *Evidence* (3rd ed.) §616, and Lord Gifford in *Shaw* v. *Wright*, 1877, 5 R. 245, at p. 247, although it is cited without disapproval in Gloag, *Contract* (2nd ed.) 717.

[60] *Shaw* v. *Wright (supra)*, L. Gifford at p. 247.

like the contract of which it forms part, may be proved *prout de jure*. The rule does not apply. to proof of the performance of obligations *ad factum præstandum*.[62]

(b) Exceptions to the Rule. Facts and circumstances which give rise to an inevitable inference that payment has been made, or that the obligation has been otherwise discharged, may be proved *prout de jure*. The principle is the same as that applicable to proof of the performance of written obligations, which have been mentioned earlier.[63] Examples of the principle in connection with oral obligations, have occurred where the relationship between the payer and the payee was such that the former was merely the "hand" of the latter in connection with the day to day administration of his affairs, and that his practice, as proved or as presumed from the circumstances, was to account daily or weekly for his intromissions without obtaining receipts. Proof *prout de jure* of such facts and circumstances were allowed, and the payments sued for were presumed to have been duly made, in the following cases:—the brother of a farmer, who was compelled to retire from active work through ill-health, lived with him and acted as farm overseer under him until his death four years later, and during the period reported all transactions orally to him from day to day:[64] a son, residing with his father, intromitted with his property and accounted to him without taking receipts, until his death,[65] and a son managing his father's affairs when he became incapax, was not sued by his younger brothers until thirteen years later:[66] a domestic servant, who collected his employer's rents and sold her corn under her oral instructions, left her employment without quarrel with her and after receiving all his wages, no action for an accounting being raised until after his death:[67] a taverner who, in accordance with custom, was presumed to account to his employer for the takings nightly or weekly, left the employer's service and continued to live in the same city for nine months before an action for accounting was raised by the employer.[68]

128. RENUNCIATION (ACCEPTILATION) OF RIGHTS

(a) Rights constituted in Writing. As a general rule the renunciation of such rights, without payment or performance by the obligant, may be proved only by the writ of the creditor or by reference to his oath.[69] As distinct from the similar rule regarding proof of performance and discharge of such obligations, which was mentioned earlier,[70] the rule in this case may

---

[61] *Burt* v. *Laing* (*supra*). As to proof of the mandate itself, see § **148**.
[62] See § **126**, sub-para. (a).
[63] See § **126**, sub-para. (d).
[64] *Russell's Trs.* v. *Russell*, 1885, 13 R. 331. See also *Stuart* v. *Maconochie*, 1836, 14 S. 412.
[65] *Lord Saltoun* v. *Fraser*, 1722 M. 11, 425.
[66] *Wilson* v. *Wilson*, 1783 M. 11, 646.
[67] *Irvine* v. *Falconer*, 1671 M. 11, 424.
[68] *Couts* v. *Couts*, 1636 M. 11, 423.
[69] Erskine, iii, 4, 8; Dickson, *Evidence* (3rd ed.) §627; Gloag, *Contract* (2nd ed.) 722.
[70] See § **125**.

perhaps be justified by regarding such unilateral renunciations as gratuitous obligations, for the proof of which writ or reference to oath is always appropriate.[71] The rule has been applied to the renunciation of an acknowledgment of trust,[72] a decree-arbitral,[73] a written lease,[74] a decree of removal,[75] the right to do diligence on a decree,[76] and a stipulation in a feu charter as to the vassal's use of the subjects.[77] Proof by writ of party[78] and reference to oath of party[79] are mentioned elsewhere.

(b) **Rights constituted Orally.** There is a conflict of opinion as to the mode of proving a renunciation of such rights, one view being that, since the right is constituted orally, its renunciation may be proved by parole evidence.[80] The other view, which has received judicial approval during this century,[81] is that the renunciation, if it takes place, not at the time of the making of the contract but after an interval, can be proved only by the writ of the creditor or by reference to his oath.[82] The last-mentioned view ought perhaps to be preferred on the ground that a renunciation of this kind is a gratuitous obligation,[71] which requires writ or reference to oath for its proof. So, for example, it was held that the renunciation of a right to half the price of a horse, which had been purchased jointly by the parties under an oral agreement, and had been sold by the defender, could be proved only by the writ or oath of the pursuer.[81]

(c) **Exceptions to the Rule.** Actings by the creditor which give rise to an inevitable inference that the right has been renounced by him, may be proved by parole evidence.[83] So, for example, proof *prout de jure* has been allowed of averments that obligatory documents have been destroyed or given up,[84] as when an IOU was handed by the creditor to the debtor for destruction in her presence,[85] or that the creditor has entered into a new contract with the debtor regarding the same subject matter.[86] Similarly,

---

[71] See § **130.**
[72] *Keanie* v. *Keanie*, 1940 S.C. 549.
[73] Dickson, *Evidence* (3rd ed.) §627.
[74] *Lord Shaw* v. *Palmer*, 1605 M. 12, 301; *Lord Craigmillar* v. *Chalmers*, 1639 M. 12, 308.
[75] *Countess of Argyle* v. *Sheriff of Moray*, 1583, M. 12, 300.
[76] *Reid* v. *Gow & Sons* (O.H.) 1903 10 S.L.T. 606.
[77] *Scot* v. *Cairns*, 1830, 9 S. 246.
[78] See §§ **302** *et seq.*
[79] See §§ **308** *et seq.*
[80] Erskine, iii, 4, 8; Gloag, *Contract* (2nd ed.) 722, note 4.
[81] *Kilpatrick* v. *Dunlop* (O.H.), 1909 2 S.L.T. 307.
[82] Dickson, *Evidence* (3rd ed.) §629. This does not apply to sums of £8 6s. 8d. or less, or to rights which are both constituted and renounced on the same occasion, when parole evidence is sufficient. See note 80 above, and Dickson, *ibid.*
[83] Dickson, *Evidence* (3rd ed.) §628.
[84] Gloag, *Contract* (2nd ed.) 722. A bill of exchange or promissory note, if delivered up to the acceptor, need not be renounced in writing: Bills of Exchange Act, 1882 (45 & 46 Vict. c. 61), s. 62 (1). As to the presumption arising from a creditor's inability to produce the document of debt, see § **66.**
[85] *Anderson's Trs.* v. *Webster*, 1883, 11 R. 35.
[86] Gloag, *Contract* (2nd ed.) 392, 722; Erskine, ii, 6, 44 (new lease); *Campbeltown Coal Co.* v. *Duke of Argyll*, 1926 S. C. 126 (new lease), L.P. Clyde at p. 131; *Edinburgh Entertainments Ltd.* v. *Stevenson*, 1926 S.C. 363 (new lease), L. J-Cl. Alness at p. 378.

proof *prout de jure* may be allowed of actings by the debtor with the consent of the creditor,[87] which are inconsistent with or contradictory of the right, and which justify an inference that the right has been renounced.[88]

129. INNOMINATE AND UNUSUAL CONTRACTS

Such contracts may be proved only by the writ of the other party or by reference to his oath.[89] The restriction of proof does not apply merely because the contract is innominate, i.e. not one of the recognised consensual contracts, and earlier statements to the contrary effect[90] have been disapproved.[89] In order that the restriction may apply, the contract, in addition to being innominate, must also be of an unusual, anomalous or peculiar character.[89] It is for the court in each case to decide whether or not the contract, as described in the averments of the party alleging it, is of this character. Proof has been restricted to writ or oath in relation to the following contracts:—an agreement by a landlord that if the tenant of the farm would remain in occupancy to the end of the lease, and pay the rent, he would repay the whole loss incurred by the tenant during the nineteen years of the lease;[91] an agreement by a person negotiating for a feu charter from a landowner, that he would pay the latter's legal expenses whether the negotiations were successful or not;[92] a confused and complex oral agreement between merchants, said to be the basis of all future business between them, that the pursuers would purport to purchase goods from the defenders, but would in fact receive only a commission on a re-sale by them to a named purchaser;[93] an agreement between two managing directors of a limited company that if one would vote for an increase in the salary of the other, the latter would pay to the former half the increase obtained;[94] an agreement by a guarantor of his son-in-law's bank overdraft that the son-in-law need relieve him of payments made under the guarantee only if his financial circumstances allowed, and that if they did not, the

[87] This part of the statement in the text is based upon the terms of the issue directed by the House of Lords in *Wark* v. *Bargaddie Coal Co.*, 1859, 3 Macq. 467 (at p. 488) for the trial of the cause:—"Whether the barrier coal worked . . . by the defenders was so worked . . . with the consent of the pursuer."

[88] *Keanie* v. *Keanie*, 1940 S.C. 549, L. Wark at p. 559; *Lavan* v. *Gavin Aird & Co.*, 1919 S.C. 345, L. J-Cl. Scott Dickson at p. 348, L. Dundas at p. 350; *Kirkpatrick* v. *Allanshaw Coal Co.*, 1880, 8 R. 327, L.P. Inglis at p. 334. This part of the statement in the text is thought to be justified by the dicta cited in this note. It seems irrelevant to consider whether an express oral renunciation, followed by actings of the kind described, may itself be proved by parole evidence, since, if the required actings must themselves justify an inference of renunciation, it is immaterial whether there was an express oral renunciation or not.

[89] *Smith* v. *Reekie*, 1920 S.C. 188; *Allison* v. *Allison's Trs.*, 1904, 6 F. 496, L.P. Kinross at p. 500; *Hendry* v. *Cowie & Son & Co.*, 1904, 12 S.L.T. 31, 261; *Forbes* v. *Caird*, 1877, 4 R. 1141, L. Deas at p. 1142; *Thomson* v. *Fraser*, 1868, 7 M. 39, L. Neaves at p. 41.

[90] Erskine, iv, 2, 20; *McFadzean's Exr.* v. *Robert McAlpine & Sons*, 1907 S.C. 1269, L.P. Dunedin at p. 1273; *Cochrane* v. *Traill & Sons*, 1900, 2 F. 794, L. Young at p. 799.

[91] *Garden* v. *Earl of Aberdeen*, 1893, 20 R. 896.

[92] *Woddrop* v. *Speirs* (O.H.), 1906, 44 S.L.R. 22.

[93] *Muller & Co.* v. *Weber & Schaer*, 1901, 3 F. 401, Lord Ordinary (Kincairney) at p. 404. The First Division adhered on different grounds.

[94] *Jackson* v. *Elphick* (O.H.) 1902, 10 S.L.T. 146.

payments would be regarded as having been made to account of his wife's interest in the guarantor's estate.[95] In respect of the following contracts the restriction of proof was not applied, and proof *prout de jure* was allowed:—an agreement by an innkeeper to stable horses for an omnibus free of charge on condition that the omnibus called at the inn on its way to and from the railway station;[96] an agreement by owners of a drifter to pay a bonus of a shilling a day to the crew, over and above wages paid by the Admiralty, while the crew and the drifter remained in Admiralty service;[97] an agreement by a defender to pay £2000 and judicial expenses on condition that the pursuer publicly abandoned his case at the conclusion of the defence evidence, so that the defender might obtain a verdict,[98] and an agreement for the compromise of a litigation by a person who was not a party, but had a material interest in it;[99] an agreement by a prospective partner to advance a sum of money to the firm on condition that it would be repaid if he decided not to become a partner;[1] an agreement to act as manager of a business for a yearly salary and a share of profits,[2] and to act as a debt collector without remuneration apart from what could be extracted from the debtors.[3] A contract to bequeath money or property by testamentary settlement may, after the testator's death, be proved only by writ, partly because it is innominate and unusual,[4] and partly because to hold otherwise would have the practical result of allowing a testamentary settlement to be proved by parole evidence.[5] A contract by a solicitor to charge only in the event of success, has been held to be anomalous and unusual, and to be proveable only by writ or oath,[6] but it has since been said that speculative actions are well known in our practice and have repeatedly received judicial recognition,[7] and, in the most recent decision, proof of such an alleged

---

[95] *Williamson* v. *Foulds* (O.H.) 1927 S.N. 164. See also *Cook* v. *Grubb*, 1963 S.L.T. 78, at pp. 81, 85, 87, 89 ("permanent employment" of motor mechanic).

[96] *Forbes* v *Caird*, 1877, 4 R. 1141.

[97] *Smith* v. *Reekie*, 1920 S.C. 188.

[98] *Jaffray* v. *Simpson*, 1835, 13 S. 1122.

[99] *Thomson* v. *Fraser*, 1868, 7 M. 39.

[1] *Hendry* v. *Cowie & Son & Co.*, 1904, 12 S.L.T. 31, 261.

[2] *Allison* v. *Allison's Trs.*, 1904, 6 F. 496.

[3] *Moscrip* v. *O'Hara, Spence & Co.*, 1880, 8 R. 36.

[4] *Fisher* v. *Fisher*, 1952 S.C. 347; *McMurrich's Trs.* v. *McMurrich's Trs.*, 1903, 6 F. 121, L. Kincairney (Ordinary) at p. 123; *Johnston* v. *Goodlet*, 1868, 6 M. 1067, L. J-Cl. Patton at p. 1072; *Edmondston* v. *Edmondston*, 1861, 23 D. 995.

[5] *Edmondston* v. *Edmondston* (*supra*), L. Jerviswoode (Ordinary) at p. 1000; *Johnston* v. *Goodlet* (*supra*), L. J-Cl. Patton, at p. 1072; *Hallet* v. *Ryrie* (O.H.) 1907 15 S.L.T. 367; *Smith* v. *Oliver*, 1911 S.C. 103, L.P. Dunedin at pp. 111-112; *Gray* v. *Johnston*, 1928 S.C. 659, L. Hunter at p. 668, L. Ormidale at p. 670; *Jackson* v. *Ogilvie* (O.H.) 1933 S.L.T. 533. With regard to some of these decisions, see § **130**, note 14.

[6] *Taylor* v. *Forbes*, 1853, 24 D. 19 (note). See also *Forbes* v. *Caird*, 1877, 4 R. 1141, L. Deas at p. 1142.

[7] *X Insurance Co.* v. *A. and B.*, 1936 S.C. 225, L.P. Normand at p. 239, L. Fleming at p. 250.

[8] *Jacobs* v. *McMillan*, 1899, 2 F. 799, per L. Kincairney (Ordinary). It was unnecessary for the Second Division to consider the mode of proof allowed, and no opinions on it were expressed. See also *A. & A. Campbell* v. *Campbell's Exrs.*, 1910. 2 S.L.T. 240, L. Skerrington (Ordinary).

contract was allowed *prout de jure*.[8] Proof by writ of party[9] and reference to oath of party[10] are dealt with later.

130. GRATUITOUS OBLIGATIONS

A unilateral gratuitous obligation or promise, for which no return is asked, as distinct from a bilateral contract in which obligations are undertaken on both sides, may be proved only by the writ of the obligant or by reference to his oath.[11] So a promise *ab ante* to renounce on a person's death the right to share in his estate *qua* next-of-kin was held proveable only by writ or oath of the person giving the promise.[12] The restriction of proof applies even when the creditor has subsequently incurred expenditure, or otherwise altered his position, in the expectation that the obligation would be implemented.[13] So a promise to bequeath a sum of money to a church in order to pay for certain buildings, was held, after the obligant's death, to be proveable only by her writ, although the church had erected the buildings in reliance upon the promise,[14] and proof restricted to writ or oath was allowed of what was construed by the court as a gratuitous promise, although the pursuer had subsequently married the obligant's daughter on the strength of it.[15] When an obligation, while *ex facie* unilateral and gratuitous, is in fact part of a bilateral onerous contract which may itself be proved by parole evidence, the obligation also may be proved *prout de jure*.[16] Proof by writ of party[17] and reference to oath of party[18] are dealt with later.

[9] See §§ **302** *et seq.*

[10] See §§ **308** *et seq.*

[11] Erskine, iv, 2, 20; Dickson, *Evidence* (3rd ed.) §598; Gloag, *Contract* (2nd ed.) 50.

[12] *Jackson* v. *Ogilvie* (O.H.) 1933 S.L.T. 533.

[13] Gloag, *Contract* (2nd ed.) 51.

[14] *Smith* v. *Oliver*, 1911 S.C. 103. See also *Gray* v. *Johnston*, 1928 S.C. 659, where the case was argued for the pursuer solely on the basis of a unilateral promise followed by actings on the faith of it, and it was held that such a promise could be proved only by writ. In *Edmondston* v. *Edmondston*, 1861, 23 D. 995, to which the Lord President in *Smith* v. *Oliver* refers, the averments disclosed a bilateral onerous contract, and proof was restricted to writ or oath, not because it was gratuitous, but because it was innominate and unusual, and, to hold otherwise, would in practice result in a testamentary settlement being proved by parole. See § **129**, note 5.

[15] *Millar* v. *Tremamondo*, 1771 M. 12, 395.

[16] *Hawick Heritable Investment Bank* v. *Hoggan*, 1902, 5 F. 75, L. Kyllachy (Ordinary) at p. 79; Dickson, *Evidence* (3rd ed.) §598; Gloag, *Contract* (2nd ed.) 52.

[17] See §§ **302** *et seq.*

[18] See §§ **308** *et seq.*

CHAPTER XII

MATTERS REQUIRING PROOF BY WRIT OR OATH
—PRESCRIPTIONS

131. PRESCRIPTIONS—GENERAL

The law of evidence is primarily concerned only with those prescriptions, more accurately described as limitations,[1] which do not extinguish an obligation or make it unenforceable, but which, after a certain lapse of time, limit or restrict the mode of proving it.   These prescriptions, which are dealt with in this chapter, are the vicennial prescription of holograph writs, the sexennial prescription of bills of exchange and promissory notes, the quinquennial prescription and the triennial prescription.   When these prescriptions apply, they result in a restriction of proof, in the case of holograph writs, to the oath of the party against whom the claim is made, and, in the case of the other prescriptions mentioned, to his writ or oath. Proof by writ of party and reference to oath of party are mentioned in the next paragraph, and more generally in later chapters.[2]

If a defender wishes to found upon one of these prescriptions he must state a plea to that effect in his defences, which the court should normally either sustain or repel before proof is allowed.   The court's decision is arrived at upon a consideration of the pursuer's averments, and of the terms of the account or other document sued upon,[3] but on a few occasions a preliminary proof has been allowed in order to determine whether or not

---

[1] *Johnson* v. *Tillie, Whyte & Co.*, 1917 S.C. 211, L. Johnston at p. 221.
[2] See §§ **302** *et seq.* (proof by writ) and §§ **308** *et seq.* (reference to oath).
[3] *Caledonian Railway Co.* v. *Chisholm*, 1886, 13 R. 773, L.P. Inglis at p. 775; *Alcock* v. *Easson*, 1842, 5 D. 356, L. J-Cl. Hope at p. 363; *Neilson* v. *Magistrates of Falkirk*, 1899, 2 F. 118, L. Kinnear at p. 125; *Ligertwood* v. *Brown*, 1872, 10 M. 832, L. Ardmillan at p. 834; *Taylor* v. *Allardyce*, 1858, 20 D. 401, L. J-Cl. Hope at p. 402; *Bracken* v. *Blasquez*, 1891, 18 R. 819, L. Adam at p. 821.

a prescription applies.[4] Unless the plea of prescription has been repelled, proof *prout de jure* on the merits of the action ought not to be allowed.[5] If, however, such a proof is allowed and acquiesced in, it is too late for the defender to raise the plea later,[6] and the court must then decide the case on the evidence led, even if the proof ought to have been restricted to writ or oath.[7]

The presenting, or concurring in, a petition for sequestration, or the lodging of a claim in a sequestration, interrupts prescription of the debt founded upon.[8]

132. PROOF OF PRESCRIBED WRITS AND OBLIGATIONS

(a) General. The general rules regarding proof by writ[9] and reference to oath[10] are dealt with later. This paragraph deals only with certain specialties arising when one of the prescriptions mentioned in this chapter is held to apply. When prescription is held to apply, it is not necessary that the creditor prove both the constitution of the debt, and its resting owing, in the same way. So, for example, the constitution of the debt may be proved by writ or by judicial admission, and its resting owing by reference to oath.[11]

(b) Judicial Admissions. A judicial admission of the holograph quality of a prescribed holograph writ, or of the constitution or resting owing of a prescribed obligation or debt, is the equivalent of proof by writ or oath of the admitted fact.[12] But, to have this effect, the judicial admission must be express, clear and unequivocal,[13] and a mere inference from averments of fact made by the defender is not sufficient. The reason for this is that, when a prescription applies, the usual presumptions from the averred actings of the parties, as to the incurring of a debt or its payment or non-payment, do not arise, and any onus which might otherwise have rested upon the debtor because of these presumptions is shifted to the creditor. The debtor need no longer prove payment or discharge, but the creditor must prove both the constitution and the subsistence of the obligation by the debtor's

---

[4] e.g. *McKinlay* v. *Wilson*, 1885, 13 R. 210; *Ross* v. *Cowie's Executrix*, 1888, 16 R. 224.
[5] *Alcock* v. *Easson* (*supra*), L. J-Cl. Hope at pp. 363-4.
[6] *Kerr* v. *Woods*, 1832, 10 S. 774. See also *Maule* v. *Sommers*, 1822, 1 S. 475, and the reference by the Lord Ordinary in *Smellie* v. *Cochrane*, 1835, 13 S. 544, at p. 546, to *Smellie* v. *Gillespie*, 1833, 12 S. 125.
[7] *Kerr's Trs.* v. *Ker*, 1883, 11 R. 108; *Wyse* v. *Wyse*, 1847, 9 D. 1405.
[8] Bankruptcy (Scotland) Act, 1913 (3 & 4 Geo. V. c. 20), s. 105.
[9] See §§ **302** *et seq.*
[10] See §§ **308** *et seq.*
[11] *Wilson* v. *Strang*, 1830, 8 S. 625; *Deans* v. *Steele*, 1853, 16 D. 317.
[12] Dickson, *Evidence* (3rd ed.) §417; *Wilson* v. *Strang* (*supra*); *Darnley* v. *Kirkwood*, 1845, 7 D. 595, L. Mackenzie at p. 598, L. Fullerton at p. 600. As to judicial admissions generally, see § **48.**
[13] *Noble* v. *Scott*, 1843, 5 D. 723, L. J-Cl. Hope at p. 727; *Darnley* v. *Kirkwood* (*supra*), L. Fullerton at p. 600.

writ or oath.[14] It should be noted in this connection that the rule of written pleading, which provides that failure to deny an averment of fact within a party's knowledge is construed as an admission of that fact,[15] does not apply when a defender pleads prescription. If a defender pleads that the pursuer must prove his case by writ or oath because a prescription applies, his failure to deny the pursuer's averments regarding constitution and resting owing is not construed as a judicial admission of them.[16] If the defender, in addition to pleading prescription, makes alternative averments of fact to meet the pursuer's case should the plea of prescription be repelled, from which, were there no prescription, an admission of the constitution of the debt might have been inferred, or states an alternative defence, such as compensation, from which a similar implied admission might have arisen, these are construed as judicial admissions only if the prescription is held not to apply.[17] If a judicial admission, although express, clear and unequivocal, is qualified, the party wishing to found upon the admission, when prescription applies, may do so only if he disproves the qualification by the debtor's writ or by reference to his oath.[18]

(c) **Proof by Writ.** There seems little doubt that the constitution of a debt may be proved by a writ dated either before or after the end of the prescriptive period.[19] In a proof of the subsistence or resting owing of a debt, however, a writ is useless unless it is dated after the end of the prescriptive period,[20] although a writ dated on the last day of the prescriptive period has been held to be sufficient.[21] When the debt has been proved

14 *Alcock* v. *Easson*, 1842, 5 D. 356, L. J-Cl. Hope at pp. 365-366; *Darnley* v. *Kirkwood* (*supra*), L. Fullerton at p. 600; *Cullen* v. *Smeal*, 1853, 15 D. 868, L .J-Cl. Hope at p. 872; *Borland* v. *Macdonald, Ltd.*, 1940 S.C. 124, L. Jamieson at p. 140.

15 As to the rule, see § **48,** sub-para. (d).

16 *Dick* v. *Aiton*, 1738 M. 12,041; *Duncan* v. *Forbes*, 1829, 7 S. 821; *Alcock* v. *Easson*, (*supra*), L. J-Cl. Hope at p. 365; *Noble* v. *Scott* (*supra*), L. J-Cl. Hope at p. 727; *Darnley* v. *Kirkwood* (*supra*), L. Fullerton at pp. 600-601.

17 *Alcock* v. *Easson* (*supra*), L. J-Cl. Hope at p. 366; *Campbell* v. *Grierson*, 1848, 10 D. 361, L. J-Cl. Hope at p. 364, L. Moncreiff at p. 366; *Cullen* v. *Smeal* (*supra*); *Miller* v. *Miller*, 1898, 25 R. 995, L. Kincairney (Ordinary) at p. 997.

18 See § **48,** sub-para. (a).

19 In *Deans* v. *Steele*, 1853, 16 D. 317, and *Kennard & Sons* v. *Wright*, 1865, 3 M. 946 (see L.P. Inglis at pp. 949,950), the writs dated within the prescriptive period would have been held sufficient if they had been in other terms. See *Stevenson* v. *Kyle*, 1850, 12 D. 673, L. Ivory (Ordinary) at pp. 674-5, L. Dundrennan at p. 675, L.P. Boyle at p. 675; *Johnson* v. *Tillie, Whyte & Co.*, 1917 S.C. 211, L. Johnston at p. 221.

20 Bell, *Commentaries*, I, 349; Dickson, *Evidence*, (3rd ed.) §§ 455, 482, 483, 516; *Deans & Moore* v. *Melvin* (O.H.) 1897, 4 S.L.T. 292; *Stevenson* v. *Kyle* (*supra*), L. Ivory (Ordinary) at p. 675, L. Dundrennan at p. 675; *Alcock* v. *Easson*, 1842, 5 D. 356, L. J-Cl. Hope at p. 365 ("the inutility of a document dated within the three years"). *Cf. Thomas* v. *Stiven*, 1868, 6 M. 777, L. Deas at p. 782. In *Johnson* v. *Tillie, Whyte & Co.* (*supra*), the contrary view was conceded by counsel and accepted by a majority of the Court. Lord Johnston, however, at pp. 221-223, in a strong dissenting opinion, refused to accept this concession, and his opinion has subsequently been mentioned with approval in *Robb & Co.* v. *Stornoway Harbour Trs.*, 1932 S.C. 290, L. Morison at p. 299; *Borland* v. *Macdonald Ltd.* 1940 S.C. 124, L. Mackay at p. 136. See also Gloag, *Contract* (2nd ed.) 744, note 1.

21 *Lindsay* v. *Moffat*, 1797 M. 11, 137; Bell, *Commentaries*, I, 420; Dickson, *Evidence* (3rd ed.) 455.

by writ to have been resting owing at a date after the end of the prescriptive period, it will usually be regarded as still subsisting at the date of the action, unless the debtor proves the contrary.[22] When the creditor relies upon payment of interest after the end of the prescriptive period as establishing the subsistence of the debt, the general rule remains applicable, and these payments must be proved by writs of the debtor.[23] In certain circumstances receipts granted by the creditor may be accepted as constructively the debtor's writs for this purpose.[24]

(d) Construction of the Oath. The construction of the oath, when the constitution or resting owing of the debt is referred to oath, is dealt with in a later chapter.[25]

133. VICENNIAL PRESCRIPTION OF HOLOGRAPH WRITS

"Holograph missive letters and holograph bonds and subscriptions in compt-books, without witnesses, not being pursued for within twenty years, shall prescrive in all time thereafter, except the pursuer offer to prove by the defender's oath the verity of the said holograph bonds and letters and subscriptions in the compt-books."[26] The prescription does not run against minors during their minority.[26] The prescription has been held to apply to all holograph writings upon which an obligation can be founded,[27] whether the writing itself expresses the obligation or is merely evidence from which an obligation can be inferred.[28] It applies to a holograph letter acknowledging the receipt of money,[29] and probably to a holograph IOU.[30] The prescriptive period runs from the date of the holograph writing even when the obligation to which it refers is future or contingent.[31] "Being pursued for within twenty years" means that within that period an action has been raised upon the holograph writ, or a plea of compensation has been founded

---

[22] Bell, *Commentaries*, I, 349; Dickson, *Evidence* (3rd ed.) § 456; *Drummond* v. *Lees*, 1880, 7 R. 452; *Johnson* v. *Tillie, Whyte & Co. (supra)*, L. Johnston at p. 222. *Cf. Storey* v. *Paxton*, 1878, 6 R. 293.

[23] Dickson, *Evidence* (3rd ed.) §§ 458, 520. The exception which, in general, allows a creditor to prove payments by his debtor *prout de jure* (see § **126,** sub-para. (c)) does not apply in cases involving prescription.

[24] See § **304,** sub-para. (c).

[25] See §§ **321-323.**

[26] Act, 1669, c. 9.

[27] Dickson, *Evidence* (3rd ed.) §423; Gloag, *Contract* (2nd ed.) 750.

[28] Bell, *Principles*, §590; *Baird* v. *Baird's Trs.* (O.H.) 1954 S.C. 290, L.P. Cooper at pp. 294-295.

[29] *Mowat* v. *Banks*, 1856, 18 D. 1093.

[30] *Macadam* v. *Findlay* (O.H.) 1911 S.C. 1366; *Dick* v. *Thomson's Trs.* (O.H.) 1929 S.L.T. 637. In *Craig* v. *Monteith's Executrix*, 1926 S.C. 123, L. Skerrington, in an *obiter* reference to his opinion in *Macadam* v. *Findlay (supra)*, observed that he had been wrong in referring to an IOU as a "bond", but adhered to his view that the prescription applies to any holograph writing on which an obligation can be founded. It seems absurd that a holograph acknowledgment of debt should prescribe, and that a typed and signed acknowledgment, which has the same result, should not. But see the reference later in this paragraph to the effect of the long negative prescription.

[31] Dickson, *Evidence* (3rd ed.) §428.

upon it in the defences to an action, or diligence has been done upon it.[32] It is not enough that there has been a mere concourse of debit and credit and an extrajudicial retention of the sum due,[33] or that the writing has been registered for execution,[34] or that interest has been paid upon the debt referred to in the writing.[35] If a reference to oath is made, the oath must prove the "verity" (the holograph quality) of the whole of the writing, except in the case of entries in account books, when proof of the authenticity of the signature is enough.[36] If the writing is shown by the oath to be holograph, it has the same effect as if the prescription had not applied.[36] The ordinary rules as to proof of payment or discharge of the obligation contained in it come into operation,[37] and there is no onus upon the pursuer, resulting at least from the prescription, to establish that the obligation has not been implemented or discharged.[38] If the oath does not establish the holograph quality of the writing, it cannot be founded upon even as an adminicle of evidence in proof of the obligation.[39]

It is thought that, with regard to most obligations founded upon holograph writings, the question of whether this prescription does or does not apply is of only academic interest. Almost all private obligations are now extinguished after twenty years by the negative prescription, even when the person against whom the negative prescription is pleaded has been in minority,[40] unless there has been interruption, which includes *inter alia* payment of interest on the debt, the payment being proved by writ.[41] This point was not mentioned in the only decisions on vicennial prescription since 1924.[42]

134. SEXENNIAL PRESCRIPTION OF BILLS OF EXCHANGE AND PROMISSORY NOTES

No bill of exchange, inland bill or promissory note is effectual as the foundation of diligence or of an action, after the expiry of a period of six

---

[32] Dickson, *Evidence* (3rd ed.) §§425, 427, 443. As to the effect of founding in a sequestration upon the debt contained in the writ, see § **131.**

[33] Dickson, *Evidence* (3rd ed.) §443.

[34] Dickson, *Evidence* (3rd ed.) §425.

[35] *Baird* v. *Baird's Trs.* (O.H.) 1954 S.C. 290, L.P. Cooper at p. 295; *Macadam* v. *Findlay* (O.H.) 1911 S.C. 1366, L. Skerrington at pp. 1367-1368; Dickson, *Evidence* (3rd ed.) §426. *Cf.* More's Notes, 271.

[36] Dickson, *Evidence* (3rd ed.) §429.

[37] As to proof of discharge or payment of such obligations, see §§ **125, 127.**

[38] Dickson, *Evidence* (3rd ed.) §431.

[39] *Baird* v. *Baird's Trs.* (O.H.) 1954 S.C. 290; *Dick* v. *Thomson's Trs.* (O.H.) 1929 S.L.T. 637.

[40] See Conveyancing (Scotland) Act, 1924 (14 & 15 Geo. V c. 27), s. 17; Conveyancing Amendment (Scotland) Act, 1938 (1 & 2 Geo. VI c. 4), s. 4; *Sutherland County Council* v. *Macdonald*, 1935 S.C. 915; *Marr's Exrs.* v. *Marr's Trs.*, 1936 S.C. 64.

[41] *Kermack* v. *Kermack*, 1874, 2 R. 156. Payment of interest does not prevent the application of the vicennial prescription of holograph writings: see note 35 above.

[42] *Baird* v. *Baird's Trs.* (*supra*); *Dick* v. *Thomson's Trs.* (*supra*). In *Dick* v. *Thomson's Trs.* there may still have been doubt as to whether the reduction of the negative prescription to twenty years applied to moveables. In the latter case there was an averment that interest had been paid, which might have prevented the application of the negative prescription.

years from the date when the sums therein become exigible.[43] The prescription does not run against minors during their minority.[44] Bank notes or bank bills payable to bearer, which circulate as money, are not affected by the prescription.[45] An action upon a bill of exchange, which was incompetent in point of form and was raised before the end of the prescriptive period, was held to prevent the application of the prescription, although incompetency was cured by amendment only after the prescriptive period had terminated.[46] By a long line of early decisions it was established, in spite of the terms of the statute, that any diligence done or action raised upon a bill within the prescriptive period, whether or not it was proceeded with, prevented the application of the prescription to the bill thereafter, even in a question with obligants other than those originally proceeded against.[47]

After the prescription has become applicable, the burden of proving the "debts contained in the said bills and promissory notes, and that the same are resting owing" may be discharged only by the writ or oath of the debtor,[45] the burden of proving both these matters resting upon the creditor.[48] Proof of prescribed claims in general has been mentioned earlier,[49] and proof of the debt in a prescribed bill is mentioned in the next paragraph.

A distinction must be made between "the debts contained in" bills of exchange, on the one hand, and, on the other hand, antecedent or contemporary contracts, such as loans[50] or contracts of sale,[51] in respect of which bills of exchange are granted as additional security to the creditor. It is only the debt contained in the bill which prescribes, and, if it is the foundation of the creditor's action, must be proved, both as to constitution and resting owing, by the writ or oath of the debtor.[52] The granting of a bill does not annul an antecedent or contemporaneous contract,[53] and the creditor may

[43] Bills of Exchange (Scotland) Act, 1772 (12 Geo. III c. 72), s. 37. (The sums become exigible on the date of the bill when it is payable on demand or at sight or on presentation, but, when it is payable otherwise, on the end of the last day of grace: Bills of Exchange Act, 1882 (45 & 46 Vict. c. 61), ss. 10-14; Dickson, *Evidence* (3rd ed.) §448.)
[44] *Ibid.* s. 40.
[45] *Ibid.* s. 39.
[46] *Bank of Scotland* v. *W. & G. Fergusson*, 1898, 1 F. 96.
[47] This line of authority is discussed and followed in *Milne's Trs.* v. *Ormiston's Trs.*, 1893, 20 R. 523. Lord Rutherfurd Clark (p. 531) doubted the soundness of the earlier view of the law and suggested that it might be reviewed on a suitable occasion. The earlier decisions are given in Dickson, *Evidence* (3rd ed.) §447. See also Gloag, *Contract* (2nd ed.) 750. As to the effect of founding on a debt in a petition for sequestration or in a claim lodged in a sequestration, see § **131.**
[48] *Darnley* v. *Kirkwood*, 1845, 7 D. 595, L. Fullerton at p. 600; *Kerr's Trs.* v. *Ker*, 1883, 11 R. 108, L.P. Inglis at p. 116.
[49] See § **132.**
[50] *MacBain* v. *MacBain*, 1929 S.C. 213; 1930 S.C. (H.L.) 72 (the proof by writ allowed was a proof of *loan*); *Nisbet* v. *Neil's Tr.*, 1869, 7 M. 1097; *Blake* v. *Turner*, 1860, 23 D. 15.
[51] *Hunter* v. *Thomson*, 1843, 5 D. 1285 (price of a horse).
[52] *Campbell's Trs.* v. *Hudson's Exr.*, 1895, 22 R. 943, L. Trayner at p. 952. "They have to prove the debt and its resting owing. What debt? The statute answers this question. It is the debt contained in the . . . bill." See also *Christie* v. *Henderson*, 1833, 11 S. 744, L. Balgray at p. 758.
[53] *Blake* v. *Turner* (*supra*), L. Neaves (Ordinary) at p. 17; *Nisbet* v. *Neil's Tr.* (*supra*), L.P. Inglis at p. 1099.

ignore the prescribed bill, and prove the other contract by the mode of proof appropriate to it, by writ or oath, for example, in the case of loan,[50] or *prout de jure* in the case of sale of goods.[51] If this course is adopted, the creditor need not prove the subsistence of the debt, since it is for the debtor to prove payment once the debt has been established.[54]

135. PROOF OF THE DEBT IN PRESCRIBED BILL OF EXCHANGE

(a) **Prescribed Bill as Adminicle of Evidence.** It has been said that "the bill may be produced in the way of adminicle as documentary evidence, but the proof on which alone judgment can proceed is the writ or oath of the debtor."[55] If the writ or oath of the debtor, apart from the bill, is necessary for judgment, it is at first sight difficult to understand what part is left for the prescribed bill to play. Equally, if the bill is allowed in any way to speak for itself, it is difficult to understand why other proof should be necessary, since the bill clearly acknowledges indebtedness. The expression "adminicle of evidence" has been used on a number of occasions in relation to prescribed bills,[56] sometimes without any clear indication of its meaning or effect. The fact that a bill was granted may be relevant in certain circumstances, and need not be ignored simply because the bill has prescribed. Thus, on a reference to oath of the constitution and resting owing of the debt in a prescribed bill, the debtor may be asked if he signed the bill, and, if so, whether he has paid it.[57] This, however, is not using the bill as an adminicle of documentary evidence. It has been said that the fact that the prescribed bill is still in the creditor's possession raises a presumption that the debt contained in it has not been paid.[58] It is thought, however, that the presumption cannot arise except in connection with an effective document of debt, which a prescribed bill is not, and that there is no place for circumstantial evidence in a proof by writ.[59] A prescribed bill may properly be used as an adminicle of evidence, however, as explaining or elucidating the other writs upon which the creditor founds in the course of a proof by writ. Thus if the creditor proves by writ *aliunde* the constitution and resting owing of a debt associated with a prescribed bill, he may refer to the bill itself to prove the amount of the debt.[60]

---

54 As to proof of payment, see § **127.**

55 Bell, *Commentaries*, I, 419. See also *Storey* v. *Paxton*, 1878, 6 R. 293, L. Ormidale at p. 298.

56 *Christie* v. *Henderson*, 1833, 11 S. 744, L. J-Cl. Boyle at p. 750; *Drummond* v. *Lees*, 1880, 7 R. 452, L. Ormidale at p. 457; *Campbell's Trs.* v. *Hudson's Exr.*, 1895, 22 R. 943, L. Trayner at p. 953; *MacBain* v. *MacBain*, 1929 S.C. 213 (affd. 1930 S.C. (H.L.) 72), L.P. Clyde at p. 216, L. Sands at pp. 217-218, L. Morison at p. 219.

57 *Christie* v. *Henderson* (*supra*), L. J-Cl. Boyle at p. 750, L. Balgray at p. 758.

58 *Campbell's Trs.* v. *Hudson's Exr.* (*supra*), L. Trayner at p. 953; *Nisbet* v. *Neil's Tr.*, 1869 7 M. 1097 (proof of loan), L.P. Inglis at p. 1099.

59 *MacBain* v. *MacBain* (*supra*), L. Sands at p. 219.

60 *MacBain* v. *MacBain* (*supra*), L. Sands at pp. 217-218. The bill was so used in *Rennie* v. *Urquhart*, 1880, 7 R. 1030, and *Wood* v. *Howden*, 1843, 5 D. 507. An attempt to use it in this way failed in *Blair* v. *Horn*, 1859, 21 D. 1004, because the other writs were not sufficiently referable to the bill in question. *MacBain* v. *MacBain* was concerned with proof of a loan (see § **119,** sub-para. (b) on this point), but L. Sand's statement appears to refer also to proof of the debt contained in a prescribed bill. It seems

LAW OF EVIDENCE

(b) Writ Sufficient for Proof of Debt in Prescribed Bill. The following are examples of writs which have been held sufficient to prove the constitution and subsistence of the debt contained in a prescribed bill of exchange or promissory note:—a note of payment of interest, signed by the debtor on the back of the prescribed promissory note seven years after its date, together with holograph entries made by the debtor, as factor on the trust estate of the deceased creditor, of payments of interest by himself for a period of six years, all of which were dated after the end of the prescriptive period, but at least twenty-one years before an action was raised:[61] a promissory note, signed by the debtor, for £36, dated after the end of the prescriptive period, bearing to be "for value received for interest," and judicially admitted to have been granted in respect of interest on the prescribed promissory note for £800, together with receipts for subsequent payments of interest for ten years which were found in the debtor's repositories after his death and were held constructively to be his writs, the prescribed promissory note remaining in the creditor's possession throughout until the raising of the action:[62] the constitution of the debt in the prescribed promissory note being judicially admitted, resting owing was held to be proved by the inventory of the deceased creditor's estate, signed and sworn by the debtor as her executor, after the end of the prescriptive period, which showed the sum contained in the prescribed promissory note as an asset of the deceased creditor's estate:[63] a letter written by the debtor to the creditor after the end of the prescriptive period, referring in general terms to a debt, asking that it be allowed to lie and stating a willingness to pay interest on it, which, under reference to the letter from the creditor to which it was a reply, was construed as an admission of resting owing of the debt in the prescribed bill.[64]

(c) Writ Insufficient for Proof of Debt in Prescribed Bill. The following are examples of writs which have been held insufficient to prove the constitution and subsistence of the debt contained in a prescribed bill of exchange or promissory note:—holograph notes by the debtor, written on the back of the prescribed promissory note, recording the payment of annual interest during the prescriptive period, together with entries in memoranda or passbooks, holograph of the debtor, recording the receipt of the sum contained in the promissory note, and the payment of yearly interest on it after the end of the prescriptive period and up to the date of the debtor's death, which was sixteen years before the raising of the action:[65] a trust disposition for behoof

probable that in both instances, when a prescribed bill exists, the bill may be referred to for the purpose suggested in the text.
61 *Drummond* v. *Lees*, 1880, 7 R. 452.
62 *Campbell's Trs.* v. *Hudson's Exr.*, 1895, 22 R. 943.
63 *Jackson* v. *Ogilvie's Exr.*, 1935 S.C. 154.
64 *Rennie* v. *Urquhart*, 1880, 7 R. 1030. See also *Wood* v. *Howden*, 1843, 5 D. 507, where there was also a receipt for interest granted by the creditor, found in the debtor's repositories at his death, and held constructively to be his writ.
65 *Storey* v. *Paxton*, 1878, 6 R. 293. It is doubtful whether this decision is now a safe guide, since the decision was partly arrived at on the outmoded view that, if the debt is shown to be subsisting after the first period of six years, a new six-year period of pre-

142

of creditors and a letter by the debtor, granted during the prescriptive period, and two letters written by the debtor after the end of the prescriptive period, all referring in general terms to the existence of debts and of liability in respect of bills of exchange, but without specific reference to the four promissory notes in question.[66]

136. QUINQUENNIAL PRESCRIPTION—ARREARS OF MINISTERS' STIPENDS, MULTURES AND RENTS—ORAL BARGAINS REGARDING MOVEABLES

(a) General. "Ministers' stipends and multures, not pursued for within five years after the same are due, and likeways mails and duties of tenants not being pursued within five years after the tenant shall remove from the lands for which the mails and duties are craved, shall prescribe in all time coming, except the said ministers' stipends, multures, mails and duties be offered to be proven to be due and resting owing by the defenders their oaths, or by a special writ under their hands, acknowledging what is resting owing; and that all bargains concerning moveables or sums of money, provable by witnesses, shall only be provable by writ or oath of party, if the same be not pursued for within five years after the making of the bargain." The prescription does not run against minors during their minority.[67] As in the case of sexennial prescription,[68] it was established by the early decisions that any judicial process raised during the prescriptive period in respect of the debt said to have prescribed, prevented the application of the prescription thereafter.[69] In an action by a tenant for the value of improvements to a farm, raised more than five years after he had removed from it, the landlord counterclaimed for rent due, and it was held that the prescription did not apply, apparently on the ground that the tenant had retained the rents in compensation of his claim.[70] Although the statute does not expressly require that debts arising from oral bargains regarding moveables, to which the prescription applies, should be proved by writ or oath to be resting owing, it has nevertheless been held that the creditor must prove the subsistence as well as the constitution of such debts, as in the case of the other debts mentioned in the statute, for which this is expressly required.[71] No difficulty seems to have arisen with regard to the use in the statute of the words "by a special writ under their hands," and the ordinary rules for

---

scription thereupon commences. See, on this point, Bell, *Principles*, §599; Dickson, *Evidence* (3rd ed.) §§447, 456; *Drummond* v. *Lees* (*supra*), L. Ormidale at p. 457.

[66] *Blair* v. *Horn*, 1859, 21 D. 1004.

[67] Act, 1669, c. 9.

[68] See § **134**, note 47.

[69] *Hogg* v. *Low*, 1826, 4 S. 708 (landlord's sequestration for arrears of rent); *McDonald* v. *Jackson*, 1826, 5 S. 26 (defence of compensation in respect of arrears of rent). *Cf.* *Cochrane* v. *Fergusson*, 1830, 8 S. 324 (where the tenant was still in occupation, and the action and arrestment were in security of rent not yet exigible). As to the effect of founding upon the debt in a sequestration, see § **131**.

[70] *Nicolson* v. *McAlister's Trs.*, 1832, 10 S. 759. This is not a very helpful decision.

[71] *Campbell* v. *Grierson*, 1848, 10 D. 361; *Kennard & Sons* v. *Wright*, 1865, 3 M. 946.

proof by writ have been applied. Proof of prescribed obligations is dealt with elsewhere.[72]

(b) Arrears of Ministers' Stipends. The prescription applies to the stipends only of parish ministers,[73] and to claims by the persons in right of such stipends during a vacancy.[74]

(c) Arrears of Rents. The prescription applies to rents due in respect of both urban and rural subjects,[75] and under both written and oral leases.[76] The prescriptive period does not commence until the tenant has removed from the lands,[67] and the prescription has thus been held not to apply to claims by a former proprietor against a tenant still in occupation,[77] or against a former tenant who had continued to occupy the land as proprietor.[78]

(d) Oral Bargains regarding Moveables. The prescription has been said to apply to all sales, locations and other consensual contracts for the constitution of which writing is not necessary,[79] and has been held to apply to the sale of a single article,[80] and to an agreement to take over the stock on a farm at valuation.[81] This wide application of the statute, which its terms would seem to justify, has been restricted by judicial decision, and the prescription has been held not to apply to any bargain which is in fact constituted by writing, such as a sale completed by correspondence.[82] It has also been held not to apply to an obligation to account as between agent and principal,[83] and to an obligation to return or to account for goods deposited for safe custody[84] or in security,[85] or removed by the defender without authority.[86]

137. TRIENNIAL PRESCRIPTION—GENERAL

(a) The Statute. "All actiones of debt for house-mailles, mennis ordinars, servands fees, merchantes comptes, and uther the like debts, that are not founded upon written obligationes, be persewed within three yeires, utherwise the creditour sall have na action, except he either preive be writ

---

[72] See § 132.
[73] It was held not to apply to teinds due to a bishop: *Hamilton* v. *Herries*, 1683 M. 11, 061.
[74] Erskine, iii, 7, 20; *Gloug* v. *Macintosh*, 1753, M. 11, 063.
[75] *Boyes* v. *Henderson*, 1823, 2 S. 169.
[76] *Nisbet* v. *Baikie*, 1729, M. 11, 059.
[77] *Strahorn* v. *Cunningham*, 1739 M. 11, 059.
[78] *Johnston's Executrices* v. *Johnston*, 1897, 24 R. 611.
[79] Erskine, iii, 7, 20.
[80] *Kennard & Sons* v. *Wright*, 1865, 3 M. 946.
[81] *Lawson* v. *Milne*, 1839, 1 D. 603.
[82] *Hunter* v. *Thomson*, 1843, 5 D. 1285; *Southesk* v. *Simpson*, 1683 M. 12, 326.
[83] *Mackinlay* v. *Mackinlay*, 1851, 14 D. 162. See also *Kilpatrick* v. *Dunlop* (O.H.) 1909, 2 S.L.T. 307.
[84] *Taylor* v. *Nisbet*, 1901, 4 F. 79.
[85] *McFarlane* v. *Brown*, 1827, 5 S. 189.
[86] *Baillie* v. *Young*, 1835, 13 S. 472.

or be aith of his partie."[87]   The minority of the creditor does not affect
the running of the prescription.[88]

(b) Debts not founded upon Written Obligations.   This qualification may
be construed as being restricted to "uther the like debts," or, alternatively,
as applying to all the categories mentioned in the statute.   In a fairly recent
decision two of the judges reserved their opinions as to which interpretation
is correct.[89]   It is thought, however, that the weight of earlier authority,
at least by implication, supports the view that the prescription does not
apply to any debt which is founded upon a written obligation.[90]   A writing,
however, in order that it may prevent the application of the prescription,
must contain, either expressly or by implication,[91] the obligation which
initiates the debt, as distinct from a later writing which merely proves the
existence of an earlier oral obligation.[92]   The following have been held to
be debts due under a written obligation to which the prescription did not
apply:—rent due under a written lease,[93] wages due under a written contract
of service,[94] a tradesman's account due under a written contract,[95] an
engineer's fee for attendance to give professional evidence based on a letter
written to him,[96] and written offers to hire sacks upon certain stated conditions.[97]   A writing by the creditor, even if orally accepted or acted upon
by the debtor, does not prevent the application of the prescription.[98]   A
writing by the debtor, on the other hand, which instructs the performance
of work or services by the creditor, and from which an obligation of payment
is inferred, would now, it is thought, be construed as a written obligation
which prevents the application of the prescription.[99] There may, however,

[87] Act, 1579, c. 83.
[88] Bell, *Commentaries*, I, 351; *Brown* v. *Brodie*, 1709 M. 11, 150.
[89] *Borland* v. *Macdonald Ltd.*, 1940 S.C. 124, L. Mackay at p. 131, L. Wark at p. 137.
[90] Dickson, *Evidence* (3rd ed.) §501; Gloag, *Contract* (2nd ed.) 741 (last line); Rankine,
   Leases (3rd ed.) 322; Millar, *Prescription*, 132, all express or imply the broader view.
   So does Bell, *Commentaries*, I, 349, but *cf.* 348. The prescription of house rents, in
   the absence of a written lease, is mentioned in More's Notes, cclxxiv, Gloag (*supra*),
   Rankine (*supra*), and *Cumming's Tr.* v. *Simpson*, 1825, 3 S. 377; and the prescribing of a
   merchant's account, if there is no written obligation, is recognised in *Douglas* v. *Grierson*,
   1794 M. 11, 116, *Chalmers* v. *Walker*, 1878, 6 R. 199, and *Broatch* v. *Jackson*, 1900,
   2 F. 968, L. M'Laren at p. 978.
[91] *Broatch* v. *Jackson* (*supra*).
[92] *Borland* v. *Macdonald Ltd.* (*supra*), L. J-Cl. Aitchison at p. 129, L. Mackay at p. 132,
   L. Wark at p. 137, L. Jamieson at p. 139; *Broatch* v. *Jackson* (*supra*), L. Kincairney
   (Ordinary) at p. 971, L.P. Balfour at p. 977; *White* v. *Caledonian Railway Co.*, 1868,
   6 M. 415, L.P. Inglis at p. 419, L. Ardmillan at p. 420; *Barr* v. *Edinburgh and Glasgow
   Railway Co.*, 1864, 2 M. 1250, L. J-Cl. Inglis at p. 1253, L. Benholme at p. 1255.
[93] See *Cumming's Trs.* v. *Simpson*, 1825, 3 S. 377.
[94] *M'Tavish* v. *Campbell*, 1777, 5 B. Supp. 543.
[95] *Watson* v. *Lord Prestonhall*, 1711 M. 11, 095; *cf. Hotson* v. *Threshie*, 1833, 11 S. 482.
[96] *Blackadder* v. *Milne*, 1851, 13 D. 820; *cf. Barr* v. *Edinburgh and Glasgow Railway Co.*
   (*supra*).
[97] *Chisholm* v. *Robertson*, 1883, 10 R. 760.
[98] *North British Railway Co.* v. *Smith Sligo*, 1873, 1 R. 309; *Chalmers* v. *Walker*, 1878,
   6 R. 199.
[99] *Broatch* v. *Jackson*, 1900, 2 F. 968; *Millar, Walker & Millar* v. *Brodie's Trs.*, 1902 4 F.
   846. The earlier decisions to the same effect are referred to in *Broatch* v. *Jackson*.

be an exception to this in relation to the purchase of goods from a merchant, instructed by a written order, which was held by some early decisions not to prevent the application of the prescription.[1] These decisions, although subjected to later criticism,[2] have not been expressly overruled, but it is thought that the rather uncertain principle underlying them[2] would not now be extended to other analogous contracts.[3]

(c) "Actions" to which Prescription Applies. The statute refers only to actions for the debts mentioned, but the application of the prescription has been extended by judicial decision to defences, such as compensation, founded upon such debts, and to a claim, similarly founded, to vote in the election of a trustee on a sequestrated estate.[4]

(d) Proof of Prescribed Debt. When the prescription is held to apply to any claim, both the constitution and the resting owing of the debt must be proved by the writ of the debtor or by reference to his oath.[5] Such proof is dealt with elsewhere.[6] In a proof by writ a letter from the defender, in reply to a letter from the pursuers which was not produced, in which she said merely that she was sorry she could not spare anything before six weeks, was held not to prove either the constitution or resting owing of the debt sued for.[7]

138. ACTION FOR RECOVERY OF DEBT DURING TRIENNIAL PERIOD

As in the sexennial[8] and quinquennial[9] prescriptions, it has been established by judicial decision that the triennial prescription does not apply to a claim which has been founded upon during the prescriptive period in any competent judicial process, even if that process has not been completed or pursued to an effectual conclusion.[10] So, the prescription was held not to

---

Cf. Wallace v. *McKissock*, 1829, 7 S. 542 (written instructions, not from debtor, but from his country agent, whose authority he denied).

[1] *Cheap* v. *Cordiner*, 1775 M. 11, 111; *Ross* v. *Shaw*, 1784 M. 11, 115; *Douglas* v. *Grierson*, 1794 M. 11, 116.

[2] See *Broatch* v. *Jackson (supra)*, L. Kincairney (Ordinary) at pp. 971-972, L.P. Balfour at pp. 975-976, L. Kinnear at p. 980; *Millar, Walker & Millar* v. *Brodie's Trs. (supra)*, L.P. Balfour at p. 848, L. McLaren at p. 849. These opinions also contain comment upon the statement in Bell, *Commentaries*, I, 349, approved by Lord President Inglis in *Chalmers* v. *Walker*, 1878, 6 R. 199, at pp. 201-202, to the effect that the prescription is excluded only by a written contract of a kind which would naturally require a written discharge.

[3] See Gloag, *Contract* (2nd ed.) 741.

[4] Dickson, *Evidence* (3rd ed.) §§509, 510, and cases there cited.

[5] Dickson, *Evidence* (3rd ed.) §511.

[6] See § **132**.

[7] *J. & D. Mitchell* v. *Moultry*, 1882, 10 R. 378.

[8] See § **134**, note 47.

[9] See § **136**, note 69.

[10] *Stock Journal Co.* v. *Clydesdale Horse Co.*, 1898, 25 R. 1016; *Eddie* v. *Monkland Railways Co.*, 1855, 17 D. 1041, L.J-Cl. Hope at p. 1045, L. Wood at pp. 1046-7, L. Cowan at p. 1048; *Dunn* v. *Lamb*, 1854, 16 D. 944. A different view was taken in some of the earlier cases: see *McLaren* v. *Buik*, 1829, 7 S. 483, L. Glenlee at p. 488, L. Pitmilly at p. 489; *Cochran* v. *Prentice*, 1841, 4 D. 76, L. J-Cl. Hope at p. 79; *Alcock* v, *Easson*,

apply when the debt had been the subject of a judicial reference during the prescriptive period, which had become abortive because of the death of the referee:[11] when a decree in absence in a foreign court, which was of doubtful validity, had been obtained in respect of it during the prescriptive period:[12] when the debt had been judicially founded upon in a counterclaim during the prescriptive period,[13] or in a claim in a process of multiplepoinding or ranking and sale.[14] The effect of founding upon the debt in a sequestration has been referred to earlier.[15]

139. PERSONAL BAR TO PLEA OF TRIENNIAL PRESCRIPTION

The prescription has been held not to be pleadable when, owing to the concealment by the debtor of the true facts or by his false representations, the creditor was unaware during the prescriptive period that he had a claim, or that it was necessary for him to pursue the claim.[16] This principle was applied when goods were falsely represented by the owner to be in a category which, under his contract with a railway company, that company was bound to carry free of charge, with the result that the railway company could not know that they were entitled to payment until after the prescriptive period had elapsed:[17] and when a domestic servant was unaware, until thirty years after the commencement of her employment, that the employer had not been depositing her wages annually to her credit in a bank, in terms of the contract between them.[18] A party has also been held to be personally barred from pleading prescription if, during the prescriptive period, he has concurred in a judicial reference concerning the claim,[19] or has admitted the debt in the course of abortive extra-judicial or quasi-judicial negotiations, which induced the creditor not to initiate judicial proceedings.[20]

140. HOUSE RENTS, BOARD AND LODGING AND ALIMENT

(a) House-Mailles. These include only the rents of urban houses, and have been held not to include the rent of a farm or of a minister's glebe.[21] Each term's rent prescribes three years after it falls due, irrespective of whether the tenant is in occupation or has removed.[21]

1842, 5 D. 356, L. J-Cl. Hope at p. 363. See also *Gobbi* v. *Lazzaroni* (O.H.), 1859, 21 D. 801, at p. 803 (action abandoned by pursuer).

11 *Dunn* v. *Lamb* (*supra*).

12 *Stock Journal Co.* v. *Clydesdale Horse Co.* (*supra*).

13 *Sloan* v. *Birtwhistle*, 1827, 5 S. 692. See also *Dunn* v. *Lamb* (*supra*), L. Ivory at p. 951, L. Rutherfurd at p. 955.

14 *Eddie* v. *Monkland Railways Co.* (*supra*), L. Wood at pp. 1046-7; *Dunn* v. *Lamb* (*supra*), L. Rutherfurd at p. 955.

15 See § **131**, note 8.

16 See Erskine, iii, 7, 36, referred to by Lord President Inglis in *Earl of Fife* v. *Duff*, 1887, 15 R. 238, at p. 253.

17 *Caledonian Railway Co.* v. *Chisholm*, 1886, 13 R. 773.

18 *Inglis* v. *Smith*, 1916 S.C. 581.

19 *Dunn* v. *Lamb*, 1854, 16 D. 944.

20 *Thomas* v. *Stiven*, 1868, 6 M. 777, L. Mure (Ordinary), at p. 779, L.P. Inglis at p. 782.

(b) Mennis Ordinars. This means the cost of board and lodging in a hotel or boarding house,[22] and has been extended to include arrears of aliment due under a contract, express or implied.[23] The prescription does not apply to claims for aliment by a mother of an illegitimate child against the father, or non-contractual claims arising *ex debito naturali*,[24] or to non-contractual claims for aliment by a *negotiorum gestor*.[25] When the claim is for aliment, alleged to have been due at fixed terms, each term's aliment prescribes three years after it falls due,[26] but when either the amount of aliment, or the times when payments were due, were not said to have been agreed upon, the prescription was held to run only from the last item of what was regarded as a continuous account.[27]

141. WAGES AND SALARIES

"Servands fees" include all wages and salaries claimed in respect of a contract of service, express or implied, and it is immaterial that the rate of remuneration may not have been agreed between the parties.[28] The prescription has been held to apply to a claim by the manager of a tweed mill for a bonus, payable out of profits and in addition to weekly salary, in respect of overtime work:[29] by an apprentice for the annual sum payable under his indenture:[30] by an official holding the public offices of sanitary inspector, burgh surveyor, firemaster and master of works, for arrears of salary:[31] by factors, chamberlains and grieves,[32] by a housekeeper or governess,[33] a shop manager,[34] and by a farm servant,[35] for salary, wages or other remuneration. Each term's payment prescribes three years after it falls due.[36]

---

[21] Dickson, *Evidence* (3rd ed.) §487; Rankine, *Leases* (3rd ed.) 322.

[22] Dickson, *Evidence* (3rd ed.) §488.

[23] *Taylor* v. *Allardyce*, 1858, 20 D. 401, L. Ardmillan (Ordinary) at pp. 401-2; *Ligertwood* v. *Brown*, 1872, 10 M. 832; *Wilson* v. *Scott* (O.H.) 1908, 15 S.L.T. 948.

[24] *Thomson* v. *Westwood*, 1842, 4 D. 833; *Ligertwood* v. *Brown* (*supra*), L. Ardmillan at p. 834, L. Kinloch at p. 836.

[25] *Davidson* v. *Watson*, 1740, 1 Pat. 288; *Thom* v. *Jardine*, 1836, 14 S. 1004, L. Fullerton (Ordinary) at p. 1006; *Longmuir* v. *Longmuir* (O.H.) 1893, 1 S.L.T. 143.

[26] Erskine, iii, 3, 17; Dickson, *Evidence* (3rd ed.) §489.

[27] *Bracken* v. *Blasquez*, 1891, 18 R. 819; *Whyte* v. *Crighton's Trs.* (O.H.) 1896, 3 S.L.T. 235.

[28] Dickson, *Evidence* (3rd ed.) §490; *Smellie* v. *Cochrane*, 1835, 13 S. 544; *Smellie* v. *Miller*, 1835, 14 S. 12; *Alcock* v. *Easson*, 1842, 5 D. 356; *Miller* v. *Miller* 1898, 25 R. 995, L. Kincairney (Ordinary) at p. 997.

[29] *Borland* v. *Macdonald Ltd.*, 1940 S.C. 124. *Cf. Allison* v. *Allison's Trs.*, 1904, 6 F. 696, where prescription held not to apply because the contract was partly one of partnership.

[30] *Crawford* v. *Simpson*, 1731 M. 11, 102.

[31] *Neilson* v. *Magistrates of Falkirk*, 1899, 2 F. 118. *Nicolson* v. *Munro*, 1747 M. 11, 080, where the prescription was held not to apply to a claim by a schoolmaster, was distinguished on the ground that, if he was a parochial schoolmaster, he held his appointment *aut vitam aut culpam*.

[32] Dickson, *Evidence* (3rd ed.) §490, and cases cited.

[33] *Smellie* v. *Cochrane* (*supra*).

[34] *Alcock* v. *Easson* (*supra*).

[35] *Miller* v. *Miller* (*supra*).

[36] Bell, *Principles*, §629; *Smellie* v. *Cochrane*, 1835, 13 S. 544; *Alcock* v. *Easson*, 1842, 5 D. 356; *Miller* v. *Miller*, 1898, 25 R. 995.

142. RETAILERS' ACCOUNTS AND ACCOUNTS FOR PROFESSIONAL CHARGES

"Merchantes comptes" has been interpreted as meaning the accounts of retail merchants[37] and tradesmen,[38] for goods supplied or work done, and accounts for professional and similar charges.[39] The prescription has thus been held to apply to the accounts of contractors and sub-contractors for work done in connection with building contracts,[40] of artificers such as wrights, masons and joiners,[41] of printers,[42] engravers,[43] surveyors,[44] architects,[45] solicitors,[46] surgeons and chemists,[47] advocates' clerks,[48] of the clerk to an arbitration,[49] and of a stockbroker for services connected with the promotion of a railway company.[50] The prescription has been held *not* to apply to mercantile transactions between manufacturer and merchant or merchant and merchant:[37] to a claim for commission by a mercantile agent on the purchase of goods by wholesale:[51] to an account-current between merchants in which there are goods furnished or services rendered on both sides of the account:[52] to what are in substance demands for accounting between mercantile,[53] or other agents or mandatories,[54] and

[37] *Brown* v. *Brown*, 1891, 18 R. 889, L. McLaren at p. 891; *Laing & Irvine* v. *Anderson*, 1871, 10 M. 74; *McKinlay* v. *McKinlay*, 1851, 14 D. 162, L. Fullerton at p. 164. See also *Sandys* v. *Lowden & Rowe*, 1874, 2 R. (J) 7.

[38] Erskine, iii, 7, 17; *McKay* v. *Carmichael*, 1851, 14 D. 207.

[39] Erskine, iii, 7, 17; *Wallace* v. *McKissock*, 1829, 7 S. 542; *White* v. *Caledonian Railway Co.*, 1868, 6 M. 415.

[40] *McKay* v. *Carmichael (supra)*; *Gordon* v. *James Ford & Son*, 1902, 39 S.L.R. 706; *Drysdale* v. *Birrell* (O.H.) 1904, 12 S.L.T. 120; *Blackadder* v. *Milne*, 1851, 13 D. 820, L. Fullerton at p. 829.

[41] *Gordon* v. *James Ford & Son (supra)*, L. Low at p. 707; *Drysdale* v. *Birrell (supra)*; *Bayn*, 1692 M. 11, 092; *Tweedie* v. *Williamson*, 1694 M. 11, 092.

[42] *Neill & Co.* v. *Hopkirk*, 1850, 12 D. 618.

[43] *Johnston* v. *Scott*, 1860, 22 D. 393.

[44] *Stevenson* v. *Kyle*, 1850, 12 D. 673.

[45] *Fairlie* v. *Earl of Breadalbane* (O.H.) 1894, 1 S.L.T. 601.

[46] *Richardson* v. *Merry*, 1863, 1 M. 940; *Deans* v. *Steele*, 1853, 16 D. 317; *Macandrew* v. *Hunter*, 1851, 13 D. 1111; *Campbell* v. *Shearer*, 1833, 11 S. 600; *Wallace* v. *McKissock*, 1829, 7 S. 542. The prescription applies to claims for commission on payments of money: *Scott* v. *Gregory's Trs.*, 1832, 10 S. 375; and for all normal disbursements made by a solicitor in his professional capacity (the test being what is covered by the solicitor's lien), including fees paid to counsel and witnesses: *Richardson* v. *Merry (supra)*, L. Curriehill at pp. 945-6. As to cash advances made in other capacities, see note 56 below.

[47] Erskine, iii, 7, 17; Bell, *Commentaries*, I. 348.

[48] *Fortune's Exrs.* v. *Smith*, 1864, 2 M. 1005.

[49] *Farquharson* v. *H. M. Advocate*, 1755 M. 11, 108.

[50] *White* v. *Caledonian Railway Co.*, 1868 6 M. 415.

[51] *Brown* v. *Brown*, 1891, 18 R. 889.

[52] *McKinlay* v. *Wilson*, 1885, 13 R. 210. See also *Brunton* v. *Angus*, 1822, 2 S. 54; *Boyes' Trs.* v. *Hamilton*, 1829, 7 S. 815; *Murray* v. *Wright*, 1870, 8 M. 722. *Cf. Batchelor's Trs.* v. *Honeyman*, 1892, 19 R. 903 (dealer's account for cows sold to farmer, giving credit for cash payments and for dung supplied by the farmer); *Gordon* v. *James Ford & Sons* 1902, 39 S.L.R. 706 (credit given for goods supplied by defenders); *Drysdale* v. *Birrell*. (O.H.) 1904, 12 S.L.T. 120 (credit given for goods supplied by defender), in all of which the prescription was held to apply.

[53] *McKinlay* v. *McKinlay*, 1851, 14 D. 162.

[54] *Grant* v. *Fleming*, 1881, 9 R. 257; *Waddel* v. *Morton*, 1825 4 S. 172; *Freer* v. *Peterson*,

their principals: to claims for relief by partners or joint adventurers *inter se* in respect of debts paid on behalf of the partnership:[55] to claims by a solicitor for cash advances, made, not in his capacity as a solicitor, but in the capacity of his client's factor, cashier or banker:[56] to fees charged by professional men, such as engineers[57] or railway contractors,[58] for giving expert evidence, or evidence otherwise associated with professional matters, when the giving of evidence is outside the normal sphere of their professional activities.[59] Despite earlier decisions to the contrary,[60] it is thought that the prescription applies to an account for the sale of a single article.[61]

143. COMPUTATION OF TRIENNIUM FOR ACCOUNTS

The prescriptive period with regard to the whole of a continuous account commences at the date of the last item.[62] The "last item" for this purpose means the last genuine item, and a fictitious item,[63] or an item such as a charge by a solicitor for rendering the account,[64] is disregarded for this purpose. An item, payment of which is no longer enforceable, because, for example, it is declared by statute to be unenforceable,[65] or because it has been separately paid by the debtor,[66] is also disregarded for this purpose.

1826, 4 S. 399; *Maxwell* v. *Welsh*, 1633 M. 11,084; *Butchart* v. *Mudie*, 1781 M. 11,113; *Hamilton & Co.* v. *Martin*, 1795 M. 11, 120; *Saddler* v. *McLean*, 1794 M. 11, 119. See also *Lamont, Nisbett & Co.* v. *Hamilton* (O.H.) 1904, 12 S.L.T. 624 (claim by marine insurance brokers for premiums paid on behalf of ship owners).

55 *Bland* v. *Short*, 1824, 3 S. 294.

56 *Richardson* v. *Merry*, 1863, 1 M. 940, L. Curriehill at pp. 945-6; *Ker* v. *Magistrates of Kirkwall*, 1827, 5 S. 742; *Moncrieff* v. *Durham*, 1836, 14 S. 830. See also note 46 above.

57 *Blackadder* v. *Milne*, 1851, 13 D. 820.

58 *Barr* v. *Edinburgh & Glasgow Railway Co.*, 1864, 2 M. 1250.

59 The earlier cases, such as *Walker* v. *McNair*, 1832, 10 S. 672 (see also the notes on these cases in *Blackadder* v. *Milne* at pp. 825-6), established the wider principle that the prescription does not apply to any charges of a professional man for work done, which, although he is qualified to do it, is of an unusual kind: e.g. a Scottish solicitor going to London to attend to the interests of a Scottish trade association. These cases are commented on in *White* v. *Caledonian Railway Co.*, 1868, 6 M. 415, L.P. Inglis at pp. 418-419, where it is indicated that the earlier principle should not be extended to facts other than those found in the existing decisions. *Ker* v. *Magistrates of Kirkwall* and *Moncrieff* v. *Durham* (mentioned in note 56 above) are examples of the same principle.

60 See the earlier decisions in Dickson, *Evidence* (3rd ed.) §493.

61 *Gobbi* v. *Lazzaroni*, 1859, 21 D. 801, L. Kinloch at p. 804; Dickson, *Evidence* (3rd ed.) §493.

62 Erskine, iii, 7, 17; Dickson, *Evidence* (3rd ed.) §498; Bell, *Principles*, §631; Gloag, *Contract* (2nd ed.) 743. It was held to be immaterial that the creditor, in his books, closed the account annually, and entered each year's indebtedness separately in the continuing account: *Whyte* v. *Currie*, 1829, 8 S. 154.

63 *Stewart* v. *Scott*, 1844, 6 D. 889; *Aytoun* v. *Stoddart*, 1882, 9 R. 631. A proof before answer has been allowed on the question of whether the final items were fictitious: *Ross* v. *Cowie's Executrix*, 1888, 16 R. 224.

64 *Tait & Johnston* v. *Hope's J.F.* (O.H.) 1904, 42 S.L.R. 17.

65 *Macpherson* v. *Jamieson*, 1901, 4 F. 218.

66 *Beck* v. *Learmonth*, 1831, 10 S. 81. The final item in an account was *not* disregarded merely because, after the debtor's death, it was paid by another person who was also liable for it: *Fisher* v. *Ure*, 1836, 14 S. 660.

An account is regarded as continuous if it is between the same parties,[67] and if it is not interrupted by the death of the debtor, which is regarded as closing the account,[68] or, possibly, by a change in the constitution of the creditor, such as a change of partnership,[69] or by a change in the agreed method of payment which results in the old account being closed and a new account opened.[70] An account does not cease to be continuous because its items vary in character and value,[71] or because there is a gap of three years between certain of the items,[72] provided that the employment or course of dealing has been continuous.[73]

[67] This may not be true if the final item, which alone prevents the prescription from applying, is a credit and not a debit item. See *Ramage* v. *Charteris*, 1782 M. 11, 113.

[68] Bell, *Commentaries*, I, 349; Gloag, *Contract* (2nd ed.) 743. Goods supplied to the widow or representatives are not regarded as included in the account: *Wilson* v. *Tours*, 1680 M. 11, 089; *Ormiston* v. *Hamilton*, 1709 M. 11, 093; *Granger's Exrs.* v. *Hamilton*, 1833, 11 S. 591 (*cf. Graham* v. *Stanebyres*, 1670 M. 11, 086); unless they were ordered by the deceased before his death: *Broughton* v. *Weston*, 1826, 4 S. 501.

[69] No certain rule on this point can be deduced from the decisions: see *Wotherspoon* v. *Henderson's Trs.*, 1868, 6 M. 1052, L. J-Cl. Patton at p. 1059, L. Neaves at p. 1061; *Stewart* v. *Scott*, 1844, 6 D. 889, L. Medwyn at pp. 893-4; *Barker* v. *Kippen*, 1841, 3 D. 965; *Torrance* v. *Bryson*, 1840, 3 D. 186.

[70] *Christison* v. *Knowles*, 1901, 3 F. 480.

[71] *Granger's Exrs.* v. *Hamilton*, 1833, 11 S. 591; *Fisher* v. *Ure*, 1836, 14 S. 660; *Ross* v. *Cowie's Executrix*, 1888, 16 R. 224; *Batchelor's Trs.* v. *Honeyman*, 1892, 19 R. 903; *Lees* v. *Jackson* (O.H.) 1925 S.L.T. 190.

[72] See Bell, *Commentaries*, I. 349.

[73] *Wotherspoon* v. *Henderson's Trs.*, 1868, 6 M. 1052.

CHAPTER XIII

PROOF OF MISCELLANEOUS MATTERS

144. GENERAL

The immediately preceding chapters have dealt with matters which must either be constituted in writing or which require writing for their proof. Apart from these, all matters of fact may in general be proved *prout de jure*, which means by oral or by written evidence, or by a combination of either or both of these with real evidence, or may be referred to the oath of the opponent.[1] Some of these matters, of which a more detailed discussion may be useful, are mentioned in this chapter. Proof in consistorial causes and in actions of affiliation and aliment is separately dealt with in the two following chapters.

145. CONTRACTS RELATING TO CORPOREAL MOVEABLES

These contracts include the sale, barter (permutation), hire (location), loan (commodate), pledge and deposit of corporeal moveables. Loan,[2] pledge[2] and deposit[3] have been described as real contracts,[4] because they require delivery or possession for their completion, as distinct from sale,[2] barter[2] and hire[2] which are included among the consensual contracts,[5] as being completed by interchange of consent. The distinction, however, is unimportant from the point of view of evidence, and the terms of each of these contracts may be proved *prout de jure*. The same rule applies to a contract of affreightment.[6] The rule may be different when the parties have committed the contract to writing.[7]

1 Reference to oath is dealt with at §§ **308** *et seq.*
2 Erskine, iv, 2, 20; Bell, *Principles*, §§89, 136, 196, 204.
3 *Taylor* v. *Nisbet*, 1901, 4 F. 79.
4 Bell, *Principles*, §17.
5 Bell, *Principles*, §16.
6 Gloag, *Contract* (2nd ed.) 191; *Rederi Aktiebolaget Nordstjernan* v. *Salvesen*, 1903,

146. INTROMISSIONS WITH MOVEABLES AND MONEY

As a general rule intromissions with corporeal moveables[8] and with money[9] may be proved *prout de jure*, and this applies whether it is the intromitter[10] or another person[11] who wishes to establish the intromissions. When, however, it is sought to establish that the intromitter received specific payments of money, the rules which govern proof of performance and discharge of written obligations,[12] or proof of payment of money,[13] have sometimes been held to apply, with the result that such payments have been held to be proveable only by writ or by writ or oath.[14] Apart, however, from doubts which have arisen as to the proof of particular payments or receipts, there seems little doubt that the fact that intromission has taken place may always be proved *prout de jure*.[15]

147. PARTNERSHIP AND JOINT ADVENTURE

Partnership[16] and joint adventure[17] are consensual contracts[18] which do not require writing for their constitution, and they may be proved *prout de jure*, or inferred from facts and circumstances, which are proved *prout de jure*. This rule may not apply to proof of the terms of the contract,[19] or of a variation of it,[20] when the contract has been reduced to writing.[21] When a partner is alleged to hold property on behalf of the firm, the question of whether this is a trust which may be proved only by the writ or oath of the partner concerned, has already been discussed.[22] Partnerships in which some of the partners have only a limited liability must be registered,[23] and while writing is not essential for their constitution, such contracts are usually reduced to writing.

6 F. 64, at p. 75 (rev. 1905, 7 F. (H.L.) 101); Dickson, *Evidence* (3rd ed.) §558. This is included in Bell, *Commentaries*, I, 342, as one of the obligations *in re mercatoria*, for which see §§ **105** *et seq.*

[7] See §§ **96** *et seq.*

[8] Dickson, *Evidence* (3rd ed.) §589; *Mitchell* v. *Berwick*, 1845, 7 D. 382.

[9] *Struthers* v. *Smith*, 1913 S.C. 1116; *Russell's Trs.* v. *Russell*, 1885, 13 R. 331; *Glasgow Royal Infirmary* v. *Caldwell*, 1857, 20 D. 1.

[10] *Chalmers* v. *Lord Craigievar*, 1628 M. 12, 368; *Struthers* v. *Smith* (*supra*).

[11] *Russell's Trs.* v. *Russell* (*supra*); *Glasgow Royal Infirmary* v. *Caldwell* (*supra*).

[12] See §§ **125, 126.**

[13] See § **127.**

[14] *Robison* v. *Rae*, 1830, 8 S. 541; *Mackenzie* v. *Elibank*, 1709 M. 12,372. *Cf. Wishart* v. *Arthur*, 1671 M. 9,978; *Baillie* v. *Menzies*, 1711 M. 9,990. See also *Cooper* v. *Donald*, 1827, 6 S. 213.

[15] Dickson, *Evidence* (3rd ed.) §593.

[16] Erskine, iii, 3, 1; Bell, *Principles*, §361; Gloag, *Contract* (2nd ed.) 191; *Morrison* v. *Service*, 1879, 6 R. 1158; *Lindsay* v. *Inland Revenue*, 1933 S.C. 33.

[17] Bell, *Principles*, §392; *Logan* v. *Brown*, 1824, 3 S. 12; *Fergusson* v. *Graham's Trs.*, 1836, 14 S. 871.

[18] Bell, *Principles*, §16.

[19] *Clark* v. *Clark's Trs.*, 1860, 23 D. 74.

[20] *Barr's Trs.* v. *Barr & Shearer*, 1886, 13 R. 1055.

[21] As to this subject in general, see §§ **96** *et seq.*, §§ **240** *et seq.*

[22] See § **123**, sub-para. (f).

[23] Limited Partnerships Act, 1907 (7 Edw. VII c. 24), s. 5.

G

148. MANDATE

(a) **The Rule.** This is one of the consensual contracts[25] which does not require writing for its constitution, and which may be proved *prout de jure*, or inferred from facts and circumstances which are proved *prout de jure*.[26] The rule applies even when the mandate relates to heritage,[27] except when it is for the purpose of executing a conveyance.[28]

(b) **Examples of the Rule.** Proof *prout de jure* has been allowed of a mandate to pay money belonging to the mandant by way of gift to a third party,[29] to destroy the mandant's will,[30] to pay the mandant's debts,[31] to invest money belonging to the mandant,[32] to purchase shares in a ship on the mandant's behalf,[33] to draw, accept or indorse bills of exchange,[34] and, in the case of a solicitor, to write letters on behalf of his client from which an acknowledgment of loan may be inferred.[35]

(c) **Circumstances from which Mandate Inferred.** A mandate to draw, accept or indorse bills of exchange has been inferred from the mandant's practice of honouring the mandatory's signature,[36] or from the custom of a particular trade which ought to be known to the mandant.[37] A mandate to receive payment of a debt, and to discharge it, may be inferred from circumstances,[38] as, for example, from the mandant's previous course of dealing,[39] but such an inference does not arise from the fact that the document of debt is in the hands of the alleged mandatory merely for the purpose of collecting the interest upon it.[40] A mandate to borrow money on behalf of a principal was held not to be inferable from the fact that the mandatory was the

---

[25] Bell, *Principles*, §16.

[26] Erskine, iii, 3, 31; Bell, *Principles*, §216; Gloag, *Contract* (2nd ed.) 184. Mandate is included in Bell, *Commentaries*, I, 342, among the examples of obligations *in re mercatoria*, as to which see §§ **105** *et seq.*

[27] *Horne* v. *Morrison*, 1877, 4 R. 977; *Whyte* v. *Lee*, 1879, 6 R. 699. See also *Caithness Flagstone Co.* v. *Sinclair*, 1880, 7 R. 1117, L.P. Inglis at p. 1120; 1881, 8 R. (H.L.) 78, L. Watson at p. 90.

[28] See sub-para. (d) below.

[29] *Mackenzie* v. *Brodie*, 1859, 21 D. 1048.

[30] *Bonthrone* v. *Ireland*, 1883, 10 R. 779.

[31] *Ross* v. *Cowie's Executrix*, 1888, 16 R. 224; *Boyd* v. *Millar*, 1933 S.N. 106; 1934 S.N. 7.

[32] *Burt* v. *Laing*, 1925 S.C. 181.

[33] *McConnachie* v. *Geddes*, 1918 S.C. 391.

[34] Dickson, *Evidence* (3rd ed.) §571; Bell, *Principles*, §§230, 321; Bell, *Commentaries*, I, 424; *Anderson* v. *Buck & Holmes*, 1841, 3 D. 975; *Swinburne* v. *Western Bank of Scotland*, 1856, 18 D. 1025.

[35] *Dryburgh* v. *Macpherson* (O.H.) 1944 S.L.T. 116.

[36] *Swinburne* v. *Western Bank of Scotland* (*supra*), L. J-Cl. Hope at p. 1028. *Cf. Ross, Skolfield & Co.* v. *State Line Steamship Co.*, 1875, 3 R. 134. The inference is not so readily drawn when the parties are not traders; *Lawson* v. *Matthew*, 1823, 2 S. 443.

[37] *Anderson* v. *Buck & Holmes* (*supra*).

[38] Dickson, *Evidence* (3rd ed.) §572.

[39] *Forbes' Exrs.* v. *Western Bank of Scotland*, 1854, 16 D. 807, L. J-Cl. Hope at p. 809.

[40] *Duncan* v. *River Clyde Trs.*, 1851, 13 D. 518; 1853, 15 D. (H.L.) 36; *Forbes' Exrs.* v. *Western Bank of Scotland* (*supra*).

principal's general agent, with written authority to draw and accept bills.[41] The mandate of a partner to bind the firm is regulated by statute.[42] An advocate appearing in a litigation is presumed to have a mandate from his client.[43] The presumption can be rebutted during the course of the litigation only by the production of a disclaimer by the client,[44] but a decree obtained against the client may be reduced, and in the course of the action of reduction the presumption may be rebutted by proof.[45] A solicitor's mandate to appear in a litigation may be inferred from his possession of the service copy of the summons or petition which has been served upon the client,[46] by the client's appearance in court in company with the solicitor,[47] by the signature of one of the pleadings by the client,[48] and, as authority for proceeding with diligence, by the client's sending to the solicitor, without directions, a bill of exchange.[49] When a solicitor's mandate is challenged by the opponent while the litigation is in progress, however, the court usually ordains the solicitor to produce a written mandate by the client.[50]

(d) Exceptions to the Rule. The rule probably does not apply when the mandate is in writing,[51] or, in practice, when the mandatory is authorised to execute a conveyance of heritage.[52] When a litigant is ordained to sist a mandatory, a written mandate,[53] signed by the litigant,[54] must be produced if it is called for by the opponent.

(e) Mandate to Vote at Meeting. The mandatory of a creditor in a sequestration must exhibit a written mandate signed by the creditor in order to be entitled to vote,[55] and the proxy of a member of a limited company, in order that he may vote on a poll at a meeting of the company, must be appointed by a written instrument signed by the person entitled to

---

41 *Sinclair, Moorhead & Co.* v. *Wallace & Co.*, 1880, 7 R. 874.
42 Partnership Act, 1890 (53 & 54 Vict. c. 39), ss. 5-8.
43 Stair, i, 12, 12; Erskine, iii, 3, 33.
44 *Oyston* v. *Turnbull*, 1875, 13 S.L.R. 69.
45 *Cowan* v. *Farnie*, 1836, 14 S. 634, L. Mackenzie at p. 645; *Young* v. *List & McHardie* 1862, 24 D. 587.
46 *Muir* v. *Stevenson*, 1850, 12 D. 512.
47 *Hepburn* v. *Tait*, 1874, 1 R. 875.
48 *Campbell* v. *Gray*, 1821, 1 S. 37.
49 *McDonald* v. *Kelly*, 1821, 1 S. 102.
50 *Ferguson, Davidson & Co.* v. *Paterson & Dobbie*, 1898, 1 F. 227; *Fischer & Co.* v. *Andersen*, 1896, 23 R. 395, L. Young at p. 399.
51 *Thompson* v. *Parochial Board of Inveresk*, 1871, 10 M. 178; 1876, 3 R. (H.L.) 1. As to this subject in general, see §§ **96** *et seq.*
52 This is not a true exception, but in practice a purchaser could not be compelled to accept a conveyance executed by an agent, or a title which included such a conveyance as a link, unless it was supported by a probative mandate from the proprietor or by a decree of court. As to leases, see Rankine, *Leases* (3rd ed.) 46.
53 *Gunn & Co.* v. *Couper*, 1871, 10 M. 116.
54 Maclaren, *Court of Session Practice*, 432; *Elder* v. *Young*, 1854, 16 D. 1003. *Cf. Bonny* v. *Gillies*, 1829, 8 S. 13, where a mandate was held insufficient, partly because it was neither solemnly executed nor holograph.
55 Bankruptcy (Scotland) Act, 1913 (3 & 4 Geo. V. c. 20), s. 59; Goudy, *Bankruptcy* (4th ed.) 192.

vote.[56] The question as to whether a proxy at a meeting, other than those abovementioned, need produce a written mandate, does not appear to have been considered by the courts, but, if produced, such a mandate need not be formally executed or holograph.[57]

149. DONATION—GENERAL

There is a strong presumption against donation. This presumption, and the standard of proof required to rebut it, are dealt with in an earlier chapter,[58] where mention is also made of the contrary presumptions which sometimes arise. It has been said that the presumption against donation *inter vivos* is stronger than the presumption against donation *mortis causa*.[59] In order to establish donation, both the intention to donate (*animus donandi*) and the conveyance, transfer or delivery of the subject of the gift, must be proved.[60]

150. ANIMUS DONANDI

Despite an earlier conflict of judicial opinion on the matter, it is well settled that the intention to make a gift either *inter vivos*[61] or *mortis causa*[62] may be proved *prout de jure*. The evidence may consist of the terms of the writing which conveys or transfers the subject of the gift,[63] or of other written evidence,[64] in which the intention to donate is expressed or implied; or of oral evidence of statements of intention made by the alleged donor;[65] or of facts and circumstances, including the actings of the alleged donor, coupled with written or oral evidence indicating an intention to donate.[66] The writings requiring most consideration by the courts in this connection have been deposit receipts made payable to the depositor or the alleged donee, or to the survivor of them, or to the alleged donee alone. The exact terms in which the deposit receipt has been taken by the depositor is always

[56] Companies Act, 1948 (11 & 12 Geo. VI. c. 38), Sched. 1, Table A, regs. 68-73.

[57] *Thompson* v. *Parochial Board of Inveresk*, 1871, 10 M. 178; 1876, 3 R. (H.L.) 1.

[58] See § 61.

[59] *Grant's Trs.* v. *McDonald*, 1939 S.C. 448, L. Normand at p. 460; *Sharp* v. *Paton*, 1883, 10 R. 1000, L. Deas at p. 1008. *Cf. Macpherson's Executrix* v. *Mackay*, 1932 S.C. 505, L.P. Clyde at p. 513.

[60] *Brownlee's Executrix* v. *Brownlee*, 1908 S.C. 232, L.P. Dunedin at p. 240; *Hubbard* v. *Dunlop's Trs.* (H.L.) 1933 S.N. 62.

[61] Dickson, *Evidence* (3rd ed.) §158.

[62] *Morris* v. *Riddick*, 1867, 5 M. 1036.

[63] e.g. *Linton* v. *Inland Revenue*, 1928 S.C. 209; *Newton* v. *Newton*, 1923 S.C. 15, L. Hunter at p. 22; *Ballantyne's Trs.* v. *Ballantyne's Trs.*, 1941 S.C. 35.

[64] e.g. the terms of the donor's testamentary settlements, if they are consistent with the intention of making the alleged gift. See *Crosbie's Trs.* v. *Wright*, 1880, 7 R. 823, L.P. Inglis at pp. 825-6. *Cf. Henderson* v. *McCulloch*, 1839, 1 D. 927, L. Gillies at p. 929; *Heron* v. *McGeoch*, 1851, 14 D. 25, L. Wood (Ordinary) at p. 28, where the terms of the testamentary settlements showed the improbability of a gift being intended. For another example of written evidence, see *Grant's Trs.* v. *McDonald*, 1939 S.C. 448.

[65] *Crosbie's Trs.* v. *Wright* (*supra*); *Anderson's Trs.* v. *Webster*, 1883, 11 R. 35; *Sharp* v. *Paton*, 1883, 10 R. 1000.

[66] *Wright's Exrs.* v. *City of Glasgow Bank*, 1880, 7 R. 527; *Crosbie's Trs.* v. *Wright* (*supra*); *Anderson's Trs.* v. *Webster* (*supra*).

relevant,[67] and may be an important element in the court's decision,[68] when construed in the light of the surrounding circumstances,[69] but the mere fact that the alleged donee is one of the persons to whom the money is payable does not of itself indicate an intention to donate, since his name may have been inserted only for the purpose of administrative convenience.[70] When oral evidence is relied upon, the intention to donate may be proved by the evidence of the donees, corroborated by the evidence of other witnesses or by facts and circumstances, but a donation may not be proved by the evidence of the donees alone.[71] Facts which have been held to throw doubt upon an alleged intention to donate are:—that the alleged gift comprised the whole or the greater part of the donor's estate;[72] that the alleged donees did not inform the donor's relatives of his ill health and prevented contact between them,[73] or supplied the donor with excessive quantities of drink;[74] and that the alleged donee was in the habit of assisting in the administration of the donor's affairs.[75]

151. CONVEYANCE, TRANSFER OR DELIVERY OF SUBJECT OF GIFT

(a) **General.** The kind of evidence by which delivery may be proved depends upon the nature of the gift, and the mode of transferring ownership appropriate to it.

(b) **Heritage and Incorporeal Rights.** A gift of heritable property may be proved only by a conveyance which has been solemnly executed[76] and completed by infeftment of the donee.[77] A gift of shares in a limited com-

---

67 *Macdonald* v. *Macdonald*, 1889, 16 R. 758, L. J-Cl. Macdonald at p. 764; *Crosbie's Trs.* v. *Wright* (*supra*), L.P. Inglis at p. 826, L. Deas at p. 830, L. Mure at p. 832, L. Shand at p. 833.

68 *Crosbie's Trs.* v. *Wright*, 1880, 7 R. 823, L.P. Inglis at p. 826, L. Mure at p. 832; *Macdonald* v. *Macdonald* (*supra*), L. J-Cl. Macdonald at p. 764; *Macpherson's Executrix* v. *Mackay*, 1932 S.C. 505; *Aiken's Exrs.* v. *Aiken*, 1937 S.C. 678.

69 *Macdonald* v. *Macdonald* (*supra*), L. Lee at p. 768.

70 *Durie* v. *Ross*, 1871, 9 M. 969, L. J-Cl. Moncreiff at p. 972.

71 *Crosbie's Trs.* v. *Wright* (*supra*), L.P. Inglis at p. 826; *Macpherson's Executrix* v. *Mackay* (*supra*), L.P. Clyde at p. 513.

72 *Sharp* v. *Paton*, 1883, 10 R. 1000, L.P. Inglis at p. 1007, L. Shand at p. 1008; *Lord Advocate* v. *Galloway*, 1884, 11 R. 541, L.P. Inglis at p. 550, L. Shand at p. 552. The apparent improbability of such a gift may be explained by the donor's state of health: *Lord Advocate* v. *McCourt*, 1893, 20 R. 488; *Grant's Trs.* v. *McDonald*, 1939 S.C. 448, L.P. Normand at p. 460.

73 *Sharp* v. *Paton* (*supra*).

74 *Ross* v. *Mellis*, 1871, 10 M. 197.

75 *Henderson* v. *McCulloch* (*supra*) (deposit receipt); *Heron* v. *McGeoch* (*supra*) (deposit receipt); *Morrison* v. *Forbes*, 1890, 17 R. 958 (deposit receipt). This was regarded as supporting the probability that the deposit receipt was taken payable to the alleged donee, not as a gift to him, but for the administrative convenience of the alleged donor.

76 *Morris* v. *Riddick*, 1867, 5 M. 1036, L.P. Inglis at p. 1041. See also *Martin's Trs.* v. *Martin* (O.H.) 1887, 24 S.L.R. 484, L. McLaren at p. 485, 2nd column. A holograph conveyance is an adequate alternative but raises practical difficulties. See § **91**, note 13, § **93**, note 31.

77 *Linton* v. *Inland Revenue*, 1928 S.C. 209; *Cameron's Trs.* v. *Cameron*, 1907 S.C. 407, L.P. Dunedin at p. 413. See also *Newton* v. *Newton*, 1923 S.C. 15. Infeftment of the

pany may be proved only by a transfer in favour of the donee and insertion of his name as owner in the company's register.[78] A gift of other incorporeal rights, when the mode of transfer is not regulated by statute, may in general be proved only by a written assignation delivered to the donee,[79] or intimated to the creditor as the equivalent of delivery.[80]

(c) Corporeal Moveables. Delivery of corporeal moveables, including money, may be proved *prout de jure*.[81] What must be proved is that the donor has divested himself of the subject of the gift and has put it in the control of the donee[82] or of another person on the donee's behalf,[83] and this general rule applies whether the gift is alleged to be *inter vivos* or *mortis causa*.[84] Physical delivery, however, has not been held essential in circumstances which made it impossible or unnecessary, as, for example, when the subject of the gift was already in the donee's possession or under his control.[85] The amount of evidence needed to prove delivery depends upon the nature of the gift and the circumstances in which it is made, and also upon the strength of the evidence of *animus donandi*, and it has been said that "weak evidence of delivery may be eked out by unmistakeable evidence of *animus donandi*."[86]

(d) Deposit Receipts. While the same general rule governs a gift of money on deposit receipt as that which governs a gift of cash, its application is necessarily different. A deposit receipt indicates by its terms the person to whom the money will be paid by the bank, and the terms of the receipt, therefore, may themselves establish whether delivery has, or has not, taken place. If a depositor takes a deposit receipt payable to himself alone, the fact that he delivers the document to the alleged donee does not establish delivery of the money, since the sole right to obtain payment from the bank remains with the depositor.[87] If, at the other extreme, a depositor takes a

granter of the deed as trustee for the donee has been held not to be an effective donation: *Cameron's Trs.* v. *Cameron* (*supra*); but doubts have been expressed about this decision: Gloag, *Contract* (2nd ed.) 74; *Carmichael's Executrix* v. *Carmichael*, 1920 S.C. (H.L.) 195, L. Shaw at p. 205.

[78] *Inland Revenue* v. *Wilson*, 1927 S.C. 733; 1928 S.C. (H.L.) 42; *Lord Advocate* v. *Galloway* 1884, 11 R. 541. See also § **116.**

[79] As to the need for delivery, see *Connell's Trs.* v. *Connell's Tr.*, 1955 S.L.T. 125. As to transfer of incorporeal rights in moveables generally, see § **116.**

[80] *Jarvie's Tr.* v. *Jarvie's Trs.*, 1887, 14 R. 411, L.P. Inglis at p. 416; Bell, *Principles*, §1462.

[81] *Milne* v. *Grant's Exrs.*, 1884, 11 R. 887, L. Young at p. 890; *Sharp* v. *Paton*, 1883, 10 R. 1000, L.P. Inglis at p. 1006.

[82] *Hubbard* v. *Dunlop's Trs.* (H.L.) 1933 S.N. 62; *Brownlee's Executrix* v. *Brownlee*, 1908 S.C. 232, L.P. Dunedin at p. 240; *Milne* v. *Grant's Exrs.* (*supra*), L. Young at p. 890; *McNicol* v. *McDougall*, 1889, 17 R. 25, L. Young at p. 28.

[83] *Hutchieson's Executrix* v. *Shearer*, 1909 S.C. 15; *National Bank of Scotland* v. *Mackie's Trs.* (O.H.) 1905, 13 S.L.T. 383.

[84] *Macpherson's Executrix* v. *Mackay*, 1932 S.C. 505, L.P. Clyde at p. 513; *McNicol* v. *McDougall* (*supra*), L. Young at p. 28.

[85] *Gibson* v. *Hutchison*, 1872, 10 M. 923 (deposit receipt already in donee's name); *Smith* v. *Smith's Trs.*, 1884, 12 R. 186 (document in possession of husband, the proper custodier of the deeds of his wife, the donee).

[86] *Macpherson's Executrix* v. *Mackay* (*supra*), L.P. Clyde at pp. 514-515.

[87] *McNicol* v. *McDougall*, 1889, 17 R. 25, L. Young at p. 28, L. J-Cl. Macdonald at p. 29.

deposit receipt payable to the alleged donee alone,[88] or to another person as trustee for the alleged donee,[89] delivery will normally be regarded as proved, even if the deposit receipt itself is retained by the depositor.[90] In principle there seems to be no reason why a deposit receipt, blank endorsed by the depositor, and handed to the alleged donee, should not have the same effect.[91] Between these two extremes is the deposit receipt which is payable either to the depositor or to the alleged donee, or to the survivor. If *inter vivos* donation is alleged in relation to such a deposit receipt, the depositor must be proved to have surrendered possession of it to the donee, or to another person on his behalf, with the practical result that, in spite of the terms of the receipt, the donee alone can demand payment from the bank.[92] If, however, donation *mortis causa* is alleged, the court in a number of cases has upheld donation although the depositor retained the deposit receipt in his possession until his death. The reason given for these decisions was either that the donee was told where the receipt was kept and how it could be obtained,[93] or, in the earlier cases, simply because the terms of the deposit receipt themselves implied some form of *de præsenti* delivery.[94]

152. FRAUD AND OTHER CRIMES OR DELICTS

Both in criminal and in civil causes these may be proved both by parole and by written evidence.[95] "The gates of justice are opened wide in the tracing of fraud."[96] This rule applies in civil causes even where, apart

---

88 *Thomson's Exr.* v. *Thomson*, 1882, 9 R. 911; *Sharp* v. *Paton*, 1883, 10 R. 1000, L.P. Inglis at p. 1006; *British Linen Co.* v. *Martin*, 1849, 11 D. 1004. See also *Gibson* v. *Hutchison* (*supra*).

89 *Boucher's Trs.* v. *Boucher's Trs.* (O.H.) 1907, 15 S.L.T. 157. Delivery does not take place if the depositor takes the deposit receipt payable to himself as trustee for the alleged donee: *Graham's Trs.* v. *Graham*, 1957 S.L.T. 43.

90 *Thomson's Exr.* v. *Thomson* (*supra*); *British Linen Co.* v. *Martin* (*supra*); *Boucher's Trs.* v. *Boucher's Trs.* (*supra*); *Graham's Trs.* v. *Graham* (*supra*), L.P. Clyde at p. 50.

91 *Grant's Trs.* v. *McDonald*, 1939 S.C. 448. In *Sharp* v. *Paton* (*supra*), where the deposit receipt was blank endorsed, the decision, which negatived donation, seems to have proceeded upon failure to prove *animus donandi*, and not upon failure to prove delivery.

92 *Watt's Trs.*, 1869, 7 M. 930. In *Durie* v. *Ross*, 1871, 9 M. 969, delivery was proved, but the alleged donee failed to prove *animus donandi*.

93 *Aiken's Exrs.* v. *Aiken*, 1937 S.C. 678.

94 *Crosbie's Trs.* v. *Wright*, 1880, 7 R. 823; *Macfarlane's Trs.* v. *Miller*, 1898, 25 R. 1201; *Scott's Trs.* v. *Macmillan*, 1905, 8 F. 214. (*Cf. Dinwoodie's Executrix* v. *Carruther's Exr.*, 1895, 23 R. 234.) It should be noted that in *Crosbie's Trs.* v. *Wright*, the leading case in this series, the deposit receipt was found on the depositor's death, not in his possession, but in the house of the donees, and there was what was described by Lord President Clyde in *Macpherson's Executrix* v. *Mackay*, 1932 S.C. 505, at p. 514, as "the equivalent of delivery." Lord McLaren in *Macfarlane's Trs.* v. *Miller*, at pp. 1211-1212, doubted the soundness of the principle attributed to *Crosbie's Trs.* v. *Wright*. *Gibson* v. *Hutchison*, 1872, 10 M. 923, and *Blyth* v. *Curle*, 1885, 12 R. 674, which were cited by L.P. Robertson in *Macfarlane's Trs.* v. *Miller*, at p. 1208, as supporting the principle attributed to *Crosbie's Trs.* v. *Wright*, both seem to be distinguishable from it.

95 Stair, iv, 3, 2 (6); Erskine, iv, 2, 21; Dickson, *Evidence* (3rd ed.) §630; *Foggo* v. *Hill*, 1840, 2 D. 1322, L. Fullerton at p. 1333; *Taylor* v. *Nisbet*, 1901, 4 F. 79, L. Moncreiff at p. 86.

96 *Tennent* v. *Tennent's Trs.*, 1868, 6 M. 840, L. Ardmillan at p. 874.

from allegations of fraud, proof would be restricted to writ or to writ or oath, as, for example, where there is a challenge of a heritable title[97] or of a contract relating to heritage[98] or of any other written contract,[99] or in a declarator of trust to which the Act, 1696, would normally apply,[1] or in proof of performance or discharge of a written obligation.[2] The standard of proof[3] for establishing allegations of fraud in civil causes, and the presumptions[4] and contrary presumptions[4] which may arise in connection therewith, have been discussed earlier.

153. AGREEMENTS FOR SETTLEMENT OF A LITIGATION

An agreement for the settlement of a pending litigation may be proved *prout de jure*,[5] and this applies even when the litigation relates to heritable property.[6] When, however, the parties choose to record their bargain in writing, as, for example, in a joint minute, parole evidence of a subsequent oral variation of the written contract is inadmissible.[7] The sanction of the court, or the interponing of its authority, is not necessary in order that a settlement of an action may be binding upon the parties.[8] An agreement not to raise an action may also usually be proved *prout de jure*,[9] but if an action, or the defence to an action, is founded upon a prior agreement which is held to be innominate and unusual,[10] or upon a prior discharge[11] or renunciation[12] of an obligation constituted in writing, or upon a prior gratuitous obligation,[13] proof by writ or oath may be necessary.

154. MARRIAGE—GENERAL

Since July 1, 1940, a marriage may be regularly constituted in one of two ways.[14] It may be solemnised by a minister of religion (*in facie ecclesiæ*),

[97] *Marshall* v. *Lyell*, 1859, 21 D. 514, L. J-Cl. Inglis at p. 521.
[98] Bell, *Principles*, §2257.
[99] Gloag, *Contract* (2nd ed.) 365.
[1] See § 123, sub-para. (d).
[2] See § 126, sub-para. (b).
[3] See § 85.
[4] See § 70.
[5] *Gow* v. *Henry*, 1899, 2 F. 48; *Love* v. *Marshall*, 1872, 10 M. 795; *Thomson* v. *Fraser*, 1868, 7 M. 39; *Jaffrey* v. *Simpson*, 1835, 13 S. 1122.
[6] *Anderson* v. *Dick*, 1901, 4 F. 68; *Torbat* v. *Torbat's Trs.* (O.H.) 1906, 14 S.L.T. 830. See also *Dewar* v. *Ainslie*, 1892, 20 R. 203. For the position when the agreement provides for the execution of a severable contract, which is itself an *obligatio literis*, see *Cook* v. *Grubb*, 1963 S.L.T. 78.
[7] *Hamilton & Baird* v. *Lewis*, 1893, 21 R. 120; *Union Canal Co.* v. *Johnston*, 1834, 12 S. 304: 1835, 1 Sh & McL. 117.
[8] *Gow* v. *Henry* (*supra*).
[9] e.g. *Downie* v. *Black*, 1885, 13 R. 271 (slander). See also *Mackintosh* v. *Mackintosh*, 1928 S.C. 83.
[10] e.g. *McFadzean's Exr.* v. *Robert McAlpine & Sons*, 1907 S.C. 1268. As to innominate and unusual contracts generally, see § 129.
[11] See §§ 125, 126.
[12] See § 128, sub-para. (a).
[13] See § 130.
[14] For further details, see Walton, *Husband and Wife* (3rd ed.) 22 *et seq.*

before two witnesses, after publication either of banns or of a statutory notice of the intended marriage by a registrar,[15] or with the licence of a sheriff.[16] It may also be contracted, in accordance with statutory provisions,[17] by declaration before a registrar in the presence of two witnesses, after publication by a registrar of notice of the intended marriage[15] or with the licence of a sheriff.[16] Since July 1, 1940, marriage may not be contracted by two of the irregular forms of marriage—declaration *de presenti* and promise *subsequente copula*,[18] but since it may still be necessary to prove marriages so contracted before July 1, 1940, a brief reference to the methods of proving them is made in a later paragraph.[19] It seems probable that marriage may still be proved to have been constituted after July 1, 1940, by cohabitation with habit and repute, an irregular form of marriage which is also referred to in a later paragraph.[20] Actions of declarator of marriage are mentioned incidentally in the following paragraphs. Proof in consistorial causes, which include actions of declarator of marriage, are dealt with generally in the next chapter.

155. REGULAR MARRIAGE

The fact that a marriage by a minister of religion, or before a registrar,[21] has been duly celebrated, may be proved *prout de jure*.[22] The law requires in each case that the marriage shall be registered, the first within three days of the ceremony,[23] and the second as soon as possible thereafter.[24] A duly authenticated extract of the entry in the register is admissible and sufficient evidence of the entry.[25] The entry in the register does not by itself establish the facts which it records,[26] but it is an adminicle of evidence, and when formal proof of a marriage is required, as in an undefended consistorial action, the courts habitually accept, as sufficient proof of the marriage, the evidence of the pursuer and the production of an authenticated extract of the entry in the register, which is identified by the pursuer as relating to the

---

15 Marriage Notice (Scotland) Act, 1878 (41 & 42 Vict. c. 43); Marriage Act, 1939 (2 & 3 Geo. VI. c. 33); Marriage (Scotland) Act, 1942 (5 & 6 Geo. VI. c. 20); Marriage (Scotland) Act, 1956 (4 & 5 Eliz. II. c. 70).

16 Marriage (Scotland) Act, 1939 (2 & 3 Geo. VI. c. 34), s. 2.

17 Marriage (Scotland) Act, 1939 (2 & 3 Geo. VI. c. 34), s. 1.

18 Marriage (Scotland) Act, 1939 (2 & 3 Geo. VI. c. 34), s. 5.

19 See § **156.**

20 See § **157.**

21 For the statutory requirements as to banns, notice, sheriff's licence and witnesses, see the previous paragraph.

22 This has always been true both of regular marriage and of irregular marriage by *de presenti* declaration of consent. See Stair, iv, 45, 19 and More's Notes, xiii; Erskine, i, 6, 5; Bell, *Principles*, §1518; Dickson, *Evidence* (3rd ed.) §543; *Walker* v. *McAdam*, 1813, 1 Dow, 148, L.Ch. Eldon at p. 185.

23 Registration of Births, etc. (Scotland) Act, 1854 (17 & 18 Vict. c. 80), s. 46. See also s. 47.

24 Marriage (Scotland) Act, 1939 (2 & 3 Geo. VI. c. 34), s. 1 (2).

25 Registration of Births, etc. (Scotland) Act, 1854 (17 & 18 Vict. c. 80), s. 58; Registration of Births, etc. (Scotland) Amendment Act, 1910 (10 Edw. VII & 1 Geo. V. c. 32), s. 1.

25 Dickson, *Evidence* (3rd ed.) §1204. See also *Stewart* v. *Stewart* (O.H.) 1930 S.L.T. 363.

marriage in question.[27] The validity of the ceremony may be challenged because of failure to comply with the statutory formalities, but, if the marriage has been registered, its validity may not be questioned in any legal proceedings on the ground that the person by whom it was celebrated or solemnised was not competent or qualified to do so.[28] The validity of the marriage may also be challenged because of a legal impediment, such as the nonage or prior subsisting marriage of one of the parties,[29] or on the ground that it was entered into under essential error, or that consent to the marriage in words but not in intention was procured by fraud or force.[30] It is thought, however, that when a regular marriage is proved to have been duly solemnised and registered, the presumption *omnia rite et sollenniter acta praesumuntur*[31] applies, so that the onus of proof rests upon the person challenging the marriage to establish its nullity.[32] There is an exception to this rule when the pursuer admits a fact, such, for example, as his own prior marriage, which itself establishes that the marriage on which he founds was a nullity, or from which its nullity must be presumed.[33] In contrast with an irregular marriage, where the matrimonial intention of the parties must be proved by the person alleging the marriage, the solemnisation of a regular marriage gives rise to a presumption that marriage was truly intended by the parties to the ceremony.[34] The view has been expressed that this presumption may be rebutted by proof that both parties took part in the ceremony without a real intention to marry,[35] and proof of such averments, before answer, has recently been allowed,[36] but there seems to be no case in Scotland where a regular marriage was annulled for this reason.[37] It

---

[27] As to extracts from the registers of the Dominions and Colonies and of foreign countries, see Walton, *Husband and Wife* (3rd ed.) 57, and the Evidence (Foreign, Dominion and Colonial Documents) Act, 1933 (23 Geo. V. c. 4), s. 1 (applied to Belgium by S.R. & O, 1933 No. 383, to France by S.R. & O. 1937, No. 515, and to Australia by S.R. & O. 1938, No. 739).

[28] Marriage (Scotland) Act, 1939 (2 & 3 Geo. VI. c. 34), s. 4.

[29] e.g. *A.B.* v. *C.B.* (O.H.) 1957 S.C. 415. See Walton, *Husband and Wife*, (3rd ed.) 5 *et seq.*

[30] *Ibid.* 45 *et seq.*

[31] As to this presumption generally, see § **60.** In England, subject to certain exceptions, there is a presumption in favour both of the formal and of the essential validity of a marriage which is proved to have been celebrated. See Phipson, *Evidence* (9th ed.) 700; Cross, *Evidence* (1958) 97, 98.

[32] See, for example, *C.B.* v. *A.B.*, 1885, 12 R. (H.L.) 36.

[33] *Sharp* v. *Sharp*, 1898, 25 R. 1132; *McDonald* v. *McDonald* (O.H.) 1924 S.L.T. 200.

[34] *Jolly* v. *McGregor*, 1828, 3 W. & S. 85, E. of Lauderdale at p. 179; *Lockyer* v. *Sinclair*, 1846, 8 D. 582, L. J-Cl. Hope at p. 602; *Robertson* v. *Steuart*, 1874, 1 R. 532, L. Deas at p. 667; *Lang* v. *Lang*, 1921 S.C. 44, L. J-Cl. Scott Dickson at p. 54.

[35] Fraser, *Husband* and *Wife*, I, 434-436; Walton, *Husband and Wife* (3rd ed.) 38. Lord Eldon in *Jolly* v. *McGregor* (*supra*), at p. 190, preferred to express no opinion on the point.

[36] *Orlandi* v. *Castelli* (O.H.) 1961 S.C. 113.

[37] *Jolly* v. *McGregor* (*supra*), which was mentioned by Lord Fraser (*Husband and Wife*, I, 431, 436) as the only example in Scotland, seems not in fact to have been an example, because it was decided by the House of Lords on the footing that the marriage was irregular, the certificate of proclamation of banns being manifestly false. See E. of Lauderdale at p. 179, E. of Eldon at p. 195, L.C. Lyndhurst at p. 202. See, however, *Orlandi* v. *Castelli* (*supra*).

seems clear that the validity of a regular marriage cannot be disturbed by proof that only one of the parties behaved in this way.[38]

156. IRREGULAR MARRIAGES—DECLARATION DE PRESENTI AND PROMISE SUBSEQUENTE COPULA

(a) **General.** Marriages constituted in either of these ways before July 1, 1940, may still be proved. If the marriage has been registered on the warrant of a sheriff following a judicial enquiry,[39] or after a decree of declarator by the Court of Session establishing the marriage,[40] the presumption of validity applies to it as in the case of a regular marriage.[41] If formal proof of such a marriage is necessary, as in an undefended consistorial action, the evidence of the pursuer and the identification by him or her, as relative to the marriage, of an authenticated extract of the entry in the register, and of an extract of any decree which may have been pronounced, is normally accepted as sufficient. If the validity of such a marriage is challenged, the onus of proof rests upon the challenger.[42] When, however, the marriage has not been registered, the person who desires to establish it must prove that all the essentials of a valid marriage were present, either in an action of declarator of marriage in the Court of Session, or in the course of a criminal prosecution for bigamy,[43] or of a civil action,[44] to which the proof of the marriage is incidental. This is dealt with in the following sub-paragraphs.

(b) **Declaration de Presenti.** The proof, both of the express interchange of consent and of the genuineness of the intention to marry, is *prout de jure*.[45] It is incompetent to refer the question to the oath of the other party.[46] If the interchange of consent was oral, it may be proved by the evidence of the persons who heard it,[47] the evidence of one of the parties to the marriage, corroborated by evidence of facts and circumstances, having been held in some cases to be sufficient.[48] If the interchange of consent was

---

[38] Fraser, *Husband and Wife*, I, 436.
[39] See Marriage (Scotland) Act, 1916 (6 Geo. V. c. 7). This Act was repealed as no longer necessary by the Marriage (Scotland) Act, 1939 (2 & 3 Geo. VI. c. 34), s. 8. As to the enquiry before the sheriff, and its purpose, see *Courtin* v. *Elder*, 1930 S.C. 68, L. Ormidale at p. 75, L. Anderson at p. 76.
[40] Such a decree must be intimated to the Registrar-General by the Principal Clerk of Session in order that the marriage may be registered: Marriage (Scotland) Act, 1939 (2 & 3 Geo. VI. c. 34), s. 6.
[41] See § **155.**
[42] See, for example, *Polack* v. *Shiels* (O.H.) 1912, 2 S.L.T. 329.
[43] *Reid* v. *H.M. Advocate*, 1934 J.C. 7.
[44] *Turnbull* v. *Wilsons and Clyde Coal Co.*, 1935 S.C. 580.
[45] Stair, iv, 45, 19 and More's Notes, xiii; Erskine, i, 6, 5; Bell, *Principles*, §1518; Dickson, *Evidence* (3rd ed.) §543; *McAdam* v. *Walker*, 1813, 1 Dow 148, L.C. Eldon at p. 185, L. Redesdale at p. 189.
[46] *Longworth* v. *Yelverton*, 1867, 5 M. (H.L.) 144.
[47] e.g. *Robertson* v. *Steuart*, 1874, 1 R. 532: 1875, 2 R. (H.L.) 80; *Davidson* v. *Davidson*, 1921 S.C. 341.
[48] *Dysart Peerage Case*, 1881, 6 App. Cas. 489, at p. 538; *Petrie* v. *Petrie*, 1911 S.C. 360; *Polack* v. *Shiels* (O.H.) 1912, 2 S.L.T. 329.

written, the writings, unless executed in accordance with the statutory formalities, must be proved to have been subscribed by the parties to the marriage.[49] An earlier interchange of consent may also be inferred from proof of the subsequent actings and admissions of the parties.[50] In contrast with a regular marriage, where the genuineness of the intention to marry is presumed, the genuineness of the apparent interchange of consent in an irregular marriage must be proved. Such proof must usually be founded upon an inference from the terms and the circumstances in which consent was apparently interchanged, or from the actings of the parties before and after the alleged marriage, or from both.[51]

(c) Promise Subsequente Copula. The opinion has been expressed that the promise must be proved by the writ of the other party to the alleged marriage, and that reference to oath is no longer competent,[52] but there is no recent judicial support for this view.[53] The writ relied upon is not inadmissible merely because it was written for the purpose of the litigation.[54] The copula, which, unless the pursuer was the defender's mistress,[55] is assumed to have occurred on the faith of the promise, may be proved *prout de jure*.[56]

157. IRREGULAR MARRIAGE—COHABITATION WITH HABIT AND REPUTE

This form of marriage is constituted neither by the cohabitation of the man and woman, nor by the fact that they hold themselves out, and are habitually regarded, as husband and wife, but by the tacit interchange of consent to marry which is inferred from these facts.[57] The facts from which the inference is drawn may be proved *prout de jure*.[58]

The Marriage (Scotland) Act, 1939,[59] which declared that no irregular marriage by declaration *de presenti* or by promise *subsequente copula* should be valid after its commencement, made no mention of an irregular marriage inferred from cohabitation with habit and repute. When the cohabitation

---

[49] *Forster* v. *Forster*, 1872, 10 M. (H.L.) 68; *Mackenzie* v. *Stewart*, 1848, 10 D. 611, L. Mackenzie at p. 638, L. Fullerton at p. 640.
[50] See, for example, *Leslie* v. *Leslie*, 1860, 22 D. 993; *Aitchison* v. *Incorporation of Solicitors*, 1838, 1 D. 42, L. Corehouse at p. 55.
[51] *Fleming* v. *Corbet*, 1859, 21 D. 1034, L. J-Cl. Inglis at p. 1044; *Imrie* v. *Imrie*, 1891, 19 R. 185; *Dunn* v. *Dunn's Trs.*, 1930 S.C. 131, L. Sands at p. 146, L. Blackburn at pp. 151-2, L. Morison at p. 159. See also the decisions cited in § **155**, note 34.
[52] Walton, *Husband and Wife* (3rd ed.) 29.
[53] See § **317**, sub-para. (b).
[54] *Lindsay* v. *Lindsay* (*supra*).
[55] See Walton, *Husband and Wife* (3rd ed.) 31.
[56] Dickson, *Evidence* (3rd ed.) 548.
[57] *Campbell* v. *Campbell*, 1867, 5 M. (H.L.) 115, at pp. 135, 140; *De Thoren* v. *Wall*, 1876, 3 R. (H.L.) 28, at pp. 29, 33; *Nicol* v. *Bell*, 1954 S.L.T. 314, L. Mackintosh at p. 326; *Lapsley* v. *Grierson*, 1845, 8 D. 34, L. J-Cl. Hope at p. 47.
[58] Bell, *Principles*, §1518; Dickson, *Evidence* (3rd ed.) §544. For a fuller discussion of the nature of the facts which must be proved, see Walton, *Husband and Wife* (3rd ed.), 34-37.
[59] (2 & 3 Geo. VI. c. 34), s. 5. The date of commencement is July 1, 1940: Marriage (Scotland) Act, 1939 (Commencement) Order, 1940.

commenced before July 1, 1940, there is no doubt that marriage may still be proved to have been constituted in this way.[60] It has been generally assumed that, even after July 1, 1940, a man and woman may become married by a tacit interchange of consent which is manifested by their cohabitation and by holding themselves out as married persons.[61]

[60] See, for example, *Nicol* v. *Bell*, 1954 S.L.T. 314.
[61] Walton, *Husband and Wife* (3rd ed.) 24; Gloag and Henderson, *Introduction to the Law of Scotland* (6th ed.) 605; *A.B.* v. *C.D.* (O.H.) 1957 S.C. 415.

CHAPTER XIV

PROOF IN CONSISTORIAL CAUSES

158. GENERAL

Consistorial actions are actions of declarator of marriage, of declarator of nullity of marriage, of declarator of legitimacy and bastardy, of separation *a mensa et thoro*, and of divorce,[1] actions of adherence,[2] an action of reduction of a decree of divorce,[3] and any other action affecting the status of the parties with regard to marriage.[3] This chapter deals with the specialties of proof and evidence which apply to these actions. It also deals more fully with the application to them of the general rules of evidence which have been mentioned elsewhere.

159. NECESSITY FOR EVIDENCE—TAKING AND RECORDING OF EVIDENCE

A decree in a consistorial cause may affect the status, not only of the parties to the action, but also of their children, and of other persons whom they may have purported to marry. It is the policy of the law, therefore, to prevent such a decree being obtained, by agreement between the parties, on what may be improper or insufficient grounds. In the Court of Session a decree may not be pronounced in a consistorial cause,[4] even if the action is undefended, until the grounds of action are substantiated by sufficient evidence.[5] In the sheriff court there is no equivalent statutory provision,[6]

[1] Court of Session Act, 1830 (11 Geo. IV. & 1 Will, IV. c. 69), ss. 33, 36.
[2] Court of Session Act, 1850 (13 & 14 Vict. c. 36), s. 16.
[3] *Acutt* v. *Acutt*, 1935 S.C. 525.
[4] For the meaning of "consistorial cause," see § **158.**
[5] Court of Session Act, 1830 (11 Geo. IV. & 1 Will. IV. c. 69), s. 36; Court of Session Act, 1850 (13 & 14 Vict. c. 36), s. 16 (adherence). As to reference to oath in a consistorial cause, see §§ **156,** sub-paras. (b) (c), **317.**
[6] The only statutory reference to such actions in the sheriff court is contained in Sheriff Courts (Scotland) Act, 1907 (7 Edw. VII. c. 51), Sch. I, Rule 23 (as amended by 2 & 3 Geo. V. c. 28). This merely excludes *inter alia* consistorial causes from a new procedure, introduced by the Act, whereby decree in absence may be obtained by a written crave

but in practice the rule applicable to the Court of Session is applied, and decrees in actions of separation and aliment and adherence and aliment are not pronounced, even when the action is undefended, until the grounds of action are substantiated by sufficient evidence.[7] The evidence in consistorial causes in the Court of Session must be recorded in full,[8] and in practice it is similarly recorded in the sheriff court. It is competent to grant a commission to examine witnesses outside Scotland even though their evidence may be the whole evidence adduced in the case.[9]

160. BURDEN AND STANDARD OF PROOF IN ACTIONS FOUNDED UPON ADULTERY, SODOMY OR BESTIALITY

The burden of proof rests upon the pursuer. So universal is this rule that even if the defender admits adultery on record and the only defence is condonation, the pursuer must lead at the proof and establish adultery before the question of condonation arises.[10] In most civil causes the burden of proof may be discharged on a balance of probabilities,[11] but adultery in an action of divorce or of separation and aliment must be proved beyond reasonable doubt.[12] Although a defender's guilt of sodomy or bestiality in an action of divorce may be proved by an extract conviction,[13] it is thought that his guilt may also be proved by evidence of the facts, whether or not the defender has been convicted, and that, when such evidence is led, proof must be beyond reasonable doubt as in a criminal cause.[14]

161. JUDICIAL ADMISSIONS

(a) **Express.** In a consistorial cause[15] decree may not be granted solely because the pursuer's averments are judicially admitted.[16] In this respect a consistorial cause differs from other civil causes.[17] There must be

endorsed on the initial writ, and apparently leaves the pursuer free to enrol and move for decree in open court. It would seem that in actions for aliment or for custody of children only, proof is not an essential prerequisite to a decree: *Christie* v. *Christie*, 1919 S.C. 576.

7 *Grant* v. *Grant*, 1908, 24 Sh.Ct.Rep. 114.
8 Conjugal Rights (Scotland) Amendment Act, 1861 (24 & 25 Vict. c. 86), s. 13; Rules of Court, 1948, Rule 133.
9 *A.B.* v. *C.B.* (O.H.) 1911, 1 S.L.T. 264; *Lawson* v. *Lawson*, 1930 S.C. 18. See §§ 400 *et seq.*
10 *Paterson* v. *Paterson*, 1938 S.C. 251, L. Mackay at p. 256, L. J-Cl. Aitchison at p. 272. See also *Bird* v. *Bird*, 1931 S.C. 731.
11 See § 85.
12 *Burnett* v. *Burnett*, 1955 S.C. 183, L.P. Clyde at pp. 186-7; *Currie* v. *Currie* (O.H.) 1950 S.C. 10, at pp. 14-15; Walton, *Husband and Wife* (3rd ed.) 58. See also *Gaskill* v. *Gaskill* [1921] P. 425, L.C. Birkenhead at p. 433; *Ginesi* v. *Ginesi* [1948] P. 179; *Preston-Jones* v. *Preston-Jones* [1951] A.C. 391, L. Simonds at p. 401, L. Oaksey at p. 409, L. Morton of Henryton at p. 412, L. MacDermott at pp. 414-415.
13 Divorce (Scotland) Act, 1938 (1 & 2 Geo. VI. c. 50), s. 1 (2).
14 As to the presumption of innocence of crime, see § 70.
15 For a list of consistorial causes, see § 158.
16 *Smith* v. *Smith*, 1929 S.C. 75, L. J-Cl. Alness at p. 82, L. Anderson at pp. 87-88; *Muirhead* v. *Muirhead*, 1846, 8 D. 786.
17 As to these, see § 48, sub-para. (a).

"sufficient evidence,"[18] but an early *obiter dictum*,[19] which suggested that, in assessing the sufficiency of the evidence, a judicial admission must be completely disregarded, is no longer approved.[20] Such an admission may help a pursuer to prove his case,[20] and may enable him to obtain a decree in his favour upon evidence which, by itself, would have been regarded as insufficient.[21] The evidence and admissions of the parties alone, however, are insufficient. There must in addition be some corroborative evidence from other witnesses. Decree of divorce for adultery was refused when the only evidence was that of the pursuer, supported by a judicial admission of adultery by the defender, although the pursuer's evidence, which demonstrated that he could not have been the father of the defender's child, was believed, and the defender's admission of adultery was clearly not collusive.[22] The value to be given to an admission, and the extent to which independent corroborative testimony is needed, depend upon the nature of the cause and the apparent risk of collusion which is associated with it, and in some cases very slight independent evidence may be enough.[23] There is less reason to suspect collusion when an action is strenuously defended.[24] It has been said that there is little risk of collusion in actions of declarator of bastardy and of marriage, and in actions of separation and aliment, whereas in actions of divorce and of declarator of nullity the risk is high.[24] With regard to actions of declarator of marriage, however, collusion may be present when the interests of third parties claiming to be the wife and legitimate children of the defender are involved,[25] and there is at least one reported case, where, although no such interests were present,[26] the defender was as anxious as the pursuer that decree should be granted.[27] With regard to actions of separation and aliment, the fact that decrees therein may now be regarded as sufficient proof of adultery or cruelty in a subsequent action of divorce,[28] may have increased the risk of collusion. An admission by a defender or a co-defender may be founded upon only against the party making it.[29]

(b) Implied. The failure of a defender to enter appearance and to lodge defences has been said to constitute an implied admission of the

---

[18] Court of Session Act, 1830 (11 Geo. IV. & 1 Will. IV. c. 69), s. 36. And see § **159.**

[19] *Muirhead* v. *Muirhead* (*supra*), L. Mackenzie at p. 786.

[20] *Macfarlane* v. *Macfarlane*, 1956 S.C. 472, L.P. Clyde at p. 481, L. Sorn at p. 483; Dickson, *Evidence* (3rd ed.) §284.

[21] *Macfarlane* v. *Macfarlane* (*supra*), L. Mackintosh (Ordinary) at p. 476; *Smith* v. *Smith*, 1929 S.C. 75, L. Moncrieff (Ordinary) at p. 77, L. J-Cl. Alness at p. 80; *Barnes* v. *Barnes*, 1935 S.C. 646. In *Smith* v. *Smith* and *Barnes* v. *Barnes* the admission was extrajudicial, but in *Macfarlane* v. *Macfarlane* the same principle was regarded as applicable to both kinds of admission.

[22] *Macfarlane* v. *Macfarlane* (*supra*).

[23] Dickson, *Evidence* (3rd ed.) §284; *Macfarlane* v. *Macfarlane* (*supra*), L. Sorn at pp. 483-484.

[24] Dickson, *Evidence* (3rd ed.) §284.

[25] Dickson, *Evidence* (3rd ed.) §284, note **(d).**

[26] *Lindsay* v. *Lindsay*, 1927 S.C. 395, L. J-Cl. Alness at p. 398.

[27] *Lindsay* v. *Lindsay* (*supra*), L. Anderson at p. 399.

[28] Divorce (Scotland) Act, 1938 (1 & 2 Geo. VI. c. 50), s. 4 (2). And see § **164.**

[29] See § **162.**

pursuer's averments, and to afford some degree of corroboration of the evidence led on his behalf.[30] These judicial dicta, however, have been disapproved,[31] and it is thought that the sufficiency or insufficiency of the evidence must be determined by the same considerations in undefended as in defended actions.

162. EXTRAJUDICIAL ADMISSIONS—GENERAL

The general rules regarding extrajudicial admissions in civil causes, which are mentioned elsewhere,[32] apply also to consistorial causes. In consistorial causes, however, unlike other civil causes, the court is concerned, not only with the relevancy, authorship, interpretation and evidential value of an admission, but also with the possibility that it may have been made collusively, in order to assist the pursuer to obtain an unwarranted decree. When clearly free from collusion, however, an admission by a defender may be an important element in the pursuer's proof,[33] and even an admission in a letter written after service of the summons, and for the purposes of the litigation, has been so regarded.[34] Other examples of written admissions, which have been accepted by the court, include a torn-up draft letter from a defender to a co-defender,[35] a letter written by the defender to the co-defender which had been stolen by the pursuer,[36] and entries in a defender's private diary.[37] Evidence of an extrajudicial admission is not necessarily inadmissible because it has not been made the subject of express averment.[38] As with judicial admissions,[39] an extrajudicial admission alone is an insufficient basis for a decree, but it may provide adequate support for evidence which, by itself, would be insufficient.[40] An admission by a defender is not corroborated by another admission by him, even if it is made in a different way.[41] An extrajudicial admission by a party, as distinct from a party's evidence *in causa*, is admissible only against the person who makes it. So an admission by the defender, made outwith the co-defender's presence, of adultery committed with the co-defender, is not admissible in

---

[30] *McDougall* v. *McDougall*, 1927 S.C. 666, L. Anderson at p. 670; *Smith* v. *Smith* (*supra*), L. J-Cl. Alness at p. 80.

[31] *Barr* v. *Barr*, 1939 S.C. 696, L.P. Normand at p. 700, L. Moncrieff at p. 701, L. Carmont at p. 702. *Cf.* Walton, *Husband and Wife* (3rd ed.) 65. As to the failure of a defender to lead evidence, or to give evidence explaining conduct which may be suspicious, as the foundation of an implied admission, see § **163**.

[32] See §§ **29, 30-34, 38**. See also § **2**, sub-para. (b).

[33] Fraser, *Husband and Wife*, II, 1170; Dickson, *Evidence* (3rd ed.) §301; *Fullerton* v. *Fullerton*, 1873, 11 M. 720.

[34] *Lindsay* v. *Lindsay*, 1927 S.C. 395 (declarator of marriage); *Smith* v. *Smith*, 1929 S.C. 75; *Barnes* v. *Barnes*, 1935 S.C. 646 (divorce for adultery).

[35] *Watson* v. *Watson*, 1934 S.C. 374.

[36] *Rattray* v. *Rattray*, 1897, 25 R. 315; *MacColl* v. *MacColl*, 1946 S.N. 80, S.L.T. 312.

[37] *Creasey* v. *Creasey*, 1931 S.C. 9.

[38] *MacColl* v. *MacColl*, 1948 S.C. 500 (oral admission).

[39] See § **161**.

[40] *Mackay* v. *Mackay*, 1946 S.C. 78. And see § **161**, note 21.

[41] *Mackay* v. *Mackay* (*supra*).

evidence against the latter, and similarly an admission by a co-defender is not admissible in evidence against a defender.[42]

163. IMPLIED EXTRAJUDICIAL ADMISSIONS

The same general principles apply to consistorial as to other civil causes.[43] What should perhaps properly be regarded as an unusual kind of implied admission occurred in an action of divorce for adultery, when the only evidence adduced by the pursuer was of regular meetings at lunch time between the defender and the co-defender in the pursuer's house during his absence, and latterly without his knowledge. The meetings for some years were concerned with the discussion of trade-union business, in which the defender and the co-defender had a common interest, but they continued for about a year after this common interest had ended. Although there was no evidence of familiarities between the defender and the co-defender, their false denial in the witness box of the continuation of the meetings after their initial purpose had ended, and their consequent inability to provide an innocent explanation for this continuation, was regarded as raising an inference that a guilty relationship had developed between them, and that adultery had taken place.[44] It has been said that this decision should be applied only in circumstances which are not only similar but are virtually identical,[45] and, in general, the failure of a defender to give evidence, or to provide an innocent interpretation of circumstances proved by the pursuer, is not to be regarded as an implied admission of guilt which may be used by the pursuer to supplement his otherwise insufficient evidence.[46]

164. CONVICTIONS AND DECREES IN OTHER CAUSES

As in other civil causes[47] a judicial admission in an earlier criminal cause, such as a plea of guilty to assault or to a charge of rape, or a judicial admission of paternity in an action of affiliation and aliment, may be founded upon by the other party in a subsequent consistorial cause as an extrajudicial admission. The fact, however, that a conviction has occurred or a decree has been pronounced in an earlier cause, is, as a general rule, irrelevant and inadmissible in evidence in a later civil cause.[47] In one case[48] the court appears to have admitted evidence of an earlier conviction of rape as being relevant to the question of the defender's adultery, although it is not clear from the report to what extent the decision was based upon this

---

[42] *Creasey* v. *Creasey*, 1931 S.C. 9; *Swapp* v. *Swapp* (O.H.) 1931 S.L.T. 199; *Rattray* v. *Rattray*, 1897, 25 R. 315, L. Trayner at p. 319, L. Moncreiff at p. 321.
[43] See § 34.
[44] *McInnes* v. *McInnes*, 1954 S.C. 396. A similar inference was drawn in *Hall* v. *Hall*, 1958 S.C. 206. See also § 168, where both these cases are referred to.
[45] *Burnett* v. *Burnett*, 1955 S.C. 183, L. Carmont at p. 188.
[46] *Bird* v. *Bird*, 1931 S.C. 731. As to whether a failure to lodge defences may be regarded as an implied admission, see § 161, sub-para. (b).
[47] See § 32.
[48] *Galbraith* v. *Galbraith* (O.H.) 1902, 9 S.L.T. 346.

evidence.[49]   Further, in two decisions,[50] evidence that a decree in an action of affiliation and aliment had been pronounced against the defender was regarded as relevant and admissible in a subsequent action of divorce for adultery.   It seems impossible to reconcile these cases with the principle that, apart from the statutory exceptions mentioned below and *res judicata*,[51] a court must have regard only to the evidence before it, and ought not to be influenced by the decision of another court pronounced on evidence of which it has no knowledge.

There are certain statutory exceptions in consistorial causes to the general rule mentioned above.   In any action of divorce, the pursuer in which has previously been granted a decree of separation *a mensa et thoro* upon the same or substantially the same facts as those averred in support of the action of divorce, the court may treat the decree of separation as sufficient proof of the adultery or cruelty in respect of which the decree was granted.[52] The pursuer must take the oath of calumny and give evidence.[52]   When the action is founded upon cruelty, however, the test to be applied is whether the pursuer can with safety to life and health live with the defender at the date when the case is heard, and the earlier decree of separation, accordingly, while relevant, is not necessarily conclusive as to the relationship between the parties at the date of the proceedings for divorce.[53]   When an action of divorce is founded upon sodomy or bestiality, the defender's guilt of sodomy or bestiality is held to be proved if an extract of a conviction therefor in any part of the United Kingdom is produced, and its application to the defender is admitted or proved.[54]

165. PARTIES AS WITNESSES

The parties to a consistorial cause and their spouses are competent and probably compellable witnesses,[55] but, like other witnesses, neither they nor an alleged paramour are liable to be asked or bound to answer any question tending to show that he or she has been guilty of adultery, unless the witness has already given evidence in the same proceeding in disproof of his or her adultery.[56]   Although a contrary opinion has been expressed,[57] more recent judicial dicta appear to support the proposition that decree in a consistorial cause may not be granted solely on the evidence of the pursuer

[49] See Lord Moncrieff's comments on the case in *McDougall* v. *McDougall*, 1927 S.C. 666, at p. 669.
[50] *Mathieson* v. *Mathieson* (O.H.) 1914, 1 S.L.T. 511; *McDougall* v. *McDougall* (*supra*), L. Anderson at p. 671.
[51] See §§ **50, 51.**
[52] Divorce (Scotland) Act, 1938 (1 & 2 Geo. VI. c. 50), s. 4 (2).   The provision applies to a decree of separation granted before the passing of the Act: *Wilson* v. *Wilson*, 1939 S.C. 102.
[53] *McFarlane* v. *McFarlane* (O.H.) 1951 S.C. 530; *Wilson* v. *Wilson* (*supra*).
[54] Divorce (Scotland) Act, 1938 (1 & 2 Geo. VI. c. 50), s. 1 (2).   And see § **160.**
[55] See § **354.**
[56] See §§ **345,** sub-para. (c), **354.**
[57] *Burrell* v. *Burrell*, 1947 S.C. 569, L. Keith at p. 579: *cf.* L. Mackintosh (Ordinary) at p. 572.

and the defender,[58] but the point has not been authoritatively decided. The practice of calling the defender as the first witness for the pursuer on the question of adultery, in an undefended action of divorce, has been criticised.[59] Despite earlier dicta to the contrary, it is admissible to lead the evidence of the spouses to establish that, although they shared a bed, intercourse between them did not occur.[60]

166. IDENTIFICATION OF DEFENDER

When the defender in a consistorial cause is not present at the proof, and it is necessary that he should be identified as the person to whom the evidence of the witnesses refers, this may be done by producing and proving the authenticity of a photograph, and showing it to the witnesses.[61] The court no longer insists upon the defender being ordered to appear, and, if necessary, apprehended.[62]

167. CORROBORATION—EVIDENCE OF SIMILAR ACTS

(a) **Adultery.** The general rules with regard to corroboration[63] apply also to consistorial causes. Thus the uncorroborated evidence of one witness cannot prove adultery,[64] but a number of witnesses each speaking to a single act of adultery between the defender and another person, whether the other person is the same[65] or different[66] on each occasion, may corroborate each other. Similarly, the evidence of a single witness to an act of adultery with a co-defender may be sufficiently corroborated by evidence of his attempted adultery or indecent conduct with another woman.[67] It is thought, however, that corroboration of a single witness in these cases is afforded only if the separate acts are similar in character, committed in similar circumstances or in a common locus, and owe their source and development to the underlying fact that, during the relevant period, the defender was abandoning himself to a mode of life which was inconsistent with his matrimonial duty.[68] The admissibility of evidence of collateral but similar acts for the purpose of attributing an adulterous significance to the actings founded upon, or as throwing light upon the conduct of the defender or his relationship with the co-defender, has been discussed earlier[69] as a relaxation in consistorial causes

---

58 *Macfarlane* v. *Macfarlane*, 1956 S.C. 472, L.P. Clyde at p. 482, L. Carmont at p. 482, L. Sorn at p. 484.
59 *Chatman* v. *Chatman* (O.H.) 1944 S.C. 494.
60 *Lennie* v. *Lennie*, 1948 S.C. 466.
61 Lewis, *Evidence*, 281; Walton, *Husband and Wife* (3rd ed.) 301.
62 See *Grieve* v. *Grieve*, 1885, 12 R. 969.
63 See §§ **381** *et seq.*
64 *Robertson* v. *Robertson*, 1888, 15 R. 1001; *Wilson* v. *Wilson*, 1898, 25 R. 788.
65 Dickson, *Evidence* (3rd ed.) §1808; *Murray* v. *Murray*, 1847, 9 D. 1556.
66 Dickson, *Evidence* (3rd ed.) §1808; *Whyte* v. *Whyte*, 1884, 11 R. 710, L. Lee (Ordinary) at p. 711 (approved on appeal).
67 *Whyte* v. *Whyte* (*supra*); *Wilson* v. *Wilson* (O.H.) 1955 S.L.T. (Notes) 81.
68 *Moorov* v. *H.M. Adv.*, 1930 J.C. 68, L. J-G. Clyde at pp. 73-74, L. Sands at p. 89. See also Hume, *Crimes*, II, 385; Alison, *Criminal Law*, II, 552.
69 See § **16,** sub-para. (b).
70 *Walker* v. *Walker*, 1953 S.C. 297; *Tullis* v. *Tullis*, 1953 S.C. 312.

of the general rule which makes such evidence inadmissible. It may some-times have to be distinguished from the value of such evidence as corroboration.

(b) Cruelty. A similar principle applies to proof of cruelty. If an isolated assault is founded upon, the evidence of the pursuer must be corroborated by other evidence relating specifically to it. A course of conduct, however, described by a pursuer, which includes a number of assaults and related incidents, if they all occur during a relatively short space of time and are attributable to some common cause or stimulus, may be sufficiently corroborated by the evidence of witnesses who speak only to some of the individual incidents. The individual incidents may for this purpose be regarded as manifestations of a continuing underlying cause, such, for example, as the defender's jealousy or intemperance or uncon-trollable temper. If against the background of the parties' married life these incidents form an apt and coherent whole, the requirements of the law as to corroboration may be satisfied, even if some of the incidents are spoken to by only one witness.[70]

168. CIRCUMSTANTIAL EVIDENCE OF ADULTERY

The general principles of circumstantial evidence, which are mentioned earlier,[71] apply also to proof of adultery in actions of divorce and separation and aliment. While direct evidence of adultery is sometimes obtainable, the court is usually asked to find adultery proved as an inference from facts and circumstances.[72] As to whether an inference of adultery arises from a defender's visits to a brothel depends upon the surrounding circumstances and the character and mode of life of the persons concerned.[73] Such an inference arises if the defender is proved to have contracted venereal disease, and intercourse with the pursuer as a possible cause is excluded.[74] Adultery is most commonly proved by evidence that the defender and co-defender shared a bed or bedroom in circumstances which exclude any other reasonable inference, or of opportunity following upon an interchange of familiarities, or expressions of passionate attachment, which lead to a moral certainty that advantage was taken of the opportunity when it occurred. Each case must be decided upon its own facts by reference to the dispositions of the persons involved as disclosed by their proved actions, there being no rigidly normal standard by which the actions of all human beings may be judged.[75]

The cases which have caused most difficulty are those in which there has been a long, and possibly indiscreet, association between a defender and a co-defender, with frequent opportunities for adultery, but with no evidence of familiarities or other indications of the existence of a passionate attach-ment. There can be a close friendship between a man and a woman without

---

[71] See §§ 8 et seq.
[72] *Walker* v. *Walker*, 1871, 9 M. 1091.
[73] See *Edward* v. *Edward*, 1879, 6 R. 1255; *Marshall* v. *Marshall*, 1881, 8 R. 702.
[74] Walton, *Husband and Wife* (3rd ed.) 60-61.
[75] See *Bennet Clark* v. *Bennet Clark*, 1909 S.C. 591, L. Kinnear at p. 609.

an immoral or guilty passion,[75] and this has been the consideration which weighed with the court in some of the reported decisions.[76] In these cases the background was regarded as being neutral, in the sense that it was consistent both with an innocent and with a guilty interpretation of the conduct of the parties, so that without evidence of familiarities the court was unable to accept a sinister interpretation of the association.[77] In other cases, however, the proved circumstances of the association, and of the opportunities available for adultery, have in themselves satisfied the court that a sexual attraction must have existed, which would inevitably result in adultery when opportunity occurred.[78] In the two cases last cited the fact that the defender and the paramour denied some of the suspicious meetings which were proved to have occurred, and were therefore unable to provide an innocent explanation of them, was regarded by the court as helping to cast a sinister light upon the association.[79]

169. INFERENCES FROM PERIOD OF GESTATION

It is sometimes possible to prove adultery as an inference from the fact that a wife has given birth to a child of which the husband could not be the father. In this connection it may be necessary to consider the length of the period of human gestation in order to ascertain whether conception could have occurred at a time when the husband had access to the wife. The older authorities accepted for this purpose arbitrary periods of six lunar months as the minimum and ten (probably calendar[80]) months as the maximum,[81] but this rule has been departed from. While the courts are regarded as having judicial knowledge of the normal period of gestation,[82] the question of whether a clearly abnormal period is a possible one is decided in each case in the light of the medical evidence led and the maturity or otherwise of the child at birth. When the period diverges largely from the normal, the burden of proving adultery or illegitimacy is more easily discharged.[83] Some of the cases in which the matter has been considered are noted below.[84] On a

---

[76] *Bennet Clark* v. *Bennet Clark (supra)*; *Ross* v. *Ross*, 1930 S.C. (H.L.) 1; *Burnett* v. *Burnett*, 1955 S.C. 183.

[77] See *Hall* v. *Hall*, 1958 S.C. 206, L. J-Cl. Thomson at p. 207.

[78] *Hall* v. *Hall (supra)*; *McInnes* v. *McInnes*, 1954 S.C. 396.

[79] *Hall* v. *Hall (supra)*, L. J-Cl. Thomson at p. 207; *McInnes* v. *McInnes (supra)*, L. J-Cl. Thomson at p. 406, L. Patrick at p. 408, L. Mackintosh at p. 410: *cf.* L. Birnam at p. 413. For the facts of *McInnes* v. *McInnes*, and another comment on this point, see § 163.

[80] Dickson, *Evidence* (3rd ed.) §136.

[81] Stair, iii, 3, 42; Erskine, i, 6, 50.

[82] *Williamson* v. *McClelland*, 1913 S.C. 678, at p. 680; *Preston-Jones* v. *Preston-Jones*, [1951] A.C. 391, at pp. 401, 406, 407, 412, 419.

[83] *Preston-Jones* v. *Preston-Jones (supra)*, at pp. 403, 419-420.

[84] Scottish Cases. *Currie* v. *Currie* (O.H.) 1950 S.C. 10; *McIntosh* v. *McIntosh*, 1947 S.N. 23; *Jamieson* v. *Dobie*, 1935 S.C. 415; *Doherty* v. *Doherty* (O.H.) 1922 S.L.T. 245; *Gray* v. *Gray* (O.H.) 1919, 1 S.L.T. 163; *Williamson* v. *McClelland (supra)*; *McDonald* v. *Main*, 1897, 34 S.L.R. 332; *Cook* v. *Rattray*, 1880, 8 R. 217; *Pitcairn* v. *Smith*, 1872, 9 S.L.R. 608. The earlier cases are given in Dickson, *Evidence* (3rd ed.) §§136-137. English Cases. *Preston-Jones* v. *Preston-Jones (supra)*; *Re S.B.* [1949] Ch. 108; *M-T* v. *M-T and Official Solr.* [1949] P. 331; *Hadlum* v. *Hadlum* [1949] P. 197; *Wood* v. *Wood* [1947] P. 103; *Clark* v. *Clark* [1939] P. 228; *Gaskill* v. *Gaskill*, [1921] P. 425.

question of whether marital intercourse did or did not take place during any period, the evidence of the spouses is admissible, and this and the question of their compellability is mentioned later.[85]

[85] See § **354.**

CHAPTER XV

PROOF IN ACTIONS OF AFFILIATION AND ALIMENT

170. GENERAL

In an action of affiliation and aliment, as in other actions, the initial onus of proof rests upon the pursuer,[1] and it must be discharged by sufficient evidence.[2] But since the alleged father of the child is not the husband of the mother, there is no presumption of paternity to assist the pursuer. Because of this, and of the consequent difficulty of obtaining sufficient evidence of paternity, some relaxation of the rules of evidence has always been allowed to a pursuer in such an action.[3] This chapter is mainly concerned with the methods whereby corroboration of the pursuer's evidence may be obtained. She herself is usually the most important witness in her own behalf, and the quantity and quality of the evidence required for her corroboration depends upon the impression formed by the court of her credibility. If her credibility is in doubt, she can succeed only if the corroborative evidence is so trustworthy and so cogent as to remove that doubt. It must satisfy the court of the probability of the truthfulness of her evidence and of the facts and circumstances from which the defender's paternity is inferred. If, however, the court believes the pursuer, the corroborative evidence necessary for a finding in her favour may be correspondingly less weighty both in quantity and quality.

171. OPPORTUNITY FOR INTERCOURSE

Evidence that the parties had opportunities for intercourse at or about the relevant times, while helpful to the pursuer's case, is not in itself sufficient corroboration of her evidence,[4] unless the circumstances or the localities of the opportunities are such as themselves to raise an inference that inter-

---

[1] *McBayne* v. *Davidson*, 1860, 22 D. 738; *Young* v. *Nicol*, 1893, 20 R. 768.
[2] *McKinven* v. *McMillan*, 1892, 19 R. 369; *Havery* v. *Brownlee*, 1908 S.C. 424, L. J-Cl. Macdonald at p. 425.
[3] Before the passing of the Evidence Act, 1853 (16 Vict. c. 20), although the parties to most actions were not allowed to give evidence, in an action of affiliation and aliment the pursuer was allowed, by her own evidence on oath, to supplement a *semiplena probatio*. See, for example, *Mann* v. *Forrest*, 1850, 12 D. 1090.
[4] *Dawson* v. *McKenzie*, 1908 S.C. 648; *Gray* v. *Marshall*, 1875, 2 R. 907.

course occurred,[5] as, for example, clandestine meetings at unreasonable hours or in suspicious circumstances.[6] Opportunity, to be of positive assistance to the pursuer, must amount to something more than the fact that the parties both resided in the same town or village.[7]

172. ACTS OF INTERCOURSE OTHER THAN THOSE FOUNDED UPON

(a) Between the Parties. Evidence of acts of intercourse between the parties, other than those alleged to have resulted in pregnancy, is admissible, and may be relevant as throwing light on the probable relationship between the parties at the date of the conception of the child.[8] This is a relaxation of the general rule[9] which makes evidence of similar acts inadmissible. An act of intercourse, which is admitted or proved to have occurred either before or after the probable date of conception, may sometimes afford sufficient corroboration of the pursuer's evidence, if opportunity at the date of conception is also proved. Whether it in fact affords this corroboration must depend upon the whole circumstances of the case, including the relationship between the parties, the nature and character of the opportunities open to them, the length of time between the act and the date of conception, and the particular circumstances in which the intercourse took place.[10] When the act of intercourse occurs *before* the date of conception, and meetings between the parties continue thereafter, ordinary experience is said to have shown that intercourse, once commenced, will probably be repeated when opportunity for it is afforded,[11] and very little further corroboration will be required.[12] The position is different when the act of intercourse occurs *after* the date of conception.[13] In some early decisions it was said that if intercourse occurred within the period of gestation, and there was opportunity at the time of conception, little or no further corroboration was required.[14] This is not now accepted as a general rule,[15] although intercourse very soon after the probable date of conception may throw a significant light on the relationship between the parties at the relevant date.[16] In general, such an act of intercourse will corroborate the pursuer only if

---

[5] *Dawson* v. *McKenzie (supra)*, L.P. Dunedin at p. 649, L. Kinnear at p. 651.

[6] *Gray* v. *Marshall (supra)*, L. J-Cl. Moncreiff at p. 908.

[7] *Buchanan* v. *Finlayson*, 1900, 3 F. 245, L. Trayner at p. 251.

[8] *Lawson* v. *Eddie*, 1861, 23 D. 876; *Ross* v. *Fraser*, 1863, 1 M. 783; *McDonald* v. *Glass*, 1883, 11 R. 57; *Scott* v. *Dawson*, 1884, 11 R. 518; *Buchanan* v. *Finlayson*, 1900, 3 F. 245; *Havery* v. *Brownlee*, 1908 S.C. 424; *Florence* v. *Smith*, 1913 S.C. 978; *Roy* v. *Pairman*, 1958 S.C. 334.

[9] See § 15.

[10] *Roy* v. *Pairman (supra)*, L. J-Cl. Thomson at p. 336.

[11] *Buchanan* v. *Finlayson (supra)*, L. Trayner at p. 251. See also L. J-Cl. Macdonald at p. 249.

[12] *Havery* v. *Brownlee (supra)*, L. J-Cl. Macdonald at p. 425.

[13] *Ross* v. *Fraser*, 1863, 1 M. 783, L. Neaves at p. 786.

[14] *Lawson* v. *Eddie*, 1861, 23 D. 876, L. Benholme at p. 880; *Ross* v. *Fraser (supra)*, L. J-Cl. Inglis at p. 785; *McDonald* v. *Glass*, 1883, 11 R. 57, L. J-Cl. Moncreiff at p. 58, L. Young at p. 59.

[15] *Florence* v. *Smith*, 1913 S.C. 978, L. Dundas at pp. 985-986.

[16] *Buchanan* v. *Finlayson*, 1900, 3 F. 245, L. J-Cl. Macdonald at p. 249, L. Trayner at p. 251.

it occurs in circumstances which indicate the probability of an earlier illicit association between the parties.[17]

(b) Between the Pursuer and Another Man. Evidence of such acts of intercourse is admissible, because it is relevant to the question of whether the defender is the father of the child.[18] If it is proved that the defender and another man had intercourse with the pursuer at or about the probable time of conception, and the evidence indicates that either of them might be the father, the pursuer fails.[19] If, on the other hand, there is evidence which makes it more probable that the defender is the father, the pursuer succeeds.[19] An example of such evidence is that menstruation took place after intercourse with the other man, and before intercourse with the defender.[20]

(c) Between the Defender and Another Woman. A judicial suggestion[21] that evidence of such acts of intercourse might be relevant and admissible, has not been adopted in practice.

173. DEFENDER'S ACTIONS AND EXPRESS OR IMPLIED ADMISSIONS

The defender's words or acts before, or at about, the time of conception, may be important as indicating the probable relationship between the parties at that time. Thus evidence of familiarities which are inconsistent with an innocent courtship, or of the defender's references to such familiarities in conversation or in letters written by him, may help to provide corroboration of the pursuer's evidence. When evidence of contemporary acts is lacking, corroboration of a truthful pursuer may be provided by what the defender does or says when he is informed of the pursuer's pregnancy, and is accused of being the cause of it. The defender's suggestions that the pursuer should procure an abortion, or for the child's adoption or future maintenance, may be consistent only with the advice to be expected from a disinterested friend. They may, on the other hand, in the circumstances in which they occur, disclose a personal and selfish interest, consistent only with an implied admission of paternity, which may afford sufficient corroboration of the pursuer's evidence. Corroboration by implied admission may also arise if the defender continues to associate with the pursuer, or if he has intercourse with her, after being charged with paternity of her child.[22] An express admission of paternity, if sufficiently proved, provides similar corroboration, even if it is subsequently denied, unless the admission is made upon a false assumption as to the probable date of conception.[23]

---

17 See *Roy* v. *Pairman*, 1958 S.C. 334.
18 *Butter* v. *McLaren*, 1909 S.C. 786. The averment regarding these acts of intercourse ought to specify the times and places and the names of the men: *Barr* v. *Bain*, 1896, 23 R. 1090.
19 *Robertson* v. *Hutchison*, 1935 S.C. 708.
20 *Sinclair* v. *Rankin*, 1921 S.C. 933.
21 *Whyte* v. *Whyte*, 1884, 11 R. 710, L. Mure at p. 711.
22 See, for example, *Roy* v. *Pairman*, 1958 S.C. 334.
23 See, for example, *Havery* v. *Brownlee*, 1908 S.C. 424, L. J-Cl. Macdonald at p. 425.

Acts of intercourse after the date of conception were mentioned above.[24] The implied admission arising from a false denial is mentioned below.[25]

174. DEFENDER'S FALSE DENIALS

(a) **The Rule.** By a rule which is peculiar[26] to actions of affiliation and aliment, the denial by a defender in the witness-box of a material fact which is proved to be true, may be accepted as corroboration of the pursuer's evidence as to the defender's paternity of her child. When the rule applies, the false denial may provide sufficient corroboration not only of the pursuer's evidence as to the occurrence of sexual intercourse at the relevant time, but also of the opportunity for it, and of the association between the parties which made it possible.[27]

(b) **Justification of the Rule.** The false denial is regarded as giving to colourless evidence a sinister complexion, or as indicating that there is something of which the defender is ashamed, or which he thinks might throw suspicion upon him, and a guilty significance is thereby given to an association which might otherwise appear to have been innocent.[28] It may also, it is thought, be regarded as an implied admission of guilt.

(c) **Proof of the Fact Denied.** The truth of the fact which the defender denies may be proved by two witnesses, of whom the pursuer may be one.[29] It has also been held, in what was described as a borderline case, that the rule applied when the defender denied two unrelated facts, each of which was spoken to by only one witness.[30] It is thought that, when the denial of a single fact is relied upon, the evidence of only one witness, however credible, is insufficient to prove its truth, at least in a case in which the only corroborative evidence consists of the defender's false denials.[31]

(d) **Materiality of the Fact Denied.** A mistake made by the defender in the witness-box on a minor detail, when his evidence on the matter is shown to be substantially accurate, does not constitute a denial of a material fact.[32] Facts which have been held to be material include:—the writing of a letter in affectionate terms by the defender to the pursuer;[33] that during the pursuer's pregnancy the defender received not only one, but two, letters from her;[34] that during the pursuer's pregnancy the defender spoke to the

[24] See § **172,** sub-para. (a).
[25] See § **174.**
[26] The effect of a false denial in consistorial causes has been mentioned earlier at §§ **163, 168.**
[27] *Macpherson* v. *Beaton,* 1955 S.C. 100, L. J-Cl. Thomson at p. 105, L. Patrick at p. 107.
[28] *Macpherson* v. *Beaton (supra),* L. J-Cl. Thomson at p. 105; *McWhirter* v. *Lynch,* 1909 S.C. 112, L.P. Dunedin at p. 113; *Dawson* v. *McKenzie,* 1908 S.C. 648, L. McLaren at pp. 650-651.
[29] *McBayne* v. *Davidson,* 1860, 22 D. 738.
[30] *Lowdon* v. *McConnachie,* 1933 S.C. 574.
[31] See *Lowdon* v. *McConnachie (supra),* L. Hunter at p. 577: *cf.* L. Anderson at pp. 578-579.
[32] *McWhirter* v. *Lynch,* 1909 S.C. 112.
[33] *Costley* v. *Little,* 1892, 30 S.L.R. 87.
[34] *Lowdon* v. *McConnachie,* 1933 S.C. 574.

pursuer's father in terms which implied an admission of sexual intercourse with the pursuer;[34] that the parties had behaved towards each other as sweethearts;[35] that the parties had been alone together on one occasion on a river bank,[36] or on three occasions, without any suggestion of impropriety, for short periods.[35] Meetings between the parties, when these are founded upon, do not need to occur at or about the date of conception, and in one fairly recent case the court accepted, as the sole corroboration of the pursuer's evidence, the defender's denial that, while returning home from a tea-party over five years before the date of conception, he had been alone with the pursuer for about an hour.[37]

175. DEFENDER AS WITNESS FOR PURSUER

Since the defender's admissions or denials in the witness-box may be of great importance to the pursuer's case, it is not unusual for the pursuer to cite the defender and to call him as one of her witnesses, in order to ensure that he gives evidence. Such a practice is unobjectionable.[38] But for this he might not tender himself as a witness, and his failure to do so is not regarded as an admission, or as corroborative of the pursuer's evidence.[39] The courts have repeatedly condemned, however, a practice of calling the defender as the *first* witness for the pursuer,[40] but in spite of this it is unfortunately still followed, at least to some extent, in the sheriff court. The practice may involve unfairness to the defender, although this may be avoided if the defender is warned of the importance and possible effect of his answers to material questions.[41] More frequently, however, it is prejudicial to the pursuer's case. Sometimes the fact that she is present in court while the defender is giving evidence, makes it impossible for the court to be completely satisfied as to the pursuer's credibility,[42] a matter which is of paramount importance for her. Not infrequently it makes it impossible to obtain the defender's admission or denial of facts emerging for the first time from the evidence of subsequent witnesses, which, although unimportant in themselves, may become material on the question of the pursuer's credibility, or the corroboration of her evidence.

[35] *Dunn* v. *Chalmers*, 1875, 3 R. 236. See also *Macfarlane* v. *Raeburn*, 1946 S.C. 67.

[36] *Macpherson* v. *Largue*, 1896, 23 R. 785.

[37] *Macpherson* v. *Beaton*, 1955 S.C. 100.

[38] *Faddes* v. *McNeish*, 1923 S.C. 443, L. Ormidale at p. 448.

[39] *Faddes* v. *McNeish* (*supra*). The position may be different if he refuses to give evidence after having been cited as a witness for the pursuer. See *Harper* v. *Paterson*, 1896, 33 S.L.R. 657, L. Moncreiff at p. 660; *Faddes* v. *McNeish*, L. J-Cl. Alness at p. 446, L. Ormidale at p. 448.

[40] *McArthur* v. *McQueen*, 1901, 3 F. 1010; *McWhirter* v. *Lynch*, 1909 S.C. 112; *Faddes* v. *McNeish* (*supra*), L. Ormidale at p. 448; *Fraser* v. *Smith*, 1937 S.N. 67, *per* L.P. Normand, L. Moncrieff. *Cf. Darroch* v. *Kerr*, 1901, 4 F. 396.

[41] See *McWhirter* v. *Lynch* (*supra*), L.P. Dunedin at p. 113.

[42] *Fraser* v. *Smith* (*supra*), *per* L. Moncrieff.

CHAPTER XVI

AUTHENTICATION OF WRITINGS SOLEMNLY EXECUTED

176. RELEVANCE TO LAW OF EVIDENCE—SCHEME OF CHAPTER

The authentication of writings in accordance with the statutory solemnities[1] has a two-fold bearing upon the law of evidence. In the first place, if a writing has the appearance, or bears the insignia, of having been authenticated in this way, it is probative, and the leading of evidence with regard to its genuineness is unnecessary. The meaning, nature and effect and essential characteristics of probative writings are dealt with first in this chapter, and this involves some discussion of the statutory solemnities themselves. In the second place, the production of a writing which has been executed in accordance with the statutory solemnities is the only means (apart from a holograph writing),[2] whereby certain matters may be founded upon in a litigation, other evidence, subject to certain exceptions, being inadmissible. The matters which can be constituted only in this way have been mentioned in an earlier chapter.[1] For this purpose the production of a probative writing is sufficient. A probative writing, however, may be reduced in an action raised for that purpose, if, despite its appearance to the contrary, it was not in fact executed in accordance with the statutory solemnities. The statutory solemnities are therefore discussed further in this connection.[3] Finally, a writing which is not probative, or which has been executed without some of the solemnities, may nevertheless be valid as if it were a solemnly executed writing if certain matters are proved.[4] This subject also is dealt with in this chapter.[5]

---

1 For the statutes prescribing the solemnities, and the deeds to which they apply, and the exceptions to the general rule, see §§ 90 *et seq.*
2 See §§ 188 *et seq.*
3 See § 182.
4 Conveyancing (Scotland) Act, 1874 (37 & 38 Vict. c. 94), s. 39.
5 See § 186.

177. RELEVANCE OF DECISIONS ON TESTAMENTARY AND HOLO-GRAPH WRITINGS

Judicial dicta and decisions having reference to testamentary writings must be read with care, since they may relate, not to the rules for the solemn execution of writings, but to the special rules regarding the revocation and amendment of testamentary and other undelivered unilateral deeds. This topic is dealt with more fully later in the chapter.[6]

Judicial decisions regarding the execution of untested holograph writings are sometimes cited as if they were relevant to the authentication of documents solemnly executed. It is thought that in general this practice is unsafe. So, for example, the signature "Connie," which has been held to be sufficient as the subscription of a holograph writing,[7] would not constitute a valid subscription of a writing solemnly executed,[8] and the rules regarding the authentication of erasures and other alterations in holograph writings must not be regarded as applicable to writings solemnly executed.[9]

178. PROBATIVE WRITING

(a) Meaning of "Probative." The word "probative" is frequently used in judicial pronouncements and in text-books to describe a writing which has been properly executed in accordance with the statutory solemnities or is the equivalent of such a writing. It is also sometimes used to describe an untested holograph writing, merely because, for certain purposes, a holograph writing is the equivalent of solemn writing.[10] It is thought, however, that the better practice is to use the word, in its original and restricted sense, as applying only to the kind of writing which affords proof of its own authenticity, and it is so used in this book. To use the word in a wider sense may lead to confusion. Thus a deed which is *ex facie* solemnly executed and therefore proves itself until reduced, may not in fact have been executed in accordance with the statutory solemnities, and would therefore not be probative if that word is used in its wider sense:[11] a deed which is not probative in the narrower sense, because some of the statutory solemnities are clearly lacking, may nevertheless be declared to be the equivalent of a solemnly executed deed:[12] and an untested holograph writing must be proved to be authentic by the party founding upon it, and is therefore never probative in the narrower sense.[13]

(b) Effect of Probative Writing. A writing[14] which appears to have been executed in accordance with the statutory solemnities proves itself. The

[6] See § 181.
[7] *Draper* v. *Thomason*, 1954 S.C. 136.
[8] See § 179, sub-para. (d).
[9] *Magistrates of Dundee* v. *Morris*, 1858, 3 Macq. 134, L.C. Chelmsford at pp. 151-2; Montgomerie Bell, *Lectures* (3rd ed.) I, 67.
[10] See § 91.
[11] *McBeath's Trs.* v. *McBeath*, 1935 S.C. 471, L.P. Clyde at p. 476; *McLaren* v. *Menzies*, 1876, 3 R. 1151, L. Deas at p. 1156; *Hamilton* v. *Lindsey-Bucknall*, 1869, 8 M. 323, L. Neaves at pp. 327-8; *Ferrie* v. *Ferrie's Trs.*, 1863, 1 M. 291, L. Curriehill at p. 298.
[12] See § 186.
[13] See § 189.

essential characteristics of such a writing are referred to in the next paragraph. When produced in a judicial proceeding the genuineness of a probative writing is assumed,[11] and the attendance of the granter and the instrumentary witnesses, to prove that he subscribed and that they witnessed, is both unnecessary and incompetent.[15] "A probative document is one which, in respect that it complies on the face of it with the prescribed legal formalities, is held to prove the verity of the legal *actus* of its author. It is important to keep in mind that, in speaking of the formalities required for the purpose of the authentication of a deed, what is meant is something in the form, or shape, or expression of the deed itself, which (when presented to the intelligent eye) provides a legal test of its authenticity. The formalities, in short, are intrinsic, not extrinsic to the deed. They are, so to speak, the legally recognisable features of honesty and genuineness which the deed carries about with it—on its face—into whosesoever hands it may pass."[16] Such deeds cease to be probative only when reduced by a decree of the Court of Session on proof, the burden of which rests upon the challenger, that they were not in fact executed according to the statutory solemnities, despite their appearance to the contrary.[11]

179. ESSENTIAL CHARACTERISTICS OF PROBATIVE WRITING

(a) **General Rule.** A writing[17] executed after October 1, 1874,[18] is probative when it bears to be subscribed[19] at the end by the granter[20] and also by two witnesses,[21] whose designations are either mentioned in a testing clause[22] or added to their signatures,[23] provided that, if the deed

---

14 A "writing" may consist, wholly or partly, of typescript, printing, lithography, photography or of other modes of representing or reproducing words in a visible form: Interpretation Act, 1889 (52 & 53 Vict. c. 63), s. 20; *Simpson's Trs.* v. *Macharg & Son*, 1902, 9 S.L.T. 398. See also § **184**, sub-para. (c). A deed is usually written in ink, but if it is written in pencil, provided the whole of the body of the deed is in pencil, there seems no reason in principle why, merely on that account, it should not be probative. See *Simson* v. *Simson*, 1883, 10 R. 1247 (tested non-holograph will, wholly in pencil, subscribed by the testatrix and witnesses in ink).

15 *Reid* v. *Kedder*, 1840, 1 Robin. App., 183; *Grant* v. *Shepherd*, 1847, 6 Bell's App., 153; *Boswell* v. *Boswell*, 1852, 14 D. 378, at pp. 382, 385, 392; *Munro* v. *Butler Johnstone*, 1868, 7 M. 250, at p. 256; Menzies, *Lectures* (Sturrock's ed.), 138; Wood, *Lectures*, 72.

16 *McBeath's Trs.* v. *McBeath*, 1935 S.C. 471, L.P. Clyde at p. 476.

17 For a definition of "writing," see § **178**, note 14.

18 Conveyancing (Scotland) Act, 1874 (37 & 38 Vict. c. 94), s. 2. As to deeds executed before October 1, 1874, see Montgomerie Bell, *Lectures* (3rd ed.) I. 23-34; Menzies, *Lectures* (Sturrock's ed.), 80 *et seq.*

19 See sub-para. (d).

20 Acts, 1540, c. 117; 1555, c. 29; 1579, c. 80; 1584, c. 4. After 1584 sealing in addition to subscription fell into disuse. Only the Sovereign may authenticate by superscription: *Foley* v. *Costello*, 1904, 6 F. 365, at p. 370; *Taylor's Executrices* v. *Thom*, 1914 S.C. 79, at p. 88.

21 Acts, 1681, c. 5; 1696, c. 15. The statutes speak of "witnesses," and custom has established that two are enough: Montgomerie Bell, *Lectures* (3rd ed.), I, 50. As to the number and designations of witnesses, see further in sub-para. (e).

22 See sub-para. (c).

23 Conveyancing (Scotland) Act, 1874 (37 & 38 Vict. c. 94), s. 38. The designations need not be written by the witnesses themselves.

is written bookwise on more than one sheet, each page must also bear to be subscribed by the granter.[24] The attested subscription of the granter and the subscriptions of the witnesses must appear at the end of the last page of the deed, [25] and not, unless linked in some way with the rest of the deed, on a following blank page.[26] A writing is also probative if it bears to have been executed in accordance with the rules for notarial execution of writings, which are mentioned later.[27]

(b) Special Rules. A deed to which a company registered under the Companies Act, 1948[28] is a party, may be validly executed on its behalf without witnesses, if it is sealed with the common seal of the company and subscribed on its behalf by two directors, or by a director and the secretary.[29] The subscriptions to a limited company's memorandum of association need be witnessed by only a single witness,[30] and a company's shares may be transferred in the manner provided by the articles of the company.[31] A deed, to which a county council, town council or district council is a party, may be validly executed on its behalf without witnesses if it is sealed with the common seal of the council and subscribed on its behalf by two members and the clerk.[32] Other statutory exceptions to the general rule include the provision that a bill of sale of a ship may be executed in the presence of, and need be attested by, only one witness.[33] Conventional, additional or reduced solemnities are mentioned later.[34]

(c) Testing Clause, Date and Place of Execution. A testing clause, when inserted, is the last clause of a deed.[35] Before October 1, 1874,[18] its inclusion was an essential solemnity. Since that date, although its inclusion is still customary, a deed does not need a testing clause in order to be probative unless it contains erasures, deletions, interlineations or other additions,[36] or unless the designations of the witnesses are not added to their signatures.[37]

---

[24] Act, 1696, c. 15. A deed written on a single sheet folded to exhibit four pages need not be subscribed by the granter on each page: *Ferguson*, 1959 S.C. 56.

[25] Act, 1696, c. 15.

[26] *Ferguson (supra); Baird's Trs.* v. *Baird*, 1955 S.C. 286.

[27] See § **185.**

[28] 11 & 12 Geo. VI, c. 38.

[29] *Ibid.*, s. 32 (4).

[30] *Ibid.*, s. 11, Sch. 1, Tables B, C, D, E.

[31] *Ibid.*, s. 73.

[32] Local Government (Scotland) Act, 1947 (10 & 11 Geo. VI, c. 43) s. 342 (1), (2). If a district council has no common seal, the subscriptions of the two members and the clerk must be attested by witnesses: s. 342 (2) (*b*).

[33] Merchant Shipping Act, 1894 (57 & 58 Vict. c. 60), s. 24 (2).

[34] See § **183.**

[35] The following is a simple form of testing clause, which includes a reference to a word written upon an erasure:—"In witness whereof these presents consisting of this and the two preceding pages are, under the declarations that the word 'shall' in the second line of page second is written on erasure and that this testing clause down to and including the word 'subscribed' was inserted before subscription, subscribed by me at Edinburgh on the third day of July nineteen hundred and sixty-two before these witnesses, John Smith and James Black, clerks to X, Y and Z, solicitors, Edinburgh."

[36] Menzies, *Lectures* (Sturrock's ed.) 171; Burns, *Conveyancing* (4th ed.) 1. See also § **180.**

[37] See sub-para. (a).

If the designations of the witnesses are placed in the testing clause and not added to the subscriptions, it is unnecessary also to mention their names in the testing clause, provided that it is clear to which subscription each designation applies.[38] Although it is customary and convenient to state in the testing clause the date and place of subscription, this is not an essential solemnity.[39] It has been judicially recognised that the part of a testing clause which refers to the place and date of subscription, and the witnesses' names and designations, cannot be written until after the deed has been executed, although by a legal fiction it is regarded as having been written at the time of execution.[40] Strictly speaking the part relating to alterations ought to be completed before subscription.[41] The testing clause may be completed by the person in possession of the deed at any time before it is founded upon in a litigation or recorded for preservation,[42] even after the death of the granter.[43] Because it is recognised that the testing clause is usually inserted after subscription, no words contained therein can restrict, alter or add to, the provisions of the deed.[44]

(d) **Subscription of Granter and Witness.** In order to be valid a subscription on a writing which purports to be solemnly executed must consist of the christened name (or forename), or the initial letter thereof, and the surname of the person subscribing.[45] Instead of the christened name or its initial letter a shortened form of the christened name may validly be used.[46] In the subscription of a married woman the surname may be her maiden

---

[38] *McDougall* v. *McDougall*, 1875, 2 R. 814 (name in testing clause written on erasure).

[39] Erskine, iii, 2, 18; Dickson, *Evidence* (3rd ed.) §§718, 722; Montgomerie Bell, *Lectures* (3rd ed.) I, 64, 65; Menzies, *Lectures* (Sturrock's ed.) 125; *Cairney* v. *Macgregor's Trs.*, 1916, 1 S.L.T., 357, L. Anderson at p. 359.

[40] *Walker* v. *Whitwell*, 1916 S.C. (H.L.) 75, L. Dunedin at p. 80, L. Shaw at p. 87; *Blair* v. *Assets Co.*, 1896, 23 R. (H.L.) 36, L. Watson at p. 47; *Smith* v. *Chambers' Trs.*, 1877, 5 R. 97, L. Deas at pp. 110-111, approving *Leith Bank* v. *Walker's Trs.*, 1836, 14 S. 332, L. Moncreiff (Ordinary) at p. 335. See also Montgomerie Bell. *Lectures* (3rd ed.)234; Menzies, *Lectures* (Sturrock's ed.) 172-3.

[41] See § **180**, sub-para. (b).

[42] *Blair* v. *Assets Co.* (*supra*), L. Watson at p. 47; Bell, *Principles*, §2226; Dickson, *Evidence* (3rd ed.) §731.

[43] *Walker* v. *Whitwell* (*supra*), L. Dunedin at p. 80; *Veasey* v. *Malcolm's Trs.*, 1875, 2 R. 748. In one case a deed was held to have been validly executed when the testing clause was inserted thirty-two years after its subscription by the granter: *Blair* v. *Earl of Galloway*, 1827, 6 S. 51.

[44] *Blair* v. *Assets Co.* (*supra*); *Smith* v. *Chambers' Trs.* (*supra*); *Reid* v. *Kedder*, 1840, 1 Robin. App., 183, L. Brougham at pp. 208, 209. Lord Gordon's *obiter* opinion to the contrary in *Smith* v. *Chambers' Trs.*, 1878, 5 R. (H.L.) 151, at pp. 168 *et seq.*, was disapproved in *Blair* v. *Assets Co.*

[45] Act, 1672, c. 21. A landowner may add the designation of his lands, prefixed by the word "of." Dickson (*Evidence* (3rd ed.) §§668, 670) accepted the view that a breach of the provisions of the Act did not invalidate the deed, but merely rendered the subscriber liable to punishment. This view has not been generally adopted. See Montgomerie Bell, *Lectures* (3rd ed.) I, 37; Menzies, *Lectures* (Sturrock's ed.) 98. The Act has been described as a definition of the word "signature" for the purposes of the authentication statutes: *Gardner* v. *Lucas*, 1878, 5 R. (H.L.) 105, L. O'Hagan at p. 114.

[46] Montgomerie Bell, *Lectures* (3rd ed.) I, 37; Menzies, *Lectures* (Sturrock's ed.) 98.

surname.[47] A surname alone, preceded by "Mr." or "Mrs.," e.g. "Mr. Smith," is not a valid subscription,[48] but the addition of "Mr." or "Mrs." to what would otherwise be a valid subscription does not render it invalid.[49] There is an exception to the general rule in favour of noblemen, who may subscribe by their titles alone,[50] and this has been extended in practice to include the eldest sons of peers who may subscribe by their courtesy titles.[51] A peeress, whether in her own right or by marriage, including the wife of a peer by courtesy, subscribes by her title or that of her husband, preceded by her christened name.[51]

A subscription by mark is not valid,[52] and a subscription adhibited by a stamp[53] or cyclostyle,[54] or typewritten,[55] is equally invalid. A deed on which the subscription of the granter or a witness consists only of initials is not probative, because in the exceptional cases in which it is has been held that such a deed was executed in accordance with the statutory solemnities, proof was necessary.[56]

---

[47] *Dunlop* v. *Greenlees' Trs.*, 1863, 2 M. 1.

[48] *Allan and Crichton*, 1933 S.L.T. (Sh.Ct.) 2. "Fullarton of that Ilk," although sustained in *Gordon* v. *Murray*, 1765 M. 16, 818, would not now be accepted as a valid subscription: Montgomerie Bell, *Lectures* (3rd ed.) I, 37; Menzies, *Lectures* (Sturrock's ed.) 98; Craigie, *Conveyancing* (2nd ed.) 66, 68.

[49] In *Ferguson*, 1959 S.C. 56, "Mme. Pion Roux" was accepted as a valid subscription.

[50] Act, 1672, c. 21. The Act allowed bishops, as well as noblemen, to subscribe by their titles. In *Drummond* v. *Farquhar*, 6th August, 1809, F.C., where the pursuer was a bishop in the Episcopal Church in Scotland, the Court of Session appointed his designation as bishop to be erased from the summons "as not recognised by the Court." On the strength of this interlocutor the Lord Lyon, writing in 1930, observed that "bishops are now obsolete": *Encyclopædia of the Laws of Scotland*, X, §298, note 4. It is understood that in practice Roman Catholic bishops in Scotland subscribe by their christened names and surnames, and bishops in the Episcopal Church in Scotland by the christened name and the name of the diocese, the signature in each case being preceded by a cross.

[51] Montgomerie Bell, *Lectures* (3rd ed.) I, 37.

[52] *Donald* v. *McGregor* (O.H.) 1926 S.L.T. 103; *Morton* v. *French*, 1908 S.C. 171; *Stirling Stuart* v. *Stirling Crawfurd's Trs.*, 1885, 12 R. 610, L. McLaren (Ordinary) at p. 617; *Crosbie* v. *Wilson*, 1865, 3 M. 870, at pp. 874, 878; Montgomerie Bell, *Lectures* (3rd ed.) I, 49; Dickson, *Evidence* (3rd ed.) §672. As to subscription by mark in connection with writs *in re mercatoria*, see § **107**, note 29. A statutory exception permits subscription by mark for the purposes of the Marriage Notice (Scotland) Act, 1878 (41 & 42 Vict. c. 43): *ibid.*, s. 16.

[53] *Stirling Stuart* v. *Stirling Crawfurd's Trs.*, 1885, 12 R. 610.

[54] *Whyte* v. *Watt*, 1893, 21 R. 165, at p. 166.

[55] *McBeath's Trs.* v. *McBeath*, 1935 S.C. 471, L.P. Clyde at pp. 476-7, L. Anderson at p. 487.

[56] Dickson, *Evidence* (3rd ed.), §671. Such a deed is also usually invalid as a solemnly executed writing, since it lacks the kind of subscription required by the authentication statutes: *Gardner* v. *Lucas*, 1878, 5 R. 638; (H.L.) 105: except perhaps in the exceptional case of a granter (but not of a witness: *Meek* v. *Dunlop*, 1707 M. 16, 806) who is either unable to write his full surname or is accustomed to subscribe by the use of initials alone. There were early decisions supporting the validity of deeds on these grounds, some of them dated after the Act, 1672, c. 21. See, for example, *Ker* v. *Gibson*, 1693 M. 16, 805; *Weir* v. *Ralston*, June 22, 1813, F.C. In one case of a bilateral contract, the onus was even placed upon the party repudiating the contract to prove that his custom was to sign *ad longum*: *Forrest* v. *Marshall*, 1701 M. 16, 805. In other cases, however, the court proceeded upon an admission that the granter had in fact adhibited his initials (see *Earl Traquair* v. *Gibson*, 1724 M. 16, 809), or insisted, in addition to

A subscription is not invalid merely because it is rude or faulty or even illegible.[57] A deed which is otherwise probative, does not cease to be probative because the granter's subscription was written upon an erasure,[58] and there seems to be no reason in principle why the position should be different if the subscription written upon an erasure is that of a witness.[59] Latent defects in the subscription of the granter of a deed are mentioned later.[60]

(e) Number and Designations of Witnesses. When there are several granters of a deed, the same two[21] witnesses, who need subscribe only once, may attest the subscriptions of those granters who sign at the same time and place.[61] One granter is not a witness to the subscription of another granter so as to make instrumentary witnesses of both subscriptions unnecessary, even when both sign at the same time and place.[62]

The designation of each witness, whether it is mentioned in a testing clause or added to the signature,[63] ought to provide such a description as will distinguish the individual who has acted as witness from all other individuals, and the most correct practice is to state the person's profession or occupation and residence.[64] In some of the older cases, however, very meagre designations were at times sustained by the Court.[65] It is customary

proof of usage, on proof, restricted to the evidence of the instrumentary witnesses, that the granter had in fact subscribed (see *Couts* v. *Straiton*, 1681 M. 16, 804). These decisions are to be regarded as exceptions to the general rule: *Gardner* v. *Lucas*, 1878, 5 R. (H.L.) 105, L. O'Hagan at p. 115. They have been described as "contrary both to the words and the spirit of the statute" (Erskine, iii, 2, 8), "led by the hardship of particular cases" (Ross, *Lectures*, I, 136). It would appear, however, that it may still be possible to have such a deed declared valid on the grounds abovementioned. See *Gardner* v. *Lucas*, 5 R. 638, L.P. Inglis at p. 645; (H.L.) 105, L.C. Cairns at p. 107; Montgomerie Bell, *Lectures* (3rd ed.) I, 49; Menzies, *Lectures* (Sturrock's ed.) 100.

57 *Stirling Stuart* v. *Stirling Crawfurd's Trs.*, 1885, 12 R. 610; *Perryman* v. *McClymont*, 1852, 14 D. 508.

58 *Brown* v. *Duncan*, 1888, 15 R. 511.

59 In *Gibson* v. *Walker*, June 16, 1809, F.C.: affd. 1814, 2 Dow, 270, however, a deed was reduced because the subscription of a witness upon an erasure was regarded as a vitiation *in essentialibus*. The instrumentary witness deponed that the signature was his, that as an official he witnessed many signatures and could not remember the circumstances in which the particular deed was subscribed, but that he would not subscribe as a witness a deed which he had not seen signed by the principal party. Those objecting to the deed founded upon the facts that the word "witness" was not in the handwriting of the witness and that his subscription was written in a different ink from that used by the granter and the other witness, and upon the proposition that both witnesses must together see the granter sign or acknowledge his signature. These are no longer valid grounds of objection to a deed.

60 See § 182, sub-para. (b).

61 Dickson, *Evidence* (3rd ed.) §704; Wood, *Lectures*, 67; *Baird's Trs.* v. *Murray*, 1883, 11 R. 153, at p. 157.

62 Montgomerie Bell, *Lectures* (3rd ed.) I. 51; Dickson, *Evidence* (3rd ed.) §693; *Miller* v. *Farquharson*, 1835, 13 S. 838, L. Corehouse (Ordinary) at pp. 839-840.

63 See sub-para. (a).

64 Montgomerie Bell, *Lectures* (3rd ed.) I, 58.

65 *Reid* v. *Brown*, 1700 (noted in *Rule* v. *Craig*, 1712 M. 16, 920) ("merchant" and "surgeon" without specification of place); *Baillie* v. *Somervel*, 1672 M. 16, 913 ("indweller in Edinburgh"); *Duncan* v. *Scrimgeour*, 1706 M. 16, 914 ("at Auchterhouse"); *Jamieson* v. *Sheriff*, 1708 M. 16, 916 ("at Leckie").

for the word "witness" to be written immediately after the signature, either by the witness himself or by another person, but this has never been a statutory requisite, and its absence does not affect the probative quality of the deed.[66] Latent defects in the attestation of the granter's signature are mentioned later.[67]

180. ALTERATIONS IN TESTED DEEDS

(a) **Unauthenticated Alterations.** The proper authentication of alterations is described in the next sub-paragraph. A writing upon which there appear erasures, deletions, interlineations or additions, which do not bear to have been properly authenticated, is not probative, because, failing agreement, a judicial declarator is necessary to determine whether it, or any part of it, is nevertheless effectual as a solemnly executed deed.[68] If the existence of an erasure or other alteration is not admitted, a proof on the point is necessary, the onus of proof of the fact of erasure in an otherwise probative deed resting upon the party who asserts it.[69] If the existence of an unauthenticated alteration is proved or admitted, there is a presumption of law, which, apart from statutory exception, [70] is irrebuttable,[71] that the alteration was made after the deed was executed.[68] This does not mean that the deed is necessarily ineffectual. When the alterations consist merely of additions, such as marginal additions, interlineations or interpolations, it may be possible, by disregarding them as *pro non scriptis*, to give effect to the rest of the deed.[72] Even when words are written upon an erasure, it may similarly be possible to disregard them as *pro non scriptis* and give effect to the rest of the deed.[73] Before this can be done, however,

---

[66] *Lord Blantyre*, 1850, 13 D. 40. The customary practice is a proper precaution for the witness's security, in order to indicate clearly the capacity in which he signs: Menzies, *Lectures* (Sturrock's ed.) 118.

[67] See § **182**, sub-paras. (c) (d).

[68] Stair, iv, 42, 19 (2); Erskine, iii, 2, 20; *Grant v. Shepherd*, 1847, 6 Bell's App. 153, L. Lyndhurst at p. 171; *Glassford's Tr. v. Glassford*, 1864, 2 M. 1317, at pp. 1324, 1326; *Munro v. Butler Johnstone*, 1868, 7 M. 250, L. Neaves at p. 256; Menzies, *Lectures* (Sturrock's ed.) 138.

[69] *Hamilton v. Lindsey-Bucknall*, 1869, 8 M. 323.

[70] The question of whether the presumption may be rebutted by parole evidence in terms of section 39 of the Conveyancing (Scotland) Act, 1874, is discussed at § **186**, sub-para. (e).

[71] *Reid v. Kedder*, 1840, 1 Robin. App., 183, L. Brougham at p. 211, L.C. Cottenham at p. 219; *Grant v. Shepherd* (*supra*), L. Lyndhurst at p. 171; *Boswell v. Boswell*, 1852, 14 D. 378; *Munro v. Butler Johnstone* (*supra*), L. Neaves at p. 256.

[72] In *Munro v. Butler Johnstone* (*supra*), the important word "not" was interpolated, without authentication, in the prohibitory clause of a deed of entail. The court disregarded the word as *pro non scripto*, and construed the rest of the deed. It was impossible, however, to spell a prohibition out of the other clauses of the deed, which as a deed of entail, was therefore held to be valueless.

[73] In *Cattanach's Tr. v. Jamieson*, 1884, 11 R. 972, there was a reference in a bond and disposition in security to another deed for a description of the subjects which were being disponed, the date of the other deed being written upon an unauthenticated erasure. The court was able to find a sufficient description of the subjects in other clauses of the bond, which was therefore held to be effectual for its purpose. For other examples, see *McDougall v. McDougall*, 1875, 2 R. 814; *Wilson v. Taylor*, 1869, 7 M. 773; *Gollan v. Gollan*, 1863, 1 M. (H.L.) 65; *Morrison v. Nisbet*, 1829, 7 S. 810.

two conditions must be satisfied. The words written upon the erasure must not be essential to the deed,[74] and it must be manifest, either by reading the erased words if they are legible, or from their context, that they were immaterial,[75] and that their deletion could not materially have altered the sense of the deed.[76] It may be possible, moreover, to hold that the clause vitiated by the unauthenticated alteration is separable from the other clauses, and, by disregarding it, to give effect to the rest of the deed.[77]

No challenge of an instrument of sasine, notarial instrument[78] or notice of title,[79] on the ground that any part of it is written on erasure, will receive effect unless it is averred and proved that the erasure was made for the purpose of fraud, or that the record in the sasine register is not conformable to the instrument as presented for registration.[80] Further, no challenge of any deed, instrument or writing recorded in any register of sasines will receive effect, on the ground that any part of the record of such deed, instrument or writing is written on erasure, unless such erasure is proved to have been made for the purpose of fraud, or the record is not conformable to the deed, instrument or writing as presented for registration.[81]

Words inserted in blanks in deeds, without authentication, are mentioned in a later paragraph.[82]

(b) Authenticated Alterations. Alterations which have been properly authenticated form part of the probative writing in which they are found, and do not deprive it of its probative quality.[83] To be properly authenticated for this purpose, the alteration must appear, from a mere reading of the deed, to have been made before the subscriptions of the granter and the witnesses were adhibited.[84] This is achieved by referring to the alteration

---

[74] *Gollan* v. *Gollan* (*supra*), L. Westbury at p. 66.

[75] Stair, iv, 42, 19 (2); *Glassford's Tr.* v. *Glassford*, 1864, 2 M. 1317, at p. 1324. In *Reid* v. *Kedder*, 1840, 1 Robin. App., 183 (name of grantee), *Howden* v. *Ferrier*, 1835, 13 S. 1097 (description of the subjects in an instrument of sasine), and *Kirkwood* v. *Patrick*, 1847, 9 D. 1361 (date before which obligation enforceable), the erasure was neld to be material, so as to invalidate either the clause in which it appeared or the whole deed. *Cf. Richardson* v. *Biggar*, 1845, 8 D. 315.

[76] *McDougall* v. *McDougall*, 1875, 2 R. 814, at pp. 819, 825.

[77] Dickson, *Evidence* (3rd ed.) §879; *Grant* v. *Shepherd*, 1847, 6 Bell's App. 153, L. Lyndhurst at p. 172; *Howden* v. *Ferrier* (*supra*); *Peddie* v. *Doig's Trs.*, 1857, 19 D. 820.

[78] See Titles to Land Consolidation (Scotland) Act, 1868 (31 & 32 Vict. c. 101), ss. 3, 144, for a definition of the various instruments covered by this provision.

[79] Conveyancing (Scotland) Act, 1924 (14 & 15 Geo. V. c. 27), s. 6 (1).

[80] Erasures in Deeds (Scotland) Act, 1836 (6 & 7 Wm. IV. c. 33); Titles to Land Consolidation (Scotland) Act, 1868 (31 & 32 Vict. c. 101), ss. 3, 144.

[81] Conveyancing (Scotland) Act, 1874 (37 & 38 Vict. c. 94), s. 54.

[82] See § **184.**

[83] Erskine, iii, 2, 20; Dickson, *Evidence* (3rd ed.) §729.

[84] At common law it is incompetent to prove this by parole evidence: *Grant* v. *Shepherd*, 1847, 6 Bell's App. 153, L. Lyndhurst at p. 171. As to whether such a proof is competent under statute, see § **186.** sub-para. (e). If the appearance of the deed itself suggests that the alteration may have been made after the deed was subscribed and attested, the presumption of law is that it was so made. Montgomerie Bell, *Lectures* (3rd ed.) I, 68. The sense of the alteration may itself disclose this, as when the recording of a deed was said to have occurred at a date (written upon an authenticated erasure) later than the date of execution of the writing in which the alteration occurred, as

in a testing clause[85] placed at the end of the body of the deed and before the subscriptions.[86] Erasures, writing on erasures,[87] interlineations or interpolations, must, by the reference in the testing clause, be adopted or acknowledged as having been made before subscription, the words or letters being quoted, and their position in the text being exactly specified by reference to page and line.[86] Marginal additions are signed by the granter with his christened name or initial on one side and his surname on the other, and must be further authenticated by a reference to them in the testing clause, as in the case of other alterations, with the additional statement that the marginal addition was signed by the granter in the presence of the witnesses.[88] An old practice, no longer followed, whereby the witnesses subscribed in the margin the granter's signature of the marginal addition, which made it unnecessary to mention the addition in the testing clause,[89] seems still to be sound in principle if the designations of the witnesses are added to their signatures.[90] Words which appear to have been inserted in blanks in the deed are mentioned in a later paragraph.[82]

The reference in the testing clause to alterations in the deed ought to have been written before the granter and witnesses subscribed,[91] unlike the date and place of execution and the witness's names and designations, which, in practice, must be written afterwards.[85] If the appearance of the deed raises an inference that the reference in the testing clause to alterations was written after the granter and the witnesses subscribed, the deed is not probative.[91] This inference might arise, if, for example, the testing clause makes reference to a date which is later than the date on which the deed is said to have been executed, or if the lines or words are so crammed together as to indicate that they were written in a space already bounded by the body of the deed above and the signatures below.[93]

disclosed by its testing clause: *Cattanach's Tr.* v. *Jamieson*, 1884, 11 R. 972.

[85] See § **179**, sub-para. (c).

[86] Dickson, *Evidence* (3rd ed.) §728; Montgomerie Bell, *Lectures* (3rd ed.) I, 68; Menzies, *Lectures* (Sturrock's ed.) 138-9, 172-3.

[87] For the position when the existence of the erasure is not admitted, see sub-para. (a) above, and note 69.

[88] Montgomerie Bell, *Lectures* (3rd ed.) I, 75; Menzies, *Lectures* (Sturrock's ed.), 139. The weight of authority seems to support the view that the granter's signature alone, without a reference in the testing clause, is insufficient for proper authentication, since without the reference it is not made to appear that the signature was attested by the witnesses. See Stair, iv, 42, 19 (3); Erskine, iii, 2, 20; Dickson, *Evidence* (3rd ed.) §734; *Smith* v. *Chambers' Trs.*, 1877, 5 R. 97, L. Deas at p. 109. Two early decisions apparently to the contrary effect (*Cuming* v. *Presbytery of Aberdeen*, 1721 Robertson's App., 364; *Spottiswood*, 1741 M. 16, 811) are discussed by Montgomerie Bell, *ibid.*, I, 76. A doubt is expressed in Burns, *Conveyancing* (4th ed.), 7.

[89] Montgomerie Bell, *Lectures* (3rd ed.) I, 77.

[90] Conveyancing (Scotland) Act, 1874 (37 & 38 Vict. c. 94), s. 38.

[91] Montgomerie Bell, *Lectures* (3rd ed.) I, 69, 234; Menzies, *Lectures* (Sturrock's ed.) 172-3; *Encyclopædia of the Laws of Scotland*, II, 270, §661 (article by John Burns, W.S.).

[92] *Cattanach's Tr.* v. *Jamieson*, 1884, 11 R. 972.

[93] Montgomerie Bell, *Lectures* (3rd ed.) I, 69, 234; Menzies, *Lectures* (Sturrock's ed.) 172, 173. In *Reid* v. *Kedder*, 1834, 12 S. 781: 1835, 13 S. 619: 1840, 1 Robinson's App., 183, the fact that the last three words of the testing clause were written over part of the granter's signature was mentioned as indicative that the signature was written first. See L. Brougham, 1 Robinson's App., at p. 209.

181. ALTERATIONS IN TESTAMENTARY WRITINGS

The rules with regard to solemn authentication are the same for testamentary as for other writings.[94] With regard to testamentary writings, however, the question which the court must frequently answer is not whether the deed was properly executed in the first place, but whether, *after* its original execution, and while still undelivered and in the possession of the granter, it was validly revoked or amended, in whole or in part, by deletions or writings which the granter made upon it. In such cases the relevant question is whether at the date of the testator's death, which is the equivalent of delivery in the case of an *inter vivos* deed, the deed as altered was or was not the effective record of his testamentary intentions. In answering this question the court is not concerned with the rules for the authentication of writings solemnly executed. The relevant rules are those which permit a testator to revoke his solemnly executed will, in whole or in part, by cancellation or deletion, if the cancellation or deletion is made with that intention (*animo revocandi*),[95] or the rules regarding holograph writings, which are sometimes so interpreted that a solemnly executed will is held to have been effectively altered after execution by what is, in effect, a holograph codicil, interlined or marginally noted in the original deed, instead of being fully expressed in a separate writing. Judicial dicta on these topics must be read with this distinction in mind, because, although sometimes pronounced in general terms, they may refer, not to the solemn execution of testamentary writings, but to their subsequent amendment.

Deletions are effective only if they are authenticated by the testator's signature or initials or are proved to have been made by him. If not thus authenticated or proved they will be ignored.[96] Marginal or interlineal additions, even if proved to be holograph of the testator, are thought to be effective only if separately authenticated by the subscription or initials of the testator.[97] Alterations to solemnly executed wills do not enjoy the relaxations extended to alterations to holograph wills.[98] The need for subscription before any holograph writing can be effective, which was mentioned by Lord McLaren in connection with holograph alterations to solemnly executed wills,[97] has been forcefully re-affirmed in recent decisions.[99] It is thought to be doubtful, therefore, whether decisions which gave effect to unauthenti-

94 *Macdonald* v. *Cuthbertson*, 1890, 18 R. 101, L.P. Inglis at pp. 104-105, L. Kinnear at p. 108; *Walker* v. *Whitwell*, 1916 S.C. (H.L.) 75, L. Dunedin at p. 79, L. Shaw at pp. 84 *et seq.*

95 McLaren, *Wills and Succession* (3rd ed.) I, §743; *Grant* v. *Shepherd*, 1847, 6 Bell's App., 153, L. Lyndhurst at p. 172; *Pattison's Trs.* v. *University of Edinburgh*, 1888, 16 R. 73; *Watson's Factor* v. *Watson* (O.H.), 1899, 7 S.L.T. 288.

96 *Pattison's Trs.* v. *University of Edinburgh* (*supra*), L. McLaren at pp. 76, 77 (propositions (1), (2)).

97 *Pattison's Trs.* v. *University of Edinburgh* (*supra*), L. McLaren at p. 77 (proposition (3)). Effect was given to such authenticated holograph additions in *Hogg's Exrs.* v. *Butcher*, 1947 S.N. 141, 190; *Caledonian Banking Co.* v. *Fraser*, 1874, 44 S.L.R. 345; *Royal Infirmary of Edinburgh* v. *Lord Advocate*, 1861, 23 D. 1213.

98 *Magistrates of Dundee* v. *Morris*, 1858, 3 Macq. 134, L. Chelmsford at p. 152. As to alterations to holograph wills, see § **192** sub-para, (b).

99 See § **191.**

cated holograph marginal additions,[1] or holograph additions in the body of the deed which were held to be authenticated by the original subscription,[2] would now be followed. For the effect of deletions, and subscribed additions or alterations, in the *copy* of a will, reference is made to the undernoted decisions.[3]

182. REDUCTION OF PROBATIVE WRITING—LATENT DEFECT IN STATUTORY SOLEMNITIES

(a) General—Onus and Standard of Proof. A probative deed,[4] the genuineness of which must be assumed,[4] may nevertheless be reduced on proof that, in fact, either the granter's subscription or the attestation was invalid.[5] Mention is therefore made in the following sub-paragraphs of the rules regarding subscription and attestation in so far as they have not been referred to earlier in this chapter. The rules for the notarial execution of deeds are mentioned later.[6]

An action of reduction of a probative deed is competent only in the Court of Session.[7] It has been said that the heavy onus which rests upon the pursuer in such an action must be discharged by clear and convincing evidence,[8] and, when the granter's signature is admitted, by evidence which is overpowering.[9] The evidence of the instrumentary witnesses alone, when they admit their signatures, but say that they do not remember seeing the granter sign or hearing his acknowledgment of his subscription, cannot discharge the onus.[10] The evidence of instrumentary witnesses, who admit their signatures but expressly deny that they either saw the granter sign or heard him acknowledge, is regarded with suspicion, partly because after a

1 *Horsbrugh* v. *Horsbrugh*, 1848, 10 D. 824.
2 *Gibson's Trs.* v. *Lamb* (O.H.), 1931 S.L.T. 22; *Gray's Trs.* v. *Dow*, 1900 3 F. 79; *Grant* v. *Stoddart*, 1849, 11 D. 860. See the doubt regarding *Grant* v. *Stoddart* expressed in Menzies, *Lectures* (Sturrock's ed.) 142.
3 *Thomson's Trs.* v. *Bowhill Baptist Church*, 1956 S.C. 217; *Lawson* v. *Lawson*, 1954 S.L.T. (Notes) 60; *Manson* v. *Edinburgh Royal Institution* (O.H.) 1948 S.L.T. 196; *MacKinnon's Trs.* v. *MacKinnon*, 1896, 3 S.L.T. 284.
4 See §§ **178, 179.**
5 Proof that the granter's signature was forged is, of course, another ground of reduction, with which this chapter is not concerned.
6 See § **185.**
7 Maclaren, *Court of Session Practice*, 82. A sheriff court has a limited power to reduce, for the purposes only of the current action, a deed or writing founded on by one party and challenged *ope exceptionis* by the other: Sheriff Courts (Scotland) Act, 1907 (7 Edw. VII. c. 51), s. 39, Rules 50, 51. This power must not be exercised if the rights of persons who are not parties to the action are affected by the deed or writing: *Donald* v *Donald*, 1913 S.C. 274. For a citation of other decisions on the point, see Dobie, *Sheriff Court Practice*, 22-24.
8 *Stirling Stuart* v *Stirling Crawfurd's Trs.*, 1885, 12 R. 610, L.P. Inglis at p. 626, L. Shand at p. 632; *Baird's Trs.* v. *Murray*, 1883, 11 R. 153, L.P. Inglis at p. 156; *Cleland* v. *Cleland*, 1838, 1 D. 254.
9 *Smith* v. *Bank of Scotland*, 1824, 2 Shaw's App., 265, L. Gifford at p. 287.
10 *Morrison* v. *Maclean's Trs.*, 1862, 24 D. 625, L. J-Cl. Inglis at p. 629; *Donaldson* v. *Stewart*, 1842, 4 D. 1215, L. J-Cl. Hope at p. 1217. See also *Smith* v. *Bank of Scotland* (*supra*), L. Gifford at p. 287; *Frank* v. *Frank*, 1793 M. 16, 822; Dickson, *Evidence* (3rd ed.) §903. As to what is required for valid attestation, see sub-paras. (c) (d) below.

lapse of time the recollection of the witnesses is not usually to be preferred to the evidence afforded by their subscriptions on the document,[11] and partly because it constitutes an admission that they had been accessories to forgery.[12] Such evidence by the instrumentary witnesses, when not supported by other evidence—that they were not in the district when the deed was signed by the granter, for example[13]—has on a number of occasions failed to satisfy the court or the jury.[14] Evidence of this nature by only one of the instrumentary witnesses, if unsupported by other evidence, can never, it is thought, discharge the onus of proof resting upon the pursuer.[15]

In some circumstances the question of whether the granter's signature was properly attested is of no practical importance. If the granter of an onerous deed delivers it to the grantee as such, and, when it is delivered, the granter's signature appears to be properly attested by two witnesses, the granter is personally barred from founding upon the latent defect that the subscribing witnesses had not in fact seen him sign or received an acknowledgment of his signature.[16] The same rule applies if the granter hands the deed to a third party in order that it may be delivered to the grantee as an onerous deed.[17]

(b) Faulty Subscription by Granter. The whole of the subscription must be adhibited by the hand of the granter, and without assistance.[18] So a deed was held invalid when the granter's hand was guided in making the subscription, although all but the last syllable was written without assistance.[19] It has also been held, however, that the subscription was not invalid when the granter's hand was held about the wrist so as to support it, no guidance being given in the formation of the letters.[20] A subscription was held invalid

---

11 *Sibbald* v. *Sibbald* 1776 M. 16, 906.
12 See Act, 1681, c. 5; *Morrison* v. *Maclean's Trs.*, 1863, 1 M. 304, L. Cowan at pp. 304-5. The instrumentary witnesses must be warned before they give evidence that they need not answer questions tending to incriminate them: Dickson, *Evidence* (3rd ed.) §§901, 904; *Frank* v. *Frank* (*supra*); *McArthur* v. *McArthur's Trs.* (O.H.) 1931 S.L.T. 463.
13 The example in the text was suggested by *Young* v. *Paton*, 1910 S.C. 63, where, however, the independent evidence as to the non-presence of the instrumentary witnesses in the district was *preferred* to the evidence of these witnesses, who deponed that it was not their practice to attest a signature without having seen it executed or heard it acknowledged.
14 *Morrison* v. *Maclean's Trs.*, 1863, 1 M. 304; *Cleland* v. *Cleland*, 1838, 1 D. 254; *Condie* v. *Buchan*, 1823, 2 S. 385; *Frank* v. *Frank*, 1793 M. 16, 822. Since neither instrumentary witness necessarily corroborates the other, the proof has also been held to fail because of a technical absence of corroboration: *McArthur* v. *McArthur's Trs.* (O.H.) 1931 S.L.T. 463.
15 *Forrest* v. *Low's Trs.*, 1907 S.C. 1240, L. Kinnear at p. 1253: 1909 S.C. (H.L.) 16, L. Dunedin and L. Shaw at p. 18. Apart from lack of cogency, the evidence must be insufficient in law through lack of corroboration: *Cleland* v. *Paterson*, 1837, 15 S. 1246.
16 *Boyd* v. *Shaw*, 1927 S.C. 414; *MacLeish* v. *The British Linen Bank* (O.H.), 1911, 2 S.L.T. 168; *National Bank of Scotland* v. *Campbell*, 1892, 19 R. 885; *Baird's Tr.* v. *Murray*, 1883, 11 R. 153. See also *Young* v. *Paton*, 1910 S.C. 63.
17 *Boyd* v. *Shaw* (*supra*); *MacLeish* v. *The British Linen Bank* (*supra*); *National Bank of Scotland* v. *Campbell* (*supra*).
18 Montgomerie Bell, *Lectures* (3rd ed.) I, 38; Menzies, *Lectures* (Sturrock's ed.) 98, 99.
19 *Moncrieff* v. *Monypenny*, 1710 M. 15, 936: 1711 Robertson's App., 26.
20 *Noble* v. *Noble*, 1875, 3 R. 74.

when it was marked in ink by the granter over words scored with a pin by another person,[21] but a subscription written free-hand by the granter herself, while she had before her a trial signature made by herself on a slip of paper below a copy of her signature made by another person, was sustained.[22] Retouching of the subscription by the granter himself, even after attestation, does not invalidate it, if the attested subscription was itself genuine and sufficient.[23] The other rules regarding the subscription of the granter of a deed were mentioned in an earlier paragraph.[24]

(c) **Competence of Instrumentary Witnesses.** Pupils,[25] blind persons[26] and persons of unsound mind[25] are not competent instrumentary witnesses. Apart from these, any person, male or female,[27] may competently act as a witness. A person who has a beneficial interest in the deed is not on that account an incompetent witness,[28] and near relatives,[29] including, it is thought, a husband or wife,[30] are not incompetent because of their relationship.

(d) **Requirements for Valid Attestation.** Attestation is not necessarily valid merely because the person subscribing as a witness was present, perhaps by accident or surreptitiously, when the deed was executed by the granter. The only persons who may validly attest are those receiving the assent, express or implied, of the granter to sign as witnesses.[31] Attestation, moreover, is invalid, and the deed will be reduced,[32] unless the witness knows the granter, and either sees him subscribe or observes his acknowledgement of his subscription at the time when he himself subscribes.[33] The witness's knowledge of the granter is sufficient if he has credible information that the person executing the writing is the person designed in it,[34] and he may receive this information from the granter himself[35] or from the introduction

---

21 *Crosbie* v. *Picken*, 1749 M. 16, 814.
22 *Wilson* v. *Raeburn*, 1800, Hume 912 (described in Montgomerie Bell, *Lectures* (3rd ed.) 38-9).
23 *Stirling Stuart* v. *Stirling Crawfurd's Trs.*, 1885, 12 R. 610.
24 See § **179**, sub-para. (d).
25 Montgomerie Bell, *Lectures* (3rd ed.) I, 50; Menzies, *Lectures* (Sturrock's ed.) 111.
26 *Cuningham* v. *Spence*, 1824, 3 S. 144.
27 Titles to Land Consolidation (Scotland) Act, 1868 (31 & 32 Vict. c. 101), s. 139; *Hannay*, 1873, 1 R. 246.
28 *Simson* v. *Simson*, 1883, 10 R. 1247; Erskine, iv, 2, 27.
29 Montgomerie Bell, *Lectures* (3rd ed.) I, 50; Menzies, *Lectures* (Sturrock's ed.) 112.
30 This seems to be implied in *Brownlee* v. *Robb*, 1907 S.C. 1302, L. Johnston (Ordinary) at p. 1310, L. McLaren at p. 1312; *Tener's Trs.* v. *Tener's Trs.*, 1879, 6 R. 1111 (over-ruled on another point in *Walker* v. *Whitwell*, 1916 S.C. (H.L.) 75).
31 *Walker* v. *Whitwell*, 1914 S.C. 560, L. Guthrie at p. 586, L. Skerrington at pp. 594-5: 1916 S.C. (H.L.) 75, L. Dunedin at p. 82, L. Shaw at pp. 90, 91.
32 *Smyth* v. *Smyth*, 1876, 3 R. 573. Lord Young's *obiter* opinion in *Geddes* v. *Reid*, 1891, 18 R. 1186, contrary to the decision in *Smyth* v. *Smyth*, that if the granter's subscription is proved, faulty attestation does not invalidate the deed, was expressly rejected in *Forrest* v. *Low's Trs.*, 1907 S.C. 1240, at pp. 1252-3 (1909 S.C. (H.L.) at p. 18).
33 Act, 1681, c. 5. The Act must now be read in the light of the decisions cited in this paragraph.
34 Dickson, *Evidence* (3rd ed.) §697; Montgomerie Bell, *Lectures* (3rd ed.) I, 52.
35 *Brock* v. *Brock*, 1908 S.C. 964, at p. 966; *Walker* v. *Adamson*, 1716 M. 16, 896; *Campbell* v. *Robertson*, 1698 M. 16, 887.

of any reliable person present.[36] The granter's acknowledgement of his subscription may be made to the witness orally, or in writing, or by his acts, or by a combination of words and acts.[37] An attestation is valid although one witness sees the granter subscribe and the other observes him acknowledge,[38] and, if neither sees him subscribe, it is valid although a separate acknowledgement is made to each witness outwith the presence of the other.[39] An attestation is not invalid because the instrumentary witnesses are unaware of the terms or nature of the deed.[40] If the pretended witnesses adhibit their subscriptions before the deed has been subscribed by the granter, so that their subscriptions do not in fact attest either that they saw the granter subscribe or that, at the time when they subscribed, the granter acknowledged his subscription, the deed is invalid and will be reduced.[32]

Questions have arisen as to where and when the instrumentary witnesses must subscribe. As to the place of signature the statute[33] is silent, and it appears to specify the time of signature only when the granter's subscription is acknowledged, in which event the witness must subscribe at the time of acknowledgement. As interpreted, however, the statute is now regarded as applying the same rule both to place and time of subscription, and as making no distinction between the occasion when the witness sees the granter sign and the occasion when the signature is merely acknowledged.[41] The rule, which must be observed as a statutory solemnity, is that the subscription or acknowledgement by the granter, and the subscription by the witness, must both take place *unico contextu*[42] as parts of a single continuous process.[43] What is said to have been intended by the rule is to ensure that the deed subscribed by the witnesses is that on which the granter's subscription was adhibited or acknowledged in their presence,[44] and that the granter's express or implied assent[31] to attestation has not been withdrawn before the witnesses subscribe.[45] In applying the rule it has been held that the witnesses need not subscribe in the presence of the granter, and the attestation was held to be valid when the witnesses, having seen the granter sign, adhibited their own subscriptions in an adjoining room, the deed having been out of their sight for a few minutes,[46] and when the witnesses, having observed the granter acknowledge his subscription in his own house, took the deed to the solicitor's office in which they were employed, where they at once adhibited their own

---

36 *Brock* v. *Brock* (*supra*).

37 *Cumming* v. *Skeoch's Trs.*, 1879, 6 R. 963; Dickson, *Evidence* (3rd ed.) §699.

38 Montgomerie Bell, *Lectures* (3rd ed.) I, 52.

39 *Hogg* v. *Campbell*, 1864, 2 M. 848.

40 Dickson, *Evidence* (3rd ed.) §701.

41 *Walker* v. *Whitwell*, 1914 S.C. 560, L. Johnston at p. 576, L. Skerrington at p. 589: 1916 S.C. (H.L.) 75, L. Dunedin at p. 83 (concurring with L. Skerrington), L. Shaw at p. 92; *Thomson* v. *Clarkson's Trs.*, 1892, 20 R. 59, L. Trayner at p. 63.

42 *Walker* v. *Whitwell* (*supra*), L. Skerrington at pp. 588, 589.

43 *Walker* v. *Whitwell* (*supra*), L. Johnston at p. 577: (H.L.) L. Shaw at pp. 89, 91; *Thomson* v. *Clarkson's Trs.* (*supra*), L. Rutherfurd Clark at p. 62, L. Kyllachy at p. 64.

44 *Thomson* v. *Clarkson's Trs.*, 1892, 20 R. 59, at pp. 61, 62.

45 *Walker* v. *Whitwell*, 1916 S.C. (H.L.) 75, L. Dunedin at pp. 81, 82, L. Shaw at p. 91.

46 *Frank* v. *Frank*, 1795 M. 16, 824: 1809, 5 Paton's App. 278. See also *Condie* v. *Buchan*, 1823, 2 S. 385.

subscriptions.[47] Since the witnesses cannot subscribe at the very moment when the granter subscribes or acknowledges his subscription, it is clear that some time must elapse between the two events, and the question of the length of time which is permissible depends upon the application of the rule to the circumstances of the particular case. Intervals of a quarter of an hour,[46] and three-quarters of an hour[47] have been held to be permissible. An attestation, however, is invalid if one of the witnesses does not subscribe until after the death of the granter.[48]

183. CONVENTIONAL ADDITIONAL OR REDUCED SOLEMNITIES

It is lawful for the parties to a contract, or for a person making a will, to stipulate or declare that solemnities different from, or in addition to, those required by law, shall be adopted in the execution of any power which they or he may confer.[49] When a person having a power of appointment under a marriage-contract purported to exercise it by directions contained in a holograph deed which was executed in accordance with the ordinary requirements of the law, the power was held not to be validly exercised because the marriage-contract required the deed to be "signed, sealed and delivered in the presence of, and attested by, two credible witnesses."[50] In one old case it was held that a holograph will, subscribed by the testator, had itself been revoked because it contained the words "in testimony of this being my last will and testament I hereby set my hand and seal," and because, when the deed was produced, the portion bearing the seal appeared to have been cut off, *animo revocandi*, by the testator.[51] Apart from contracts which parties have committed unnecessarily to writing, a topic which has been mentioned earlier,[52] there appear to be no recent reported decisions on additional conventional solemnities.

A reduction in the solemnities required by the general law is authorised in some cases by statute, and examples of this are given in an earlier paragraph.[53] A testator, in his solemnly executed will, may direct that testamentary effect shall be given to future informal writings which lack some or all of the statutory solemnities, and he may prescribe what is necessary for their validity.[54] Such a direction usually refers to "any writing under my hand." It seems to be settled that if the word "writing" is used, the document founded upon must be solemnly executed or holograph,[55] unless the word is

[47] *Thomson* v. *Clarkson's Trs.* (*supra*).
[48] *Walker* v. *Whitwell*, 1916 S.C. (H.L.) 75.
[49] *Campbell's Trs.* v. *Campbell*, 1903, 5 F. 366, at pp. 370, 371, 373.
[50] *Campbell's Trs.* v. *Campbell* (*supra*).
[51] *Nasmyth* v. *Hare*, 1821, 1 Sh. App. 65. It has been said that this decision applies *a fortiori* to the omission or obliteration of a conventional additional solemnity from any deed which declares that the additional solemnity is necessary to prove the consent of the parties to it. See Dickson, *Evidence* (3rd ed.) §748.
[52] See §§ 96 *et seq.*
[53] See § 179, sub-para. (b).
[54] *Fraser* v. *Forbes' Trs.*, 1899, 1 F. 513, at p. 519.
[55] *Waterson's Trs.* v. *St. Giles Boys' Club*, 1943 S.C. 369, at pp. 375-6 (Seven Judges). The earlier decisions of *Ronald's Trs.* v. *Lyle*, 1929 S.C. 104, and *Gillespie* v. *Donaldson's Trs.*, 1831, 10 S. 174, were over-ruled.

qualified or used in a context which shows that an informal document is sufficient.[56] But this does not apply to such words as "letters," "jottings," "memoranda" and the like.[55] It is settled that the words "under my hand" mean "signed by me,"[55] unless the testator has indicated, expressly or by implication, that an unsigned document is sufficient.[57] It may yet have to be decided, however, whether an unsigned document can ever be made effective as a testamentary writing by a direction in the testator's earlier will.[58]

184. BLANKS IN DEEDS

(a) **General.** During the sixteenth and seventeenth centuries a practice was sanctioned of executing deeds containing blanks, and this early practice has left its mark upon the law relating to authentication of deeds. But for its distorting effect, the rules for the authentication of erasures[59] and writings on erasures[59] would, it is thought, apply equally to blanks and writings on blanks.

Until 1847, when the practice became unnecessary,[60] the name of the bailie of a superior or disponer was left blank in a precept of sasine, when the feu charter or disposition containing it was executed. This enabled the vassal or disponee to whom it was delivered to insert the name of a person selected by himself as the bailie from whom sasine was formally taken.[61] The concept underlying this practice, *viz.* that the subscription of the granter of a solemnly executed deed not only warranted what the deed contained, but also gave authority to another person to complete the deed at an unspecified future time, is a departure from the general rules for the authentication of solemnly executed documents.

A similar departure from these general rules was sanctioned by practice during the seventeenth century in connection with solemnly executed bonds in which the name of the creditor was left blank. This enabled the bonds to be passed from hand to hand like bank notes,[62] or the modern postal order, until a holder, who wished to obtain payment from the granter, inserted his own name in the bond as the creditor under it. The practice, which was brought to an end in 1696 by statute,[63] appears to have been suggested by that part of the law merchant which dealt with bills of exchange, a matter

---

[56] e.g. *Waterson's Trs.* v. *St. Giles Boys' Club* (*supra*) ("any informal writing"); *Fraser* v. *Forbes' Trs.* (*supra*) ("although the same may not be formal"). The qualification "formal or informal" is frequently added.

[57] *Crosbie* v. *Wilson*, 1865, 3 M. 870 ("a writing under my hand *or* any writing subscribed by me however informal"). The implication was that "under my hand" was intended to mean "written by me." See also *Lamont* v. *Magistrates of Glasgow*, 1887, 14 R. 603 ("writing under my hand *or* signed by me"); *Baird* v. *Jaap*, 1856, 18 D. 1246 ("any jotting under my hand" . . . "any writing signed by me"). This was the way in which these three cases were explained in *Waterson's Trs.* v. *St. Giles Boys' Club* (*supra*).

[58] *Waterson's Trs.* v. *St. Giles Boys' Club* (*supra*), at p. 376.

[59] See **§ 180**.

[60] Infeftment Act, 1845 (8 & 9 Vict. c. 35); Lands Transference Act, 1847 (10 & 11 Vict. c. 49).

[61] See Erskine, ii, 3, 33.

[62] Bell, *Commentaries*, II, 15.

[63] Act, 1696, c. 25, the effect of which is discussed in sub-para. (d).

now regulated by statute.[64] The signature of a bill of exchange which is left blank in any material particular operates as authority to the person in possession of the bill to fill up the blank in any way he thinks fit,[65] and a signature on a blank stamped paper may operate as authority to the person to whom it is delivered to fill it up as a complete bill of exchange for any amount the stamp will cover, using the signature for that of the drawer or acceptor or indorser.[65] The burden of proving that the bill was incomplete when delivered, and was completed contrary to his instructions, rests upon the person who signed the incomplete bill, and it is not for the holder of the bill to establish that it is in order.[66]

Although the leaving of blank spaces in solemnly executed deeds is no longer sanctioned as a general practice, the concept that the subscription of such a deed may authorise its subsequent completion in accordance with the express or implied consent of the granter has figured occasionally in later cases,[67] and has been approved judicially in the sheriff court as recently as 1962.[68] It is thought, however, that this concept is inconsistent with the rules for the authentication of solemnly executed writings. If these rules are applied, any part of a deed which is inserted after the granter has subscribed is effectual only if the person founding upon it is able to establish that the granter, by his actings, is personally barred from disputing its validity, or has entered into some new agreement which has the same result.[69] When pleas of this kind are sustained, the question of whether the deed is ineffectual, merely because it is improperly authenticated, becomes academic.

(b) Probative Nature of Deed containing Blanks—Onus of Proof. This chapter of law has never been properly explored, and any views expressed must be tentative. It is thought, however, that the principles applicable to probative deeds,[70] and in particular to alterations made before or after execution,[71] apply in general to deeds in which blanks are left when the deed is first engrossed.

If the blanks have not been completed when the deed is founded upon, the deed is clearly not probative, and the question whether it is nevertheless

---

[64] Bills of Exchange Act, 1882 (45 & 46 Vict. c. 61).

[65] *Ibid.*, s. 20 (1). See *Russell* v. *Banknock Coal Co.*, 1897, 24 R. 1009.

[66] *Anderson* v. *Somerville, Murray & Co.*, 1898, 1 F. 90.

[67] *Earl of Buchan* v. *Scottish Widows' Fund*, 1857, 19 D. 551, L. J-Cl. Hope at p. 555, L. Cowan at p. 556; *Carsewell's Trs.* v. *Carsewell* (O.H.) 1896, 3 S.L.T. 218.

[68] *British Wagon Co. Ltd.* v. *Russell*, 1962 S.L.T. (Sh.Ct.) 55. See also *United Dominions Trust (Commercial) Ltd.* v. *Lindsay*, 1959 S.L.T. (Sh.Ct.) 58, *per* the sheriff at p. 60, where it was averred in connection with a solemnly executed hire-purchase contract, partly printed and partly in writing, that the written portions were blank when the hirer subscribed. The opinion was expressed that at common law, unless the hirer could prove fraud, he was bound by the writing inserted over his signature in the blank spaces, just as a cheque signed in blank binds the drawer in a question with the person to whom he hands it.

[69] The pleas associated with personal bar in cases of this kind are mentioned later. See sub-para. (e) below.

[70] As to the meaning of "probative," see § **178**, sub-para. (a). For the essential characteristics of a probative deed, see § **179**.

[71] See § **180**.

effectual, in whole or in part, depends upon the materiality of the clause which contains the blank, and whether or not it is separable from the rest of the deed. What has been said in this connection about unauthenticated alterations[71] is thought also to apply to blanks.

When it is admitted or proved that what was originally a blank space in a deed has been completed at a later date,[72] it is thought that the deed is not probative unless the inserted words are mentioned in a testing clause just as if they were words written upon an erasure.[73] Unless so mentioned, the presumption is that the words were written after the execution of the deed,[74] and the onus of establishing, by admission or proof, that they were in fact inserted before execution, or that, if inserted thereafter, they were inserted with the consent of the granter, rests upon the party founding upon it.[75]

(c) **Partly Printed Deeds.** Printed forms, having blank spaces which are later completed in writing, are frequently used for wills, hire-purchase and similar contracts, cautionary obligations and bail bonds. If the rules mentioned in the earlier sub-paragraphs are applied to them, they would be valueless as probative documents, because the persons founding upon them would be required to prove in each case that the blanks had been filled in before execution, or possibly, if after execution, with the consent of the granter.[76] It is thought, however, that special statutory provision is made for these deeds in the following terms: "All deeds . . . having a testing clause may be partly written and partly printed or engraved or lithographed: Provided always that in the testing clause the date, if any . . . shall be engrossed at length, and all such deeds shall be as valid and effectual as if they had been wholly in writing."[77] The effect of the statute appears to be that, if the requirement of a testing clause is complied with,[78] the rules regarding blanks do not apply to partly printed deeds, and they are as effectual as if they were wholly in writing.[79] It seems to follow that the onus of reducing

---

[72] If this is not obvious from ocular inspection, the burden of proving that the words were inserted in a blank space rests upon the person who asserts that they were. See *Hamilton* v. *Lindsey-Bucknall*, 1869, 8 M. 323 (word written on erasure).

[73] *Sinclair* v. *Sinclair*, 1746 M. 11, 559; Dickson, *Evidence* (3rd ed.) §659. See also *Earl of Buchan* v. *Scottish Widows' Fund*, 1857, 19 D. 551, L. Murray at p. 555. For the general rule regarding alterations to a deed, see § **180.**

[74] As to the general rule, see § **180,** sub-para. (a).

[75] In *Earl of Buchan* v. *Scottish Widows' Fund* (*supra*), it was admitted that the redemption sum in a redeemable bond was inserted in a blank space after the deed had been executed. The defenders, who were founding on the deed as completed, were made to take a counter-issue as to whether the words were inserted with the authority of the granters. The relevancy of the defences was not challenged.

[76] See sub-para. (b) above.

[77] Titles to Land Consolidation Act, 1868 (31 & 32 Vict. c. 116), s. 149, as modified by the Conveyancing (Scotland) Act, 1874 (37 & 38 Vict. c. 94), s. 38. The effect of this clause upon the deeds referred to in the text has not been considered in any reported decision.

[78] But see Lord Kyllachy's opinion, in *Simpson's Trs.* v. *Macharg & Son*, 1902, 9 S.L.T. 398, that the section should now be read as follows:—"All deeds may be partly written and partly printed, and all such deeds shall be valid and effectual in the same manner as if they had been wholly in writing."

[79] This appears to gain support from *Nisbet*, 1897, 24 R. 411, where, in connection with such a deed, a proof under section 39 of the 1874 Act was allowed, not because blanks had been filled in, but because the witnesses were not designed.

the deed, if it is otherwise probative, rests upon the person who asserts that the blanks were completed after execution.[80]

(d) Blanks in Name of Creditor, Assignee or Disponee. The statute[63] which prohibited the practice[81] of executing personal bonds blank in the creditor's name, also created a new and exceptional rule for the authentication of certain solemnly executed deeds. It applies to all bonds, assignations, dispositions or other deeds which are subscribed when blank in the name of the person or persons in whose favour they are conceived. Any such deed is null, unless the name of the creditor, assignee or disponee is inserted, either at the time of subscription or before delivery, in the presence of the witnesses who attested the granter's subscription. The statute does not apply to the indorsation of bills of exchange or the notes of a trading company. The onus of proving that the name of the creditor, assignee or disponee was blank when the deed was executed, rests upon the party challenging the deed. When that onus has been discharged, the party founding upon the completed deed must then undertake the onus of proving that the name was inserted before delivery of the deed, and in the presence of the original instrumentary witnesses.[82] Although the statute provides that the whole deed shall be null, it has been held that the nullity applies only to the names inserted in the blanks and to the clauses which are directly and specially affected thereby.[83] This may or may not have the effect of nullifying the whole deed. Thus the invalid insertion in a blank of the name of only one of a number of legatees, each receiving a separate legacy, would invalidate only the legacy with which the blank was concerned.[84] The invalid insertion in a blank of a sole disponee would nullify the whole disposition, but an invalidity in connection only with a substitute heir in a deed of entail nullifies the destination to that heir, but does not nullify the destination to the institute or to earlier substitutes.[83] In a disposition to trustees, when the names of all the trustees were inserted invalidly in blanks, the whole trust deed was held null in terms of the statute,[85] but it is thought that if only some of the trustees are invalidly nominated on blanks, the disposition in favour of the other trustees would be upheld.[86]

(e) Blanks in Other Material Parts. If, at the time when a deed is founded upon in a litigation, there is a blank in a material part, the question as to whether the whole deed, or only the part affected by the blank, is ineffectual

---

[80] This assertion is frequently made in connection with hire-purchase contracts.
[81] See sub-para. (a) above.
[82] *Donaldson* v. *Donaldson*, 1749 M. 9080.
[83] *Abernethie* v. *Forbes*, 1835, 13 S. 263, L. Jeffrey at pp. 267, 268; *Kennedy* v. *Arbuthnot*, 1722 M. 1681.
[84] *Abernethie* v. *Forbes* (*supra*), L. Jeffrey at p. 267.
[85] *Pentland* v. *Hare*, 1829, 7 S. 640. The deed was also held null at common law upon another ground. It is thought that an appointment of trustees would now be made by the court in terms of the Trusts (Scotland) Act, 1921 (11 & 12 Geo. V. c. 58), s. 22. See *Pattullo*, 1908, 16 S.L.T. 637; *Auld*, 1925 S.L.T. 83.
[86] See *Robertson* v. *Ogilvie's Trs.*, 1844, 7 D. 236 (an attested holograph deed in which the names of some of the trustees were written on erasures).

is governed, it is thought, by the principles applying to unauthenticated erasures in the same connection.[87] A cautionary obligation, in which the cautioner guaranteed payment up to a sum, which was left blank, of any arrears owed to a supplier by the person selling his goods on commission, was held to bind the cautioner, on the view that the omission to complete the blank did not cancel the obligation but merely left it unlimited in amount.[88] On the other hand, a trust disposition and settlement which provided *inter alia* that the trust funds should be accumulated until they amounted to a sum, which was left blank, and should then be used for charitable purposes concerned with the education of a number of boys of a specified class, the number also being blank, was held to be wholly ineffectual.[89]

If, when a deed is founded upon in a litigation, spaces which were blank when the deed was executed have been filled in, the words inserted in the blanks (other than the creditors' names)[90] ought to be ignored, and the deed construed as if the spaces were still blank.[91] No other view seems to be supportable if the general rules for the authentication of solemnly executed documents are applied.[92] Thus when a trust-deed was executed with all the trust purposes left blank, and the blanks were later filled in, in terms approved by the granter, the whole deed was held to be ineffectual at common law.[93]

As with other defects in the authentication of writings, different rules of law may operate to prevent the granter of a deed, or his successor in title, from founding upon the invalid authentication of the part containing the blank. The same point has been mentioned in connection with the plea of personal bar,[94] and with the revocation or amendment of undelivered unilateral deeds, such as testamentary writings.[95] When, several years after the death of the creditor, the granter of a bond sought to reduce it on the ground that when it was signed by him it was blank in the amount, the action was held to lack foundation because he had not averred that the sum was blank when the deed was delivered.[96] The reasons for the decision are not reported, but it is thought to have been an application of the principle of personal bar. In a similar action, when the blank concerned the sum for

---

[87] Dickson, *Evidence* (3rd ed.) §650; Menzies, *Lectures* (Sturrock's ed.) 144. As to the general principles, see § **180**, sub-para. (a).

[88] *Buchanan* v. *Dickie*, 1828, 6 S. 986.

[89] *Ewen* v. *Ewen's Trs.*, 1830, 4 W. & S. 346 (reversing the Court of Session in 1828, 6 S. 479).

[90] As to the exceptional rule for creditors' names, see sub-para (d) above.

[91] *Earl of Buchan* v. *Scottish Widows' Fund*, 1857, 19 D. 551, L. J-Cl. Hope at p. 555. In this case, however, the court contemplated the possibility that effect might be given to the words. The possible grounds of decision are mentioned later in the paragraph.

[92] The general rule is that a deed is validly executed only in so far as its terms are subscribed by the granter and his subscription is properly attested, anything added or altered after execution being ignored. For the application of the general rule to unauthenticated alterations, see § **180**, sub-para. (a).

[93] *Pentland* v. *Hare*, 1829, 7 S. 640.

[94] See § **182**, sub-para. (a) (deed properly attested when delivered).

[95] See § **181**.

[96] *Baillie* v. *Scott*, 1828, 6 S. 1016. This may, however, have been a decision on the facts. Absolvitor was pronounced, and there is a vague reference to evidence in the argument.

which a bond of annuity was redeemable, the court approved a counter issue as to whether the blank had been completed after execution with the authority or consent of the granter or his duly qualified agent.[97] While the exact ground upon which the defence was thought to be relevant is not easily deduced from the opinions, the redemption clause was clearly regarded as ineffectual unless the defenders undertook the onus of establishing that the pursuer, by his subsequent actings, had barred himself from challenging the sum which had been inserted in the blank space. In very special circumstances, when a will was written to the testator's dictation above his signature, and he then and there in the presence of the witnesses, who then added their own subscriptions, acknowledged that the writing correctly set forth his wishes, it was held that, the whole proceedings constituting one act, and there being express acknowledgement by the testator, the will was valid.[98]

185. NOTARIAL EXECUTION OF WRITINGS

Since January 1, 1925,[99] any deed, instrument or writing, whether relating to land or not, may be validly executed on behalf of a granter, who for any cause, permanent or temporary, is blind[1] or unable to write, by a solicitor,[2] notary public, justice of the peace, or, as regards testamentary writings, by a parish minister acting in his own parish,[3] or his assistant (or colleague)[3] and successor so acting.[4] The person executing the deed on the granter's behalf is referred to as the "notary" in this paragraph. The granter must declare that he is blind or unable to write,[5] and the onus of proving that this declaration was untrue rests upon the person seeking to reduce the deed.[6] The writing must be read over to the granter, and it must then be subscribed on his behalf, in his presence, and by his authority, all before two witnesses, who have heard the writing read over to the granter and have heard or seen his authority given.[4] The witnesses, by subscribing, attest not only the subscription of the notary, but also the fact that the deed was

[97] *Earl of Buchan* v. *Scottish Widows' Fund*, 1857, 19 D. 551.
[98] *Carsewell's Trs.* v. *Carsewell* (O.H.) 1896, 3 S.L.T. 218.
[99] As to deeds executed before that date, see Conveyancing (Scotland) Act, 1874 (37 & 38 Vict. c. 94), s. 41 and Montgomerie Bell, *Lectures* (3rd ed.) I, 39 *et seq*; Menzies, *Lectures* (Sturrock's ed.) 102 *et seq.*
[1] If a blind person can write, his deed is probably valid when executed by him personally: Burns, *Conveyancing* (4th ed.) 9; Montgomerie Bell, *Lectures* (3rd ed.) I, 46-47.
[2] "Law agent" (the term formerly used) is now deemed to mean a solicitor enrolled, or deemed to have been enrolled, in pursuance of the Solicitors (Scotland) Act, 1933 (23 & 24 Geo. V. c. 21) (see ss. 49, 50 of that Act); and includes every person entitled to practise as a solicitor in a court of law in Scotland: Conveyancing (Scotland) Act, 1924 (14 & 15 Geo. V. c. 27), s. 2 (6). He may act as notary without having taken out an annual certificate authorising him to practise: *Stephen* v. *Scott*, 1927 S.C. 85.
[3] The power is also given to a minister of the Church of Scotland who has been appointed to officiate as minister to a charge without limit of time or for a period of years in any parish in which his charge, or any part of it, is situated: Church of Scotland (Property and Endowments) Amendment Act, 1933 (23 & 24 Geo. V, c. 44), s. 13 (1). A certificate of a principal clerk of the General Assembly is conclusive evidence of the parish in which the charge is situated: s. 13 (2). "Assistant and successor" includes "colleague and successor": s. 13 (3) (4).
[4] Conveyancing (Scotland) Act, 1924 (14 & 15 Geo. V. c. 27), s. 18 (1).

read over to the granter and that he gave authority for its execution on his behalf.[7] A holograph docquet, in statutory form,[5] or in any words to the like effect,[8] must precede the signatures of the notary and the witnesses.[4] The docquet must be written on the last page of the deed, and it is unnecessary for the notary to sign above as well as below the docquet.[9] The earlier pages, if any, must be authenticated in the usual manner[10] by the subscription of the notary.[9] The designations of the witnesses, as with other solemnly executed deeds,[10] must be either mentioned in a testing clause or added to their signatures,[9] and, if there is no testing clause,[11] a specification of the place and date[11] of signing may be added, if desired, to the docquet.[9] The docquet must be written by the notary in the presence of the granter and witnesses, and the subscriptions of the notary and witnesses must be adhibited in the presence of the granter of the deed and of each other.[12] In order to avoid the risk of challenge, it is probably desirable, when the parties to a bilateral deed execute notarially, that each party should be represented by a separate notary. It is by no means certain, however, that the deed is invalid because one notary executes on behalf of both parties.[13]

A writing which appears to have been executed by a notary in accordance with the rules mentioned above is a probative writing.[14] In common with other probative writings, a notarially executed deed may be reduced on the ground that the statutory rules have not in fact been complied with. A notarially executed deed may also be reduced if the notary has a beneficial interest in it.[15] A notarially executed writing which is not probative or

---

5 *Ibid.* Sch. I. The docquet is in the following terms:—Read over to, and signed by me for and by authority of the above-named *A. B.* (*without designation*), who declares that he is blind (*or* is unable to write) all in his presence, and in presence of the witnesses hereto subscribing. *C. D.*, solicitor (*or* notary public), Edinburgh (*or as the case may be*). *M. N.*, witness. *P. Q.*, witness.

6 Dickson, *Evidence* (3rd ed.) §683. The granter is personally barred from seeking reduction of his own deed on the ground that his declaration was untrue: Dickson, §684.

7 Montgomerie Bell, *Lectures* (3rd ed.) I, 57; *Farmer* v. *Myles*, 1760 M. 16, 849.

8 Conveyancing (Scotland) Act, 1924 (14 & 15 Geo. V. c. 27), s. 18 (1). See also *Watson* v. *Beveridge*, 1883, 11 R. 40; *Atchison's Trs.* v. *Atchison*, 1876, 3 R. 388.

9 *Ibid.*, Sch. I, note. The note has been regarded as explanatory of the section: *Hynd's Tr.* v. *Hynd's Trs.*, 1955 S.C. (H.L.) 1, at pp. 9, 11, 27. For the proposition that the deed need not be signed above as well as below the docquet, see also *Mathieson* v. *Hawthorns & Co. Ltd.*, 1899, 1 F. 468.

10 See § **179**, sub-para. (a).

11 See § **179**, sub-para. (c).

12 *Hynd's Tr.* v. *Hynd's Trs.*, 1955 S.C. (H.L.) 1.

13 A bilateral contract, subscribed on behalf of each party by the same notary, was held invalid in *Craig* v. *Richardson*, 1610 M. 16, 829. In *Graeme* v. *Graeme's Trs.*, 1868, 7 M. 14, however, the earlier case was not accepted as laying down a general rule even for contracts between strangers, and was held not to apply to a mutual will.

14 See §§ **176, 178.**

15 *Crawford's Trs.* v. *Glasgow Royal Infirmary* (O.H.) 1955 S.C. 367; *Gorrie's Tr.* v. *Stiven's Executrix*, 1952, S.C. 1; *Finlay* v. *Finlay's Trs.*, 1948 S.C. 16; *Newstead* v. *Dansken* (O.H.) 1918, 1 S.L.T. 136. The opinion has been expressed that a deed is not invalid merely because the notary's employers had a beneficial interest in the deed: *Hynd's Tr.* v. *Hynd's Trs.*, 1955 S.C. (H.L.) 1, at pp. 13-14, 21. As to the validity in Scotland of a will notarially executed in England, in accordance with English law, by a solicitor who had a beneficial interest, see *Irving* v. *Snow*, 1956 S.C. 257. In the last-mentioned

which has been executed without some of the solemnities, may nevertheless be valid as if it had been solemnly executed if certain matters are proved.[16]

186. VALIDITY OF INFORMALLY EXECUTED DEED—CONVEYANCING (SCOTLAND) ACT, 1874, SECTION 39

(a) General. At common law a solemnly executed deed is valid for its purpose only if the solemnities of execution are complied with. The fact that they have been complied with must be manifest from a mere scrutiny of the writing itself. If the insignia of a probative deed are lacking, their place cannot be taken by proof that the solemnities were in fact observed, such proof being incompetent.[17] A limited exception to this rule is authorised by a statutory provision,[18] which is in the following terms:—"No deed, instrument or writing subscribed by the granter or maker thereof, and bearing to be attested by two witnesses subscribing, - - - shall be deemed invalid or denied effect according to its legal import because of any informality of execution; but the burden of proving that such deed, instrument or writing so attested was subscribed by the granter or maker thereof, and by the witnesses by whom such deed, instrument or writing bears to be attested, shall lie upon the party using or upholding the same; and such proof may be led in any action or proceeding in which such deed, instrument or writing is founded on or objected to, or in a special application to the Court of Session, or to the sheriff within whose jurisdiction the defender in any such application resides, to have it declared that such deed, instrument or writing was subscribed by such granter or maker and witnesses".

(b) Essential Requirements for Operation of Section. The section provides that, in spite of what would otherwise be a fatal informality of execution, a deed may nevertheless be valid and effective as a solemnly executed deed. Before this can occur, however, two essential conditions must be complied with.

The first condition, which relates to the appearance of the deed, is that it must be validly subscribed by the granter and by the two persons who bear, on the face of the deed, to attest the granter's signature. The requirements of a valid subscription have been mentioned earlier.[19] Thus the deed remains invalid, in spite of the section, if the subscription of the granter or one of the witnesses was "Mr. Smith," even if it were proved that Mr. Smith had in fact adhibited that subscription,[20] or if the subscriptions of the granter and witnesses appear, not on the last page of the deed itself or linked with it, but on a following blank page.[21]

---

case the opinion was expressed that some aspects of the earlier decisions may need reconsideration.

[16] Conveyancing (Scotland) Act, 1874 (37 & 38 Vict. c.94), s. 39; Conveyancing (Scotland) Act, 1924 (14 & 15 Geo. V. c. 27), s. 18 (2). This subject is dealt with at § **186**.

[17] See § **178**, sub-para. (b). For the insignia of a probative deed, see § **179**.

[18] Conveyancing (Scotland) Act, 1874 (37 & 38 Vict. c. 94), s. 39.

[19] See § **179**, sub-para. (d).

[20] *Allan and Crichton*, 1933 S.L.T. (Sh.Ct.) 2.

[21] *Baird's Trs.* v. *Baird*, 1955 S.C. 286, at pp. 293, 295. For the rule as to the position of the attested subscription, see § **179**, sub-para. (a).

The second condition, which relates to the fact of execution as distinct from the mere appearance of the deed, is a proof by the party upholding the deed that it was in fact subscribed by the granter and two witnesses[22] in such a way as to constitute a validly attested subscription.[23] Proof that the granter and witnesses in fact subscribed is not enough, if the purported attestation by the witnesses was invalid. The rules for valid attestation have been mentioned earlier.[24] So the proof required by the section fails, and the deed is invalid, if one of the subscribing witnesses neither saw the granter sign nor heard him acknowledge,[25] or subscribed before the granter,[26] or subscribed after the death of the granter,[23] or had not received the granter's assent to his acting as a witness.[27]

(c) Informality as to Designations of Witnesses. The absence of the designations of the witnesses, either after their signatures or in a testing clause,[28] is an informality to which the section has been held to apply, and if the proof required by the section is satisfactory, the deed is valid in spite of the lack of this solemnity.[29] The section applies similarly if the informality consists in the misspelling in the testing clause of the names of one of the witnesses, provided that there is no doubt that the accompanying designation applies to the subscription of the witness whose subscription is in question.[30]

(d) Informality as to Subscription of Pages. A deed consisting of more than one sheet is improbative unless each page is subscribed by the granter.[31] This solemnity is necessary in order to authenticate the pages other than the last page as forming part of the deed to which the attested subscription relates. If, in spite of the absence of this solemnity, the proof required by the section satisfies the court that the earlier unauthenticated pages formed part of the "deed, instrument or writing" when the granter and the witnesses subscribed, the deed is valid in terms of the section.[32]

(e) Informality as to Authentication of Alterations. A deed is improbative if it contains erasures, deletions, interlineations or additions which have

---

[22] Proof of subscription by the granter is not enough: *Bisset*, 1961 S.L.T. (Sh.Ct.) 19.
[23] *Walker* v. *Whitwell*, 1916 S.C. (H.L.) 75.
[24] See § **182**, sub-para. (d).
[25] *Forrest* v. *Low's Trs.*, 1907 S.C. 1240, L. Johnston (Ordinary) at pp. 1246-7, L. Kinnear at pp. 1252-3.
[26] *Smyth* v. *Smyth*, 1876, 3 R. 573.
[27] *Walker* v. *Whitwell* (*supra*), at pp. 83, 90.
[28] For the rule as to this, see § **179**, sub-paras. (a), (c), (e).
[29] *Inglis' Trs.* v. *Inglis*, 1901, 4 F. 365; *Nisbet*, 1897, 24 R. 411; *Thomson's Trs.* v. *Easson*, 1878, 6 R. 141; *Addison*, 1875, 2 R. 457.
[30] *Richardson's Trs.*, 1891, 18 R. 1131.
[31] See § **179**, sub-para. (a).
[32] *Inglis' Trs.* v. *Inglis* (*supra*); *Brown*, 1883, 11 R. 400; *McLaren* v. *Menzies*, 1876, 3 R. 1151. The underlying principle is thought to be the same as that applying to the informality mentioned in sub-para. (e) below. Recent examples of the application of the section to this kind of informality may be found in *Bisset*, 1961 S.L.T. (Sh.Ct.) 19; *Bogie's Exrs.* v. *Bogie*, 1953, 69 Sh.Ct.Rep. 128; *Manson* v. *Campbell*, 1948, 64 Sh.Ct.Rep. 28; *Shiell*, 1936 S.L.T. 317.

not been properly authenticated.[33] The solemnity is necessary because, without it, it does not appear that the alterations formed part of the deed when it was subscribed by the granter and witnesses. Despite an early doubt on the point,[34] it is thought to be clear that a deed, lacking this solemnity, may nevertheless be valid in terms of the section, if, as a result of the proof which the section requires, the court is satisfied that the un-authenticated alterations in fact formed part of the deed when the granter and witnesses subscribed. The section provides for proof that the "deed, instrument or writing" was subscribed by the granter and witnesses. Unless the deed, instrument or writing which the granter and witnesses are said to have subscribed is identified by reference to its terms, the proof, and the finding of the court following thereon, are meaningless.[35] In a petition presented under the section in respect of a trust-disposition in which the trustees' names had been altered without authentication, the court was asked *inter alia* to declare that the deed was valid and entitled to effect according to its legal import. The court directed that this part of the prayer should be deleted by amendment, presumably because it went beyond the terms of the section. Thereafter, however, following the proof required by the section, the court found and declared that the trust-disposition mentioned in the petition, i.e. the deed containing the unauthenticated alterations, was sub-scribed by the granter and by the witnesses.[36] More recently it has been a matter of express decision that the informality arising from unauthenticated alterations may competently be a subject of proof under the section.[37]

(f) Informality in Notarially Executed Writing. Since January 1, 1925,[38] the section applies not only to a deed executed by the granter, but also to a notarially executed deed, which for the purpose of the section is deemed to be a deed subscribed by the granter or maker.[39] In order that the section may apply, however, the deed must have been executed in accordance with section 18 (1) of the Conveyancing (Scotland) Act, 1924,[39] the provisions of which have been referred to earlier.[40] Thus the section does not apply, and the deed is invalid, if the holograph docquet, together with the signatures of the notary and the two witnesses, were not made *unico contextu* in the presence of the granter.[41] Similarly, it is thought, the section does not apply if, in spite of what is said in the docquet, the granter did not in fact declare that he was blind or unable to write, or the writing was not read over to him

---

[33] See § **180**, sub-para. (a).

[34] *McLaren* v. *Menzies* (*supra*), L. Curriehill, *obiter*, at p. 1173.

[35] The necessity of identifying the terms of the deed to which the proof relates arises in the same way in connection with the absence of a subscription on each page when there is more than one sheet. See sub-para. (d) above. The underlying principle is thought to be the same in both instances.

[36] *Addison*, 1875, 2 R. 457.

[37] *Elliot's Exrs.* (O.H.) 1939 S.L.T. 69. See also Menzies, *Lectures* (Sturrock's ed.) 133; Burns, *Conveyancing* (4th ed.) 3.

[38] Conveyancing (Scotland) Act, 1924 (14 & 15 Geo. V. c. 27).

[39] *Ibid.*, s. 18 (2); *Hynd's Tr.* v. *Hynd's Trs.*, 1954 S.C. 112, at pp. 121, 125 (affd. 1955 S.C. (H.L.) 1).

[40] See § **185**.

[41] *Hynd's Tr.* v. *Hynd's Trs.*, 1955 S.C. (H.L.) 1.

in the presence of the witnesses, or the witnesses did not see or hear him authorise the notary to sign.[40] All these solemnities, it is thought, are essential to a valid notarial execution, [42] and there can be no room for the operation of the section unless they have been complied with. It has been held that the section applied although the words "who declares that he is unable to write," or words to the like effect, were omitted from the holograph docquet.[43] It is thought, however, that, if the principle underlying this decision were carried to its logical conclusion, it would be possible to dispense with the docquet altogether by proving the truth of what should have been contained in it by parole evidence. It seems clear that this would not be an admissible use of the section.[44] It is thought, on the analogy of a deed signed by the granter, that informalities as to the designations of the witnesses,[45] the subscription of pages other than the last page in a deed consisting of more than one sheet,[46] and, possibly, unauthenticated alterations,[47] may competently be the subject of proof under the section, with the result that despite the informalities, the deed may yet be valid.

187. ADOPTION OF INVALID DEED BY SUBSEQUENT DEED

A deed which is invalid, because it lacks some or all of the statutory solemnities, may become effective, as if it had been solemnly executed, if it is adopted by, or recognised as genuine and authentic in, a subsequent deed which itself complies with the statutory solemnities.[48] The underlying principle is the same as that applying to the adoption of invalid deeds by subsequent holograph writings, a subject which is mentioned later.[49]

---

[42] The corresponding essential requirements for the application of the section to a deed executed by the granter, are mentioned in sub-para. (b) above.

[43] *Shiels* v. *Shiels*, 1951, 67 Sh.Ct.Rep. 54; *cf. Cameron* v. *Holman*, 1951, Scottish Land Court Reps., 14.

[44] See *Hynd's Tr.* v. *Hynd's Trs. (supra).* In *Watson* v. *Beveridge*, 1883, 11 R. 40, where the section was not referred to, proof before answer was allowed of an averment that the deed had in fact been "read over" to the granter, although the words used in the docquet were merely that it had "been previously gone over and explained" to him. The majority did not commit themselves to a view as to whether the informality in the docquet was an insuperable flaw in the deed. Lord Rutherfurd Clark, in a strong dissenting opinion, thought that even if the notary had read every word of the deed to the granter, the correct wording of the docquet was a solemnity, the absence of which could not be cured by extraneous evidence.

[45] See sub-para. (c) above.

[46] See sub-para. (d) above.

[47] See sub-para. (e) above.

[48] *Callander* v. *Callander's Trs.*, 1863, 2 M. 291. See also § **285.**

[49] See § **190,** sub-paras. (c) (d).

CHAPTER XVII

AUTHENTICATION OF HOLOGRAPH WRITINGS

188. EFFECTIVENESS OF UNTESTED HOLOGRAPH WRITING

A valid holograph writing, although not executed in accordance with the statutory solemnities,[1] is the equivalent of a writing so executed.[2] A writing, not holograph of the granter, which has been adopted as holograph by him, is equally effective for this purpose.[3] The reason for relaxing, in the case of holograph writings, the rules for the authentication of solemnly executed documents is that the forgery of the whole of a hand-written deed is more difficult, and less likely to be attempted, than the forgery of a mere signature.[4]

189. IMPROBATIVE NATURE OF UNTESTED HOLOGRAPH WRITING

Unlike a solemnly executed writing, an untested holograph writing is not probative,[5] although it is sometimes so described.[6] Unless its genuineness is admitted, it must be proved to be holograph before it can be founded upon.[7] Because of the practice, in unopposed applications in the commissary courts, of granting confirmation without proof of the holograph nature of the testamentary writing founded upon, if it contains within it (*in gremio*) a statement that it was written by the granter, it was at one time thought that such a statement in any writing placed upon the person disputing it the burden of proving the contrary. It is now authoritatively decided that such a statement does not have this effect,[7] except perhaps in a case where it is admitted that the deed was executed by the granter, but disputed that the whole of it was written by him.[8]

---

[1] As to the nature of the solemnities, see §§ **176** *et seq.*

[2] As a matter of conveyancing practice this would not be true of a holograph not-tested disposition of heritage. See § **91**, note 13.

[3] See § **190**, sub-paras. (c), (d).

[4] Stair, iv, 42, 6; Erskine, iii, 2, 22; Montgomerie Bell, *Lectures* (3rd ed.) I, 78; Bell, *Dictionary* (7th ed.), 509; *Callander* v. *Callander's Trs.*, 1863, 2 M. 291, L. Cowan at p. 301. For a decision which appears to destroy the justification for the relaxation, see § **190**, sub-para. (a), note 20.

[5] For the meaning of "probative," see § **178**, sub-para. (a).

[6] *Cranston*, 1890, 17 R. 410, L. McLaren at p. 415.

[7] *Harper* v. *Green*, 1938 S.C. 198; *Cranston* (*supra*); *Anderson* v. *Gill*, 1858, 20 D. 1326: (H.L.) 7: 3 Macq. 180. As to what must be proved, see the next paragraph.

190. CHARACTERISTICS AND PROOF OF HOLOGRAPH WRITING

(a) **General Rule.** In order to be the equivalent of a solemnly executed writing an untested holograph writing must be proved by the person founding upon it to be wholly, or in the essential parts,[9] written by the granter and subscribed by him.[10] Writings expressly or impliedly adopted as holograph, which have the same effect, are mentioned later.[11]

A writing which complies with the rule does not cease to be valid merely because it is written in pencil,[12] or partly in pencil and partly in ink,[13] unless the pencil writing consists only of unauthenticated alterations to a document written originally in ink, which, if construed as merely deliberative, are ignored.[14] A writing which purports to be solemnly executed, but is defective in some of the solemnities, as where the witnesses did not see the granter sign or hear him acknowledge his signature,[15] or their designations are not added to their signatures or mentioned in a testing clause,[16] will nevertheless be sustained as a valid holograph writing if it complies with the rule mentioned above. And an otherwise valid holograph writing will not be held invalid merely because it concludes with the words "before these witnesses," and was not in fact attested.[17] A document written by a partner, and signed by him with the firm name, binds the firm,[18] and a document holograph of, and signed by, a duly authorised agent on behalf of his principal, binds the principal.[19]

In one case,[20] a will which was wholly in typewriting except for the testator's signature, and which was untested, was held to be valid as a holograph will in the following circumstances: (1) the will was admittedly

---

[8] In such a case the effect of the *in gremio* statement may place upon the person disputing the genuineness of the writing, the burden of proving that, although it was the granter's deed, he did not in fact write all of it himself. See *Harper* v. *Green* (*supra*), L. Carmont at p. 205.

[9] A testamentary writing, subscribed by the testator, of which only the introductory words "To my Executors," were holograph, was held not to be holograph in the essential parts: *Maitland's Trs.* v. *Maitland*, 1871, 10 M. 79. For other examples of what are, or are not, essential parts, see the next sub-para.

[10] Bell, *Principles*, §20; approved in *Tucker* v. *Canch's Tr.*, 1953 S.C. 270, at pp. 274, 276; *Bridgeford's Exr.* v. *Bridgeford*, 1948 S.C. 416, at pp. 419-20; *Macdonald* v. *Cuthbertson*, 1890, 18 R. 101, at p. 106. As to what constitutes an adequate subscription, see § **191**. For the statutory provisions regarding proof of holograph testamentary writings, see sub-para. (e) below.

[11] See sub-paras. (c), (d) below.

[12] *Muir's Trs.*, 1869, 8 M. 53; *Tait's Trs.* v. *Chiene*, 1911 S.C. 743.

[13] *Manson* v. *Edinburgh Royal Institution for the Education of Deaf and Dumb Children* (O.H.) 1948 S.L.T. 196.

[14] See § **192**, sub-para. (b).

[15] *Yeats* v. *Yeats' Trs.*, 1833, 11 S. 915.

[16] *Lorimer's Exrs.* v. *Hird* (O.H.) 1959 S.L.T. (Notes) 8.

[17] *Gunnell's Trs.* v. *Jones* (O.H.) 1915, 1 S.L.T. 166.

[18] *Nisbet* v. *Neil's Tr.*, 1869, 7 M. 1097; *Buchanan* v. *Dennistoun*, 1835, 13 S. 841.

[19] *Whyte* v. *Lee*, 1879, 6 R. 699, at pp. 704, 705. Cf. *Scottish Lands and Buildings Co. Ltd.* v. *Shaw*, 1880, 7 R. 756 (offer to purchase heritage, purporting to be written and signed by offerer, and in fact written and signed by his brother with his authority, held not binding).

[20] *McBeath's Trs.* v. *McBeath*, 1935 S.C. 471.

typewritten by the testator himself and subscribed in his handwriting: (2) it contained a statement, also in typewriting, that it was typed by the testator and accepted as holograph by him: (3) it was admitted that owing to physical infirmity the testator's handwriting had become indecipherable, and that he invariably used a typewriter for all communications. The decision to uphold the validity of the deed was by a majority of Seven Judges, the dissenting minority consisting of the Lord President (Clyde), the Lord Justice-Clerk (Aitchison) and Lord Murray, and Lord Morison, in an addendum to his opinion, appeared to concede that, apart from the very special circumstances of the particular case, the minority view was correct. This decision has since been held to rule only in cases where the essential facts are identical.[21] The absence, in an untested typewritten will, of a statement that it was typed by the granter and accepted as holograph by him, was regarded as a sufficient ground of distinction.[21] The sole justification for relaxing the statutory solemnities in favour of holograph writings[22] would seem to be destroyed if a deed which contains no handwriting except the signature may be sustained as a holograph deed. Typewriting, while it may afford evidence of the identity of the machine used, does not help to identify the person using it. Handwriting, on the other hand, by its mere appearance, enables the writer of the body of the deed to be identified with the writer of the subscription, and as the granter of the deed. This distinction, upon which, in principle, the rule regarding holograph documents is founded, was the foundation of the minority view in *McBeath's Trs.* v. *McBeath*,[20] a view with which, in general, Lord Morison finally concurred. It is thought, accordingly, that the general rule has not been affected by the decision.

Except in the case of testamentary writings, which are mentioned later,[23] and of a holograph acceptance of intimation of an assignation,[24] untested holograph writings, although proved to be genuine, are not probative of the dates they bear.[25] When the date is of importance, it must be proved to be the true date by the party founding upon the writing.[26] The right of challenging the date, however, is open only to third parties, since the granter and grantee are barred *personali exceptione* from challenging it on that ground.[27]

(b) Deeds partly Printed and partly Holograph. All the reported decisions on deeds of this kind relate to the difficulties which have arisen when a testator completes the blanks in a printed form of will, in ignorance of the fact that, unless the deed is solemnly executed, there is a grave risk that it

---

[21] *Chisholm* v. *Chisholm* (O.H.) 1949 S.C. 434. The averment that the will was valid as a holograph document because it had been typed by the testator was held to be irrelevant, and the action, in so far as founded on this averment, was dismissed.

[22] See § **188**, note 4.

[23] See sub-para. (e) below.

[24] Bell, *Principles*, §1465; Dickson, *Evidence* (3rd ed.) §775.

[25] Erskine, iii, 2, 22; Dickson, *Evidence* (3rd ed.) §770.

[26] *Dyce* v. *Paterson*, 1847, 9 D. 1141 (sequestration); *Waddell* v. *Waddell's Trs.*, 1845, 7 D. 605 (insanity). The date appearing in the writing is not to be disregarded. It is an item of evidence to be considered in relation to the whole circumstances: Dickson, *Evidence* (3rd ed.) §772.

[27] Dickson, *Evidence* (3rd ed.) §774.

will be invalid. What is said in this sub-paragraph, therefore, refers in terms only to testamentary writings, but there seems no reason why the principles underlying the decisions should not apply to other untested deeds which are partly holograph and partly printed. They apply also to a deed which is partly holograph and partly typewritten or written by the hand of another person.[28]

The general rule is that a deed may be valid as a holograph writing if *in the essential parts* it is written by the granter.[29] This part of the general rule has been expanded by decision in its relation to testamentary deeds of the kind mentioned above. In order that such a testamentary deed may be valid as a holograph writing all the essential parts must be in the testator's writing.[30] The printed parts must be purely formal or superfluous, so that, if they are struck out or disregarded, there still remains a complete expression of the writer's intention.[31] But the printed parts must not be entirely disregarded. However clear the expression of intention in the written parts may seem to be, no effect can be given to them if any of the printed parts add to, detract from or qualify what is expressed by the written words.[32] It would seem that once it is held that a writing is essentially holograph because it complies with the principles mentioned above, then effect may properly be given to the whole document, printed and written.[33]

The principles are easy to state, but their application is frequently difficult. The question of whether a particular deed is essentially holograph is said to be one of fact,[31] which must be decided in the first place by construing the holograph parts of the deed.[34] Deeds were held to be holograph when the portions in the testator's writing consisted of the following:—(i) "[testator's name and address]"—"to my sisters [A and B] £40 each: to Mr. and Mrs. [C] £10 each"—"Residue divided into 4 equal parts to [D, E, G, F]"—"Reverend [H]"—"[the date]"—"[testator's signature]."[35] (ii) "[testator's name and address and the date]"—"[a name and address]"—"[a name and address]"—"[house at 19 Upper Grove Place," "Furniture, bed and table linen in fact everything in the house, also my insurances, and pay all my debts at my death, all other money left by me to be divided among the family." "[testator's signature], 19 Upper Grove Place, Edinburgh."[36] (iii) "[testator's name and address and the date]"—"[two names and addresses]"—"Jane Carmichael (nee Clark), as long as she remains a faithful and dutiful wife, all my houses, lands, all money that is or may be mine

---

28 *Macdonald* v. *Cuthbertson*, 1890, 18 R. 101, at p. 109.
29 See sub-para. (a) above.
30 *Gillies* v. *Glasgow Royal Infirmary*, 1960 S.C. 439, L.P. Clyde at p. 442.
31 *Macdonald* v. *Cuthbertson* (*supra*), L. Kinnear at p. 108; approved in *Bridgeford's Exr.* v. *Bridgeford*, 1948 S.C. 416, at pp. 420, 437; *Tucker* v. *Canch's Tr.*, 1953 S.C. 270, at pp. 274, 277.
32 *Bridgeford's Exr.* v. *Bridgeford*, 1948 S.C. 416, at pp. 420, 421, 438.
33 *Tucker* v. *Canch's Tr.* (*supra*), at p. 278; *Bridgeford's Exr.* v. *Bridgeford* (*supra*), at p. 438.
34 For a discussion of what may, and what may not be, read into incompleted sentences in the testator's handwriting, see *Cameron's Trs.* v. *Mackenzie*, 1915 S.C. 313, L.P. Strathclyde at pp. 318-319; *Gillies* v. *Glasgow Royal Infirmary* (*supra*), at pp. 442, 443.
35 *Gillies* v. *Glasgow Royal Infirmary* (*supra*).
36 *Bridgeford's Exr.* v. *Bridgeford* (*supra*).

[and an enumeration of household goods]. I desire at the decease of my wife and myself that the whole of the estate be divided as follows:—[exact instructions for the division of the capital of the estate, appointment of executors, and testator's signature]."[37]   Deeds were held *not* to be holograph when the portions in the testator's writing consisted of the following:— (i) "[testator's name and address]"—"to my daughter Enid. . . . Revoke former will," "[testator's signature]"—"[the date]"—"[testator's signature]."[38] (ii) "[testator's name and address]"—"my two brothers [naming them] equally and jointly, if one deceased to the survivor only"—"their"—"[a name and address]"—"[the testator's name]"—"[the date]"—"[testator's signature]."[39]

(c) Express Adoption as Holograph. A deed which is printed, typewritten or written by the handwriting of another, may become the equivalent of a deed holograph of the granter if he adds below it, in his own handwriting, the words "adopted as holograph" and his signature.[40] This applies even when the holograph docquet appears immediately after the signature, instead of immediately before it.[40] The operative part of such a deed is the holograph docquet,[41] by which the granter agrees to be bound by a writing which would not otherwise be binding upon him.[42] The use of such docquets makes it possible for all the parties to a deed to be bound by it as if it were holograph of each of them. It may be written and subscribed by one of the parties and adopted as holograph by the other, or it may be printed, typewritten or written by another person, and adopted as holograph by each of the parties by a docquet written and subscribed by himself.[43]

[37] *Carmichael's Exrs.* v. *Carmichael*, 1909 S.C. 1387.
[38] *Tucker* v. *Canch's Tr.*, 1953 S.C. 270. It was contended that, even if the holograph portion of the deed failed to dispone anything to the person named, the will at least effectively revoked earlier wills. This contention was unsuccessful. Such a deed must receive effect as a whole, or not at all.
[39] *Macdonald* v. *Cuthbertson*, 1890, 18 R. 101.
[40] *Gavine's Tr.* v. *Lee*, 1883, 10 R. 448. Other words accepting or adopting what appears above the docquet, such as "I agree to the above," produce the same result. See Dickson, *Evidence* (3rd ed.) §756; *Maitland's Trs.* v. *Maitland*, 1871, 10 M. 79, L. Kinloch at p. 84.
[41] *McBeath's Trs.* v. *McBeath*, 1935 S.C. 471, L.P. Clyde at p. 477.
[42] *Campbell's Trs.* v. *Campbell*, 1903, 5 F. 366, L. McLaren at p. 372. In *Harvey* v. *Smith*, 1904, 6 F. 511, an offer was signed in circumstances which cast grave doubts upon the serious intention of the offeror to enter into a contract. It was held that the writing and subscribing of the words "adopted as holograph" was not binding unless the offeror understood that, by so doing, he made the deed irrevocably binding upon him. For doubts about this decision, see Gloag, *Contract* (2nd ed.) 95-96. Whatever the *ratio decidendi* may have been, it is thought that it cannot mean that a person is not bound by such a docquet unless he understands the literal meaning of the words "adopted as holograph." A person entering into a contract which is unintelligible to him, is bound by its true construction as ascertained by the court: *Laing* v. *Provincial Homes Investment Co.*, 1909 S.C. 812. See also *Bell Bros.* v. *Reynolds*, 1945 S.C. 213, at p. 221.
[43] Dickson, *Evidence* (3rd ed.) §756. The authorities cited by Dickson are not exactly in point, but the statement seems to be clearly right in principle. A deed holograph of one of the parties is not holograph of the others who merely sign it: *Miller* v. *Farquharson*, 1835, 13 S. 838. (Opinions to the contrary in *Dickson* v. *Blair*, 1871, 10 M. 41, L. Deas at p. 46, and *Weir* v. *Robertson*, 1872, 10 M. 438, are thought to be wrong in

(d) Implied Adoption as Holograph. Although not expressly adopted as holograph, a deed which is printed, or typewritten or written by the hand of another, may be adopted as holograph by implication if it is referred to and recognised in a later holograph writing as a valid and subsisting writ.[44] The principle is the same as that applicable to solemnly executed deeds which make reference to earlier improbative writings as if they were valid.[45] So a non-holograph acceptance of an offer to purchase heritage was given holograph effect by the covering holograph letter with which it was enclosed, in which reference was made to "my acceptance of your offer."[44] What remained of a solemnly executed will, after parts had been deleted, and most of the testing clause and the signatures of the testator and witnesses had been cut off, was held to be valid as if it were holograph, because a holograph note, written in the margin and subscribed by the testator, mentioned certain of its provisions in such a way as to show that they were still effective.[46] A will, written to the testator's dictation by his wife, was held to be valid as a holograph writing because in a holograph note, subscribed by the testator, at the top of the other side of the page, there was a reference to "my Trustees," which was construed as a recognition of the valid appointment of trustees, and of the trust purposes, in the non-holograph writing.[47] A non-holograph will, in which *inter alia* each grandchild was given a legacy of £25, was held to have been impliedly adopted as holograph, because in a holograph codicil, subscribed by the testator, one of the grandchildren was "fined" £12 for his failure to repay a loan, "leaving balance £13 as his share."[48]

A similar principle applies to a holograph writing which is invalid, as such, because it is not subscribed. This also may, by implication, be adopted as holograph, if it is unmistakably identified by, and incorporated by reference in, another writing which is both holograph and subscribed.[49] So an unsigned holograph will was held to have been adopted as valid by a later subscribed holograph writing, which commenced with the words "In addition to will made before my father's death":[50] and by a subscribed holograph docquet, on the back of one of the pages, which appointed two named executors "of this my Will".[51] The adoption is effective, however, only in so far as the unsigned document is consistent with the terms of the adopting document.[52] A mere subscription on the envelope containing the unsigned writing is not sufficient to render the latter valid as a holograph writing.[53]

principle.) And it is not binding even upon the party who wrote it, if his liability depends upon all being bound: Gloag, *Contract* (2nd ed.) 201.
[44] *McGinn* v. *Shearer*, 1947 S.C. 334, at pp. 344, 346.
[45] See the reference to *Callender* v. *Callender's Trs.*, 1863, 2 M. 291, in *McGinn* v. *Shearer* (*supra*).
[46] *Liddle* v. *Liddle* (O.H.) 1898, 6 S.L.T. 218.
[47] *Cross' Trs.* v. *Cross* (O.H.) 1921, 1 S.L.T. 244.
[48] *Craik's Executrix* v. *Samson* (O.H.) 1929 S.L.T. 592.
[49] *Stenhouse* v. *Stenhouse*, 1922 S.C. 370, L.P. Clyde at pp. 372-373.
[50] *Fraser's Executrix* v. *Fraser's C.B.*, 1931 S.C. 536.
[51] *Campbell's Exrs.* v. *Maudslay* (O.H.) 1934 S.L.T. 420. See also *Muir* v. *Muir* (O.H.) 1950 S.L.T. (Notes) 40.
[52] *Macphail's Trs.* v. *Macphail*, 1940 S.C. 560.

(e) Proof and Date of Testamentary Writings—Statutory Provisions.
Any testamentary writing on which confirmation of executors nominate was
issued prior to July 1, 1938, is deemed to be probative.[54] Any other testamentary writing may be proved to be in the proper handwriting of, and
signed with the proper signature of, the deceased testator in an action in
the sheriff court for declarator that the writing is holograph of the testator,
in the course of which the sheriff may accept as evidence of these facts the
affidavits of two or more persons, who depone that they are well acquainted
with the handwriting and signature of the testator.[55] Persons may so depone
although they have a patrimonial interest in the estate.[55] The sheriff may
call for further affidavits, or may appoint the relevant facts to be proved
by the ordinary rules of evidence.[55] The affidavits may be endorsed on the
testamentary writing or an extract thereof, or may be contained in separate
documents referring *in gremio* to the testamentary writing or extract.[56] The
affidavits may be taken before a magistrate, commissioner for oaths, justice
of the peace or notary public, not being the solicitor for the pursuer or one
of his partners or servants, or before any commissioner whom the sheriff
may appoint.[56] Every holograph writing of a testamentary character is,
in the absence of evidence to the contrary, deemed to have been executed
or made of the date it bears.[57]

191. SUBSCRIPTION OF HOLOGRAPH WRITING

To be effectual a holograph writing must be subscribed by the granter,
since without subscription the writing is understood to be an incomplete
act from which he has resiled.[58] So when a holograph writing is only super-
scribed,[59] or bears the granter's signature down the left side of the last
page,[60] the whole deed is ineffectual, and, when there is writing both above
and below the signature, only the writing above the signature is effectual.[61]
Subscription of the last page of the writing is sufficient, and if it is not clear
from the writing itself to which pages the subscription applies, this may be
established by parole evidence.[62] An exception to the general rule was
sustained when an unsubscribed holograph offer was delivered for the purpose

---

53 *Macphail's Trs.* v. *Macphail* (*supra*), at p. 567. See also *Stenhouse* v. *Stenhouse*, 1922
   S.C. 370 ("will and testament of Joseph Stenhouse" on the envelope).
54 Conveyancing Amendment (Scotland) Act, 1938 (1 & 2 Geo VI. c. 24), ss. 11, 12.
55 A. S., July 19, 1935, s. 1 (2). Apart from the exceptional procedure provided by the
   Act of Sederunt, the action proceeds as an ordinary action: s. 1 (4). The initial writ
   must be served on the heir at law, and on such other persons interested as the sheriff
   may direct: s. 1 (1).
56 *Ibid.*, s. 1 (3).
57 Conveyancing (Scotland) Act, 1874 (37 & 38 Vict. c. 94), s. 40. This is an exception
   to the general rule regarding the dates of holograph writings. See sub-para. (a) above.
58 Stair, iv, 42, 6. See also § **190**, sub-para. (a).
59 *Taylor's Executrices* v. *Thom*, 1914 S.C. 79; *Foley* v. *Costello*, 1904, 6 F. 365.
60 *Robbie* v. *Carr* (O.H.) 1959 S.L.T. (Notes) 16.
61 *McLay* v. *Farrell*, 1950 S.C. 149. *Cf. Fraser's Executrix* v. *Fraser's C.B.*, 1931 S.C. 536,
   (mentioned with doubt in *McLay* v. *Farrell*), where the writing after the signature was
   preceded by the letters "P.S."
62 *Cranston*, 1890, 17 R. 410, at pp. 411, 415; *Speirs* v. *Home Speirs*, 1879, 6 R. 1359.

of being acted upon, and was met by a subscribed holograph acceptance[63] or its equivalent.[64] It was held that in these circumstances a contract had been validly concluded and was binding on both parties. In one of these cases[64] the court was influenced to some extent by the fact that the name of the granter of the unsubscribed writing appeared *in gremio* of it, a consideration which is no longer relevant.[59] There has been no recent consideration by the Court of Session of the effect of an unsubscribed holograph writing of a contractual, as distinct from a testamentary, character, but the opinion has been expressed that, in general, the same rules apply to holograph writings of both classes.[65]

The requisites of a valid subscription of solemnly executed writings have been discussed in an earlier chapter.[66] Since valid holograph writings may include such informal documents as letters, notes or jottings, a corresponding informality is permitted in their subscription, and the rule for solemnly executed documents does not apply.[67] A subscription of a holograph writing is valid if it is the form of subscription ordinarily used by the granter for the kind of writing in question. So a holograph letter was held to be validly subscribed in one case by initials alone,[68] and in another case by a shortened form of the christened name without the surname,[69] it being proved or admitted in each case that the writer was accustomed to sign letters in that way. As in the case of solemnly executed writings, a subscription is not invalid merely because it is preceded by "Mr." or "Mrs."[70] It has been said, however, that "yr. loving mother" is not a valid subscription.[71]

192. ALTERATIONS TO HOLOGRAPH WRITING

(a) **Non-Holograph Alterations.** An alteration, whether it be a deletion or an addition, made or written by a person other than the granter of the deed, is of no effect and will be ignored.[72] The only possible exception to this statement would be an alteration written *aliena manu*, which was subscribed by the granter of the holograph writing and attested in accordance with the statutory solemnities, which would be, in effect, a solemnly executed codicil to a holograph writing.

(b) **Testamentary Writings.** When a holograph testamentary writing is found to contain deletions or erasures which appear to have been made by the testator, or holograph additions, the date when these were made is usually of little importance.[73] In particular it is usually of little moment whether they were made before or after the subscription of the deed.[74] What must

---

63 *Caithness Flagstone Quarrying Co.* v. *Sinclair*, 1880, 7 R. 1117 (the opinions on the point were *obiter*).
64 *Weir* v. *Robertson*, 1872, 10 M. 438.
65 *McGinn* v. *Shearer*, 1947 S.C. 334, L. Moncrieff at pp. 343-4.
66 See § **179,** sub-para. (d).
67 *Draper* v. *Thomason*, 1954 S.C. 136, at p. 140.
68 *Speirs* v. *Home Speirs*, 1879, 6 R. 1359.
69 *Draper* v. *Thomason* (*supra*) ("Connie").
70 *Manson* v. *Edinburgh Royal Institution* (O.H.) 1948 S.L.T. 196 ("Mrs. Elizabeth Campbell or Rigg"). See also § **179,** sub-para. (d).
71 *Pentland* v. *Pentland's Trs.* (O.H.) 1908, 16 S.L.T. 480, L. Skerrington at p. 481.

be proved by the party founding upon the writing in its altered form is that the alterations were in fact made by the hand of the testator, and that they were made with the deliberate intention of revoking or amending the parts of the deed to which they refer. That they were made with this intention will be assumed if they are separately authenticated by the testator's signature or initials. Such authentication, however, is not essential. In this respect alterations to holograph writings, consisting of writing on erasure, interpolations, interlineations and marginal additions, are to be distinguished from similar alterations to solemnly executed writings,[75] and unauthenticated alterations made by the testator in his own handwriting to a holograph deed are in the same position as alterations in a solemnly executed writing which are authenticated by being mentioned in the testing clause.[76] Whether a deletion was made by the testator accidentally or deliberately is a question of fact to be ascertained by evidence.[77] Subject to any doubt on this question, however, there is a presumption of fact, when holograph testamentary writings containing alterations are found apparently undisturbed in the repositories of the testator, that the alterations were made by him with testamentary intention.[78] This presumption does not apply when the original writing is in ink and the alterations are in pencil. In these circumstances the pencil alterations are presumed to be merely deliberative in character and effect will not be given to them,[79] unless this presumption can be rebutted by evidence.[80] It has been said that a word which has been deleted, but is still legible, may be looked at in order to see what the testator originally intended, and to give a meaning to the parts of the writing left undeleted.[81]

(c) **Obligatory Delivered Writings.** *Inter vivos* deeds are thought to be in a different position from testamentary writings from this point of view. Since the writing is intended to leave the granter's possession during his life-

---

[72] This seems too obvious to require authority, but if authority is necessary it can be found in *Pattison's Trs.* v. *University of Edinburgh*, 1888, 16 R. 73, L. McLaren at p. 77 (proposition (2)).

[73] If the date is important it must be proved, because the date of the alteration is not presumed to be that of the original writing: Dickson, *Evidence* (3rd ed.) §760.

[74] In *Reid's Exrs.* v. *Reid* (O.H.) 1953 S.L.T. (Notes) 51, effect was given to an unauthenticated holograph addition above the signature of a holograph will, which was manifestly made more than two years after the signature was adhibited. The testator had added the dates both of the original writing and of the addition.

[75] *Magistrates of Dundee* v. *Morris*, 1858, 3 Macq. 134, L. Chelmsford at p. 152. As to alterations of solemnly executed wills, see § **181.**

[76] *Robertson* v. *Ogilvie's Trs.*, 1844, 7 D. 236, L. Mackenzie at p. 242 (approved in *Magistrates of Dundee* v. *Morris* (supra)); *Hogg's Exrs.* v. *Butcher*, 1947 S.N. 141, L. Mackintosh (Ordinary) at pp. 142-3 (*affd.* 1947 S.N. 190). See also McLaren, *Wills and Succession* (3rd ed.) I, 288.

[77] *Magistrates of Dundee* v. *Morris* (supra), at p. 153.

[78] *Milne's Exr.* v. *Waugh*, 1913 S.C. 203, L.P. Dunedin at p. 208; *Allan's Executrix* v. *Allan*, 1920 S.C. 732.

[79] *Currie's Trs.* v. *Currie*, 1904 ,7 F. 364; *Munro's Exrs.* v. *Munro*, 1890, 18 R. 122; *Lamont* v. *Magistrates of Glasgow*, 1887, 14 R. 603, at pp. 607, 609.

[80] *Lamont* v. *Magistrates of Glasgow* (supra), L. Shand at p. 608, L. Adam at p. 609.

[81] *Magistrates of Dundee* v. *Morris*, 1858, 3 Macq. 134, L. Cranworth at p. 164, followed reluctantly in *Chapman* v. *Macbean*, 1860, 22 D. 745, L. J-Cl. Inglis at p. 747.

time, there is no room for the presumption that unauthenticated alterations were made by him before the deed became effective by delivery. It is thought, therefore, that deletions, to be effective, must be authenticated by the granter's subscription or initials, that additions, even if holograph, must be similarly authenticated, and that unauthenticated erasures are fatal to the deed, or to the clause in which they occur.[82]

[82] See Montgomerie Bell, *Lectures* (3rd ed.) I, 73. It may be possible to hold that the clause in which the vitiation occurs is separable from the other clauses, and, by disregarding it, to give effect to the rest of the deed. See § **180,** sub-para (a).

CHAPTER XVIII

PUBLIC AND OFFICIAL WRITINGS—EXTRACTS AND COPIES—BUSINESS BOOKS

193. SCOPE OF CHAPTER

This chapter deals with documents,[1] not as constituting or proving obligations, but as evidence of the facts stated in them. It is proposed to consider various types of documents from one or both of two aspects: (1) whether the document itself requires to be proved; and (2) whether and to what extent it is evidence of the facts stated in it.

194. STATUTES

(a) **Public General Statutes.** These consist of the Acts of the Parliament of Scotland down to 1707, and thereafter the Acts of the Parliament of the United Kingdom. They need not be proved.[2] Should any question arise

---

[1] It also includes maps, plans and tombstones.
[2] *Macmillan* v. *McConnell*, 1917 J.C. 43, L. J-Cl. Scott Dickson at p. 47; *Herkes* v. *Dickie*, 1958 J.C. 51, at pp. 55, 57, 58.

as to the precise terms of a Scots Act the Record Edition[3] would probably rule, subject to this that these Acts were revised in 1906.[4] In the case of a United Kingdom statute the matter is resolved by production of a copy bearing to be printed by the Queen's Printer or under the authority of H.M. Stationery Office.[5] Statements and narrative in public statutes are mentioned later.[6]

(b) **Private Statutes.** Since 1850, every Act[7] is deemed to be a Public Act and is to be judicially taken notice of unless the contrary is expressly provided.[8] Accordingly, it is now unnecessary, as a rule, to prove such an Act and, as in the case of a Public Act, its terms are established by production of a copy bearing to be printed by the Queen's Printer or under the authority of H.M. Stationery Office.[9] A Private Act which was passed before 1850 and which does not contain a clause to the effect that it is to be judicially noticed as a Public Act should be proved by a copy sworn to be collated with the Parliament Roll.[10] Statements and narrative in private statutes are mentioned later.[6]

195. PRIVATE ACTS OF THE SCOTTISH PARLIAMENT

These consist of decrees of the Parliament when acting in a judicial capacity, and of grants of land, titles and immunities or ratifications of Crown grants. Their terms, it is thought, are sufficiently established by the Record Edition.[11] The evidential effect of such a decree is presumably the same as that of any other decree.[12] Grants were made *salvo jure cujuslibet*,[13] so that statements in them would appear to be of little value in evidence.

196. LEGISLATION OF THE PARLIAMENT OF NORTHERN IRELAND

Since 1922 there has been a subordinate legislature in Northern Ireland.[14] The legislation of that body is for evidential purposes treated as if Northern

3 *The Acts of the Parliaments of Scotland* (ed. Thomson and Innes 1844-75); but in *Kemp v. Glasgow Corporation.* 1920 S.C. (H.L.) 73, the Record Edition was not referred to.
4 Statute Law Revision (Scotland) Act, 1906 (6 Edw. VII c. 38), s. 1. This statute does not deal with Private Acts nor with Public Acts of a constitutional nature.
5 Dickson, *Evidence* (3rd ed.) §1105. See also Phipson, *Evidence* (9th ed.) 572; *Encyclopædia of the Laws of Scotland*, xiv, §518. The Evidence Act, 1845 (8 & 9 Vict. c. 113), does not apply to Scotland.
6 See § **197.**
7 Even if the Act in its application is private. As to the classes of such Acts see *Encyclopædia of the Laws of Scotland*, xiv, §519.
8 Interpretation Act, 1889 (52 & 53 Vict. c. 63), s. 9.
9 See sub-para. (a).
10 Dickson, *Evidence* (3rd ed.) §1105.
11 *The Acts of the Parliaments of Scotland* (ed. Thomson and Innes, 1844-75). The only previous *official* collection was the "*Black Acts,*" 1566: *Sources and Literature of Scots Law* (Stair Society) 3-15.
12 See § **205.**
13 Act, 1606, c. 68; see *Earl of Lauderdale* v. *Scrymgeour Wedderburn*, 1910 S.C. (H.L.) 35, at p. 42.
14 Government of Ireland Act, 1920 (10 & 11 Geo. V c. 67), s. 1.

Ireland were a British possession within the meaning of Evidence (Colonial Statutes) Act, 1907.[15] At the same time[16] the provisions of the Documentary Evidence Acts, 1868[17] and 1882,[18] were made applicable to Northern Ireland.

197. HEADINGS, PUNCTUATION AND NARRATIVE IN STATUTES

The title, which is regarded as part of the statute, and the headings which introduce fascicles of sections, may be used in construing the Act,[19] and, although it has been said that marginal notes, brackets and punctuation must be ignored in construction,[20] the proper view would appear to be that they cannot be wholly disregarded.[21]

Statements and narrative in public statutes are evidence of the facts narrated,[22] but their effect is not conclusive,[23] and consequently may be contradicted by other evidence.[24] Such matters in Private Acts, even when rendered public for the purposes of judicial knowledge either by an *in gremio* provision to that effect or by virtue of the Interpretation Act, 1889,[25] are not evidence except in peerage cases, and even then only in relation to Private Acts which, as in the past, proceeded on evidence approved by the judges.[26] Statements in Private Acts appear, however, to be admissible to prove reputation in questions of public or general right.[27]

198. ORDERS AND PROCLAMATIONS

(a) **Orders in Council.** Orders in Council are acts of subordinate legislation made by the Crown by virtue of the prerogative, or by a minister of the Crown by virtue of statute. Since 1948 they have been classed as

---

15 Government of Ireland (Adaptation of Enactments) (No. 3) Order, 1922, S.R. & O. 1922, No. 183, para. 38 (1); see also § **203**.

16 *Ibid.*, para. 38 (2).

17 31 & 32 Vict. c. 37.

18 45 & 46 Vict. c. 9.

19 *Magistrates of Buckie* v. *Countess of Seafield's Trustees*, 1928 S.C. 525; *Millar & Lang Ltd.*, v. *Macniven & Cameron Ltd.*, (O.H.) 1908, 16 S.L.T. 56.

20 Because they were not considered by parliament: Craies, *Statute Law* (5th ed.) 183; *cf.* Gloag & Henderson, *Introduction to the Law of Scotland* (6th ed.) 5-6.

21 "While notice may, therefore, in my view be taken of punctuation in construing a statute, a comma or the absence of a comma must, I think, be disregarded if to give effect to it would so alter the sense as to be contrary to the plain intention of the statute": *Alexander* v. *Mackenzie*, 1947 J.C. 155, L. Jamieson at p. 166; *Dormer* v. *Newcastle-upon-Tyne*, [1940] 2 K.B. 204, at p. 214.

22 Not *qua* statute, but *qua* public document: Phipson, *Evidence* (9th ed.) 347; Dickson, *Evidence* (3rd ed.) §1108.

23 Dickson, *Evidence* (3rd ed.) §1108.

24 *Ibid.*

25 52 & 53 Vict. c. 63, s. 9.

26 Dickson, *Evidence* (3rd ed.) §1108.

27 *Ibid.*; Phipson, *Evidence* (9th ed.) 310, 316. In a recent English case dealing with a fair or wake it was held that in the absence of evidence to the contrary the narrative in a Private Act must be very strong evidence of the truth of a matter long beyond the reach of living memory: *Wyld* v. *Silver*, [1962] 3 W.L.R. 841.

statutory instruments[28] and are proved as such.[29] Of Orders before that year *prima facie* evidence exists when there is produced a copy of the *Gazette*[30] purporting to contain the order;[31] or a copy purporting to be printed by the government printer,[32] or under the superintendence of H.M. Stationery Office,[33] or a certified copy or extract.[34] In Scotland, apart from such *prima facie* evidence, it would appear that an Order must be proved by production of the original or of a copy sworn to be a true copy.[35] Orders in Council pursuant to statute are within judicial knowledge.[36]

(b) **Royal Proclamations.** A royal proclamation is the vehicle of legislation by the Crown in these matters where the Crown has a discretionary authority either by virtue of the prerogative or statute. Proclamations are also in use to declare war and peace, lay embargoes on shipping, and to summon and dissolve parliament. They are "valid in law" if published in the *Gazette*,[37] and are part of judicial knowledge as if they had been enacted by Parliament.[38]

(c) **Statutory Instruments.** A statutory instrument is any document by which Her Majesty exercises a power conferred on her exercisable by Order in Council or a minister exercises a power conferred on him exercisable by statutory instrument.[39] The term also includes any document by which a rule-making authority under the Rules Publication Act, 1893,[40] exercises its powers since 1948.[41] While a statutory instrument does not require to be proved,[42] its terms in case of doubt are established under the Documentary Evidence Acts,[43] and its date of issue by a list issued by the Stationery Office.[44]

199. PRE-1708 SCOTTISH SUBORDINATE LEGISLATION

Before its abolition in 1708,[45] the Scottish Privy Council was the principal executive organ as well as a superior judicatory, and the Acts of Privy Council were analogous to the English Orders in Council. Such Acts—and decrees

---

[28] Statutory Instruments Act, 1946 (9 & 10 Geo. VI c. 36), s. 1 (1).
[29] See sub-para. (c).
[30] See § **208.**
[31] Documentary Evidence Act, 1868 (31 & 32 Vict. c. 37), s. 2 (1).
[32] *Ibid.,* s. 2 (2).
[33] Documentary Evidence Act, 1882 (45 & 46 Vict. c. 9), s. 2.
[34] Documentary Evidence Act, 1868 (31 & 32 Vict. c. 37), s. 2 (3).
[35] Phipson, *Evidence* (9th ed.) 563, 575; *Encyclopædia of the Laws of Scotland*, vi, par. 916.
[36] *Macmillan* v. *McConnell*, 1917 J.C. 43; *Bradley* v. *Arthur*, 1825, 4 B. & C. 292, at p. 304.
[37] Crown Office Act, 1877 (40 & 41 Vict. c. 41), s. 3. See § **208.**
[38] Phipson, *Evidence* (9th ed.) 574.
[39] Statutory Instruments Act, 1946 (9 & 10 Geo. VI c. 36), s.1.
[40] 56 & 57 Vict. c. 66, s. 4.
[41] Statutory Instruments Act, 1946 (9 & 10 Geo. VI c. 36), s. 1 (2).
[42] *Macmillan* v. *McConnell*, 1917 J.C. 43, L. J-Cl. Scott Dickson at p. 47.
[43] Documentary Evidence Act, 1868 (31 & 32 Vict. c. 37), s. 2; Documentary Evidence Act, 1882 (45 & 46 Vict. c. 9), s. 2.
[44] Statutory Instruments Act, 1946 (9 & 10 Geo. VI c. 36), s. 3 (1).
[45] Act, 6 Anne, c. 6, s. 1.

when the Privy Council was acting in a judicial capacity—are, it is thought, adequately proved by production of the manuscript of the Register of the Privy Council[46] or by an extract therefrom certified by the Keeper of the Records.[47]

200. BYE-LAWS AND REGULATIONS

A bye-law or regulation, as presently considered, is "an ordinance affecting the public, or some portion of the public, imposed by some authority clothed with statutory powers."[48] Where the statute authorising the bye-law or regulation provides that it shall have the same effect as if it were contained in the Act,[49] or shall have the effect of an Act of Parliament,[50] no proof of it is required.[51] Statutory instruments[52] and orders founded on in a summary prosecution[53] are mentioned elsewhere. The statute authorising the making of an order may also provide how the terms of the order are to be proved, e.g., by a certificate.[54] Where there is no statutory method of certifying the terms of a bye-law, a witness would be required to prove the accuracy of the copy.[56]

201. ACTS OF SEDERUNT AND ACTS OF ADJOURNAL

Acts of Sederunt and Acts of Adjournal are authenticated respectively by the signature of the Lords of Council and Session and the Lords Commissioners of Justiciary.[57] The legislation instituting the College of Justice provided for royal ratification of Acts of Sederunt,[58] but the Act of 1540 gave power to the Lords of Session to make such Acts by themselves.[59] The latter statute would appear to give an Act of Sederunt statutory effect. After 1893 Acts of Sederunt and Acts of Adjournal were statutory rules[60] and are now since 1948 statutory instruments.[61] As such they are part of

[46] This work has been largely calendared and printed in *Register of the Privy Council of Scotland*, H.M.S.O.
[47] Public Records (Scotland) Act, 1937 (1 Edw. VIII & 1 Geo. VI c. 43), s. 9.
[48] *Kruse* v. *Johnson*, [1898] 2 Q.B. 91, at p. 96.
[49] *Institute of Patent-Agents* v. *Lockwood*, 1894, 21 R. (H.L.) 61, at pp. 67, 70, 71.
[50] *Hamilton* v. *Fyfe*, 1907 S.C. (J.) 79.
[51] *Herkes* v. *Dickie*, 1958 J.C. 51, at pp. 55, 57.
[52] § **198,** sub-para. (c).
[53] § **209.**
[54] Local Government (Scotland) Act, 1947 (10 & 11 Geo. V c. 43), s. 303; Agricultural Wages (Scotland) Act, 1949 (12, 13 & 14 Geo. VI c. 30), s. 15. As to the limitations of such certificates, see *R.* v. *Governor of Brixton Prison, ex parte Shuter*, [1960] 2 Q.B. 89. As to statutory certificates, see § **206.**
[56] Dickson, *Evidence* (3rd ed.) §§ 1316, 1317.
[57] Normally the president of each court signs, and the accession of the other lords is testified by the addition of "*I. P. D.*", *in praesentia dominorum: Maclean of Ardgour* v. *Maclean*, 1941 S.C. 613, at p. 708.
[58] Act, 1532, c. 2; Act of Sederunt, May 27, 1532.
[59] Act, 1540, c. 10.
[60] Rules Publication Act, 1893 (56 & 57 Vict. c. 66), s. 4.
[61] Statutory Instruments Act, 1946 (9 & 10 Geo. VI c. 36), s. 1 (2); see also § **198,** sub-para. (c).

the general law and do not require proof.[62]

The position of these Acts before 1893 is lacking in authority. Although they do not appear to come within the ambit of the Act of 1868,[63] which gives certain orders *prima facie* value, it is thought that in the absence of challenge, copies of Acts of Sederunt and Acts of Adjournal would be received without proof, but if challenged—and there appears to be no reported case of challenge—the books of sederunt or books of adjournal would be produced by their custodier or an extract given by the clerk of court or by the keeper of the records to whom the books have been transmitted for custody.

202. ACTS OF ASSEMBLY

Acts of Assembly are the vehicle of legislation of the General Assembly of the Church of Scotland. There appears to be no distinction between the legislative and other powers of the church courts (including the General Assembly) in relation to proof of an Act. This may be done by producing the original minutes, if these are authenticated according to the forms observed by the church,[64] or an extract attested by the clerk which will be received in evidence.[65] There are various church records embodying the earlier Acts of Assembly,[66] the more recent being printed by authority of the Assembly.

203. DOMINION, COLONIAL AND FOREIGN STATUTES

Dominion, colonial and foreign statutes are not part of the general law and therefore, unlike British statutes, do not prove themselves by mere citation. Dominion and Colonial statutes may be proved by production of certified copies or of a print, copies certified by the clerk or other proper officer of a legislative body in any colony being *prima facie* evidence.[67] They may also be proved by copies purporting to be printed by the government printer of the colony.[68] Such prints are received in evidence in all courts in the United Kingdom without proof that they were so printed. The Act applies to statutes passed by the legislature of any British possession (including local legislatures where they exist) and the Act may be extended to

---

[62] See §§ **52, 53.**

[63] Documentary Evidence Act, 1868 (31 & 32 Vict. c. 37), s. 2.

[64] In particular, authentication by the *timeous* subscription of the moderator and clerk is not essential: the Act, 1686 c. 4, "ordaining Interlocutors to be subscribed by the Judges" does not apply to church matters: *Fergusson* v. *Skirving*, 1850, 12 D. 1145, affd. 1 Macq. 232 (presbytery); Cox, *Practice* (4th ed.) 71 *et seq.* The inspection and subscription of the minutes is normally done half yearly: see also § **221**, sub-para. (d).

[65] As to the form, see Cox, *Practice and Procedure in the Church of Scotland* (4th ed.) 73 *et seq.*

[66] *Ibid.*, 190 *et seq: Sources and Literature of Scots Law* (Stair Society) 156-7.

[67] Colonial Laws Validity Act, 1865 (28 & 29 Vict. c. 63), s. 6; *King* v. *Governor of Brixton Prison, ex parte Percival*, [1907] 1 K.B. 696, at p. 707.

[68] Evidence (Colonial Statutes) Act, 1907 (7 Edw. VII c. 16), s. 1.

apply to protectorates.[69] It seems likely that in almost all cases it will be more convenient to prove colonial statutes in this way rather than under the Act of 1865, except that no one but an expert can be sure that the printer's copy tendered is the latest version of the local law.[70]

Foreign statutes may be proved in the same way as any other matter of foreign law by the evidence of witnesses skilled in the law of the country concerned.[71]

Foreign, dominion and colonial documents are dealt with elsewhere.[72]

204. CROWN CHARTERS, LETTERS PATENT, ETC.

Crown charters are grants made by the Crown usually under the great seal[73] or otherwise according to the forms prescribed by statute.[74] The variety of names, such as letters patent, pardons, commissions, given to these grants refers to the subject matter of the grant rather than the form. A charter is a probative document if executed in the normal way. Usually, royal charters were engrossed in the Register of the Great Seal,[75] but until 1672[76] failure to register was not attended by any penalty and omissions were common.[77] The register was not probative until 1809,[78] and before then booking usually preceded sealing, thus affording *locus pœnitentiæ*.[79] It is admissible for a witness to testify that he has examined the register and produce his copy thereof; and an extract by an official having a commission to that effect from the Clerk Register is admissible evidence.[80] Despite their imperfections these royal registers are of great weight.

A royal charter is not always proof of the facts narrated therein. Thus a remission is not proof that a crime has been committed,[81] nor a gift of

---

[69] The Act of 1907 has been extended to various protectorates by orders. For the purposes of the Act, Northern Ireland is treated as if it were "a British possession": see § **196.**

[70] *R.* v. *Governor of Brixton Prison ex parte Shuter*, [1960] 2 Q.B. 89.

[71] Dickson, *Evidence* (3rd ed.) §1107. See § **415.**

[72] See § **220.**

[73] Grants of lesser rights were normally given under the privy seal; in addition writs under the privy seal were also precepts for the execution of a grant under the great seal. The necessity for a privy seal precept was removed in 1809 by 49 Geo. III c. 42, s. 13, and of a signature as warrant for a grant by Titles to Land Consolidation (Scotland) Act, 1868 (31 & 32 Vict. c. 101), s. 63. For the former practice, see Menzies, *Lectures* (Sturrock's ed.) 837-844.

[74] *e.g.* Titles to Land Consolidation (Scotland) Act, 1868 (31 & 32 Vict. c. 101), s. 83, as amended by Conveyancing (Scotland) Act, 1874 (37 & 38 Vict. c. 94), s. 57.

[75] After about 1808 this is called the *Register Magni Sigilli*. There was also a Register of the Privy or Secret Seal: Livingstone, *Guide to the Public Records of Scotland.*

[76] Act, 1672, c. 16.

[77] Hector McKechnie, *Pursuit of Pedigree*, 62-63.

[78] 49 Geo. III c. 42, s. 15.

[79] Erskine, iv, 1, 22; Dickson, *Evidence* (3rd ed.) §§1151, 1302; *cf.* Titles to Land Consolidation (Scotland) Act, 1868 (31 & 32 Vict. c. 101), ss. 78, 87. A precept under the privy seal, which was formerly a necessary warrant for a great seal charter, does not prove such a grant under the great seal: *Mags. of Sanquhar* v. *Officers of State*, 1864, 2 M. 499.

[80] Titles to Land Consolidation (Scotland) Act, 1868 (31 & 32 Vict. c. 101), s. 87. See § **227.**

[81] *Baird* v. *Baird*, 1662 M. 12, 630.

escheat that the person escheated was a bastard,[82] although bastardy may be established by a legitimation.[83] British and United Kingdom peerages may also be proved by production of entries in the House of Lords Journals.[84]

Letters patent for inventions are now regulated by the Patents Act, 1949, and they are within judicial knowledge, without proof, if sealed with the seal of the Patent Office.[85] Further a certificate purporting to be signed by the comptroller and certifying that an entry which he is authorised to make has or has not been made, or that any other thing he is authorised to do has or has not been done, is *prima facie* evidence of the matters so certified;[86] and a copy of any entry in any register or of any document kept in the Patent Office or of any patent or an extract from any such register or document purporting to be certified by the comptroller and to be sealed with the seal of the Patent Office is admitted in evidence without further proof and without production of the original.[87]

Records of chancery, although granted under the great seal or the analogous "quarter seal", differ from other Crown grants under seal in that they are not special grants *de novo* of particular rights, but are rather deliverances or decrees in the judicial process initiated by brieve, which process was largely superseded by procedure by summons. The chief part of these records of chancery are the retours and decrees of services of heirs.[88] The retour of service was the verdict of an inquest or assize held by virtue of a brieve issued out of chancery for trying certain matters, such as the propinquity of the claimant's ancestor, and whether the ancestor was seized of lands. The verdict of the assize was "retoured," or returned, to chancery and an extract retour was given out under seal.[89] The book of engrossed retours begins in 1830, but they are often incomplete or inaccurate. However, these books and other records of chancery may be of importance in pedigree cases.[90] Extracts from chancery are equivalent to extract retours.[91]

Procedure by brieve and retour has now been superseded by petition and service;[92] and an extract registered decree of service is equivalent in effect to the former retour.

205. JUDICIAL RECORDS

Interlocutors, decrees, verdicts and other steps in procedure are proved

---

[82] *Cunningham* v. *Montgomery*, 1670 M. 12, 637.
[83] *King's Advocate* v. *Crow*, 1669 M. 12, 637.
[84] *Barony of Saye & Sele*, 1848, 1 H.L.C. 507.
[85] Patents Act, 1949 (12, 13 & 14 Geo. VI c. 87), s. 21 (1).
[86] *Ibid.*, s. 77 (1).
[87] *Ibid.*, s. 77 (2).
[88] See generally, Thomas Thomson, *Abridgment of Retours* (1811) preface; Dickson, *Evidence* (3rd ed.) §§ 1144-1150.
[89] Originally the principal retour was given out.
[90] Hector McKechnie, *Pursuit of Pedigree*, 18-22.
[91] Titles to Land Consolidation Act, 1868 (31 & 32 Vict. c. 101), ss. 36, 37; Balfour, *Practicks* (1754) 420, "Na persoun can pretend or alledge ignorance of ony retour or evident that is past or extractit furth of the chancellarie."
[92] Service of Heirs Act, 1847 (10 & 11 Vict. c. 47), s. 2; Titles to Land Consolidation Act, 1868 (31 & 32 Vict. c. 101), s. 27.

by the original, authenticated by the judge or the clerk of court, as the case may be, or by extracts[93] certified by the proper officer, who, in the case of records in the custody of the court, is the clerk of court or the extractor,[94] and, in the case of records which have been transmitted to his custody, the Keeper of the Records of Scotland.[95]

As between the parties or their successors these records, unless impugned on some extrinsic ground, are conclusive of all facts stated in them which fall properly within the record.[96] But they are not conclusive as to extraneous matters. Persons who had been fined by magistrates for attending conventicles brought an action founded on subsequent legislation to recover the fines. The decree imposing the fines bore that the money had been applied to the use of the town. This statement was held not to be within the record and therefore not probative *per se* of the fact.[97] It was not decided that it had no evidential value. When the parties are not the same, the findings in one cause would appear to have no evidential value in another unless the first was an action *in rem*.[98]

Admissions on record and confessions by plea are dealt with elsewhere.[99]

206. STATUTORY CERTIFICATES

The statutory provisions which allow certificates to take the place of oral testimony are variously expressed, and since they introduce an exception to the general rule which excludes writing as evidence of the facts stated in it, their precise terms are important.[1] Where a certificate is "conclusive evidence" of the matter certified, evidence to contradict it is inadmissible.[2] A provision that a certificate shall be "sufficient evidence" renders corroboration unnecessary, and its natural meaning would appear to be that "the Court might act upon it if they thought fit."[3] It has, however, been held that in the absence of evidence in exculpation such a certificate is conclusive,[4] and the opinion has been expressed that a provision "where the court is satisfied by a certificate" renders the certificate conclusive.[5] In any event, where such a certificate is sufficient only if the other party does not require that the granter be called as a witness, and he is called, his uncorroborated oral evidence is not sufficient to establish a crucial fact.[6] *"Prima facie* evidence"

---

[93] Dickson, *Evidence* (3rd ed.) §1286.

[94] *Ibid.*, §§ 1286, 1288.

[95] Public Records (Scotland) Act, 1937 (1 Edw. VIII & 1 Geo. VI c. 43), s. 9, as amended by Public Registers and Records (Scotland) Act, 1948 (11 & 12 Geo. VI c. 57), s. 1. See also § 227. As to judgments of the House of Lords, see § 207.

[96] See §§ 50, 51.

[97] *Stuart* v. *Mags. of Edinburgh*, 1697 M. 12, 536.

[98] See §§ 50, 51.

[99] See § 32.

[1] *Bisset* v. *Anderson*, 1949 J.C. 106, at p. 111.

[2] *Jamieson* v. *Dow*, 1899, 2 F. (J.) 24; *Henderson* v. *Wardrope*, 1932 J.C. 18.

[3] *Garbutt* v. *Durham Joint Committee*, [1906] A.C. 291, at p. 294, quoted in *Bisset* v. *Anderson* (*ut supra*). See also *Callan* v. *MacFadyen*, 1950 J.C. 82, at p. 87.

[4] *Chalmers* v. *McMeeking*, 1921 J.C. 54.

[5] *Kemp* v. *Ballachulish Estate Co.*, 1933 S.C. 478, at p. 491.

[6] *Callan* v. *MacFadyean* (*supra*). As to crucial facts see § 382.

means the same as "sufficient."[7] It has been held that where a certificate signed by an analyst is made "evidence" of the facts therein stated it merely comes in place of the analyst's oral testimony and is therefore insufficient, unless corroborated, to establish a crucial fact.[8] But a provision that a certificate "shall, until the contrary is proved, be evidence"[9] seems to imply that it is sufficient, although granted by one person. The phrase "admissible in evidence" is defined in the Merchant Shipping Act, 1894,[10] to mean evidence of the matters stated,[11] but even without such definition it is difficult to attach any other meaning to the phrase.

Some statutes provide expressly that no proof of the handwriting of the granter of the certificate or of his official position shall be required,[12] and other statutes require merely a certificate "purporting" to be signed by the proper official.[13] But even when there are no such provisions, proof of the authenticity of the certificate is unnecessary, unless it is challenged.[14]

207. NON-LEGISLATIVE RECORDS OF PARLIAMENT

The non-legislative records of both houses of Parliament include the Journals, speeches from the throne and addresses to the Crown. These are *prima facie* evidence of the proceedings which they record, but generally not of any facts to which they refer.[15] A copy judgment of the House of Lords, if certified by the proper officer, is adequate proof.[16]

208. GAZETTE

The official organs of the state are the *Gazettes* of Edinburgh, London and Belfast (formerly Dublin).[17] These are admissible evidence of the *public* matters contained in them.[18] Thus the *Gazette* is *prima facie* evidence of any proclamation, order or regulation issued by the Crown, the Privy Council or any of the principal departments of state,[19] but not of minor acts of officials.[20] Matters in the *Gazette* relating to questions of *private* right or affecting

---

7 *Bisset* v. *Anderson* (*ut supra*).
8 *Bisset* v. *Anderson* (*supra*). As to crucial facts see § **382.** Some recent statutes provide that in Scotland the certificate and the evidence of the person signing it, if he be called as a witness, shall be "sufficient" evidence: e.g., Road Traffic Act, 1962 (10 & 11 Eliz. II c. 59), s. 2 (3).
9 Local Government (Scotland) Act, 1947 (10 & 11 Geo. VI c. 43), s. 303.
10 57 & 58 Vict. c. 60.
11 See § **215.**
12 e.g. Agricultural Wages (Scotland) Act, 1949 (12, 13 & 14 Geo. VI c. 30), s. 15; Mental Health (Scotland) Act, 1960 (8 & 9 Eliz. II c. 61), s. 57 (2).
13 Motor Spirit (Regulation) Act, 1948 (11 & 12 Geo. VI c. 34), s. 11.
14 *Henderson* v. *Wardrope* (*supra*).
15 Dickson, *Evidence* (3rd ed.) §1110; Bell, *Principles*, §2210.
16 Dickson, *Evidence* (3rd ed.) §1110; *Aberdeen Railway Co.* v. *Blaikie*, 1854, 16 D. 470.
17 Documentary Evidence Act, 1868 (31 & 32 Vict. c. 37), s. 5; Government of Ireland (Adaptation of Enactments) (No. 3) Order, 1922, S.R.&O. 1922, No. 183, para. 38 (2) (c).
18 Phipson, *Evidence* (9th ed.) 349-50; Dickson, *Evidence* (3rd ed.) §§1112, 1113.
19 Documentary Evidence Act, 1868 (31 & 32 Vict. c. 37), s. 2; Documentary Evidence Act, 1882 (45 & 46 Vict. c. 9), s. 2.
20 Phipson, *Evidence* (9th ed.) 349.

individuals are in a different position: the *Gazette* is only evidence of the fact of publication not of the facts contained in the notice,[21] unless statute enjoins otherwise.[22]

209. ADMINISTRATIVE DOCUMENTS IN CRIMINAL PROCEDURE

In addition to the rules already mentioned relative to the evidential effect of public documents in criminal procedure further special rules have been made by statute,[23] Thus, in summary procedure, any letter, minute or other official document issuing from the office or in the custody of any of the departments of state or government in the United Kingdom is, when produced, *prima facie* evidence of the matters contained in it without being produced or sworn to by any witness. A copy of such document bearing to be certified by any person having authority to certify it is held as equivalent to the original. No proof of signature or of authority to certify is required.[24] Further, any order by any department of state or government or any local authority or public body made under statutory powers, or a print or copy of such order, is when produced in summary prosecution received in evidence of the due making, confirmation and existence of such order without being sworn to by any witness and without further or other proof; but the accused may challenge the order on the ground that it is *ultra vires*.[25] The words "when produced" appear to be ambiguous. When the order founded upon has been given the status of an Act of Parliament by the statute which authorised the making of it, there is no need for it to be "produced" in the technical sense, or "received in evidence" because it is used merely to remind the court of what the law is.[26] The position is otherwise when the order lacks this statutory status and it must then be produced and made part of the evidence in the cause.[27] The opinions of Lord Johnston and Lord Skerrington in *Macmillan* v. *McConnell*[26] also imply that there is a distinction between orders which contain the law and those which establish a fact, and that the latter must be " produced " and " received in evidence ", while the former need not be. The distinction, however, is rather one of procedure than of evidence. In solemn procedure, in a notice of previous convictions relative to aggravation of a charge[28] on indictment, the convictions are held to apply to the accused in the absence of challenge by him.[29]

21 Dickson, *Evidence* (3rd ed.) §§ 1112, 1113.
22 e.g., Banking (Scotland) Act, 1845 (8 & 9 Vict. c. 38), s. 3 (conclusive evidence).
23 Summary Jurisdiction (Scotland) Act, 1954 (2 & 3 Eliz. II c. 48), s. 35 (3). Certain military documents are also given evidential value: e.g., Army Act, 1955 (3 & 4 Eliz. II c. 18), s. 198.
24 *Ibid.*, s. 35 (1).
25 *Ibid.*, s. 35 (2): contrast the position of orders or bye-laws not having the force of statute: Renton & Brown, *Criminal Procedure* (3rd ed.) 433.
26 *Herkes* v. *Dickie*, 1958, J.C. 51, at pp. 55, 57, 58; *Macmillan* v. *McConnell*, 1917 J.C. 43, at pp. 47, 53.
27 *Herkes* v. *Dickie* (*supra*). It seems doubtful whether the regulations in *Macmillan* v. *McConnell* (*supra*) in fact possessed this status, but in both cases the opinions cited proceeded upon the assumption that they did.
28 Previous convictions used, not in aggravation, but in support of a substantive charge, must now be proved to apply to the accused even in the absence of previous challenge.

210. REGISTERS OF DEEDS AND OTHER WRITINGS

Private deeds may be registered for one or more of three purposes:
(1) for preservation; (2) for execution; and (3) for publication. The
appropriate registers are the books of the courts and the register of sasines.
Generally, an extract from these registers is probative evidence of the tenor
of the original deed except in case of forgery.

211. REGISTRATION FOR PRESERVATION

Any deed of private parties, whether it contains a clause of consent for
registration for preservation or not,[30] may be registered in the books of
Council and Session[31] or in the books of the sheriff court.[32] The purpose
here is to guard against loss or destruction of the deed. The principal
deed is retained by the keeper of the register, but an extract may be given out
to interested parties.[33] Such extract is probative evidence of the tenor of
the deed.[34]

212. REGISTRATION FOR EXECUTION

Private deeds may be registered in the books of a court for execution.[35]
The effect of such registration is to dispense in advance with an action to set
up the obligation contained in the deed. An extract of the deed is equivalent
to a decree of the court, and execution can be done on the extract. The
principal deed is now retained in the register and only extracts are given
out.[36] Registration for execution requires a clause of consent for registration
in the deed, except in the case of bonds in favour of the Crown.[37] As with
registration for preservation, the competent court books available for
registration for execution have been limited to the books of Council and
Session and the sheriff court books.[38] An extract or official copy of a deed
registered for execution is probative evidence of the tenor of the deed.[39]

The opposite view was adopted in *H.M. Advocate* v. *Gillan*, 1910 S.C. (J.) 49; *O'Donnell*
v. *H.M. Advocate*, 1930 J.C. 1, but the part of section 66 of the Criminal Procedure
(Scotland) Act, 1887, upon which these views were based has now been repealed:
Criminal Justice (Scotland) Act, 1949 (12, 13 & 14 Geo. VI c. 94), s. 79, Sch. 12.

[29] Criminal Justice (Scotland) Act, 1949 (12, 13 & 14 Geo. VI c. 94), s. 39.

[30] The common law requirement for such a clause was removed by the Act, 1698 c. 4:
Dickson, *Evidence* (3rd ed.) §1140.

[31] Initiated 1554 when styled "Register of Deeds."

[32] The former multiplicity of court books in which registration was competent was restricted by the Act, 49 Geo. III c. 42: Dickson, *Evidence* (3rd ed.) §1141.

[33] Dickson, *Evidence* (3rd ed.) §1139.

[34] Act, 1698 c. 4.

[35] For the historical development of registration for execution, see Dickson, *Evidence*
(3rd ed.) §1136; *Encyclopædia of the Laws of Scotland*, xii, §762.

[36] Registration of Writs (Scotland) Act, 1868 (31 & 32 Vict. c. 34), s. 2. The principal
deed may be given out on the order of a judge.

[37] Court of Exchequer (Scotland) Act, 1856 (19 & 20 Vict. c. 56), s. 38.

[38] Act, 49 Geo. III c. 42.

[39] Registration of Writs (Scotland) Act, 1868 (31 & 32 Vict. c. 34), s. 2.

213. REGISTRATION FOR PUBLICATION

The system of registration for publication[40] of deeds creating heritable rights was introduced by the Act, 1617 c. 16, which instituted a universal system of registration of deeds, consisting of a general, or nation-wide, register of sasines (arranged in county divisions) and particular or local registers. Registration of the deed in the appropriate register constitutes infeftment. The principal deed is returned to the ingiver after recording, and extracts of the register are to "make faith" with the principal except in questions of forgery.[41] Nevertheless, in conveyancing practice, these sasine extracts are not as highly regarded as extracts from the registers appropriate to preservation and execution where the original deeds are retained.[42] The present registers are governed by legislation which instituted a new general register of sasines and abolished the particular registers.[43] The Burgh Registers which had been outwith the Act of 1617 until 1681,[44] were to be gradually discontinued after 1926.[45]

214. OTHER REGISTERS

There are other public registers kept by the state analogous to the preceding three which deal not only with land rights but also with personal obligations and diligences. Some of these have been considered elsewhere.[46]

(a) The Register of Inhibitions and Adjudications[47] is the only diligence register now in use.[48] Inhibition is the interdiction of a person from dealing with his estate; and adjudication is the procedure whereby a creditor may obtain a title to heritable estate of his debtor in satisfaction of the debt.

(b) The Register of Inhibitions (General[49] and Particular[50]) was[51] the appropriate register for interdictions and letters of inhibition. Such registration was necessary to make the diligence effective against all the lieges.

(c) The Particular Register of Hornings was kept locally and then

---

[40] For the historical development of registration for publication, see *Encyclopœdia of the Laws of Scotland*, xii, §773; McKechnie, *Pursuit of Pedigree*, 23, n. 2.

[41] Act, 1617 c. 16; Titles to Land Consolidation (Scotland) Act, 1868 (31 & 32 Vict. c. 110), s. 142.

[42] Burns, *Conveyancing Practice* (4th ed.) 204. *Cf.* Conveyancing (Scotland) Act, 1924 (14 & 15 Geo. V c. 27), s. 2 (2). Until 1845 it was not the deed transferring the land which was registered but a notarial instrument which narrated the deed and the ceremony of taking sasine.

[43] Land Writs Registration (Scotland) Act, 1868 (31 & 32 Vict. c. 64), s. 8.

[44] Act, 1681 c. 13.

[45] Burgh Registers (Scotland) Act, 1926 (16 & 17 Geo. V c. 50), s. 1.

[46] e.g. Crown Charters, for which see § **204.**

[47] McKechnie, *Pursuit of Pedigree*, 39-41; Land Writs Registration (Scotland) Act, 1868 (31 & 32 Vict. c. 64), s. 17.

[48] Earlier registers of apprisings (or comprisings) are preserved in H.M. General Register House: Livingstone, *Guide to the Public Records of Scotland*; Land Writs Registration (Scotland) Act, 1868 (31 & 32 Vict. c. 64), ss. 16, 17.

[49] Act, 1597 c. 36.

[50] Act, 1581 c. 24.

[51] Discontinued by Land Writs Registration (Scotland) Act, 1868 (31 & 32 Vict. c. 68), ss. 16, 17.

transmitted to the treasurer. It contained letters of horning (or outlawry) for debt.[52]

Extracts from these registers are probative both at common law[53] and statute.[54]

215. RECORDS, ETC., RELATIVE TO SHIPS

Under the Merchant Shipping Act, 1894,[55] various documents, some of which are mentioned later in this paragraph, are "admissible in evidence." This phrase is defined to mean evidence of the matters stated therein in pursuance of the Act or by any officer in pursuance of his duties as such officer.[56] It has hitherto been assumed that such a document is sufficient evidence of the facts stated in it, although uncorroborated,[57] but the question does not seem to have been considered since the decision in *Bisset* v. *Anderson*.[58] In any event, the document is not conclusive and may be rebutted.[59]

The entry in a register book of British ships is evidence of ownership of a ship or of shares therein and of mortgages.[60] The same is true of a certificate purporting to be signed by the registrar.[60] An entry in the official log-book is admissible in evidence;[61] and in a prosecution for an offence against the Act, but not in a civil claim,[62] the log-book must, if practicable, be produced: otherwise the court may refuse to receive evidence.[63] It seems to be implied in two English decisions[64] that the entry in the log-book is sufficient evidence for a conviction, but it is doubtful whether this view would be taken in Scotland. All documents duly authenticated for the Ministry of Transport are admissible in evidence.[65] In a claim in respect of the death of a passenger the entry of the deceased's name in the passenger list is evidence that he was a passenger.[66] A deposition on oath made outside the United Kingdom is admissible in evidence on proof that the witness cannot be found in the United Kingdom and, in a criminal trial, provided it was made in presence of the accused.[67]

---

[52] Act, 1579 c. 13.

[53] *Williamson* v. *Threapland*, 1682 M. 12, 548 (inhibition).

[54] Act, 1581 c. 24 (inhibition); Act, 1579 c. 13 (horning).

[55] 57 & 58 Vict. c. 60.

[56] s. 695.

[57] *Duffus & Lawson* v. *Mackay*, 1857, 19 D. 430, where the certificate of registry was signed presumably by the registrar only.

[58] 1949 J.C. 106. See § **206.**

[59] *Watson* v. *Duncan*, 1879, 6 R. 1247. See also *Duthie* v. *Aiken*, 1893, 20 R. 241. *Duffus & Lawson* v. *Mackay* (*supra*) may depend on the fact that the proceedings were summary, and some of the observations have been doubted: *Bell* v. *Gow*, 1862, 1 M. 183.

[60] ss. 26, 31, 32, 64 (2).

[61] s. 239. See *Williams* v. *Dobbie*, 1884, 11 R. 982, at pp. 983, 988.

[62] *Sharp* v. *Rettie*, 1884, 11 R. 745.

[63] s. 228 (d).

[64] *Robinson* v. *Robson*, [1943] 1 K.B. 401; *Patterson* v. *Robinson*, [1929] 2 K.B. 91.

[65] s. 719. As to the transfer of function from the Board of Trade, see Halsbury, *Laws of England*, vol. 35, p. 33.

[66] s. 507.

The ship's log and other logs, which are not kept under the statute, are not evidence, but they may, like reports, be used to refresh the memory of the person who made the entry or for purposes of cross-examination.[68]

216. REGISTERS OF BIRTHS, DEATHS AND MARRIAGES

Before the operation on January 1, 1855, of the Registration of Births, Deaths and Marriages Act, 1854,[69] there was no statutory system of registration of vital statistics. The only records were those of the parishes instituted in the sixteenth century by virtue of the legislation of the provincial council of the Catholic Church, and thereafter regulated by acts of assembly of the Reformed Church between 1574 and 1816.[70] This system of parish registration operated with varying degrees of accuracy and completeness. The chief defects were that not all parishes kept registers;[71] as a rule only members of the established church were considered; and the events recorded were baptisms (not births), weddings in established churches—sometimes merely banns—and burials rather than deaths. Thus, for example, the recording of a burial is evidence of burial but not of the age at death.[72] The registers are admissible evidence of the facts contained in them, the degree of credit being proportionate to their regularity.[73] The absence of an entry relating to an event raises no presumption against its occurrence.[74]

217. REGISTRATION OF BIRTHS, DEATHS AND MARRIAGES ACT, 1854

The registration of births, deaths and marriages is now governed by the Act of 1854[69] and subsequent legislation,[75] which instituted a regular public system of registration administered on the basis of registration districts, which originally corresponded to parishes. The registers are kept by registrars, who derive their information from persons who give it under penalty for falsehood. An extract given out locally by the district registrar or centrally from the General Registry Office is admissible as evidence without further proof of the entry.[76] The entry is not evidence of the facts stated in it, but it may be evidence of **a** statement against interest of the person proved

---

[67] s. 691.

[68] *Admiralty* v. *Aberdeen Steam Trawling & Fishing Co.*, 1909 S.C. 335, at p. 341. See also, *Palestine Transport Shipping Co.* v. *Greenock Dockyard Co.*, (O.H.), 1947 S.N. 162.

[69] 17 & 18 Vict. c. 80.

[70] Dickson, *Evidence* (3rd ed.) §§1168-1204.

[71] In 1801 only 99 out of 850 parishes had registers.

[72] *Watson* v. *Glass*, 1837, 15 S. 753.

[73] Dickson, *Evidence* (3rd ed.) §1173.

[74] *Ibid.*

[75] Collectively entitled Registration of Births, Deaths and Marriages (Scotland) Acts, 1854-1938.

[76] Registration of Births, Deaths and Marriages (Scotland) Act, 1854 (17 & 18 Vict. c. 80), s. 58.

[77] *Stewart* v. *Stewart*, (O.H.) 1930, S.L.T. 363; *Alexander* v. *Alexander*, 1920, S.C. 327; *Mathieson* v. *Mathieson* (O.H.), 1914, 1 S.L.T. 511; *Duncan* v. *Duncan*, 1893, 30 S.L.R. 435. It may provide hearsay evidence: *Tennent* v. *Tennent*, 1890, 17 R. 1205 (a case of an English entry). See § 372.

to have signed it.[77] Proof of regular marriage by evidence of an extract certificate of marriage is dealt with elsewhere.[78]

218. PROFESSIONAL AND MILITARY REGISTERS

Authorised copies of registers or lists kept under statute relative to the practice of certain professions or certificates granted by persons appointed to keep these records are generally *prima facie* evidence; the appearance of a person's name in them is evidence of his name having been duly registered or entered. Absence of a person's name from the list or a certificate to that effect is equally evidence of non-registration of that person. Examples of professions whose registers or rolls are in this position are architects,[79] dentists,[80] medical practitioners,[81] nurses,[82] pharmaceutical chemists,[83] veterinary surgeons[84] and midwives.[85] Any list purporting to be issued by the Council of the Law Society, and to contain the names of solicitors who have obtained practising certificates for the current year, is, until the contrary is proved, evidence that the persons named in the list hold current certificates; and the absence of a name, until the contrary is proved, is evidence that the person is not entitled to practise under a current certificate; and an extract from the roll of solicitors certified as correct by the registrar shall be evidence of the facts appearing in the register.[86]

A similar evidential effect is given to documents purporting to be issued by or on behalf of the Army Council, Admiralty or Air Council relative to the status, rank and appointment of the members of H.M. Forces appearing therein; and records and certificates signed by a commanding officer are, for certain purposes, evidence of the facts stated therein.[87]

219. OFFICIAL RECORDS

Books kept by public officials for the purpose of recording certain facts

[78] See § 155.
[79] Architects (Registration) Act, 1931 (21 & 22 Geo. V c. 33), s. 3 (4).
[80] Dentists Act, 1957 (5 & 6 Eliz. II c. 28), s. 16 (4).
[81] Medical Act, 1858 (21 & 22 Vict. c. 90), s. 27; Medical Act, 1950 (14 Geo. VI c. 29), s. 35, Sch. 2.
[82] Nurses (Scotland) Act, 1951 (14 & 15 Geo. VI c. 55), s. 2 (3).
[83] Pharmacy Act, 1954 (2 & 3 Eliz. II c. 61), s. 6 (2).
[84] Veterinary Surgeons Act, 1881 (44 & 45 Vict. c. 62), s. 3 (2); Veterinary Surgeons Act, 1948 (11 & 12 Geo. VI c. 52), s. 6 (6).
[85] Midwives (Scotland) Act, 1951 (14 & 15 Geo. VI c. 54), s. 3 (5).
[86] Legal Aid and Solicitors (Scotland) Act, 1949 (12 & 13 Geo. VI c. 63), s. 19, Sch. 5, para. 6; similar provisions obtain in England: Solicitors Act, 1957 (5 & 6 Eliz. c. 27), s. 17.
[87] Army Act, 1955 (3 & 4 Eliz. II c. 18), s. 198; Army Reserve Act, 1950 (14 Geo. VI c. 32), s. 21, as amended by Revision of Army and Air Force Acts (Transitional Provisions) Act, 1955 (3 & 4 Eliz. II c. 20), s. 3, Sch. 2; Air Force Act, 1955 (3 & 4 Eliz. II c. 19), s. 198; Air Force Reserve Act, 1950 (14 Geo. VI c. 33), s. 21, as amended by Revision of Army and Air Force Acts (Transitional Provisions) Act, 1955 (3 & 4 Eliz. II c. 20), s. 3, Sch. 2; but these certificates are limited to the purposes specified in the relevant acts: *Robson Scott's Trs.* v. *Robson Scott*, 1945 S.C. 52, L.P. Normand at p. 55; *Hannay*, 1949 S.C. 304—both cases under Confirmation of Executors (War Service) (Scotland) Act, 1940 (3 & 4 Geo. VI c. 41), ss. 1, 2.

are admissible as *prima facie* evidence of those facts, but not of extraneous matters which may have been entered.[88] A jail book exhibited by the clerk to the jail was evidence of the date of an execution. In the same case an extract from the books of the War Office would have been admitted to prove where a unit was stationed at a particular time, if the person who made the extract had been adduced to prove its accuracy.[89] Records of lighthouse keepers are admissible as evidence of the weather.[90] The appointment of a burgh official is sufficiently proved by an entry in the burgh books.[91]

220. FOREIGN, DOMINION AND COLONIAL DOCUMENTS

At common law the contents of public registers of countries outwith Scotland require to be proved. However, the Evidence (Foreign, Dominion and Colonial Documents) Act, 1933,[92] authorised the making of Orders in Council whereby, subject to any conditions specified in the Order[93] and any requirements of rules of court, a document purporting to be issued in the country[94] to which the Order relates as an official copy of an entry in a register specified in the Order and purporting to be authenticated as such in the manner specified in the Order as appropriate in the case of such a register, shall without evidence as to the custody of the register or inability to produce it, and without any further or other proof, be received as evidence that the register contains such an entry.[95] And a certificate purporting to be given in the country to which the Order relates as an official certificate of any such class as is specified in the Order, and purporting to be signed by the officer, and to be authenticated in the manner specified in the Order as appropriate in the case of a certificate of that class, shall be received as evidence of the facts stated in the certificate.[96] Orders have been made in respect of many countries.

221. MINUTES OF MEETINGS: GENERAL

(a) **Introductory.** The best evidence of what took place at a meeting is the testimony of those who were present, and on strict principle a written account is inadmissible except as evidence against those who have accepted it as accurate. The principle has, however, been impinged upon by statute[97] and there are dicta suggesting that, even at common law, minutes may

---

[88] Dickson, *Evidence* (3rd ed.) §1209; *cf.* Army Act, 1955 (3 & 4 Eliz. II c. 18), s. 198.

[89] *Kay* v. *Rodger*, 1832, 10 S. 831.

[90] *Williams* v. *Dobbie*, 1884, 11 R. 982.

[91] *Hunter* v. *Hill*, 1833, 11 S. 989.

[92] 23 Geo. V c. 4.

[93] The requirements specified in the order must be complied with: *Motture* v. *Motture*, [1955] 1 W.L.R. 1066.

[94] "Country" means "a Dominion, the Isle of Man, any of the Channel Islands, a British Colony or Protectorate, a foreign country, a colony or a protectorate of a foreign country, or any mandated territory": Evidence (Foreign, Dominion and Colonial Documents) Act, 1933 (23 Geo. V c. 4), s. 1 (4).

[95] *Ibid.*, s. 1 (2) (c).

[96] *Ibid.*, s. 1 (2) (d).

[97] See § 222.

234

acquire general evidential value.[98] Any such value is, it is thought, confined to the minute of a corporation, or possibly of persons meeting under a common duty, such as trustees, but not to that of a meeting of individuals who voluntarily meet to discuss a matter.[99] The other main distinction appears to be in the method of approving the minute.[1]

While a minute may be written and approved at the meeting, the normal practice is to compile a draft minute from notes taken at the meeting and present it for approval at the next meeting. There are thus three writings, the notes, the draft minute and the approved minute.

(b) **Before Approval.** The notes, like any other notes made at the time,[2] may be used to refresh the memory of the person who took them while he is giving evidence.[3] A ruling that the witness might use the draft minute for the same purpose was excepted to, with, it is thought, some justification, but the case was settled.[3]

(c) **After Approval.** Unless under statute[4] or in matters of great antiquity[5] or in exceptional circumstances[6] the principal, if not the only, evidential value of an approved minute is as the writ of party[7] or as a statement against interest.[8] Where the meeting was one of individuals held to discuss a common project, the minute can be evidence against one of the individuals only if he has approved it. This he may do either by signing it or assenting to its signature by the chairman of that or a subsequent meeting.[9] But a minute of meeting of a corporation or firm is evidence against it if it has been approved at a subsequent meeting, even although not composed of the same individuals.[10] It is the assent, not the signature, which is vital. Signature by a chairman who has no authority has no effect,[11] and conversely an unsigned minute was held to be evidence against a firm.[12]

---

98 *City of Glasgow Bank Liquidators*, 1880, 7 R. 1196, at p. 1199. But it is not easy to see the value of the minute if the facts have been proved *aliunde*. *Cf. Johnston* v. *Scott*, 1860, 22 D. 393, at p. 402, where it is said that a minute is not evidence at all, but may be an adminicle of evidence. See also *A.* v. *B.*, 1858, 20 D. 407.

99 *Johnston* v. *Scott (ut supra)*, at pp. 402, 403; Dickson, *Evidence* (3rd ed.) §1216.

1 See sub-para. (c).

2 See § **341.**

3 *Wilson* v. *G. & S.W. Rly.*, 1851, 14 D. 1. *Cf. Mathers* v. *Laurie*, 1849, 12 D. 433.

4 See § **222.**

5 Dickson, *Evidence* (3rd ed.) §1217.

6 *A.* v. *B.*, 1858, 20 D. 407. The minutes incorporated hearsay of a person who died before the proof, and the tenor of a letter later lost.

7 See § **303.**

8 See § **29.**

9 *Devlin* v. *McKelvie*, 1915 S.C. 180, where the pursuer failed to prove that the defender had assented to signature by the chairman; *Cameron* v. *Panton's Trs.*, 1891, 18 R. 728, where the pursuer did not sign the minute; *Johnston* v. *Scott (supra)* at pp. 399-404, where the defenders neither signed nor assented to the chairman's signature.

10 *Cf. Hill* v. *Lindsay*, 1847, 10 D. 78, where all the shareholders signed the minute and proof was allowed only because the minute was not clear.

11 *Mackenzie* v. *Macartney*, 1831, 5 W. & S. 504: *Devlin* v. *McKelvie (supra)*.

12 *Ivison* v. *Edinburgh Silk Yarn Co.*, 1846, 9 D. 1039. This was a joint stock company; but the Private Act establishing it expressly excluded its incorporation.

An approved minute may, however, have a wider evidential value owing to the operation of some extrinsic rule. So, for example, the minutes of a kirk session have been admitted (1) as proof of the tenor[13] of a letter engrossed in them, the principal having been lost and (2) as hearsay[14] of the minister who had died, provided that they might require to support them the evidence not only of the clerk who wrote them, but also of others present at the meeting.[15]

(d) Kirk Sessions and other Church Courts. The minutes of these bodies of the Established Church[16] sometimes take the form of, or include, decrees in an ecclesiastical process. Such decrees are probably admissible where they have been authenticated according to the forms of the church, which at one time seem to have been somewhat irregular.[17] In other situations it appears that these minutes are not in general admissible as evidence.[18] The records of dissenting congregations are not admissible.[20]

222. MINUTES OF MEETING: STATUTORY

(a) Local Authorities. The minute books of local authorities are "received in evidence" without further proof.[21] This, it is thought, makes the minutes evidence of decisions and orders therein recorded. It has been held that the minutes of road trustees are the only competent evidence of their proceedings.[22] It has been doubted whether an order by road trustees was valid *quoad* third parties where the minute recording it was unsigned, though approved at a subsequent meeting.[23]

(b) Limited Companies. A company's articles may render the minutes conclusive evidence of the fact that a resolution has been carried or lost,[24] but they may be supplemented by other evidence, at least so as to show that the proper procedure was followed.[25] Apart from these special provisions

---

13 See § 233.

14 See § 373.

15 *A.* v. *B.*, 1858, 20 D. 407, at pp. 417, 418.

16 A kirk session is not a corporation: *Kirk Session of North Berwick* v. *Sime*, 1839, 2 D. 23.

17 *Ferguson* v. *Skirving*, 1850, 12 D. 1145; affd. 1852, 1 Macq. 232; see also *Dalhousie's Tutors*, 1890, 17 R. 1060, where the admissibility of the minute was not in issue and it was held competent to lead evidence to explain the decree, but not to contradict it. As to the mode of authentication of minutes, etc., and their inspection by superior church courts, see Cox, *Practice and Procedure in the Church of Scotland* (4th ed.) pp. 70, 72, 75. See also § 202.

18 *A.* v. *B.* (*ut supra*).

20 Dickson, *Evidence* (3rd ed.) §1216. *Mathers* v. *Laurie*, 1849, 12 D. 433 (Free Church).

21 Local Government (Scotland) Act, 1947 (10 & 11 Geo. VI c. 43), Sch. 3, Part IV, para. 6.

22 *McGhie* v. *McKirdy*, 1850, 12 D. 442. Doubted by Dickson, *Evidence* (3rd ed.) §1215.

23 *L. Blantyre* v. *Dickson*, 1885, 13 R. 116; *Forbes* v. *Morison*, 1851, 14 D. 134; *cf. Ivison* v. *Edinburgh Silk Yarn Co.*, 1846, 9 D. 1039, where unsigned minutes of a firm were admitted against the firm.

24 Companies Act, 1948 (11 & 12 Geo. VI c. 38), Sch. I, Table A, Reg. 58.

25 *Fraserburgh Commercial Co.*, 1946, S.C. 444.

the minutes of a general meeting of a company and of directors,[26] purporting to be signed by the chairman at that or the next succeeding meeting, are evidence of the proceedings.[27] They are not expressly either conclusive or exhaustive, and in England, while the absence of any reference to a matter in the minutes is evidence that it was not discussed, a transaction may be proved though not inserted in the minutes.[28] Where, however, a resolution for voluntary winding up had been intimated to the Registrar and recorded in a minute, as directed by statute, and acted upon by the Court, evidence to supplement the terms of the resolution, as recorded in the minute, was held inadmissible.[29]

(c) Sequestrations. The Bankruptcy (Scotland) Act, 1913,[30] requires minutes to be kept of the first statutory meeting of creditors, but there is no express provision as to their effect. In the normal case, where the sheriff is not present, the preses reports the proceedings to him by lodging the minutes authenticated by himself.[31] These have been said to be the only legitimate evidence of the proceedings,[32] but this statement is not supported by the authorities cited[33] and cannot be reconciled with opinions which imply that a creditor may object to the accuracy of the minutes before they have been acted on.[34] The Act makes no express provision for minutes of the second statutory meeting or of any special meetings of creditors or of meetings of commissioners, but probably the same rules would apply. The accuracy of the minutes can be challenged only if they have not been acted on by the sheriff[34] or by the creditors themselves.[35]

The trustee must keep a sederunt book recording minutes of creditors and commissioners, states of accounts, etc.[36] Under the earlier Acts extracts from it were received in evidence, but this provision was repealed in 1839 and not re-enacted.[37] The principal minutes of meetings of creditors and commissioners have, it is thought, the same effect whether they are recorded in the sederunt book or not,[38] and the trustee's account of a matter does not

26 Companies Act, 1948 (11 & 12 Geo. VI c. 58), s. 15.
27 *Ibid.*, s. 145 (2).
28 *Re Fireproof Doors*, [1916] 2 Ch. 142; Palmer, *Company Law* (20th ed.) 488; Buckley, *Companies Acts* (13th ed.) 339.
29 *City of Glasgow Bank Liquidators*, 1880, 7 R. 1196, at p. 1199.
30 3 & 4 Geo. V c. 20.
31 *Ibid.*, ss. 64, 66.
32 Goudy, *Bankruptcy* (4th ed.) 197, 198.
33 Bell, *Commentaries* (7th ed.) 312, merely says that the minutes are legal evidence; and in *Gascoyne* v. *Manford*, 1848, 10 D. 376, the accuracy of the minutes was not challenged, though the interlocutor may go further.
34 *Brown* v. *Lindsay*, 1869, 7 M. 595. In a later passage Goudy says (p. 226) that the minutes are good *prima facie* evidence and cannot be contradicted by parole proof.
35 *Lea* v. *Landale*, 1828, 6 S. 350, where other creditors in reliance on a resolution had refrained from sequestrating.
36 Bankruptcy (Scotland) Act, 1913 (3 & 4 Geo. V c. 20), s. 80.
37 Act, 33 Geo. III c. 74, s. 53; Bankrupts Estates (Scotland) Act, 1839 (2 & 3 Vict. c. 41), s. 63.
38 *Smith* v. *Mackay*, 1835, 13 S. 323, which proceeded on the minutes, which in fact were recorded in the sederunt book.

become evidence, except against himself, merely because he has recorded it in the sederunt book.[39] It is thought that this restricted proposition is more in accordance with principle than the statement that the sederunt book constitutes *prima facie* proof of the matters contained in it relating to the estate, except when founded on by the trustee in his own favour.[40]

223. HISTORIES AND PRIVATE RECORDS

In ancient matters, such as peerage and pedigree cases, contemporary chronicles and histories are admissible evidence on the ground that the authors were acquainted with the facts and that their compilation was not made with a view to litigation.[41] The weight to be given to these works depends on the reputation of the historian.[42] Modern compilations, such as peerage books, because they are secondary works based on primary sources which are still extant, are not admissible.[43] Private muniments, such as cartularies, old inventories of writs and tacks of land are admissible,[44] as are entries in family bibles, memoranda in church registers, tombstone inscriptions,[45] and minutes.[46]

224. MAPS AND PLANS

Under the Ordnance Survey Act, 1841,[47] in order to enable the general survey to be completed, procedure was laid down for ascertaining and marking the "reputed boundaries" of counties, towns and parishes,[48] but nothing done under the Act alters boundaries, and all right and title remain as if the Act had not been passed.[49] This last provision does not seem to have been brought to the notice of the court in two cases where, however, it was held that the Ordnance Survey map is insufficient to establish a parish boundary.[50] It is, however, good evidence of natural features.[51] The weight to be attached to a cartographer's map depends on his reputed accuracy.[52] An estate map or plan is good evidence if it can be shown that it was impartial, e.g., that it was made by or for the common author of the parties, or at least that it has been so used that it would probably have been challenged

---

[39] *Mansfield* v. *Maxwell*, 1835, 13 S. 721.

[40] Goudy, *Bankruptcy* (4th ed.) 340; Dickson, *Evidence* (3rd ed.) §1214.

[41] *Report on the Trial of Earl of Stirling*, 1839 (ed. Swinton).

[42] Dickson, *Evidence* (3rd ed.) §1220; Stair, iv, 42, 16; Erskine, iv, 2, 7.

[43] Dickson, *Evidence* (3rd ed.) §1220. The *Statistical Accounts* of 1796 and 1845 "are not, strictly, evidence"; *Meacher* v. *Blair-Oliphant*, 1913, S.C. 417, at pp. 430, 432, 437.

[44] McKechnie, *Pursuit of Pedigree*, 41-43; see also, *Mags. of Sanquhar* v. *Officers of State*, 1864, 2 M. 499 (charter in collection in Advocates' Library); *Proceedings before the Committee of Privileges* (H.M.S.O.): *Dudhope Peerage*, 1952; *Earldom of Dundee*, 1953.

[45] Dickson, *Evidence* (3rd ed.) § 1222.

[46] *Ibid.*, §1217. See also §§ **221, 222.**

[47] 4 & 5 Vict. c. 30.

[48] Ordnance Survey Act, 1841 (4 & 5 Vict. c. 30), ss. 1, 2, 6.

[49] *Ibid.*, s. 12.

[50] *Meacher* v. *Blair-Oliphant*, 1913 S.C. 417; *Gibson* v. *Bonnington Sugar Refining Co.*, 1869, 7 M. 394. It does establish distances: *Morrison* v. *McCowan*, 1939 J.C. 45.

[51] *Meacher* v. *Blair-Oliphant* (*supra*), at p. 437.

[52] *Meacher* v. *Blair-Oliphant* (*supra*), at p. 430; and the evidence before him: *ibid.*, at p. 437.

if inaccurate. A plan of unknown origin belonging to the pursuer was rejected, or at least held of no evidential value.[53] On the other hand, where a plan had been handed by the defender's author to his trustees in bankruptcy during negotiations for sale of the property, it was admitted and used as evidence against the defenders,[54] and the same was held with regard to a plan which had been used in settling a question between predecessors of the parties.[55]

225. NOTARIAL INSTRUMENTS

A notarial instrument is a narrative under the hand of a notary detailing procedure which has been transacted by or before him in his official capacity,[56] and being a tested writ, is probative of the act which it is in the province of the notary to perform, but not of extraneous facts narrated in the instrument.[57] Notarial power has by statute been accorded to consuls-general and consuls appointed by the Crown abroad.[58] A notarial instrument can only be contradicted by way of reduction.[59]

226. CITATIONS AND EXECUTIONS

Some documents, although neither probative nor privileged according to the rules of execution of writs, are nevertheless competent and conclusive evidence of the matters which they narrate, when they have been signed by the appropriate officer—messenger at arms, sheriff officer or solicitor.[60] These are chiefly citations of witnesses, parties, jurors and havers,[61] and executions, which narrate the fact of citation having been carried out.[62] An *ex facie* regular execution is probative of these facts, but not of extraneous matter,[63] and is generally exclusive evidence of the citation. But there are exceptions: parole evidence was allowed where the debtor had destroyed the execution of the charge necessary to constitute notour bankruptcy,[64] and the execution of citation of parties, witnesses and havers in Small Debt actions,[65] and the service of complaints, warrants and other proceedings in summary criminal procedure may be proved by the oath of the officer.[67]

53 *Place* v. *Earl of Breadalbane*, 1874, 1 R. 1202.
54 *Reid* v. *Haldane's Trs.*, 1891, 18 R. 744.
55 *Brown* v. *N.B. Rly.*, 1906, 8 F. 534.
56 Dickson, *Evidence* (3rd ed.) §§1233-1238, 1244, 1245; Bell, *Law Dictionary* (7th ed.) 744. A notice of title is now equivalent to a notarial instrument: Conveyancing (Scotland) Act, 1924 (14 & 15 Geo. V c. 27), s. 6 (1).
57 Stair, iv, 42, 9; Erskine, ii, 3, 34; iv, 2, 5; Bell, *Principles*, §2221; Dickson, *Evidence* (3rd ed.) §1233; *Balfour* v. *Lyle*, 1832, 10 S. 853.
58 Act, 6 Geo. IV c. 87, s. 20; Commissioners for Oaths Act, 1889 (52 Vict. c. 10), s. 6.
59 Dickson, *Evidence* (3rd ed.) §1244.
60 *Ibid.*, §§1246, 1247.
61 *Ibid.*, §§1253-1261.
62 *Ibid.*, §§1261-1284.
63 *Ibid.*, §§1263, 1279.
64 *Drummond* v. *Clunas Tiles & Mosaics Ltd.*, 1909, S.C. 1049.
65 Small Debt (Scotland) Act, 1837 (7 Will. & 1 Vict. c. 41), s. 3.
67 Summary Jurisdiction (Scotland) Act, 1954 (2 & 3 Eliz. II c. 48), ss. 18, 22.

227. EXTRACTS AND COPIES

The best evidence of a document is the document itself, and accordingly copies of a document are generally inadmissible.[68] The rule suffers exception in a few cases, the chief of these being extracts. Extracts are official copies extracted from public or official records by or on behalf of the custodier of the record, or the person empowered to give out extracts, and authenticated by that person. The admissibility of extracts rests on their preparation under official care and their authentication by the proper officer[69]. An *ex facie* regular extract proves itself because the extract is presumed by law to conform to the interlocutors or other warrants for it, and to be signed as required by law.[70] These rules apply principally to judicial extracts and extracts from registers of private deeds. Modern statutes have extended the area where extracts are admissible to such documents as extracts of entries in the registers of births, deaths and marriages.[71] Copies of certain documents, such as those relating to shipping,[72] when certified in the manner prescribed, are deemed to be equivalent to principals. Entries in bankers books have, on the grounds of convenience, the statutory privilege of being proved by sworn copies.[73]

As has been mentioned elsewhere[74] where a document is required to be proved in order to create rights, an action of proving the tenor is generally necessary; but where writings are merely evidence of facts recourse may be had to secondary evidence, including copy documents, where it is "not reasonably practicable and convenient to produce the primary evidence."[75] Thus where it is impracticable for a party to produce a writing, e.g., a tombstone inscription, a copy will be admissible.[76] Admission of secondary evidence in this situation also applies in criminal cases.[75]

Copies may also be received when recovered under a commission and diligence granted by the court in circumstances which make it inconvenient or a breach of confidence to give up the whole record;[77] but the party should first exhaust his power to recover the principals.[78]

It is competent in civil litigation, where the principal document is not material, for the parties to agree to accept a copy as equivalent to the

[68] See § 229.
[69] Dickson, *Evidence* (3rd ed.) §1285; Stair, iv, 42, 10. There is no apparent reason why the same principle should not apply to the extracts from the records of courts or from registers which have ceased to function, such as courts of parliament or privy council or register of entails. Indeed fees are prescribed for extracts from these records: Act of Sederunt, 20 March, 1934.
[70] Stair, iv, 42, 10. *Cf. Mathers* v. *Laurie*, 1849, 12 D. 433 (extract minute of a court not recognised by law not admissible.)
[71] See § 217.
[72] See § 215.
[73] See §§ 301, 368.
[74] See §§ 230, sub-para. (b), 231.
[75] *MacLeod* v. *Woodmuir Miners Welfare Society Social Club*, 1961, J.C. 5, at p. 9.
[76] Dickson, *Evidence* (3rd ed.) §239; see also § 221, sub-para. (e).
[77] Dickson, *Evidence* (3rd ed.) §§1318, 1376.
[78] *Caledonian Rly. Co.* v. *Symington*, 1912, S.C. 1033. *Cf. Sleigh* v. *Glasgow & Transvaal Options Ltd.*, 1903, 5 F. 332.

principal.[79] The admission of copy documents in criminal procedure is mentioned elsewhere.[80]

In practice, the copy telegram issued by the Post Office to the addressee is treated as equivalent to the original telegram handed in by the sender; but the original may always be recovered from the Post Office.[81]

228. BUSINESS BOOKS

(a) Introductory. Entries in business books may be the writ of the person by whom, or on whose behalf, they are kept,[82] or they may be evidence of a statement against interest.[83] This paragraph is concerned with the principle on which they may be evidence, and along with other evidence sufficient evidence, in his favour.

(b) Origin and History of the Principle. The admissibility of such entries appears to be a relic of the time before 1853[84] when a party was not an admissible witness, and to have been formulated in 1672 as a method of avoiding the injustices resulting to merchants from the exclusion. A merchant, suing for the price of goods, tendered, as proof of delivery, his compt book bearing the particulars and one witness, and in supplement offered his own oath upon the verity of his account.[85] The Lords found the same sufficient in respect of the great prejudice that merchants might sustain if they were restricted to a full probation.[86] Founding on that case Erskine states the principle thus: "No merchant's books can be full evidence in his own favour; but if they be regularly kept, and contain his whole transactions, they ought to afford at least a *semiplena probatio*; and therefore, if they be supported by one witness, in articles which admit of parole evidence, they will be received as legal proof, provided the merchant himself, if required, make oath in supplement that the transaction is there fairly stated." Early in the nineteenth century the Court of Session found delivery of three parcels of goods proved, although there was no witness to the first and second at all, and the evidence of the sole witness to the third was very vague. The House

---

[79] Where parties admit that hospital records apply to the pursuer, that admission does not extend to facts or opinions contained in the records: *McHugh* v. *Leslie*, (O.H.) 1961 S.L.T. (Notes) 65.

[80] See § 49.

[81] *Somervell* v. *Somervell*, 1900, 8 S.L.T. 112, where the Lord Ordinary repelled the objection to the granting of commission on the ground of confidentiality but sustained it on the ground that, in the absence of information of the office of issue of the telegrams, undue efforts would be required by the Post Office to search out the telegrams; *Mowat* v. *Caledonian Banking Co.*, 1895, 3 S.L.T. 108.

[82] See § 303.

[83] See § 29.

[84] See § 348, sub-para. (b).

[85] Similar devices were applied in actions of affiliation and aliment (see § 170) and in actions on the Edict (Erskine, iii, 1, 29; Bell, *Commentaries* (7th ed.) I. 500).

[86] *Wood* v. *Kello*, 1672, M. 12, 728, Erskine's only authority, iv, 2, 4. Stair reported the case, but did not cite it in his *Institutions*. He says "Count-books are probative against those who made them . . .; but they prove not for them": iv, 42, 14.

[87] *Ivory & Co.* v. *Gourlay*, 1816, 4 Dow, 467.

of Lords reversed on the ground that the books were not kept with sufficient regularity, but said nothing about the absence of other evidence.[87] This silence seems to have encouraged attempts to prove a debt by the pursuer's books alone, but a bank's claim failed where it renounced probation and relied entirely on its own books.[88] Where the defence depended on proving that goods had been obtained from a third party, it was held that mere production of the third party's account was insufficient.[89] The principle has been extended beyond merchant's books to include at least those of a bank,[90] and there is some authority for the view that books kept by a party in connection with an executry might be evidence in his favour.[91] In one case there was an apparent relaxation of the principle as explained by Erskine. In an action for payment of tolls on carts the decree expressly proceeded on the accounts and books produced and the pursuer's oath in supplement, but in fact direct evidence had been led.[92] An explanation of the principle, which, though historically unsound, is more in accordance with modern practice, was given by Lord Medwyn.[93] "If regularly kept, bank's or merchant's books are admitted to supplement or support a proof in such matters as, from their minuteness and multiplicity, it cannot be that the testimony of witnesses, unaided by reference to them, could be expected to supply the requisite evidence."

(c) **The Principle.** Books if apparently regularly kept and sworn to as an accurate record are admissible evidence. If the entries are supported by independent evidence, the proof is in law sufficient. The direct testimony of one witness is sufficient independent evidence for this purpose,[86] but it is thought that other evidence might well be, e.g., proof of an extra-judicial admission.

[88] *British Linen Co.* v. *Thomson*, 1853, 15 D. 314, at pp. 318, 320.
[89] *Hatton* v. *Buckmaster & Co.*, 1853, 15 D. 574. As the third party was an admissible witness he could speak both to the verity of the account and to delivery of the goods.
[90] *British Linen Co.* v. *Thomson* (*supra*); *Grant* v. *Johnston*, 1845, 7 D. 390, L. Medwyn at p. 393.
[91] *Fisher's Trs.* v. *Fisher*, 1850, 13 D. 245, at p. 252. See also *Macfarquhar* v. *McKay*, 1869, 7 M. 766, where an account of the pursuer's disbursements on behalf of the defender, sworn to by him, was held sufficient in the absence of counter evidence.
[92] *Balfour* v. *Sharp*, 1833, 11 S. 784.
[93] *Grant* v. *Johnston* (*ut supra*).

CHAPTER XIX

PROOF OF TERMS OF DOCUMENT NOT PRODUCED

229. BEST EVIDENCE RULE

Secondary or substitutionary evidence is inadmissible when primary or original evidence is, or ought to be, available.[1] One example of this rule is the exclusion of secondary hearsay evidence.[2] The other main example, so far as affects the admissibility of evidence,[3] is the exclusion of secondary evidence of a document. Except in the circumstances mentioned below,[4] it is incompetent incidentally in the course of a proof or trial to establish the terms of a document not produced by secondary evidence, i.e., by parole evidence,[5] or, unless of consent or under statutory authority,[6] by production of a copy.[7] What the rule excludes is secondary evidence, and it does not mean that because a fact could be proved by production of a document it cannot be proved by other primary evidence. Where an agreement could have been proved by a letter of undertaking, the pursuer was allowed to prove it by letters and entries in the defenders' books.[8] Births, deaths and marriages may be proved by parole without extracts from the register.[9] Further, it is competent to prove that the document exists[10] and also to prove a practice founded on instances occurring in documents, such as leases and insurance policies, without producing them.[11]

If a document is not in a party's possession and could not have been recovered by him, its terms may, in certain circumstances,[4] be proved incidentally in the course of a depending action either in the Court of Session

---

1 Dickson, *Evidence* (3rd ed.) §195.
2 See § **370**. Another occurs with real evidence. See § **420**.
3 A somewhat different form of the best evidence rule may still be of importance in connection with the sufficiency or probative value of evidence, when, for example, circumstantial evidence is relied on, though direct evidence is available. See § **8**.
4 See § **230**.
5 *Malley* v. *L.M.S. Railway*, 1944 S.C. 129, L.P. Cooper at p. 138; *Aitchison* v. *Robertson*, 1846, 9 D. 15; *Gibson* v. *Anderson*, 1846, 9 D. 1.
6 See § **227**.
7 *Summers* v. *Fairservice*, 1842, 4 D. 347; Dickson, *Evidence* (3rd ed.) §227.
8 *Thom* v. *North British Banking Co.*, 1850, 13 D. 134, L. Fullerton at p. 143.
9 Dickson, *Evidence* (3rd ed.) §210. See also § **217**.
10 *Ibid.*, §216.
11 *Ibid.*, §221.

or in the sheriff court.[12]   Except in these circumstances the terms of the document can be proved only in an action of proving the tenor,[13] which is competent only in the Court of Session[14] or the Teind Court.[15]

230. INCIDENTAL PROOF OF TERMS OF DOCUMENT

(a) General.   Except in the case of one class of document,[16] incidental proof of the terms of a document is usually allowed when it is not in the party's possession and could not have been recovered by him in spite of all due exertion.[17]   The extent of the exertion required, or, in more technical terms, the precision of the proof of the *casus amissionis*, varies with the nature and importance of the document.[18]   But the condition of due exertion will probably be held satisfied if the document is in the possession of the opposite party and he has failed to produce it when called on to do so.[19] Such incidental proof has been allowed not only in the case of letters and other documents which were merely adminicles of evidence,[20] but also in the case of documents which formed the only competent evidence of a party's case or of part of it.[21]   There does, however, seem to be this distinction between these different types of document.   When a party moves for proof without being able to produce a document which normally would be essential for his case, he must make averments sufficient to shew that he is entitled to prove its terms incidentally.   Proof has been refused,[22] or at least ought not to have been allowed,[23] owing to the insufficiency of such averments.   On the other hand, where the document was merely an adminicle of evidence, so far at least as the reports shew, there were no particular averments, and proof was led without notice.[20]   Although this distinction has not been expressly noticed, it appears to be of some importance.   In a criminal trial the terms of a writing may be proved by parole evidence if its production is impracticable.[24]

(b) Excepted Documents.   If the pursuer's title is constituted by a will not produced, the tenor of the will can be proved only in an action of proving

---

12 *Elliott* v. *Galpern*, 1927 S.C. 29.

13 See § **231.**

14 *Dunbar & Co.* v. *Scottish County Investment Co.*, 1920 S.C. 210.

15 *Alexander* v. *Oswald*, 1840, 3 D. 40.

16 See sub-para. (b).

17 *Clements* v. *Macaulay*, 1866, 4 M. 543; *Dowgray* v. *Gilmour*, 1907 S.C. 715; *Clark* v. *Clark's Trs.*, 1860, 23 D. 74.   In the first case due exertion was proved; in the others it was not.   See also *McIntosh* v. *Chalmers*, 1883, 11 R. 8, L.O. at p. 12.

18 *Walker* v. *Nisbet*, 1915 S.C. 639.   See further § **234.**

19 *Elliott* v. *Galpern*, 1927 S.C. 29; *Young* v. *Thomson*, 1909 S.C. 529; *Mitchell* v. *Berwick*, 1845, 7 D. 382.

20 *Clements* v. *Macaulay* (*supra*); *A.* v. *B.*, 1858, 20 D. 407, at p. 415; *Ritchie* v. *Ritchie*, 1857, 19 D. 505.

21 *Young* v. *Thomson* (*supra*) (receipt for payment of money); *Drummond* v. *Clunas Tiles and Mosaics, Ltd.*, 1909 S.C. 1049 (execution of charge); *Elliott* v. *Galpern* (*supra*) (written offer and acceptance).

22 *Walker* v. *Nisbet* (*supra*).

23 *Mackinnon's Trustee* v. *Bank of Scotland*, 1915 S.C. 411, L. Hunter at p. 423.

24 *MacLeod* v. *Woodmuir Miners Welfare Society Social Club*, 1961 J.C. 5.

the tenor,[25] and this applies probably to all documents which constitute rights, as opposed to documents which are merely evidence of them.[26] In two cases the title of the claimant depended on a written contract of copartnery. In one[27] an action of proving the tenor was held necessary; in the other[28] it was not. These decisions are reconcilable on the view that in the former the writing was regarded as constituting the contract,[29] while in the latter it was regarded merely as evidence of it.[30] In an action by one granter of a promissory note, who had paid, against another for relief, incidental proof of the terms of the note was refused. While this decision is said to rest on the ground that the note was "the basis of the pursuer's case," the opinions are open to the construction that the true ground was the insufficiency of the explanation for the failure to produce in view of the nature of the document.[18]

231. ACTION OF PROVING THE TENOR

(a) **General.** "The purpose of an action of proving the tenor is to replace a lost document by a new document [*viz.* a decree] in precisely the same terms, and with the same legal effect."[31] The action may also be used to restore parts of a document which have been destroyed, obliterated or mutilated.[32] Anyone with an interest, however slight, has a title to sue,[33] and all parties interested must be called as defenders.[34] If the pursuer alone has an interest, the lieges need not be called.[34] Where the representatives of the granter of the deed cannot be found, they have been called as "the heir and representatives of" A.B., but the decree, in that event, is not *res judicata* against them.[35] The conclusion is "For declarator that (*the lost deed*) was of the tenor following (*set out the terms of the lost deed*) and that the decree to be pronounced herein shall be equivalent to the original deed."[36]

(b) **Averments and Proof.** To obtain decree the pursuer must aver and prove (1) the execution of the document,[37] (2) its tenor or terms[38] and (3) the *casus amissionis*.[39] But these three matters may not be wholly independent. For example, if it is proved that the document was destroyed by

---

25 *Gilchrist* v. *Morrison*, 1891, 18 R. 599.
26 *Elliott* v. *Galpern* (*supra*), at p. 33.
27 *Shaw* v. *Shaw's Trs.*, 1876, 3 R. 813.
28 *Clark* v. *Clark's Trs.* (*supra*), where the Lord Justice-Clerk clearly implied, and L. Cowan expressly said, that an action of proving the tenor was unnecessary.
29 The Lord President used the word "constitute."
30 On this distinction see § **96.**
31 *Rannie* v. *Ogg*, 1891, 18 R. 903, L. Kinnear at p. 909. The effect of a decree is considered in detail at § **236.**
32 See § **235.**
33 *Browne* v. *Orr*, 1872, 10 M. 397; *Winchester* v. *Smith*, 1863, 1 M. 685.
34 Rules of Court, 1948, Rule 197.
35 *Pollok* v. *Jones' Heir*, 1899, 1 F. 394.
36 Rules of Court, 1948, Appendix, Form 2 (b).
37 See § **232.**
38 See § **233.**
39 See § **234.**

someone with an adverse interest, who had no right to destroy it (the *casus amissionis*), the burden of proving its execution and tenor may be reduced,[40] and strong evidence that a deed of the nature alleged was executed may lead the court to accept slight evidence of its tenor.[41] Clear proof of authenticity and tenor reduces the burden of proving the *casus amissionis*, and *vice versa*.[42] It is therefore unwise to isolate the evidence on one matter in a previous decision and assume that the same result will follow in another cause where the evidence on that matter is similar. The evidence on the other matters may be different.

(c) **Procedure.** Until 1913[43] the Lord Ordinary made great avizandum. Now the cause proceeds as an ordinary action, provided that if the action is undefended there must be proof.[44] But if it is defended, it may be dismissed as irrelevant without proof.[45]

232. EXECUTION: AVERMENT AND PROOF

An averment of execution is naturally essential. Since the document *ex hypothesi* cannot be produced and spoken to, the proof must be by inference.[46] Evidence that a deed of the nature alleged was executed[47] or existed[48] is sufficient. Where the pursuers had possessed property for over eighty years and there was a statement in a disposition in favour of a neighbouring proprietor suggesting that he had granted a disposition in favour of the pursuers, the Court doubted whether execution was proved, but refused decree on another ground.[49] In a case where the pursuer failed to prove the *casus amissionis* the judges differed as to whether execution was proved.[50]

233. TENOR: PROOF

Since the alleged terms of the document are set forth in the conclusion, they need not be repeated in the condescendence. While it is not necessary

---

40 *Young* v. *Thomson*, 1909 S.C. 529, at p. 536; *Leckie* v. *Leckie*, 1884, 11 R. 1088; *Borland* v. *Andrew's Judicial Factor*, 1901, 4 F. 129; *Ritchie* v. *Ritchie*, 1871, 9 M. 820; *Rintoul* v. *Boyter*, 1833, 6 W. & S. 394. In the first three cases parole evidence of the tenor was held sufficient.

41 *Leckie* v. *Leckie* (*supra*); *Rintoul* v. *Boyter* (*supra*).

42 *Graham* v. *Graham*, 1847, 10 D. 45, at p. 49.

43 C.A.S. c. IV. 5.

44 Rules of Court, 1948, Rule 199. The rule is peremptory. It appears that however irrelevant the averments, the Lord Ordinary must allow proof.

45 This was done in *Clyde* v. *Clyde*, 1958 S.C. 343.

46 As to the possible distinction between direct and indirect evidence of the fact of execution, where a subsequent action of reduction is brought on the ground of forgery, see § **236**.

47 *Young* v. *Anderson*, 1904, 4 F. 128 (evidence that deceased's solicitor called on him on the night of his death, and entry in the solicitor's books "getting will executed").

48 *Leckie* v. *Leckie*, 1884, 11 R. 1088; *Rintoul* v. *Boyter*, 1833, 6 W. & S. 394 (in both of which the will had been seen and read); *Pollok* v. *Jones' Heir*, 1899, 1 F. 394 (instrument of sasine following on lost disposition).

49 *Incorporation of Skinners and Furriers in Edinburgh* v. *Baxter's Heir*, 1897, 24 R. 744.

50 *Smith* v. *Ferguson*, 1882, 9 R. 866.

to prove the *ipsissima verba* of the document, it must be established that it was substantially to the effect alleged.[51] The most satisfactory proof is by written adminicle, e.g. an extract, a draft or a copy, supported by parole evidence to connect it with the original. The rule is that written adminicles must be averred, but all this appears to mean is that, if the pursuer is relying on written adminicles, he must set forth these sufficiently to shew that he has a relevant case.[52] There is no decision that a pursuer is not entitled to rely on a written adminicle at the proof because he has not averred it. Where it was proved that a person had executed a will on the day he died and an alleged copy which bore to have been compared was produced, the copy was held sufficient proof of the tenor.[53] The terms of a disposition were held proved where the description and other clauses peculiar to the deed were taken from the instrument of sasine following on it, and the clauses of style from the forms in use at the time.[54] The terms of an ante-nuptial marriage contract and of a post-nuptial marriage contract were established from a draft of the latter and an instrument of sasine following on it.[55] In all these cases parole evidence was led to establish the circumstances, e.g. by whom a document had been written, and evidence was also produced of entries in solicitors' books. The tenor of a report dated 1629 was proved by a copy established by expert evidence to be in seventeenth century hand-writing.[56] On the other hand, decree was refused where it was doubtful whether the disposition had ever been granted and the pursuers had framed its alleged clauses from the titles of neighbouring properties.[57] But, although written adminicles are the most satisfactory form of proof, they are not essential. While in some cases they are to be expected, e.g. a draft of a disposition,[58] in others they are not, e.g. draft or copy of a composition contract.[59] Parole proof may be sufficient if the document is of a simple nature and has been unlawfully destroyed.[60]

234. CASUS AMISSIONIS: AVERMENT AND PROOF

The pursuer must aver and prove loss of the document "in such a manner as implied no extinction of the right of which it was the evident,"[61] and

---

[51] *Leckie* v. *Leckie*, 1884, 11 R. 1088.

[52] *Jenkinson* v. *Campbell*, 1850, 12 D. 854.

[53] *Young* v. *Anderson*, 1904, 7 F. 128.

[54] *Pollok* v. *Jones' Heir*, 1899, 1 F. 394. A more extreme form of this was figured by L. McLaren in *Rannie* v. *Ogg*, 1891, 18 R. 903, at p. 909.

[55] *McLeod* v. *Leslie*, 1865, 3 M. 840.

[56] *Richmond* v. *Officers of State*, 1869, 7 M. 956. See also *A.* v. *B.*, 1858, 20 D. 407, copy of letter in kirk session minutes.

[57] *Incorporation of Skinners and Furriers in Edinburgh* v. *Baxter's Heir*, 1897, 24 R. 744. *Cf. Maxwell* v. *Reid*, 1863, 1 M. 932.

[58] *Rannie* v. *Ogg* (*supra*), at p. 909.

[59] *Winton & Co.* v. *Thomson & Co.*, 1862, 24 D. 1094.

[60] *Young* v. *Thomson*, 1909 S.C. 529; *Leckie* v. *Leckie* (*supra*).

[61] *Winchester* v. *Smith*, 1863, 1 M. 685, at p. 689, quoted in *Clyde* v. *Clyde*, 1958 S.C. 343, at p. 345, and in *Mackinnon's Tr.* v. *Bank of Scotland*, 1915 S.C. 411, at p. 423, where a cautioner paid the amount due, received the bond and, as he was entitled to do, destroyed it, and the Bank was not allowed to prove its terms. *Cf. Drummond* v. *Clunas*

the precision of the averment and the weight of the proof required thus depend on the nature of the lost document.[62] If it is of a kind which is usually destroyed when it has served its purpose, e.g. a bill,[62] or an I.O.U.,[63] or of a kind which is revocable, e.g. a will,[64] what is called a special *casus amissionis* must be averred and proved. The pursuer must then establish the actual, or at least probable, cause of the loss, and one not inconsistent with the continued existence of the right. The reason for this is that the granter of the I.O.U. may have paid the money and recovered and destroyed the document, while the granter of the will may have decided to revoke it and simply burnt it. The action failed where the will was proved to have been destroyed without authority[65] or on the testator's instructions[66] and where a letter of guarantee was delivered to the cautioner after payment and destroyed by him.[67] On the other hand, where a person has taken infeftment and possessed for a long time, he is unlikely to destroy his own title.[68] In such a case a general *casus amissionis* will probably suffice, which usually means averment and proof merely that the document cannot be found.[62] But the nature of the document is not conclusive, because the circumstances may render the general rule inapplicable. Where it was proved that the testator died on the day a will was said to have been executed and his estate had been administered for over fifty years on the basis of the will, the court was satisfied with a general statement that the will could not be found.[69] The same result was reached where a bond had been founded on in previous proceedings,[70] and also, apparently on the evidence of the annuitant (pursuer) that he had not destroyed it, where a bond of annuity had disappeared.[71] On the other hand, a special *casus amissionis* was required in the case of a long lease[72] and in that of a deed of entail[73] because the circumstances were suspicious.

235. MUTILATED DOCUMENTS

An action of proving the tenor is competent to restore any obliterated

Tiles and Mosaics, Ltd., 1909 S.C. 1049, where a debtor was charged and paid and received the execution, which he destroyed, but the creditor was allowed to prove the terms of the execution. *Cf.* also *Smith's Trs.* v. *Smith*, 1904, 6 F. 775, which is difficult to reconcile with the general rule. *Russell's Trs.* v. *Russell*, 1862, 24 D. 1141, provides a practical illustration of the specification required.

[62] *Walker* v. *Nisbet*, 1915 S.C. 639, at pp. 643, 645.
[63] *Borland* v. *Andrew's Judicial Factor*, 1901, 4 F. 129. See also *Smith* v. *Ferguson*, 1882, 9 R. 866.
[64] *Clyde* v. *Clyde* (*supra*).
[65] *Cullen's Exr.* v. *Elphinstone*, 1948 S.C. 662, and *Falconer* v. *Stephen*, 1849, 11 D. 1338 (both unauthorised destruction of a will after testator's death).
[66] *Bonthrone* v. *Ireland*, 1883, 10 R. 779.
[67] *Mackinnon's Trustee* v. *Bank of Scotland*, 1915 S.C. 411.
[68] *Pollok* v. *Jones' Heir*, 1899, 1 F. 394.
[69] *Young* v. *Anderson*, 1904, 7 F. 128.
[70] *Mackenzie* v. *Lord Dundas*, 1835, 14 S. 144.
[71] *Brodie* v. *Brodie*, 1901, 4 F. 132, a doubtful decision. Lord Moncreiff dissented.
[72] *Paterson* v. *Houston*, 1837, 16 S. 225.
[73] *Graham* v. *Graham*, 1847, 10 D. 45; *Marquis of Annandale* v. *Lord Hope*, 1733, 1 Pat. App. 108.

part of a document.[74] Where the damage is clearly due to natural causes, wear and tear or damp, or was accidental, and there are no suspicious circumstances, there is little difficulty.[75] If there are suspicious circumstances, the opposite is true.[76] Where the document has been deliberately mutilated, the result depends on whether the person had the right to do so. If he had no right, the mutilation has no legal effect.[77] If he had, the effect depends on his intention. The question in fact is the same as that which has been raised in other types of cases, such as declarators, reductions, multiplepoindings and special cases. Indeed, it was observed that an action of proving the tenor was inapplicable to a case where issues were raised as to the right of a granter of a document to mutilate it and *quo animo* she had done so.[78]

236. EFFECT OF DECREE

The modern conclusion for declarator ends with the words "and that the decree to be pronounced herein shall be equivalent to the original deed."[79] The earlier form was for declarator that the decree "shall be in all respects as valid and effectual a document to the pursuer, in all cases, improbation as well as others, as the original deed, if extant, would be. . . ."[80] All the decisions on this question turn on the earlier form, but it is thought that they still apply, notwithstanding the disappearance of the words "improbation as well as others." Lord Kinnear's dictum,[81] that the decree replaces the lost document and has the same legal effect, must mean the same legal effect as the document had when executed. It is replaced only because authorised cancellation has been negatived by proof of some other *casus amissionis*. Where Lord Deas had proposed an interlocutor reserving all questions as to who could take benefit under the deed and whether the act which destroyed it was wrongful or legal, Lord President Inglis (then Lord Justice-Clerk) observed that such a reservation is necessarily implied in all decrees of proving the tenor.[82] But this observation must refer to the first proposed reservation only. Otherwise proof of the *casus amissionis* would be irrelevant, and seven judges had just preceded the Lord President, four holding as the ground of their opinions that the destruction of the document was wrongful and three that it was legal. An express dictum that a decree did not preclude defenders, who had appeared, from maintaining (in a subsequent process)

---

[74] *Duke of Athole*, 1880, 7 R. 1195; *Winchester* v. *Smith*, 1863, 1 M. 685.

[75] *Duke of Athole* (*supra*); *Duke of Argyll* v. *Campbell*, 1873, 11 M. 611; *Cousin* v. *Gemmill*, 1862, 24 D. 758.

[76] *Graham* v. *Graham*, 1847, 10 D. 45 (deed of entail with a great part of the testing clause torn off, under reduction on the ground of forgery).

[77] *Cunningham* v. *Mouat's Trustees*, 1851, 13 D. 1376 (unauthorised deletion of signature by solicitor); *Ronald*, 1830, 8 S. 1008 (unauthorised deletion of clause); *Falconer* v. *Stephen*, 1849, 11 D. 1338 (will destroyed by solicitor after death of testator).

[78] *Winchester* v. *Smith* (*supra*), at p. 698.

[79] Rules of Court, 1948, Appendix, Form 2 (*b*). See § **231**, sub-para. (a).

[80] See *Smith* v. *Smith's Trs.*, 1904, 6 F. 775.

[81] See § **231**, sub-para. (a).

[82] *Winchester* v. *Smith*, 1863, 1 M. 685, at p. 700.

that the persons who destroyed the deed were entitled to do so, appears irreconcilable with all principle.[83]   The decree, however, is open to attack on grounds on which the document itself might have been attacked, e.g. incapacity of the granter, facility and circumvention or fraud.   According to Dickson[84] reduction on the ground of forgery is also competent, but there is an obvious difficulty.   Decree cannot be granted in an action of proving of the tenor unless the court is satisfied that the deed was executed by the alleged granter, and *prima facie* a reduction on the ground of forgery would be met by a plea of *res judicata*, unless the decree were in absence.[85] Stair[86] and Erskine,[87] however, appear to take the view that reduction would be open unless the proof of execution in the proving of the tenor was by direct evidence.

[83] *Smith* v. *Smith's Trs. (supra)*, at p. 778.   The rubric is misleading.   None of the judges concurred in Lord Trayner's dictum.   Lord Moncreiff was absent.
[84] *Evidence* (3rd ed.) §1356.
[85] See § **231,** sub-para. (a).
[86] iv, 32, 11.
[87] iv, 1, 59.

CHAPTER XX

STAMPING OF DEEDS

237. GENERAL

Stamping is a statutory requirement designed to raise revenue, and one of its sanctions is the inadmissibility in evidence of an instrument not duly stamped. Admissibility thus depends on the terms of the statutory provisions. Unless it is stamped *pendente processu*,[1] "an instrument executed in any part of the United Kingdom, or relating, wheresoever executed, to any property situate, or to any matter or thing done or to be done, in any part of the United Kingdom, shall not, except in criminal proceedings, be given in evidence, or be available for any purpose whatsoever, unless it is duly stamped in accordance with the law in force at the time when it was first executed."[2] Unless the instrument falls under the statutory description, no question of stamping arises, since our courts do not enforce the revenue law of foreign states.[3] It has been held in England that if there is a trace of a stamp, the instrument will be presumed to have been duly stamped,[4] and the same presumption arises if the original document cannot be produced and its terms are proved by secondary evidence.[5] It is the duty of the judge to take notice of the omission,[6] and the decision of a judge of the Court of Session that the stamp is sufficient or that the instrument does not require a stamp is final,[7] but a decision to the opposite effect is not.[8] Inadmissibility in evidence of the instrument is, apart from the penalty, the only sanction. The party may prove his case by any other competent evidence available.[9]

238. COLLATERAL PURPOSE

There is no doubt that an instrument not duly stamped is inadmissible

---

1 See § 239.
2 Stamp Act, 1891 (54 & 55 Vict. c. 39), s. 14 (4).
3 *Stewart* v. *Gelot*, 1871, 9 M. 1057, at pp. 1062, 1064, 1065; *Valery* v. *Scott*, 1876, 3 R. 965, at p. 967.
4 Dickson, *Evidence* (3rd ed.) §978.
5 Dickson, *Evidence* (*ut supra*): Bell, *Commentaries* (7th ed.) 1, 340, note 1. But it must be impossible to produce the original: *Cowan* v. *Stewart*, 1872, 10 M. 735.
6 *Cowan* v. *Stewart* (*supra*). But it has been said that a judge is not compelled to raise doubtful points: *Don Francesco* v. *De Meo*, 1908 S.C. 7, L. Ardwall at p. 11. See *Foster* v. *Driscoll*, [1929] 1 K.B. 470.
7 Court of Session Act, 1868 (31 & 32 Vict. c. 100), s. 41.
8 *Simpson's Trs.* v. *Simpson*, 1933 S.C. 128.
9 *Fraser* v. *Bruce*, 1857, 20 D. 115; *Greenock Bank* v. *Darroch*, 1834, 13 S. 190.

to establish the obligation which it was intended to constitute or prove. But under the statutes in force before 1891[10] the courts evolved a rule that "an instrument, if it contains evidence of a fact foreign to the purpose for which it was executed, may be admitted as evidence of that fact notwithstanding the terms of the Stamp Act."[11] "Unintended effect" would thus be a better description than "collateral purpose," the phrase by which this exception is known. An instrument not duly stamped was held admissible as evidence of the state of mind of the granter,[12] and in the same case there are dicta that such an instrument might be used for a comparison of handwriting or as evidence that a signatory was alive at its date.[13] In an action of damages for wrongous use of diligence an unstamped agreement between the defender and a third party was admitted as evidence that the defender had probable cause. The ruling was excepted to, and the case settled.[14] In two cases the instrument founded on was separate from the instrument which was not duly stamped.[15]

In the statutes under which these decisions were pronounced the sanction was in this or similar form: "no instrument shall be pleaded or given in evidence or admitted to be good, useful, or available in law or equity."[16] Section 14 (4) of the Stamp Act, 1891, however, adds the words "or be available for any purpose whatsoever," which suggests a deliberate intention to put an end to the "collateral purpose" exception. In Scotland that result has been hinted at *obiter*,[17] and an opinion to that effect has been expressed in England.[18] Nevertheless, it has been held that an unstamped agreement might be looked at, not as an agreement, but as evidence of its terms,[19] and that an insufficiently stamped promissory note could be used to extract an admission from the granter.[20]

238. AFTERSTAMPING

An instrument not duly stamped may be received in evidence on payment of the duty, the penalty and one pound, if it may legally be stamped after execution.[21] This course has been allowed after proof and before judgment,[22]

10 Stamp Act, 1891 (54 & 55 Vict. c. 39).
11 *Durie's Executrix* v. *Fielding*, 1893, 20 R. 295, L. Kinnear at p. 299. On the previous decisions L. McLaren's view seems too restricted.
12 *Mackenzie* v. *Crawford*, 1839, 1 D. 1091.
13 *Ibid.*, at pp. 1094, 1096.
14 *Henning* v. *Hewatson*, 1852, 14 D. 1084. See also *Paton* v. *Earl of Zetland*, 1843, 5 D. 1049, where the court founded on the part of the document which, if it had stood alone, would not have required a stamp.
15 *Matheson* v. *Ross*, 1849, 6 Bell's App., 374, where a state of settlement was admitted and an unstamped receipt appended to it disregarded; *Fraser* v. *Bruce*, 1857, 20 D. 115, where notes of interest payments on the back of an unstamped promissory note were admitted.
16 Stamp Act, 1870 (33 & 34 Vict. c. 97), s. 17.
17 *Watson* v. *Watson*, 1934 S.C. 374, L. Murray at pp. 378, 379.
18 *Fengl* v. *Fengl*, [1914] P. 274.
19 *Mason* v. *Motor Traction Co.*, [1905] 1 Ch. 419, at p. 425. No reasons were given.
20 *Birchall* v. *Bullough*, [1896] 1 Q.B. 325. The procedure is obscure to a Scots lawyer, and the judges seem to have overlooked the last words of s. 14 (4).
21 Stamp Act, 1891 (54 & 55 Vict. c. 39), s. 14 (1).

and also on appeal.[23]   Where the pursuer's case depended on an unstamped document which was not admitted, a new trial was granted, the pursuer having had the document duly stamped.[24]   But if a judgment has become final, it cannot be suspended on the ground that it proceeded on a document which ought to have been stamped.[25]   The Act seems to contemplate payment at the time,[26] but the court has sisted process to enable payment to be made,[27] or it may admit the instrument on an undertaking that it will be duly stamped and the penalty paid.[28]

[22] *Weinschel*, (O.H.) 1916, 2 S.L.T. 346.
[23] *Simpson's Trs.* v. *Simpson*, 1933 S.C. 128.
[24] *Ivison* v. *Edinburgh Silk Yarn Co.*, 1845, 8 D. 236.
[25] *Napier* v. *Carson*, 1828, 6 S. 500. See also *Barbour* v. *Grierson*, 1828, 6 S. 860.
[26] *McTaggart* v. *McEachern's Judicial Factor*, (O.H.) 1949 S.C. 503, at p. 504. See *Muirhead* v. *Meikle*, 1917 S.C. 554.
[27] *Bankier* v. *Robertson*, 1864, 2 M. 1153.
[28] *Simpson's Trs.* v. *Simpson* (*supra*), at p. 132.

CHAPTER XXI

CONTRADICTION, EXPLANATION OR VARIATION OF WRITINGS BY EXTRINSIC EVIDENCE

240. GENERAL RULE

As a general rule it is incompetent to contradict, modify or explain writings by parole or other extrinsic evidence.[1] In so far as contradiction and modification are concerned the general rule in Scotland appears to be the same as the equivalent English rule, which provides that extrinsic evidence is inadmissible to contradict, vary, add to or subtract from the terms of a writing.[2] The English statement of the rule differs from the Scottish in that, subject to exceptions, it admits extrinsic evidence for the purpose of explaining or interpreting a writing. The distinction between the two statements of the rule, however, is theoretical rather than practical, because the excep-

---

[1] Dickson, *Evidence* (3rd ed.) §1015.
[2] *Bank of Australasia* v. *Palmer*, [1897] A.C. 540, L. Morris at p. 545; Phipson, *Evidence* (9th ed.) 599.

tions to this part of the Scottish rule are so numerous and extensive that little harm would probably result if the English method of statement were to be adopted. The traditional Scottish statement of the rule is nevertheless helpful in that it emphasises the important principle that the court, when seeking the intention of the writer, must find it in the words which he has used in the writing. "The duty of the court in dealing with the document is not to discover the abstract or secret intention of the parties as contradistinguished from what they have expressed, but to construe and give effect to the words in which they have deliberately set forth their final intention."[3]

241. SCHEME OF THE CHAPTER

While it is possible to state broadly the general rule[4] and the nature of the extrinsic evidence to which it applies,[5] this chapter is largely concerned with the occasions when, despite the rule, extrinsic evidence has been considered by the courts. The classes of writing to which the rule does[6] and does not[7] apply are mentioned first, with a reference to the implied terms of a written contract[8] and to the position of a writing which is *ex facie* incomplete or defective.[9] Examples of the application of the general rule are also given.[10] Then follows a discussion of the general exceptions to the rule,[11] the exceptions connected with the explanation of a writing,[12] and finally the exceptions which in certain circumstances allow the variation of a writing to be proved by extrinsic evidence.[13]

242. MEANING OF EXTRINSIC EVIDENCE

"Extrinsic evidence," as used in the general rule, includes parole evidence, but is not confined to it. It extends to all evidence, written or oral, extraneous to the document. Thus it includes parole testimony given by the parties themselves, evidence of statements which they have made orally or in writing by way of admission, or as to their intention in executing the document, or as to their understanding of its meaning and effect, and evidence of the actings of the parties or course of dealing before and after the execution of the document, including the evidence of any writings dealing with these actings. An oath on reference, although not evidence, is also mentioned in this chapter.

243. WRITINGS TO WHICH GENERAL RULE APPLIES—DEFINITION

The writings to which the general rule applies have been described as

3 Dickson, *Evidence* (3rd ed.) §1043. This topic is mentioned again at § 267, sub-para. (a).
4 See §240.
5 See §242.
6 See §§243, 245-253.
7 See §244.
8 See §251.
9 See §254.
10 See §255.
11 See §§256-266.
12 See §§267-277.
13 See §279.

those which the parties have constituted as the only outward and visible expression of their meaning, and deliberately prepared as the record of a transaction.[14] They have been said to include all documents which embody the terms of contracts, and which are really designed for recording and proving the final intentions of the parties.[15] "The whole doctrine of the exclusion of parole testimony with regard to . . . a written document rests upon this, that the document is intended to be a final and conclusive statement of the whole transaction between the parties."[16] These statements do not amount to a definition of the documents to which the general rule applies, but they indicate the principles which must underly an attempted definition. In England, where the underlying principles appear to be the same, a succinct and comprehensive definition has been suggested,[17] which can be used with advantage in Scotland. In accordance with this definition the general rule applies to any transaction which has been reduced to, or recorded in, writing, either by requirement of law, or agreement of the parties. The definition includes the discharge, as well as the creation, of obligations.[18] Writings to which the general rule does not apply are mentioned in the next paragraph.

244. CONTRACTS ONLY PARTLY IN WRITING—RULE INAPPLICABLE

When a contract is intended by the parties to be partly oral and partly in writing,[19] or is an oral contract in which a writing is incorporated,[20] all the oral stipulations may be proved by parole evidence. This is accordingly not an exception to the general rule, but a statement of circumstances in which, by definition, the general rule does not apply.[21] So, in a case which concerned a contract for the supply of iron pipes of certain dimensions at a specified price per yard, all specified in writing, proof of an oral stipulation as to the quantity to be supplied would have been allowed, if the court had been satisfied that the writing was intended only to give particulars of dimensions and price, in relation to a contract, the obligatory provisions of which had been agreed upon orally.[22] A sale of turnips by public roup, during which the auctioneer read excerpts from a document described as an agreement of sale, which had been signed only by the exposer, was held to be essentially an oral contract, and proof of an additional stipulation, said to have been announced by the auctioneer, was accordingly allowed.[23] Such a case must be distinguished from a sale regulated by formal articles of roup, which are properly authenticated at every stage and are finally executed by both exposer

14 Dickson, *Evidence* (3rd ed.) §1015.
15 Dickson, *Evidence* (3rd ed.) §1016. See also Dickson, *Evidence* (3rd ed.) §1043.
16 *McAdam* v. *Scott*, 1912, 50 S.L.R. 264, L. Kinnear at pp. 266-7.
17 Phipson, *Evidence* (9th ed.) 599.
18 See §249.
19 See the examples in Dickson, *Evidence* (3rd ed.) §1033.
20 Dickson, *Evidence* (3rd ed.) §1037.
21 See §243.
22 *Pollock & Dickson* v. *McAndrew*, 1828, 7 S. 189, L. Glenlee at p. 191. This case is also referred to at §263, notes 19-22.
23 *Christie* v. *Hunter*, 1880, 7 R. 729.

and purchaser.[24] When it is averred that, during the execution of an oral contract, invoices or similar documents have passed between the parties containing printed or written conditions which contradict some of the conditions of the contract, the court must consider the whole history of the transaction in order to discover whether the contract was fundamentally oral or fundamentally written. In such circumstances proof before answer is usually necessary.[25] A sale note, correctly recording the terms of an oral contract, has been held not to convert the oral contract into a written contract so as to make the general rule apply.[26] The general rule is also thought not to apply when a written offer is met by an oral acceptance which is subject to conditions or which constitutes a counter offer. This matter is discussed in a later paragraph.[27]

In one case which does not properly find a place in this paragraph, but which is difficult to classify, the general rule was not applied. Two bilateral written contracts were executed by the same parties, each providing for the sale of a ship. It was held competent to prove that the written contracts were intended merely as pieces of machinery for the implementing of an earlier oral agreement for the sale of both ships together, and not as superseding that agreement.[28] Before bills of sale could be executed in implement of the written contracts, one of the ships was requisitioned by the Government, and the purchasers were held entitled to refuse to accept a bill of sale of the other ship in spite of the separate written contract regarding it.[29]

245. WRITING AS REQUIREMENT OF LAW

The general rule applies to all documents embodying transactions which the law requires to be constituted in writing. These include contracts relating to heritage,[30] contracts of service for more than one year,[31] sub-

---

[24] *Ibid.*, L.P. Inglis at p. 730. For examples of sales regulated by articles of roup, which were held to be written contracts, see *Stevenson* v. *Moncrieff*, 1845, 7 D. 418 (sale of heritage); *Lang* v. *Bruce*, 1832, 10 S. 777 (sale of cattle).

[25] In *Buchanan & Co.* v. *Macdonald*, 1895, 23 R. 264, a printed notice as to terms of credit, on the invoice sent with each consignment of goods, was said to conflict with the oral contract, in terms of which all the consignments were supplied. After proof it was held that the invoices were intended only to indicate the quantity of goods despatched, and not to vary or express the terms of the contract, which remained oral throughout. In *Woodrow* v. *Patterson*, 1845, 7 D. 385, proof before answer was allowed of an averment that invoices accompanying goods, which stated that they had been "bought" at the price indicated, were not intended to vary or qualify the underlying oral agreement that the goods were supplied on sale or return.

[26] *Ireland & Son* v. *Rosewell Gas Coal Co.*, 1900, 37 S.L.R. 521, L. Kyllachy (Ordinary) at p. 522 approved.

[27] See § **248.**

[28] In Gloag, *Contract* (2nd ed.) 369, note 4, it is observed that this could be said of every case where a contract, written or oral, is followed by a conveyance.

[29] *Claddagh Steamship Co.* v. *Steven & Co.*, 1919 S.C. (H.L.) 132. This seems to go beyond what is thought to be the true ground of decision of the analogous case of *Duke of Fife* v. *Great North of Scotland Railway Co.*, 1901, 3 F. (H.L.) 2 (see § **250**, sub-para. (c), note 79), and to be truly a departure from, rather than an exception to, the general rule. It was apparently followed in *Wann* v. *Gray & Son*, (O.H.) 1935 S.N. 8.

[30] See § **93.**

[31] e.g. *Dumbarton Glass Co.* v. *Coatsworth*, 1847, 9 D. 732. See § **95.**

missions and decrees-arbitral in arbitrations,[32] and testamentary settlements.[33] It also applies to obligations which are declared by statute to be enforceable only if they are in writing, such as cautionary obligations[34] and certain hire-purchase and credit-sale agreements,[35] to marine insurance[36] and most other contracts of insurance,[36] to transfers of incorporeal rights in moveables,[37] and to declarations of trust.[37a]

246. WRITING BY AGREEMENT OF PARTIES

The general rule applies to all writings in which, by agreement of the parties, their obligations have been constituted[38] or an earlier oral or informal agreement has been subsequently embodied in a formal and effective written contract with the intention that it should take the place of the earlier agreement.[39] "The principle is well established that, when communings are followed by a written contract, it is not competent to allow any part of the communings, or even of letters that may have passed between the parties, to be held as part of the written contract, or to refer to them so as to enlarge or control the terms of the contract."[40]

247. INFORMAL WRITINGS

The application of the general rule is not confined to solemnly executed or holograph writings. It applies to informal writings *in re mercatoria*,[41] including bills of exchange,[42] and to a joint minute for the settlement of an action, signed by counsel without witnesses.[43] It also applies to a writing, which, because it is neither solemnly executed nor holograph, would be ineffective but for the fact that it has been homologated or *rei interventus* has followed upon it, such as a memorandum for a lease for nineteen years, signed by the parties without witnesses, and followed by possession.[44] The rule was even applied to a mere draft lease upon which possession had

---

[32] *Highland Railway Co.* v. *Great North of Scotland Railway Co.*, 1896, 23 R. (H.L.) 80. As to arbitrations generally, see §§101-103.
[33] See §§104, 253, sub-para. (b).
[34] e.g. *McPherson* v. *Haggart*, 1881, 9 R. 306. See §113.
[35] See §114.
[36] See §115, where an exception to the general rule in relation to marine insurance is noted.
[37] See §116.
[37a] *Pickard* v. *Pickard*, 1963 S.L.T. 56.
[38] See §97.
[39] *Inglis* v. *Buttery & Co.*, 1877, 5 R. 58, L. Gifford at p. 69: approved 1878, 5 R. (H.L.) 87, L. Blackburn at p. 102. See also §98.
[40] *Walker* v. *Caledonian Railway Co.*, 1858, 20 D. 1102, L. J-Cl. Hope at p. 1105.
[41] e.g. *Inglis* v. *Buttery & Co.*, 1878, 5 R. (H.L.) 87. As to writings *in re mercatoria* generally, see §§105 *et seq.*
[42] *National Bank of Australasia* v. *Turnbull & Co.*, 1891, 18 R. 629, L.P. Inglis at p. 634, L. McLaren at p. 638. For a statutory exception to the application of the general rule to bills of exchange, see §112.
[43] *Hamilton & Baird* v. *Lewis*, 1893, 21 R. 120. Proof of an oral agreement to vary the terms of the joint minute was refused. As to proof of agreements for the settlement of actions, see §153.
[44] *Pratt* v. *Abercromby*, 1858, 21 D. 19.

followed.[45] The general rule also applies to discharges, even where, as in the case of receipts,[46] these are informal. Contracts which are constituted by correspondence between the parties are mentioned in the next paragraph.

248. CORRESPONDENCE BETWEEN PARTIES: OFFER AND ACCEPTANCE

The general rule applies to a contract constituted by letters passing between the parties.[47] When the matter is one which requires writing for its constitution, as in the case of missives for the sale of heritage, the offer and acceptance must be holograph of, or adopted as holograph by, the respective parties.[48] The general rule applies also, however, when the offer and acceptance are contained in correspondence, not because the law requires it, but merely because the parties chose to constitute their contract in this way.[49] The general rule also extends to a written offer which is completed by an unqualified oral acceptance,[50] or by actings from which an unqualified acceptance was implied.[51] If it is averred that, instead of an unqualified acceptance of the written offer, there was an acceptance subject only to conditions, or a counter offer, it is difficult to understand how, in principle, the general rule can apply, since the terms of the contract must then be sought, not in the writing alone, but partly in the writing and partly in the oral communings following thereon. In such circumstances, it is thought, parole proof is not only admissible but essential.[52]

249. UNILATERAL WRITINGS

The general rule applies[53] to unilateral writings which constitute or create or discharge obligations on the part of the granter,[54] or from which such obligations or their discharge are inferred. It thus applies to personal and heritable bonds and discharges thereof,[55] to bills of exchange, cheques

[45] *Wight* v. *Newton*, 1911 S.C. 762. See also *Bathie* v. *Lord Wharncliffe*, 1873, 11 M. 490.
[46] See §249.
[47] Dickson, *Evidence* (3rd ed.) §1016.
[48] See §93.
[49] *Riemann* v. *John Young & Co. Ltd.*, (O.H.) 1895, 2 S.L.T. 426 (contract of employment terminable at short notice).
[50] *Pollock & Dickson* v. *McAndrew*, 1828, 7 S. 189 (argued on both sides on footing that contract was in writing).
[51] *Muller & Co.* v. *Weber & Schaer*, 1901, 3 F. 401 (sold-notes, granted by pursuers and admittedly retained by defenders without timeous rejection, which pursuers themselves sought to qualify by reference to an earlier oral agreement). See also *Croudace* v. *Annandale S. S. Co.*, (O.H.) 1925 S.L.T. 449, where a letter confirming an oral contract was ambiguous, and it was not clear whether the contract ever ceased to be oral, and proof of the conversations between the parties was allowed.
[52] Gloag, *Contract* (2nd ed.) 364, however, does not make this distinction. In *Thomson* v. *Garioch*, 1841, 3 D. 625, the general rule was applied, although it was averred by the defender that the oral acceptance of the written offer was subject to additional provisions which the pursuers in turn accepted orally. The terms of the interlocutor, however, indicate that parole proof was held to be incompetent because what the defender wished to prove was illegal. A similar point arose in *Cuthbertson* v. *Lowes*, 1870, 8 M. 1073.
[53] Dickson, *Evidence* (3rd ed.) §1016.
[54] As to these generally, see §100.
[55] *Wallace* v. *Henderson*, 1867, 5 M. 270; *Drysdale* v. *Johnstone*, 1839, 1 D. 409,

and promissory notes,[56] and to cautionary obligations.[57]   It has also been applied to a deed of appointment of a factor,[58] a mandate to buy shares from which an obligation to pay stockbroker's commission was implied,[59] and scrip notes obliging the granter to deliver iron to bearer.[60] In two cases[61] relating to a notice to remove from, or a notice of intention to leave, a farm, it was contended that the general rule applied to the document.   It was held that parole evidence was admissible to prove that one co-proprietor or co-tenant signed, not only on his own behalf, but also on behalf of the other proprietor or tenant, but it was not made clear in the opinions whether this was regarded as an exception to the general rule, or whether the general rule was regarded as not applicable to such a document.

The general rule has been applied to a discharge by creditors of all debts due to them prior to a certain date,[62] and by an employer of all sums due by his factor,[63] and to receipts for payment of sums due to the granters, such as receipts written on the back of a bill of exchange for payments to account of the sum due under it,[64] a receipt for payment of a sum due by the insurers under a policy of insurance,[65] and a receipt in the body of a disposition of heritage in respect of payment of the price.[66]   It has also been applied to a receipt which acknowledged, not only the payment of money, but also the terms of a bilateral contract in respect of which the payment was made,[67] such as a receipt for a sum of money "in payment of purchase price of 150 shares . . . the transfer for which will be sent you for signature in due course."[68]   Other decisions with regard to receipts and discharges are mentioned later.[69]

250. CONVEYANCES OF HERITAGE

(a) General. These deeds have been subjected to a special extension of the general rule. ∗ Before a purchaser of heritage obtains a title to the property it is usual for the parties to enter into a written contract, which may consist

---

[56] As to the application of the general rule to bills of exchange, cheques and promissory notes, and the exceptions thereto, see § 112.

[57] See § 245, note 34.

[58] *Hilson* v. *Otto*, 1870, 9 M. 18.

[59] *Stevenson* v. *Manson*, 1840, 2 D. 1204.

[60] *Mackenzie* v. *Dunlop*, 1853, 16 D. 129.

[61] *Walker* v. *Hendry*, 1925 S.C. 855; *Graham* v. *Stirling*, 1922 S.C. 90. These cases should probably be regarded merely as examples of the rule of the law of principal and agent which allows the authority of a principal to be proved by parole evidence. See § 260, sub-para. (b).

[62] *Harris* v. *Churchill*, 1822, 1 S. 348.

[63] *Spence* v. *Duncan*, 1706 M. 12, 333.

[64] *Macfarlane* v. *Watt*, 1828, 6 S. 556.

[65] *Anderson* v. *Forth Marine Insurance Co.*, 1845, 7 D. 268.

[66] *Gordon* v. *Trotter*, 1833, 11 S. 696.

[67] It appears that in England the general rule is not applied to such receipts, on the ground that they are not intended by the parties as contracts or binding legal instruments or as necessarily including all the terms of the agreement between them. See Phipson, *Evidence* (9th ed.) 602.

[68] *Lindsay* v. *Craig*, 1919 S.C. 139.

[69] See §§ 255, sub-para. (c), 259.

of solemnly executed articles or memorandum of sale, or of an informal interchange of letters (missives), which are holograph or adopted as holograph. In both cases the general rule applies to the written contract. It is an express or implied condition of all such contracts, however, that the seller shall grant to the purchaser a disposition, which, when recorded in the Register of Sasines, gives him a real, instead of merely a personal, title to the property. When such a disposition has been delivered to and accepted by the purchaser, in implement of the obligations of the contract, the original contract is at an end, and is superseded by the disposition, which becomes the sole measure of the contracting parties' rights. Thereafter the general rule applies to the disposition.[70]

The general rule has been applied on the same principle to a feu charter, which was preceded by a personal bond granted by the prospective feuar for payment of the feu duty which would later become due under the feu charter. It was held that once the feu charter was executed the liability of the debtor under the personal bond was discharged, and was superseded by the liability of the vassal for the time being under the feu charter.[71] The general rule applies also to a solemnly executed lease which must be regarded as superseding earlier less formal missives of lease.[72]

(b) Exception in Multiple Contract. When a disposition follows upon a multiple contract, which provides not only for the sale of heritage but for other matters as well, the disposition supersedes the original contract only in so far as it relates to the sale of heritage, and the original contract continues to be otherwise effective.[73] The disposition is final and conclusive in regard only to the rights which it was intended and adapted to carry, namely the heritage.[74] With regard to the other matters, the granting of the disposition does not "exhaust the contract between the parties."[75] So, when a contract provided for the performance of building work on,[73] or the sale of moveable fittings in,[76] the premises sold, as well as for the sale of the premises themselves, it was held that the acceptance of the disposition did not preclude the purchaser from enforcing that part of the contract which dealt with performance of work or sale of moveables.

(c) Exceptional Decisions in Special Circumstances. It has been held in what, it is thought, must be regarded as very special circumstances, that

[70] *Edinburgh United Breweries Ltd.* v. *Molleson*, 1894, 21 R. (H.L.) 10, L. Watson at p. 16; *Orr* v. *Mitchell*, 1893, 20 R. (H.L.) 27, L. Watson at p. 29; *Lee* v. *Alexander*, 1883, 10 R. (H.L.) 91, at pp. 96, 97, 98, 100. This statement was re-affirmed in *Butter* v. *Foster*, 1912 S.C. 1218, at p. 1225, and by Lord Reid in *Anderson* v. *Lambie*, 1954 S.C. (H.L.) 43, at p. 62.

[71] *King's College of Aberdeen* v. *Lady Hay*, 1852, 14 D. 675. This result was achieved by reading the documents together. It is thought that, since the decision of *Lee* v. *Alexander* (*supra*), the same result would be reached without considering the terms of the earlier documents, which the feu-contract would be regarded as superseding.

[72] *Robertson's Trs.* v. *Lindsay*, 1873, 1 R. 323, L. Deas at p. 327.

[73] *McKillop* v. *Mutual Securities Ltd.*, 1945 S.C. 166, L. Moncrieff at p. 172. For another example of a multiple contract, see *Gibb* v. *Cunningham & Robertson*, (O.H.) 1925 S.L.T. 608 (contract for sale both of shares and of heritage).

the parties may agree, before the disposition is granted, that the general rule shall not apply, and that, for certain purposes, the original contract shall continue to govern their rights and obligations.[77] In one case, where a disposition was granted in implement of a decree arbitral,[78] the opinion was expressed that, the governing instrument being the decree arbitral and the disposition having been granted for the sole purpose of constituting a feudal title, the terms of the former deed, which the disposition purported to repeat but repeated inaccurately, continued to regulate the obligations of the parties.[79] An analogous exception to the general rule was permitted in connection with an oral contract for the sale of two ships, which was held to govern the two written contracts, each relating to one ship, which followed upon it.[80]

When a solemn lease was executed after the tenant had been in possession for some time under an informal agreement, and the solemn lease was said to differ in its provisions from the informal agreement, the solemn lease was not applied to anything done by the parties prior to the date of its execution, although it bore to be effective retrospectively from the date of entry. In such a case the party founding upon the informal agreement is allowed to prove that it differs in its terms from the subsequent lease, and that the question at issue between the parties relates to the period prior to the execution of that lease.[81]

251. IMPLIED TERMS OF A CONTRACT

The general rule applies not only to the express terms of a written contract, or of a conveyance of heritage following upon a written contract, but also to terms which, apart from express stipulation in the writing itself,

[74] *Jamieson* v. *Welsh*, 1900, 3 F. 176, L. Kinnear at p. 182. The other rights are thought to arise from collateral agreements, properly so described. As to these, see § **262**.

[75] *Butter* v. *Foster*, 1912 S.C. 1218, L. Mackenzie at p. 1225.

[76] *Jamieson* v. *Welsh* (*supra*). The same principle was mentioned with approval in *Forth Bridge Railway Co.* v. *Incorporation of the Guildry of Dunfermline*, 1909 S.C. 493, at p. 502, where it was observed that a disposition might be regarded as only partly implementing a decree-arbitral, if that document dealt also with other matters not covered by the disposition. *Wann* v. *Gray & Son*, (O.H.) 1935 S.N. 8, which is difficult to understand, may also be partly explicable on the same principle.

[77] *Fraser* v. *Cox*, 1938 S.C. 506; *Young* v. *McKellar Ltd.*, 1909 S.C. 1340; *Wood* v. *Magistrates of Edinburgh*, 1886, 13 R. 1006. As to the first two of these decisions, see Lord Wark in *Norval* v. *Abbey*, 1939 S.C. 724, at p. 730.

[78] In Gloag, *Contract* (2nd ed.) 369, it is doubted whether, or to what extent, the general rule applies to conveyances which follow decrees-arbitral. See *Guthrie* v. *Glasgow and South-Western Railway Co.*, 1858, 20 D. 825.

[79] *Duke of Fife* v. *Great North of Scotland Railway Co.*, 1901, 3 F. (H.L.) 2, L. Macnaghten at pp. 12-13. It is thought that the true ground of decision in this case was that the clause in the disposition was an "ungrammatical and . . . unintelligible" sentence, and that it was therefore permissible to look at the decree-arbitral in order to discover its meaning. See Lord Low's opinion (at pp. 4-5), which was substantially affirmed by the House of Lords, and the comments of Lord Dundas (Ordinary) thereon in *Forth Bridge Railway Co.* v. *Incorporation of the Guildry of Dunfermline* (*supra*), at pp. 497-8.

[80] *Claddagh Steamship Co.* v. *Steven & Co.*, 1919 S.C. (H.L.) 132, mentioned more fully at § **244**.

[81] *Korner* v. *Shennan*, 1950 S.C. 285.

are implied by law. A tenant under a written agricultural lease was not allowed to prove an oral agreement which would have the effect of adding to the obligation, placed by implication of law upon the landlord, to put the buildings into proper repair at the commencement of the lease.[82] It was held to be an implied term of a joint minute in which two defenders undertook to pay a sum of money to the pursuer in settlement of an action, all questions of relief between the co-obligants being expressly reserved, that each defender should be liable for half, and proof of an oral agreement to the contrary was refused.[83] When a deed, which *ex facie* is solemnly executed, is delivered by the granter, implied authority is thereby given to the grantee to insert a testing clause when necessary, and proof of an intention that there should be no testing clause is incompetent.[84] The conveyance of a building having a mutual gable which overlapped a neighbouring building stance gave to the disponee an implied right to recover half the value of the gable from the owner of the stance when he came to build upon it. The opinion was expressed that this implied right could not be displaced by reference to a contrary provision in the missives which preceded the disposition.[85] Reference is made later in the chapter to implied terms arising in special circumstances, which, by an exception to the general rule, may be proved by extrinsic evidence.[86]

252. STATUTE, JUDICIAL DECREE AND SIMILAR WRITINGS

The general rule applies to rights and obligations constituted by such writings as it does to those constituted by private writings. It was applied to an obligation imposed by statute upon a railway company to accept a lease of a railway line on terms and conditions specified in the statute,[87] and to a right of inheritance constituted by statute;[88] to a right to a lump sum payment under a small debt decree;[89] to a liquidator's right to remuneration in terms of a resolution recorded in a minute, the making of which was directed by statute;[90] and to the boundaries of a glebe as fixed by a decree or minute of a presbytery.[91]

---

[82] *Barclay* v. *Neilson*, 1878, 5 R. 909. See also *Wight* v. *Newton*, 1911 S.C. 762.

[83] *Union Canal Co.* v. *Johnston*, 1834, 12 S. 304: 1835, 1 Sh. & McL. 117. It is thought that the decision would have been otherwise but for the express reference in the joint minute to the obligations of the co-obligants *inter se*, which made it necessary for the court to decide this matter on a construction of the writing. In general the liabilities of co-obligants *inter se* may be proved *prout de jure*. See § 261.

[84] *Shaw* v. *Shaw*, 1851, 13 D. 877, at p. 879.

[85] *Baird* v. *Alexander*, 1898, 25 R. (H.L.) 35, L. C. Halsbury at p. 37. Lord Herschell, at p. 39, reserved his opinion. Lord Shand, at p. 41, thought the missives might be looked at to see if they contained a discharge of the right.

[86] See § 273, sub-para. (d).

[87] *Stirling & Dunfermline Railway Co.* v. *Edinburgh & Glasgow Railway Co.*, 1852, 14 D. 747: 1853, 15 D. (H.L.) 48.

[88] *McMurrich's Trs.* v. *McMurrich's Trs.*, 1903, 6 F. 121, L. McLaren at pp. 125-6.

[89] *Lavan* v. *Gavin Aird & Co.*, 1919 S.C. 345. See also *Watson* v. *Gardner*, 1834, 12 S. 588.

[90] *City of Glasgow Bank Liquidators*, 1880, 7 R. 1196; Companies Act, 1862 (25 & 26 Vict. c. 89), s. 67; now Companies Act, 1948 (11 & 12 Geo. VI, c. 38), s. 145 (1).

[91] *Dalhousie's Tutors* v. *Minister of Lochlee*, 1890, 17 R. 1060: affd. 1891, 18 R. (H.L.) 72.

253. INCORPORATION BY REFERENCE OF OTHER WRITINGS

(a) **General.** The application of the general rule to a particular document does not exclude consideration by the court of other writings, if the terms of the document show, by express reference or clear implication, that the other writings are intended to be incorporated in it, or to be looked at in construing it.[92] In accordance with this principle the courts have considered, in conjunction with the terms of the principal document, plans,[93] schedules or specifications,[94] estate rules in connection with leases,[95] and the rules of an Association of which only one of the contracting parties was a member.[96] In some cases it was held that the other writing was incorporated in the principal document for a limited purpose only.[97] If another writing is held to have been incorporated by express reference or clear implication in the principal document, extrinsic evidence is admissible to identify the other writing.[98] The mere exhibition by one of the parties to the other of a writing, such as a plan,[99] or a list of articles to be used in connection with the contract,[1] does not necessarily incorporate it in the written contract subsequently executed, and estate regulations which were expressly incorporated in the lease of a sitting tenant were held not to be incorporated by implication in missives of lease of the same property to the same tenant, which were to take effect on the expiry of the existing lease.[2] And the mere reference in the principal document to an earlier holograph agreement, even when it is expressly stated to be in implement of that agreement, does not have the effect of incorporating the earlier agreement in the principal document, or of allowing it to be founded upon as controlling or qualifying the terms of that document.[3] In two earlier decisions this principle was not applied. In one, the court considered the terms of an advertisement and of articles of

---

[92] Dickson, *Evidence* (3rd ed.) §1047.

[93] *Burrell & Son* v. *Russell & Co.*, 1900, 2 F. (H.L.) 80, L. C. Halsbury at p. 84 (express incorporation); *Edinburgh Tramways Co.* v. *Black*, 1873, 11 M. (H.L.) 57, L. Chelmsford at p. 58 (private Act—implied incorporation); *Shearer* v. *Peddie*, 1899, 1 F. 1201; *Boyd* v. *Hamilton*, 1907 S.C. 912 (feu disposition—implied incorporation).

[94] *Aberdeen Railway Co.* v. *Blaikie*, 1851, 13 D. 527 (schedule expressly incorporated in contract); *Wilson* v. *Glasgow and South-Western Railway Co.*, 1851, 14 D. 1 (specification expressly incorporated in contract).

[95] *Lyon* v. *Irvine*, 1873, 1 R. 512 (general regulations expressly incorporated); *Pratt* v. *Abercromby*, 1858, 21 D. 19 (general regulations expressly incorporated for limited purpose). For other cases, see Rankine, *Leases* (3rd ed.) 108.

[96] *Stewart, Brown & Co.* v. *Grime*, 1897, 24 R. 414: distinguished in *McConnell & Reid* v. *Smith*, 1911 S.C. 635, at p. 638.

[97] *Barr* v. *Robertson*, 1854, 16 D. 1049 (plan); *Pratt* v. *Abercromby* (*supra*) (estate rules); *Shearer* v. *Peddie* (*supra*) (plan); *Boyd* v. *Hamilton* (*supra*), at p. 919 (plan); *Goodwins Jardine & Co. Ltd.* v. *Brand & Son*, 1905, 7 F. 995 (arbitration clause in contract between one of parties and a third party).

[98] Dickson, *Evidence* (3rd ed.) §1049.

[99] *Boyd* v. *Hamilton* (*ut supra*); *Gordon* v. *Marjoribanks*, 1818, 6 Dow, 87, at pp. 112 *et seq.*; *Heriot's Hospital* v. *Gibson*, 1814, 2 Dow, 301, at pp. 306, 311-2. In the two House of Lords decisions cited, the earlier speech of Lord Mansfield to the contrary effect in *Deas* v. *Magistrates of Edinburgh*, 1772, 2 Pat. 259, was found unacceptable.

[1] *Walker* v. *Caledonian Railway Co.*, 1858, 20 D. 1102.

[2] *Stewart* v. *Maclaine*, (H.L.) 1899, 37 S.L.R. 623.

[3] *Lee* v. *Alexander*, 1883, 10 R. (H.L.) 91, L. Watson at p. 96.

roup, to which reference was made in a disposition, in order to discover the boundaries of the subjects disponed, apparently upon the ground that the advertisement and articles of roup were statutory prerequisites of the sale.[4] In the other, the court construed the terms of a submission to an arbiter in the light of an earlier agreement between the parties.[5] It is thought that the view subsequently expressed in the House of Lords[3] would now be followed, and that an earlier agreement, even if mentioned in the principal document, would not be considered by the court, unless this were allowed by one of the recognised exceptions to the general rule.[6]

(b) **Testamentary Writings.** The principle applicable to testamentary writings is similar to that applying to other writings, although what is described in the last sub-paragraph as "the principal document" may, in the case of testamentary writings, consist of several documents. All the un-revoked testamentary writings, or parts of testamentary writings, of the testator must be read together as if they were one document.[7] The testator may, by reference to it in his testamentary writings, incorporate therein another writing, which may be informal, and parole evidence is admissible to identify the other writing to which the testamentary writings refer.[8] A reference to "such bequests as I may instruct . . . in a letter signed by me of this date" was held to have the effect of incorporating the letter in the will.[8] The question of whether it is competent to look at testamentary writings which have been revoked is discussed later in this chapter.[9]

254. WRITINGS EX FACIE INCOMPLETE OR DEFECTIVE

When a writing, which is founded upon by one of the parties as constituting a right, is construed by the court as incomplete or defective for this purpose, evidence of facts extrinsic to the writing, purporting to show that the

---

4 *Davidson* v. *Magistrates of Anstruther Easter*, 1845, 7 D. 342, at pp. 352, 353. L. Fullerton (pp. 354-355) dissented on the view that evidence regarding the advertisement and articles of roup was inadmissible, unless it could be brought within a recognised exception to the general rule.

5 *Renton* v. *North British Railway Co.*, 1847, 9 D. 1209. Lord Fullerton (p. 1217) dissented in this case also. In *Leith Heritages Co.* v. *Edinburgh and Leith Glass Co.*, 1876, 3 R. 789 (action of damages for breach of warrandice), L. Gifford (at p. 794) stated that a minute of sale was "embodied" in a disposition because it was referred to in the narrative. In L. Ormidale's opinion (at p. 799), however, the earlier deed could be looked at only because of an ambiguity in the dispositive clause of the disposition, and Lord Neaves and the Lord Justice-Clerk proceeded upon other and special grounds of decision.

6 The exceptions to the general rule are mentioned later in this chapter. See also § **250**, sub-para. (c), notes 77, 79.

7 *Magistrates of Dundee* v. *Morris*, 1858, 3 Macq. 134; *Horsbrugh* v. *Horsbrugh*, 1847, 9 D. 329, at pp. 340-1, 353, 359-360; *Tronson* v. *Tronson*, 1884, 12 R. 155, at pp. 156, 157, 158. See also *Wingate* v. *Wingate's Trs.*, 1921 S.C. 857. Whether a testamentary writing revokes or qualifies all the earlier testamentary writings, or only some of them, depends upon the construction of the writings by the court: *Bankes* v. *Bankes' Trs.*, 1882, 9 R. 1046.

8 *Inglis* v. *Harper*, 1831, 5 W. & S. 785.

9 See §**274** sub-para (c).

right was nevertheless constituted, is inadmissible.[10] A decree-arbitral was *ex facie* invalid because it bore to be signed, not only by the two arbiters, but also by the oversman, who was entitled to arbitrate only if the arbiters disagreed and devolved the submission upon him. It was held incompetent to prove by parole evidence that the oversman did not in fact act, and that the award was that of the arbiters alone.[11] An alleged written contract for the sale of heritage, consisted of what, for practical purposes, may be regarded as a written offer to sell,[12] and a written acceptance subject to conditions which were not mentioned in the offer. The alleged acceptance, as construed by the court, did not meet the offer so as to constitute a binding contract. It was held incompetent to prove by parole evidence that the additional conditions attached to the acceptance were not truly conditions, because they related, not to the subject matter of the written contract, but to certain oral representations, collateral to the contract, which had been made by the other party.[13]

The position is different when the court is unable, from a mere perusal of the terms of the writing, to decide whether or not a binding contract has been effected. When, for example, a contract of sale is alleged to have been made by written offer and acceptance, the question may turn upon whether or not the offer was accepted within a reasonable time. What is a reasonable time in a particular case may depend upon the nature of the article sold, and whether its market price fluctuated quickly or was relatively static. In such cases, if the surrounding circumstances are not admitted or within judicial knowledge, they must be proved.[14] And when from the terms of what is alleged to be a testamentary writing it is not clear whether it was intended as a will, or merely as a draft or note of instructions for the preparation of a will, extrinsic evidence of the surrounding circumstances is admissible.[15] When, however, no doubt arises on the face of the will, and it bears to express a completed testamentary intention, proof of an averment that it was delivered to a solicitor for some purpose other than as a valid will, or for cancellation or destruction, is incompetent.[16]

255. EXAMPLES OF APPLICATION OF THE GENERAL RULE

(a) **Explanation of the Writing.** Examples of the application of the general rule in this connection are mentioned later.[17]

---

[10] A missing term in a written contract which has been acted upon, may, in certain circumstances, be proved by extrinsic evidence. See §263.

[11] *Davidson* v. *Logan*, 1908 S.C. 350, L. Ardwall (Ordinary) at pp. 364-5, L. Low at p. 367, L. J-Cl. Macdonald at p. 369.

[12] *Johnston* v. *Clark*, 1855, 18 D. 70, L.P. McNeill at p. 72.

[13] *Johnston* v. *Clark* (*supra*).

[14] *Wylie & Lochhead* v. *McElroy*, 1873, 1 R. 41; *Glasgow, etc., Steam Shipping Co.* v. *Watson*, 1873, 1 R. 189.

[15] *Young's Trs.* v. *Henderson*, 1925 S.C. 749; *Wilson* v. *Hovell*, 1924 S.C. 1; *Sprot's Trs.* v. *Sprot*, 1909 S.C. 272; *Whyte* v. *Hamilton*, 1882, 9 R. (H.L.) 53.

[16] *Robb's Trs.* v. *Robb*, 1872, 10 M. 692, L.P. Inglis, L. Deas at p. 697; *Wilson* v. *Hovell* (*supra*), L. Constable (Ordinary) at pp. 5-6. See also *MacLaren's Trs.* v. *Mitchell & Brattan*, (O.H.) 1959 S.C. 183.

[17] See §267, sub-para. (b).

(b) Addition to Written Contract. Extrinsic evidence was *disallowed* or *disregarded* of the following *suggested additions* to written contracts:—an obligation upon a landlord to execute fencing and draining, which was provided for in an earlier informal agreement but was not mentioned in the written lease;[18] an obligation to pay a landlord the cost of cultivating the summer fallow left upon the farm by the former tenant, said to have been agreed to orally by the new tenant, but not mentioned in his lease;[19] an alleged condition in a sale of heritage that the price was to be wholly paid within six years, which was not mentioned in the missives;[20] and a provision, said to have been agreed to orally, but not mentioned in the written contract, that a specified number of pipes were to be delivered in terms of the contract.[21] Examples relating to custom or usage of trade are given later.[22]

(c) Contradiction of the Writing. Extrinsic evidence for the purpose of *contradicting* the terms of a writing was *disregarded* or *disallowed* in respect of the following:—an oral agreement that goods delivered in terms of a written contract of sale were to be accepted by the purported purchasers on a commission basis for re-delivery to another named buyer;[23] an oral agreement that a bond and disposition in security would not be called up at its due date except upon certain conditions;[24] an oral agreement by a landlord to repair fences although the lease placed the obligation upon the tenant;[25] an oral agreement that the purchaser under a written contract of sale of the seller's interest in his father's estate was entitled to withhold £1,000 of the price, and to retain this sum if he was the ultimate loser on a realisation of the property;[26] a statement by a landlord's factor, when showing a prospective tenant the boundaries of a farm, that these included a small portion of land which the lease, when it was executed, showed to be excluded;[27] an understanding between the original parties to a feu contract that the feu should not extend to a road which the feu contract specified as the boundary;[28] an oral agreement guaranteeing a minimum period of employment in spite of a written contract which enabled the employment to be terminated on one month's notice on either side[29] or by the employer at any time;[30] an averment that certain buildings, which were stated in a lease

---

18 *Norval* v. *Abbey*, 1939 S.C. 724. The defender was not the original landlord but a purchaser from him. This, however, did not form part of the ground of judgement. See also note 25 below.
19 *Alexander* v. *Gillon*, 1847, 9 D. 524.
20 *General Assembly of Baptist Churches* v. *Taylor*, 1841, 3 D. 1030.
21 *Pollock & Dickson* v. *McAndrew*, 1828, 7 S. 189. See also *Walker* v. *Caledonian Railway Company*, 1858, 20 D. 1102. Both these cases are mentioned again at §263.
22 See §276.
23 *Muller & Co.* v. *Weber & Schaer*, 1901, 3 F. 401. This case is mentioned again at § 259, sub-para. (a).
24 *Wallace* v. *Henderson*, 1867, 5 M. 270.
25 *McGregor* v. *Lord Strathallan*, 1862, 24 D. 1006. See also note 18 above.
26 *Pattinson* v. *Robertson*, 1844, 6 D. 944: affd. 1846, 5 Bell's App., 259.
27 *Gregson* v. *Alsop*, 1897, 24 R. 1081.
28 *Shaw Stewart* v. *Macaulay*, 1864, 3 M. 16.
29 *Riemann* v. *John Young & Co. Ltd.*, (O.H.) 1895, 2 S.L.T. 426.
30 *Hilson* v. *Otto*, 1870, 9 M. 18.

to have been valued at a certain sum, had not in fact been valued prior to the execution of the lease;[31] an averment that a particular debt had not in fact been paid or particular sums had not been accounted for, in contradiction of a general discharge of "all debts due"[32] or of "all intromissions";[33] an averment, in contradiction of a receipt for a sum of money, that no money in fact passed,[34] and, of a discharge, that the debt had not been paid;[35] an oral agreement that two of three co-guarantors of a bank overdraft would be freed of their obligation under the guarantee on the occurrence of a certain event;[36] and, in a question between co-obligants under a bond and disposition in security and the creditor therein, an averment that a letter of relief granted by one of the co-obligants to the others had been drafted by the creditor's solicitor, with the result that, despite the terms of the bond and disposition in security, the creditor had agreed that two of the co-obligants were cautioners only, and not principals:[37] an averment, held to contradict a recognised rule of construction, that a testator, who had bequeathed to a legatee a house, which at the date both of the bequest and of his death was burdened with a recorded bond and disposition in security, had demonstrated by his actings that he intended the legatee to receive the house disburdened of the bond.[38] Examples relating to custom or usage of trade[39] and to agency[40] are given later.

(d) Variation of Writing by Oral Agreement. Evidence has been *disregarded* or *disallowed* of the following oral agreements to vary the terms of a writing:—an agreement that a house, which in terms of a lease the tenant was bound to build of stone and lime, could be built of stone and clay;[41] an agreement that annual balance sheets, which in terms of a deed of copartnery became final if not objected to within two months, should be regarded as only provisional;[42] an agreement that a lump sum, to which the creditor was entitled in terms of a small debt decree, might be paid by instalments;[43] an agreement that wages due under a contract of employment

---

[31] *Lawson* v. *Murray*, 1825, 3 S. 371.

[32] *Harris* v. *Churchill*, 1822, 1 S. 348.

[33] *Spence* v. *Duncan*, 1706 M. 12, 333.

[34] *Anderson* v. *Forth Marine Insurance Co.*, 1845, 7 D. 268. *Cf. Smith* v. *Kerr*, 1869, 7 M. 863, mentioned at § **259**, sub-para. (a). For other decisions regarding receipts, however, see §§ **249, 259**, sub-paras. (a) (b).

[35] *Macfarlane* v. *Watt*, 1828, 6 S. 556.

[36] *McPherson* v. *Haggart*, 1881, 9 R. 306, L. J-Cl. Moncreiff at p. 317. This dictum is *obiter*, because there was no relevant averment that the other cautioner had been a party to the alleged agreement. For the exception to the general rule which allows the liability of co-obligants *inter se* to be proved by extrinsic evidence, see § **261**.

[37] *Drysdale* v. *Johnstone*, 1839, 1 D. 409. The position is different in a question between the co-obligants themselves: see § **261**.

[38] *Brand* v. *Scott's Trs.*, 1892, 19 R. 768.

[39] See § **276**.

[40] See § **260**.

[41] *Skinner* v. *Lord Saltoun*, 1886, 13 R. 823.

[42] *Barr's Trs.* v. *Barr & Shearer*, 1886, 13 R. 1055.

[43] *Lavan* v. *Gavin Aird & Co.*, 1919 S.C. 345.

should be reduced;[44] an agreement that during part of the currency of a lease the rent should be reduced;[45] and an agreement that the pursuers would accept certain guarantee insurance policies in place of the sum of money payable to them in terms of a joint minute signed by counsel for the parties.[46]

256. EXCEPTIONS TO THE GENERAL RULE

The rest of this chapter is concerned with the many exceptions to the general rule. The more important exceptions have acquired subsidiary rules of their own. An attempt has been made to group the decisions into defined classes, but in doubtful cases an arbitrary classification has been necessary. In these instances a reference in the notes indicates similar or analogous decisions which have been placed in other classes. The statutory exception which admits parole evidence in connection with bills of exchange has been mentioned earlier.[47] Reference to oath of averments which seek to explain,[48] contradict[48] or vary[49] writings, is mentioned in this chapter, although an oath on reference is not, strictly speaking, evidence.

257. FRAUD, ESSENTIAL ERROR OR ILLEGALITY

The general rule does not apply when it is sought to reduce a writing on the ground of fraud,[50] essential error[51] or illegality.[52] In these cases the question is not whether the written contract can be construed, contradicted or modified by extrinsic evidence, but whether it is binding upon the parties.[53] Thus extrinsic evidence was *admitted* of a conversation with the granter of a conveyance of heritage, in an action of reduction of the deed on the ground that it had been impetrated by circumvention when he was of weak and facile mind;[54] of false statements said to have been made by servants of the owners of two motor cars as to the roadworthiness of the vehicles, in a reduction *ope exceptionis* of a written hire-purchase agreement, which included an acknowledgment by the hirer that he had examined the vehicles, and had satisfied himself as to their roadworthiness;[55] of an averment that, to the knowledge of the disponee and his solicitor, the owner of

---

[44] *Dumbarton Glass Co.* v. *Coatsworth*, 1847, 9 D. 732. As to the possible exception when there is homologation or *rei interventus*, see §279, sub-para. (d).

[45] *Turnbull* v. *Oliver*, 1891, 19 R. 154; *Law* v. *Gibsone*, 1835, 13 S. 396. As to the possible exception when there is homologation or *rei interventus*, see §279, sub-para. (d).

[46] *Hamilton & Baird* v. *Lewis*, 1893, 21 R. 120.

[47] See §112.

[48] See §§266, sub-para. (c), 272, sub-para. (b).

[49] See §279.

[50] See § 125. This includes written contracts induced by misrepresentation: *Bell Brothers (H.P.) Ltd.* v. *Aitken*, 1939 S.C. 577, L.P. Normand at p. 585.

[51] *Steuart's Trs.* v. *Hart*, 1875, 3 R. 192, at p. 201; *Stewart* v. *Kennedy*, 1890, 17 R. (H.L.) 25.

[52] This includes writings, which, in themselves innocent, were executed to promote an illegal or immoral purpose. See Dickson, *Evidence* (3rd ed.) §§1038-1040; Gloag, *Contract* (2nd ed.) 563.

[53] Gloag, *Contract* (2nd ed.) 365.

[54] *Napier* v. *Sharp*, 1851, 14 D. 313.

[55] *Bell Brothers (H.P.) Ltd.* v. *Aitken* (*supra*).

heritable property granted a disposition of it in the belief that it was burdened with a cumulo feu-duty of £9 15/-, the truth being that only 3/- of the cumulo duty was a burden upon the property;[56] and of the unwarranted belief of the seller of entailed property, induced by the agent of the purchaser, that the contract was conditional upon the court approving of the whole terms of the bargain as fair and reasonable.[57]

258. BLUNDERS BY DRAFTSMEN

When one party to a written contract avers that, as a result of a drafting error, the writing misrepresents the agreement and intention of both parties, he will be allowed to prove his averment by parole or other extrinsic evidence. A disposition of heritage, which conveyed a farm and a neighbouring colliery, was reduced as a result of extrinsic evidence which established that the parties had only the farm in mind when they made their bargain, and that the colliery was included because of a conveyancing blunder on the part of both the solicitors concerned.[58] A feu contract was reduced in so far as it imposed an obligation on the superiors to form certain roads coloured brown on a plan appended to the deed, because it was proved by extrinsic evidence that these roads had been coloured brown erroneously, and contrary to the agreement of the parties as disclosed by the missives.[59] It has been said, in connection with recorded titles to heritage, that a Scottish court has no power to make a new bargain for the parties or to alter the deed in order to make it conform to the missives or to the real intention of the parties.[60] The reduction of the deed is the only competent remedy, although a partial reduction may be competent if the reduced part is clearly severable from the rest.[61] In an earlier case, however, not concerned with a title to heritage, a remedy was given in similar circumstances without reducing the deed. Proof was allowed of an averment that in a formal minute of agreement for *inter alia* the payment to a hotel manager of one-fifth part of the profits of the hotel, "one-fifth" had been inserted, by an arithmetical error on the part of a clerk, as being the half of one-tenth.[62] And the opinion was expressed that an insurance company could competently be proved to have made a clerical blunder in the terms of an insurance policy, which failed to give effect to the instructions of the insured who had requested the policy.[63]

259. WHEN REAL NATURE OF WRITTEN CONTRACT IN ISSUE

(a) **General.** The general rule does not apply, and extrinsic evidence is

---

[56] *Steuart's Trs.* v. *Hart (supra).*
[57] *Stewart* v. *Kennedy (supra).*
[58] *Anderson* v. *Lambie,* 1954 S.C. (H.L.) 43.
[59] *Glasgow Feuing & Building Co.* v. *Watson's Trs.,* 1887, 14 R. 610.
[60] *Anderson* v. *Lambie (supra),* L. Morton at p. 50, L. Reid at p. 61, L. Keith at p. 67; *Steuart's Trs.* v. *Hart,* 1875, 3 R. 192, at p. 200.
[61] *Anderson* v. *Lambie (supra),* L. Reid at pp. 60-61. See also *Glasgow Feuing & Building Co.* v. *Watson's Trs. (supra); Waddell* v. *Waddell,* 1863, 1 M. 635.
[62] *Krupp* v. *Menzies,* 1907 S.C. 903. See also *Carricks* v. *Saunders,* 1850, 12 D. 812.
[63] *North British Insurance Co.* v. *Tunnock & Fraser,* 1864, 3 M. 1, L. J-Cl. Inglis at p. 5,

admissible, when it is alleged that the writing was not intended to be a true record of the contract, but was merely a cover for some ulterior transaction of a different nature.[64] Although in a Scottish case in the House of Lords[65] it was said that a Court of Equity may always give effect to a transaction different from what the deeds represent its character to be, such a general statement of the exception appears to leave no content to the general rule, and it was not followed in a subsequent case,[66] where the exception, had it been of general application, ought to have been allowed. In that case a written contract for the sale of goods was alleged to be only *pro forma*, the true contract being that the consignees accepted the goods as agents on a commission basis for sale to a third party. Despite this allegation the general rule was applied, and extrinsic evidence was disallowed.[66]

It is thought that the exception to which this paragraph relates must in general be restricted to transactions where there is an element of collusion or deceit.[64] The exception which allows extrinsic evidence in relation to fraud or illegality, which has been mentioned earlier,[67] is an example of the same principle. In a declarator of marriage founded upon a written acknow-ledgment, the defender may prove that the writing was not executed for the purpose of constituting marriage, but collusively in order to deceive.[68] In two cases concerning receipts, where the circumstances were rather special, but where an element of collusion or deceit existed, extrinsic evidence was allowed when it was alleged:—that a receipt by a minor, with the consent of her curators, was granted for the purpose, not of acknowledging the receipt of money, but of enabling the trustees to settle the Government duties on her father's estate;[69] that a receipt for payment of rent in the tenant's possession, which he founded upon as a valid receipt, had been sent to him by the landlord merely as a reminder that the rent was due, and not as an acknowledgment of payment.[70] In the last mentioned case the proof was said to be allowed in order to discover whether the receipt came into the debtor's possession as a "delivered evident," i.e., as an effective receipt.[70] In the statutory examples mentioned in the next sub-paragraph an element of collusion is present in most cases.

[64] Dickson, *Evidence* (3rd ed.) §1038.
[65] *Scottish Union Insurance Co.* v. *Marquis of Queensberry*, 1842, 1 Bell's App., 183. *Ex facie* absolute assignations were held to be truly in security only. It was later said, however, that the real nature of the transaction was implied by the terms of the deeds themselves, and to be "stamped from the beginning as a transaction of loan": *Anderson* v. *Lambie*, 1954 S.C. (H.L.) 43, L. Keith at pp. 68-69.
[66] *Muller & Co.* v. *Weber & Schaer*, 1901, 3 F. 401.
[67] See §257.
[68] Dickson, *Evidence* (3rd ed.) §1038; *Imrie* v. *Imrie*, 1891, 19 R. 185; *Maloy* v. *Macadam* 1885, 12 R. 431; *Fleming* v. *Corbet*, 1859, 21 D. 1034, L. J-Cl. Inglis at p. 1044. As to proof of irregular marriages generally, see §§ 156, 157. As to collusion regarding a regular marriage, see *Orlandi* v. *Castelli* (O.H.) 1961 S.C. 113, and §155.
[69] *Smith* v. *Kerr*, 1869, 7 M. 863. *Cf. Anderson* v. *Forth Marine Insurance Co.*, 1845, 7 D. 268.
[70] *Henry* v. *Miller*, 1884, 11 R. 713, L.P. Inglis at p. 716. This case may perhaps also be regarded as an example of a condition attached to the delivery of a writing, which may be proved by extrinsic evidence. As to this, see § 264. For other decisions on receipts and discharges, see the next sub-para., and §§ 249, 255, sub-para. (c).

(b) Statutory Exceptions: Sale of Goods: Bill of Exchange. When a transaction in the form of a contract of sale of goods, whether oral[71] or written,[72] is alleged to have been intended to operate by way of mortgage, pledge, charge or any other security,[73] without delivery of the goods to the creditor, this may be proved by extrinsic evidence. "The reality of the transaction must be inquired into, and if, contrary to the form of the contract, and even the declaration of the parties, it appears from the whole circumstances that a true sale was not intended, it will be held that the property has not passed, and that no effectual security has been acquired."[74] On these grounds extrinsic evidence was *admitted* in the following circumstances:—by a written contract the owner of certain horses and wagons purported to sell them subject to a condition that he could buy them back within a year at the original purchase price with interest at 6 per cent., and the goods remained in the seller's possession;[75] a debtor in a sum of money granted a receipt for that sum which bore to be the price of certain articles of furniture, and it was averred that no money passed and that the furniture remained in the debtor's possession;[76] a receipt was granted for £79 which bore to be the price of certain machinery, and on the same day the machinery was hired back to the purported seller at a rent equal to interest at 4½ per cent. on £79 (with mutual rights of redemption);[77] the recipient of a loan of money gave the creditor a receipted invoice for bicycles at a specified price which was averred not to have been paid.[78]

In two cases[79] raising questions similar to those mentioned above, which were decided before the Sale of Goods Act, 1893,[73] proof was allowed in spite of the fact that the contract was in writing. In each case the question turned upon whether, in terms of section 1 of the Mercantile Law (Scotland) Amendment Act, 1856,[80] goods had in fact been sold, although not delivered to the purchaser, with the result that the subsequent sequestration of the seller did not defeat the purchaser's right to obtain delivery, or whether, on the other hand, the transaction was in reality an unsuccessful attempt to grant a security *retenta possessione*. It is possible to regard these as additional examples, apart from statute, of the exception described generally in the last sub-paragraph. On the other hand, Lord Watson doubted whether, in

[71] *Scottish Transit Trust* v. *Scottish Land Cultivators*, 1955 S.C. 254; *Newbigging* v. *Ritchie's Tr.*, 1930 S.C. 273. Although these cases are concerned with oral contracts, the opinions are thought to apply also to written contracts. The same statutory provision governs both.
[72] *Gavin's Tr.* v. *Fraser*, 1920 S.C. 674; *Hepburn* v. *Law*, 1914 S.C. 918; *Rennet* v. *Mathieson*, 1903, 5 F. 591; *Jones & Co.'s Tr.* v. *Allan*, 1901, 4 F. 374; *Robertson* v. *Hall's Tr.*, 1896, 24 R. 120.
[73] Sale of Goods Act, 1893 (56 & 57 Vict. c. 71), s. 61 (4).
[74] *Robertson* v. *Hall's Tr.* (*supra*), L. Moncreiff at p. 134.
[75] *Gavin's Tr.* v. *Fraser* (*supra*). It was held after proof that the agreement was in fact a contract of sale.
[76] *Hepburn* v. *Law* (*supra*) (held not to be a sale).
[77] *Rennet* v. *Mathieson* (*supra*) (held not to be a sale).
[78] *Jones & Co.'s Tr.* v. *Allan* (*supra*) (held not to be a sale).
[79] *McBain* v. *Wallace*, 1881, 8 R. (H.L.) 106; *Liddell's Tr.* v. *Warr*, 1893, 20 R. 989. See also *Pattison's Tr.* v. *Liston*, 1893, 20 R. 806.
[80] 19 & 20 Vict. c. 60. Section 1 of this Act was repealed by the Sale of Goods Act.

such a case, when the writing was unambiguous, it was competent to consider extrinsic evidence.[81]

Another statutory exception to the general rule, which allows parole evidence in relation to bills of exchange, has been mentioned earlier.[82]

260. PRINCIPAL AND AGENT

(a) **Liability of Apparent Principal.** When a person, who has signed a contract ostensibly on his own behalf, alleges that he was acting for an undisclosed principal, and is accordingly not liable, the general rule applies in a question between himself and the creditor in the obligation. Solicitors who signed missives for the sale of heritage,[83] and a chartered accountant who signed a receipt for the price of shares,[84] were not allowed to prove by extrinsic evidence that, in spite of the unqualified terms of their written obligations, they had acted only as agents for other persons. Exceptions to the general rule have been allowed, however, in the circumstances mentioned in the next sub-paragraph.

(b) **Rights and Obligations of Undisclosed Principal.** By an exception to the general rule it is competent to prove that a person who was not a signatory of a writing was in fact the principal of one of the signatories, and is entitled to sue or is liable to be sued upon it.[85] When notice to a tenant to remove was given by only one of two co-proprietors, the other co-proprietor was held entitled to prove that the notice had been signed on his behalf and with his authority.[86] Conversely, when one of two co-tenants gave notice of intention to remove, the proprietors were allowed to prove that the notice had been given on behalf of, and with the authority of, the other tenant.[87] This exception is said to be justified because it does not discharge any liability appearing *ex facie* of the writing, but merely adds a party to it.[88] This is not an adequate justification because the general rule excludes additions to the writing as well as contradictions. In reality the position here appears to be that a rule of the law of principal and agent conflicts with, and takes precedence over, the general rule of the law of evidence.[89]

---

[81] *McBain* v. *Wallace* (*supra*), L. Watson at pp. 114-5. It has been suggested that section 61 (4) of the Sale of Goods Act was enacted because of doubts such as those expressed by Lord Watson, and to provide that, in spite of the form of the contract, the intention of the parties might be proved by extrinsic evidence: see *Robertson* v. *Hall's Tr.* (*supra*), L. Moncreiff at p. 135.

[82] See § 112.

[83] *Gibb* v. *Cunningham & Robertson*, (O.H.) 1925 S.L.T. 608.

[84] *Lindsay* v. *Craig*, 1919 S.C. 139. In *Welsh's Trs.* v. *Forbes*, 1885, 12 R. 851, where a proof in similar circumstances was allowed, it is thought that L. Rutherfurd Clark's dissenting opinion, at p. 862, was correct.

[85] Gloag, *Contract* (2nd ed.) 127. There are exceptions to the exception, for which see Gloag.

[86] *Walker* v. *Hendry*, 1925 S.C. 855.

[87] *Graham* v. *Stirling*, 1922 S.C. 90.

[88] Gloag, *Contract* (2nd ed.) 127; *Graham* v. *Stirling* (*supra*), L. Ashmore (Ordinary) at p. 98.

[89] *Anderson* v. *Gordon*, 1830, 8 S. 304, where the general rule was applied in these circumstances, would presumably not now be followed.

261. CO-OBLIGANTS AND CO-CREDITORS INTER SE

Extrinsic evidence is admissible to establish that the contractual relationship between co-obligants is different from that expressed or implied in the writing which constitutes their contractual relationship with the creditor.[90] Such evidence is not, of course, competent in a question between the co-obligants and the creditor.[91] Thus a co-cautioner was allowed to prove an agreement, contrary to the implied term of a cautionary obligation, that he was not bound to communicate to his co-cautioners the benefit of a security which he had obtained from the principal debtor;[90] a co-acceptor of a bill of exchange was allowed to prove, contrary to the presumption that two co-obligants *inter se* are each liable for half, that she was a cautioner only in relation to the other acceptor and was entitled to relief against him for the whole sum due under the bill which she had paid to the creditor;[92] and extrinsic evidence was allowed to prove that, as between two joint tenants, only one of them owned the crop and stock on the farm,[93] or was concerned in the active working of the quarries which were the subject of the lease.[94] An earlier case,[95] where proof was refused of an oral agreement between two defenders as to the allocation *inter se* of their liability under a joint minute for payment of a sum of money to the pursuers, is thought to be distinguishable, because the question of relief between the co-obligants was expressly mentioned in the joint minute and fell, therefore, to be decided on a construction of its terms.

The same principle was applied to a case of co-creditors under an insurance policy. Two persons in contemplation of marriage agreed to effect an insurance on their joint lives, the proceeds to be payable to the survivor on the death of either of them. The insurance policy, when issued, made the proceeds payable, not to the survivor, but to the "executors, administrators and assigns" of the two assured. The opinion was expressed that it was competent to prove the insured persons' own agreement *inter se* as to the disposal of the proceeds of the policy in respect of which they were joint creditors.[96]

262. COLLATERAL AGREEMENTS

By an exception to the general rule, agreements which are collateral to a

---

[90] *Hamilton & Co.* v. *Freeth*, 1889, 16 R. 1022. See also *Thow's Tr.* v. *Young*, 1910 S.C. 588, L. Skerrington (Ordinary) at p. 593, L.P. Dunedin at pp. 595-6.

[91] *Drysdale* v. *Johnstone*, 1839, 1 D. 409.

[92] *Crosbie* v. *Brown*, 1900, 3 F. 83.

[93] *Kilpatrick* v. *Kilpatrick*, 1841, 4 D. 109.

[94] *Moore* v. *Dempster*, 1879, 6 R. 930.

[95] *Union Canal Co.* v. *Johnston*, 1834, 12 S. 304; 1835, 1 Sh. & McL., 117. In *McPherson* v. *Haggart*, 1881, 9 R. 306, where proof of such an agreement was also held to be inadmissible, it was observed that there was no relevant averment that the other co-cautioner had been a party to it.

[96] *North British Insurance Co.* v. *Tunnock & Fraser*, 1864, 3 M. 1, L. Benholme at p. 5. Lord Benholme described the agreement between the spouses as a "collateral contract." This was not, however, a collateral agreement in accordance with Dickson's definition (Dickson, *Evidence* (3rd ed.) §1033), because, in a question between the insured and the insurance company, it clearly contradicted the terms of the written contract. As to collateral agreements, see §262.

writing may be proved by extrinsic evidence. The title of the paragraph, however, must be carefully defined. Some of the cases appear to indicate that any agreement may be proved as collateral which is not found in the writing, and is not directly contradictory of anything found there, but this has been said to leave very little content to the general rule.[97] It is thought that the exception must be strictly confined to the kind of collateral agreement described by Dickson[98] in general terms.

Dickson defines the word "collateral" in relation to this exception in the following terms:—"The rule by which extrinsic evidence is inadmissible to add to the stipulations of a deed does not apply to matters collateral to the document; because on these there is no written agreement between the parties. In such questions, therefore, the nature and object of the writing must be considered, so that on the one hand obligations or conditions may not be added to a deed designed for recording all the agreement which the parties made on a particular subject, while, on the other hand, a writing intended to embrace only certain branches or stipulations of an agreement ought not to be stretched to matters beyond its purview; for, if it were, extrinsic evidence would be excluded on matters which the parties purposely left to be expiscated by that means."[98] What are described by Dickson[98] as the "most prominent" illustrations of this exception are cases where the writing is a short memorandum in which only certain points of the contract are recorded: e.g., a pencil note "Six weeks at two guineas," which was regarded as recording only *some* of the terms of a contract for the hire of a horse, leaving the remaining terms to be proved by parole evidence.[99]

So defined, the scope of this exception is rightly to be regarded as very limited indeed. It includes only agreements between the parties or their successors in title which are shown by the terms of the writing, as construed by the court, not to form part of the matter with which the writing was properly concerned. One example, mentioned above, is a writing which was clearly intended to record only some of the terms of a contract.[99] Another is a conveyance of heritage following upon a multiple contract, which provides not only for a sale of heritage but also for other matters, such as the performance of work or the sale of moveables. Since these other matters do not properly fall to be mentioned in a conveyance of heritage, they may be proved by extrinsic evidence.[1] Another example is an agreement, entered into during the currency of a lease, in terms of which the landlord, on the termination of the lease, must pay to the tenant all his loss during the nineteen years of his tenancy.[2] Proof[3] of the agreement was allowed because (*a*) it could not have

---

[97] Gloag, *Contract* (2nd ed.) 371.

[98] Dickson, *Evidence* (3rd ed.) §1033. See *Norval* v. *Abbey*, 1939 S.C. 724, L. Wark at p. 730, L. Jamieson at p. 734. Many of the examples given by Dickson do not fall within his own general definition.

[99] As to this kind of writing, see §**244.**

[1] For the decisions, see §**250,** sub-para. (b).

[2] *Garden* v. *Earl of Aberdeen*, 1893, 20 R. 896. See also *British Workman's etc., Assurance Co. Ltd.*, (O.H.) 1900, 8 S.L.T. 67, where the collateral agreement did not take effect until the termination of the written contract. The case is difficult to fit into one of the recognised exceptions.

[3] Proof was restricted to writ or oath only because the agreement was held to be innominate and unusual.

been included in the lease, since it was entered into after the lease had commenced, and (*b*) it did not seek to contradict or vary the lease, since it did not commence to operate until after the lease had terminated. An example of this kind has been described as " the constitution of an original and independent agreement by parole."[4]

The following are examples of agreements which fall outside the definition of "collateral agreement" suggested above. An oral agreement, confirmed in writing, was entered into between landlords and prospective tenants with regard to fencing, on the strength of which the tenants accepted a lease which did not refer to the agreement. In a question between the original tenants and disponees of the original landlords, the tenants' averments with regard to the agreement were held to be irrelevant, because proof of them would result in adding to the lease terms which were not, but which ought to have been, contained therein.[5] An oral agreement was said to have been made *unico contextu* with the execution of a formal lease of certain premises for a period of five years. The oral agreement provided for payment by the tenants to the landlords of the sums which the latter would have had to disburse in respect of owners' rates and property tax during the currency of the lease. The landlord's averments regarding the oral agreement were held irrelevant because they related, not to a collateral agreement, but to an agreement which purported to add to, or to alter, the express stipulations of the lease regarding the payments to be made by the tenants.[6]

The exception regarding collateral agreements must be considered along with, and distinguished from, the following other exceptions, which are mentioned elsewhere:—the exception relating to the liability of co-obligants and co-creditors *inter se*,[7] which does not affect the relationship between the parties to the written contract; the exception relating to proof of a missing term in a written contract,[8] whereby a term, essential to the fulfilment of a contract which has been acted upon, may be proved by extrinsic evidence; and the exception relating to a condition attached to the delivery or execution of a writing,[9] which suspends the operation of the whole contract until the condition is fulfilled.

263. MISSING TERM IN WRITTEN CONTRACT

A limited exception to the general rule is allowed in the following circumstances. When a written contract has been acted upon, and it appears, as

---

[4] *Kirkpatrick* v. *Allanshaw Coal Co.*, 1880, 8 R. 327, L.P. Inglis at p. 332, quoted by L. Trayner in *Garden* v. *Earl of Aberdeen* (*supra*), at p. 899. Another example of a collateral agreement may be found in *McAlister* v. *Gemmil*, 1862, 24 D. 956: affd. 1863, 1 M. (H.L.) 1, and possibly in *Merrow & Fell* v. *Hutchison & Brown*, 1873, 10 S.L.R. 338.
[5] *Norval* v. *Abbey*, 1939 S.C. 724.
[6] *Perdikou* v. *Pattison*, 1958 S.L.T. 153. See also *McGregor* v. *Lord Strathallan*, 1862, 24 D. 1006 ("an attempt to engraft on the lease a clause not to be found in it": L. J-Cl. Inglis at p. 1010); *Stewart* v. *Clark*, 1871, 9 M. 616.
[7] See § 261. For the use of the word "collateral" in *North British Insurance Co.* v. *Tunnock & Fraser*, 1864, 3 M. 1, see note 96 to that paragraph.
[8] See § 263.
[9] See § 264. For the description of such a condition as a "collateral agreement" in *Semple* v. *Kyle*, 1902, 4 F. 421, see note 29 to that paragraph.

construed by the court, that one of the terms essential for its fulfilment as a concluded contract is not expressed in the writing,[10] or is expressed only imperfectly or incompletely,[11] and must necessarily have been the subject of oral agreement between the parties, the missing or incompletely expressed term may be proved by parole or other extrinsic evidence. On the other hand, an unexpressed term which is not essential for the fulfilment of the contract, even if oral agreement upon it would seem to be probable, may not be proved.[12] Evidence of a custom of trade may in certain circumstances be admissible, when a contract is silent on the matter to which it relates.[13]

The following are examples of circumstances in which the exception was allowed. When, in a lease of land for experimental bulb growing, it was essential to know the date of entry and thus the date of termination of the lease, and neither was stated in the writing, parole evidence as to the date of entry agreed upon by the parties was admitted.[14] When, in an agricultural lease, the provisions with regard to rotation of crops and a yearly reduction of rent in respect of repairs done by the tenant, made it clear that the duration of the let was a period of years, without specifying the number of years, the extrinsic evidence of an advertisement, which stated that the farm was to be let for eighteen years, was admitted in order to supply the missing term.[15] In a written contract for the sale of a pawnbroking business on a condition, which was purified, that the purchaser should be accepted as tenant for the remaining ten years of the seller's lease, the seller undertook to allow her capital "to remain on loan" to the purchaser, without the duration of the loan being specified. The purchaser averred an oral agreement that the loan should endure until the expiry of the lease. But for the fact that the parties were held, by their actings, to have indicated their agreement as to the missing term, it seems probable that parole evidence would have been allowed with regard to it.[16] The actings of parties[17] are, in any event, extrinsic evidence. By written contract the defender undertook to assign to the pursuer certain businesses and plant in consideration of there being allotted to him 1,750 preference shares of £1 each, bearing a specified rate of interest, in "your

---

10 *McAllister* v. *McGallagley*, 1911 S.C. 112. "Well here is one vital stipulation as to which we are not at one. In such circumstances, in order to expiscate the matter, the court would have been driven . . . to find out *aliunde* what the term of the loan was to be": L.P. Dunedin, at p. 118. "A perfectly good averment that there was one term of the bargain which was left, so far as the writing was concerned, unsettled, and that the settling of that term might be arranged verbally": L.P. Dunedin at p. 117. "It is, I think, [a question] of explaining an ambiguous agreement and supplying a necessary term which is awanting": L. Johnston at pp. 121-2.
11 *Renison* v. *Bryce*, 1898, 25 R. 521.
12 *Walker* v. *Caledonian Railway Co.*, 1858, 20 D. 1102. The parties are bound by the true construction of the terms of the contract as these shall be ascertained by the court: *Laing* v. *Provincial Homes Investment Co. Ltd.*, 1909 S.C. 812, at pp. 822, 826.
13 See §276.
14 *Watters* v. *Hunter*, 1927 S.C. 310.
15 *Russell* v. *Freen*, 1835, 13 S. 752. See, in particular, the opinion of L. Corehouse (Ordinary), at p. 754. For another similar example, see *McLeod* v. *Urquhart*, 1808 Hume, 840, explained by L.P. Dunedin in *McAllister* v. *McGallagley (supra)*, at pp. 117-8.
16 *McAllister* v. *McGallagley (supra)*, L.P. Dunedin at p. 118, L. Johnston at pp. 121-2. L. Kinnear, at p. 120, reserved his opinion on this, but agreed that the parties had resolved the question by their actings.

proposed limited company." The limited company, when formed by the pursuer, had a capital of £10,000 of which the preference shares represented £9,500. The defender averred an oral agreement that the proposed company should have a share capital not exceeding £5,000. It was held that "your proposed limited company" required elucidation, and that since the capital of the proposed company was a matter of great importance in relation to the value of the shares to be allotted to the defender, and had not been specified in the writing, proof of the oral agreement was permissible.[18]

In the following cases, on the other hand, the general rule was applied. In a written contract for the supply of iron pipes of certain dimensions at a specified price per yard, no reference was made to minimum or maximum quantities. The purchasers averred that the sellers had agreed orally to supply a specified quantity. Proof of the oral agreement was refused,[19] on the ground that there was nothing "palpably defective"[20] about the contract which would prevent it being carried into effect without explanation,[20] and that the court must not make a new contract for the parties[21] in place of their own written contract, which left each party free to stop the contract when he chose.[22] In somewhat similar circumstances, where the written contract was for the performance of the horse haulage work on a railway company's lines for three years, at a specified rate per day for each horse and man, the contract to be worked to the satisfaction of the company's goods manager, the contract did not provide for the supply or employment of any particular number of horses. The contractor averred that the contract was executed with special reference to a list of the number of horses to be supplied at each station, which had been shown to him. Proof of the prior communings of the parties and of the list was refused, apparently on the ground that the missing term was not essential to the execution of the contract.[23] It was observed that "if such evidence is to be admitted, there would be an end to the rule of written contracts altogether. It would be open to any party to raise questions as to the construction of a contract he found to be working against him. . . . If the pursuer stipulated for the constant employment of a certain number of horses . . . that was a most important part of the stipulation, and ought to have been embodied in the contract."[24]

264. CONDITIONAL DELIVERY OR EXECUTION OF WRITING

In England it is permissible to prove by extrinsic evidence that a written contract, *ex facie* unconditional, was delivered or signed subject to a condition that it was not to take effect until the condition was purified.[25] On a few

---

[17] Cases in which the actings of parties may be proved in order to explain the contract are mentioned later. See §275, sub-para. (c).
[18] *Renison* v. *Bryce*, 1898, 25 R. 521.
[19] *Pollock & Dickson* v. *McAndrew*, 1828, 7 S. 189. See also §244, note 22.
[20] *Ibid.*, L. Pitmilly at p. 191.
[21] *Ibid.*, L. Alloway, L. J-Cl. Boyle, at p. 191.
[22] *Ibid.*, L. J-Cl. Boyle at p. 191.
[23] *Walker* v. *Caledonian Railway Co.,* 1858, 20 D. 1102.
[24] *Ibid.*, L. J-Cl. Hope at p. 1105.
[25] Phipson, *Evidence* (9th ed.) 608; Cross, *Evidence* (1958) 477.

occasions this English exception to the general rule has been applied in Scotland.[26] The only purpose for which such a proof can be allowed is to suspend the operation of the whole contract until the condition is fulfilled.[27] Proof of such a condition has been *allowed* in the following circumstances:— when it was averred that a written contract, to take advertising space from advertising contractors for a period of two years, was signed by the defenders' managing director subject to the orally expressed condition that the contract was not to be regarded as binding until it was approved by his co-directors;[28] when it was averred that a cheque, *ex facie* unqualified, was delivered subject to the condition that it would be stopped unless the drawer received on that day a cheque for the same amount from a named person;[29] when a receipt was sent by a landlord to a tenant merely as a reminder that the rent was due, and subject to the condition that he should either send the money or return the receipt.[30] When a written contract of employment followed upon a written application by the employee, in which he undertook not to interfere with the employer's business on the termination of the employment, it was held that the undertaking, which was not mentioned in the contract, was a collateral undertaking on the faith of which the applicant obtained employment.[31]

265. QUESTIONS WITH THIRD PARTIES

It has been held in certain circumstances that the general rule does not apply in a question between persons who are not parties to the writing, but have an interest, or between such persons and one of the parties.[32] The most frequent examples are declarators of trust. A third party with an interest may prove *prout de jure* that subjects held on an *ex facie* absolute title by one party are really held in trust for another,[33] although in a question between the parties

---

26 Gloag, *Contract* (2nd ed.) 371. See also L. Bramwell, *obiter*, in *N.B. Rly. Co.* v. *Wood*, 1891, 18 R. (H.L.) 27, at pp. 36-37.

27 *Norval* v. *Abbey*, 1939 S.C. 724, L. Wark at p. 731.

28 *Abrahams & Sons* v. *Robert Miller (Denny) Ltd.*, 1933 S.C. 171. For another similar example, see *Dodds* v. *Walker*, 1822, 2 S. 73 (acceptance by agent of offer to take a lease to be binding only if approved by principal).

29 *Semple* v. *Kyle*, 1902, 4 F. 421. The condition was held proved, and the drawer, who was sued on the cheque by an endorsee for value who had known that the cheque was dishonoured, was assoilzied. Despite L. Kinnear's opinion to the contrary (at p. 424), it is thought that the condition *did* qualify the meaning and effect of the writing, and that it was not, accordingly, a collateral agreement. As to collateral agreements, see §262.

30 *Henry* v. *Miller*, 1884, 11 R. 713, as described by L. Shand at p. 718. This case is also mentioned in §259, sub-para. (a).

31 *British Workman's etc. Insurance Co. Ltd.* v. *Wilkinson*, (O.H.) 1900, 8 S.L.T. 67. This was a departure from the general rule which is difficult to fit into one of the recognised exceptions.

32 Gloag, *Contract* (2nd ed.) 377, 390. In England the exception appears to be limited to rights arising independently of the writing. When the third party's rights originate in the relations established by the writing, the general rule applies. See Phipson, *Evidence* (9th ed.) 602. But it has been said that the authorities are too scanty to allow of any generalisation about the exception. See Cross, *Evidence* (1958) 480-1.

33 *Hastie* v. *Steel*, 1886, 13 R. 843; *Lord Advocate* v. *McNeill*, 1864, 2 M. 626, L. Deas at p. 634; *Lord Elibank* v. *Hamilton*, 1827, 6 S. 69. In *Scott* v. *Miller*, 1832, 11 S. 21,

to the writing the trust must be proved by the writ or oath of the alleged trustee.[34] And the acceptor of a bill was held entitled, as a third party to the transaction, to prove against an assignee who had charged him on it, that the assignee held the bill in trust for another person who had discharged his claim in respect of it.[35]

For the purpose of this exception a person deriving title from a party to the writing is not, in general, a third party.[36] Differing opinions have been expressed as to whether a trustee on the sequestrated estate of one of the parties to the writing, as representing his creditors, can be regarded as a third party for this purpose.[37] In one case proof *prout de jure* was allowed in a declarator of trust between the trustees on the sequestrated estates of the two parties to the writing.[38] It has been said that the decisions which turn upon the application of section 61 (4) of the Sale of Goods Act, 1893,[39] where a transaction in the form of a contract of sale is alleged to have been intended to operate by way of a security, are also examples of the exception mentioned in this paragraph, since they must invariably arise in a question with the trustee on the sequestrated estate, or with a creditor, of one of the parties.[40] These cases have been mentioned earlier.[41]

266. WRITING ADMITTEDLY INACCURATE

(a) **General.** When the party founding upon a writing admits on record, or by writ or oath, that it does not contain a true account of the transaction, the door is opened to extrinsic proof of the facts.[42] "When both parties are agreed that the writing does not express the contract, and yet differ as to what the real contract is, then, unless evidence were admissible, there would be a complete *impasse*—no solution being possible."[43]

(b) **Judicial Admission.** When the creditor in a bond and disposition in

there were conflicting opinions. The cases are discussed in McLaren, *Wills and Succession* (3rd ed.) II, 1070-1.
[34] See §§ **122, 123.**
[35] *Middleton* v. *Rutherglen*, 1861, 23 D. 526.
[36] Gloag, *Contract* (2nd ed.) 377. In *Norval* v. *Abbey*, 1939 S.C. 724, the general rule was applied between one party and the singular successors of the other.
[37] *Wink* v. *Speirs*, 1867, 6 M. 77. L. J-Cl. Patton (p. 80) and L. Benholme (p. 82) thought that the trustee in bankruptcy was a third party: *contra* L. Cowan at p. 81: *dubitanti* L. Neaves at p. 82. The trustee in a sequestration is at the same time an agent of the general body of creditors and a representative of the bankrupt, taking his estate *tantum et tale* as it stood in him. See Goudy, *Bankruptcy* (4th ed.) 336, 249.
[38] *Wallace* v. *Sharp*, 1885, 12 R. 687.
[39] 56 & 57 Vict. c. 71.
[40] Gloag, *Contract* (2nd ed.) 378. In three cases mentioned by Gloag, of which the leading case was *McBain* v. *Wallace*, 1881, 8 R. (H.L.) 106, decided before the passing of the Sale of Goods Act, proof was allowed. The fact that creditors, who might or might not have been regarded as third parties, were involved, was nowhere stated as one of the reasons for allowing a proof. These decisions are also mentioned in § **259**, sub-para. (b).
[41] See § **259**, sub-para. (b).
[42] Dickson, *Evidence* (3rd ed.) §1035; *Norval* v. *Abbey*, 1939 S.C. 724, L. Wark at p. 730.
[43] *Grant* v. *Mackenzie*, 1899, 1 F. 889, at p. 894.
[44] *Hotson* v. *Paul*, 1831, 9 S. 685.

security for £900, who had charged on the bond, admitted that only £300 had been advanced, extrinsic evidence was admitted to prove the amount actually advanced, and no evidence on this point having been adduced by the creditor, the charge was suspended except to the extent of the sum admitted by the debtor, which was £5.[44] A person who had some years earlier granted a disposition containing a discharge for the price of £120, which was stated to have been paid, sued the disponee for £80 on an averment that only £40 of the price had in fact been paid. Since the disponer had admitted that the statements in the disposition were inaccurate, the disponee was allowed to prove by extrinsic evidence that, although *ex facie* absolute, the disposition was truly in security for advances made to the disponer which were still outstanding.[45] Conversely when a disponee admitted that the price actually paid by him was not the price which was stated in the disposition to have been paid, the disponer was allowed to prove by extrinsic evidence that the disposition, although *ex facie* absolute, was truly in security only.[46] Employers, who were bound under a written contract of employment to pay a weekly wage of forty shillings, averred that by oral agreement between the parties this had been reduced to thirty-five shillings. When the employee admitted the reduction, subject to the explanation that the balance was to be accumulated to provide a retirement pension, it was held that proof of the true terms of the oral agreement was permissible.[47] When a person who had charged upon a bill of exchange admitted that the bill had not been granted for value received, and that it was an accommodation bill in respect of a joint adventure in which the acceptor was alleged to have an interest, it was held that summary diligence on the bill was incompetent, and the process of suspension of the charge was sisted to enable the charger to prove, in any action of accounting which he might raise, the existence of the joint adventure which was denied by the acceptor of the bill.[48] Following missives of let of a furnished house the landlord sued the tenant for damages because he had opened certain repositories in breach of an alleged oral agreement that they should be kept locked. The tenant, while denying the oral agreement, admitted that at the request of the landlord certain repositories were in fact kept locked throughout the tenancy, and this was held sufficient to justify parole evidence as to what the true agreement was.[49]

(c) **Admission on Reference to Oath.** When the party founding upon a writing admits on a reference to his oath that the true contract between the parties was of a different nature from that described in the writing, the latter may be disregarded as being inconsistent with the true contract.[50] It is then competent to prove *prout de jure* the terms of the true contract, and any

---

[45] *Miller* v. *Oliphant*, 1843, 5 D. 856.
[46] *Miller* v. *Miller*, (O.H.) 1905, 12 S.L.T. 743. In *Grant's Trs.* v. *Morison*, 1875, 2 R. 377, the position was the same, except that there was in addition a back letter, which was also admitted by the disponee to be inaccurate. *Cf. Leckie* v. *Leckie*, 1854, 17 D. 77.
[47] *Campbell* v. *Arbuthnot*, 1904, 12 S.L.T. 438. For variation of a writing, see § **279**.
[48] *Blackwood* v. *Hay*, 1858, 20 D. 631.
[49] *Miller* v. *Wilson*, (O.H.) 1919, 1 S.L.T. 223.
[50] Dickson, *Evidence* (3rd ed.) §1035.

breach of them, if the contract is of a kind which permits of such proof.[51] This appears to be permissible even without an averment of collusion or deceit.[52] It was held competent for a debtor in a bond recording a loan of money to refer to the creditor's oath an averment that the contract was in truth a contract of apprenticeship,[53] or for the sale of a horse,[54] and, if the oath were affirmative of the reference, to prove *prout de jure* the terms of the contract and any failure to implement them.

It is thought that the position is otherwise when what is referred to oath is concerned, not with the nature of the contract as a whole, but with its interpretation or explanation in point of detail. In the latter event, when what is referred to oath, for example, is a specific interpretation of some word or words in the contract, it is thought that the party referring to oath must accept the deponent's admission or denial in accordance with the ordinary rules relating to reference to oath.[55]

267. EXPLANATION OF THE WRITING

(a) **General.** In accordance with the general rule the intention of the parties to a writing must be discovered from the writing itself, and from it alone.[56] When the language of the writing is clear and applies without doubt or difficulty to the facts of the case, extrinsic evidence is neither necessary nor admissible for its interpretation.[57] Even when, because there is an ambiguity,[58] the exception applies, the purpose of extrinsic evidence is not to discover the writer's intention apart from the words used in the writing, but to ascertain the proper meaning of these words.[59] "We must seek the meaning of the writer, but we must find it in his words; and we must seek the meaning of the words, but they must be *his* words, the words as he used them, the meaning which they have in his mouth."[60]

---

[51] Dickson, *Evidence* (3rd ed.) §1035; Gloag, *Contract* (2nd ed.) 377. It has been said that this result also follows if the admission is contained in a writing subsequent to the date of the writing in question: Gloag, *Contract* (2nd ed.) 376-377. It is doubted whether this is sound in principle unless there is ambiguity in the original writing. As to this, see §275, sub-para. (a).

[52] Proof *prout de jure* is competent when there is collusion or deceit, reference to oath being then unnecessary. See §259.

[53] *Aikman*, 1665 M. 12, 311.

[54] *Kinnaird* v. *McDougal*, 1694, 4 Brown's Supp., 184. See also *Sim* v. *Inglish*, 1674 M. 12, 321, the first report of which supports the statement in the text, whereas the second report appears to contradict it, but is difficult to understand.

[55] As to this, see §272, sub-para. (b).

[56] See §240.

[57] Bell, *Commentaries* (7th ed.) I, 456; *Blair* v. *Blair*, 1849, 12 D. 97, L. Moncreiff at p. 107; *Higgins* v. *Dawson*, [1902] A.C. 1. See also *Nasmyth's Trs.* v. *National Society for Prevention of Cruelty to Children*, 1914 S.C. (H.L.) 76, L. Loreburn at p. 82, L. Atkinson and L. Shaw at p. 83, L. Parmoor at p. 84: *dub.* L. Dunedin at pp. 82-83; Phipson, *Evidence* (9th ed.) 630.

[58] "Ambiguity" is used in this chapter to mean any doubt as to the meaning of the words or their application to the facts, including inaccuracies and misdescriptions.

[59] Dickson, *Evidence* (3rd ed.) §1043.

[60] Graves, 28 Amer. L. Rev., 323 (quoted in Phipson, *Evidence* (9th ed.) 633).

(b) Basic Rules of Construction. Before it can be decided in a particular case whether extrinsic evidence is admissible or not, certain basic rules of construction may have to be considered.[61] There is a presumption that the words of a writing are to be understood according to their plain, ordinary and obvious acceptation,[62] unless the law has attached to them a recognised meaning, in which case they are presumed to bear that meaning.[63] The words are to be construed neither by strictly etymological nor by vulgar and inaccurate standards, but in accordance with the meaning which persons of ordinary intelligence would naturally attribute to them.[64] If, however, it is clear from some parts of the writing[65] under construction that the writer has used certain words in a particular sense, or even in a peculiar or in-accurate sense, they will be so construed in each part of the writing in which they occur in the same connection or apparently with the same signification.[66] On this ground the word "heirs"[67] was construed as meaning "heirs of the body" instead of the persons entitled to the succession by operation of law,[68] "money" was construed as including the testator's whole moveable estate[69] and "will" was construed as including a marriage contract.[70]

If by applying these basic rules of construction the court has been able to give an intelligible meaning to the writing, then failing a relevant averment that the writing, so construed, cannot reasonably be applied to the facts,[71] extrinsic evidence purporting to show that some other meaning was intended is inadmissible. Extrinsic evidence was held inadmissible on these grounds in the following circumstances. In a mercantile contract, because "acre" was defined by statute to mean imperial acre, evidence of an oral agreement that it should mean a Scotch acre was excluded,[72] and an assignation of rents in a disposition of a farm, the assignation being in statutory form and interpreted by statute, was construed by the court without reference to earlier articles of sale which made special provision for the disposal of the rents.[73] The

---

[61] There are conflicting views as to whether the admissibility of extrinsic evidence is part of the law of evidence, or whether, since it relates to construction, it is part of substantive law. For a discussion of the subject, see Phipson, *Extrinsic Evidence in Aid of Interpretation* (1904) 20 L.Q.R. 245, at pp. 246-7.

[62] Bell, *Principles*, §524; Dickson, *Evidence* (3rd ed.) §1052; Wigram's First Proposition (Wigram, *Extrinsic Evidence in Aid of the Interpretation of Wills* (5th ed.) 11).

[63] Bell, *Principles*, §1694; *Blair* v. *Blair*, 1849, 12 D. 97, at pp. 109-111; *Brand* v. *Scott's Trs.*, 1892, 19 R. 768 (recognised rule of construction). The presumption may be irrebuttable if the meaning has been prescribed by statute. See *Thomson* v. *Garioch*, 1841, 3 D. 625; *McDowall & Neilson's Tr.* v. *J. B. Snowball & Co. Ltd.*, 1904, 7 F. 35, at pp. 44, 45.

[64] Bell, *Commentaries* (7th ed.) I, 456; Dickson, *Evidence* (3rd ed.) §1052.

[65] or writings. See §**253.**

[66] Dickson, *Evidence* (3rd ed.) §1053; *Lee* v. *Alexander*, 1883, 10 R. (H.L.) 91, at p. 93; Wigram's First Proposition (Wigram, *ut cit.*, 11-12).

[67] *Hunter* v. *Nisbett*, 1839, 2 D. 16; *Anderson* v. *Anderson*, 1829, 7 S. 743.

[68] For the usual interpretation, see McLaren, *Wills and Succession* (3rd ed.) II, §§1379, 1381.

[69] *Easson* v. *Thomson's Trs.*, 1879, 7 R. 251.

[70] *Dunsmure* v. *Dunsmure*, 1879, 7 R. 261.

[71] See §**268.**

[72] *Thomson* v. *Garioch*, 1841, 3 D. 625. *Cf. Miller* v. *Mair*, 1860, 22 D. 660 (mentioned at §**272**, note 32).

[73] *Butter* v. *Foster*, 1912 S.C. 1218, at p. 1225.

word "heirs" in a will was held to have a recognised legal meaning when used in relation to moveable estate as importing a destination to the heirs *in mobilibus*, and there being nothing in the will to indicate a different construction, evidence of a memorandum of instructions purporting to show that the testatrix intended to benefit the heir-at-law was held to be inadmissible.[74] The word "interest" in a lease was held to have a definite, unambiguous and well-known meaning, both in common and legal parlance, and evidence that it was used by landlords and tenants to mean annual rent-charges, including repayments of capital, was held to be inadmissible.[75] In articles of roup of heritage the expression "rents falling due from and after Martinmas" was held to be unambiguous in law and in practice, and evidence of earlier communings purporting to show that it was intended to mean "falling due *before* and payable *after* Martinmas" was held to be inadmissible.[76] In a mercantile contract "cash on delivery less 2½ per cent. in fourteen days as usual" was held to have no technical or unusual significance,[77] and "sharp fresh water sand" was held incapable of meaning sand made by grinding down stone chips,[78] and in both cases extrinsic evidence to indicate a different construction was disallowed. The word "residue" in a will, although capable of including heritage, was construed by reference to other parts of the will as being intended to exclude it, and evidence of the testator's instructions to his solicitors, purporting to show an intention contrary to the construction placed upon the word by the court, was held to be inadmissible.[79] In a question as to whether a disposition of *inter alia* "all other lands and others" included a particular midsuperiority, it was held, on a proper construction of the deed as a whole, that there was no ambiguity, and evidence of prior communings between the parties was held to be inadmissible.[80] A submission and the decree arbitral following thereon were concerned with the question of whether the receipts of the traffic exchanged between two railway companies under a statute were to be divided between the two companies in accordance with their respective mileage, and it was held that "traffic" was quite unambiguous, and that evidence purporting to show that the word was not intended to include passenger traffic was inadmissible.[81]

[74] *Blair* v. *Blair*, 1849, 12 D. 97, at p. 108.

[75] *Sinclair* v. *McBeath*, 1868, 7 M. 273, at pp. 277, 278.

[76] *Stevenson* v. *Moncrieff*, 1845, 7 D. 418. For a reference to other decisions relating to sales by auction, see §244, notes 23, 24.

[77] *Towill & Co.* v. *The British Agricultural Association*, 1875, 3 R. 117.

[78] *Parochial Board of Greenock* v. *Coghill & Son*, 1878, 5 R. 732. See also *Miller* v. *Miller*, 1822, 1 Shaw's App., 308, L. C. Eldon at p. 317.

[79] *Farquhar* v. *Farquhar's Exrs.*, 1875, 3 R. 71. *Cf. Cathcart's Trs.* v. *Bruce*, (O.H.) 1923 S.L.T. 722, where a letter of instructions was looked at only for the purpose of discovering the testator's state of knowledge.

[80] *Lee* v. *Alexander*, 1883, 10 R. (H.L.) 91. See also *Barclay* v. *Neilson*, 1878, 5 R. 909, where the court felt able to put a construction upon a blundered clause in an agricultural lease relating to new buildings and repairs, and where evidence of an oral agreement upon the matter was held inadmissible. As to the inadmissibility of evidence of possession to contradict or explain an unambiguous bounding title in a disposition or similar deed, see *Dalhousie's Tutors* v. *Minister of Lochlee*, 1890, 17 R. 1060; *North British Railway Co.* v. *Moon's Trs.*, 1879, 6 R. 640.

[81] *Highland Railway Co.* v. *Great North of Scotland Railway Co.*, 1896, 23 R. (H.L.) 80.

268. WHEN EXTRINSIC EVIDENCE IN EXPLANATION IS ALLOWED

If, after the basic rules of construction have been applied,[82] the language of a writing still requires elucidation, either because it appears to the court, or it is averred by the parties, that its meaning is uncertain, or that there is uncertainty about its application to the facts, extrinsic evidence, subject to one qualification, is in general admissible to explain and clarify.[83] The qualification relates to evidence of direct declarations of intention or understanding, which, in general, is inadmissible.[84] It is thought to be immaterial whether the ambiguity is patent or latent, extrinsic evidence being generally admissible in both cases. The supposed distinction between patent and latent ambiguities is mentioned in the next paragraph.

269. SUPPOSED DISTINCTION BETWEEN PATENT AND LATENT AMBIGUITIES

In England a distinction, based upon a rule of pleading propounded by Lord Bacon, was at one time made between patent and latent ambiguities. A patent ambiguity is apparent on the face of the writing, whereas a latent ambiguity arises, not from the words of the writing, which are clear and comprehensible, but from their attempted application to the facts. The rule was supposed to be that a latent ambiguity might competently be resolved by extrinsic evidence, whereas a patent ambiguity might not. If this were once the rule in England, it appears to be so no longer.[85] "The only patent ambiguities that are not open to explanation by extrinsic evidence appear to be those which, in the nature of things, are incapable of explanation, as, for example, where the name of a legatee is left wholly blank."[86]

In two early House of Lords decisions in Scottish cases Lord Chancellor Brougham pronounced this English distinction to be part of the law of Scotland.[87] Lord Brougham's statements in these two cases have been quoted without qualification or comment in one Scottish text-book,[88] and in at least one later Scottish decision,[89] but the distinction has been described as not always very satisfactory or easy to apply.[90] In practice the distinction appears never to have been applied in Scotland, and in a number of reported cases patent ambiguities have been resolved by the admission of extrinsic evidence.

---

[82] For the basic rules of construction, see § 267, sub-para. (b).

[83] Wigram's Fifth Proposition (Wigram *ut cit*, 14); Phipson, *Evidence* (9th ed.) 630.

[84] See § 270.

[85] Phipson, *Evidence* (9th ed.) 635-6; *Watcham* v. *East African Protectorate*, [1919] A.C. 533.

[86] Phipson, *Evidence* (9th ed.) 635-6. *Phipson* (at p. 632) mentions *Higgins* v. *Dawson*, [1902] A.C. 1, as an example of a patent ambiguity where circumstantial extrinsic evidence was excluded. In fact extrinsic evidence was excluded only because no ambiguity of any kind was found to be present.

[87] *Morton* v. *Hunter & Co.*, 1830, 4 W. & S. 379, L. Brougham at pp. 386-7; *Logan* v. *Wright*, 1831, 5 W. & S. 242, L. Brougham at p. 247. In *Logan* v. *Wright*, however, L. Brougham conceded that extrinsic evidence was admissible when there was a doubt as to the identity of the subject matter of the writing.

[88] Bell, *Principles*, §§524, 1871. For the treatment of this topic in Dickson, McLaren and Gloag, see the next paragraph.

[89] *Ritchie* v. *Whish*, 1880, 8 R. 101, L.P. Inglis at p. 104.

The following are examples of cases in which extrinsic evidence was admitted to resolve a *patent* ambiguity. In a letter addressed to "James Riddell, agent, The Clydesdale Bank, Limited" in connection with an assignation of insurance policies, the granter directed that the policies should be held in security of "any advances or obligations I may at present or at any future time be under to you." The writings were described by Lord Ardwall as "ambiguous in their terms." The ambiguity was patent and was caused by the fact that the word "agent" might be merely descriptive of the assignee as an individual, or might, on the other hand, describe the character in which he received the policies. Proof of the circumstances in which the deeds were executed was held to have been rightly allowed.[91] In a disposition of minerals it was not clear from the terms of the writing, which included a provision for payment of annual surface damages, whether or not the disponees were entitled to work the coal in such a way as to bring down the surface. Proof of the circumstances existing at the date of the deed was allowed.[92] In a solemnly executed writing it was not clear whether the words "I hand over my life policy" were intended to be an assignation of the policy or merely a record of its delivery to the person named. Evidence of direct declarations of intention by the granter was thought to be inadmissible, but extrinsic evidence of the surrounding circumstances was admitted and considered by the court.[93] In a contract to supply "all your requirements,"[94] or "your usual requirements"[95] of a particular commodity, the ambiguity of the expressions quoted was patent on a reading of the contract, but extrinsic evidence was allowed in order to show their proper interpretation. In each of two testamentary writings there was a legacy of £6,000 to the same legatee. The ambiguity, as to whether one or two legacies was intended, arose clearly on the face of the writings themselves. It was held nevertheless, that, although evidence of direct declarations of intention must not be looked at, extrinsic evidence of the testator's circumstances at the dates when the deeds were executed was admissible.[96]

It is thought that the supposed distinction between patent and latent ambiguities may now be ignored in practice, except perhaps in connection with direct declarations of intention or understanding, which are mentioned in the next paragraph.

270. DIRECT DECLARATION OF INTENTION OR UNDERSTANDING—EQUIVOCATION

Both in England[97] and in Scotland[98] evidence of direct statements by

---

90 Gloag, *Contract* (2nd ed.) 372.
91 *Robertson's Tr.* v. *Riddell*, 1911 S.C. 14.
92 *Anderson* v. *McCracken Brothers*, 1900, 2 F. 780.
93 *Brownlee* v. *Robb*, 1907 S.C. 1302, at pp. 1311, 1313, 1314.
94 *Von Mehren & Co.* v. *Edinburgh Roperie & Sailcloth Ltd.*, 1901, 4 F. 232.
95 *Blackstock* v. *Macarthur*, 1919 S.C. 57.
96 *Trustees of the Free Church of Scotland* v. *Maitland*, 1887, 14 R. 333, at pp. 338, 341, 343, 344. For a similar case, where even a direct declaration of intention was apparently considered, see *Livingston* v. *Livingston*, 1864, 3 M. 20. As to direct declarations of intention, however, see the next paragraph.
97 Phipson, *Evidence* (9th ed.) 635.

the writer as to what he intended the writing to mean, or as to his understanding of its meaning, is in general inadmissible. In a Scottish case in the House of Lords it was said that the irrelevancy of averments regarding statements of this kind is too obvious to need argument.[99] There would be a risk, if such statements were admitted, that the parole evidence of the parties to a written contract might take the place of the writing, or that hearsay evidence of what a testator said might take the place of the will.[1] This risk does not arise to the same extent from the admission of circumstantial evidence of the granter's intention, which, when there is an ambiguity, is always accepted.[2]

There is an exception to the exclusion of direct declarations of intention in the case of equivocation, an English conception which appears to have been accepted as part of the law of Scotland.[3] An equivocation arises when the language of the writing, though intended to apply to one person or one thing only, is equally applicable in all its parts to two or more, and it is impossible to gather from the context which was intended.[4] When there is an equivocation, it is said, direct declarations of the granter's intention are admissible to solve it.[4]

The supposed distinction between patent and latent ambiguities was mentioned in the last paragraph. While referring to the general terms of Lord Brougham's pronouncements on this topic, most of the Scottish text-book writers[5] appear to have altered and restricted the application of the distinction. In the first place, the tendency has been to restrict the use of the term *latent ambiguity* to that particular kind of latent ambiguity which in England is called an *equivocation*.[6] In the second place, when speaking of the use of extrinsic evidence in the case of latent ambiguities, thus defined,

[98] *Devlin's Trs.* v. *Breen*, 1943 S.C. 556, at pp. 570, 582, 586: affd. 1945 S.C. (H.L.) 27; *Campbell's Trs.* v. *Adamson*, 1911 S.C. 1111; *Brownlee* v. *Robb*, 1907 S.C. 1302, at pp. 1311, 1314; *Johnstone* v. *Haviland*, 1896, 23 R. (H.L.) 6, L. Watson at p. 6, L. Shand at p. 11; *Trustees of the Free Church of Scotland* v. *Maitland*, 1887, 14 R. 333, L.P. Inglis at p. 338, L. Shand at p. 343, L. Adam at p. 344; *Farquhar* v. *Farquhar's Exrs.*, 1875, 3 R. 71, L. Gifford at p. 74: *cf.* L. J-Cl. Moncreiff at p. 73. In only one case (*Livingston* v. *Livingston*, 1864, 3 M. 20), a letter expressly declaratory of a testator's intention was considered by the court.

[99] *Devlin's Trs.* v. *Breen*, 1945 S.C. (H.L.) 27, L. Macmillan at p. 38.

[1] The reason for the exclusion of direct declarations of intention appears not to have been discussed in Scotland. In England, whence the doctrine was accepted, the distinction is arbitrarily made, and its origins seem to be obscure. See Phipson, *Evidence* (9th ed.) 632-633; Cross, *Evidence* (1958) 491, 492.

[2] See § 271.

[3] *Charter* v. *Charter*, 1874 L.R. 7, H.L. 364, L.C. Cairns at pp. 376-7, applied in *Devlin's Trs.* v. *Breen*, 1943 S.C. 556, at pp. 570, 582, 586 (affd. 1945 S.C. (H.L.) 27).

[4] Wigram's Seventh Proposition (Wigram *ut cit.*, 14); Phipson, *Evidence* (9th ed.) 675; Cross, *Evidence* (1958) 490, 491, 493 *et seq.* There appears to be no logic in allowing direct declarations of intention in a case of equivocation and refusing them in a case of misdescription. See Phipson, *ut cit.*, 631, 632. The distinction in England is said to have been due to "special reasons. which are partly historical and partly precautionary, but wholly arbitrary": Phipson, *Extrinsic Evidence in Aid of Interpretation* (1904) 20 L.Q.R. 245, at p. 253.

[5] Bell, *Principles*, §§524, 1871, appears to be the only exception.

[6] See Dickson, *Evidence* (3rd ed.) §§1075, 1077, 1078; McLaren, *Wills and Succession* (3rd ed.) I, §715. Both writers define latent ambiguity as if it meant equivocation.

they say, not that it is admissible in the case of latent and inadmissible in the case of patent ambiguities, but that, in the case of latent ambiguities, extrinsic evidence of *intention* is admissible, whereas in the case of patent ambiguities it is not.[7] It is made clear that, in the case of both kinds of ambiguity, *circumstantial* evidence of intention is admissible,[2] and that it is only with regard to *direct declarations* of intention that any distinction exists.[7] The distinction at one time recognised between patent and latent ambiguities appears, therefore, to have been replaced by a distinction, relevant only in connection with direct declarations of intention, between the particular kind of latent ambiguity known as an equivocation and all other ambiguities, whether latent or patent.

In view of the opinions cited above it must be accepted that, in theory at least, direct declarations of intention or understanding are admissible in evidence, when, but only when, there is an equivocation. There seems to be no reported decision in Scotland, however, in which the question has arisen. In one case,[8] where, strangely enough, the ambiguity was patent, evidence of what might be regarded as a declaration of intention was considered.[9] Attempts to found on such evidence in other cases involving patent ambiguities were not unnaturally unsuccessful.[10]

271. CIRCUMSTANTIAL OR INDIRECT EVIDENCE OF INTENTION

Although evidence of direct declarations of intention made by the granter of a writing are in general excluded,[11] circumstantial evidence of his intention is in general admissible.[12] The purpose of the evidence is not to establish intention apart from the writing, but to discover the meaning of

---

7   Dickson, *Evidence* (3rd ed.) §§1079, 1081, 1083; McLaren, *Wills and Succession* (3rd ed.) I, §§717, 720, 723; Gloag, *Contract* (2nd ed.) 372. The examples given by Gloag of extrinsic evidence held admissible in cases of latent ambiguities, are, however, examples of circumstantial evidence which would have been equally admissible if the ambiguities had been patent. In one of them (*Robertson's Tr.* v. *Riddell*, 1911 S.C. 14) the ambiguity was in fact patent and not latent.

8   *Livingston* v. *Livingston*, 1864, 3 M. 20. What was described (p. 27) as an express declaration of intention was in fact a letter of obligation, granted by the testator after the execution of one testamentary writing, and before the execution of another. All three documents were looked at by the court as if they constituted one series of testamentary writings. See, for a similar approach, *Campbell's Trs.* v. *Adamson*, 1911 S.C. 1111, L. Johnston at p. 1117; *Ritchie* v. *Whish*, 1880, 8 R. 101.

9   Another very early example, *Weir* v. *Steele*, 1745 M. 11, 359, was later described as contrary to all legal principle: *Blair* v. *Blair*, 1849, 12 D. 97, at pp. 108, 109.

10   *Brownlee* v. *Robb*, 1907 S.C. 1302; *Trustees of the Free Church of Scotland* v. *Maitland*, 1887, 14 R. 333. The facts in these cases were mentioned in the last paragraph. See also *Farquhar* v. *Farquhar's Exrs.*, 1875, 3 R. 71, at p. 74 ("conversations of the testator . . . are not admissible").

11   See § 270.

12   Dickson, *Evidence* (3rd ed.) §1083; McLaren, *Wills and Succession* (3rd ed.) I, §§689 *et seq.*, 707, 712. The rule in England appears to be identical. See Phipson, *Evidence* (9th ed.) 633-4, 637, 654; Phipson, *Extrinsic Evidence in Aid of Interpretation* (1904), 20 L.Q.R. 245, at 255 (with quotations from Hawkins, Graves, Thayer); Cross, *Evidence* (1958), 489. Circumstantial evidence is said to be inadmissible only when (*a*) there is no ambiguity, (*b*) the language is so imperfect as to be a nullity, (*c*) the words will not bear the meaning suggested. See Phipson's article, cited above, at p. 268.

the words which the granter used in the writing,[13] and the evidence is admissible only when there is an ambiguity.[14] Circumstantial or indirect evidence may consist of evidence of special or technical meanings of words or of the granter's habits of speech,[15] of the circumstances antecedent to and surrounding the execution of the writing,[16] of the granter's actings subsequent to the execution of the writing,[17] and of custom or usage of trade.[18] The admissibility of revoked or superseded writings or clauses is doubtful.[19] The purpose of the evidence is to resolve the ambiguity and to identify the thing or the person or the nature or extent of the right or liability about which there is a doubt.[20]

272. MEANING OF WORDS USED

(a) General. As stated earlier, the words used in a writing are to be understood according to their plain, ordinary and obvious acceptation, or according to any recognised meaning attached to them by law.[21] When, however, the characters in which the document is written are difficult to decipher, or are in a foreign language, expert evidence is admissible to declare what the characters are or to translate the foreign words.[22] The same principle applies when the words used, although decipherable and apparently in English, are peculiar[23] or are used in a peculiar way.[24] If the peculiar use or meaning of the word is not obvious, it must be specially averred before extrinsic evidence becomes admissible to establish it.[25] So extrinsic evidence is admissible to provide the meaning of trade or technical terms,[26] such as "soum" in connection with an area of pasture,[27] "cutting-shop" in the glass-cutting trade,[28] "statuary" in the carrying trade,[29] "Scotch iron of best quality" in the iron casting trade,[30] "St. Lawrence" in a contract of marine

---

[13] See §267, sub-para. (a).
[14] See §§267, sub-para. (a), 268.
[15] See §272.
[16] See §273.
[17] See §275.
[18] See §276.
[19] See §274.
[20] See §277.
[21] See §267, sub-para. (b).
[22] Wigram's Fourth Proposition (Wigram *ut cit.*, 13); Dickson, *Evidence* (3rd ed.) §1058; Phipson, *Evidence* (9th ed.) 407.
[23] Dickson, *Evidence* (3rd ed.) §§1058, 1059.
[24] Dickson, *Evidence* (3rd ed.) §1060.
[25] *Sutton & Co.* v. *Ciceri & Co.*, 1890, 17 R. (H.L.) 40, at p. 43; Dickson, *Evidence* (3rd ed.) §1063. Extrinsic evidence, to show that the word "effects" in a will was intended to include heritage, was disallowed because it was not averred that the word had a technical meaning in British Guiana, where the will was made; *Griffith's J.F.* v. *Griffith's Exrs.*, 1905, 7 F. 470.
[26] *Buttery & Co.* v. *Inglis*, 1877, 5 R. 58, at p. 67: 1878, 5 R. (H.L.) 87, at p. 90; Gloag, *Contract* (2nd ed.) 365.
[27] *McKenzie* v. *McCrae*, 1825, 4 S. 147.
[28] *Watson* v. *Kidston & Co.*, 1839, 1 D. 1254.
[29] *Sutton & Co.* v. *Ciceri & Co.* (*supra*), at pp. 40-41.
[30] *Fleming & Co.* v. *Airdrie Iron Co.*, 1882, 9 R. 473.

insurance,[31] and "stone" in connection with the local price of cheese, used as a means of fixing the rent in a lease.[32] It seems probable that, as in England,[33] evidence would be admitted to show that the writer was in the habit of designating certain persons or things by peculiar terms or nicknames, as in a case where, a legacy having been left to "Mrs. G.," it was proved that the testator was accustomed to address a Mrs. Gregg by that abbreviation.[34]

(b) Reference to Oath. Although the deponent under a reference to oath does not give evidence, extrinsic or otherwise, it seems appropriate to mention in this paragraph that it is competent to refer to the opponent's oath an averment that the words in a writing were used with a special meaning, or that the writing failed in some specific way to record the true facts or the true or full intention of the parties.[35] When this occurs the ordinary rules with regard to reference to oath apply, and the party who refers perils this part of his case on being able to elicit the desired admission.[36] It was thus held competent to refer to the oath of a tenant a landlord's averment that the word "interest" in a written lease was intended to mean a composite annual payment comprising both repayment of capital and interest in the usual sense of that word,[37] and that a mill was included in a lease by mistake;[38] to refer to the debtor's oath an averment that a sum of money, which in a disposition was acknowledged to have been received, had not in fact been paid;[39] and, in an action of damages for breach of warrandice, to refer to the disponer's oath an averment that it had been intended to include in the disposition the land from which the pursuer had been evicted.[40]

273. CIRCUMSTANCES SURROUNDING EXECUTION OF WRITING

(a) General. When there is an ambiguity[41] in a writing, extrinsic evidence is admissible to show the circumstances which surrounded the granter when he subscribed it, as well as those which were antecedent to or coincident with

---

[31] *Birrell* v. *Dryer*, 1884, 11 R. (H.L.) 41. The evidence being inconclusive as to whether the river or the gulf was intended, the House of Lords construed the words in the light of the extrinsic facts known to both parties.

[32] *Miller* v. *Mair*, 1860, 22 D. 660. The Weights and Measures Acts, which made the use of imperial measure obligatory, were held not to apply, because the contract was not a sale or for the performance of work, or with regard to any matter relating to a weight or measure. *Cf. Thomson* v. *Garioch*, 1841, 3 D. 625 (mentioned at § 267, sub-para. (b)).

[33] Phipson, *Evidence* (9th ed.) 634; Cross, *Evidence* (1958) 483, 489.

[34] Dickson, *Evidence* (3rd ed.) §1059; McLaren, *Wills and Succession* (3rd ed.) I, 382.

[35] Dickson, *Evidence* (3rd ed.) §1100; Gloag, *Contract* (2nd ed.) 376.

[36] Dickson, *Evidence* (3rd ed.) §1414. See § **308.** The position is different when what is referred to oath is an averment that the contract as a whole was of a different nature from that contained in the writing. As to this, see § **266,** sub-para. (c).

[37] *Sinclair* v. *McBeath*, 1869, 7 M. 934.

[38] *Lawson* v. *Murray*, 1829, 7 S. 380.

[39] *Gordon* v. *Trotter*, 1833, 11 S. 696. See also *Spence* v. *Duncan*, 1706 M. 12, 333 (general discharge of factor's intromissions).

[40] *Stewart* v. *Ferguson*, 1841, 3 D. 668, L. Ivory (Ordinary) at p. 674.

[41] For the meaning of "ambiguity," see § 267, note 58. Evidence is inadmissible if there is no ambiguity: see § 267, sub-para. (a).

its execution.[42] The purpose of the evidence is to enable the court to examine the writing as nearly as possible from the point of view from which the granter saw it, and to learn the appropriate meaning of the words when used by a person in that situation.[42] The evidence is relevant only in so far as the circumstances were known to the granter, or are presumed to have been known to him, at the date of the execution of the writing. Clauses revoked or rejected during negotiations,[43] and the granter's actings subsequent to the execution of the writing[44] are mentioned separately later.

(b) **Contracts.** "Where a term which might have two or more meanings is used in a mercantile contract, it is competent to prove the circumstances surrounding the parties, the character of their business, and the previous course of dealing, if any, between them, for the purpose of determining the true construction of the language used."[45] This principle was applied to a contract for the supply, for a fixed period and at a fixed price, of "your usual requirements" or "all your requirements" of a commodity, when there was a dispute as to whether the words quoted included requirements resulting from an expansion of the purchaser's business.[46] When a charter-party provided that the lump sum payable by way of freight should be reduced if the vessel was unable to carry the tonnage guaranteed, and it was alleged that the failure to carry the guaranteed tonnage was due to the bulky nature of the cargo tendered by the charterers, it was held "competent to investigate the whole facts and circumstances attendant upon the execution of the charter-party, with the view of ascertaining what particular kind of goods, if any, it was then in the contemplation of both parties should be shipped and carried, that being the cargo with reference to which it must be presumed, in the absence of express or implied stipulation to the contrary, that the guarantee was given and accepted."[47] In connection with unilateral discharges of obligations it has been said that "the general words in a release are limited always to that thing or those things which were specially in the contemplation of the parties at the time when the release was given."[48] The principle was applied in construing the words "I hand over" in a deed relating to a policy of insurance,[49] and was also said to apply to a clause in a disposition of heritage which reserved the right to work, win and carry away coal, there being a doubt as to whether this allowed the owner of the coal to bring down the surface.[50]

---

[42] Dickson, *Evidence* (3rd ed.) §1067; Wigram's Fifth Proposition (Wigram, *ut. cit.* 14).

[43] See §274.

[44] See §275.

[45] *Von Mehren & Co.* v. *Edinburgh Roperie & Sailcloth Ltd.*, 1901, 4 F. 232, at p. 239. See also *Buttery & Co.* v. *Inglis*, 1877, 5 R. 58, L. Ormidale at p. 67: approved 1878, 5 R. (H.L.) 87, at p. 102.

[46] *Blacklock & Macarthur* v. *Kirk*, 1919 S.C. 57; *Von Mehren & Co.* v. *Edinburgh Roperie & Sailcloth Ltd.* (*supra*).

[47] *MacKill & Co.* v. *Wright Brothers & Co.*, 1888, 16 R. (H.L.) 1, at p. 6.

[48] *London & South Western Railway Co.* v. *Blackmore*, 4 E. & I. App., 610, L. Westbury at p. 623, quoted with approval by L. Kinnear in *McAdam* v. *Scott*, 1912, 50 S.L.R. 264, where proof was allowed in order to define and identify the claims mentioned in a discharge, which were said to be ambiguously described.

[49] *Brownlee* v. *Robb*, 1907 S.C. 1302.

There is some authority for the view that, although earlier communings or negotiations are superseded by the execution of a written contract,[51] and are inadmissible for the purpose of showing *intention*, they may legitimately be looked at in order to discover the *knowledge* of the parties as to the then existing facts or circumstances, in the light of which they executed the contract.[52] This was said with regard to prior correspondence between the parties to a marriage contract, in a question as to whether the husband's estate was liable to make good an annuity from a military pension fund, which, under the rules of that fund, had ceased on a widow's second marriage. It was said that the earlier documents might be looked at in order to discover what the pension was and what knowledge the parties had of it.[53]

(c) **Testamentary Writings.** In every case of ambiguity[41] in a testamentary writing "the court has a right to ascertain all the facts which were known to the testator at the time he made his will, and thus to place itself in the testator's position, in order to ascertain the bearing and application of the language which he uses, and in order to ascertain whether there exists any person or thing to which the whole description given in the will can be, reasonably and with sufficient certainty, applied."[54] The court has been held entitled to know the amount of the estate at each relevant period according to the testator's own estimate,[55] the relationship of the persons claiming to be legatees and the way in which the testator was accustomed to design them,[56] the circumstances of the testator's family and the history of his provision for them,[57] the testator's knowledge that his daughter had only one illegitimate child and was beyond the age of child bearing,[58] the fact that, when his will was made, a Scottish testator's bequest to the National Society for Prevention of Cruelty to Children, an English institution, would, by an agreement between the two institutions subsequently departed from, have been handed over to the *Scottish* National Society for the Prevention

---

[50] *Bank of Scotland* v. *Stewart*, 1891, 18 R. 957, L.P. Inglis at p. 960. In fact, however, the First Division ignored the proof which had been led, and construed the deed without its assistance.

[51] See §§ **246, 250.**

[52] Dickson, *Evidence* (3rd ed.) §1069.

[53] *Forlong* v. *Taylor's Exrs.*, 1838, 3 Sh. & Macl., 177, L. Cottenham at p. 210. In *Leith Heritages Co.* v. *Edinburgh & Leith Glass Co.*, 1876, 3 R. ¦789, L. Ormidale, at p. 797, thought that the mere existence of an ambiguity in a disposition entitled the court to look at an earlier minute, which was superseded by the disposition, in order to learn the true meaning of the ambiguous words. This case was mentioned earlier, along with other special cases, at §253, sub-para. (a).

[54] *Charter* v. *Charter*, 1874 L.R. 7 (H.L.) 364, L. C. Cairns at p. 377: applied in *Devlin's Trs.* v. *Breen*, 1943 S.C. 556, at pp. 570, 582, 586 (affd. 1945 S.C. (H.L.) 27). See also McLaren, *Wills and Succession* (3rd ed.) I, 388.

[55] *Trustees of the Free Church of Scotland* v. *Maitland*, 1887, 14 R. 333, L.P. Inglis at p. 338. See also *Craw's Trs.* v. *Blacklock*, 1920 S.C. 22 (relative values of moveable and heritable estate); *McGowan* v. *Anstruther's Trs.*, 1827, 5 S. 276 (gradual increase of testator's wealth); *Livingston* v. *Livingston*, 1864, 3 M. 20 (purchase of heritage).

[56] *Cathcart's Trs.* v. *Bruce*, (O.H.) 1923 S.L.T. 722.

[57] *Milne* v. *Scott*, 1880, 8 R. 83, at pp. 86, 88.

[58] *Scott's Trs.* v. *Smart*, 1954 S.C. 12 (meaning of "children").

of Cruelty to Children,[59] and, in a question as to whether heritage, disentailed by the testator or held under a special destination, has been carried by a subsequent general testamentary disposition, the testator's actings in relation to his estate and with his succession generally.[60] In general, direct declarations of the testator's intention as distinct from circumstantial evidence as to the meaning of the words used in the writing, are inadmissible in evidence.[61]

Except perhaps in the case of equivocation,[62] it seems clear that the evidence not only of oral statements by the testator, but also of letters of instructions to a solicitor, or drafts or copies of wills, is inadmissible for the purpose of explaining what the will is intended to mean.[63] In a more recent case in the Outer House, where a description in the will did not apply to any known person, but was an apparent misdescription of one of two persons, evidence of the testator's letter of instructions to his solicitor was admitted in order to discover the testator's state of knowledge of the two persons and their families.[64]

(d) Implied Term of Contract or Testamentary Writing.

Extrinsic evidence is inadmissible to contradict, modify or explain a term of a writing which is implied by law.[65] Conversely, however, an implied term may arise only because of the extrinsic circumstances, and, in this event, it is competent to allow proof of these circumstances. In a written contract for sale of goods, for example, it is a condition implied by statute, where the buyer expressly or by implication makes known to the seller the particular purpose for which the goods are required, and the goods are of a description which it is in the course of the seller's business to supply, that the goods shall be reasonably fit for that purpose.[66] When it is averred that the facts giving rise to the implied condition existed, proof of them is admissible.[67] Similarly, in the case of a testamentary writing, the question of whether it is impliedly revoked by the subsequent birth of a child, in virtue of the *conditio si testator sine*

---

59 *Nasmyth's Trs.* v. *National Society for Prevention of Cruelty to Children*, 1914 S.C. (H.L.) 76. The Second Division (pp. 77-81) decided in favour of the Scottish Society on these and similar considerations. The House of Lords reversed, largely on the view that, since there was no ambiguity, the evidence was irrelevant, or, in the case of L. Dunedin, that since the words used exactly described the English Society, and did not describe the Scottish Society with complete accuracy, the evidence was insufficient to displace the obvious and natural meaning to be attributed to the words.

60 *Gray* v. *Gray's Trs.*, 1878, 5 R. 820, L.P. Inglis at p. 824. On this topic, which at one time gave rise to much conflict of judicial opinion, see also *Campbell* v. *Campbell*, 1878, 6 R. 310: 1880, 7 R. (H.L.) 100; *Glendonwyn* v. *Gordon*, 1870, 8 M. 1075: 1873, 11 M. (H.L.) 33; *Catton* v. *Mackenzie*, 1870, 8 M. 1049.

61 See §270.

62 McLaren, *Wills and Succession*, I, 396. As to declarations of intention and equivocation, see §270.

63 *Blair* v. *Blair*, 1849, 12 D. 97, L. Moncreiff at pp. 107 *et seq.*, L. Cockburn at p. 112; *Farquhar* v. *Farquhar's Exrs.*, 1875, 3 R. 71, at p. 73.

64 *Cathcart's Trs.* v. *Bruce*, (O.H.) 1923 S.L.T. 722.

65 See §251.

66 Sale of Goods Act, 1893 (56 & 57 Vict. c. 71), s. 14 (1).

67 *Jacobs* v. *Scott & Co.*, 1899, 2 F. (H.L.) 70, at pp. 78, 80.

68 *Hughes* v. *Edwardes*, 1892, 19 R. (H.L.) 33, L. Watson at p. 35.

liberis decesserit, is "one wholly dependent upon the circumstances of the case,"[68] and the extrinsic circumstances may therefore be proved.[69]

274. REVOKED OR REJECTED CLAUSES

(a) General. Although, when there is ambiguity in connection with a writing, evidence of the surrounding circumstances is in general admissible,[70] there is a doubt as to whether the court may legitimately take cognisance of the fact that clauses suggested for inclusion in the writing were deliberately cancelled or rejected by the parties before the writing was executed. Contracts and testamentary writings are mentioned separately in this connection in the following sub-paragraphs.

(b) Contracts. In a written contract shipbuilders undertook, for a lump sum payment, to *repair* the hull plating of a ship. In the specification relative thereto the words "but if any new plating is required the same to be paid for extra" had been deleted before the contract was executed.[71] The question at issue was whether the obligation to repair included an obligation to *renew* defective plating when this was found to be necessary. The Lord Justice-Clerk was of the opinion that the court was entitled to consider, as part of the antecedent circumstances, the fact that the quoted words had been deliberately deleted, and also to look at the correspondence between the parties relating to the deletion. In reliance upon this evidence he construed the obligation to repair as including an obligation to renew without additional charge.[72] The House of Lords was unanimously of opinion that it was quite improper, in attempting to discover the meaning of the contract, to consider the deleted words or any part of the antecedent communings between the parties.[73] In a more recent case in the Court of Session, however, in which the circumstances appear to be almost identical, the majority found themselves able to distinguish the earlier case, and, in a charter-party, they construed the standard exception for "restraint of princes" in the light of the fact that the words "including interferences of Government Authorities" had been deliberately deleted by the parties before the deed was executed.[74]

(c) Testamentary Writings. It has been said that, while a revoked will cannot be referred to as having any testamentary intention, "it may be used

[69] *Stuart-Gordon* v. *Stuart-Gordon,* 1899, 1 F. 1005; *McKie's Tutor* v. *McKie,* 1897, 24 R. 526; *Elder's Trs.* v. *Elder,* 1895, 21 R. 704; *Millar's Trs.* v. *Millar,* 1893, 20 R. 1040. The rule with regard to the *conditio si institus sine liberis decesserit,* may well be different. See *Devlin's Trs.* v. *Breen,* 1945 S.C. (H.L.) 27, at pp. 32, 33, 35, 38.
[70] See §273.
[71] *Inglis* v. *Buttery & Co.,* 1877, 5 R. 58: 1878, 5 R. (H.L.) 87.
[72] L. Ormidale construed the contract without reference to the evidence, but was of opinion that, if it were admissible, it pointed in the same direction. It seems probable that he considered the deleted words and the communings between the parties to be inadmissible. L. Gifford thought that reference to the deleted words and the communings was wholly inadmissible.
[73] 5 R. (H.L.) 87, at pp. 90, 96, 97, 98, 99, 102, 105.
[74] *Taylor* v. *John Lewis Ltd.,* 1927 S.C. 891, L. J-Cl. Alness at pp. 897-8, L. Anderson at p. 901. L. Hunter, *contra,* at pp. 899-900.

to show what the testator knew when he wrote it, and also what was his will at the time, though he has since revoked it."[75] This was applied in a subsequent case where the question at issue was whether a bequest was intended as a mere repetition of a legacy for the same amount in an earlier and still effective will, or whether two legacies were intended. In resolving the ambiguity, the court held itself entitled to look at the whole history of the bequest, including the reference to it in a number of revoked wills.[76] And, to resolve a doubt as to whether "failing such children" meant failing their coming into existence or failing their survival of the parent, it was held legitimate to use a revoked will as a glossary, in order to determine the meaning of the words used in the effective deed.[77] The two last-mentioned cases were later said to show that there are "certain strictly limited purposes for which a court of construction may look at a revoked will,"[78] these purposes being the identification of the subject matter of the gift and the identification of the beneficiary.[79] In the House of Lords, however, it was doubted whether, even for these purposes, reference to a revoked will is admissible.[80]

275. SUBSEQUENT ACTINGS OF PARTIES

(a) **General.** Even when there is an ambiguity,[81] evidence regarding the actings of the parties, or of the granter, *after* the execution of the writing is, strictly speaking, irrelevant, except in so far as it throws light retrospectively upon the circumstances prevailing at the time of execution. The purpose of extrinsic evidence is to discover the meaning which the writer intended the words to have at the time when the words were used, which is the time when the writing was executed.[82] Subsequent actings which merely reflect a change of circumstances or a change in the writer's intention are of course irrelevant. Evidence of subsequent actings has been admitted in construing old writings, contracts and testamentary writings, and these are mentioned separately in the following sub-paragraphs. It cannot be pretended that the distinction mentioned above has been scrupulously noticed in every decision.

(b) **Old Writings.** "It is a well established principle of law that writings,

---

75 *Magistrates of Dundee* v. *Morris*, 1858, 3 Macq. 134, L. Wensleydale at p. 171. A contrary opinion was expressed by L. Watson in *Gordon* v. *Gordon's Trs.*, 1882, 9 R. (H.L.) 101, at p. 105.

76 *McLachlan* v. *Seton's Trs.*, 1937 S.C. 206, at pp. 223-4, 236-7.

77 *Currie's Trs.* v. *Collier*, 1939 S.C. 247. See L. Watson, *contra*, in *Gordon* v. *Gordon's Trs., ut cit.*

78 *Devlin's Trs.* v. *Breen*, 1943 S.C. 556, L. J-Cl. Cooper at p. 571.

79 *Ibid.*, L. Wark at pp. 582-3, L. Jamieson at p. 586.

80 *Devlin's Trs.* v. *Breen*, 1945 S.C. (H.L.) 27, L. Thankerton at p. 32. The doubt was *obiter*, because the *conditio* under consideration was held not to be a presumption rebuttable by evidence—there was, that is to say, no ambiguity—but to be a rule of construction arising in a certain class of wills. Evidence, therefore, was irrelevant, and the question of its admissibility did not truly arise. L. Macmillan, at p. 38, said merely that the evidence was inadmissible "for the present purpose."

81 For the meaning of "ambiguity," see § 267, note 58. As with other extrinsic evidence, evidence of subsequent actings is inadmissible if there is no ambiguity. See *Scott* v. *Howard*, 1881, 8 R. (H.L.) 59, L. Watson at p. 67.

82 See § 267, sub-para. (a).

even Acts of Parliament, more especially those of ancient date, the terms of which leave their true meaning and effect doubtful or obscure, may be cleared up and interpreted—not controlled or altered—by the usage or possession which has followed upon them."[83] In so far as Acts of Parliament are concerned, the principle applies only to those enacted "one or two centuries ago."[84] The principle has been applied, not only to the identification of the subject matter of the writing, but also to ambiguities regarding the extent of the obligations undertaken, even when a presumptive rule of construction applies.[85] The justification for the principle is that the actings following the writing, being the parties' own exposition of their language and intentions, is the best mode of explaining obscure or obsolete expressions.[86]

Evidence of subsequent actings has been admitted and considered in construing the following:—ancient charters and statutes relating to a university in order to discover whether women had a right of membership;[83] a lease granted a hundred years earlier and a sub-lease granted thirty years earlier, to resolve an ambiguity as to the nature of the public burdens in respect of which one of the parties was entitled to relief;[87] a feu contract granted one hundred and eighty-four years earlier, to resolve an ambiguity as to whether an obligation to relieve from teind duties included an obligation to relieve from augmentations of stipend;[88] a disposition granted one hundred and forty years earlier for behoof of the poor of the parish, in order to discover whether this meant the legal poor or the occasional poor;[89] a feu charter granted sixty-seven years earlier, in order to discover whether an obligation to relieve from all burdens included an obligation to relieve from minister's stipend.[90]

(c) **Contracts.** In a written contract for the sale of a business it was provided that the seller should take bills from the purchaser for the price, no date for payment of the price being specified. Promissory notes repayable on demand were granted. When five years later the seller charged on these for payment, the purchaser contended that there was an antecedent agreement that the price should not be payable until the termination of a lease which was still current. It was held that, although the written contract was silent as to the date when the price should be paid, the parties had solved this question for themselves by their actings. By granting and accepting promissory notes payable on demand, they had shown that the price was payable when

---

[83] *Jex-Blake* v. *Senatus of Edinburgh University*, 1873, 11 M. 784, at pp. 813, 820-821, 825.

[84] *Clyde Navigation Trs.* v. *Laird & Son*, 1883, 10 R. (H.L.) 77, L. Watson at p. 83.

[85] *Welwood's Trs.* v. *Mungall*, 1921 S.C. 911, L.P. Clyde at p. 926; *North British Railway Co.* v. *Magistrates of Edinburgh*, 1920 S.C. 409, L.P. Strathclyde at p. 428. See also *Jopp's Trs.* v. *Edmond*, 1888, 15 R. 271.

[86] Dickson, *Evidence* (3rd ed.) §1087.

[87] *Jopp's Trs.* v. *Edmond* (*supra*); *North British Railway Co.* v. *Magistrates of Edinburgh* (*supra*); *Masters of Dundee* v. *Wedderburn*, 1830, 8 S. 547.

[88] *Welwood's Trs.* v. *Mungall* (*supra*).

[89] *Inspector of Kinglassie* v. *Kirk Session of Kinglassie*, 1867, 5 M. 869. See also *Flockhart* v. *Kirk Session of Aberdour*, 1869, 8 M. 176; *University of Aberdeen* v. *Irvine*, 1868, 6 M. (H.L.) 29.

[90] *Heriot's Hospital* v. *McDonald*, 1830, 4 W. & S. 98.

the seller chose to demand it.[91] Similarly when a written contract of employment was silent as to the dates when an annual salary should be paid, it was held that the contract fell to be construed in accordance with the practice of the parties under it.[92] After an action had been raised in England against an English company, a Scottish firm, in an agreement constituted by correspondence, obliged themselves to pay the defendants' costs and damages on condition that the conduct of the defence was left in their hands. The defendants having been unsuccessful, the Scottish firm contended that in terms of the agreement the English company was obliged to concur in an appeal. In construing the agreement, the court relied upon later correspondence between the parties, at the time when the appeal was being discussed, as indicating that neither party regarded the original agreement as remaining effective beyond the court of first instance.[93] When there was a doubt as to the meaning of "Whitsunday" in relation to the commencement and termination of an agricultural lease, it was held that the parties, by their subsequent actings, showed that they had intended it to mean 26th May, the old term, and not 15th May, which was the legal term.[94] In a question under a feu contract as to whether a feuar had a permanent right of access from a lane which was the boundary of her feu, the interlocutor found that "under the terms of the feu-contract libelled, as explained by the subsequent actings of the parties," she had such a right.[95] It was said that "the true interpretation of a boundary description . . . is to be arrived at, not only from the terms of the description in reference to the other clauses of the grant, but also with reference to facts and circumstances at the time when the grant was made, and the conduct of the parties immediately after the grant."[96] The actings of parties have also been mentioned earlier in connection with proof of a missing term in a contract.[97]

(d) **Testamentary Writings.** Direct statements by a testator, made orally or in notes or correspondence after the date of his will, are in general[98] inadmissible in order to show his intention, or his understanding of its meaning.[99] The subsequent actings of the testator, however, as distinct

---

[91] *McAllister* v. *McGallagley*, 1911 S.C. 112, L.P. Dunedin at p. 119, L. Kinnear at p. 120, L. Johnston at p. 122. This case was mentioned earlier in connection with proof of a missing term. See § **263.**

[92] *Macgill* v. *Park*, 1899, 2 F. 272.

[93] *Boyle & Co.* v. *Morton & Sons*, 1903, 5 F. 416, L. J-Cl. Macdonald at p. 421, L. Young at p. 422, L. Trayner at pp. 422-3, L. Moncreiff at p. 423.

[94] *Hunter* v. *Barron's Trs.*, 1886, 13 R. 883.

[95] *Boyd* v. *Hamilton*, 1907 S.C. 912.

[96] *Ibid.*, L. Kinnear at p. 923.

[97] See § **263.**

[98] The only occasion on which direct declarations of intention or understanding may be admissible in evidence is mentioned at § **270.**

[99] *Trustees of the Free Church of Scotland* v. *Maitland*, 1887, 14 R. 333, L.P. Inglis at p. 338, L. Shand at p. 343; *Farquhar* v. *Farquhar's Exrs.*, 1875, 3 R. 71, L. Gifford at p. 74: *cf.* L. J-Cl. Moncreiff at p. 73; *Catton* v. *Mackenzie*, 1870, 8 M. 1049, L. Kinloch at p. 1062. The admissibility of correspondence for this purpose was doubted in *Glendonwyn* v. *Gordon*, 1873, 11 M. (H.L.) 33, L. Colonsay at p. 42.

from his direct statements, are thought to be admissible in evidence.[1] When the question in issue was whether, on the assumption that an entail was invalid, the testator, who was the heir in possession, intended to include the entailed subjects in the conveyance of his whole property, heritable and moveable, contained in his general disposition and settlement, Lord President Inglis said:—"We are entitled to look at every deed executed by him, dealing with the entailed and unentailed lands, to see whether it was in his mind to convey the entailed estate by the general words of conveyance, or whether, *after the deed was made*, it was in his mind that he had conveyed it."[2] The court, largely on the evidence of the testator's whole dealings with the entailed lands before and after the general settlement, and of the deeds relating thereto, held that it was not his intention to include the entailed lands in the general conveyance. The same principle has been applied when the question in issue was whether a special destination in a title to heritage was revoked by a general disposition of the whole estate in the testator's will.[3]

276. CUSTOM OR USAGE OF TRADE

(a) **General.** Evidence of custom or usage is admissible in four cases, (1) where the writing expressly refers to and incorporates the custom,[4] (2) on a point for which the writing makes no provision, express or implied,[5] (3) where it is averred that words or phrases are used with an unusual meaning and there is some ambiguity,[6] and (4) to modify the rights and obligations which the law would normally infer.[7] It must, however, be admitted that it is difficult to distinguish cases which have been held to fall under one of those classes from others which have not. While no effect can be given to a custom which would render a contract *pactum illicitum*[8] or which contradicts an express statutory enactment,[9] a custom must often to some extent run counter to the general law.[10] Otherwise proof of it would be useless. The custom must be clearly and precisely averred.[11] To render a custom binding the evidence must show that it is certain, uniform, reasonable and, except

---

[1] *Catton* v. *Mackenzie* (*supra*), at pp. 1055, 1059, 1060, 1062; *Glendonwyn* v. *Gordon* (*supra*), L. Colonsay at p. 42: *contra* L. C. Selborne at p. 42; *Farquhar* v. *Farquhar's Exrs.* (*supra*), L. Gifford at pp. 73-4.

[2] *Catton* v. *Mackenzie* (*supra*), at p. 1055. See also *Thoms* v. *Thoms*, 1868, 6 M. 704.

[3] *Glendonwyn* v. *Gordon* (*supra*).

[4] *Strathlorne S.S. Co. Ltd.* v. *Hugh Baird & Sons, Ltd.*, 1915 S.C. 956, at pp. 973, 981: reversed on the ground that the custom was not proved; 1916 S.C. (H.L.) 134.

[5] See sub-para. (b).

[6] See sub-para. (c). As to the meaning of "ambiguity" see §267, note 58.

[7] See sub-para. (d).

[8] *Ronaldson* v. *Drummond & Reid*, 1881, 8 R. 956.

[9] *Magistrates of Dunbar* v. *Duchess of Roxburghe*, 1835, 1 Sh. & Macl., 134, L. Brougham at p. 195.

[10] Gloag's statement to the contrary (*Contract* (2nd ed.) 379) is not supported by the authorities cited. L. Rutherfurd-Clark thought such proof admissible: *Nisbet* v. *Mitchell-Innes*, 1880, 7 R. 575, at p. 578.

[11] *Nisbet* v. *Mitchell-Innes* (*ut supra*); *Sutton & Co.* v. *Ciceri & Co.*, 1890, 17 R. (H.L.) 40, L. Watson at p. 43.

in the first class of case referred to,[4] known to both parties or at least so notorious that they must be taken to have known of it.[12]

(b) **No Provision in Writing.** In a lease of a furnished house, which made no provision as to rates, it was held that there was incorporated a custom that the landlord was obliged to relieve the tenant of occupier's rates.[13] Where lace manufacturers had contracted to make lace for other manufacturers from designs supplied by the latter, it was held that, in accordance with a custom of trade, it was an implied term that lace should not be manufactured from the designs except with the consent of the manufacturers who supplied them.[14] But if the writing does provide for the point, evidence of custom is inadmissible. Where bills of lading provided that delivery should be "from the ship's tackles," no effect could be given to a custom of delivery into shed at the cost of the consignees.[15] A contract to deliver "in about two weeks" could not be varied by a custom allowing an extension of time.[16] Even if the writing is not express, it may deal with the matters to which the custom relates so fully as to negative the suggestion that the parties contracted with reference to the custom.[17]

(c) **Special Meaning of Words.** Evidence was held admissible to show that by custom of trade "pig iron delivered f.o.b. Glasgow" meant pig iron from particular ironworks,[18] and that in a contract for sale of a ship the chronometer was not included.[19] But if the word or phrase is unambiguous,[20] proof of modifying custom is not allowed. So it was refused where the word was "interest" in a lease[21] and "approved acceptance" in a contract of sale.[22] It would probably also be refused if the word is defined by statute.[23]

(d) **Modification of Implied Terms.** In the case of sale it is expressly provided that where any right, duty or liability would arise by implication of law it may be negatived or varied by usage.[24] This rule is of general application.[25] Where a tenant repaired his house, effect was given to an

---

12 *Strathlorne S.S. Co. Ltd.* v. *Hugh Baird & Sons, Ltd.* (*supra*), at 1916 S.C. (H.L.) pp. 135, 136. Proof of what generally happens is not necessarily a proof of usage: *Brown* v. *McConnell*, 1876, 3 R. 788, at pp. 788, 789; *Cazalet* v. *Morris*, 1916 S.C. 952.
13 *Sturrock* v. *Murray*, 1952 S.C. 454.
14 *William Morton & Co.* v. *Muir Brothers & Co.*, 1907 S.C. 1211.
15 *Hogarth & Sons* v. *Leith Cotton Seed Oil Co.*, 1909 S.C. 955. See also *Duthie & Co.* v. *Merson & Gerry*, 1947 S.C. 43.
16 *P. & W. MacLellan, Ltd.* v. *Peattie's Trs.*, 1903, 5 F. 1031.
17 *Buchanan* v. *Riddell*, 1900, 2 F. 544, at p. 549; *Gordon* v. *Thomson*, 1831, 9 S. 735; Dickson, *Evidence* (3rd ed.) §1092.
18 *Mackenzie* v. *Dunlop*, 1853, 3 Macq. 22 (the proof failed).
19 *Armstrong & Co.* v. *McGregor & Co.*, 1875, 2 R. 339, L. Ardmillan at p. 343 (the proof failed).
20 As to the meaning of "ambiguity," see §**267**, note 58.
21 *Sinclair* v. *McBeath*, 1868, 7 M. 273.
22 *McDowall & Neilson's Tr.* v. *J. B. Snowball & Co., Ltd.*, 1904, 7 F. 35.
23 *Hunter* v. *Barron's Trs.*, 1886, 13 R. 883, at p. 890, but not concurred in by the other judges.
24 Sale of Goods Act, 1893 (56 & 57 Vict. c. 71), s. 55.
25 Gloag, *Contract* (2nd ed.) 379.

admitted local custom under which the landlord was bound at the end of the lease to pay him the value of the wood used.[26] An averment that articles heritable in law were by a local custom not included in a sale of heritage, if relevantly stated, might have been remitted to proof.[27]

277. IDENTIFICATION OF SUBJECT OR PERSON OR NATURE OF OBLIGATION OR RIGHT

(a) **General.** When there is an ambiguity,[28] the purpose of admitting circumstantial evidence[29] is to resolve the ambiguity and to identify the subject of the writing, the person mentioned in it, or the nature and extent of any obligation or right created by it, about which there is a doubt.[30] The party who desires to lead evidence must specify the words which are claimed to be ambiguous and the precise meaning which he desires to attribute to them.[31] It is probably unnecessary to state that when the writing itself refers to extrinsic matters in order to identify a thing, person or right, proof of the extrinsic matter is not only admissible but essential, not because the writing is ambiguous, but because the extrinsic facts are incorporated by reference in it. So when, in a lease, the subjects let were described by reference to what was "tenanted by" a previous tenant, proof was necessary of what in fact the previous tenant tenanted,[32] and the same principle applied when in a feu-contract there were reserved to the adjoining feuars the whole rights and privileges "which they at present possess."[33]

(b) **Identification of Subject or Thing.** When an estate is described in the title deeds by a general name or in general terms, so that its extent and boundaries cannot be ascertained from the title deeds themselves, extrinsic evidence is admissible to establish what has been possessed under the general name or general descriptive words for the prescriptive period.[34] The same principle was applied in defining "the estate of Dallas"[35] and "the property known as the Royal Hotel,"[36] in missives of sale, and when the boundaries of land disponed were described partly by reference to a pier, evidence as to

26 *Learmonth* v. *Sinclair's Trs.*, 1875, 5 R. 548.
27 *Nisbet* v. *Mitchell-Innes* (*supra*).
28 For the meaning of "ambiguity," see § 267, note 58. When there is no ambiguity extrinsic evidence is inadmissible. See § 267, sub-paras. (a), (b).
29 See § 271.
30 Wigram's Fifth Proposition (Wigram, *Extrinsic Evidence in Aid of the Interpretation of Wills* (5th ed.) 13-14). See also Dickson, *Evidence* (3rd ed.) §1070; McLaren, *Wills and Succession* (3rd ed.) I, 378 *et seq.*; Gloag, *Contract* (2nd ed.) 372. Wigram adds to what is stated in the text:—"The same is true, it is conceived, of every other disputed point respecting which it can be shown that a knowledge of extrinsic facts can in any way be made ancillary to the right interpretation of a testator's words."
31 *Sutton & Co.* v. *Ciceri & Co.*, 1890, 17 R. (H.L.) 40, L. Watson at p. 43.
32 *Earl of Ancaster* v. *Doig*, 1960 S.C. 203. See also *Gregson* v. *Alsop*, 1897, 24 R. 1081.
33 *Argyllshire Commissioners of Supply* v. *Campbell*, 1885, 12 R. 1255.
34 *North British Railway Co.* v. *Hutton*, 1896, 23 R. 522, L. McLaren at p. 525. See also *Brown* v. *North British Railway Co.*, 1906, 8 F. 534, L. Kyllachy at p. 543.
35 *Houldsworth* v. *Gordon Cumming*, 1909 S.C. 1198: 1910 S.C. (H.L.) 49.
36 *Macdonald* v. *Newall*, 1898, 1 F. 68.

the extent of the pier was held admissible.[37] Evidence has also been regarded as admissible to define the following ambiguous expressions relating to the subject matter of a writing:—in a will, the words "residue," when it was uncertain whether this included heritage,[38] "the gas companies' shares that were lately bought by me from Mrs. J. Bruce's trustees for £300," when the testator was averred to have bought no shares for £300, but only shares to a total value of £798,[39] and "my black horse" when the testator was averred to have only a white one;[40] in a feu-contract, the expression "water-side grass";[41] in a contract regarding the assignation and allotment of shares in limited companies, the expression "your proposed limited company,"[42] and in a mercantile contract the expressions "your requirements,"[43] "all your requirements,"[44] and a "thousand" rabbits,[45] when there was a doubt as to the extent or number of the subjects so described; in a mercantile contract, the words "best quality," in relation to the goods to be supplied, which were averred to have a special meaning in the particular trade;[46] in a contract of carriage the word "statuary,"[47] and, in a policy of marine insurance, the expression "no St. Lawrence," when there was a doubt as to whether this meant the river or the gulf of that name.[48]

(c) **Identification of Person.** In testamentary writings extrinsic circumstantial evidence has been regarded as admissible to identify the beneficiary, or the person with reference to whom the beneficiary was identified in the writing, when the following ambiguous expressions were used:—"heirs"[49] and "children,"[50] which have a variety of possible meanings; nicknames such as "Mrs. G.";[51] "my late brother James's son," when the brother James had only a daughter;[52] "General Alexander Fairlie Bruce" when no person of that name existed, but there had existed a Major-General Alexander James Bruce and an Alexander Fairlie Bruce;[53] "William Keiller, confectioner in Dundee" when the only claimants were William Keiller, a confectioner in Montrose, and James Keiller, a confectioner in Dundee;[54] and "the National Society for the Prevention of Cruelty to Children," when it was

---

37 *Davidson* v. *Magistrates of Anstruther*, 1845, 7 D. 342.
38 *Craw's Trs.* v. *Blacklock*, 1920 S.C. 22 (evidence to show that legacies exceeded moveable estate).
39 *Bruce's Trs.* v. *Bruce*, 1875, 2 R. 775.
40 McLaren, *Wills and Succession* (3rd ed.) I, 384, quoting from Wigram.
41 *Logan* v. *Wright*, 1831, 5 W. & S. 242, L. C. Brougham at p. 246.
42 *Renison* v. *Bryce*, 1898, 25 R. 521.
43 *Blackstock* v. *Macarthur*, 1919 S.C. 57.
44 *Von Mehren & Co.* v. *Edinburgh Roperie & Sailcloth Ltd.*, 1901, 4 F. 232.
45 An English example quoted in Dickson, *Evidence* (3rd ed.) §1061. The averment was that in the particular trade a thousand rabbits meant twelve hundred.
46 *Fleming & Co.* v. *Airdrie Iron Co.*, 1882, 9 R. 473.
47 *Sutton & Co.* v. *Ciceri & Co.*, 1890, 17 R. (H.L.) 40.
48 *Birrell* v. *Dryer*, 1884, 11 R. (H.L.) 41.
49 Erskine, iii, 8, 47; Dickson, *Evidence* (3rd ed.) §1083.
50 *Scott's Trs.* v. *Smart*, 1954 S.C. 12.
51 Dickson, *Evidence* (3rd ed.) §1059; McLaren, *Wills and Succession* (3rd ed.) I, 382.
52 *Macfarlane's Trs.* v. *Henderson*, 1878, 6 R. 288.
53 *Cathcart's Trs.* v. *Bruce*, (O.H.) 1923 S.L.T. 722.

averred that the testator intended to benefit the *Scottish* National Society for the Prevention of Cruelty to Children.[55]

(d) **Extent of Obligation or Right.** The admission of extrinsic evidence to explain the general words in a release or discharge, in order to discover the nature of the claims or other matters to which the release or discharge relates, has been mentioned earlier.[56] Examples of particular writings which were construed in the light of surrounding circumstances have also been given earlier.[57] In a number of cases, when a will contained a bequest to a particular beneficiary, and it was doubtful, after full effect had been given to every indication of intention arising from the terms of the deed itself, whether this was intended to be in addition to, or in substitution of, a bequest of an identical sum of money in an earlier unrevoked will, extrinsic circumstantial evidence[58] was admitted to resolve the ambiguity.[59] Extrinsic evidence as to a testator's actings has been admitted in order to discover whether a special destination in a title to heritage was intended to be revoked by a general disposition of his whole estate contained in his will.[60] When the question at issue was whether an obligation in a marriage contract to make good an annuity from a military pension fund continued to be exigible although, under the rules of the fund, the pension ceased to be payable on the beneficiary's second marriage, extrinsic evidence of surrounding circumstances was held admissible.[61]

278. FAILURE TO RESOLVE AMBIGUITY

If after all admissible extrinsic evidence has been led, the court is unable to determine what the granter intended by the words which he used, the writing will be held void from uncertainty.[66] "A court cannot construe a contract which is so vague as to be no contract at all,"[67] and further extrinsic

---

[54] *Keiller* v. *Thomson's Trs.*, 1826, 4 S. 730. See also *Keiller* v. *Thomson's Trs.*, 1824, 3 S. 279. Dickson (*Evidence* (3rd ed.) §1073) thought that the descriptions in these cases were so erroneous, that the court, in effect, made a bequest which the testator intended, but had not expressed.

[55] *Nasmyth's Trs.* v. *National Society for the Prevention of Cruelty to Children*, 1914 S.C. (H.L.) 76. See the critical comments in the House of Lords upon the nature of the evidence admitted and relied upon in the Court of Session.

[56] See §273, sub-para. (b), note 48.

[57] See §273.

[58] Direct declarations of intention are of course inadmissible: *Johnstone* v. *Haviland*, 1896, 23 R. (H.L.) 6, L. Watson at p. 9, L. Shand at p. 11. See, on this question, § 270.

[59] *McLachlan* v. *Seton's Trs.*, 1937 S.C. 206; *Royal Infirmary of Edinburgh* v. *Muir's Trs.*, 1881, 9 R. 352, L.P. Inglis and L. Mure at p. 356; *Milne* v. *Scott*, 1880, 8 R. 83, L.P. Inglis at p. 86, L. Mure at p. 88, L. Shand at p. 88; *McGowan* v. *Anstruther's Trs.*, 1827, 5 S. 276. See also Dickson, *Evidence* (3rd ed.) §1085. *Cf. Arres' Trs.* v. *Mather*, 1881, 9 R. 107; *Horsbrugh* v. *Horsbrugh*, 1847, 9 D. 329.

[60] See §275, sub-para. (d).

[61] *Forlong* v. *Taylor's Exrs.*, 1838, 3 Sh. & Macl. 177.

[66] Dickson, *Evidence* (3rd ed.) §1076; Wigram's Sixth Proposition (Wigram, *ut cit.*, 14).

[67] Quoted in Bell, *Principles*, §524. A party cannot, however, escape liability under a contract by saying merely that it was unintelligible to him. He is bound by the true construction of the terms of the contract as these shall be ascertained by the court. See *Laing* v. *Provincial Homes Investment Co. Ltd.*, 1909 S.C. 812, at pp. 822, 826.

evidence is thus inadmissible for the purpose of filling in a name left blank, of reconciling conflicting clauses in a will, or where the language used is so imperfect that to admit further evidence would be not to interpret the document but virtually to make a new one.[68]

279. VARIATION OF THE WRITING

(a) **General.** The proper mode of varying a written contract is the execution of a new written contract. Examples of the general rule, which excludes extrinsic evidence for the purpose of proving an oral agreement to vary the terms of a written contract, have been given earlier.[69]

The decisions regarding the exceptions to the rule are difficult to reconcile, and it is not easy to deduce general principles from them. The position of a party, who is sued for a breach of contract in which the pursuer is said to have acquiesced, is mentioned here,[70] but is doubtfully relevant to the subject matter of this paragraph. There is authority for the view that when it is admitted on record that some variation of the written contract was agreed upon, proof *prout de jure* of the exact terms of the agreement is admissible.[71] With regard to alleged oral agreements for the permanent variation of a written contract, it is thought that an attempt must be made to distinguish contracts which require writing for their constitution[72] from written contracts which the law does not require to be in writing.[73] In both kinds of contract an agreement to vary may be proved as an inference from facts and circumstances.[74] Apart from this, while in both cases an agreement to vary must be proved by writ or oath,[75] it is necessary also, when a variation of the first kind of contract is in question, to aver and prove actings which constitute homologation or *rei interventus*.[76] Mention is also made in this paragraph of difficulties which have arisen from the undefined use of the expression *rei interventus*,[77] and from certain *obiter dicta* in *Wark* v. *Bargaddie Coal Co.*[78] Building and engineering contracts are dealt with separately.[79]

(b) **Acquiescence in Breach of Contract.** It seems to be settled that when, in answer to an action for breach of contract, the defender avers that the pursuer agreed to, or acquiesced in, the breach in question, the agreement or acquiescence may be proved *prout de jure*, and, if proved, constitutes a good

---

[68] Dickson, *Evidence* (3rd ed.) §1076; Phipson, *Evidence* (9th ed.) 637.
[69] See §255, sub-para. (d).
[70] See sub-para. (b).
[71] *Campbell* v. *Arbuthnot*, 1904, 12 S.L.T. 438. For the facts of this case, see § 266, sub-para. (b).
[72] For contracts of this kind, see §§93 *et seq.*
[73] For some contracts of this kind, see §§ 144 *et seq.*
[74] See sub-para. (g).
[75] See sub-paras. (d), (f).
[76] See sub-para. (d).
[77] See sub-para. (c).
[78] See sub-para. (e).
[79] See sub-para. (h).

defence to the action.[80] This topic is not concerned with attempts to prove a variation of a written contract, and is therefore not strictly speaking relevant to his paragraph.

(c) Meaning of Rei Interventus. The task of deducing principles from the opinions dealing with this topic is made more difficult by the use of the expression *rei interventus* in two distinct senses.[81] In this chapter its use is restricted to the "proceedings" referred to in Bell's definition,[82] which take place in the knowledge and with the permission of the obligor on the faith of the agreement as if it were perfect, which are unequivocally referable to the agreement, and which produce alteration of circumstances, loss or inconvenience to the obligee.[82] This meaning of the expression presupposes an imperfectly constituted agreement, which, if not judicially admitted, must be proved by writ or oath.[83] The definition, moreover, speaks of *any* proceedings.[82] This implies that the proceedings, although on the faith of the agreement and referable to it, need not necessarily be inconsistent with the terms of the original contract or concerned with the execution of the new agreement. Thus an oral agreement to reduce the rent under a written lease for a term of years, if proved by writ or oath, could, it is thought, be completed by parole proof that the tenant, relying, to the landlord's knowledge, on the agreement, had purchased another farm or business with borrowed money.

In some of the opinions, however, which deal with the subject matter of this paragraph, the expression *rei interventus* is used as if it meant simply any actings from which an alleged new agreement must necessarily be inferred, whether or not the parties had put their agreement expressly into words.[84] When the expression is used in this sense the actings must not only be inconsistent with the original written contract,[85] but they must be concerned with the execution of the new agreement, and must manifest its terms.[86]

(d) Variation of Contracts requiring Writing for their Constitution. When a party avers that a contract which requires writing for its constitution[72] has been permanently altered by oral agreement, not only is parole evidence of the agreement inadmissible, but a reference of the agreement to the oath of

---

[80] *Wark* v. *Bargaddie Coal Co.*, 1859, 3 Macq. 467; *Sutherland* v. *Montrose Shipbuilding Co.*, 1860, 22 D. 665, at p. 671; *Walker* v. *Flint*, 1863, 1 M. 421, L. Benholme at p. 422, L. Neaves at p. 423; *Kirkpatrick* v. *Allanshaw Coal Co.*, 1880, 8 R. 327, at pp. 334, 336; *Carron Co.* v. *Henderson's Trs.*, 1896, 23 R. 1042, L. McLaren at p. 1054. *Wark* v. *Bargaddie Coal Co.* is discussed in sub-para. (e).
[81] In Gloag, *Contract* (2nd ed.) 46-47, the two meanings are distinguished.
[82] Bell, *Principles*, §26.
[83] See §§ **280, 281.**
[84] It is used in this sense in Bell, *Principles*, §946; Gloag, *Contract* (2nd ed.) 396; *Kirkpatrick* v. *Allanshaw Coal Co.*, 1880, 8 R. 327, at pp. 332, 333, 337; *Lavan* v. *Gavin Aird & Co.*, 1919 S.C. 345, at p. 350.
[85] *Lavan* v. *Gavin Aird & Co.*, 1919 S.C. 345, at pp. 348, 349.
[86] Actings of this kind are mentioned in sub-para. (g) below.

the other party is incompetent,[87] unless there are also averments of actings consequent upon the oral agreement which are relevant to infer *rei interventus*[88] or homologation.[89] From the point of view of proof the oral agreement is regarded as if it were a new and independent contract which requires writing for its constitution.[90] If the oral agreement is established by writ or oath or judicial admission, the averments of *rei interventus* or homologation may then be proved *prout de jure*.[91] What is required to establish *rei interventus* or homologation is mentioned later.[91] This principle was applied when a tenant under a written lease for a term of years averred that the landlord had agreed orally to construct a new road, and that on the faith of this agreement the tenant had incurred expenditure in reclaiming certain moorland to which the new road was intended to give access;[92] and when a tenant under a written lease averred an oral agreement by the landlord to provide steam for heating purposes on the faith of which the tenant incurred expenditure in the installation of plant and machinery.[93] The principle was also applied in the following circumstances, when proof of the oral agreement by writ or oath being held essential, and not having been tendered, the question of *rei interventus*[88] or homologation could not arise:—in response to a claim for rent, it was averred that the landlord had orally agreed to accept, and had in fact accepted for several years, a rent which was less than that stipulated in the lease;[94] a feu-contract provided that no building on the feu should be used as a public house, and the vassal averred that the superior had agreed orally that a particular house might be used in this way;[95] an employee, who for a number of years had accepted a wage which was less than that stipulated for in a written contract of service, was averred by the employers to have agreed orally that the contract should be varied by reducing the wage.[96]

The question of whether this principle has been qualified by certain dicta in *Wark* v. *Bargaddie Coal Co.*,[97] is discussed in the next sub-paragraph.

---

[87] *Perdikou* v. *Pattison*, 1958 S.L.T. 153 (lease of heritage), L. J-Cl. Thomson at p. 157, L. Patrick at p. 158, L. Mackintosh and L. Blades at p. 159. On this point generally, see §**92**, sub-para. (c).

[88] For the meaning of *rei interventus*, see sub-para. (c).

[89] See §**92**, sub-paras. (b), (c). See also Dickson, *Evidence* (3rd ed.) §1103.

[90] *Carron Co.* v. *Henderson's Trs.*, 1896, 23 R. 1042, L. Kyllachy (Ordinary) at pp. 1048-9, L. McLaren at p. 1054.

[91] See §§**282, 283**. It was also mentioned at sub-para. (c) above.

[92] *Philip* v. *Gordon Cumming's Exrs.*, 1869, 7 M. 859. In spite of a suggestion in the Lord Justice-Clerk's opinion that the averments of *rei interventus* were irrelevant, the court adhered to the Lord Ordinary's interlocutor, which allowed proof of the oral agreement by writ or oath on the assumption that there were relevant averments of *rei interventus*.

[93] *Stewart* v. *Clark*, 1871, 9 M. 616. The reference in the argument, and in the Lord Ordinary's opinion, to *Walker* v. *Flint*, 1863, 1 M. 417, seems to make it clear that proof of the agreement by writ or oath was allowed on the footing that *rei interventus* was relevantly averred.

[94] *Rattray* v. *Leslie's Tr.*, 1892, 19 R. 853. See also *Turnbull* v. *Oliver*, 1891, 19 R. 154; *Law* v. *Gibsone*, 1835, 13 S. 396; *Gibb* v. *Winning*, 1829, 7 S. 677.

[95] *Scot* v. *Cairns*, 1830, 9 S. 246.

[96] *Dumbarton Glass Co.* v. *Coatsworth*, 1847, 9 D. 732.

[97] *Wark* v. *Bargaddie Coal Co.*, 1859, 3 Macq. 467.

Variation of the contracts mentioned in this sub-paragraph may also be proved as an inference from facts and circumstances.[74]

(e) Dicta in Wark v. Bargaddie Coal Co. Some confusion has been caused by statements made in *Wark* v. *Bargaddie Coal Co.*[97] by Lord Chelmsford, who was one of the two Law Peers whose speeches are reported. The pursuer in the case under appeal had concluded (a) for reinstatement of a barrier of coal which, in contravention of the terms of the mineral lease, the defenders had broken, and (b) for interdict against further contravention in the future. The decision of the House of Lords did not affect the interdict against future contraventions which had been granted by the Court of Session. With regard to contraventions in the past, which were said to have been acquiesced in by the pursuer, the House of Lords merely remitted to the Court of Session to direct an issue as to whether the barrier had been broken with the pursuer's consent. The actual decision and the speech of Lord Cranworth, the other Law Peer,[98] dealt only with the alleged right of a landlord to sue a tenant in respect of a breach of contract in which he had acquiesced.[99] Lord Chelmsford, however, commenced his speech[1] with a statement of what he understood to be the law of Scotland regarding the effect of *rei interventus* in excluding *locus pænitentiæ*, following an oral agreement which requires writing for its constitution. His statement is founded upon Bell's well-known definition.[1] He appears, however, not to have appreciated the distinction made in the law of Scotland, and by the Court of Session[2] in the case under appeal, between the constitution of such an agreement, which, as he rightly states, may be oral, and its proof, which, apart from judicial admission, is restricted to writ or oath. That the law of Scotland requires the oral agreement in these circumstances to be proved by writ or oath was apparent to the Court of Session then, and despite the decision of the House of Lords in *Wark* v. *Bargaddie Coal Co.*, has since been affirmed in numerous decisions.[3] It has been suggested[4] that, as a result of Lord Chelmsford's speech, an anomalous exception has been created which affects only an oral agreement to vary, as distinct from an oral agreement to constitute such a contract, with the result that the oral agreement to vary, as well as the *rei interventus* which follows it, may be proved by parole evidence. It is difficult to understand why one speech in the House of Lords, not related to the actual judgment, should be thought to have justified such a departure from a well-recognised principle of the law of Scotland.[5]

(f) Variation when Writing Not Required. When a contract is in writing,

---

[98] *Ibid.*, L. Cranworth at pp. 486-7.
[99] See Lord McLaren in *Carron Co.* v. *Henderson's Trs.*, 1896, 23 R. 1042, at p. 1054.
[1] *Ibid.*, L. C. Chelmsford at pp. 477-479. For references to Bell's definition, see sub-para. (c) above.
[2] *Wark* v. *Bargaddie Coal Co.*, 1856, 18 D. 772, at pp. 774-5.
[3] See, for example, *Sutherland's Tr.* v. *Miller's Tr.*, 1888, 16 R. 10; *Gibson* v. *Adams*, 1875, 3 R. 144; *Philip* v. *Gordon Cumming's Exrs.*, 1869, 7 M. 859 (the rubric is misleading); *Paterson* v. *Earl of Fife*, 1865, 3 M. 423; *Walker* v. *Flint*, 1863, 1 M. 417.
[4] Rankine, *Leases* (3rd ed.) 110.
[5] For the general principle, see §§ **280** *et seq.*

although the law does not require writing for its constitution,[73] an oral agreement to vary it must be proved by writ or oath. It would appear, however, that it is not necessary, in addition, to establish *rei interventus*[88] or homologation.[6] When it was averred that a beneficiary, who was entitled to the whole of an estate in terms of a private Act of Parliament, had agreed to modify his claim to a half share, it was held that the alleged oral agreement could be proved by writ or oath,[7] and the same rule was applied when it was alleged that written instructions to a stockbroker were later altered orally.[8]

Variation of this kind of contract may also be proved as an inference from facts and circumstances. This is mentioned in the next sub-paragraph.

(g) **Agreement Inferred from Facts and Circumstances.** When there is no express oral agreement to vary a written contract, or when it is impossible to prove such an agreement by writ or oath, it may sometimes be possible to aver facts and circumstances which are explicable only on the assumption that such an agreement, express or implied, in fact existed.[9] In such a case the written contract is "altered *rebus et factis* for the past and for the future by acts of the parties necessarily and unequivocally importing an agreement to alter."[10] "It is a delicate thing to infringe on the terms of a written contract, but when the parties have been acting so as to alter it by their conduct, then we must give effect to the change."[11] Averments of this kind may be proved by parole evidence.[10]

Of necessity the actings relied upon for this purpose must be at variance with the terms of the written contract,[12] and they must be more compelling than those required to establish *rei interventus*[13] or homologation.[14] It is thought that they should be sent to proof only if they are relevant to establish beyond reasonable doubt the variation of the written contract which it is desired to infer from them.[15] Unlike averments of *rei interventus*, moreover, the actings with which this sub-paragraph are concerned must, by their own nature, manifest a particular variation of the written contract.[13]

If the facts and circumstances themselves establish that a written contract has been varied in a particular way, it is immaterial whether or not they are preceded by an express oral agreement. The parole proof of such an express agreement, if it existed, as an incident of the proof of facts and circumstances,

---

6 Dickson, *Evidence* (3rd ed.) §1103.
7 *McMurrich's Trs.* v. *McMurrich's Trs.*, 1903, 6 F. 121.
8 *Stevenson* v. *Manson*, 1840, 2 D. 1204. It is implied by the Lord Ordinary's opinion that it is unnecessary to prove *rei interventus* or homologation as well.
9 Dickson, *Evidence* (3rd ed.) §1029; Erskine (Nicolson's ed.) iii, 2, 3, note (*d*).
10 *Carron Co.* v. *Henderson's Trs.*, 1896, 23 R. 1042, L. Kyllachy (Ordinary) at p. 1049.
11 *Baillie* v. *Fraser*, 1853, 15 D. 747, L. Robertson at p. 750.
12 Gloag, *Contract* (2nd ed.) 396; *Kirkpatrick* v. *Allanshaw Coal Co.*, 1880, 8 R. 327, L. Mure at pp. 337, 338; *Lavan* v. *Gavin Aird & Co.*, 1919 S.C. 345. In these opinions actings of this kind are sometimes described as *rei interventus*. As to the meanings of this expression, see sub-para. (c) above.
13 See sub-para. (c) above.
14 *Wark* v. *Bargaddie Coal Co.*, 1859, 3 Macq. 467, L. C. Chelmsford at p. 480.
15 See the analogous rule for the discharge of written obligations by an inference from facts and circumstances, which is mentioned in §126, sub-para. (d).

is therefore unobjectionable. "Where there are averments of acquiescence in operations inconsistent with the terms of the written contract they may be admitted to proof, and if it appear that the acquiescence was the consequence of a previous arrangement . . . it is then competent to prove that arrangement."[16] The success of the proof in these circumstances depends primarily upon the cogency of the inferences arising from the actings of the parties, and only incidentally from the existence of the earlier oral agreement.[17]

(h) Building and Engineering Contracts. In these and similar executory contracts it is usual for the contract itself to give express power to the architect or engineer to order extras or deviations, subject, it may be, to a proviso that the contractor shall not be entitled to extra payment unless a written order for the extra work has been given to him.[18] If such a power is given, but there is no provision that the architect's orders must be given in writing, the inference is that they may be given orally.[19] Without such a provision the contractor is not entitled to deviate from the terms of the written contract, even on the order of the architect or engineer.[20] When some such power is given to the architect or engineer in the written contract, the question of whether he exceeded his authority, in ordering a particular deviation or extra, must turn upon the construction put upon the terms of the contract. A power to "increase, lessen or omit any part of the work," for example, does not give authority to the architect to give directions which would be inconsistent with the works specified in the contract; "his authority is to control the performance of the contract, not to make it or vary it."[21] And a provision in the contract that the work must be done "to the entire satisfaction of the architect in every respect" does not give the architect authority to dispense with performance of the express provisions of the contract: his approval applies only to the mode of fulfilling these express provisions.[22] When there is no express power to authorise deviations, it seems doubtful whether, even in an executory contract, it is relevant to aver that a deviation was authorised orally by the owner's supervisor or representative in charge, and that he did not interfere when he knew that the work was proceeding in accordance with the deviation.[23]

[16] *Sutherland* v. *Montrose Shipbuilding Co.*, 1860, 22 D. 665, L. J-Cl. Inglis at p. 673.
[17] In *Baillie* v. *Fraser*, 1853, 15 D. 747, where a variation of a written lease was held proved by the actings of the parties, it is made clear in the Lord Ordinary's opinion that no express agreement had taken place. Had there been such an agreement, however, it could competently have been proved along with the actings. See the comment on this case in Gloag, *Contract* (2nd ed.) 393, note 2.
[18] For the usual terms of these contracts, and the decisions regarding them, see *Encyclopædia of the Laws of Scotland*, II, §§943 *et seq.*
[19] Gloag, *Contract* (2nd ed.) 397, founding upon *Forrest* v. *Scottish County Investment Co.*, 1915 S.C. 115: affd. 1916 S.C. (H.L.) 28.
[20] *Steel* v. *Young*, 1907 S.C. 360.
[21] *Forrest* v. *Scottish County Investment Co.*, 1916 S.C. (H.L.) 28, L. Parmoor at pp. 37-8, L. Wrenbury at p. 39.
[22] *Ramsay & Son* v. *Brand*, 1898, 25 R. 1212, L.P. Robertson at p. 1215.
[23] Gloag, *Contract* (2nd ed.) 396-7; *Burrell & Son* v. *Russell & Co.*, 1900, 2 F. (H.L.) 80, L. C. Halsbury at pp. 86-7, L. Morris at p. 87, L. Davey at p. 88.

CHAPTER XXII

REI INTERVENTUS: HOMOLOGATION

280. INTRODUCTORY

Certain agreements and obligations, of which the most important are those relating to heritage, require for their constitution and proof writing either solemnly authenticated or holograph. Without such writing there is *locus pænitentiæ*, and either party may resile.[1] But if the agreement or obligation is established by judicial admission, or by writ or by oath on reference, and actings have followed on it, the right to resile may be cut off, or, in other words, the agreement or obligation may become binding. When the actings are those of the person seeking to enforce the agreement or obligation they are known as *rei interventus*; when they are those of the person seeking to resile they are known as homologation.[2] Not infrequently both parties take some action following on an imperfect agreement, and both *rei interventus* and homologation are pleaded and may support each other.[3] Two of the more recent authorities[4] are in that position, and since between them they raise nearly all the points of importance, their facts are fully stated later,[5] together with some observations on the decision of the House of Lords in *Mitchell*.[2] *Rei interventus* and homologation may also have the effect of completing an agreement, although the parties have not expressly agreed to all the terms.[6] Further, they may render binding an informal agreement to vary a written contract.[7]

281. REI INTERVENTUS: GENERAL

Although the term is sometimes used in a wide sense to cover the whole principle, viz. the agreement and the actings following thereon, its precise meaning is a real change of position[8] by the creditor. Bell's description has

---

[1] See § 92. Certain informalities may be cured by proof under the Conveyancing (Scotland) Act, 1874 (37 & 38 Vict. c. 98), s. 39. See § 186.
[2] *Mitchell* v. *The Stornoway Trustees*, 1936 S.C. (H.L.) 56, at p. 63; *M'Calman* v. *M'Arthur*, 1864, 2 M. 678, at p. 682.
[3] *Bathie* v. *Lord Wharncliffe*, 1873, 11 M. 490, at p. 496; *Kinnear* v. *Young*, 1936 S.L.T. 574.
[4] *Mitchell* v. *The Stornoway Trustees* (*supra*); *Danish Dairy Co.* v. *Gillespie*, 1922 S.C. 656.
[5] See § 286.
[6] The cases are discussed at § 282, sub-para. (c).
[7] See § 279, sub-para. (g).
[8] Bell, *Principles*, §27A.

frequently been approved. "*Rei interventus* raises a personal exception, which excludes the plea of *locus pœnitentiæ*. It is inferred from any proceedings not unimportant on the part of the obligee, known to and permitted by the obligor to take place on the faith of the contract as if it were perfect,[9] provided they are unequivocally referable to the agreement and productive of alteration of circumstances, loss or inconvenience, though not irretrievable."[10] Although Bell refers only to contract, the principle applies also to unilateral obligations such as a cautionary obligation,[11] provided that all the cautioners have signed.[12] It also applies to prevent the granter of a deed from founding on the fact that his signature was not properly attested.[13] Since *rei interventus* raises a personal exception the doctrine is really part of the general doctrine of personal bar.[14]

282. PROOF OF AGREEMENT

(a) General. Subject to the exception mentioned in sub-paragraph (c), no amount of *rei interventus* is of any avail unless the agreement, or obligation, is established by competent evidence.[15] Although it has frequently been laid down that the agreement can be established only by writ or oath,[16] this is not exhaustive. It can also be established by admission on record[17] or by a combination of these. Thus a partial admission on record may be completed by writ or oath.[18] The suggestion that the actings can be founded on as evidence of the nature of the agreement[19] is difficult to reconcile with principle or authority.[20]

9 i.e. executed with the necessary formalities.
10 Bell, *Principles*, §26. For the use of the phrase to mean actings from which a new agreement must be inferred, see §279, sub-para. (c).
11 *National Bank of Scotland* v. *Campbell*, 1892, 19 R. 885; *Church of England Fire and Life Assurance Co.* v. *Wink*, 1857, 19 D. 1079.
12 *Paterson* v. *Bonar*, 1844, 6 D. 987. But *cf. Craig* v. *Paton*, 1865, 4 M. 192, where a cautioner signed and delivered the bond knowing that a co-cautioner refused to sign, and was held liable. Attestation may not be necessary: see §113.
13 *National Bank of Scotland* v. *Campbell* (*supra*). See also *Baird's Trustee* v. *Murray*, 1883, 11 R. 153.
14 *Boyd* v. *Shaw*, 1927 S.C. 414, and *Baird's Trustee* v. *Murray* (*supra*), raised substantially the same question as *National Bank of Scotland* v. *Campbell* (*supra*) and *Church of England Fire and Life Assurance Co.* v. *Wink* (*supra*), but they were decided on general pleas of personal bar.
15 *Stobo, Ltd.* v. *Morrisons (Gowns) Ltd.*, 1949 S.C. 184; *East Kilbride Development Corporation* v. *Pollok*, 1953 S.C. 370; *Buchanan* v. *Duke of Hamilton*, 1878, 5 R. (H.L.) 69 (where it turned out that there was no *consensus in idem*). If the agreement was made by an agent, his authority must be implied, admitted or proved: *Pratt* v. *Abercromby*, 1858, 21 D. 19.
16 *Sutherland's Trustee* v. *Miller's Trustee*, 1888, 16 R. 10 (decided in the sheriff court on oath and in the Division on writ); *Gibson* v. *Adams*, 1875, 3 R. 144; *Philip* v. *Gordon-Cumming's Executors*, 1869, 7 M. 859 (the rubric is misleading); *Walker* v. *Flint*, 1863, 1 M. 417.
17 *Church of England Fire and Life Assurance Co.* v. *Wink*, 1857, 19 D. 1057.
18 *Paterson* v. *Earl of Fife*, 1865, 3 M. 423.
19 *Seller* v. *Aiton*, 1875, 2 R. 381, L. Shand at p. 390.
20 *Mitchell* v. *The Stornoway Trustees*, 1936 S.C. (H.L.) 56, L. Macmillan at p. 66. See note 35. But see §279 (g) (variation of written contract inferred from actings).

(b) Proof by Writ.[21] The writ founded on need not be one to which the opponent was a party,[22] and some of the terms may be proved by one writ and some by another.[23] The following have been held sufficient:—a docquet in a building plan,[24] a return under the Valuation Acts,[25] entries in the landlord's books,[26] an offer from the tenant,[27] an adjusted draft[28] and a receipt for feu-duty which stated the area of the ground.[29] From the example last cited a receipt for a year's rent must be distinguished, since it does not indicate the endurance of the lease.[30]

(c) Incomplete Agreement. Express agreement on every term is, generally speaking, not necessary. In lease, for example, if the four essentials, parties, subjects, duration and rent, are established by writ, oath or judicial admission, and nothing has been said about the other terms, the lease is binding if *rei interventus* or homologation has followed; and the clauses usual and necessary in a lease of its kind are added by the court, after a remit, if necessary, to a conveyancer.[31] The same course is competent in a sale of heritage.[32] It cannot, however, be followed if, in the circumstances, more than the usual and necessary clauses require to be added. Where the essentials of sale of heritage were agreed, but it was clear that various reservations and servitudes would be required, which had not been discussed, it was held that there was no sufficient agreement.[33] If, on the other hand, an additional term has been discussed, but there is no competent evidence that it has been agreed to, the result appears to depend upon the importance attached to the term by the parties in their communings, "a question of degree, of the relative importance of the point left unsettled."[34] In a sale of heritage the question of the servitudes to be imposed on the ground, described by Lord Deas as "of vital importance," and by Lord Shand as "of vital consequence," was discussed, but no agreement reached, and it was held that there was no contract.[35] Where, however, only "petty details" remained unsettled, the bargain was held complete, the details being left for subsequent settlement.[36]

---

[21] As to proof by writ generally, see §§ 302 *et seq.*
[22] *Emslie* v. *Duff*, 1865, 3 M. 854.
[23] *Wilson* v. *Mann*, 1876, 3 R. 527.
[24] *Mitchell* v. *The Stornoway Trustees* (*supra*).
[25] *Emslie* v. *Duff* (*supra*).
[26] *Wares* v. *Duff Dunbar's Trustees*, 1920 S.C. 5.
[27] *Forbes* v. *Wilson*, 1873, 11 M. 454.
[28] *Bathie* v. *Lord Wharncliffe*, 1873, 11 M. 490. See also *Lang* v. *Lang's Trustees*, 1889, 16 R. 590 (marriage contract).
[29] *Stodart* v. *Dalzell*, 1876, 4 R. 236.
[30] *Gowans' Trustees* v. *Carstairs*, 1862, 24 D. 1382.
[31] *Wight* v. *Newton*, 1911 S.C. 762, at pp. 772, 775; *Erskine* v. *Glendinning*, 1871, 9 M. 656.
[32] *Westren* v. *Millar*, 1879, 7 R. 173, at p. 178.
[33] *Stobo, Ltd.* v. *Morrisons* (*Gowns*) *Ltd.* (*supra*).
[34] Gloag, *Contract* (2nd ed.) p. 40.
[35] *Heiton* v. *Waverley Hydropathic Company*, 1877, 4 R. 830. *Cf. Colquhoun* v. *Wilson's Trustees*, 1860 22 D. 1035, doubted in so far as it proceeded on the view that the actings are evidence of the contract in *Mitchell* v. *The Stornoway Trustees*, 1936 S.C. (H.L.) 56. L. Macmillan at p. 66, and in *East Kilbride Development Corporation* v. *Pollok*, 1953 S.C. 370, at p. 374.
[36] *Westren* v. *Millar* (*supra*).

A draft lease contained a clause about fencing, to which the tenant objected. He amended it, but the landlord did not agree. The tenant took possession and was held entitled to a lease excluding altogether any mention of fencing.[37]

283. THE ACTINGS

(a) General. The actings, or the abstention from action, which may be equally effective,[38] may be judicially admitted[39] or proved by parole evidence.[40] But they do not constitute *rei interventus* so as to render the agreement effectual unless they are performed in reliance on the agreement, known to the obligor to be so performed, and productive of some loss to the obligee. Although all three conditions must be proved, they may have a bearing on each other.[41] The more extensive the actings, the more likely they are to be known to the obligor, and the more expensive they are, the more likely they are to have been performed in reliance on the agreement. The averments must be sufficiently specific to shew that the actings fulfilled these conditions.[42]

(b) Reliance on Agreement. The acts must be such as would not have been done except in reliance on the agreement. "Unequivocally referable to the agreement" are Bell's words, and the phrase "not unimportant"[43] refers, not to the extent of the acts, but to their nature or significance[43] in shewing reliance on the agreement.[44] Obviously the acts must be subsequent in date to the agreement.[45] Most of the cases deal with leases, and it must be plain that the acts are referable to a lease for a term of years and not equally referable to a lease for a year.[46] When a tenant pulled down buildings and drove tiles for draining, both obligations mentioned in a draft lease, and also spent a considerable amount on lime and manure, these actings were held to have been done in reliance on the draft lease for nineteen years.[47] Where there was an informal agreement for a lease, followed by a probative lease, which was reduced, the tenant's entry and other actings were held to be

[37] *Wight* v. *Newton* (*supra*). The pursuer (the tenant) concluded for a lease as amended by himself, and the Lord Ordinary held that he was not entitled to it and assoilzied. The Division reversed, holding that the conclusions were wide enough to enable them to grant declarator of a lease in modified form.

[38] *Danish Dairy Co.* v. *Gillespie*, 1922 S.C. 656, at pp. 666, 670, 672.

[39] *Beardmore & Co.* v. *Barry*, 1928 S.C. 101, point not raised in House of Lords, 1928 S.C. (H.L.) 47.

[40] *Mitchell* v. *The Stornoway Trustees*, 1936 S.C. (H.L.) 56, at p. 63. See §**286.**

[41] *Buchanan* v. *Harris & Shelden*, 1900, 2 F. 935, at p. 939; *Danish Dairy Co.* v. *Gillespie* (*ut supra*).

[42] *Van Laun & Co.* v. *Neilson, Reid & Co.*, 1904, 6 F. 644, at p. 653. But somewhat vague averments passed in *National Benefit Trust, Ltd.* v. *Coulter*, 1911 S.C. 544.

[43] The word used by the Lord President in *Bathie* v. *Lord Wharncliffe*, 1873, 11 M. 489, at p. 496, and by Lord Macmillan in *Mitchell* v. *The Stornoway Trustees* (*supra*), at p. 66.

[44] *Buchanan* v. *Harris & Shelden* (*ut supra*).

[45] *Pollok* v. *Whiteford*, 1936 S.C. 402; *Van Laun & Co.* v. *Neilson, Reid & Co.* (*supra*); *Mowat* v. *Caledonian Banking Co.*, 1895, 23 R. 270.

[46] *Pollok* v. *Whiteford* (*supra*); *Mowat* v. *Caledonian Banking Co.* (*supra*).

[47] *Bathie* v. *Lord Wharncliffe* (*supra*); *Sutherland's Trustee* v. *Miller's Trustee*, 1888, 16 R. 10.

referable to the lease and not to the informal agreement.[48] Where there was a binding agreement for renewal of a lease, and the tenant sought to establish an additional oral agreement, it was held that the acts founded on were ordinary acts of tenancy and so referable to the lease.[49] There was a great difference of opinion on this point in *Mitchell* v. *The Stornoway Trustees*.[40]

(c) **Obligor's Knowledge and Permission.** The actings must be permitted to take place on the faith of the contract as if it were perfect. It is necessary, accordingly, either that the obligor should know of the actings and allow them to take place as if there was a binding contract,[50] or at least that the actings should be such as would naturally be expected to follow on the agreement.[51] Thus it was held irrelevant to aver that the obligee had given up a business in order to take possession under a lease, without averring knowledge by the obligor.[52] Knowledge and permission by an agent are sufficient, but only if the agent has implied or express authority to enter into the agreement,[53] or to permit the acts.[54] It may be more difficult to establish knowledge of abstention from acting than knowledge of positive acts.[53] A singular successor may be bound not only by knowledge of the informal agreement, but also by knowledge of facts which should put him on his inquiry.[55]

(d) **Consequent Loss or Inconvenience.** The entire phrase is "productive of alteration of circumstances, loss or inconvenience, though not irretrievable," and with it is coupled in many opinions the earlier words "proceedings not unimportant." The importance depends on the size of the transaction,[56] and in most of the cases the point has been clear one way or the other. The seller or landlord withdrawing the subjects from the market, and the purchaser or tenant taking possession and expending money on the subjects are frequent examples. The only case in which there was a real question seems to be *Mitchell* v. *The Stornoway Trustees*,[57] where there was a great difference of opinion on this point also.

---

[48] *Gardner* v. *Lucas*, 1878, 5 R. 638, point not raised in House of Lords, 1878, 5 R. (H.L.) 105.

[49] *Philip* v. *Gordon Cumming's Executors*, 1869, 7 M. 859. The rubric is misleading.

[50] *Bell* v. *Goodall*, 1883, 10 R. 905; *Stewart* v. *Burns*, 1877, 4 R. 427, where the pursuer (the seller) warned out a tenant at the defender's request.

[51] *Gardner* v. *Lucas* (*supra*), at pp. 650, 656; *Danish Dairy Co.* v. *Gillespie* (*supra*), at pp. 666, 670; *National Bank of Scotland* v. *Campbell*, 1892, 19 R. 885; *Boyd* v. *Shaw*, 1927 S.C. 414 (pleaded as personal bar, but similar to *National Bank of Scotland* v. *Campbell*).

[52] *Gardner* v. *Lucas* (*supra*).

[53] *Danish Dairy Co.* v. *Gillespie* (*supra*).

[54] *Heiton* v. *Waverley Hydropathic Co.*, 1877, 4 R. 830.

[55] *Stodart* v. *Dalzell*, 1876, 4 R. 236. In *Wilson* v. *Mann*, 1876, 3 R. 527, it was held that a lease constituted by informal writ and *rei interventus* was good against a singular successor, whether he knew of the *rei interventus* or not. But knowledge of a mere personal right is irrelevant; *Wallace* v. *Simmers*, 1961 S.L.T. 34; *Morier* v. *Brownlie & Watson*, 1895, 23 R. 67.

[56] *Kinnear* v. *Young*, (O.H.) 1936 S.L.T. 574.

[57] 1936 S.C. (H.L.) 56. For the facts see §286.

284. HOMOLOGATION

(a) **General.** Homologation has a wider scope than *rei interventus*. Not only may it exclude *locus pænitentiæ* from an imperfectly constituted agreement, but it may also bar reduction of a properly constituted agreement voidable on some extrinsic ground such as error.[58] Although this latter application of homologation falls outside the law of evidence, the decisions are used interchangeably as authorities in both branches.[59] Bell's definition covers the aspect of homologation here dealt with. Homologation is "an act approbatory of a preceding engagement, which is itself defective or informal, either confirming it or adopting it as binding. It may be express or inferred from circumstances. It must be absolute and not compulsory, nor proceeding on error or fraud, and unequivocally referable to the engagement; and must imply assent to it, with full knowledge of its extent, and of all the relative interests of the homologator."[60] Homologation thus differs from *rei interventus* in one important respect. No prejudice to anyone need be established, except the loss of the right to resile.[61] Where the deed is a conveyance defective *in substantialibus* there seems to be no room for homologation.[62]

(b) **Preceding Engagement.** The preceding engagement must be established by writ[63] or oath[64] or judicial admission.[64] The following have been held to be sufficient proof by writ: the docquetting of building plans;[65] an acknowledgment of loan neither holograph nor tested;[66] an informal offer to lease;[67] an informal submission and award;[68] an improbative award;[69] improbative offer and acceptance of a lease.[70]

(c) **The Approbatory Act.** Naturally this must be subsequent to the

---

58 Gloag, *Contract* (2nd ed.), deals with the first application of homologation at pp. 171 *et seq.* and with the second at pp. 544 *et seq.*

59 In *Danish Dairy Co.* v. *Gillespie*, 1922 S.C. 656 (defective writings relating to lease), L.P. Clyde at p. 664, cited *Gardner* v. *Gardner*, 1830, 9 S. 138 (reduction *ex capite lecti*).

60 *Principles,* §27.

61 *Mitchell* v. *The Stornoway Trustees*, 1936 S.C. (H.L.) 56, at p. 67. Professor Rankine's statement, *Personal Bar*, at p. 144, is at least misleading.

62 *Boswell* v. *Boswell*, 1852, 14 D. 378 (deed of entail: homologation not pleaded, though mentioned in headnote); *Robertson* v. *Ogilvie's Trustees*, 1844, 7 D. 236, at pp. 242, 244 (trust disposition and settlement); *Grant* v. *Shepherd*, 1847, 6 Bell's App. 153 (deed of entail). But there may be adoption. See §285.

63 *Mitchell* v. *The Stornoway Trustees* (*supra*), at p. 64 (where this is taken for granted).

64 There is no direct authority for this, but it seems sound in principle.

65 *Mitchell* v. *The Stornoway Trustees* (*supra*). The docquet followed on other writings. See §286.

66 *M'Calman* v. *M'Arthur*, 1864, 2 M. 678. Since the decision in *Paterson* v. *Paterson*, 1897, 25 R. 144, the document alone would have sufficed without proof of homologation. See §§118 *et seq.*

67 *Forbes* v. *Wilson*, 1873, 11 M. 454.

68 *Bremner* v. *Elder*, 1875, 2 R. (H.L.) 136. The criticism in the House of Lords of the interlocutor of the Court of Session is difficult to reconcile with its own action in sustaining the appellant's fifth plea.

69 *Robertson* v. *Boyd and Winans*, 1885, 12 R. 419.

70 *Danish Dairy Co.* v. *Gillespie* (*supra*).

engagement.[71] Since the act is evidence of consent it must be that of one capable of consenting. A pupil or an idiot cannot homologate,[72] nor can a minor without the consent of his curators.[73] Further, the party must know that he has a right to resile.[74] Where an heir performed acts apparently approbatory of a deed of entail it was held in a reduction *ex capite lecti* that he had not homologated because he did not know that the deed was reducible.[75] An act after an action has been raised has probably no effect,[76] nor has one done under reservation or protest.[77] The following have been held to be approbatory acts: assistance by the superiors' factor in proceedings before the Dean of Guild brought by the vassal and based on an informal feu contract;[78] acceptance of rent for fifteen years under an informal lease;[79] payments under an informal award.[80] If the act is that of an agent it has no effect unless the agent had authority to conclude the contract or the principal authorised the act.[81]

285. ADOPTION

Although the word "adopting" appears in Bell's definition of homologation,[82] adoption proper differs from homologation. An imperfectly constituted obligation may be adopted, and so validated, if it is repeated, confirmed or corroborated in a properly authenticated writing, which is in effect a new obligation. No knowledge of the original defect is necessary, and the obligation takes effect from the date of the adoption, not, as in homologation, from the date of the imperfect obligation.[83] An heir of entail in possession granted a bond of provision in favour of his younger children. The bond was not properly authenticated, and the succeeding heir of entail, the debtor in the bond, brought an action of declarator of nullity. The defenders pleaded that the granter had confirmed the bond, and this plea

---

71 *Mitchell* v. *The Stornoway Trustees* (*supra*), at pp. 62, 63.

72 Erskine, iii, 3, 47.

73 *Brodie* v. *Brodie*, 1827, 5 S. 900 (reduction *ex capite lecti*).

74 *Shaw* v. *Shaw*, 1851, 13 D. 877 (defective execution of missive of lease); not an easy report to follow, but Lord Cockburn states the principle clearly.

75 *Gardner* v. *Gardner*, 1830, 9 S. 138, cited by L.P. Clyde in *Danish Dairy Co.* v. *Gillespie*, 1929 S.C. 656.

76 *Harkness* v. *Graham*, 1833, 11 S. 760 (reduction on the ground of minority and lesion). There was ratification, not homologation, by the minor after he attained majority and after the action had been raised. Apparently the minor was bankrupt and had no interest in the outcome of the case. A litigant is not likely to perform an approbatory act against his own interest, and one in his own favour could not be taken into account.

77 *Miller & Son* v. *Oliver & Boyd*, 1906, 8 F. 390, where the pursuers were held not to have consented to the enlargement of the scope of a reference because they had protested timeously.

78 *Mitchell* v. *The Stornoway Trustees* (*supra*).

79 *Forbes* v. *Wilson* (*supra*).

80 *Bremner* v. *Elder* (*supra*), where the Court of Session proceeded more definitely on homologation; *Robertson* v. *Boyd and Winans* (*supra*).

81 *Danish Dairy Co.* v. *Gillespie* (*supra*). In *Forbes* v. *Wilson* (*supra*) the agent had authority, but in addition the landlord had knowledge.

82 See § **284**, sub-para. (a).

83 Bell, *Principles*, §27

was sustained by a majority of the whole court on the ground that the granter had in subsequent properly authenticated deeds "adopted," "affirmed," or "reiterated" the bond, or that these deeds were equivalent to a bond of corroboration.[84] All the judges who mentioned homologation, which was not pled, rejected it on various grounds.[85] The only person who could homologate was the debtor, the pursuer. Another reason, stressed in argument,[86] but not mentioned in the opinions, was that the granter did not know of the defect. Adoption proper thus depends, in this connection,[87] on the construction and effect of later deeds, not on any question of evidence.

286. LEADING AUTHORITIES

(a) **Mitchell v. The Stornoway Trustees.**[88]   The pursuer wished to feu a piece of ground from the defenders for building purposes. After negotiation the defenders intimated in writing to the pursuer that they were prepared to feu him a piece of ground, not precisely defined, the feuduty to be at the rate of £12 an acre. A site plan was prepared, and the defenders' factor docquetted it as approved. This docquet was held in the House of Lords to constitute proof by writ of the agreement. It does not appear from the report that the site plan contained any terms of the feu, and the House must have regarded the docquet as confirming the terms of the earlier writings, as seems to be implied in the speech of Lord Blanesburgh. The pursuer then presented a petition for a lining, and the burgh surveyor, who had a difficulty about the plans, obtained a satisfactory assurance from the defenders' factor. This assistance given by the factor was held to amount to homologation, described by Lord Thankerton as a somewhat narrow ground. *Rei interventus* was also pleaded, and was said to consist in three acts by the pursuer, (1) a journey to Glasgow to see contractors with a view to the erection of buildings on the site, (2) his purchase of a motor lorry, and (3) the presentation of the petition for lining. In the Court of Session all three were rejected as *rei interventus*, the first because the defenders did not know of it and were not bound to anticipate it, the second because the purchase took place two days before the agreement, and the third on two grounds (*a*) that it was equally referable to a desire by the pursuer to start building as soon as his agreement with the defenders should be constituted and (*b*) that a few shillings for court fees was not sufficient loss or inconvenience. It is not very clear whether the House of Lords agreed with this or not. The first two grounds disappeared, but Lord Macmillan found sufficient *rei interventus* in the third. Lord Thankerton and Lord Maugham expressly disagreed with him on the same grounds as the Court of Session. Lord Atkin agreed with Lord Macmillan's opinion, and Lord Blanesburgh's

---

[84] *Callander* v. *Callander's Trustees*, 1863, 2 M. 291. Gloag, *Contract* (2nd ed.) 171, seems to treat this as a case of homologation.

[85] *Ibid.*, at pp. 311, 317, 324.

[86] *Ibid.*, at p. 298.

[87] Evidence may be of importance where it is pled that a void deed, e.g. a forged deed, has been adopted; *Muir's Executors* v. *Craig's Trustees*, 1913 S.C. 349.

[88] 1936 S.C. (H.L.) 56.

speech is capable of being read as referring only to homologation. It may be significant that no reference to *rei interventus* appears in headnote or rubric.

(b) **Danish Dairy Co. v. Gillespie.**[89] The pursuers were tenants from the defender under a lease which expired at Whitsunday, 1920. By 1st December, 1919, parties' solicitors had agreed on the terms of a new lease to begin at Whitsunday, 1920, but their letters were not holograph or adopted as holograph. On 10th March, 1920, the defender purported to resile, and the pursuers raised an action of damages. They founded on both *rei interventus* and homologation. The *rei interventus* was alleged to consist in the fact that they had not looked for new premises between 1st December and 10th March. This was rejected on the ground that it was not proved that the defender knew of, or ought to have anticipated, their abstention. It was a term of the agreement that the pursuers should pay the whole expenses of the new lease. The pursuers' solicitor paid these to the defender's solicitor, who sent a receipt and cashed the cheque. This was relied on as homologation, but was rejected on the ground that the defender knew nothing about the payment, that it was not proved that the defender's solicitor had authority to conclude a lease, and therefore that his act did not bind the defender.

[89] 1922 S.C. 656.

CHAPTER XXIII

RECOVERY AND PRODUCTION OF DOCUMENTS

287. GENERAL

The court has power to compel the production of documents which may have a bearing on the issues. A party may be ordered to produce a document,[1] but the power is usually exercised by approving a specification of documents[2] and granting diligence for their recovery.[3] Only documents are recovered in this way, not things,[4] and diligence is not granted for recovery of public documents or documents in the custody of a court, the proper procedure being to cite the custodier to exhibit them at the trial.[5] In some cases, where a document is in possession of a third party, diligence is refused, and the possessor must be cited as a witness and required to bring the document with him.[6] Although a diligence may be granted before the record is closed[7] to enable the party to make his averments specific,[8] and has been granted in slander actions to enable the pursuer to frame an issue,[9] the usual purpose is to enable a party, after proof has been allowed or issues approved, to recover documents for use at the proof or trial.[10] Since any documents recovered must be lodged as a production, diligence has been refused on the ground

---

1 *Reavis* v. *Clan Line Steamers*, 1926 S.C. 215. This decision proceeded on the statutory rule that a party must produce documents on which he founds in his pleadings. See also Sheriff Courts (Scotland) Act, 1907, Rule 68 (*a*), as amended by A.S. of 16th July, 1936.
2 See § **297.**
3 As to the special procedure for bankers' books see §**301.**
4 *Mactaggart* v. *Mackillop*, (O.H.) 1938 S.L.T. 559; *H.M. Advocate* v. *Fleming*, 1864, 2 M. 1032. See §**418.**
5 *Maitland* v. *Maitland*, 1885, 12 R. 899, at p. 903. Rules of Court, 1948, Rule 127.
6 See §**289** (b).
7 In the Court of Session it may be granted before calling; Rules of Court, 1948, Rule 120 (*a*). See *Braby & Co.* v. *Story*, (O.H.) 1896, 3 S.L.T. 325.
8 See §**296.**
9 *Graeme-Hunter* v. *Glasgow Iron & Steel Co., Ltd.*, (O.H.) 1908, 16 S.L.T. 15; *Stephen* v. *Paterson*, 1865, 3 M. 571.
10 A diligence has been granted during a proof; *Baroness Grey* v. *Richardson*, 1874, 1 R. 1138, and after appeal to the House of Lords, when the petition had not been served; *Tulloch* v. *Davidson's Exrs.*, 1858, 20 D. 1319.

that any documents recovered could not be lodged timeously.[11] Diligence is normally granted when proof by writ has been allowed, and has been granted in a petition for service,[12] but it was refused for use at a reference to oath, which is not a proof.[13] The court exercises the power in accordance with rules of practice and always subject to confidentiality,[14] and may refuse a diligence as matter of discretion.[15] A specification must pass the several tests mentioned in the following paragraphs, and approval of it implies that it has passed them all. On the other hand, refusal may be on one of several grounds, including confidentiality and discretion, and it is not clear in some of the decisions on which ground the court proceeded.[16] A number of the reported cases were decided in Single Bills or on the Motion Roll with little or no citation of authority, and opinions are brief or non-existent. When the documents are in the possession of a third party he has no opportunity of raising any objection when the diligence is asked for, but he is not compelled to produce if he can establish confidentiality[17] or show that production will cause him substantial prejudice.[18]

288. AVERMENTS AS TEST

A diligence will not be granted for the recovery of documents unless the documents will, or at least may, have a bearing on the averments remitted to proof.[19] So strictly was this rule applied that where the Lord Ordinary had allowed the pursuers a proof of their averments and to the defenders a conjunct probation, the defenders, owing to the form of the interlocutor, could not recover documents bearing on a separate substantive defence.[20] On the other hand, a Lord Ordinary found that, owing to the form of his interlocutor allowing proof, he had to grant a diligence much against his will.[21] *Ogston & Tennant Ltd.* v. *The "Daily Record," Glasgow, Ltd.*,[22] is an example of close comparison between averment (or its equivalent) and the specification. In a river pollution case diligence was granted to recover the books of the defenders that excerpts might be taken of entries showing the materials used by them in the mill, but not excerpts to show their expenditure on buildings (for the purpose of showing that the value of the mill had increased) or the amount of paper manufactured. Diligence was also refused for recovery of plans of the mill.[23] On the other hand, where the

---

[11] *Murphy* v. *Clyde Navigation Trustees*, 1900, 4 F. 653.
[12] *Irving's Trs.* v. *Irving*, (O.H.) 1894, 1 S.L.T. 665.
[13] *Miller's Trs.* v. *McDonald*, (O.H.) 1931 S.L.T. 601.
[14] See §§ 391 *et seq.*
[15] *Macqueen* v. *Mackie & Co., Distillers, Ltd.*, 1920 S.C. 544. See also *Young* v. *National Coal Board*, 1957 S.C. 99.
[16] See § 392
[17] See §§ 391 *et seq.*
[18] *North British Railway Co.* v. *R. & J. Garroway*, 1893, 20 R. 397, at p. 401.
[19] *British Publishing Co.* v. *Hedderwick & Sons*, 1892, 19 R. 1008. As to diligence in a proof by writ, see § 305.
[20] *Scott, Simpson & Wallis* v. *Forrest & Turnbull*, 1897, 24 R. 877.
[21] *Brown* v. *Evered*, (O.H.) 1904, 12 S.L.T. 121.
[22] 1909 S.C. 1000.
[23] *Duke of Buccleuch* v. *Cowan*, 1866, 4 M. 475, at p. 483.

issue was whe ther the coeration in a lease was merely the mone y rent, or included also certain services by the tenant, a diligence was granted for recovery of the tenant's books that excerpts might be taken showing his profits. These might show that the money rent was inadequate.[24] The pursuer's objection that this did not bear directly on the issue, which seems a strong one, was overruled. Where coalmasters presented an application to the Railway and Canal Commissioners for an order declaring that an increase of freight charges was unreasonable, which placed on the railway company the onus of establishing that the increase was reasonable, the court refused a diligence for recovery of the coalmaster's books showing, *inter alia*, their profits, on the ground that their profits had no bearing on the question whether the rates were unreasonable.[25] In an action of damages arising out of a tramway accident a diligence for recovery of the defenders' time tables, etc., was refused on the ground that there was no averment that the tram was not running to time.[26] Subsequent doubts about the relevancy of the averments remitted to proof is not a ground for refusing recovery, if the documents bear on the averments.[27]

289. PURPOSE OF RECOVERY AS TEST

(a) **Preliminary.** It is often said that a document which is to be used for cross-examination only is not recoverable by diligence,[28] but this proposition is far too wide. Documents are frequently recovered for that purpose.[29] It has also been said that "the proper use of diligence is to recover writings of the nature of evidence, and capable of being used as evidence in the cause: we must be satisfied that the writings are of such a kind that they may be used in evidence."[30] But this dictum has little value as a practical guide. First, the question whether a document is recoverable has been said no longer to depend on whether it is evidence or could be used in evidence.[31] Secondly, neither in the older nor in the modern cases is there any explanation of the meaning in this connection of the terms "of the nature of evidence," "used as evidence" and "used in evidence."[32] Third, the decision in *Livingstone*,[30]

---

[24] *Robertson* v. *Earl of Dudley*, 1875, 2 R. 935.

[25] *John Watson, Ltd.* v. *Caledonian Railway Co.*, 1901, 3 F. 791.

[26] *Burrows* v. *Corporation of Glasgow*, (O.H.) 1916, 1 S.L.T. 420. For other examples, see *Earl of Morton* v. *Fleming*, (O.H.) 1921, 1 S.L.T. 205; *Northern Garage, Ltd.* v. *North British Motor Manufacturing Co.*, Ltd., (O.H.) 1908, 16 S.L.T. 573.

[27] *Duke of Hamilton's Trustees* v. *Woodside Coal Co.*, 1897, 24 R. 294.

[28] Dickson, *Evidence* (3rd ed.) §1361; Lewis, *Evidence*, 191; *Encyclopædia of the Laws of Scotland*, III, 551.

[29] *Young* v. *National Coal Board*, 1957 S.C. 99, L. J-Cl. Thomson at p. 105; *Black* v. *Bairds & Dalmellington*, 1939 S.C. 472, L. J-Cl. Aitchison at p. 478; *Admiralty* v. *Aberdeen Steam Trawling and Fishing Co.*, Ltd., 1909 S.C. 335, L. McLaren at p. 341; *Emslie* v. *Alexander*, 1862, 1 M. 209, L. J-Cl. Inglis at p. 210.

[30] *Livingstone* v. *Dinwoodie*, 1860, 22 D. 1333, at p. 1334.

[31] *Young* v. *National Coal Board (supra)*, L. Blades at p. 108; *Black* v. *Bairds & Dalmellington (ut supra)*; *Admiralty* v. *Aberdeen Steam Trawling and Fishing Co.*, Ltd. *(supra)*, L.P. Dunedin at p. 340.

[32] Some judges seem to have thought that counsel were trying to recover the writings of living persons in order to use them as evidence of the facts stated in them: at least they contrasted them with the writings of a deceased person: *County Council of Fife* v.

which forms the basis of the first proposition and from which the second is taken, was much more limited than they suggest.[33]

(b) Suggested Rule. It is thought that the rule justified by the decisions can be stated most precisely in negative form. A document is not recoverable if it has not been communicated to or by one of the parties and if it can be used only to provide material for the examination in chief or in cross of a witness who is not a party. To state the rule positively, and at the same time comprehensively, is more difficult, but it is thought that it may be stated thus. Subject to confidentiality[34] and relevancy,[35] a document is recoverable if it is a deed granted by or in favour of a party or his predecessor in title, or a communication sent to, or by or on behalf of, a party, or a written record kept by or on behalf of a party. The distinction between what is and what is not recoverable by diligence has been assimilated to the distinction between documents which, both in the Court of Session and in the sheriff court, must be lodged in process before the proof and those which may be produced for the first time at the proof.[36] Although a document in the second category is not in general recoverable by diligence, a witness who has it in his possession may be cited to bring it with him to the proof.[37]

(c) Documents not Recoverable. It has been said of *Livingstone* v. *Dinwoodie*,[30] to the dicta in which later pronouncements have paid lip service as establishing a rule, that "all that was decided . . . was that the court will not grant a diligence for the recovery of documents in the possession of persons who had no interest whatever in the case, and had nothing to do with it except that they might probably be called as witnesses."[33] It is thought that the accident of who happens to possess the document is not the sole deciding feature and that the question of who wrote it, and to whom, is of at least equal importance. In *Livingstone* v. *Dinwoodie*[30] the letters were written by one third party to another. Subject to this, however, the dictum provides a general guide to the later decisions, and forms the basis of the negative statement of the suggested rule. In accordance with that rule

---

Thoms, 1898, 25 R. 1097, L. J.-Cl. Macdonald at p. 1098; *Hogg* v. *Campbell*, 1864, 2 M. 1158, L. Deas and L. Ardmillan at p. 1161. But a document is evidence that the writer has committed the statement to writing and so may be of use in cross-examining him: *Maitland* v. *Glasgow Corporation*, 1947 S.C. 20; in that case the court would not have granted a diligence for the recovery of Mrs. Smith's letters to her sister to see what account of the accident she had given in them. In *Mackinnon* v. *National S.S. Co.*, (O.H.) 1904, 12 S.L.T. 411, and *Devlin* v. *Spinelli*, (O.H.) 1906, 14 S.L.T. 9, a diligence to recover letters from the defenders to their servants was refused, but the reasons are not convincing. Confidentiality was not stated as the reason.

[33] *Admiralty* v. *Aberdeen Steam Trawling and Fishing Co., Ltd.* (*supra*), L. Kinnear at p. 343; *Watson* v. *Watson*, 1934 S.C. 374, at p. 380.

[34] See §§ **391** *et seq.*

[35] See § **288.**

[36] See § **300.**

[37] *Livingstone* v. *Dinwoodie* (*supra*), at p. 1334; *Hogg* v. *Campbell* (*supra*), at p. 1161; *Steven* v. *Nicoll*, 1875, 2 R. 292, at p. 293; *North British Railway Co.* v. *R. & J. Garroway*, 1893, 20 R. 397, at p. 403; *Watson* v. *Watson* (*ut supra*). For form of citation, see Encyclopædia, Scottish Legal Styles, II, Forms 516, 518.

the following documents have been held not to be recoverable: correspondence relating to the state of mind of a deceased testator passing between one of his servants and another person, neither of whom was a party to the action:[30] reports made to the defenders' contractors, who were not parties to the action, by their superintendent of works;[38] communications passing between the pilot and the master of the defenders' vessel in a claim for salvage;[39] the business books of a bankrupt's creditors, who were not parties to the action;[40] diaries of living persons who were not parties to the action.[41]

(d) Documents Recoverable.[42] Documents which, if their authenticity is presumed or averred, constitute written evidence, are clearly recoverable. These include probative writings,[43] holograph writings,[44] writings *in re mercatoria*,[45] writings to be tendered in a proof by writ,[46] writings by a deceased person,[47] documents which by statute are made evidence, such as a ship's log,[48] and minutes of meeting of a company.[49] Other writings are recoverable in general if they have been written to or by a party. These include business books and records and other writings by or on behalf of a party which may contain an extrajudicial admission or statement against interest,[50] or may throw light on his state of mind,[51] as, for example, his mental condition[52] or fraudulent intent.[53] They also include communications received by a party which may disclose his state of knowledge at a particular time or contain a "contemporaneous record" of events,[54] as, for example, reports received by a party from his contractors[55] or from his employees.[56] In an action by a trustee in bankruptcy for reduction of an assignation granted by the bankrupt, diligence was granted for recovery of the bankrupt's

---

[38] *Sutherland* v. *John Ritchie & Co.*, (O.H.) 1900, 8 S.L.T. 100.

[39] *Devlin* v. *Spinelli* (*supra*).

[40] *Steven* v. *Nicoll* (*supra*). *Cf. Porter* v. *Phœnix Assurance Co.*, 1867, 5 M. 533, where the defenders recovered the business books of third parties to instruct sales for the pursuer, whose own books were said to have been destroyed by fire.

[41] *Hogg* v. *Campbell* (*supra*); *McNeill* v. *Campbell*, 1880, 7 R. 574. *Cf. Fraser* v. *Fraser's Trustees*, (O.H.) 1897, 4 S.L.T. 228 (doctor's diary recovered: a doubtful decision).

[42] Subject to relevancy and confidentiality.

[43] See § **178.**

[44] See § **188.**

[45] See § **105.**

[46] See § **305.** *Caledonian Rly. Co.* v. *Crockett & Co.*, (O.H.) 1902, 10 S.L.T. 89.

[47] See § **371.**

[48] *Admiralty* v. *Aberdeen Steam Trawling and Fishing Co.* (*supra*), L.P. Dunedin at p. 340.

[49] Companies Act, 1948 (11 & 12 Geo. VI. c. 48), s. 145 (2).

[50] See § **29.** The decisions in *Jenkins* v. *Glasgow Corporation*, (O.H.) 1934 S.L.T. 53, and *French* v. *Purnell*, (O.H.) 1931 S.L.T. 85, are difficult to reconcile with principle.

[51] See § **375.**

[52] *Mackintosh* v. *Fraser*, 1859, 21 D. 783, at p. 792.

[53] *Strachan* v. *Barlas*, (O.H.) 1894, 2 S.L.T. 59.

[54] This, however, is limited to medical or other scientific reports: *Black* v. *Bairds & Dalmellington* (*supra*), L. J-Cl. Aitchison at p. 477, L. Wark at p. 483.

[55] *Sutherland* v. *John Ritchie & Co.*, (O.H.) 1900, 8 S.L.T. 100; *Sneddon* v. *Glasgow Corporation*, (O.H.) 1935 S.L.T. 74.

[56] *Tannett, Walker & Co.* v. *Hannay & Sons*, 1873, 11 M. 931.

public examination.[57] This may be explained on the view that the examination was public and that the answers were to questions by or on behalf of the pursuer. In many of these cases the practical result of recovery is to provide material for the cross-examination of the person making the report.

290. REPORTS BY SERVANTS

While communications made to a party are in their nature recoverable, recovery may be refused on the ground that they were made after the dispute had arisen, or was at least in contemplation, and are therefore confidential.[58] But there is an arbitrary exception in the case of reports to a party by his servants present at the incident, and made at or about the time of it.[58]

291. PARTICULAR CASES: DAMAGES

(a) **Recovery from Pursuer.** Most of the cases are actions for damages for slander involving injury to business. The defender usually recovers the pursuer's business books for entries showing his profits before and after the slander.[59] Receipts for income tax have been recovered.[60] They have also been refused.[61] Where a pursuer alleged that as a result of personal injury his business had suffered, the defenders recovered his business books for three years for excerpts showing his profits, and also his income tax receipts.[62] In an action of damages for illegal detention of a ship, the defenders obtained a wide diligence for recovery of documents relating to the history of the ship, which they alleged had been carrying on a smuggling trade.[63]

(b) **Recovery from Defender.** In an action of damages for breach of promise the pursuer was refused a recovery of the defender's books as unnecessary, but there was a difference of opinion as to whether they were

---

[57] *Emslie* v. *Alexander*, 1862, 1 M. 209. The report of *Fife County Council* v. *Thoms*, 1898, 25 R. 1097, is obscure, but the decision is not surprising. The letters were obviously confidential, as the defender argued, and the diligence was obviously fishing and should never have been agreed to.

[58] *Young* v. *National Coal Board*, 1957 S.C. 99, Lord Ordinary at p. 101, L. J-Cl. Thomson at p. 105, L. Mackintosh at p. 106; *Anderson* v. *St. Andrews Ambulance Association*, 1942 S.C. 555, L.P. Normand at p. 557, L. Moncrieff at p. 559; *Black* v. *Bairds & Dalmellington*, 1939 S.C. 472, L. Mackay at p. 482, L. Wark at p. 483, where a limited specification was approved in special circumstances. See further on this subject § 395, sub-para. (b).

[59] *Gray* v. *Wyllie*, 1904, 6 F. 448; *Aitchison & Sons, Ltd.* v. *McEwen*, 1903, 5 F. 303; *Christie* v. *Craik*, 1900, 2 F. 1287; *Rhind* v. *Kemp*, (O.H.) 1894, 1 S.L.T. 434.

[60] *Macdonald* v. *Hedderwick & Sons*, 1901, 3 F. 674 (this reads like a deliberate statement of practice, but *Christie* v. *Craik* (*supra*), was not cited).

[61] *Christie* v. *Craik* (*supra*) (no opinions were delivered); *Gray* v. *Wyllie* (*supra*) (a special reason was given for refusing a diligence for income tax returns, which may have applied to the receipts, though they are not mentioned in the opinion); *Keir* v. *George Outram & Co. Ltd.*, (O.H.) 1913, 2 S.L.T. 165.

[62] *Johnston* v. *Caledonian Railway Co.*, 1892, 20 R. 222, where *Craig* v. *North British Railway Co.*, 1888, 15 R. 808, was distinguished, and the decision explained to rest on the excessive period; *Irvine* v. *Glasgow and South Western Railway Co.*, (O.H.) 1913, 2 S.L.T. 452.

[63] *Van Engers, Roeclofs & Co.* v. *Ellis Hughes*, (O.H.) 1898, 6 S.L.T. 90.

ever recoverable in such a case.[64]   Recovery was allowed in three subsequent cases in the Outer House.[65]   In an action of damages for slander against a newspaper the pursuer recovered books to show its average circulation in the month when the alleged slander was published.[66]   In an action of damages for slander it is competent to prove in aggravation actual malice on the part of the defender, and recovery has been allowed for that purpose.[67]

(c) Recovery from Third Parties.   In most cases involving personal injuries, when the pursuer has been in hospital, the hospital records are recovered from the Regional Hospital Board after intimation to the Lord Advocate.[68]   Although diligence for recovery of income tax returns has been refused at the instance of a party,[69] a more recent decision seems to show that it would be granted if the Lord Advocate does not object.[70]

292. PARTICULAR CASES: SLANDER

(a) General.   Damages have already been dealt with.[71]   Where a written slander is alleged, the pursuer is, as a general rule, entitled to recover the original writing or a copy.[72]   If the defender does not plead *veritas*, he cannot recover the pursuer's books except so far as they bear on damages.[73]

(b) Newspaper: Anonymous Letter.   If the publishers refuse to disclose the name of the author and thus assume responsibility, the general rule is that diligence is not granted to discover it.[74]   But if it is averred that the publishers themselves composed the letter, a diligence has been allowed to recover evidence as to the true authorship.[75]

(c) Fair Comment.   Where the defence was fair comment the defender recovered documents tending to establish the facts on which he had commented, but not other facts unconnected with them,[76] and where the comment

---

[64] *Somerville* v. *Thomson*, 1896, 23 R. 576.
[65] *Robertson* v. *Hamilton*, 1915, 2 S.L.T. 195; *Stroyan* v. *McWhirter*, 1901, 9 S.L.T. 242; *Brodie* v. *McGregor*, 1900, 8 S.L.T. 200.
[66] *Macdonald* v. *Hedderwick & Sons* (*supra*).   See also *Brown* v. *Evered*, (O.H.) 1904, 12 S.L.T. 121 (damages for infringement of patent).
[67] *Cunningham* v. *Duncan & Jamieson*, 1889, 16 R. 383, distinguished in *Morrison* v. *Smith & Co.*, 1897, 24 R. 471 (referred to at note 74);   *Reid* v. *Johnston & Co.*, 1912 S.C. 187.
[68] *Glacken* v. *National Coal Board*, 1951 S.C. 82.
[69] *Gray* v. *Wyllie* (*supra*).
[70] *Henderson* v. *McGown*, 1916 S.C. 821. *Cf. Jenkins* v. *Glasgow Corporation*, (O.H.) 1934 S.L.T. 53.
[71] See § **291.**
[72] *Mathieson* v. *Scottish Trade Protection Society*, (O.H.) 1897, 5 S.L.T. 213.
[73] *Aitchison & Sons, Ltd.* v. *McEwan*, 1903, 5 F. 303.
[74] *Morrison* v. *Smith & Co.*, 1897, 24 R. 471.
[75] *Cunningham* v. *Duncan & Jamieson*, 1889, 16 R. 383, distinguished in *Morrison* v. *Smith & Co.* (*supra*) and followed in *Greig* v. *Balfour & Co.*, (O.H.) 1897, 5 S.L.T. 175, and *Falconer* v. *Docharty*, (O.H.) 1893, 1 S.L.T. 96.
[76] *Wheatley* v. *Anderson and Miller*, 1927 S.C. 133.

was alleged to be based on letters received by the defenders, the pursuer was granted a diligence to discover whether the letters existed.[77]

293. PARTICULAR CASES: FRAUD

A wider recovery is allowed where fraud is in issue. A shareholder of the City of Glasgow Bank was discharged by the liquidators on the footing that he had disclosed all his assets. In a reduction of the discharge the pursuers averred that he had fraudulently concealed certain specific property and also other assets (unspecified) to the value of £40,000. The court granted a sweeping diligence involving an enquiry into the whole of the shareholder's affairs.[78] In an action of damages against bank directors for fraudulently inducing the pursuer to take shares, and for fraudulent concealment, very wide recovery was allowed, though fraud is not specifically mentioned in the opinions.[79] A document not uttered is in many cases not recoverable,[80] but where the defender was accused of fraud, his diary was held recoverable as possible evidence of his state of mind.[81]

294. PARTICULAR CASES: TITLES

It has been laid down that a diligence will be granted to recover from the opposite party only specific documents for a specific purpose,[82] and in the interlocutor pronounced, the court gave effect to that view. But in an earlier case[83] what was characterised by the defenders, with some justification, as a fishing diligence, was granted. Attempts to recover third parties' titles have failed.[84]

295. OBJECTION BY GOVERNMENT

Diligence will almost certainly be refused if a Minister objects that recovery would be contrary to the public interest, but this probably applies only where the document is in the possession of the department or its agent.[85] Indeed, the objection has little point otherwise. The court has power to overrule the objection,[86] but, in considering whether to do so or not, it must accept the Minister's opinion and decide whether, in spite of it, it will allow recovery.[87] A practice of ordering production under seal so that the court itself may consider the danger to the public interest has been disapproved.[88]

---

[77] *Ogston & Tennant, Ltd.* v. *The "Daily Record," Glasgow, Ltd.*, 1909 S.C. 1000.

[78] *Assets Co., Ltd.* v. *Shirres' Trustees*, 1897, 24 R. 418. See also *Wilson's Trustees* v. *Bank of England*, (O.H.) 1925 S.L.T. 81.

[79] *Dobbie* v. *Johnston*, 1860, 22 D. 1113: *Tulloch* v. *Davidson's Trustees*, 1858, 20 D. 1319.

[80] *Watson* v. *Watson*, 1934 S.C. 374, L. Murray at p. 378.

[81] *Strachan* v. *Barlas*, (O.H.) 1894, 2 S.L.T. 59.

[82] *Richardson* v. *Fleming*, 1867, 5 M. 586; *Earl of Lauderdale* v. *Scrymgeour Wedderburn*, 1905, 7 F. 1045, at p. 1048.

[83] *Riggs* v. *Drummond*, 1861, 23 D. 1251. No opinions are reported.

[84] *Riggs* v. *Drummond* (supra); *Fisher* v. *Bontine*, 1827, 6 S. 330.

[85] *Whitehall* v. *Whitehall*, 1957 S.C. 30.

[86] *Glasgow Corporation* v. *Central Land Board*, 1956 S.C. (H.L.) 1.

[87] *Ibid.*, at p. 18, 1955 S.C., at p. 75; *Henderson* v. *McGown*, 1916 S.C. 821, at p. 825.

[88] *Rogers* v. *Orr*, 1939 S.C. 492, at p. 498; *Admiralty* v. *Aberdeen Steam Trawling and Fishing Co. Ltd.*, 1909 S.C. 335, at pp. 340, 342, 344.

Nevertheless, it is difficult to see how the court can avoid forming some view as to the extent of the public danger, and there are traces of this in the case referred to.[89] In a subsequent case[85] the Lord President observed that the circumstances in which the courts might disregard the Minister's certificate would vary, according to the grounds on which that certificate was based. The peculiar circumstances of that case forced the Minister to disclose his grounds, but in the normal case he need not do so.[90] In any event, the court will over-rule the objection only for some compelling reason,[91] and there is no case, at least since 1844, where it has done so.[92] The objection must be by the Minister, not by a litigant.[93] The objection was sustained *quoad* the following, the court in more than one case observing that recovery was not vital to the litigant[94]:— Crown precognitions and communications between the procurator-fiscal and the Crown office;[95] communications by a private individual to the police;[96] probably statements made to Post Office investigators;[97] a report by the police to a procurator-fiscal;[98] a report by a naval officer to the Admiralty following a collision;[99] medical history sheets of a soldier;[1] income tax returns;[2] instructions issued to officers of excise;[3] communications between the Central Land Board and district valuers.[86] An objection to produce a telegram by the Postmaster General, was upheld, not on the ground of public policy, but on account of the difficulty of finding it.[4] The objection was over-ruled *quoad* a Post Office Savings Bank account, and sustained *quoad* the inventory of an estate.[5]

296. ON OPEN RECORD

A diligence may be granted for the recovery of documents to enable a

---

[89] 1956 S.C. (H.L.) at p. 18, 1955 S.C. at p. 77, where Lord Russell referred to the compelling reasons for the objection in the leading English case.

[90] *Glasgow Corporation* v. *Central Land Board*, 1956 S.C. (H.L.), at p. 19, 1955 S.C., at p. 66.

[91] *Ibid.*, at pp. 20, 25.

[92] 1955 S.C. at p. 77. *Halcrow* v. *Shearer*, 1892, 20 R. 216, is inconclusive, the report in question having been made to the County Council.

[93] *Henderson* v. *Robertson*, 1853, 15 D. 292. In *Sheridan* v. *Peel*, 1907 S.C. 577, although the question of the Lord Advocate's consent was mentioned, diligence was refused on other grounds. In *Muir* v. *Edinburgh and District Tramways*, 1909 S.C. 244, no reason was given, in the absence of objection by the Lord Advocate, for refusing recovery of police reports.

[94] *Glasgow Corporation* v. *Central Land Board*; *Henderson* v. *McGown*; *Rogers* v. *Orr* (*supra*); *Caffrey* v. *Lord Inverclyde*, 1930 S.C. 762.

[95] *Arthur* v. *Lindsay*, 1895, 22 R. 417; *Donald* v. *Hart*, 1844, 6 D. 1255. *Cf. Mills* v. *Kelvin & James White, Ltd.*, 1912 S.C. 995, where the Lord Advocate did not object.

[96] *Rogers* v. *Orr* (*supra*). Contrast *Sheridan* v. *Peel* (*supra*), where the Lord Advocate consented to recovery.

[97] *Downie* v. *H.M. Advocate*, 1952 J.C. 37.

[98] *Hastings* v. *Chalmers*, 1890, 18 R. 244; *McKie* v. *Western S.M.T. Co.*, 1952 S.C. 206 (report by police officer to his superior).

[99] *Admiralty* v. *Aberdeen Steam Trawling and Fishing Co., Ltd.* (*supra*).

[1] *Caffrey* v. *Lord Inverclyde* (*supra*).

[2] *Henderson* v. *McGown* (*supra*). See *Shaw* v. *Kay*, (O.H.) 1904, 12 S.L.T. 359.

[3] *Tierney* v. *Ballingall & Son*, 1896, 23 R. 512.

[4] *Somervell* v. *Somervell*, (O.H.) 1900, 8 S.L.T. 112.

[5] *Forrest* v. *MacGregor*, (O.H.) 1913, 1 S.L.T. 372.

party to make his averments specific. It has been said that he must first have set forth his case in general terms, and not be merely trying to discover whether he has a case. But it has never been explained how, if from the documents recovered a pursuer discovers another case, he is to be prevented from pleading it, since the record is open. A strictly limited recovery appears to be the best safeguard. In an action of damages the pursuer averred that fires had been caused on his land by sparks from railway engines, which were not provided with proper spark arresters. The defenders called on him to specify which engines did not have proper spark arresters, and the pursuer moved for a diligence for recovery of records showing the identification marks of all engines operated at the material time on the particular stretch of line. The diligence was granted as an assistance to specification of the engine concerned,[6] the pursuer's intention being to follow it with a motion for an order to view.[7] On the other hand, where the action was alternatively against a bank or the bank agent as an individual, and on alternative grounds, a diligence was refused on the view that the pursuer was merely trying to find out what ground of action he had, and against whom it should be directed.[8] Diligence has been refused on the ground that the averments are already sufficiently specific.[9] This might lead to a complication. Unless the opposite party is barred by his attitude on the Motion Roll, he may raise the question of specification again on the Debate Roll and, even if the Lord Ordinary remains of the same mind, may succeed in the Inner House. The question of recovery would then arise again, but this time in order to amend. The court refused diligence to enable a party to make an amendment specific,[10] but this is a different thing from amending to make more specific averments which are already on the record. It has been held that a sheriff has power to grant a diligence before the record is closed.[11]

297. THE SPECIFICATION

The normal method[12] of recovering documents is to lodge a specification with a motion for its approval and for the appointment of a commissioner to execute the diligence. The specification consists, or at least should consist, of a detailed and articulate statement of the particular documents, or classes of documents, which are sought to be recovered.[13] Where a call is for books tending to show the truth of some averment it should be "in order that excerpts may be taken therefrom at the sight of the commissioner," unless there is a special reason for requiring the books themselves. The specification concludes with a call "failing principals, drafts, copies or duplicates of the

---

6 *MacRae* v. *British Transport Commission*, 1957 S.C. 195. See also *Donaldson* v. *Bannatyne*, 1828, 7 S. 130.
7 See §**418**, sub-para. (b).
8 *Greig* v. *Crosbie*, 1855, 18 D. 193.
9 *Jamieson* v. *Jamieson*, (O.H.) 1928 S.L.T. 427; *Dalgleish's Trustees* v. *Mathieson's Trustees*, (O.H.) 1902, 10 S.L.T. 56.
10 *Thomson* v. *Gordon*, 1869, 7 M. 687.
11 *Orr* v. *Orr*, 1937, 53 Sh.Ct.Rep. 89. *Cf. Prentice* v. *Kirkwood*, 1949, 65 Sh.Ct.Rep. 207.
12 As to special orders, see §**287**.
13 Rules of Court, 1948, Rule 120 (*b*); *Paterson* v. *Paterson*, (O.H.) 1919, 1 S.L.T. 12.

above." But approval of a specification containing such a call does not entitle the party to obtain copies, etc., until he has made a reasonable attempt and failed to recover the principals.[14] If the court refuses part of the specification, the deletion ought to be authenticated by the judge, or presiding judge, or the clerk of court.[15]

298. EXECUTION OF COMMISSION

When the commissioner has fixed the diet, the haver, i.e. the person thought to be in possession of the documents, is cited to it and informed of the documents he is expected to produce by sending him a copy of the specification, as approved, or of the part which affects him. It appears to be impossible to enforce the attendance of a haver furth of Scotland, since the English court has decided that the Evidence by Commission Act, 1843,[16] applies only to witnesses and will therefore not enforce the attendance of havers.[17] The same rule presumably applies to other countries under the Evidence by Commission Acts, 1859,[18] and 1885.[19] The haver is put on oath by the commissioner and questioned by the solicitor who has cited him, or by counsel. The only legitimate purposes of the examination are to recover the document and if the haver does not have it, to discover why. If the haver answers that he has the document, and has no objection to delivering it, he hands it over to the commissioner, and that ends the matter. But if he says he does not have it, he may then be asked if he ever had it. If that is answered in the affirmative, he may be asked what he has done with it. If he has destroyed it,[20] he may be asked when, where, how and why, and if he has handed it to someone else, to whom.[21] Questions as to the contents of the documents[22] or as to the merits of the cause[23] are incompetent. The haver, who has had no opportunity to object to the terms of the specification, is entitled at this stage to refuse to answer or to produce, either on the ground of confidentiality[24] or on the ground that to do so will cause him serious prejudice.[25] It is the duty of the commissioner to decide the question, and if an appeal is taken, to seal up the documents for the decision of the court,[26] or in case of special difficulty he may report to the court.[25] Where

---

[14] *Caledonian Railway Co.* v. *Symington*, 1912 S.C. 1033. *Cf. Sleigh* v. *Glasgow and Transvaal Options, Ltd.*, 1903, 5 F. 332.

[15] *Thomson & Co.* v. *Bowater & Sons*, 1918 S.C. 316.

[16] 6 & 7 Vict. c. 82.

[17] *Burchard* v. *Macfarlane*, [1891] 2 Q.B. 241. In *Blaikie* v. *Aberdeen Rly. Co.*, 1851, 13 D. 1307, a puisne judge enforced the diligence in England.

[18] 22 Vict. c. 20.

[19] 48 & 49 Vict. c. 74.

[20] This statement by a haver may be used as evidence at the trial; *Home* v. *Hardy*, 1842, 4 D. 1184; *Falconer* v. *Stephen*, 1849, 11 D. 1338.

[21] *Somervell* v. *Somervell*, (O.H.) 1900, 8 S.L.T. 84 (a clear and very helpful account of how a haver should be examined); *Gordon* v. *Davidson*, 1865, 3 M. 938; *Cullen* v. *Thomson and Kerr*, 1865, 1 M. 284.

[22] *Somervell* v. *Somervell* (*supra*).

[23] *Dye* v. *Reid*, 1831, 9 S. 342.

[24] See §391.

[25] *North British Railway Co.* v. *R. & J. Garroway*, 1893, 20 R. 397.

[26] *Stewart, Govan & Co.* v. *Birrell*, 1897, (O.H.) 5 S.L.T. 174.

excerpts only are to be taken, except of consent the commissioner alone may see the books, but he may have the assistance of an accountant.[27] In the Court of Session it is competent before executing the commission to serve on the person from whom documents are sought to be recovered a notice requiring him to produce the documents and an affidavit stating that he has produced all the documents he has, or that he has none, and who, if anyone, has other documents.[28]

Special rules apply in the Court of Session to the appointment of the commissioner, and to the lodging of his report and the documents recovered, and intimation thereof.[29]

299. OTHER TRIBUNALS

(a) **Criminal.** The High Court may grant a diligence for recovery at the instance of an accused person.[30] It has never been decided whether the sheriff has this power.[31]

(b) **Church Courts.** The sheriff has power to grant warrant for the citation of witnesses to the courts of the Church of Scotland[32] and possibly to those of other churches.[33] Presumably, therefore, he has power to grant commission and diligence for recovery of documents for use before these courts.

(c) **Arbitrations.** The proper procedure is that the arbiter, if so advised, approves the specification, and application is then made to the court for a diligence.[34] If a haver refuses to produce on the ground of confidentiality, the arbiter or the party may apply to the court, which must consider whether the objection is well founded before pronouncing an order.[35]

300. PRODUCTION OF DOCUMENTS

(a) **At Calling or Tabling.** In the Court of Session the pursuer must lodge along with the summons any deeds or documents founded on in the summons.[36] A document is "founded on" if it appears from the condescendence that the pursuer's case is to any extent based on it,[37] but the rule is not strictly enforced unless the defender insists.[38] A similar obligation lies on

---

27 *Municipal Council of Johannesburg* v. *Stewart & Co.*, (O.H.) 1911, 1 S.L.T. 359.
28 Rules of Court, 1948, Rule 121.
29 *Ibid.*, Rule 122.
30 *Downie* v. *H.M. Advocate*, 1952 J.C. 37. No decision was given, but the suggestion that the accused's right to recover depended on her satisfying the Crown that the documents were material has been criticised; Renton and Brown, *Criminal Procedure* (3rd ed.) 77.
31 Renton and Brown, *Criminal Procedure* (*ut supra*).
32 *Presbytery of Lews* v. *Fraser*, 1874, 1 R. 888.
33 *Ibid.*, at p. 894.
34 *Blaikie* v. *Aberdeen Rly. Co.*, 1851, 13 D. 1307; *Crichton* v. *North British Railway Co.*, 1888, 15 R. 784.
35 *Blaikie* v. *Aberdeen Rly. Co.*, 1852, 14 D. 590.
36 Rules of Court, 1948, Rule 106 (*d*).
37 *Western Bank* v. *Baird*, 1863, 2 M. 127.
38 *Reavis* v. *Clan Line Steamers*, 1926 S.C. 215.

the defender.[39] In the sheriff court a party must, if required, lodge before the record is closed any document founded on so far as in his power.[40]

(b) Before Proof or Trial. In the Court of Session all documents "intended to be used or put in evidence at the proof" or trial must be lodged on or before the seventh day prior to the diet.[41] Notwithstanding the generality of the words "used at the proof," this rule is not applied to documents written by a witness who is not a party and used merely to test the credibility of that witness,[42] or to refresh his memory. Such a document may be produced at the diet,[42] or the witness may be cited to produce it.[43] In the sheriff court documents intended to be used or put in evidence at a proof must be lodged by the fourth day before the diet,[44] with presumably an exception of documents written by a witness not a party.

301. BANKERS' BOOKS

A copy of any entry in a banker's book is *prima facie* evidence of such entry and of the matters there recorded,[45] provided it is proved that the book was at the time of making the entry one of the ordinary books of the bank, that the entry was made in ordinary course of business, and that the book is in the custody or control of the bank. This proof may be by a partner or officer of the bank and may be oral or by affidavit.[46] It must further be proved that the copy is correct.[47] A court or judge may authorise a litigant to inspect, and take copies of, entries in a banker's book for the purpose of the proceedings.[48] "Bank" and "banker" mean any person, persons, partnership or company carrying on the business of banking, a savings bank and a post office savings bank.[49]

[39] Rules of Court, 1948, Rule 109 (c).
[40] Sheriff Courts (Scotland) Act, 1907 (7 Edw. VII. c. 51), Rule 47.
[41] Rules of Court, 1948, Rules 129, 141.
[42] *Paterson & Sons* v. *Kit Coffee Co. Ltd.*, 1908, 16 S.L.T. 180. It is understood that this is the prevailing practice.
[43] See § **289**, sub-para. (b).
[44] Sheriff Courts (Scotland) Act, 1907 (7 Edw. VII. c. 51), Rule 68, as amended. Rule 142, which refers to jury trials, is slightly differently phrased.
[45] Bankers Books Evidence Act, 1879 (42 & 43 Vict. c. 11), s. 3.
[46] *Ibid.*, s. 4.
[47] *Ibid.*, s. 5.
[48] *Ibid.*, ss. 7, 8.
[49] *Ibid.*, s. 9; Companies Act, 1948 (11 & 12 Geo. VI. cap. 38), s. 432.

CHAPTER XXIV

WRIT OF PARTY

302. GENERAL

Proof of an obligation by writ of party means proof of the obligation by unequivocal[1] inference from documents which are actually[2] or constructively[3] his writ.[4] Accordingly, even after it has been admitted or proved that the writ or writs are those of the party, the question remains whether they are sufficient to justify the inference.[5] In drawing the inference it may be necessary to take into account the relevant circumstances, which may be either those in which the document was written[6] or its history.[7] Dicta suggesting that the writ must be intended as an acknowledgment to the creditor are inconsistent with the decisions.[8]

Each reported decision was naturally given in relation to a particular statute or rule of the common law, and in some cases the court has founded on the words of the relevant statute, but, generally speaking, decisions under one statute or common law rule have been cited, both in argument and by the court, in cases under another,[9] and it appears convenient, subject to the above observation, to deal with the subject as one.

303. ACTUAL WRIT OF PARTY

Where the party's signature is admitted or proved the writ need not be holograph or tested.[10] If, however, it is not admitted that he appended his signature to the words appearing on the document, parole proof is com-

---

1 A word much stressed in *Seth* v. *Hain*, 1855, 17 D. 1117 (trust).
2 See § 303.
3 See § 304.
4 *Robb & Co.* v. *Stornoway Pier and Harbour Commission*, 1932 S.C. 290, L.P. Clyde at p. 297, L. Blackburn at p. 298 (triennial).
5 For examples, see §§ 119 (loan), 122 (trust), 132, sub-para. (c) (prescription), 135 (sexennial), 137, sub-para. (d) (triennial), 282 (*rei interventus*), 284, sub-para. (b) (homologation).
6 See § 307, sub-para. (e). See also § 273.
7 See § 305.
8 See § 305.
9 *MacBain* v. *MacBain*, 1930 S.C. (H.L.) 72, L.C. Hailsham at p. 75 (sexennial); *Paterson* v. *Paterson*, 1897, 25 R. 144, at pp. 168, 174, 175, 190 (loan); *Fisher* v. *Fisher's Trustees*, 1952 S.C. 347, where, in a case concerning a contract relating to heritage, reference was made to a decision on loan.
10 *Paterson* v. *Paterson*, 1897, 25 R. 144 (loan).

petent to show that he did.[11] Entries in a party's business books are his writ.[12] Even unsigned jottings in books may be writ if they are admitted or proved to be holograph.[13] The authenticity of the signature or the fact that the writing is holograph may be proved by parole evidence.[14] Markings by the debtor on the back of a bill of interest paid are his writ,[15] and so may be a minute of meeting approved by him.[16] Even when the debtor is in a sense acting on behalf of the creditor, a writ granted by him in that capacity is his. Where the debtor acted as factor on the trust estate of the creditor, entries by the factor in the trust cash book were held to be his writ,[15] and an inventory which included a debt due by the executor, was, when signed by him, his writ.[17] Where the defender had signed and delivered an unqualified acknowledgment of receipt of money, a proof was allowed before answer of his averment that he was acting only as an agent.[18] With regard to one case[19] it is doubtful whether the loan was proved by the actual writ of the borrower or her constructive writ, or as to whether it was a case of proof by writ at all.[20]

304.   CONSTRUCTIVE WRIT OF PARTY

(a) **General.** A document written by another person may be the writ of the party, and parole evidence is competent to show that it is.

(b) **Agent.** The most obvious example is the writ of an authorised agent, solicitor,[21] banker,[22] factor,[23] partner[24] or cashier.[24] But the agent's authority, if not admitted, must be proved,[25] and it must be shown that his authority was either specific or otherwise sufficient to bind the principal.[26]

---

[11] *Christie's Trustees* v. *Muirhead*, 1870, 8 M. 461 (loan); *Mackenzie* v. *Stewart*, 1848 9 D. 611, at pp. 633, 639, 641, 645 (proof of promise of marriage), referred to in *Thoms* v. *Thoms*, 1867, 6 M. 174, at p. 177 (relief).

[12] *Jackson* v. *Ogilvie's Executor*, 1935 S.C. 154, at p. 163 (sexennial); *Hope* v. *Derwent Rolling Mills Co., Ltd.*, 1905, 7 F. 837 (loan); *Thomson* v. *Lindsay*, 1873, 1 R. 65 (trust); *Walker* v. *Buchanan, Kennedy & Co.*, 1857, 20 D. 259 (trust); *Seth* v. *Hain*, 1855, 17 D. 1117 (trust: the proof failed).

[13] *Storeys* v. *Paxton*, 1878, 6 R. 293 (sexennial: the proof failed); *Wink* v. *Speirs*, 1868, 6 M. 657 (loan: the proof failed).

[14] *Borland* v. *Macdonald, Ltd.*, 1940 S.C. 124, at pp. 137, 138 (triennial); *Dunn's Trustee* v. *Hardy*, 1896, 23 R. 621, at p. 633 (loan).

[15] *Drummond* v. *Lees*, 1880, 7 R. 452 (sexennial and vicennial).

[16] *Devlin* v. *McKelvie*, 1915 S.C. 180 (relief). As to minutes, see § 221.

[17] *Jackson* v. *Ogilvie's Executor* (*supra*) (sexennial).

[18] *Welsh's Trustees* v. *Forbes*, 1885, 12 R. 851 (loan: a decision unlikely to be extended: see L. Rutherfurd Clark at p. 862, L. Craighill at p. 863).

[19] *Laidlaw* v. *Shaw*, 1886, 13 R. 724 (loan).

[20] See *Dunn's Trustee* v. *Hardy* (*supra*), at p. 634, and *Paterson* v. *Paterson* (*supra*), at pp. 180, 187.

[21] *Dryburgh* v. *Macpherson*, (O.H.) 1944 S.L.T. 116 (loan), approved and distinguished in *Fisher* v. *Fisher's Trs.*, 1952 S.C. 347 (heritage: unusual and innominate contract).

[22] *Clark's Executrix* v. *Brown*, 1935 S.C. 110, at pp. 116, 118, 122 (loan).

[23] *Smith* v. *Falconer*, 1831, 9 S. 474 (triennial).

[24] *Bryan* v. *Butters Brothers & Co.*, 1892, 19 R. 490 (loan).

[25] *Smith* v. *Smith*, 1869, 8 M. 239 (loan).

[26] *McGregor* v. *McGregor*, 1860, 22 D. 1264 (sexennial).

While an express admission on record of the subsistence of the obligation renders proof unnecessary,[27] pleadings signed by counsel or solicitor are not, unless specially authorised, the writ of the party.[27] They therefore cannot be used merely as a basis for an inference.[27]

(c) Creditor's Writ. Documents granted by the creditor and received and retained by the debtor become constructively the debtor's writ. He is taken to have retained them for his own proper purposes. This rule was applied to the following documents retained by a debtor: receipts granted by the creditor,[28] a letter from the creditor acknowledging receipt of interest,[29] and a letter from the creditor explaining the trust.[30] A letter from the creditor to which the debtor's letter is a reply may be looked at to explain the latter, and so becomes the debtor's writ.[31] Diligence has been granted to recover the creditor's letter to which the debtor's is an answer.[32]

305. DELIVERY

Whether delivery is necessary depends on the terms of the writ. If it is merely an unqualified acknowledgment of receipt of money, no inference of liability to repay arises without delivery.[33] But if it actually acknowledges the obligation or is so expressed as to justify an inference of liability, delivery is unnecessary. Entries in an alleged debtor's books may be his writ, although the creditor knew nothing about them until long after they were made,[34] and the creditor may obtain a diligence for recovery of writs on which he hopes to rely.[34] A letter written by a landlord to the inspector of taxes was held to be his writ in a question with a person claiming the tenancy of a farm.[35] In the same case Lord President McNeill expressed the opinion that a letter written to a third party refusing a lease on the ground that the farm was already let to A.B. could be founded on by A.B.[36] This decision was not cited in a subsequent case[37] where the writ founded on was the inventory of a

---

27 *Darnley* v. *Kirkwood*, 1845, 7 D. 595, at pp. 598, 600, 602 (sexennial); *Campbell* v. *Grierson*, 1848, 10 D. 361 (quinquennial and triennial); *Cullen* v. *Smeal*, 1853, 15 D. 868, at p. 879 (triennial). See also § **132**, sub-para. (b).

28 *Campbell's Trs.* v. *Hudson's Exr.*, 1895, 22 R. 943, at pp. 948, 953 (sexennial); *Wood* v. *Howden*, 1843, 5 D. 507 (sexennial).

29 *Wood* v. *Howden* (*supra*).

30 *Thomson* v. *Lindsay*, 1873, 1 R. 65 (trust).

31 *MacBain* v. *MacBain*, 1930 S.C. (H.L.) 72 (sexennial); *Rennie* v. *Urquhart*, 1880, 7 R. 1030 (sexennial). As to the importance of producing the whole correspondence, see *McKeen* v. *Adair*, 1864, 2 M. 392 (loan).

32 *Stevenson* v. *Kyle*, 1849, 11 D. 1086 (triennial). See *Fiske* v. *Walpole*, 1860, 22 D. 1488 (triennial).

33 See § **62**.

34 *Hope* v. *Derwent Rolling Mills Co., Ltd.*, 1905, 7 F. 837 (loan); *Walker* v. *Buchanan, Kennedy & Co.*, 1857, 20 D. 259 (trust). As to diligence, see *Paterson* v. *Paterson*, 1897, 25 R. 144, at p. 184; *Walker* v. *Buchanan, Kennedy & Co.* at p. 260; *Seth* v. *Hain*, 1855, 17 D. 1117, at p. 1118 (trust).

35 *Emslie* v. *Duff*, 1865, 3 M. 854 (lease). See also *Wilson* v. *Scott*, (O.H.) 1908, 15 S.L.T. 948 (triennial: admission in letter to third party).

36 *Cf. Wink* v. *Speirs*, 1868, 6 M. 657, L. Neaves at p. 658.

37 *Jackson* v. *Ogilvie's Exr.*, 1935 S.C. 154 (sexennial).

deceased person's estate, and the opinion of the Lord President, though not those of the other judges, suggests that delivery or some equivalent was required. But, although delivery of a writ in such terms is not necessary, it must be clear from the writ itself and the surrounding circumstances that the writer is committing himself seriously[38] to a statement from which the relevant admission of liability or of the obligation may be inferred. A letter from the alleged debtor to his brother saying, "I am sorry I cannot help you, as I already owe Aunt Mary £1,000 myself," is much stronger proof of the debt to Aunt Mary than a holograph scrap of paper bearing the words, "I owe Aunt Mary £1,000," found in a box of Christmas decorations and possibly a relic of a family game. Entries in regularly kept books, taken into account in balancing, are better evidence than an isolated note, the purpose of which is doubtful.[39]

306. WRIT OF TRUSTEE OR EXECUTOR

If a creditor has a claim against the estate, his action must be against the executor,[40] and as he is the pursuer's "party" there seems no reason in principle why his writ as executor should not be evidence against him in that capacity. There does not seem to be any reported decision to that effect, but an executor was held to have homologated an informal acknowledgment of loan by the deceased.[41] A decree against the executor, however, may still leave open the question whether he is entitled as against the beneficiaries to take credit for the amount in the decree.[40] A different situation arises in a multiplepoinding where the executor is not a claimant. He is not the "party" of any of the claimants, and they cannot use his writ in the competition. The position might be different if a trustee or an executor were a claimant.[42]

307. PAROLE EVIDENCE

(a) General. The phrase, "writ sufficient to let in parole proof," or similar words, used in some of the cases,[43] is very general and may be misleading. It was explained by Lord Kinnear:— "If the documents are insufficient to prove the alleged loan, I am unable to see upon what grounds

---

38 "For the purpose of being acted on as true debts"; *Briggs* v. *Swan's Exrs.*, 1854, 16 D. 385, L. Wood at p. 394.

39 *Storeys* v. *Paxton*, 1878, 6 R. 293 (sexennial and vicennial).

40 *Briggs* v. *Swan's Exrs.*, 1854, 16 D. 385, L. J-Cl. Hope at p. 389 (interruption of long negative prescription).

41 *McCalman* v. *McArthur*, 1864, 2 M. 678 (loan). Since the decision in *Paterson* v. *Paterson*, 1897, 25 R. 144 (loan) the informal writing would have been enough without homologation.

42 This was pointed out by L. Shand in *Farquhar* v. *Farquhar*, 1886, 13 R. 596, where in a multiplepoinding a claimant proposed to refer to the oath of trustees, the real raisers. In *Dunn's Trustee* v. *Hardy*, 1896, 23 R. 621 (loan), a multiplepoinding, the court held that a claimant could not use the writ of a deceased trustee or that of competing claimants, the latter partly on the ground that it was not probative, an untenable view since *Paterson* v. *Paterson* (*supra*).

43 e.g. by L. Deas in *Williamson* v. *Allan*, 1882, 9 R. 859, at p. 865 (loan). This decision is explained in *Dunn's Trustee* v. *Hardy*, 1896, 231 R. 621, at p. 634 (loan).

they should be held sufficient to let in parole evidence. The rule is that loans cannot be proved except by the writ of the borrower. It is quite consistent with the rule to admit parole evidence of facts extrinsic to the writing, in order to prove that it is in truth and in law the borrower's writ. It may be necessary, and it is perfectly competent, to prove handwriting, or to prove delivery, or, it may be, to prove the authority of an agent. . . . But parole evidence is not admissible except for the purpose of enabling the creditor to prove the loan, not by the parole evidence itself, but by his debtor's writ."[44] In some cases,[45] where proof had been led, the Inner House considered it without deciding that it was competent. In addition to proving that the writ is actually[46] or constructively[47] that of the debtor, there appear to be four purposes for which parole evidence is competent.

(b) Amount of Debt. Once the existence of the obligation has been established by writ, the amount of the debt may be proved by parole evidence.[48] In the case of a solicitor's business account this is done by taxation.[49] A conclusion for declarator of trust may be accompanied by conclusions for an accounting, in which objections may be supported by parole.[50] Where the writ admits some debt, and there is no debt other than that sued for to which the admission could apply, the identification is sufficient.[51]

(c) Date of Writ. This may be proved by parole evidence.[52]

(d) Delivery. Where necessary,[53] this may be proved by parole evidence.[44]

(e) Circumstances. "In any proof *scripto* the court must have before it the circumstances which called for the writings and which were before the parties when they were written. In the case of correspondence particularly, it may be impossible to understand the effect of the alleged debtor's letters without taking into account, not only the terms of the letters to which they are an answer, but also the circumstances in which the alleged debtor wrote them."[54] Although this passage is expressed in general terms, "parole

---

[44] *Dunn's Trustee* v. *Hardy* (*supra*), at p. 633.
[45] *Thomson* v. *Geekie*, 1861, 23 D. 693 (loan).
[46] See §303.
[47] See §304.
[48] *Borland* v. *Macdonald, Ltd.*, 1940 S.C. 124, at pp. 130, 138 (triennial); *Johnson* v. *Tillie, Whyte & Co.*, 1917 S.C. 211 (triennial); *Wilson* v. *Scott*, (O.H.) 1908, 15 S.L.T. 948 (triennial); *Stevenson* v. *Kyle*, 1850 12 D. 673 (triennial); *Rutherford's Exrs.* v. *Marshall*, 1861, 23 D. 1276 (loan), in which no opinions are reported, seems to be a contrary decision.
[49] *Macandrew* v. *Hunter*, 1851, 13 D. 1111 (triennial).
[50] *Walker* v. *Buchanan Kennedy & Co.*, 1857, 20 D. 259 (trust); *Seth* v. *Hain*, 1855, 17 D. 1117 (trust). The terms of the trust may be proved parole. See §122.
[51] *Rennie* v. *Urquhart*, 1880, 7 R. 1030 (sexennial); *Fiske* v. *Walpole*, 1860, 22 D. 1488 (triennial). Contrast *Blair* v. *Horn*, 1859, 21 D. 1004 (sexennial), where there were other debts to which the writ could have applied.
[52] *Williamson* v. *Allan* (*supra*), where an IOU bore an incorrect date and the true date was proved; *Evans* v. *Craig*, 1871, 9 M. 801, at p. 803 (loan).
[53] See §305.

evidence is not admissible except for the purpose of enabling the creditor to prove the loan, not by the parole evidence itself, but by his debtor's writ."[55] It is not easy to illustrate the extent of the rule. In *Robb & Co.*[54] the parole evidence appears to have been used to establish (1) that the letters were actually or constructively those of the defender and (2) that they had passed between the parties. In *Jackson*,[56] where the inventory of a deceased's estate signed by the executor was held to be the writ of the executor as an individual, the only disputed circumstance appears to have been whether the executor acquiesced in the inclusion of his debt in the inventory, and understood the effect of so doing. This suggests that if the solicitors had included the debt without saying anything to the executor, and he had signed without noticing it, the inventory would, or at least might, not have been held to be his personal writ. Where the writ was partly in the handwriting of the creditor, but included a receipt and signature by the debtor, proof was allowed as to whether the document was in "its present state" when signed by the defender.[57]

(f) Interlocutor allowing Proof. A difference of opinion arose in *Clark's Executrix* v. *Brown*[58] as to the correct form of interlocutor. The majority held that the appropriate interlocutor sanctioned by practice is to allow proof *habili modo*. This leaves all questions of admissibility to be settled at the proof or, more usually, to be reserved. The Lord Justice-Clerk (Aitchison) strongly dissented, holding that the interlocutor ought to specify what the parole proof was to be about. It is true that practice does sanction the general form, though in at least two cases the court pronounced a precise interlocutor.[57] But in a more recent case the sheriff-substitute specifically allowed the pursuer to adduce any competent evidence to show that the documents were the authentic writs of the defender. This interlocutor was read by the Lord Justice-Clerk (Thomson) in the course of his opinion and he made no adverse comment on it.[59] There seems little doubt that it is better expressly to limit the parole proof to such of the disputed averments as require, and are capable of, such proof.

---

[54] *Robb & Co.* v. *Stornoway Pier and Harbour Commission*, 1932 S.C. 290, L.P. Clyde at p. 296 (triennial). See also §273.

[55] *Dunn's Trustee* v. *Hardy* (*ut supra*).

[56] *Jackson* v. *Ogilvie's Exr*, 1935 S.C. 154 (sexennial).

[57] *Christie's Trustees* v. *Muirhead*, 1870, 8 M. 461 (loan); *Johnston* v. *Scott*, 1860, 22 D. 393, at p. 395. *Cf. Hope* v. *Derwent Rolling Mills Co., Ltd.*, where a proof, apparently *prout de jure*, was allowed, and at the end the court picked out the writs on which loan was held proved.

[58] 1935 S.C. 110 (loan). See also observations in *Gill* v. *Gill*, 1907 S.C. 532 (loan).

[59] *Hamilton* v. *Hamilton's Executrix*, 1950 S.C. 39 (sexennial).

CHAPTER XXV

OATH OF PARTY

308. GENERAL

Reference to the oath of party is a form of procedure peculiar, it is thought, to Scotland[1] and competent only in civil causes.[2] Under it a litigant is entitled, except in certain circumstances,[3] to require his opponent to answer on oath as to the truth of his case, or some specific part of it. Briefly, the procedure is that the party referring lodges a minute specifying the matters referred to his opponent's oath; the court sustains or refuses the minute; if the minute is sustained, the opponent must appear, take the oath and depone; and should he fail to do so, he is held as confessed, though he may be reponed.[4] Reference to oath has been described as a contract under which, if the reference is sustained, the party to whose oath reference is made must depone on pain of being held as confessed and the party referring undertakes to be bound by his opponent's answers.[5] These answers are thus not evidence in the ordinary sense, since, in spite of stray dicta about believing the deponent, they must be accepted—challenge or contradiction is incompetent,[5] and even the conviction of the deponent for perjury does not affect the matter.[6] The procedure was developed when a party was not a competent witness in his own cause, and it enabled a litigant to appeal against the apparent effect of the evidence of competent witnesses to the conscience

---

[1] *Longworth* v. *Yelverton*, 1867, 5 M. (H.L.) 144, at p. 145; *Paterson* v. *Paterson*, 1897, 25 R. 144, at p. 152.
[2] Bell, *Principles*, §2263. See also §117.
[3] See §§314 *et seq.*
[4] See §319.
[5] *Longworth* v. *Yelverton*, 1865, 3 M. 645, at pp. 656-683, where the matter was fully considered, 1867, 5 M. (H.L.) 144. For the facts of this case, see §317, sub-para. (c).
[6] Bell, *Principles*, §2265; *Penney* v. *Aitken*, 1927 S.C. 673, at p. 681.

of his opponent.[7] It was expressly saved when parties became competent witnesses.[8]

309. STAGE OF CASE

Reference to oath is competent at any time after preliminary pleas have been disposed of until extract of the final judgment, including that of the House of Lords.[9] In one exceptional case[10] a reference was with difficulty sustained before the record was closed on the ground of the party's advanced age. The practice of allowing a reference "before answer"[11] is "wholly inconsistent with the notion of a proper reference to oath of party,"[12] and is not likely ever to be revived.[13] A minute tendered under reservation of an objection to the other party's title was refused.[14] If a party states a preliminary plea, but, before it is disposed of, depones on a reference to his oath, he is held to have abandoned it.[15]

Reference after judgment had passed was allowed where decree on the merits had been extracted, but the auditor's report on expenses had not been approved,[16] and where, after absolvitor and decree for the taxed expenses, the process was transmitted to the extractor, but extract had not been issued.[17] In a suspension a reference is competent before issue of the certificate of refusal,[18] and where after a reclaiming motion the cause has been remitted to the Lord Ordinary to deal with expenses.[19] If the reference is sustained after judgment and the effect of the oath is to contradict the decree granted, the court must recall its own decree.[20]

---

[7] *Pattinson* v. *Robertson*, 1846, 9 D. 226, at p. 229; *Adam* v. *Maclachlan*, 1846, 9 D. 560, at p. 576. In *Murray* v. *Murray*, 1839, 1 D. 484, the defenders obtained a verdict. The cause was then referred to their oath, their oath was held affirmative of the pursuer's case, and decree passed against them. Moreover, they were found liable in the whole expenses, including those of the jury trial, on the ground that they had "all along been maintaining a plea contrary to equity and good conscience."

[8] Evidence (Scotland) Act, 1853 (16 Vict. c. 20), s. 5. See also §117.

[9] *Longworth* v. *Yelverton*, 1865, 3 M. 645, at pp. 660, 666, 672, 5 M. (H.L.) 144, at pp. 145 (but the closing of the record is not necessarily the correct *terminus a quo*), 150.

[10] *Riley* v. *McLaren*, 1853, 16 D. 323. In spite of the rubric and what Dickson says (*Evidence* (3rd ed.) §1423), it does not appear that the oath was to lie *in retentis*, in the sense that if the party survived till the appropriate stage of the case his oath would be taken again.

[11] *Anstruther* v. *Wilkie*, 1856, 18 D. 405, where L. Cowan's dissent was thinly veiled; *Grant* v. *Marshall, Ramsay & Co.*, 1851, 13 D. 500.

[12] *Adam* v. *Maclachlan*, 1847, 9 D. 560, L. J-Cl. Hope at p. 572.

[13] Dickson, *Evidence* (3rd ed.) §§1423, 1424.

[14] *Turnbull* v. *Borthwick*, 1830, 7 S. 735. The hints in the opinions that the defender might have deponed under reservation of his plea of "no title to sue" are inconsistent with *Adam* v. *Maclachlan* (*supra*).

[15] *Henderson* v. *Smith*, 1852, 14 D. 583.

[16] *Drew* v. *Drew*, 1855, 17 D. 784.

[17] *Aikman* v. *Aikman's Trustees*, 1867, 6 M. 277. Consignation of expenses was made a condition.

[18] *Macdonald* v. *Cooper*, 1848, 10 D. 740.

[19] *Brown* v. *Ferguson*, 1852, 14 D. 841.

[20] See *Brown* v. *Edgley*, 1843, 5 D. 1087, interlocutor of the sheriff-substitute at p. 1089; *Hamilton's Exrs.* v. *Struthers*, 1858, 21 D. 51, interlocutor at p. 56.

310. MINUTE OF REFERENCE: PROCEDURE

The procedure must be initiated by lodging a minute referring to the opponent's oath,[21] and this is the stage for stating any objection. If a party allows the minute to be sustained and appears and depones without objection, he cannot afterwards maintain that the reference ought not to have been sustained,[22] but if an objection is taken and repelled, it may be repeated on appeal, although the party has deponed.[23] In the Court of Session, if the reference is after judgment, it must be by petition or note,[24] and the minute, petition or note is signed by counsel, whose general mandate is sufficient.[25] In the sheriff court the minute may be signed either by the party or by his solicitor.[26] It has been held that the solicitor requires an express written mandate.[27] If the minute is sustained, there must be an interlocutor to that effect.[28]

311. MINUTE OF REFERENCE: TERMS

(a) **General.** Since the oath is, or at least ought to be, interpreted under reference to the minute,[29] the framing of the minute is a matter for careful consideration.[30] It must on the one hand be sufficiently wide that an affirmative oath will establish what must be proved by oath.[31] This need not be the party's whole case. Part may be admitted,[32] or proved by writ,[33] or already decided,[34] or capable of proof by parole evidence.[35] On the other hand, by including unnecessary matter the party takes the risk that some

---

21 *Brown* v. *Mason*, 1856, 19 D. 137, L. Curriehill at p. 138.

22 *Turnbull* v. *Borthwick*, 1830, 8 S. 735; *Hewit* v. *Pollock*, 1821, 1 S. 167.

23 *Hamilton* v. *Hamilton's Executrix*, 1950 S.C. 39; *Dewar* v. *Pearson*, 1862, 4 M. 493. But cf. *Broom* v. *Edgley*, 1843, 5 D. 1087, a decision to the opposite effect.

24 *Longworth* v. *Yelverton*, 1865, 3 M. 645, at pp. 660, 666; *Winton & Co.* v. *Thomson & Co.*, 1862, 24 D. 1094.

25 Dickson, *Evidence* (3rd ed.) §1444.

26 Sheriff Courts (Scotland) Act, 1907 (7 Edw. VII. c. 51), Rule 64.

27 *Grahams* v. *Ferguson*, 1775, M. 12, 249: *Inglis* v. *Fuller*, 1712, M. 12,249; *Hardie* v. *Allan*, 1709, M. 12,248.

28 *Pollok* v. *Whiteford*, 1936 S.C. 402; *Fraser* v. *Bruce*, 1857, 20 D. 115, where the court refused to consider the deposition because there was no minute, and consequently no interlocutor sustaining a minute.

29 See §321.

30 *Penney* v. *Aitken*, 1927 S.C. 673, where there was a difference of opinion as to the meaning of the minute.

31 *Megget* v. *Brown*, 1827, 5 S. 343. It is difficult to see how in *Penney* v. *Aitken* (*supra*) an oath which merely affirmed that the pursuer had paid the defender £100, as the sheriffs and L. Hunter held, led to decree.

32 *Darnley* v. *Kirkwood*, 1845, 7 D. 595, L. Mackenzie at p. 598, L. Fullerton at p. 600. See §132, sub-para. (b).

33 *Deans* v. *Steele*, 1853, 16 D. 317 (resting owing referred to defender's oath on assumption that constitution proved by writ).

34 *Cameron* v. *Armstrong*, 1851, 13 D. 1256 (birth of child proved parole: paternity referred to defender's oath); *Campbell* v. *Turner*, 1822, 1 S. 500 (bill for £150 reduced to £120 and onerosity of balance referred to oath).

35 *Finlay* v. *Outram*, 1851, 14 D. 48 (terms of contract proved by pursuer's oath and defective performance proved by parole: L. J-Cl. Hope criticised with some justification the form of the minute of reference and the use made of the deposition by the majority).

point which he could have established *aliter* is decided against him on the oath.[36] The minute must state distinctly what is referred, making clear the point to which the party referring desires an affirmative answer.[37] No fact can be referred unless it has been averred,[38] and, *a fortiori*, a party cannot refer a fact inconsistent with his own averments.[39] Where pursuers abandoned a conclusion for implement of a contract to feu and obtained an issue on their alternative conclusion for damages for deterioration to the ground caused by the defenders' occupation, a reference of the contract to the defenders' oath was refused.[40] When the whole cause is referred, the reference is of the facts on which the parties are at issue on record.[41]

(b) **What must be Referred.** Where the triennial, quinquennial or sexennial prescription applies, the statutes require that both constitution and resting owing must be proved by writ or oath, with a qualification in the case of the sexennial prescription.[42] Accordingly, in the absence of writ or explicit judicial admission, both constitution and resting owing must be referred, except in some cases to which the sexennial prescription applies.[42] Where prescription does not apply, but for some reason the pursuer elects, or is compelled, to try to prove an obligation by the defender's oath, he need refer only constitution, leaving it to the defender, if his oath is affirmative, to prove discharge by any competent mode.[43] In spite of *obiter* dicta to the contrary,[44] it is thought that this rule applies to loan. According to the institutional writers it is "the borrowing of money" which cannot be proved by witnesses,[45] and Gloag uses the phrase "the fact that money has been lent."[46] There is no actual decision, but in three cases the court proceeded on a reference of constitution only.[47] The point is not of great importance *quoad* loan, since the court regards a deposition of payment as intrinsic.[48]

---

[36] *Fraser* v. *Bruce*, 1857, 20 D. 115, where loan was proved *scripto* and the pursuer made an incompetent attempt to refer resting owing to the defender's oath, unnecessarily as the Lord Ordinary observed.
[37] *Finlay* v. *Outram (supra)*, at p. 53. In *Sinclair* v. *McBeath*, 1869, 7 M. 934, there is an example of how a fact ought to be referred.
[38] *McFarlane* v. *Scott*, 1828, 6 S. 1095.
[39] *Napier* v. *Graham*, 1874, 1 R. 906, L. Neaves at p. 909.
[40] *Gordon* v. *Stewart*, 1868, 7 M. 248. The rubric and the last sentence of the Lord President's opinion are wrong. The conclusion was not for damages for breach of contract. It assumed that no contract was proved.
[41] *Penney* v. *Aitken (supra)*, at pp. 677, 682.
[42] See §134.
[43] *Fraser* v. *Bruce (supra)*, where, the constitution of loan having been proved *scripto* and decree granted, the court allowed the defender to lodge a minute of reference to the pursuer's oath, to prove repayment.
[44] *Gow's Exrs.* v. *Sim*, 1866, 4 M. 578, L. Cowan at p. 581; *Chrystal* v. *Chrystal*, 1900, 2 F. 373, L.P. Balfour at p. 378; *Penney* v. *Aitken (supra)*, L. Ormidale at p. 679.
[45] Stair, iv, 43, 4; Erskine, iv, 2, 20.
[46] *Contract* (2nd ed.), 192.
[47] *Chrystal* v. *Chrystal (supra)*, at p. 374; *Newlands* v. *McKinlay*, 1885, 13 R. 353; *Mackay* v. *Monro*, 1871, 8 S.L.R. 438, where the rubric is inaccurate. The reference was of constitution only, and the majority so treated it, holding that the oath disclosed an intrinsic qualification.
[48] See §321, sub-para. (c).

(c) After Judgment. Although it has been said that after judgment the whole case must be referred,[49] this does not appear to be universally true. A separate point may be referred,[50] if an affirmative oath would overturn the judgment, even although not leading to a final decision in favour of the party referring.[51]

312. RETRACTION OF REFERENCE

A party may withdraw the reference at any time before his opponent has deponed,[52] on cause shown,[53] or at least unless the reference was made from improper motives, e.g., to obtain delay,[54] or the opponent would be prejudiced.[55] It is usually a condition that the party referring pays all expenses.[54]

313. DEFERENCE

If the party to whose oath reference is made alleges that he cannot speak distinctly to the facts, he may defer to the oath of his opponent. It is then for the court to decide which party should depone.[56] If the deference is sustained the case is decided on the oath of the party originally referring.[57] The latest reported case mentioning deference was in 1828.[58]

314. REFUSAL OF REFERENCE: GENERAL

While it is the general right of a party to refer to his opponent's oath, there are circumstances in which the court will refuse to sustain the reference. Attempts have been made to distinguish the reasons for refusal depending on competency from those depending on the exercise of discretion, but it is of little practical importance.[59] The interlocutors frequently merely refuse the reference, leaving the reason to be gathered from the opinions or speeches, sometimes a task of difficulty.[60] It is proposed therefore in this

---

[49] *Longworth* v. *Yelverton*, 1865, 3 M. 645, at pp. 660, 666, 681; 1867, 5 M. (H.L.) 144.
[50] *Sinclair* v. *McBeath*, 1869, 7 M. 934.
[51] *Broom* v. *Edgley*, 1843, 5 D. 1097.
[52] Dickson, *Evidence* (3rd ed.) §1445.
[53] *Galbraith* v. *McNeill*, 1828, 7 S. 63.
[54] *Jameson* v. *Wilson*, 1853, 15 D. 414, L.O. at p. 415.
[55] *Dick* v. *Hutton*, 1876, 3 R. 448.
[56] Dickson, *Evidence* (3rd ed.) §1447; Stair, iv, 44, 13; Erskine, iv, 2, 8.
[57] *Ridland* v. *Sinclair*, 1613, Court Book of Orkney and Shetland, edited by Barclay, p. 82. The pursuer sued for £8, the price of goods sold to the defender, and referred his claim to the defender's oath. The defender deferred, and the pursuer's oath established his claim to the extent of £5 6s. 8d.
[58] *Galbraith* v. *McNeill*, 1828, 7 S. 63.
[59] There are some clear cases of incompetence, e.g., where the party has already called his opponent and examined him as a witness, and in such cases the court obviously *must* refuse the reference.
[60] In *Longworth* v. *Yelverton*, 1865, 3 M. 645, 1867, 7 M. (H.L.) 144, the majority in the Court of Session refused the reference as matter of discretion. Lord Deas, who dissented, must have thought it competent, and Lord Ardmillan expressly said so, but in the House of Lords the Lord Chancellor, with whom Lord Cranworth agreed, held that the reference was incompetent on the strength of Lord President McNeill's opinion

and the next four paragraphs to consider the grounds on which references are refused, without enquiring closely in every case into the theoretical background.

Where it is sought to establish a right which can only be constituted by writing, a reference is useless and therefore refused. So an oath cannot take the place of a feudal conveyance,[61] or of a lease for a term of years,[62] or of a will. A local custom cannot be referred to oath.[63] It is incompetent to refer to oath a matter which parties have agreed to submit to the decision of a judicial referee or an arbiter.[64] The obvious reason is that if parties have agreed that the question at issue shall be decided in one way, one of them cannot be compelled to change to a different method. It is a good reason for refusing a reference that the oath may prejudice the interests of a third party.[65]

315. QUESTION OF LAW

Since the purpose of a reference is to elicit facts, a reference on a question of law will be refused.[66] Where a plea of *res judicata* was sustained on the pleadings, a reference was refused on the ground that the question was one of law.[67] But a mixed question of fact and law may be referred, leaving the court to make the distinction in construing the oath.[68] What began as a reference of mixed fact and law (whether the sum claimed was due) was on one occasion neatly turned by the Lord Ordinary into a reference of pure fact (what was the agreement and whether it was erroneously stated in the lease).[69]

316. PARTY EXAMINED AS WITNESS

A litigant who has called and examined his opponent as a witness may not refer the cause "or any part of it" to his oath.[70] The purpose of this is that the party should not be re-examined on the same subject.[71] So where

in the Court of Session. Lord Westbury gave no opinion, and the Lord President, who had meantime become Lord Colonsay, impliedly repudiated the Lord Chancellor's construction of his opinion.

[61] Bell, *Principles*, §2263.
[62] *Perdikou* v. *Pattison*, 1957 S.L.T. 153. The position may be different if there is *rei interventus* or homologation. See §§ 280 *et seq.*
[63] Dickson, *Evidence* (3rd ed.) §1426.
[64] *McLaren* v. *Shore*, 1883, 10 R. 1067. The ground of decision of the majority was narrower, but Lord Shand proceeded on the view stated in the text, and Lord Mure agreed with it.
[65] *Longworth* v. *Yelverton* (*supra*). For the facts of this case, see § 317, sub-para. (c).
[66] *Conacher* v. *Robertson*, 1829, 8 S. 141.
[67] *Sawers* v. *Clark*, 1892, 19 R. 1090, at p. 1092. See also *Kirkpatrick* v. *Bell*, 1864, 2 M. 1396, where there was a difference of opinion as to whether there was any relevant fact in dispute. For the sequel see 1864, 3 M. 252.
[68] This is a possible explanation of *Anstruther* v. *Wilkie*, 1856, 18 D. 405, where the reference was allowed "reserving all questions as to the relevancy and sufficiency of the averments offered to be proved." See § 309.
[69] *Lawson* v. *Murray*, 1829, 5 S. 380, commended in *Sinclair* v. *McBeath*, 1869, 7 M. 934.
[70] Evidence (Scotland) Act, 1853 (16 & 17 Vict. c. 20), s. 5.
[71] *Dewar* v. *Pearson*, 1866, 4 M. 493.

part of the pursuer's case was provable by parole and he adduced the defender and examined him on that part, it was held competent to refer the other part of the case, which was provable only by writ or oath, to the defender's oath.[71] Again, where a person was called and examined by the pursuer in the course of a proof by writ, but only as to whether the writ was that of the defender, and later was herself sisted as defender *qua* executrix of the original defender, the court sustained a reference of the whole cause to her oath.[72] A party was called and examined by his opponent in a proof which was later held to be incompetent, and a reference to his oath was sustained.[73] It appears to have been assumed that examination of an opponent on commission would not bar a reference to his oath.[74] Although the Act does not deal with the case of a party who has given evidence on his own behalf, the court will not, unless in exceptional circumstances, allow a reference to his oath, if his opponent has cross-examined him on the merits.[75]

317. CONSISTORIAL CAUSES

(a) **General.** The whole cause cannot be referred to oath.[76] This decision proceeds on section 36 of the Court of Session Act, 1830,[77] and therefore applies to all consistorial causes enumerated in the Act.[78]

(b) **Marriage by Promise Subsequente Copula.**[79] *Longworth* v. *Yelverton*[76] does not in terms cover this, since part of the case may be proved by parole evidence. It was firmly established that the promise might be proved either by the defender's writ or by his oath, and it does not seem to have occurred to Lord Justice-Clerk Inglis that the 1830 Act made any difference to that rule.[80] The opinion, however, has been expressed that in view of *Longworth*[76] proof of the promise by oath is incompetent.[81] This is certainly not a well recognised doctrine,[82] and in the latest case opinions were reserved.[83]

(c) **Longworth v. Yelverton.** In this leading case[76] the pursuer concluded for declarator that she and the defender were married. Before the action was raised, but after the date of the alleged marriage, the defender had gone through a ceremony of marriage with a Mrs. Forbes, who lived with him as his wife and bore him children. The Lord Ordinary assoilzied the defender,

---

[72] *Hamilton* v. *Hamilton's Executrix.*, 1950 S.C. 39.
[73] *Swanson* v. *Gallie*, 1870, 9 M. 208.
[74] *Laing* v. *Nixon*, 1866, 4 M. 327. It is stated in the rubric, though not expressly in the body of the report, that the pursuer waived his right to refer to the defender's oath.
[75] *Macleay* v. *Campbell*, 1876, 3 R. 999.
[76] *Longworth* v. *Yelverton*, 1867, 5 M. (H.L.) 144.
[77] 11 Geo. IV. and 1 Will. IV. c. 69.
[78] Declarators of marriage and of nullity, of legitimacy and bastardy, and divorce and judicial separation. See § **158.**
[79] Incompetent since 1st July, 1940: Marriage (Scotland) Act, 1939 (2 & 3 Geo. VI. c. 34), s. 5: Marriage (Scotland) Act, 1939 (Commencement) Order, 1940. See § **156,** sub-para. (c)
[80] *Ross* v. *Macleod*, 1861, 23 D. 972.
[81] Walton, *Husband and Wife* (3rd ed.), 29.
[82] *Mackie* v. *Mackie*, 1917 S.C. 276.
[83] *Lindsay* v. *Lindsay*, 1927 S.C. 395.

and his judgment, reversed by the Inner House, was restored by the House of Lords. When the Division was moved to apply the judgment of the House of Lords the pursuer referred the whole cause to the defender's oath. The latter opposed the reference on four grounds, (1) that after a judgment of the House of Lords it was incompetent, (2) that it might compel the defender to admit the crime of bigamy,[84] (3) that the interests of Mrs. Forbes and her children were involved, and (4) that it was incompetent in a consistorial action. Oddly enough, although this fourth was the main ground of decision of the majority in the House of Lords,[85] it does not seem to have been pressed in the Court of Session, and opinions were expressed against it. The first ground found no support at all. The Lord President did not commit himself on the second, but the other judges rejected it on the ground that all the defender would be asked to admit would be the marriage with the pursuer, which was not bigamous. The fact that he would *ipso facto* admit that his marriage to Mrs. Forbes was bigamous was regarded as irrelevant. It is not clear what the House of Lords thought about this. The decision of the Division (Lord Deas dissenting) was founded almost exclusively on the third ground, the interests of Mrs. Forbes and her children. In the House of Lords it formed an additional reason.

318. INCRIMINATION

It is a good ground for refusing a reference that the deponent might have to admit a crime. A reference was refused where the defenders might have had to admit that they had uttered forged letters[86] or that they had committed an assault,[87] and where the pursuer might have had to admit that he had granted receipts for less than he had received in order to defraud the revenue.[88] The matter must be criminal. A reference was sustained as to whether the defender had written a defamatory letter, which was not a criminal act, but refused as to whether he had written a threatening one, which was.[89] On principle it would appear that the objection would disappear if the party has been tried and either convicted or acquitted, or has been called as a witness for the prosecution, and two old cases support this view.[90]

319. HOLDING AS CONFESSED AND REPONING

If a person cited to appear and depone fails to appear he will be held as confessed, but if he can offer a good excuse he may be reponed.[91] He may also be held as confessed if he refuses to answer a proper question.[92]

---

84 As to incrimination, see § **318.**
85 The Lord Chancellor and Lord Cranworth. Lord Westbury gave no opinion, and Lord Colonsay did not commit himself. See § **314,** note 60.
86 *McEachern* v. *Ewing & Co.*, 1824, 3 S. 9.
87 *Miller and Smellie* v. *Brown*, 1828, 6 S. 561.
88 *Thomson* v. *Young*, 1828, 7 S. 32. As to bigamy see § **317,** sub-para. (c).
89 *McCallum* v. *McCall*, 1825, 3 S. 551.
90 *Jantzen* v. *Easton*, Feb. 3, 1814, F.C.; *Gordon* v. *Gordon*, 1731, 1 Pat. App. 60.
91 Erskine, iv, 2, 17; *Mitchells* v. *Moultrys*, 1882, 10 R. 378; *Miller* v. *Cooper*, 1835, 13 S. 369; *Drummond* v. *Gilmour*, 1832, 10 S. 266.
92 *Murray* v. *Murray*, 1839, 1 D. 484; *Longworth* v. *Yelverton*, 1867, 5 M. (H.L.) 144, at p. 148.

320. CONDUCT OF REFERENCE

(a) **General.** In the Court of Session the deposition is taken before a judge or a commissioner.[93] In the sheriff court the deposition is normally taken before the sheriff, and on a strict reading of the Act[94] he is not entitled to appoint a commissioner. It is for the commissioner to decide whether the deponent is physically and mentally fit to depone,[95] but where it was subsequently discovered that the deponent was unfit the deposition was withdrawn.[96] The deponent takes the oath or affirms, and is examined by counsel or solicitor for the party referring. He must answer all competent questions under penalty of being held as confessed,[97] and any statement volunteered by him must be received.[98] Documents may be put to him to refresh his memory.[99] The judge or commissioner may put questions,[1] but counsel or solicitor for the deponent has no such right,[2] though he may suggest questions to the judge,[2] refer the deponent to documents[3] and object to incompetent questions.[4] The commissioner must authenticate the report.[5]

(b) **Mode of Examination.** Although the deponent is examined on behalf of his opponent, it is not cross-examination, which is successful if either the witness makes admissions or is shown to be unreliable. Merely to show that the deponent on a reference to oath is unreliable does not advance matters. Accordingly, the examiner's purpose is not to catch him out in inaccuracies, but to induce him to admit the truth. This is done by proceeding from special to general, that is to say by putting questions on particular points, which it is anticipated he will have to admit, and leading him on till in view of these admissions he must admit the general point which has been referred to his oath.[6] If he does not make this general admission, either he

---

93 Evidence (Scotland) Act, 1866 (29 & 30 Vict. c. 112), s. 3. It seems doubtful whether the Act authorises the appointment of a commissioner, but it is done; *Cowbrough & Co.* v. *Robertson*, 1879, 6 R. 1301.

94 Sheriff Courts (Scotland) Act, 1907 (7 Edw. VII. c. 51), Rules 64, 65, 70. These provisions distinguish between a deposition (Rule 64) and evidence (Rule 70), and Rule 65 does not by necessary implication obliterate this distinction.

95 *Kirkpatrick* v. *Bell*, 1864, 2 M. 1396. The deponent in that case turned out to be unfit and unlikely ever to be fit to depone, and the reference was disregarded: 1864, 3 M. 252.

96 *Campbell* v. *Arnott*, 1836, 14 S. 505.

97 *Longworth* v. *Yelverton*, 1867, 7 M. (H.L.) 144, at p. 148; *Murray* v. *Murray*, 1839, 1 D. 484, at p. 485.

98 *Paterson* v. *Cowie's Exr.*, 1904, 7 F. (J.) 68.

99 *Boyd* v. *Kerr*, 1843, 5 D. 1213. Documents cannot be recovered under a diligence for this purpose; *Miller's Trustees* v. *McDonald*, (O.H.) 1931 S.L.T. 601. As to the use of documents in interpreting the oath, see § 321, sub-para. (b).

1 *Soutar* v. *Soutar*, 1851, 14 D. 140.

2 *Heslop* v. *Runcie*, 1894, 22 R. 83.

3 *Blair* v. *McPhun*, 1856, 18 D. 1202.

4 Dickson, *Evidence* (3rd ed.) §1486.

5 *Cleland* v. *P. & W. McLellan*, 1851, 13 D. 504.

6 Dickson's explanation of the practice (*Evidence* (3rd ed.) §1490) is that if the general question is put first and answered, any questions which involve contradiction of the answer are incompetent as involving the party in the risk of perjury. He founds on passages from Erskine and More's Notes to Stair, but both were dealing, not with the original examination, but with re-examination, i.e., a second and separate examination.

is in the awkward position of standing self-confessed as a liar, or the court may disregard his general denial and proceed on the inevitable inference from his previous admissions.[7] The court has taken this course even where the general question was put first.[8] In spite of the rules laid down as to the proper mode of examination, they are not always strictly observed,[8] and there does not seem to be any reported decision where an objection to a special question has been sustained on the ground that the answer would, or might, contradict the answer already given to a general question at that diet of examination. The true reason for the rule, or practice, it is thought, is that it is the most likely method to elicit the truth, as Stair himself says.[9]

(c) **Re-examination.** A second examination at a new diet may be allowed where the original deposition did not exhaust the reference[10] or was unintelligible,[11] where books referred to by the deponent should be produced,[12] to give the deponent an opportunity to consult books,[13] and where the party referring was excusably absent from the diet.[14] It seems to be settled by decision that at a re-examination the deponent cannot be asked any question the answer to which might contradict his answers at the first examination,[15] but this rule appears to rest on the erroneous theory that if a person contradicts himself when on oath he is guilty of perjury.[16] Even if the theory were sound, it is difficult to see why the court should intervene to protect a person who is prepared to commit perjury.[17]

321. INTERPRETATION AND EFFECT OF OATH

(a) **Credibility.** Since the only question is, what has the deponent sworn,[18] the question of credibility arises only in two cases. First, a general denial may be disregarded if the previous specific admissions lead to the inference that it is untrue.[19] Secondly, if the deponent, professing forgetfulness or ignorance, depones *non memini* or *nihil novi*, the reply is as a rule treated as negative, in the sense that it does not establish the matter referred.[20] But

To aver that a witness has contradicted himself is not a relevant charge of perjury: Hume, Crimes, I, 372 Macdonald, *Criminal Law* (5th ed.). 164.

7 *Heddle* v. *Baikie*, 1841, 3 D. 370, at pp. 373, 376, reversed on a construction of the minute and oath: 1843, 15 S. Jur. (H.L.) 559; *Murray* v. *Murray* (*supra*), at p. 485; *Hunter* v. *Geddes*, 1835, 13 S. 369, at p. 378.
8 *Heddle* v. *Baikie* (*supra*).
9 Stair, iv, 44, 11.
10 *Thomson* v. *Thomson*, 1830, 8 S. 571.
11 *Cooper* v. *Marshall*, 1877, 5 R. 258.
12 *Gordon* v. *Pratt*, 1860, 22 D. 903; *Young* v. *Pollock*, 1832, 10 S. 570.
13 *Anstruther* v. *Lewis*, 1851, 13 D. 841.
14 *Hill* v. *Cameron*, 1835, 13 S. 764.
15 Erskine, iv, 2, 15.
16 See note 6 (*supra*).
17 An analogous view was expressed in *Laing* v. *Nixon*, 1866, 4 M. 327, L.P. Inglis at p. 328.
18 See § 308.
19 See § 320, sub-para.(b).
20 Dickson, *Evidence* (3rd ed.) §1499; Erskine, iv, 14, 2. Both writers say that after a *non memini* the party referring may fall back on other proof, presumably competent proof.

where the fact is recent and such that the deponent must almost certainly have known about it and can hardly have forgotten, his answer may be disbelieved. He is then treated as if he had refused to answer and held as confessed, unless he can show some good reason for his ignorance or forgetfulness.[20]

(b) **General.** Where a deponent depones that he believes a fact to be true (sometimes called the "oath of credulity"[21]) he must state some good reason for his belief,[22] and if he admits facts which lead to a particular legal result his unsupported general statement to the opposite effect is disregarded.[23] It is incompetent to supplement the oath by the deponent's averments,[24] though when the reference is in general terms it may be necessary to look at the pleadings of the party referring in order to discover what was referred, and in that way to interpret the oath.[25] No effect can be given to admissions obtained of facts not averred by the party referring.[26] Further, the oath cannot be supplemented, qualified, contradicted or explained by documents, even if these are produced and referred to,[27] but a document may be shown to the deponent so that in light of it he may, if so advised, amend his answer.[28] On the other hand, the contents of documents may be made part of the oath if they are placed in the hands of the deponent and he is questioned on them.[29] This was achieved in one case by putting his own pleadings in the deponent's hands and asking him whether the statements in them were true.[30] If the deponent refers to a document as supporting his statement and it does not do so, the court will reject that part of the oath.[31]

(c) **Qualified Oath.** This means a deposition containing an admission coupled with a qualification. If the qualification is intrinsic, it receives effect as part of the oath; if it is extrinsic, it is disregarded. A qualification is intrinsic if it completes the answer to the question referred. If the terms of a contract are referred, everything deponed to as part of the bargain is intrinsic,[32] but statements as to what happened afterwards are not,[33] though

---

[21] *Cooper* v. *Hamilton*, 1824, 2 S. 728, 1825, 2 W. & S. 59.
[22] See § 323.
[23] *Hamilton's Exrs.* v. *Struthers*, 1858, 21 D. 51. See also § 320, sub-para. (b).
[24] *Penney* v. *Aitken*, 1927 S.C. 673, at pp. 678, 680, 682.
[25] *Penney* v. *Aitken (supra)*; *Napier* v. *Graham*, 1874, 1 R. 906.
[26] *Napier* v. *Graham (supra)*. In *Grant* v. *Marshall, Ramsay & Co.*, 1851, 13 D. 500, the deponent admitted facts not averred, a second suspension was brought founded on these facts, and a second reference allowed.
[27] *Broatch* v. *Dodds*, 1892, 19 R. 855; *Gordon* v. *Pratt*, 1860, 22 D. 903; *Heddle* v. *Baikie*, 1847, 9 D. 1254, at pp. 1260, 1263.
[28] *Boyd* v. *Kerr*, 1843, 5 D. 1213.
[29] *Jackson* v. *Cochrane*, 1873, 11 M. 475; *Broatch* v. *Dodds (supra)*.
[30] *Jackson* v. *Cochrane (supra)*. The deponent said that they were true, and his oath was held negative. A bank account was made part of the oath in *Hunter* v. *Geddes*, 1835, 13 S. 369.
[31] *Hunter* v. *Geddes (supra)*; *Cooper* v. *Hamilton*, 1824, 2 S. 728, 1825, 2 W. & S. 59, at p. 64.
[32] *Halliday* v. *Halliday*, 1826, 5 S. 116, L.P. Hope at p. 119. This is mainly illustrated under constitution. See § 322.
[33] See § 323.

they may establish an alteration in its terms. An exception, however, is recognised in the case of loan, where an assertion of payment is treated as intrinsic, though the payment may take place long afterwards.[34]

322. CONSTITUTION

(a) General. This is established by the admission of facts which give rise to the obligation. But if the deponent adds that it was agreed at the time that the normal obligation should not arise, that is an intrinsic qualification, and the oath is negative. In a claim for wages for services a qualification that it was agreed that the services should be rendered in return for board and lodging or gratuitously is intrinsic.[35] So also in a claim for payment for goods supplied is a qualification that they were supplied on the credit of a third party[36] or that the deponent had rejected them.[37] A deponent admitted granting a lease for two years, on which possession had followed, but added that this was conditional on security for the rent being found, which was not done, and this was held intrinsic.[38] Where a bill was prescribed and the granter deponed that he signed it to enable another bill to be retired, but that without his knowledge it had been discounted with a bank, the granter came under no obligation to the bank.[39]

(b) Loan. Although only constitution need be referred, a statement that the loan has been repaid is treated as intrinsic, and the oath is therefore negative.[40]

323. RESTING OWING

A deposition that the debt has been discharged by payment negatives resting owing.[41] A deposition of discharge in some other way has the same effect, but only if the deponent states that the creditor agreed to this method of discharge either when the obligation was incurred[42] or at some later time.[43] Resting owing was negatived where the debtor deponed that the creditor had

---

[34] *Gow's Executors* v. *Sim*, 1866, 4 M. 578, L. Neaves at p. 583. In *Mackay* v. *Monro*, 1871, 8 S.L.R. 438, L. Deas seemed to have some doubt about this departure from principle and proceeded on the ground that the advance and the repayment were part of the same transaction. The other judges did not concur in the Lord President's view that in the minute of reference "constitution" should be read as resting owing, a view inconsistent with the sanctity attached to the minute in *Bertram & Co.* v. *Stewart's Trustees*, 1874, 2 R. 255. The decision in *Newlands* v. *McKinlay*, 1885, 13 R. 353, where constitution was referred and payment held intrinsic, confirms the exception. See also §**118.**

[35] *Anderson* v. *Halley*, 1847, 9 D. 1222. See also *Knox* v. *McCaul*, 1861, 24 D. 16, where the employment of a solicitor was admitted, but subject to his recovering his fees from the other side.

[36] *Meyer & Mortimer* v. *Lennard*, 1851, 14 D. 99.

[37] Stair, iv, 44, 14.

[38] *Greig* v. *Boyd*, 1830, 8 S. 382; *Robertson* v. *Thomson*, 1824, 3 S. 182.

[39] *Drummond* v. *Crichton*, 1848, 10 D. 340.

[40] *Newlands* v. *McKinlay*, 1885, 13 R. 353. See further §§ **311,** sub-para. (b), **321,** sub-para. (c).

[41] *Fyfe* v. *Carfrae*, 1841, 4 D. 152. As to loan, see §§ **118, 311,** sub-para. (b), **321,** sub-para. (c),

[42] *Thomson's Exr.* v. *Thomson*, 1921 S.C. 109.

agreed to take payment in goods,[42] by collecting accounts due to the debtor,[43] and by withholding wages due to the debtor's son,[44] and had in each case so obtained payment. But a mere statement by the debtor that the creditor owes him money without adding that the creditor agreed to compensate the debts does not negative resting owing.[45] Since, however, the burden is on the party referring to prove resting owing,[46] the oath may be negative even if the deponent can only say that he believes the debt to have been discharged, provided he can give sound reasons for his belief.[47]

324. CREDITOR'S OATH AS TO EXTINCTION

If the creditor denies discharge, the oath is negative. If he admits receipt of money, not in discharge of the debt, but for some other reason, such as payment of another debt, the oath is still negative.[48] But if he admits receipt of the money and says he used it to pay another debt or in some other way for the debtor's benefit, the oath is affirmative, unless he adds that the debtor agreed to his action.[49]

325. SPECIALTIES OF PARTIES: GENERAL

In what may be called the normal case the litigation is between two individuals, and a reference to the oath of party is an appeal to the conscience of the person who knows the facts and whose pocket is affected by the construction placed on his oath.[50] A great deal of trouble would have been avoided if the oath on reference had been confined to that situation, and little injustice would have resulted, since in a very large number of cases it is the referring party's own fault that he has to resort to the procedure.[51] Nevertheless, it has been extended to deal with joint obligants, and, a much greater extension, reference has been allowed to the oath of persons who have no personal interest in the action.

326. CO-OBLIGANTS

(a) General. Where the obligation[52] is not constituted in writing all the alleged obligants subject to the jurisdiction of the Scottish courts must be called as defenders.[53] Any reference must, as a general rule,[54] be to the

---

[43] *Cowbrough & Co.* v. *Robertson*, 1879, 6 R. 1301, L. Deas at p. 1312.
[44] *Law* v. *Johnston*, 1843, 6 D. 201.
[45] *Cooper* v. *Marshall*, 1877, 5 R. 258; *Fenning* v. *Meldrum*, 1876, 4 R. 148. See also *Stewart* v. *Robertson*, 1852, 15 D. 12.
[46] *Cowbrough & Co.* v. *Robertson* (*supra*), L. Deas at p. 1311.
[47] *Mackay* v. *Ure*, 1849, 11 D. 982, where the grounds of belief were held sufficient; *Crichton* v. *Campbell*, 1857, 19 D. 661, where they were not.
[48] *Beattie* v. *Haliburton*, 1827, 5 S. 236.
[49] Erskine, iv, 2, 12; Dickson, *Evidence* (3rd ed.) §1520.
[50] *Adam* v. *Maclachlan*, 1847, 9 D. 560, L. J-Cl. Hope at p. 567, L. Medwyn at p. 574.
[51] *Christie* v. *Henderson*, 1833, 11 S. 744, at p. 753.
[52] This refers to joint and several obligations. If the obligation is several, each debtor's oath will affect only his own share.
[53] *Neilson* v. *Wilson*, 1890, 17 R. 608.
[54] It is unnecessary to refer to the oath of a defender who admits the debt on record or against whom decree in absence has passed; *Boyd* v. *Fraser*, 1853, 15 D. 342.

oaths of all the defenders, and if one of them depones that the debt has been paid, all are freed,[55] and so are any who do not admit constitution.[56] Where only some of the co-obligants under a prescribed bill were sued and all the defenders admitted constitution, but none could depone to payment, resting owing was held proved, although a co-obligant not called might have paid the debt.[57]

(b) **Partners.** These differ from other co-obligants because the obligation is primarily that of the firm,[58] but since the firm cannot take an oath the reference must be to the oath of the partners. *Prima facie* the reference ought to be to the oaths of all the partners; otherwise the referring party might single out the partner whose oath is likely to be most favourable to him.[59] Whether it is necessary to cite and examine all the partners depends on circumstances. The oath cannot as a rule be held affirmative unless all the partners have had an opportunity to depone.[59] But if it is averred that there was only one acting partner or one particularly acquainted with the subject matter of the reference, it may be enough to refer to his oath.[60] Should his oath not establish this averment, presumably, if affirmative, it would not bind the firm. It might be thought that, as in the case of other co-obligants, where one partner was cited and deponed negative that would end the matter. Where, however, a charge on a bill was given by a firm and no value referred to oath by the suspender, and one partner appeared and deponed that value had been given, Lord President Boyle made it a ground for remitting back that the other partner had not deponed.[61]

327. AGENCY: CORPORATE BODIES

As a general rule it is incompetent in an action to which the principal is party to refer to the oath of his agent.[62] There is, however, some support for the view that where principals have delegated their powers to a manager, reference to his oath is competent on a matter falling within his authority.[63]

---

55 Stair, iv, 44, 8; Dickson, *Evidence* (3rd ed.) §1470; *Darnley* v. *Kirkwood*, 1845, 7 D. 595, at p. 603; *Christie* v. *Henderson*, 1833, 11 S. 744, L.P. Hope at p. 750. Erskine (iv, 2, 10) is doubtful.
56 *Duncan* v. *Forbes*, 1831, 9 S. 540.
57 *Christie* v. *Henderson* (*supra*), a doubtful decision, conflicting with what appears to be the rule in partnership (*infra*). It is described as a whole court decision, but it was decided by five to four. It was followed in *Black* v. *Black*, 1838, 16 S. 1220, explained in *Darnley* v. *Kirkwood*, 1845, 7 D. 595, at p. 599, explained away in *Drummond* v. *Crichton*, 1848, 10 D. 340, at pp. 346, 347, 348, 352, doubted in *Boyd* v. *Fraser* (*supra*), at p. 344, and by Dickson (*Evidence* (3rd ed.) §468), and not mentioned in *Campbell's Trustees* v. *King's Trustees*, (O.H.) 1897, 4 S.L.T. 265.
58 *Nisbet's Trustees* v. *Morrison's Trustees*, 1829, 7 S. 307, L. Pitmilly at p. 310.
59 *McNab* v. *Lockhart*, 1843, 5 D. 1014; *Broom* v. *Edgley*, 1843, 5 D. 1087. In both cases the partnerships had been dissolved, but the dicta included existing firms.
60 *McNab* v. *Lockhart* (*supra*), L. Medwyn at p. 1020.
61 *Cleland* v. *McLellan*, 1851, 13 D. 504. It is difficult to see how the deposition of the other partner could benefit anyone. None of the other judges concurred with this ground of judgment, and two of them doubted it.
62 *Sawers* v. *Clark*, 1892, 19 R. 1090; *Bertram & Co.* v. *Stewart's Trustees*, 1874, 2 R. 255, decided on the words of the Act; Bell, *Principles*, §2263.

This extension does not seem to have been applied where the principal was an individual, but reference was allowed, apparently without objection, to the oath of a bank agent as representing the bank in an action by the bank,[64] to that of the clerk to road trustees, who was, however, himself the charger,[65] and to that of the Treasurer of Edinburgh Royal Infirmary.[66] On the other hand, a reference was refused to the oath of the directors, secretaries, solicitors and treasurers (all named) of a railway company.[67] A reference is not allowed to a corporation,[68] but was allowed, apparently without objection, to the oath of the managing director of a limited company.[69]

328. TRUSTEES AND EXECUTORS

In an action against an executor for a debt said to have been due by the deceased, reference to the oath of the executor should *prima facie* be allowed, since he is the pursuer's party. But in some old cases cited by Dickson[70] the court, while sustaining the reference, qualified the interlocutor with a view to protecting the interests of beneficiaries. In two cases they required the referring party to find caution to repay, should he obtain decree, any amount due to legatees or other creditors,[71] and in another the reference was allowed for constituting the debt so far as it affected the executor's own part in the inventory, "but no ways to prejudge the nearest of kin, nor the creditors."[72] The explanation of these qualifications probably is that when these cases were decided an executor nominate, as such, had a beneficial right to one-third of the estate,[73] and the reference was designed to affect that share only. The decisions accordingly have no bearing now when the office of executor is no longer a benefit.[74] A reference has been allowed to the oath of an executrix, and it was not suggested that this course was wrong as such,[75] and it is thought that such an oath would be conclusive as regards the estate. Where the executor has no knowledge of the debt, as may frequently happen, and depones accordingly, the oath is negative.[76] If there is any reason to

---

63 *McNab* v. *Lockhart*, 1843, 5 D. 1014, L. Medwyn at p. 1020.

64 *Dickson* v. *Ker*, 1830, 9 S. 125, referred to in *Bertram & Co.* v. *Stewart's Trustees* (*supra*), at p. 258.

65 *Dykes* v. *Hill*, 1828, 6 S. 479.

66 *White* v. *Caledonian Railway Co.*, 1869, 7 M. 583, at p. 588. This is the only reference to the case, and the Treasurer may have been a party.

67 *White* v. *Caledonian Railway Co.* (*supra*). No reasons were given for this decision. The pursuer's averments brought him very near Lord Medwyn's rule. See note 63.

68 *White* v. *Caledonian Railway Co.* (*supra*).

69 *Borland* v. *Macdonald, Ltd.*, 1940 S.C. 124, 140 (interlocutor).

70 *Evidence* (3rd ed.) §1464.

71 *Ker* v. *Lady Corrington*, 1627 M. 12,478; *Scott* v. *Cockburn*, 1627 M. 12,477.

72 *Cockburn* v. *McKalla*, 1681, 3 Br. Supp. 407. But the interlocutors in *Ross* v. *Guthrie*, 1839, 2 D. 6. seem to suggest that an affirmative oath by an executrix might lead to a decree for the whole amount of the estate remaining in her hands.

73 Abolished by Intestate Moveable Succession (Scotland) Act, 1855 (18 & 19 Vict. c. 23), s. 8, amending the Act. 1617, cap. 14, "Anent Executors."

74 *Smart* v. *Smart*, 1926 S.C. 392.

75 *Hamilton* v. *Hamilton's Executrix*, 1950 S.C. 39. On the other hand it has been assumed that when the alleged debtor is dead proof by oath is impossible; *Philip* v. *Gordon Cumming's Exrs.*, 1869, 7 M. 859.

suppose that the executor may depone falsely because of a personal interest, the court would probably exercise its discretion to refuse.[77]

In this connection trustees appear to be in a similar position to executors. The court allowed a reference to the oath of trustees, reserving all questions as to the effect of the oath when taken.[78] But in a later case, decided on another point, the judges had no doubt about a reference to the oath of trustees, not only of debts incurred by themselves, but also of those incurred by the deceased.[79] But where trustees or executors are not parties, e.g., when they are merely pursuers and not claimants in a multiplepoinding, a claimant cannot refer to their oaths to establish his claim.[80]

It appears competent to refer his ancestor's obligations to an heir, and if his oath is affirmative, to hold him liable to the extent of the succession.[81]

329. TUTORS, CURATORS AND JUDICIAL FACTORS

It is competent to refer to the oath of a tutor conducting an action on behalf of a pupil, but only as to matters which fell within his administration.[82] Where the litigant is a minor the reference is to his oath, not that of his curator.[83] Probably a reference would not be allowed to the oath of a judicial factor, he having no personal interest.[84]

330. HUSBAND AND WIFE

Since the abolition of the *jus mariti* it is difficult to see how any question can arise except as to two classes of debt contracted by the wife. In the case of her ante-nuptial debts the husband is liable to the extent of the value of property received by him from, through or in right of her.[85] To establish that liability both constitution and resting owing must be referred to the husband's oath.[86] Where the wife is alleged to have contracted debts falling within the *præpositura*, constitution may be referred to the oath of the wife, but, according to the most recent authority, to render the husband liable resting owing must be referred to his oath.[87]

[76] But further proof may be competent. See §321, note 20.

[77] *Murray* v. *Lawrie's Trustees*, 1827, 5 S. 515.

[78] *Murray* v. *Lawrie's Trustees* (*supra*). The dissenting judge (L. Alloway) made some pointed criticisms of the decision, which has been described as not deciding much; *Forsyth's Trustees* v. *McLean*, 1854, 16 D. 343.

[79] *Bertram & Co.* v. *Stewart's Trustees*, 1874, 2 R. 255. The nature of the decision referred to by L. Deas suggests that the difficulty he and L. Ardmillan had in view was that, on a proper reference, the trustees might emit oaths of credulity (see § 321, sub-para. (b)), not that any question as to the beneficiaries would arise.

[80] *Farquhar* v. *Farquhar*, 1886, 13 R. 596, L. Shand at p. 598.

[81] *Darnley* v. *Kirkwood*, 1845, 7 D. 595, 1846, 8 D. 441. See also *Phillpotts* v. *Rae*, 1847, 9 D. 1427.

[82] Dickson, *Evidence* (3rd ed.) §1460.

[83] *Ibid.* §1461.

[84] *Ibid.* §1462.

[85] Married Women's Property (Scotland) Act, 1877 (40 & 41 Vict. c. 29), s. 4.

[86] *Mitchells* v. *Moultrys*, 1882, 10 R. 378. See also *Morrice* v. *Munro & Son*, 1829, 8 S. 156.

[87] *Mitchells* v. *Moultrys* (*supra*). The wife's oath was, however, considered sufficient in *Young, Trotter & Co.* v. *Playfair*, 1802 M. 12486, not cited in *Mitchells* v. *Moultrys* (*supra*).

331. ASSIGNEES; ARRESTEES; BANKRUPTS

Until intimation of the assignation, payment or any other exception to the debt may be proved by the oath of the cedent, but after intimation it can be proved only by that of the assignee, unless the subject has been rendered litigious before intimation or the assignee admits either that the assignation is gratuitous or in trust for the cedent.[88] An arrestee may prove by the common debtor's oath any defence to payment of the debt arrested.[89] The arrester may refer the resting owing of that debt to the arrestee's oath, but the arrestee's denial does not affect the common debtor.[90] As a bankrupt has usually no interest in the estate, there cannot be a reference to his oath either by a creditor of his claim[91] or by a party sued by the trustee of his defence.[92] On the other hand, the trustee may refer a claim to the oath of a claimant.[93] Possibly there may be a reference to the oath of a debtor who has granted a trust deed, but only if a surplus is expected.[94]

[88] *Lang* v. *Hislop*, 1854, 16 D. 908, at p. 913; *Campbell* v. *Campbell*, 1860, 23 D. 159, interlocutor of 15th March, 1859.
[89] Dickson, *Evidence* (3rd ed.) §1477.
[90] *Ibid.*, § 1478; *Hogg* v. *Low*, 1826, 4 S. 702.
[91] *Adam* v. *Maclachlan*, 1847, 9 D. 560.
[92] *Thomson* v. *Duncan*, 1855, 17 D. 1081, at p. 1090.
[93] *Jackson* v. *McIver*, 1875, 2 R. 882.
[94] Dickson, *Evidence* (3rd ed.) §1481; *Robertson* v. *Thom*, 1848, 21 Sc. Jur. 96.

CHAPTER XXVI

ATTENDANCE OF WITNESSES

332. GENERAL

All courts have power to compel the attendance of witnesses residing within their jurisdiction.[1] Attendance is ordered by citation and, if the witness is in Scotland, may be enforced by apprehension. A person cited is not entitled to disregard the citation on the ground that he is not a competent witness.[2] A peer must obey a citation.[3] It is doubtful whether the lower courts may issue warrant for the apprehension of a peer, but the Court of Justiciary or the Court of Session, as the case might be, would grant the necessary authority.[4]

333. CRIMINAL

For a trial in the High Court warrant to cite witnesses is issued by the Clerk of Justiciary; where the trial is on indictment in the sheriff court it is issued by the sheriff-clerk of the district where the second diet is to be called.[5] The warrant may be executed by a messenger-at-arms, sheriff officer or police constable[6] at any place in Scotland.[7] The accused does not appear to have a right to the services of the police for this purpose,[8] and therefore, if the police will not act, he must, to ensure valid citation, employ a messenger-at-arms or a sheriff officer. But if a judge or sheriff were satisfied before the jury was empanelled that a material witness for the defence had been warned in some formal way, e.g., by registered letter, and had failed to appear, that might be sufficient reason for adjourning the trial. Where a witness regularly cited, fails to appear, warrant may be granted for his apprehension and

---

[1] A warrant of citation issued in a sheriff court may be executed in any sheriffdom without endorsation: Sheriff Courts (Scotland) Act, 1907 (7 Edw. VII. c. 51), Rule 10.

[2] *Bryce*, 1844, 2 Broun 119.

[3] *Fraser* v. *Nicholl*, 1840, 2 D. 1254.

[4] Dickson, *Evidence* (3rd ed.) §1691.

[5] Criminal Procedure (Scotland) Act, 1887 (56 & 57 Vict. c. 35), s. 23.

[6] *Ibid.*, s. 24. If the witness is in prison citation is by an officer of the prison on a request by the prosecutor or the defending solicitor: Prisons (Scotland) Act, 1952 (15 & 16 Geo. VI. & 1 Eliz. II. c. 61), s. 61. See Renton and Brown, *Criminal Procedure* (3rd ed.), 87.

[7] Criminal Law (Scotland) Act, 1830 (11 Geo. IV. and 1 Will. IV. c. 37), s. 8.

[8] It is the duty of a police constable to execute any warrant, citation or deliverance, but only if it is issued by a judge: Police (Scotland) Act, 1956 (4 & 5 Eliz. II. c. 26), s. 4 (1) (c). It is understood that in some areas the police are willing to cite defence witnesses.

detention until the trial,[9] and the same course may be followed if a witness is likely to abscond.[10] A witness in England or Northern Ireland may be cited to attend a trial in Scotland.[11] While failure to obey the citation may be punished by the appropriate English or Northern Irish court,[11] there seems to be no power to enforce attendance. In case of a summary trial the Act is a sufficient warrant for the citation of witnesses,[12] which means that no other warrant is required. Citation may be at any place in Scotland by any officer of law.[13] A witness who has been cited and fails to appear may be punished[14] and may be apprehended and kept in custody till the trial.[15] A witness in England may be cited if the complaint is endorsed by a court of summary jurisdiction there.[16]

334. COURT OF SESSION

The interlocutor fixing a proof or a jury trial is warrant to cite witnesses in Scotland.[17] The citation may be by messenger-at-arms, or in a county where there is no resident messenger-at-arms or in an island, by sheriff officer,[18] or by post.[19] If the witness fails to attend, he may be apprehended on letters of second diligence. If the witness is in England or Northern Ireland a special warrant may be granted by the Lord Ordinary or the court.[20] The application may require to be supported by an affidavit,[21] and the granting is entirely a matter of discretion.[22] Warrant is not granted if the witness is to

9 *H.M. Advocate* v. *Bell*, 1936 J.C. 89 (narrative of earlier proceedings).
10 Hume, II, 375.
11 Writ of Subpœna Act, 1805 (45 Geo. III. c. 92), s. 3; Supreme Court of Judicature (Northern Ireland) Order, 1921 (S.I. 1921, no. 1802), s. 3; General Adaptation of Enactments (Northern Ireland) Order, 1921 (S.I. 1921, no. 1804), s. 5. The 1805 Act mentions only the Court of Justiciary, but its terms seem wide enough to include the lower courts.
12 Summary Jurisdiction (Scotland) Act, 1954 (2 & 3 Eliz. II. c. 48), s. 18 (1).
13 *Ibid.*, s. 22. "Officer of law" includes sheriff officer and police officer, but as there is no warrant issued by a judge, the police are under no obligation to cite witnesses. See note 8 *supra*.
14 *Ibid.*, s. 33 (1).
15 *Ibid.*, s. 19.
16 *Ibid.*, s. 22; Summary Jurisdiction (Process) Act, 1881 (44 & 45 Vict. c. 24), ss. 4, 8. This Act contemplates a warrant issued by a court, which was necessary in 1881. Since under the 1954 Act no warrant is issued by the court, the two Acts do not fit, but this is concealed by the device of having the order assigning a diet signed by the sheriff or magistrate instead of the clerk of court.
17 Court of Session Act, 1850 (13 & 14 Vict. c. 36), s. 43. This section applies to jury trials, but the practice in proofs is the same; Maclaren, *Court of Session Practice*, 343.
18 Execution of Diligence (Scotland) Act, 1926 (16 & 17 Geo. V. c. 16), s. 1.
19 Citation Amendment (Scotland) Act, 1882 (45 & 46 Vict. c. 77).
20 Attendance of Witnesses Act, 1854 (17 & 18 Vict. c. 34), s. 1; General Adaptation of Enactments (Northern Ireland) Order, 1921 (S.I. 1921, No. 1804), s. 5.
21 *Macdonald* v. *Highland Railway Co.*, 1892, 20 R. 217 (affidavit required); *Pirie* v. *Caledonian Railway Co.*, 1890, 17 R. 608 (affidavit not required, but certificate by solicitor lodged).
22 *Henderson* v. *North British Railway Co.*, 1870, 8 M. 833; *Gellatly* v. *Law*, 1865, 4 M. 267.
23 *Macdonald* v. *Highland Railway Co.* (*supra*); *Gilmour* v. *North British Railway Co.*, 1893, 1 S.L.T. 370.

opinion only.[23] If the witness does not obey the citation he may be punished by the court of his own residence,[24] but his attendance cannot be enforced.

335. SHERIFF COURT

A copy of an interlocutor certified by the sheriff clerk allowing a proof or fixing the date for a jury trial is sufficient warrant to cite witnesses.[25] It may be executed in any part of Scotland, without endorsement,[26] by sheriff officer personally or at the dwelling house, or by sheriff officer or solicitor by post.[27] If a witness after citation fails to attend, he may be apprehended on warrant for second diligence, and detained until he finds caution for his appearance.[28] There is no method for effective citation of witnesses furth of Scotland.

336. OTHER TRIBUNALS

(a) **Arbitrations.** Arbiters have no power to compel the attendance of witnesses. A warrant to cite must be obtained from the Court of Session or the sheriff,[29] and compliance with the citation may be enforced by the sheriff.[30] An application for warrant to cite a witness in England was refused, apparently on the ground that the Act[31] does not apply to arbitrations.[32] Where the witness is in England or Northern Ireland the Court of Session will grant a commission to take his evidence,[33] and his attendance before the commissioner may be enforced by the English court under the Evidence by Commission Act, 1843.[34] In one case the court granted commission to take evidence to lie *in retentis*.[35]

(b) **Church Courts.** The sheriff may grant warrant to cite witnesses to attend the courts of the Church of Scotland and, if necessary, letters of second diligence,[36] and the opinion has been expressed that he may also do so in the case of voluntary churches.[37]

(c) **Statutory Tribunals.**[38] A civilian witness to a court martial is cited

---

[24] Attendance of Witnesses Act, 1854 (17 & 18 Vict. c. 34), s. 3.
[25] Sheriff Courts (Scotland) Act, 1907 (7 Edw. VII. c. 51), Rule 71.
[26] *Ibid.*, Rule 10.
[27] *Ibid.*, Rule 72.
[28] *Ibid.*, Rule 73.
[29] Dickson, *Evidence* (3rd ed.) §1704; *Caird*, 1865, 3 M. 851.
[30] *Blaikie* v. *Aberdeen Railway Co.*, 1852, 14 D. 590.
[31] Attendance of Witnesses Act, 1854 (17 & 18 Vict. c. 34).
[32] *Highland Railway Co.* v. *Mitchell*, 1868, 6 M. 896.
[33] *John Nimmo & Son*, 1905, 8 F. 173.
[34] 6 & 7 Vict. c. 82, s. 5.
[35] *Galloway Power Co.* v. *Carmichael*, 1937 S.C. 135.
[36] *Presbytery of Lews* v. *Fraser*, 1874, 1 R. 888.
[37] *Ibid.*, at p. 894.
[38] Most of these have power to cite, and some at least have power to punish failure to attend, but few have power to order apprehension. The main ground of the decision in *Presbytery of Lews* v. *Fraser*, (*supra*), that the sheriff may on the application of a presbytery grant letters of second diligence, was that a presbytery is a court recognised by law. The same reasoning appears to apply to statutory tribunals.

in writing, and if he fails to attend he may be punished by the civil courts.[39] Where a tribunal is set up to enquire into a definite matter by resolution of both Houses of Parliament, and the Tribunals of Enquiry (Evidence) Act, 1948, is made applicable, the tribunal has the powers of the Court of Session to enforce the attendance of witnesses.[40] This presumably includes power to issue letters of second diligence. In addition, the Court of Session may punish any witness who fails to obey a citation.[41] The General Commissioners may cite witnesses under the Income Tax Act,[42] and fine them for failure to obey.[42] In proceedings against a solicitor before the Disciplinary Committee the Court of Session or the sheriff may grant warrant to cite witnesses and letters of second diligence.[43]

[39] Naval Discipline Act, 1957 (5 & 6 Eliz. II. c. ¡53), ss. 64, 65; Army Act. 1955 (3 & 4 Eliz. II. c. 18), ss. 103, 101; Rules of Procedure (Army) 1956 (S.I. 1956, No. 162), Rule 91; Air Force Act, 1955 (3 & 4 Eliz. II. c. 19), ss. 103, 101; Rules of Procedure (Air Force) 1956 (S.I. 1956, No. 163), Rule 91.
[40] Tribunals of Inquiry (Evidence) Act, 1948 (11 & 12 Geo. V. c. 11), s. 2 (1).
[41] *Ibid.*, s. 2 (2).
[42] 15 & 16 Geo. VI. & 1 Eliz. II. c. 10, s. 59.
[43] Solicitors (Scotland) Act, 1933 (23 & 24 Geo. V. c. 21), s. 29.

CHAPTER XXVII

ORAL EVIDENCE—GENERAL

337. THE OATH

(a) **General.** Every witness before giving evidence must take the oath,[1] unless he is a child[2] or feeble minded[3] or affirms,[4] and may be punished if he refuses to do so.[5] If a witness is called merely to be shown to the jury he must be sworn, since the other side may wish to question him.[6] The witness swears with right hand uplifted,[7] and the form of oath is: "I swear by Almighty God, and as I shall answer to God at the great day of judgment, that I will tell the truth, the whole truth and nothing but the truth." The whole oath must be administered,[8] except that the words "and as I shall answer to God at the great day of judgment" may be omitted. If the witness states, expressly or impliedly,[9] that that manner of taking the oath is not appropriate to his religious belief, the oath is administered in the appropriate manner. Thus a Jew takes the oath with his head covered, and a Mohammedan on the Koran, while a Chinese breaks a saucer. But if a witness takes the oath in Scots form, either without objection or having declared it to be binding on him, it is no defence to a charge of perjury to say that it was not binding on him.[10] If he does object, but it is not reasonably practicable without inconvenience and delay to administer the oath in the appropriate manner, the witness may be required to affirm.[11]

---

1   *McLaughlin* v. *Douglas and Kidston*, 1863, 4 Irv. 273, 286, 287. A statutory exception is made by section 34 of the Summary Jurisdiction (Scotland) Act, 1954 (2 & 3 Eliz. II. c. 48), which applies where the witness is examined in several trials at the same diet for offences against the same statute.
2   See § 349.
3   See § 350.
4   See sub-para. (b).
5   *Bonnar* v. *Simpson*, 1836, 1 Swin. 39. See generally Stringer, *Oaths* (4th ed.).
6   Dickson, *Evidence* (3rd ed.) §1765; *Milne*, 1866, 5 Irv. 229.
7   Recognised in Oaths Act, 1888 (51 & 52 Vict. c. 46), s. 5.
8   *McLaughlin* v. *Douglas and Kidston* (*supra*), where the oath omitted the words "the whole truth."
9   A Jew usually silently covers his head.
10 False Oaths (Scotland) Act, 1933 (23 & 24 Geo. V. c. 21), s. 7.
11 Oaths Act, 1961 (9 & 10 Eliz. II. c. 21), s. 1.

(b) Affirmation. If a witness objects to being sworn and states as the ground of his objection either that he has no religious belief or that the taking of an oath is contrary to his religious belief, he may affirm.[12] The affirmation is administered to him in these words, with right hand uplifted: "I . . . do solemnly, sincerely, and truly declare and affirm that I will tell the truth, the whole truth, and nothing but the truth."[13] The words must be strictly adhered to. In a case under the Act anent Quakers the words "and truly" had been omitted from an affidavit, which was therefore held invalid.[14] A person wilfully affirming falsely is liable to punishment.[15]

338. CONDUCT OF PROOF OR TRIAL

(a) Civil Proof or Jury Trial. Each party[16] in turn leads evidence both to support his own averments and to rebut those of his opponent,[17] and usually the witnesses are cross-examined and re-examined. Except with permission of the judge, re-examination must be confined to matters raised in cross-examination. If permission is granted, the judge usually allows cross-examination on the new point. The judge may himself put questions, but it has been held in a prosecution that if he elicits some new and material evidence he must give an opportunity for cross-examination on that point,[18] and probably the same view would be taken in a civil case. As a general rule, that concludes the evidence, but it is competent, though most unusual, to allow the pursuer a proof in replication with regard to any matter of which notice has not been given on record or of which it may fairly be said proof in anticipation could not be expected.[19] Proof in replication was allowed where, if it had not been allowed, one party would have had no opportunity to meet his opponent's case.[20] It has also been allowed in a slander action to prove malice[21] or to meet *veritas*.[22] The court may on the motion of either party permit a witness to be recalled.[23] This was allowed, technically on the motion of the pursuer, but actually on the suggestion of the Lord Ordinary, to enable a witness to speak more clearly to acts of adultery,[24] and it has also been allowed to enable the witness to be asked[25] whether he had on an occasion before he gave evidence made a statement inconsistent with his evidence.[26] But recall was refused where the contradictory statement was alleged to have been made after he had

---

[12] Oaths Act, 1888 (51 & 52 Vict. c. 46), s. 1.
[13] *Ibid.*, s. 2.
[14] *McCubbin* v. *Turnbull*, 1850, 12 D. 1123.
[15] Oaths Act, 1888 (51 & 52 Vict. c. 46), s. 3.
[16] Usually the pursuer begins, but the defender may be appointed to lead.
[17] *Dick & Stevenson* v. *Mackay*, 1880, 7 R. 778, L. Shand at p. 791.
[18] *McLeod* v. *H.M. Advocate*, 1939 J.C. 68.
[19] *Dick & Stevenson* v. *Mackay* (*supra*); *Wilson* v. *Thomas Usher & Son*, 1934 S.C. 332, at p. 338; *Gairdner* v. *Youngs*, 1874, 2 R. 173.
[20] *Gairdner* v. *Youngs* (*supra*).
[21] *Rankine* v. *Roberts*, 1873, 1 R. 225.
[22] *Kessack* v. *Kessack*, 1899, 1 F. 398.
[23] Evidence (Scotland) Act, 1852 (15 Vict. c. 27), s. 4.
[24] *A.* v. *B.*, 1856, 20 D. 407, at pp. 413, 418.
[25] Under section 3 of the Evidence (Scotland) Act, 1852 (15 Vict. c. 27).

given evidence.[27] It is competent to agree that a witness is to be held as concurring in chief and in cross with another witness. The second witness is sworn and gives his name, age and designation, and, if he is an expert witness, his qualifications.

(b) Criminal Trial. Evidence for the prosecution, upon whom the burden of proof always rests, is led first, followed by the evidence, if any, for the defence. After each witness has been examined, cross-examined and re-examined, the judge may put questions, but if he elicits any new and material evidence he must give an opportunity to cross-examine on that evidence.[18] Proof in replication is incompetent,[28] but it is competent to allow the prosecutor to recall a witness before,[29] but not after,[30] his case is closed. It is also competent for the judge at any time, even after both cases are closed, to recall a witness to clear up a point left ambiguous or obscure.[31] But probably if the judge elicits any new and material evidence he must give an opportunity to cross-examine.[18] It is incompetent to hold a witness as concurring with another witness.[32]

339. QUESTIONS

(a) General. Questions should be clear and unambiguous and as short as possible, each raising a single point. A long and involved question may confuse the witness and give an unjustified bad impression, or it may lead to an incomplete answer. A cross-examiner may obtain what appears to him at the time a favourable answer, only to find, possibly on appeal, that the question was ambiguous and that the court is unwilling to rely on the answer because the witness may have taken the other meaning from the question.

(b) Leading Questions. A leading question is one which suggests the answer desired. Except for introductory narrative and on non-controversial matters evidence should not be elicited in examination in chief by such questions. Thus a witness should be asked not "Was the march at Yernup one of the marches of the common?" but "What were the marches of the common in that quarter?";[33] not whether certain named persons were present, but who was present;[34] not whether she formed a certain impression,

---

[26] *Dyet* v. *National Coal Board*, 1957 S.L.T. (Notes) 18; *Hoey* v. *Hoey*, 1884, 11 R. 578; *Robertson* v. *Steuart*, 1874, 1 R. 532, at pp. 586, 588. See also *Begg* v. *Begg*, 1887, 14 R. 497.

[27] *Begg* v. *Begg* (*supra*).

[28] *McNeilie* v. *H.M. Advocate*, 1929 J.C. 50; *Docherty and Graham* v. *McLennan*, 1912 S.C. (J.) 102.

[29] *Todd* v. *MacDonald*, 1960 J.C. 93.

[30] *McNeilie* v. *H.M. Advocate* (*supra*).

[31] *Todd* v. *MacDonald* (*supra*), L. Sorn at p. 96; *Davidson* v. *McFadyean*, 1942 J.C. 95, where dicta in earlier cases, which would justify such recall for wider purposes, were doubted: *Collinson* v. *Mitchell*, 1897, 24 R. (J.) 52, 2 Adam 277; *Saunders* v. *Paterson*, 1905, 7 F. (J.) 58, 4 Adam 468.

[32] *Cafferty* v. *Cheyne*, 1939 J.C. 1.

[33] *Hunter* v. *Dodds*, 1832, 10 S. 833.

[34] *Mackenzie* v. *Murray*, 1819, 2 Mur. 155.

but what impression she formed;[35] not whether she was employed to find lodgings for the pursuer and a young woman, but whether she had been employed to find lodgings, and, if so, for whom.[36] Leading questions on any point of importance ought to be objected to, though the mere putting of the question usually does the damage, and in a proof it is often better just to have the evidence recorded as question and answer, so as to enable the judge and any appeal court to see how the evidence was elicited. It may then be treated as of little weight.[37] But circumstances may be mentioned to the witness to direct his mind to the facts to which he is to speak. Thus a fact may be stated to remind the witness of a date.[38]

(c) **Hypothetical Questions.** This phrase has two meanings. First, the hypothesis may be that something happened which did not happen. In some cases such a question is essential, e.g. in a reduction on the ground of misrepresentation. The pursuer must be asked what he would have done if he had known the truth.[39] A recent disapproval in the Outer House[40] of such questions cannot be of universal application and is difficult to reconcile with an earlier Inner House decision.[41] Secondly, the hypothesis may be that something has been, or will be, proved. Such a question should not be asked unless evidence has been led to support the hypothesis or it is intended to lead such evidence. In any event, evidence depending on an unproved hypothesis is useless.[42]

(d) **Double Questions.** This form of question makes an implied assumption and the witness cannot answer it directly without affirming the truth of the assumption. The hackneyed example is, "Have you stopped beating your wife?" Questions of this nature are often put unintentionally by a cross-examiner so certain of his facts that he does not notice that the witness has not admitted them, and they are unfair and should be objected to. An affirmative and a negative answer may be almost equally damaging, and a perfectly honest witness may give a bad impression because he cannot answer directly, but has to enter on an explanation. Dickson[43] gives two examples, asking a person why he did something before asking whether he did it, and asking how much was paid before asking whether any payment was made.

(e) **Questions Usurping Function of Court.** In many cases the fact in issue is really a matter of inference from other facts, and it is for the court, not the witnesses, to draw the inference. So it is incompetent in an action

---

35 *King* v. *King*, 1842, 4 D. 490.
36 *Baillie* v. *Bryson*, 1818, 1 Mur. 331.
37 *McKenzie* v. *McKenzie*, 1943 S.C. 108; *Bishop* v. *Bryce*, 1910 S.C. 426.
38 *Auchmutie* v. *Ferguson*, 1817, 1 Mur. 212.
39 *A. W. Gamage Ltd.* v. *Charlesworth's Trustee*, 1910 S.C. 257, L. Kinnear at p. 265; *Boyd & Forrest* v. *G. & S.W. Rly.*, 1915 S.C. (H.L.) 20, at pp. 24, 26, 38, 42; *McWilliams* v. *Sir William Arrol & Co. and Lithgows, Ltd.*, 1961 S.C. 134, at p. 144.
40 *A.B.* v. *C.D.*, 1957 S.C. 415.
41 *Bairner* v. *Fels*, 1931 S.C. 674.
42 As to the effect on expert evidence, see § 413, sub-para. (b).
43 *Evidence* (3rd ed.) §1771.

arising from a traffic accident to ask a witness, even in cross, whether in his opinion the driver was to blame.[44] It is also incompetent to ask a witness his opinion as to the meaning of a contract, that being for the court.[45] A witness may not be asked his impression from the facts known to him; it is for the court to form its impression on the whole evidence.[46] So evidence of a witness's impression that a wife's distressed condition on a particular occasion was due to her husband's ill treatment was rejected since it was based on her knowledge of the husband's previous conduct towards his wife.[46] On the other hand, evidence of an impression produced at the moment by the facts then observed is competent.[47] Where a witness in an action of divorce for adultery had given evidence that on entering a room at midnight she found the defender and a man not her husband lying together on a sofa,[48] it was held competent to ask her what her impression was.[49]

340. OBJECTIONS TO QUESTIONS

In a civil jury trial in the Court of Session usually one counsel is heard for the objector, then one for the opposite party and finally the original counsel in reply, but in cases of difficulty and moment more counsel than one may be heard.[50] The party dissatisfied with the ruling may have the ruling and his objection recorded in the notes of evidence.[51] Failure to state an objection may prejudice an application for a new trial on the ground of surprise.[52] In a civil jury trial in the sheriff court exception to the sheriff's rulings on admission of evidence must, if required by the party taking the exception, be recorded to the sheriff's dictation in the shorthand notes.[53]

In a proof in the Court of Session an objection should be recorded in the notes of evidence, together with the grounds of it, the decision and the Lord Ordinary's reasons for his decision.[54] If an objection is sustained to a line of evidence, counsel should state, if it be the fact, that that line would have been pursued with other named witnesses. This ensures that if the ruling is reversed there will be no confusion as to what additional evidence may be led.[54] In a proof in the sheriff court any objection must, if desired, be noted in the notes of evidence to the sheriff's dictation.[55] A very general

---

[44] *Gunn* v. *Gardner*, 1820, 4 Mur. 194. See also § 411, sub-para. (b).
[45] *Milne* v. *Samson*, 1843, 6 D. 355.
[46] *A.B.* v. *C.D.*, 1848, 11 D. 289, at p. 293.
[47] *King* v. *King*, 1842, 4 D. 590, at p. 596; *A.B.* v. *C.D.*, 1848, 11 D. 289, at pp. 292, 295.
[48] The evidence is narrated at 4 D. 575.
[49] *King* v. *King* (*supra*). The question was put in an improper leading form, viz. whether her impression was that criminal intercourse had taken place.
[50] C.A.S. F. II. 3.
[51] Rules of Court, 1948, Rule 143.
[52] *Wilson* v. *Thomas Usher & Son*, 1934 S.C. 332, at p. 338.
[53] Sheriff Courts (Scotland) Act, 1907 (7 Edw. VII. c. 51), Rule 139. The restriction of the right to the party taking the exception is disregarded in practice.
[54] *Hewat* v. *Edinburgh Corporation*, 1944 S.C. 30.
[55] Sheriff Courts (Scotland) Act, 1907 (7 Edw. VII. c. 51), Rule 74. The Rule is badly framed. It appears to imply that the evidence objected to is to be led even if the objection is sustained, but the practice of allowing such evidence under reservation has made it unnecessary to attempt to attach a definite meaning to the Rule. It also confines to the objector the right to have the objection noted.

practice, however, is to allow the evidence under reservation as to its admissibility and leave the point for decision later.[56]   If the statutory procedure is followed and a decision given, an appeal lies with leave to the sheriff,[57] and an appeal to the Court of Session is incompetent unless there has first been an appeal to the sheriff.[58]   A ruling on confidentiality may be appealed with leave to the sheriff.[59]

In a criminal jury trial the objection and the ruling are recorded in the notes of the proceedings,[60] but failure to object does not necessarily bar an appeal on the ground that incompetent evidence was led.[61]   In a summary criminal trial any objection to the competency or admissibility of evidence must, if either party desires it, be entered in the record.[62]   If the accused is legally represented, no conviction may be set aside in respect of such objections unless they have been timeously stated at the trial.[63]   But if they have been timeously stated, it is no bar to the appeal that they have not been entered in the record.[64]   The opinion has been expressed, *obiter*, that in a summary criminal trial when an objection is taken the evidence ought to be allowed under reservation,[65] but in a subsequent case the suggestion received no encouragement.[66]

341.   EVIDENCE IN CHIEF

(a) **Leading Questions.**   This subject has already been dealt with.[67]

(b) **Refreshing Memory.**   As a general rule a witness must speak from his own recollection, but he is usually allowed to refresh his memory by looking at notes made by himself at the time of the events to which he is speaking, or very shortly thereafter.   It is everyday practice for police officers to refer to their notebooks for details of measurements and positions, and for any statement made by an accused person.   The notes, though not themselves evidence, become part of the witness's oral testimony, and the other side is entitled to see them.[68]   If the witness does not use them, the other side is not entitled to see them.[69]   A witness seeing a motor car knock down a pedestrian and drive on, may write down the number of the car and, if

---

[56] *McDonald* v. *Duncan,* 1933 S.C. 737, at p. 744.
[57] Sheriff Courts (Scotland) Act, 1907 (7 Edw. VII. c. 51), Rule 75.
[58] *Jackson* v. *McKay,* 1923 S.C. 286.
[59] Sheriff Courts (Scotland) Act, 1907 (7 Edw. VII. c. 51), Rule 76.
[60] Criminal Appeal (Scotland) Act, 1926 (16 & 17 Geo. V. c. 15), s. 11 (1); Act of Adjournal, 22nd March, 1935.
[61] Macdonald, *Criminal Law* (5th ed.), 358. See also § 1.
[62] Summary Jurisdiction (Scotland) Act, 1954 (2 & 3 Eliz. II. c. 48), s. 38.
[63] *Ibid.,* s. 73 (1); *Maciver* v. *MacKenzie,* 1942 J.C. 51.
[64] *McDonalds, Ltd.* v. *Adair,* 1944 J.C. 119.
[65] *Clark* v. *Stuart,* 1950 J.C. 8.
[66] *McLeod* v. *Woodmuir Miners Welfare Society Social Club,* 1961 J.C. 5.
[67] See § 339, sub-para. (b).
[68] *Niven* v. *Hart,* 1898, 25 R. (J.) 89.   The Lord Justice-General referred with approval to a practice that, where notes contain private memoranda irrelevant to the case, they are handed to the judge, who reads out what is material.
[69] *Hinshelwood* v. *Auld,* 1926 J.C. 4.

unable at the trial to remember the number, may recall it to memory from his note. The privilege is primarily confined to the original notes, but in two old cases witnesses were allowed to refer to secondary documents. A witness was allowed to refer to a draft minute of meeting framed by him from notes made apparently partly by himself and partly by some one else.[70] In such circumstances it is advisable to have the original notes available for inspection. Where a witness was using a printed report which he alleged was in substance the same as his notes, an objection was repelled on the ground that no attempt was made to discredit the statement by calling for the notes.[71] Presumably if the notes had been called for and were not available, the objection would have been sustained, and in a subsequent case the objection was sustained on that ground.[72] In that case Lord Fullerton distinguished two kinds of original note. First there are notes of a temporary state of affairs, e.g. the height of a flood; second there are notes of permanent features, e.g. the width of a bridge. Lord Fullerton thought that the former kind, if called for, must be produced but not the latter. Presumably the distinction is that the width of the bridge can be checked at any time, whereas the height of the flood at a particular moment cannot. The purpose of the notes or other writing is to refresh, stimulate or excite the memory of the witness. They are not a substitute for his memory.[73] An exception is made, however, even where the witness is wholly dependent on his note, provided that it is proved to have been accurately made, and, in a solemn criminal trial, that it is a production.[74] A shopkeeper whose shop has been broken into may read from the list of missing property made by him as soon as possible. There is also an exception in the case of medical and other expert reports. These may be read by the witness who made them as part of his evidence.[75] A witness may also refer to documents or books written under his direction or perused by him so that he was then satisfied of their accuracy.[76] The document itself need not be admissible in evidence. A witness has been allowed to look at an unstamped document.[77]

(c) **Hostile Witness.** This expression has no technical meaning in Scotland. When a witness gives evidence damaging to the case of the party calling him, the counsel or solicitor of that party is free to challenge his

---

[70] *Wilson* v. *Glasgow & South Western Railway*, 1851, 14 D. 1. This ruling was excepted to, but the case was settled. As to minutes generally, see § 221.

[71] *MacKenzie* v. *Horne*, 1838, 16 S. 1286; 1839, McL. & Rob., 977. In *Wilson* v. *Glasgow & South Western Railway* (*supra*), the witness was not asked to produce the original notes.

[72] *Campbell* v. *Macfarlane*, 1840, 2 D. 663. Another ground for refusing to allow the witness to use the report was that the copy proposed to be used had been made by a third party, who was not a witness, and had not been checked by the witness himself.

[73] *Macpherson*, 1845, 2 Broun, 450.

[74] *Macpherson* (*supra*) (where the writing was not lodged); *Gibb*, 1871, 2 Coup. 35 (where it was).

[75] *Black* v. *Bairds and Dalmellington*, 1939 S.C. 472, L. J-Cl. Aitchison at p. 477. The observations on that opinion in *Anderson* v. *St. Andrew's Ambulance Association*, 1942 S.C. 555, appear to relate to the question of recovery.

[76] Dickson, *Evidence* (3rd ed.) §1784.

[77] *Dickson* v. *Taylor*, 1816, 1 Mur. 142. But see § 238.

evidence by suggesting to him that in specified respects it is mistaken, unreliable or untruthful, and may ask the court to disbelieve any part of it.[78] He does not require the leave of the court to do this.[78] The same rule applies in a prosecution.[79] A witness may be asked, in order to explain his apparent reluctance, whether an attempt has been made to intimidate him.[80]

342. CROSS-EXAMINATION: GENERAL

(a) **Introductory.** Cross-examination has two purposes, first to test the veracity of the witness and the accuracy of his evidence, and secondly to obtain from him evidence on points on which he has not been questioned and which may support the cross-examiner's case.[80a] It follows that in so far as the opposing counsel or solicitor is satisfied that the witness is veracious and that his evidence in chief is accurate and complete, cross-examination is useless. It may even be harmful to the cross-examiner by emphasising the evidence already given or suggesting to the jury that the cross-examiner has a weak case. But if a party intends to lead evidence to contradict what a witness has said he is at least wise to challenge the witness's statements by cross-examination.[81]

(b) **Accuracy of Evidence.** Inaccuracy in evidence may be due to deliberate lying, to reckless over-confidence, or to the unconscious substitution of imagination for genuine recollection. Many a witness really believes that he is describing exactly what he has seen or heard, when in fact he only remembers certain parts, and the rest of his evidence consists of what he thinks must have happened or must have been said. Frequently, a detailed cross-examination will lead the witness (whatever the cause of his inaccuracy) to contradict himself or other witnesses on the same side, or to contradict some fact established by other evidence. Opinions have differed as to the proper course for the cross-examiner when there is an apparent inconsistency in the evidence of the witness. Is he entitled to leave the inconsistency and found on it, or must he give the witness an opportunity to explain it?[82] Opinions have also differed as to whether a cross-examiner, having received a general answer negativing his case, must proceed to put further detailed questions which can only be answered in the negative.[83] There appears to be some risk in omitting the additional questions in both cases.[81]

(c) **Credibility of Witness.** This may be tested by cross-examination as to interest,[84] e.g. relationship,[85] motive (whether, for example, he has made

[78] *Avery* v. *Cantilever Shoe Co.*, 1942 S.C. 469; *Lowe* v. *Bristol Motor Omnibus Co.*, 1934 S.C. 1.
[79] *Frank* v. *H.M. Advocate*, 1938 J.C. 17.
[80] *Manson* v. *H.M. Advocate*, 1951 J.C. 49.
[80a] See C.A.S. F. II. 4.
[81] On the effect of failure to cross-examine, see § **346.**
[82] *Macfarlane* v. *Raeburn*, 1946 S.C. 67, at pp. 73, 76.
[83] *Wilson* v. *Thomas Usher & Son*, 1934 S.C. 332, at pp. 337 and 338.

a claim against the defenders arising from the same accident), or prejudice.[86] Subject to privilege,[87] the witness may be cross-examined on his character,[88] e.g. as to convictions for crime inferring dishonesty. It was held competent to ask a witness, who was warned that she need not answer, whether she had been found fault with by previous mistresses for telling lies.[89] Since the evidence of a prostitute[90] and of an accomplice[91] is suspect, it must be competent to ask a witness if she or he holds that character. But if questions are apparently put merely to annoy the witness, the court may refuse to allow them.[92] Lastly, it is competent to ask a witness whether he has not made a previous statement inconsistent with his evidence, as to which see the next paragraph.

(d) **New Matter.** The second purpose of cross-examination is to elicit from the witness evidence on matters as to which he has not been asked in examination in chief, but which may be within his knowledge. Frequently in a trial on a charge of careless driving a prosecution witness is asked in cross-examination whether there was not in the vicinity another vehicle, which he has not mentioned, but the presence of which may be important. Failure to put such a question to the appropriate witnesses is prejudicial to a defence founded on the alleged presence of the other vehicle.[81] Where the court is to be asked to draw an inference from the facts, the inference must be put in cross-examination, if it is an inference as to the witness's actions or intentions, to that witness,[93] and. if it is a scientific inference, to the expert witnesses.[94] The witness may have an explanation destroying, or at least throwing doubt on, the inference.[81] It has been held that where a witness's own conduct is called in question he ought to be given an opportunity to explain it.[95]

343. CROSS-EXAMINATION: PREVIOUS STATEMENTS

(a) **General.** At common law it was competent to ask a witness whether

---

[84] The Attorney-General for Ireland, having elicited, by two questions, that a defence witness lived next door to the prisoner, sat down. Maurice Healy, *The Old Munster Circuit*, p. 93.

[85] *Roxburgh* v. *Watson*, 1868, 7 M. 19.

[86] *King* v. *King*, 1841, 4 D. 124, where it was held competent, not only to cross-examine a witness as to expressions of hostility to a party, but also to prove these by other evidence.

[87] See §345.

[88] Evidence of character in the case of rape is dealt with at §20, and of slander at §18.

[89] *King* v. *King*, 1842, 4 D. 590.

[90] *Tennant* v. *Tennant*, 1883, 10 R. 1187.

[91] *Dow* v. *McKnight*, 1949 J.C. 38.

[92] *Falconer* v. *Brown*, 1893, 21 R. (J.) 1. See §20, note 43.

[93] *Ryan* v. *Mills*, 1948 J.C. 28, at p. 35; *McCann* v. *Adair*, 1951 J.C. 127, at p. 130; *Cambo Shipping Co.* v. *Dampskibselskabet Carl*, 1920 S.C. 26, at p. 30.

[94] *Crawford* v. *Granite S.S. Co., Ltd.*, 1906, 8 F. 1013, at p. 1025.

[95] *Turner* v. *Board of Trade*, 1894, 22 R. 18; *Watson* v. *Board of Trade*, 1892, 19 R. 1078. Both cases deal with enquiries into shipping casualties and are therefore special. In an ordinary action any explanation would normally be given in re-examination.

he had on a previous occasion made a statement different from his evidence, but if he denied doing so, evidence could not be led to contradict the denial.[96] By statute it is now "competent to examine any witness . . . as to whether he has on any specified occasion made a statement . . . different from the evidence given by him"; and it is "competent . . . to adduce evidence to prove that such witness has made such different statement on the occasion specified."[97] These provisions do not apply to statements made by a witness after he has given evidence.[98] Evidence cannot be adduced under the second part of the section unless the witness has been specifically asked, in terms of the first part, whether he made the statement.[99] Accordingly, if a pursuer or a prosecutor wishes to take advantage of the section he probably must call the witness himself and put the statement to him.[1] Section 4 of the Evidence (Scotland) Act, 1852,[97] empowers a judge to allow a witness to be recalled, and it has been suggested that a pursuer might be allowed to recall a witness to speak to a statement alleged to have been made by a defence witness and denied by him.[2] It has been held incompetent for a prosecutor to recall a witness for this purpose after the prosecution case is closed,[3] but a defender was allowed to recall a witness for the pursuer after the pursuer's case was closed in order to cross-examine her on statements alleged to have been made by her,[4] and in another case the same course would probably have been followed if the statement and the occasion had been averred with greater specification.[98] The previous statement may have been made while giving evidence in another case or in the statutory examination of the witness as a bankrupt,[5] or in answer to a questionnaire,[6] or probably in the witness's pleadings in another case to which he was a party,[7] or merely in conversation,[8] or before a commissioner.[9]

96 *Livingstone* v. *Strachan, Crerar & Jones*, 1923 S.C. 794, L. Murray at p. 818; *Gall* v. *Gall*, 1870, 9 M. 177.
97 Evidence (Scotland) Act, 1852 (15 & 16 Vict. c. 27), s. 3.
98 *Begg* v. *Begg*, 1887, 14 R. 497.
99 *Livingstone* v. *Strachan, Crerar & Jones (supra); Gall* v. *Gall (supra); McTaggart* v. *H.M. Advocate*, 1934 J.C. 33. Cf. *Common*, 1860, 3 Irv. 632, which has been doubted; *Kerr* v. *H.M. Advocate*, 1958 J.C. 14.
1 *Gall* v. *Gall (supra); McTaggart* v. *H.M. Advocate (supra).*
2 *Livingstone* v. *Strachan, Crerar & Jones (supra),* at pp. 801, 810.
3 *McNeilie* v. *H.M. Advocate*, 1929 J.C. 50. This is a rule of criminal procedure; *Todd* v. *McDonald*, 1960 J.C. 93, at p. 96
4 *Robertson* v. *Steuart*, 1874, 1 R. 532, at pp. 586, 595; *Hoey* v. *Hoey*, 1884, 11 R. 578; *Dyet* v. *N.C.B.*, 1957 S.L.T. (Notes) 18.
5 *Emslie* v. *Alexander*, 1862, 1 M. 209; *Forrests* v. *Low's Trustees*, 1907 S.C. 1240, at p. 1248.
6 *Maitland* v. *Glasgow Corporation*, 1947 S.C. 20. See also *Healey* v. *A. Massey & Son*, (O.H.) 1961 S.C. 198.
7 *Jackson* v. *Glasgow Corporation*, 1956 S.C. 354, L.P. Clyde at p. 358, L. Russell at p. 362; *Stewart* v. *Gelot*, 1871, 43 Sc. Jur. 578, where an exception against the admission of cross on such pleadings was abandoned. But averments, like precognitions, are the pleader's version of the witness's statement. As to precognitions, see sub-para. (b).
8 *Robertson* v. *Steuart (supra),* at p. 595.
9 *Forrests* v. *Low's Trustees (supra),* where the evidence was taken to lie *in retentis,* and it was held that the report of the commissioner could not be used to contradict the witness, since she had appeared and given evidence at the proof.

(b) Precognition. As Dickson himself pointed out,[10] there is no limitation in section 3 as to the nature of the previous occasion, nor is there any exception of previous statements made on precognition, and there is authority,[11] seldom, if ever, referred to, that statements made on precognition are not excepted. Nevertheless, modern practice[12] has introduced such an exception, which, possibly because the point never seems to have been fully argued, is supported on various grounds and is therefore difficult to define. First, the exception applies to a statement "made under the confidential circumstances of precognition."[13] The word "precognition" is here used as an abstract term to mean the act of taking a statement from a person for the purpose of discovering what his evidence is to be in a cause commenced or at least decided upon.[14] Accordingly, a statement made during police enquiries was held not to be made on precognition in civil proceedings connected with the same facts.[15] If no statement made under precognition is admissible, a witness to an alibi cannot be asked whether he told a police officer sent to take his statement that he had never even heard of the accused. Such a rule is certainly precise.

Another reason given for the exception is that a written precognition (the term here used in a concrete sense) is the precognoscer's version, probably inaccurate, of the witness's statements "put into consecutive narrative form."[16] There are two sufficient reasons for refusing to allow a precognition to be read. First, by definition it does not contain the actual statements of the witness. Secondly, except in the special case of a doctor or other expert, a witness is not allowed to incorporate a written statement into his testimony as evidence of the facts stated in it.[17] The exception is thus easy to justify where the essential preliminary of cross-examination has been omitted[18] or in *obiter* dicta.[19] But it can be applied at the proper

[10] (1st ed.) §1808 (published in 1855). In the second edition (1864), after several decisions, the editor left the text unchanged. The editor of the third edition, in another part of the book (§265), stated that the balance of authority is against the competency of contradicting a witness by what he said on precognition. But this balance was created by taking into account decisions to the effect that precognitions could not be used as hearsay of a deceased person. See *Livingstone* v. *Strachan, Crerar & Jones*, 1923 S.C. 794, L. Murray at p. 818.

[11] *Leckie*, 1895, 1 Adam 538; *Robertson*, 1873, 2 Coup. 495; *Inch* v. *Inch*, 1856, 18 D. 997. *Contra, O'Donnell and McGuire*, 1855, 2 Irv. 236. Doubtful, *Luke*, 1866, 5 Irv. 293.

[12] But in *Livingstone* v. *Strachan, Crerar & Jones (supra)* L. Murray expressed his disagreement with the practice and L. J-Cl. Alness reserved his opinion, and in *McTaggart* v. *H.M. Advocate (supra)* all the opinions were inconsistent with it.

[13] *McNeilie* v. *H.M. Advocate*, 1929 J.C. 50, L. J-G. Clyde at p. 53, who expressed no disapproval of the fact that the witness had been cross-examined as to a statement made on precognition.

[14] *Ibid.* and L. Sands at p. 54; *Kerr* v. *H.M. Advocate*, 1958 J.C. 14, L. J-Cl. Thomson at p. 19.

[15] *Gilmour* v. *Hansen*, 1920 S.C. 598.

[16] *Kerr* v. *H.M. Advocate (supra)*, L. J-Cl. Thomson at p. 19.

[17] *Black* v. *Bairds and Dalmellington*, 1939 S.C. 472, L. J-Cl. Aitchison at p. 477. See also *Gibson* v. *National Cash Register Co.*, 1925 S.C. 500, where the letter written by the witness was certainly not substituted for his oral testimony.

[18] As in *Kerr* v. *H.M. Advocate (supra)*.

[19] As in *Binnie* v. *Black*, (O.H.) 1923 S.L.T. 98, and *Black* v. *Bairds and Dalmellington (supra)*, L. Wark at p. 484.

beginning, viz. cross-examination,[20] only by assuming (first) that the witness will deny making the statement[21] and therefore that the person taking the precognition will be called, (second) that that person will be unable to remember any statement, however simple,[22] and (third) that an account written by the witness may be substituted for his sworn testimony.[17] In the only modern case[22] in which the question arose and was decided at that stage the first assumption was overlooked, and the Lord Ordinary made the second and third, holding that "in very many cases the person taking the precognition cannot be expected to remember what was said and the most reliable evidence would be . . . the precognition." These considerations suggest that section 3 ought not to be excluded by the mere fact that a precognition has been taken, and that the matter is one of credibility. If the witness and the precognoscer differ as to what was said, the evidence of the latter may be suspect,[16] but that is not nowadays a reason for excluding it.[22a]

344. CROSS-EXAMINATION: SEVERAL PARTIES

(a) Civil Causes. Cases where pursuers have conflicting interests must be rare, but in one case where salvage actions were conjoined the court expressly gave the pursuers the right to cross-examine each other's witnesses.[23] An opinion by Lord Shand that one defender has no right, apart from agreement, to cross-examine a witness called for another defender, was not concurred in by the other judges, and it was held in that case that there was implied agreement to hold all the evidence as evidence in the cause.[24] In modern practice proofs and trials are conducted on that footing.[25]

(b) Criminal Trials. The right of one co-accused to cross-examine another co-accused, or a witness called by another co-accused, is discussed in the next chapter.[26]

345. PRIVILEGE OF WITNESS

(a) General. A witness is entitled to refuse to answer a question if a true answer may lead to his conviction for a crime or involves an admission of adultery. The privilege is that of the witness, not of a party. "The

---

20 See sub-para. (a) (*supra*).
21 In *Kerr* v. *H.M. Advocate* (*supra*), when the witness was ultimately cross-examined, he practically admitted having made the statement.
22 In *Connolly* v. *National Coal Board*, (O.H.) 1953 S.C. 376, the statement was that a pin in the short arm of a piece of machinery had come out. However forgetful solicitors and police officers may be in their work, a confectioner can remember gossip six years old: *Robertson* v. *Steuart* (*ut supra*).
22ª See §348, sub-para. (b).
23 *Boyle* v. *Olsen*, 1912 S.C. 1235.
24 *Ayr Road Trustees* v. *Adams*, 1883, 11 R. 326.
25 Otherwise there could have been no question of granting a diligence to one defender for the recovery of documents in the hands of another; *Anderson* v. *St. Andrew's Ambulance Association*, 1942 S.C. 555.
26 See §§359-362.

common law interposes to protect the witness, not to give an advantage to the defender,"[27] or, it may be added, to the pursuer, the prosecutor or the accused. It is the duty of the judge to tell the witness that he need not answer such a question, but if the judge does not realise the situation and the witness apparently does not understand his rights, it is proper for counsel to point these out to the judge.[27] The opinion has been expressed that it is not incompetent to raise the point in the form of an objection, i.e. an objection by a party,[28] and in two criminal trials[29] it was raised by objections by the prosecutor. The privilege applies only to the particular question, and a witness has no right to refuse to be sworn or to answer any question because he anticipates an incriminating question.[30]

(b) Incrimination. "It is a sacred and inviolable principle . . . that no man is bound to incriminate himself."[31] The privilege applies not only to a direct question as to whether he has committed a specified crime, but to examination on facts which indirectly infer guilt or may form links in a chain of evidence.[32] But there is no privilege if the witness cannot be prosecuted for the crime, either because he has been called as a witness for the prosecution in the trial of another person for the same crime,[33] or because he has already been convicted of the crime. If asked, he must state whether he has been convicted,[34] but his answer, if negative, cannot be contradicted by parole evidence.[34] Since the only legitimate purpose of this type of question is to shake credibility, it is confined to crimes inferring dishonesty, such as theft or perjury, or possibly extreme depravity.[35]

(c) Adultery. At common law a witness is not bound to answer a question tending to show that he has committed adultery. This applies both in civil causes[36] and criminal trials[37] and is not confined to cases where adultery is the issue.[37] The section which made the parties to any proceeding instituted in consequence of adultery, and the husbands and wives

---

[27] *Kirkwood* v. *Kirkwood*, 1875, 3 R. 235, L.P. Inglis at p. 236.

[28] *Ibid.*, L. Deas at p. 236.

[29] *Dickie* v. *H.M. Advocate*, 1897, 24 R. (J.) 82; *Kennedy* v. *H.M. Advocate*, 1896, 23 R. (J.) 28.

[30] *Don* v. *Don*, 1848, 10 D. 1046.

[31] *Livingstone* v. *Murrays*, 1830, 9 S. 161, L. Gillies at p. 162.

[32] Dickson, *Evidence* (3rd ed.) §1789.

[33] *Macmillan* v. *Murray*, 1920 J.C. 13; *McGinley* v. *MacLeod*, 1963 S.L.T. 2.

[34] *Dickie* v. *H.M. Advocate* (*supra*), L. J-Cl. Macdonald at p. 83; *Kennedy* v. *H.M. Advocate* (*supra*), L. J-Cl. Macdonald at p. 30. In the former of these passages there is a dictum to the effect that if the witness denies the conviction it may be proved by production of an extract. But the extract would still have to be applied, and the course suggested is not followed in practice. See, however, Macdonald, *Criminal Law* (5th ed.) 310.

[35] Dickson, *Evidence* (3rd ed.) §1618.

[36] *Kirkwood* v. *Kirkwood* (*supra*), where the Evidence Further Amendment (Scotland) Act, 1874 (37 & 38 Vict. c. 64), s. 2, was founded on, but the Lord President's opinion was based on common law; *Muir* v. *Muir*, 1873, 11 M. 529.

[73] *Stephens*, 1839, 2 Swinton 348 (rape) where a doctor, who had attended the woman, and gave evidence of her modesty, was asked in cross whether he had had intercourse with her himself, and was told that he need not answer.

of such parties, competent witnesses in such proceeding, went on to provide "that no witness to any proceeding, whether a party to the suit or not, shall be liable to be asked or bound to answer any question tending to show that he or she has been guilty of adultery, unless such witness shall have already given evidence in the same proceeding in disproof of his or her alleged adultery."[38] Since the words are "witness to any proceeding," not "to any such proceeding," this would appear to be merely a restatement of the common law. Provided that the witness is made fully aware of his rights, and is willing to answer, the evidence is competent.[39] If he refuses to answer, this should not be recorded,[40] and the refusal cannot be founded on.[41] If he answers in the negative, he may be cross-examined to test credibility.[42]

346. FAILURE TO CROSS-EXAMINE

(a) **Civil Causes.** The most serious practical result of failure to cross-examine, or to cross-examine fully,[43] appears after the proof is closed. It may be a ground for setting aside a verdict,[44] and it may provide a substantial ground of decision on a proof.[45] If the point arises during a proof, the defect is more likely to be curable. In theory a defender who has failed to cross-examine the pursuer's witnesses may be stopped from leading evidence to contradict them, but there does not seem to be any modern instance of this, and it is usual to allow the evidence to be led either merely for what it is worth or with a right to the pursuer to recall his witnesses to contradict it, or to have his witnesses recalled for cross-examination before the evidence is led.[46] Failure to cross-examine does not supply corroboration. A single witness does not become sufficient in law because he is not cross-examined.[47] The contrary view[48] seems to have arisen from a misunderstanding of the decision in *Keenan* v. *S.C.W.S.*[44]

(b) **Criminal Trials.** Since the burden of proof lies on the prosecutor throughout, the defence need not cross-examine, but may simply rely on the

---

[38] Evidence Further Amendment (Scotland) Act, 1874 (37 & 38 Vict. c. 64), s. 2.
[39] *McDougall* v. *McDougall*, 1927 S.C. 666; *Bannatyne* v. *Bannatyne*, 1886, 13 R. 619; *Kirkwood* v. *Kirkwood* (*supra*).
[40] *Cook* v. *Cook*, 1876, 4 R. 78.
[41] *Hunt* v. *Hunt*, (O.H.) 1893, 1 S.L.T. 157.
[42] *Muir* v. *Muir* (*supra*).
[43] See § 342, sub-para. (b).
[44] *Wilson* v. *Thomas Usher & Son*, 1934 S.C. 332 (where the cross was held sufficient); *Keenan* v. *S.C.W.S.*, 1914 S.C. 959 (where on a crucial point there was contradictory evidence, and the pursuer, who did not cross the defenders' witnesses on it, was held to have admitted that his witnesses were discredited).
[45] *Bishop* v. *Bryce*, 1910 S.C. 426 (where a finding in fact made by the sheriff was on appeal held not to be proved because the defender had not been cross-examined on it); *Jordan* v. *Court Line*, 1947 S.C. 29, L. Carmont at p. 36.
[46] *Bishop* v. *Bryce* (*supra*), L.P. Dunedin at p. 431; *Wilson* v. *Thomas Usher & Son*, 1934 S.C. 332, L. J-Cl. Aitchison at p. 338.
[47] *Stewart* v. *Glasgow Corporation*, 1958 S.C. 28; *Moore* v. *Harland & Wolff*, 1937 S.C. 707, at pp. 715, 729.
[48] Lewis, *Evidence*, 226.

prosecution evidence not reaching the necessary standard. As in civil causes, absence of cross-examination does not supply corroboration.[49] The fact that the defence has not cross-examined one witness on a particular matter, though it may be subject of comment, does not prevent cross-examination of another witness on that matter.[50] The point does not seem to have arisen with regard to defence witnesses.

347. RECORDING OF EVIDENCE

In the Court of Session evidence in a proof, whether taken before a judge or on commission, is recorded by a sworn shorthand writer and certified by him, with power to the court to make such alterations as appear to be necessary.[51] The same applies in civil jury trials.[52] The rule in the sheriff court is similar,[53] except that in a summary cause the evidence is not recorded unless the sheriff so orders.[54] In solemn criminal procedure shorthand notes are taken of the proceedings, including the evidence.[55] In summary criminal procedure the evidence is not recorded, though the notes taken by the sheriff or other judge might be used to refresh his memory if occasion arose.[56]

[49] *Wilson* v. *Brown*, 1947 J.C. 81, L. Mackay at pp. 94, 95, L. Jamieson at pp. 96, 97; *Morton* v. *H.M. Advocate*, 1938 J.C. 50, L. J-Cl. Aitchison at p. 54.
[50] *McPherson* v. *Copeland*, 1961 J.C. 74.
[51] Rules of Court, 1948, Rule 133.
[52] *Ibid.*, Rule 150.
[53] Sheriff Courts (Scotland) Act, 1907 (7 Edw. VII. c. 51), Rules 65, 66 and 137. In spite of the terms of Rule 137 notes are in practice taken only of the evidence and the charge.
[54] *Ibid.*, s. 8.
[55] Criminal Appeal (Scotland) Act 1926 (16 & 17 Geo. V. c. 15), s. 11; Act of Adjournal, 22nd March, 1935, s. 1.
[56] See *Davidson* v. *McFadyean*, 1942 J.C. 95, where the fact that the sheriff had written "sworn" after the name of a witness was held to be evidence that the witness had taken the oath.

CHAPTER XXVIII

ORAL EVIDENCE: SPECIALTIES OF WITNESSES

348. INTRODUCTORY

(a) **General.** A witness is competent unless he is excluded by a rule of law, and compellable unless he is entitled on some legal ground to refuse to give evidence. As a general rule any person is a competent and compellable witness, but some are not competent, and some, though competent, are not compellable. Further, a witness may be competent and compellable, but his evidence may not be admissible for all purposes or against all the parties.[1] This chapter deals with these exceptional cases.

(b) **The Old Law.** Under early practice there were numerous grounds on which persons were held to be incompetent as witnesses.[2] Of these some have been abolished by, or as the result of, statute, and others have been abandoned. An atheist may now affirm,[3] and outlawry has been abolished.[4] A party to a civil action and, subject to limitations, the husband or wife of such party are competent.[5] So is an accused person and, again

---

1 *Young* v. *H.M. Advocate*, 1932 J.C. 63, at p. 73. Where several parties are associated on the same side of a case, e.g. several co-accused tried together (§§ 359-362) or several pursuers or defenders, a witness incompetent as to one is incompetent as to all, *quoad* any part of the case in which they are mutually interested: Dickson, *Evidence* (3rd ed.) §1611. See *Gavin* v. *Montgomerie*, 1830, 9 S. 213, where the court was divided as to whether the witness's husband had an interest.
2 Dickson, *Evidence* (3rd ed.) §§1542-1611.
3 Oaths Act, 1888 (51 & 52 Vict. c. 46), s. 1.
4 Criminal Justice (Scotland) Act, 1949 (12, 13 & 14 Geo. VI. c. 94), s. 15.
5 Evidence (Scotland) Act, 1853 (16 Vict. c. 20), s. 3; Evidence Further Amendment (Scotland) Act, 1874 (37 & 38 Vict. c. 64), ss. 2, 3. As to the limitations, see §§ **354, 355.**

subject to limitations, the husband or wife of such person.[6] Relationship,[7] except as between husband and wife, agency and partial counsel,[8] conviction of crime[8] and interest[8] no longer disqualify. There has not been a reported objection on the ground of malice and enmity[9] or of bribery[10] for a century, and the court refused to set aside a conviction on the ground that a witness had told another witness about to be called the answers he had given in cross-examination.[11] The development of the law is described in general terms in *Dow* v. *MacKnight*,[12] where it is pointed out "that moral turpitude or interest is a ground of criticism not of the admissibility of the witness but of the reliability of his evidence."[13]

(c) **Penuria Testium.** The old grounds of objection to a witness were so numerous that it might be impossible to find competent witnesses to prove a case. This situation was known as *penuria testium* and justified the admission of witnesses who would normally have been incompetent.[14] Since the abolition of the old objections the phrase has now no technical meaning, but is sometimes loosely used to describe a situation where in the nature of the case there must be a paucity of witnesses, with the implication that slight corroboration is sufficient, or to justify the admission of hearsay.[15]

349. CHILDREN

A child is admissible if he appears to be able to understand what he has seen or heard and to give an account of it and to appreciate the duty to speak the truth.[16] It is for the judge to determine whether a child should be examined, after a preliminary interrogation of the child and, if necessary, after hearing other evidence.[17] A child of three was rejected in a murder trial, mainly because she had not made a *de recenti* statement,[18] while one of three and a half was admitted when she had made a *de recenti* statement, and the charge was of assault on her.[19] Children of from four to seven have been admitted in criminal cases,[20] but a child of six was rejected as a

---

6 Criminal Evidence Act, 1898 (61 & 62 Vict. c. 36), ss. 1, 4. As to the limitations, see §§ **352, 353, 355.**
7 Evidence (Scotland) Act, 1840 (3 & 4 Vict. c. 59), s. 1.
8 Evidence (Scotland) Act, 1852 (15 Vict. c. 27), s. 1; Evidence (Scotland) Act, 1853 (16 Vict. c. 20), s. 2.
9 *Wilson*, 1861, 4 Irv. 42.
10 *Crichton* v. *Fleming*, 1840, 3 D. 313.
11 *Campbell* v. *Cadenhead*, 1884, 11 R. (J.) 61.
12 *Dow* v. *MacKnight*, 1949 J.C. 38, at pp. 42, 56.
13 *Ibid.*, at pp. 56, 57. As to cross-examination on these points, see § **342**, sub-para. (c).
14 *Surtees* v. *Wotherspoon*, 1872, 10 M. 866; *Dow* v. *MacKnight* (*supra*), at pp. 53, 56.
15 *Moorov* v. *H.M. Advocate*, 1930 J.C. 68, at p. 79; *McKie* v. *Western Scottish Motor Traction Co.*, 1952 S.C. 206, at p. 209 (reclaimers' argument). See § **170** (affiliation).
16 Dickson, *Evidence* (3rd ed.) §1543.
17 *Ibid.*, §1548.
18 *Thomson*, 1857, 2 Irv. 747.
19 *Miller*, 1870, 1 Coup. 430.
20 Bell's Notes, 247.

result of examination.[21]   There do not appear to be any reported civil cases where such young children have been admitted, but there seems to be no reason why they should not be.   A boy of nearly seven was rejected in an action of divorce on the ground of adultery "on account of the nature of the case."[22]   Where a child or young person is called as a witness in any case involving indecency or immorality the court may be cleared while he is giving evidence.[23]   Children under twelve are not put on oath, but admonished to tell the truth, children over fourteen are usually sworn. The oath is not administered to children between these ages unless the judge is satisfied that the child understands its nature.[24]   The matter is one for the discretion of the judge.[25]

350.   MENTAL INCAPACITY

This is a question of degree,[26] and the competency of the witness depends on the nature and extent of the incapacity.[27]   The decision is for the judge, and it is competent,[28] and may be necessary,[29] to lead evidence, including possibly that of the witness himself,[30] as to the state of his mind.   In solemn criminal procedure witnesses may be called for this purpose although they are not on the crown or defence lists.[28]   A witness who is insane at the time of the trial is usually rejected,[31] but an exception has been permitted.[32] The mere fact that the witness is an inmate of a mental hospital does not exclude.[33]   It is stated by Hume[34] that a witness who suffers from periodic derangements may be examined regarding any matter observed by him during a period of sanity, but that if a period of subsequent insanity has intervened before the trial, he is inadmissible for this purpose.   In the latter of two cases,[35] in which a witness was rejected because he had been insane between the incident and the trial, the judges were of opinion that this part of the rule should be reconsidered, and it is extremely doubtful whether it would now be applied.   Something may turn on the nature of the evidence proposed to be taken from a witness.   A mentally defective witness was rejected when she was to be asked why the title to shares had been taken in a particular way.[36]   The effect of examination on a mentally defective

---

21 *McBeth*, 1867, 5 Irv. 353.
22 *Robertson* v. *Robertson*, 1888, 15 R. 1001.
23 Children and Young Persons |(Scotland) Act, 1937 (1 Edw. VIII. & 1 Geo. VI. c. 37), s. 45.
24 Dickson, *Evidence* (3rd ed.) §1549.
25 *Anderson* v. *McFarlane*, 1899, 1 F. (J.) 36.   Modern scientific opinion is that children develop earlier than they used to, and account may have to be taken of this.
26 *Black*, 1887, 1 White, 365.
27 Dickson, *Evidence* (3rd ed.) §1550.
28 *Black (supra): Stott*, 1894, 1 Adam 386.
29 *McKenzie*, 1869, 1 Coup. 244; *Stott (supra)*.
30 *O'Neil and Gollan*, 1858, 3 Irv. 93.
31 Macdonald, *Criminal Law* (5th ed.) 288.
32 *Stott (supra)*.
33 *Littlejohn*, 1881, 4 Coup. 454.
34 II, 340.
35 *Sheriff*, 1866, 5 Irv. 226; *McKenzie*, 1869, 1 Coup. 244.
36 *Buckle* v. *Buckle's Curator*, (O.H.) 1907, 15 S.L.T. 98.

witness must be kept in view,[37] and this might apply also to an insane witness. An imbecile was rejected apparently on the ground that she did not understand the nature of an oath,[38] but in a later case it was held that that was not a sufficient reason for rejecting such a witness, and that, in a fitting case, a witness of defective capacity might be admonished to tell the truth, like a child.[39] When commission is granted to take the evidence of a witness of doubtful mental capacity, it is for the commissioner to decide whether he should be examined.[40]

351. DEAF, DUMB AND INARTICULATE WITNESSES

A deaf mute of normal mental capacity who understands the nature of an oath is treated as an ordinary witness, except that he is sworn and his evidence is taken through an interpreter using the deaf and dumb alphabet, or, if the witness does not know the alphabet, by written question and answer.[41] Where neither method is possible the witness may communicate by signs if these can be understood[42] and interpreted. In neither of these cases[42] was the witness put on oath. An inarticulate witness was examined through a person who understood her means of expression.[43] Where it was not clear whether the disability was physical or mental the witness was rejected.[44]

352. HUSBAND OR WIFE OF ACCUSED: WITNESS FOR DEFENCE

At common law the spouse of an accused person was not a competent witness. In certain statutory offences, however, it was provided by the statutes[45] concerned that, if the accused person thought fit, his wife or husband, as the case might be, might be called, sworn, examined and cross-examined as an ordinary witness in the case, or in like manner as any other witness. The phrases used seem to indicate that the spouse is not only competent but compellable. These statutes have not been repealed, but, by a later statutory provision[46] which applies to every criminal cause, the husband or wife of the accused person was made a competent witness for

---

[37] *Tosh* v. *Ogilvy*, 1873, 1 R. 254, at p. 257; *Kilpatrick Parish Council* v. *Row Parish Council*, (O.H.) 1911, 2 S.L.T. 32.

[38] *Murray*, 1866, 5 Irv. 232. See also *McGilvray*, 1830, Bell's Notes, 264.

[39] *Black (supra)*.

[40] *Tosh* v. *Ogilvy (supra); McIntyre* v. *McIntyre*, (O.H.) 1920, 1 S.L.T. 207.

[41] Dickson, *Evidence* (3rd ed.) §1556; Macdonald, *Criminal Law* (5th ed.) 289; *Martin*, 1823, Shaw, 101; *Reid*, 1835, Bell's Notes, 246.

[42] *Rice*, 1864, 4 Irv. 493; *Montgomery*, 1855, 2 Irv. 222.

[43] *Howison*, 1871, 2 Coup. 153. See also *Mark*, 1845, 7 D. 882.

[44] *O'Neil and Gollan*, 1858, 3 Irv. 93.

[45] Explosive Substances Act, 1883 (46 & 47 Vict. c. 3), s. 4 (2); Criminal Law Amendment Act, 1885 (48 & 49 Vict. c. 69), s. 20; Merchandise Marks Act, 1887 (50 & 51 Vict. c. 28), s. 10; Betting and Loans (Infants) Act, 1892 (55 & 56 Vict. c. 4), s. 6.

[46] Criminal Evidence Act, 1898 (61 & 62 Vict. c. 36), s. 1. As to the words in the section "at every stage of the proceedings," see § **356**, note 88. The spouse must be called as a witness at the trial and before the defence evidence is closed: *Clark & Bendall* v. *Stuart*, 1886, 13 R. (J.) 86, at pp. 92-93 (a case under the Criminal Law Amendment Act, 1885 (48 & 49 Vict. c. 69)).

the defence. He or she may not be called as a witness except upon the application of the accused,[47] and his or her failure to give evidence must not be the subject of comment by the prosecutor.[48] The provision applies whether the accused is charged solely or jointly with another person. One co-accused may not call the spouse of another accused as a witness,[49] and the evidence of a spouse called by one accused is not evidence for or against another.[50] The question as to whether the spouse can be compelled by the accused to give evidence against his or her will does not seem to have arisen for decision.[51] Notice of the intention to call the husband or wife as a defence witness must be given to the prosecutor in the usual way.[52] A provision in a later section[53] of the same statute, which seems to indicate that the spouse of the accused may be called as a witness for the defence "without the consent of the person charged," is difficult to understand, and it is thought that for practical purposes it may be ignored. The question of confidential communications between the spouses is mentioned later.[54]

353. HUSBAND OR WIFE OF ACCUSED: WITNESS FOR PROSECUTION

At common law, with a single important exception, one spouse is not a competent witness against the other.[55] It is immaterial that the marriage has been irregular, but the incompetency of the witness would probably not be sustained unless the fact of the marriage is instantly verifiable.[56] The exception applies when the husband or wife is the alleged victim, in which case he or she is both a competent and a compellable witness.[55] In order to make the spouse a competent witness the crime need not involve physical injury. A husband is competent and compellable when his wife is charged with uttering cheques on which his signature was forged,[57] or with stealing his property,[58] and a wife is competent and compellable when her husband is charged with falsely accusing her of trying to poison him.[59]

[47] *Ibid.*, s. 1 (c).
[48] *Ibid.*, s. 1 (b). See, *mutatis mutandis*, § 357.
[49] *Ibid.*, s. 1 (c). The spouse of the person charged shall not be called except upon the application of the accused.
[50] Alison, II, 621, 622; *Young*, 1932 J.C. 63, at p. 74.
[51] See § 353, note 60.
[52] Criminal Evidence Act, 1898 (61 & 62 Vict. c. 36), s. 5.
[53] *Ibid.*, s. 4. The general permission has already been given in sec. 1, and its repetition is unnecessary, unless, by allowing the spouse to be called without the consent of the accused, it was intended to give to a defending solicitor the power enjoyed by counsel of conducting the defence as he thinks proper, irrespective of his client's wishes. See *Batchelor* v. *Pattison and Mackersy*, 1876, 3 R. 914, at p. 918. But the grammatical inelegance in the omission of the words "for the" before "defence" gives rise to the suspicion that the words "or defence" were added as a result of an ill-considered and last minute amendment. The bill was much altered in its passage through Parliament.
[54] See § 355.
[55] *Harper* v. *Adair*, 1945 J.C. 21; *Foster*, 1932 J.C. 75. This exception is not affected by the statutory provisions: Criminal Evidence Act, 1898 (61 & 62 Vict. c. 36), s. 4 (2); Criminal Law Amendment Act, 1912 (2 & 3 Geo. V. c. 20), s. 7 (6).
[56] *Reid*, 1873, 2 Coup. 415; *Muir*, 1836. 1 Swin. 402.
[57] *Foster* (*supra*).
[58] *Harper* v. *Adair* (*supra*).
[59] *Millar*, 1847, Ark. 355.

P

By statute a husband or wife of the accused, while not compellable,[60] is a competent witness for the prosecution, without the consent of the accused, when the accused is charged with an offence under one of the following enactments:—Criminal Law Amendment Act, 1885;[61] Mental Health (Scotland) Act, 1960;[62] Children and Young Persons (Scotland) Act, 1937;[63] National Assistance Act, 1948;[64] Immoral Traffic (Scotland) Act, 1902;[65] National Insurance Act, 1946;[66] Workmen's Compensation (Supplementation) Act, 1951,[67] or with any of the following crimes or offences:—any offence in respect of a child or young person which constitutes the crime of incest,[63] any offence involving bodily injury to a child or young person,[63] and the crime of bigamy.[68] The confidentiality of communications between husband and wife is dealt with later.[69]

354. HUSBAND OR WIFE OF PARTY: CIVIL CAUSES

At common law the husband or wife of a party was not a competent witness. The Evidence (Scotland) Act, 1853,[70] provided that it should be competent to adduce the husband or wife of a party, but no person is compellable to answer any question tending to criminate himself or herself, and the confidentiality of communications during marriage is safeguarded.[71] The Act did not apply to consistorial actions,[72] but that limitation was

---

60 The enactments mentioned in notes 66, 67, expressly provide that the spouse is not compellable, but the remaining statutes which are included in, or have been added to, the Schedule to the Criminal Evidence Act, 1898, or which are similar in terms to sec. 4 of that Act, do not. There is no reported Scottish decision exactly in point, but in an unreported case, where the accused was charged with assault on his wife and child, Lord Fleming held the wife competent and compellable *quoad* the assault on herself, and competent, but not compellable, *quoad* the assault on the child. In *R.* v. *Leach*, [1912] A.C. 305, the House of Lords held that a spouse was not compellable under the statute, and the practice of warning a spouse that he or she need not give evidence (*H.D.*, 1953 J.C. 65) indicates that this interpretation is accepted in Scotland. *Fraser*, 1901, 3 F. (J.) 67, does not decide the point, because the statute in question there expressly provided that the spouse was not compellable.

61 Criminal Evidence Act, 1898 (61 & 62 Vict. c. 36), s. 4 (1) and Sch. This is the only unrepealed statute mentioned in the original Schedule which applies to Scotland.

62 Mental Health (Scotland) Act, 1960 (8 & 9 Eliz. II. c. 61), s. 96 (5).

63 Children and Young Persons (Scotland) Act, 1937 (1 Edw. VIII. & 1 Geo. VI. c. 37), Sch. 1, as applied by the Criminal Procedure (Scotland) Act, 1938 (1 & 2 Geo. VI. c. 48), s. 11. "Offence involving bodily injury" includes lewd practices (*H.M. Advocate* v. *Lee*, 1923 J.C. 1) and assault by attempting to strike (*H.M. Advocate* v. *Macphie*, 1926 J.C. 91).

64 National Assistance Act, 1948 (11 & 12 Geo. VI. c. 29), s. 51; National Assistance (Adaptation of Enactments) Regulations, 1952 (S.I. 1952, No. 1334), Sch. pt. II.

65 Immoral Traffic (Scotland) Act, 1902 (2 Edw. VII. c. 11); Criminal Law Amendment Act, 1912 (2 & 3 Geo. V. c. 20), s. 7 (6).

66 National Insurance Act, 1946 (9 & 10 Geo. VI. c. 67), s. 53 (5).

67 Workmen's Compensation (Supplementation) Act, 1951 (14 & 15 Geo. VI. c. 22), s. 4 (5).

68 Criminal Justice Administration Act, 1914 (4 & 5 Geo. V. c. 58), s. 28 (3). At common law the spouse of a person charged with bigamy was not competent: *Armstrong*, 1844, 2 Broun 251.

69 See § 355.

70 16 Vict. c. 20.

71 s. 3. See § 355.

removed by section 2 of the Evidence Further Amendment (Scotland) Act, 1874,[73] which further provided that no witness should be asked or bound to answer any question tending to shew that he or she has been guilty of adultery, unless the witness has already given evidence in the same proceeding in disproof of his or her alleged adultery. Apart from the confidentiality of communications during marriage,[74] the privilege of a husband or wife is thus the same as that of any other witness.[75] The evidence of a husband or wife is admissible to prove that intercourse did or did not take place between them during any period, but neither is compellable to give such evidence.[76] It does not appear to have been decided whether one spouse is, as a general rule, a compellable witness against the other. The limited form of the proviso, which applies only to communications, suggests that the intention of the leading part of the section is to make such a witness compellable, but it has been decided in a criminal case[77] that implication is not a safe ground for holding that the common law has been altered and that therefore a wife, though competent, is not compellable.

355. HUSBAND AND WIFE: CONFIDENTIAL COMMUNICATIONS

(a) **General.** The rule that communications between husband and wife during the subsistence of the marriage are privileged and may not be given in evidence is not a sacred principle of the common law, but entirely the creation of the statutes which made parties and their spouses competent witnesses.[78] Accordingly its scope depends, not on the underlying principle,[79] but on the words of the statutes.

(b) **Civil Causes.** The Evidence (Scotland) Act, 1853,[80] provides that nothing in the Act "shall in any proceeding render any husband competent or compellable to give against his wife[81] evidence of any matter communicated by her to him during the marriage, or any wife competent or compellable to give against her husband[81] evidence of any matter communicated by him to her during the marriage." Since both the words "competent" and "compellable" are used, it would appear that either the party or the witness may object. The communication may be oral or written,[82] and the rule applies even if the marriage has been dissolved by death or divorce.[79] In spite of the generality of the words there is a recognised exception where the action is concerned with the conduct of the spouses towards each other,

[72] s. 4.
[73] 37 & 38 Vict. c. 64.
[74] See §355.
[75] See §345.
[76] Law Reform (Miscellaneous Provisions) Act, 1949 (12, 13 & 14 Geo. VI. c. 100), s. 7
[77] *Leach* v. *R.*, [1912] A.C. 305. See §353, note 60.
[78] *Sawers* v. *Dalgarnie*, 1858, 21 D. 153, L. Benholme at p. 157.
[79] Dickson, *Evidence* (3rd ed.) §1660.
[80] 16 Vict. c. 20, s. 3.
[81] Otherwise the rule does not apply: *Sawers* v. *Dalgarnie* (*supra*), L. Cowan at p. 156.
[82] Dickson, *Evidence* (3rd ed.) § 1661: *MacKay* v. *MacKay*, 1946 S.C. 78 (letter to husband confessing adultery); *Gallacher* v. *Gallacher*, 1934 S.C. 339 (letters to wife inciting her to commit adultery).

as in actions of divorce.[82] Since only the husband and wife are mentioned in the Act it is impossible to accept Dickson's view[79] that it is incompetent to examine third parties as to communications in their presence between husband and wife. The authorities cited by him have no bearing, and a communication in presence of third parties can hardly be said to have been "confided by one of the spouses to the bosom of the other." The rule does not apply to a wife examined as a witness in the bankruptcy of her husband.[83]

(c) **Criminal Trials.** The corresponding provision of the Criminal Evidence Act, 1898,[84] appears, oddly enough, as a proviso to section 1, although one would have thought that its main importance was in relation to section 4. The proviso, however, bears to affect the whole Act. "Nothing in this Act shall make a husband compellable to disclose any communication made to him by his wife during the marriage, or a wife compellable to disclose any communication made to her by her husband during the marriage." There is one marked contrast with the provision of the Evidence (Scotland) Act, 1853,[80] the words "competent or" do not appear. The objection is therefore open only to the witness. In two modern statutes it is expressly provided that a wife or husband shall not be compellable to disclose communications made during the marriage.[85] So far as applicable, the questions raised under the Evidence (Scotland) Act, 1853,[80] would receive the same answer here. The communication may be oral or written,[82] the rule applies even if the marriage has been dissolved,[79] and the evidence of third parties as to such communications is competent.

356. ACCUSED PERSON: GENERAL

At common law an accused person was not a competent witness at his own trial. Hence the former importance of a prisoner's declaration,[86] his only opportunity of telling his own story. Under sec. 1 of the Criminal Evidence Act, 1898,[87] every person charged with an offence is a competent witness for the defence at every stage of the proceedings,[88] whether he is charged solely or jointly with any other person. In solemn procedure his name need not be included in the list of witnesses for the defence.[89] He may

---

[83] Bankruptcy (Scotland) Act, 1913 (3 & 4 Geo. V. c. 20), ss. 86, 87; *Sawers* v. *Dalgarnie* (*supra*).
[84] 61 & 62 Vict. c. 36, s. 1, proviso (d).
[85] National Insurance Act, 1946 (9 & 10 Geo. VI. c. 67), s. 53 (5); Workmen's Compensation (Supplementation) Act, 1951 (14 & 15 Geo. VI. c. 22), s. 4 (5).
[86] Macdonald, *Criminal Law* (5th ed.) 201, 328. See §31.
[87] 61 & 62 Vict. c. 36. This is a United Kingdom statute, and some of its provisions do not apply in Scotland, e.g. ss. 1 (h) and 3. In *Young* v. *H.M. Advocate*, 1932 J.C. 63, the Lord Justice-General observed that the difficulties which attend the application of the Act to the law and practice of Scotland have only disclosed themselves as experience of its operation has accumulated. Although a further thirty years have passed, it is still necessary to rely largely on English authority.
[88] While these words are presumably inserted to cover any preliminary hearing in England, they would include a proof as to the accused's fitness to plead or as to the admissibility of a statement by him: *Manuel* v. *H.M. Advocate*, 1958 J.C. 41, at p. 49.
[89] *Kennedy*, 1898, 1 F. (J.) 5.

be called only on his own application.[90] Accordingly, one co-accused cannot call another.[91] If he is the only witness to the facts called by the defence, he must be called immediately after the close of the evidence for the prosecution.[92] This provision does not seem to have been considered in any reported case, and the only method of enforcing it, viz., by refusing to allow the evidence of the accused if he has already called, for example, an expert witness, seems drastic. Unless otherwise ordered by the court, he gives his evidence from the witness box.[93] He is not bound to disclose any communication made to him by his wife during the marriage.[94] He may be asked in cross-examination any question notwithstanding that it would tend to criminate him as to the offence charged.[95]

357. ACCUSED PERSON: COMMENT ON FAILURE TO TESTIFY

The accused's failure to give evidence must not be made the subject of comment by the prosecutor.[96] It has been held in two summary causes[97] that such comment by the prosecutor is not in itself a ground for setting aside a conviction. None of the judges said so, but a fairly obvious reason is that a magistrate, and certainly a sheriff, is bound to notice that the accused has not given evidence and may be expected to give that fact its proper effect in the circumstances, whatever the prosecutor may say. The matter, however, is different in solemn procedure. A jury may well be influenced by such comment, and, if it were made, a verdict of guilty would probably be quashed, though a firm correction by the judge might save it.[98] The provision, however, does not deprive the judge of the right to comment to the jury on the accused's failure to give evidence, but he should do so only in exceptional circumstances, and not with undue emphasis.[99] It may be proper to direct the jury that on the facts they are entitled in the absence of any explanation by the accused to draw an inference of guilt.[1] It would also seem proper, where innocent explanations for the accused's conduct have been suggested unsuccessfully in cross-examination or suggested in the speech for the defence, for the judge to point out to the jury that such explanations would have come better from the accused, who would have been liable to cross-examination.[2] For that reason alone it might be unwise to follow the suggestion[3] that the rule should be altered.

[90] Criminal Evidence Act, 1898 (61 & 62 Vict. c. 36), s. 1 (a).
[91] See §360.
[92] Criminal Evidence Act, 1898 (61 & 62 Vict. c. 36), s. 2.
[93] *Ibid.*, s. 1 (g).
[94] *Ibid.*, s. 1 (d). See §355.
[95] *Ibid.*, s. 1 (e). This provision must be read subject to limitation. See § 358.
[96] Criminal Evidence Act, 1898 (61 & 62 Vict. c. 36), s. 1 (b).
[97] *Ross* v. *Boyd*, 1903, 5 F. (J.) 64; *McAttee* v. *Hogg*, 1903, 5 F. (J.) 67.
[98] *Ross* v. *Boyd* (*supra*).
[99] *Scott*, 1946 J.C. 90.
[1] *Hardy*, 1938 J.C. 144.
[2] See observations of L. Carmont in *Maitland* v. *Glasgow Corporation*, 1947 S.C. 20, at p. 28.
[3] *Scott* (*supra*), L. Moncrieff at p. 97.

358. ACCUSED PERSON: EVIDENCE OF ANOTHER OFFENCE OR OF BAD CHARACTER

(a) **General.** The accused must not be asked, and if asked must not be required to answer, any question tending to show that he has committed or been convicted of, or been charged with, any offence other than that with which he is then charged, or is of bad character, except in one or other of four cases.[4] This leading provision raises several points. (i) In contrast, for example, with proviso (e) of the same section, it is in negative form, and the mere fact that one of the exceptions applies does not necessarily establish the admissibility of a question on one of the prohibited subjects. It may be inadmissible on more general grounds.[5] Even if the accused has given evidence against another person charged with the same offence, evidence that he himself has been previously charged with another offence, of which he has been acquitted, if it neither affects his credibility nor bears on the offence for which he is on trial, is irrelevant, and so inadmissible.[5] But evidence of a charge followed by an acquittal *may* be admissible as a preliminary to relevant questions, e.g., as to evidence given by the accused in a previous trial when he was acquitted.[6] (ii) The mere asking of the question may be fatal even if it is disallowed or withdrawn.[7] This may explain the practice of applying to the judge before putting the question.[8] (iii) Cross-examination on the accused's own statement is not prohibited. If he gives evidence that he has never been charged,[9] he may be cross-examined on that, even although the charge resulted in an acquittal.[10] (iv) The judge has a discretion. The evidence which satisfies the particular exception may be so trivial, and the evidence which it is proposed to take from the accused so serious, that it would be unfair to allow it.[11] (v) An appeal may succeed even if no objection is taken at the trial.[12] (vi) Breach of the prohibition does not necessarily lead to the quashing of the conviction.[12]

(b) **Admissibility as Evidence of Guilt.** The prohibition does not apply if proof that the accused has committed or been convicted of the other offence is admissible to show that he is guilty of the offence charged. Part of the proof of certain offences consists of proof of previous convictions,[13] and a previous conviction may be admissible in proof of reset.[14] The

---

[4] Criminal Evidence Act, 1898 (61 & 62 Vict. c. 36), s. 1 (f). For the four cases, see sub-paras. (b) to (e).
[5] *Maxwell* v. *Director of Public Prosecutions*, [1935] A.C. 309, at p. 319.
[6] *Ibid.*, at p. 320.
[7] *Barker* v. *Arnold*, [1911] 2 K.B. 120.
[8] *O'Hara*, 1948 J.C. 90, at p. 92.
[9] i.e. accused before a court: *Stirland* v. *Director of Public Prosecutions*, [1944] A.C. 315, at pp. 323, 327.
[10] *Ibid.*, at pp. 326, 327.
[11] *O'Hara (supra)*, at pp. 99, 102.
[12] *Stirland* v. *Director of Public Prosecutions (supra)*, at p. 327.
[13] Prevention of Crimes Acts, 1871 (34 & 35 Vict. c. 112) and 1908 (8 Edw. VII. c. 59); Road Traffic Act, 1960 (8 & 9 Eliz. II. c. 16), s. 110.
[14] Prevention of Crimes Act, 1871 (34 & 35 Vict. c. 112), s. 19.

situation under the Criminal Law Amendment Act, 1922,[15] is analogous. The defence of reasonable cause to believe that the girl was over sixteen is open only to an accused who has not been charged before, and cross-examination as to a previous charge would be competent.[16] In England such cross-examination has been held competent to meet a defence of accident.[17]

(c) **Attempt to Establish Good Character.** The actual words of this exception are that "he has personally or by his advocate asked questions of the witnesses for the prosecution with a view to establish his own good character,[18] or has given evidence of his good character."[4] It does not therefore in terms cover the case where the accused has led evidence of witnesses to his good character, but this point does not appear to have been raised.

(d) **Imputation on Character of Prosecution Witnesses.** This exception is that "the nature or conduct of the defence is such as to involve imputations on the character of the prosecutor or the witnesses for the prosecution." The generality of these words has been restricted by decision. "Nature or conduct of the defence" mean the way it is conducted, not its substance, and the imputations on the character of witnesses must be in matters extraneous to the charge.[19] So where a person charged with assaulting two constables pleaded self defence and gave evidence that one of the constables was the aggressor and was drunk, it was held that this formed part of the substance of the defence and was not extraneous to the charge and did not open the way to cross-examination of the accused on his character.[20] On the other hand, to suggest to a constable that he had been reduced from inspector for a breach of discipline would probably do so. A suggestion that a witness, when assaulted at a previous time, had been engaged on some criminal business, was held to do so.[21]

(e) **Evidence against Person Charged with Same Offence.** This cannot apply to evidence given for the prosecution in prior proceedings because the accused could not himself be tried for the offence.[22] It might apply where in prior proceedings the accused had been called for one accused and in the course of his evidence had said something against another. But the most likely event is that an accused, in the course of giving evidence on his own behalf, implicates a co-accused charged with the same offence. If A and B are charged with assault and B gives evidence that A was kicking the victim and he (B) was trying to protect him, B may be asked whether

15 12 & 13 Geo. V. c. 56.
16 *Maxwell* v. *Director of Public Prosecutions* (*supra*), at p. 321.
17 *Ibid.*, at p. 318. See also §**28.**
18 "Good character" probably includes both general reputation and actual moral disposition: *Stirland* v. *Director of Public Prosecutions* (*supra*), at p. 324.
19 *O'Hara* (*supra*), at p. 98.
20 *O'Hara* (*supra*).
21 *Fielding* v. *H.M. Advocate*, 1959 J.C. 101.
22 *Macmillan* v. *Murray*, 1920 J.C. 13.

he has previously been convicted of theft, and such question may be put either on behalf of A or by the prosecutor.[23] There does not seem to be any reported case in which this exception has been founded on for the purpose of putting such a question, but since it recognises that one co-accused has the right to cross-examine another, it is the foundation of the rule that evidence given by one co-accused is evidence against another.[24]

359. CO-ACCUSED CALLED ON OWN APPLICATION

In this and the three following paragraphs[25] the expression "co-accused" is used in its widest sense to signify persons who are indicted on the same indictment or charged on the same complaint. It thus includes persons who are charged with separate offences and persons who are not tried together.

When a co-accused on trial with others is called as a witness on his own application in terms of the Criminal Evidence Act, 1898,[26] sec. 1, the admissibility and effect of his evidence *quoad* himself are the same as if he were on trial alone.[27] The Act does not deal expressly with the admissibility and effect of his evidence *quoad* his co-accused on trial with him, and the law has been derived by implication from sec. 1 (f) (iii). Where there is a joint defence the evidence of one of the co-accused is in the ordinary case admissible for and against the others.[28] No authority was cited for this proposition, but it presumably rests on the leading provision of sec. 1, "every person charged with an offence . . . shall be a competent witness for the defence . . ., whether the person so charged is charged solely or jointly with any other person." A joint defence involves a single representation, so that no question of cross-examination on behalf of the other accused arises. Where there are separate defences and separate representation, the evidence of each accused is admissible against the others.[29] "In the ordinary case, therefore, once one of the accused goes into the box in support of his separate defence, the door opens for a general cross-examination by his co-accused for the purpose of vindicating their own separate defences."[29] The Lord Justice-General was concerned only with the effect of the evidence against the co-accused, but his dictum clearly means that cross-examination may be used to obtain evidence favourable to the co-accused, including new matter.[30] But it must be read subject to the rule that an accused has no right to cross-examine unless the evidence incriminates him.[31] So long as

---

[23] *Hackston* v. *Millar*, 1906, 8 F. (J.) 52.
[24] *Young* v. *H.M. Advocate*, 1932 J.C. 63. See § 359
[25] §§ 360-362.
[26] 61 & 62 Vict. c. 36.
[27] See §§ 356, 358. In *R.* v. *Rowland*, [1910] 1 K.B. 458, A and B were tried together for the same offence, and A called B as a witness, B apparently not objecting. B gave evidence in favour of A and was cross-examined as to his own part. This was held proper under sec. 1 (*e*), but the decision is doubtful, since B, not having been called on his own application, was not a witness in pursuance of the Act.
[28] *Young* v. *H.M. Advocate*, 1932 J.C. 63, at p. 72.
[29] *Ibid.*, at p. 74.
[30] One of the purposes of cross-examination: see § 342, sub-para. (d).

that rule stands unqualified, the law is left in this position that if one co-accused gives evidence tending to incriminate another, however slightly, he may be fully cross-examined like any other witness; otherwise he cannot be cross-examined at all.[32] In any event, the prosecutor is entitled to cross-examine last.[33] Two conditions attach to the application of sec. 1 (f) (iii). First, the witness must be called "in pursuance of this Act," i.e., inter alia, on his own application.[34] Secondly, the "other person" must be "charged with the same offence."[35]

360. CO-ACCUSED CALLED AS WITNESS FOR ANOTHER

Since an accused person, i.e., a person on trial, was not at common law a competent witness and since by statute he can be called only on his own application,[36] one accused cannot call another if they are being tried together.[37] But at common law it is competent for one co-accused to call another, if their trials have been separated,[38] or if the co-accused to be called pleads guilty during the trial,[39] or, a fortiori, has pled guilty at an earlier diet. It would seem to follow that if the prosecutor withdraws the charge against one co-accused, another may call him, and it has been so held.[40] The opposite result was reached in another case,[41] apparently on the ground that the accused ought to have asked for a separation of trials. As the wish to call a co-accused as a witness is not, now at least,[42] regarded as a compelling reason for separating trials,[43] it is thought that the earlier decision would probably be followed. A co-accused called as a witness by another accused is in the same position as any other witness called for the defence, and is subject to cross-examination, e.g., on previous convictions, but since he is an accomplice, his evidence may require close scrutiny.[44]

---

[31] *Gemmell and McFadyen* v. *MacNiven*, 1928 J.C. 5. This decision is alleged to follow *Hackston* v. *Millar*, 1906, 8 F. (J.) 52, but it goes beyond it. *Hackston* decided only that a co-accused is entitled to cross-examine if the evidence incriminates him. It did not decide that that was the limit of his right. See also *Townsend* v. *Strathern*, 1923 J.C. 66, and *Morrison* v. *Adair*, 1943 J.C. 25, referred to at §361.

[32] But the evidence of a witness called for one co-accused, as distinct from that of the co-accused himself, is never evidence against another. This common law rule is not affected by the Act. See *Young* v. *H.M. Advocate* (*supra*), at p. 73.

[33] This right was expressly recognised both by the judges and by defence counsel at the trial which preceded *Young* v. *H.M. Advocate* (*supra*).

[34] See note 27 for comment on *R.* v. *Rowland.*

[35] See §361 as to co-accused tried together for separate offences.

[36] Criminal Evidence Act, 1898 (61 & 62 Vict. c. 36), s. 1 (*a*).

[37] See *R.* v. *Rowland*, [1910] 1 K.B. 458, commented on at §359, note 27.

[38] *Bell and Shaw* v. *Houston*, 1842, 1 Broun 49; *Morrison* v. *Adair*, 1943 J.C. 25. But *cf. Mitchell*, 1887, 1 White 320, where L. Young refused to allow witnesses to be examined for the defence because they were charged with the same crime, though on a separate indictment.

[39] *Thomson*, 1892, 3 White 321; *Wilson*, 1860, 3 Irv. 623.

[40] *Henderson*, 1850, J. Shaw 394, at p. 422.

[41] *McCabe*, 1857, 2 Irv. 599.

[42] In *Nicolson*, 1887, 1 White 307, L. Young said that he would have regarded it as a good reason for separating trials.

[43] *Morrison* v. *Adair* (*supra*).

[44] See §363, note 58.

It has never been decided that in solemn procedure notice must be given of the intention to call him,[45] but in the only reported case since 1887 where the defence proposed to call a co-accused, notice was given.[46] The reports of the earlier cases do not mention this point. Although it appears to have been obligatory to give notice of defence witnesses, the Crown ordinarily abstained from founding on an omission to do so.[47]

361. CO-ACCUSED ON TRIAL ON SEPARATE CHARGES

There are here two possible situations. The first occurs when A and B are tried together on separate charges,[48] and therefore sec. 1 (f) (iii) of the Criminal Evidence Act, 1898,[49] does not apply. At common law the evidence of a witness called for one co-accused is not admissible against another,[50] and it follows that when a co-accused gives evidence, his evidence, apart from the Act, is not admissible against another.[50] Accordingly, there is no need for a right to cross-examine on such evidence. But if one co-accused thinks that he can obtain evidence in his favour from another he appears to be entitled to cross-examine him for that purpose. Two bus drivers were charged on the same complaint with separate acts of negligence leading to separate collisions. The accused moved for a separation of trials on the ground that each wished to call the other as a witness. The sheriff-substitute refused the motion, and the High Court declined to interfere, mainly on the ground that in the circumstances it was probable that both accused would give evidence. The plain implication of the Lord Justice-General's opinion is that each could obtain by cross-examining the other the evidence he hoped to obtain by examining him as a witness. While this evidence might come out in examination in chief it was more likely to be brought out fully in cross. Moreover, the penultimate paragraph of the opinion makes it clear that evidence led for one co-accused is admissible for the other.[51]

The second situation arises where A and B are on trial for the same offence and B is also on trial for a separate and unconnected offence. May the prosecutor cross-examine A with a view to obtaining evidence against B on the separate charge against him? This question does not seem to have been expressly considered, but Lord Justice-General Clyde may have had it in view when he said "It may well be that a prosecutor is not entitled, under the cloak of cross-examination, to examine an accused upon matters

[45] Criminal Procedure (Scotland) Act, 1887 (50 & 51 Vict. c. 35), s. 36.
[46] *Thomson (supra)*.
[47] Hume, II., 399.
[48] This is competent at least where the charges relate to incidents closely connected in time, place and circumstances: *Matthewson* v. *Ramsay*, 1936 J.C. 5.
[49] 61 & 62 Vict. c. 36.
[50] *Young* v. *H.M. Advocate*, 1932 J.C. 63, at p. 73. In *Parker and Barrie* v. *H.M. Advocate*, 1888, 16 R. (J.) 5, where the masters of two ships were charged with separate acts of negligence causing a collision, the Lord Justice-Clerk made it clear that he intended to charge the jury to that effect.
[51] *Morrison* v. *Adair*, 1943 J.C. 25. The rule that one co-accused may cross-examine another only if the evidence incriminates him (§ 359) was not mentioned in the opinion.

irrelevant to the question of his own guilt, and extraneous to any evidence he has given, in order to make him an additional witness against his co-accused."[52] It is not quite clear whether the Lord Justice-General was proceeding on the construction of the statute or on the general discretion of the judge to disallow cross-examination, but if it was the latter he might have added that such evidence would be elicited by the prosecutor after counsel for the co-accused had exhausted his normal rights of cross-examination. Moreover, such cross-examination would give the prosecutor an advantage not enjoyed by the other co-accused since their rights of cross-examination are limited. In these circumstances it is thought that a prosecutor would not be allowed to cross-examine for the purpose stated.

362. WITNESS CALLED FOR CO-ACCUSED

If the defence is joint each defence witness is a witness for all the accused. But a difficulty may arise if there are separate defences and two of the co-accused wish to call the same witness. The common law is that the evidence of a witness led for one co-accused is not evidence against another, who should therefore have no right to cross-examine. But if he has no right to cross-examine, he may be unable to bring out evidence which he expects the witness to give in his favour. It would appear that the judges are not prepared to press the technical rules to the point of unfairness.[53]

363. ACCOMPLICES

This term may apply to a person in at least five situations: (1) a person on trial along with others on the same or a related charge,[54] i.e. a co-accused,[55] (2) a co-accused whose trial has been separated,[55] (3) a co-accused who has pleaded guilty during the trial,[55] (4) a person who has previously pleaded guilty to, or been convicted of, the charge or a related[54] charge and (5) a witness who admits his own guilt of the charge or a related[54] charge.[56] It is not settled whether the term applies to a person, other than an accused, who has neither admitted nor been convicted of the charge, but to whom the evidence points as an associate.[57] An accomplice may be inadmissible on the ground that he is a co-accused,[55] but, apart from that, he is admissible either for the prosecution or the defence. His evidence, however, is received with suspicion, and a jury must be specifically directed that it is their duty to apply to it "a special scrutiny over and above the general examination which a jury has to apply to all the material evidence."[58]

52 *Young* v. *H.M. Advocate* (*supra*), at p. 74.
53 *Morrison* v. *Adair*, 1943 J.C. 25.
54 Theft and reset of the same property are related charges: *H.M. Advocate* v. *Murdoch*, 1955 S.L.T. (Notes) 57.
55 As to the admissibility of such persons as witnesses, see, § 360.
56 *H.M. Advocate* v. *Murdoch* (*supra*). Admission of guilt, art and part, of a statutory charge would be enough: Criminal Justice (Scotland) Act, 1949 (12, 13 & 14 Geo. VI. c. 94), s. 31.
57 *Wallace* v. *H.M. Advocate*, 1952 J.C. 78, L. Keith at p. 83.
58 *Ibid.*, L. J-G. Cooper at p. 82. This has been laid down only *quoad* witnesses for the prosecution, and the question has not been raised whether it is proper to give a similar direction as regards a defence witness. See § 360.

Subject to that, the evidence of an accomplice, if believed, has the same effect in law as that of any other witness. Accordingly, a conviction resting entirely on the evidence of two accomplices was sustained.[59]

364. PUBLIC PROSECUTOR

While it has been laid down emphatically that a prosecutor, i.e., the person who conducts the prosecution, can never be a competent witness,[60] some doubt has been thrown on that opinion.[61]

365. JUDGES AND ARBITERS

(a) **Supreme Courts.** While there is no actual decision, it is plain from the opinions in the undernoted case[62] that it is incompetent to call a judge as a witness as to judicial proceedings which took place before him, though he might be a witness as to an extraordinary event such as a riot, or possibly an assault. In view of these opinions it is thought that some earlier cases[63] where judges were examined of consent, both of themselves and of parties, are now of no importance.

(b) **Inferior Courts.** Judges of inferior courts are competent witnesses to the proceedings before them[64] and are frequently called in trials for perjury to testify as to the evidence given in their courts.[65]

(c) **Arbiters.** The arbiter is a competent witness in an action for enforcement or reduction of his award, but only certain evidence may be taken from him. His evidence is competent on any matter which would entitle the court to interfere with his award.[66] He may be asked about the procedure he adopted, to find out whether he has transgressed the rules of natural justice.[66] He may be asked how he construed the submission, for if he misconstrued it, his award may be reduced.[67] He may be asked what factors he has taken into account, because if he took into account some irrelevant factor, again his award may be reduced.[67] But he cannot be asked to give his reasons for his award, unless it is averred that he has erred in some way which entitles the court to interfere, such as those mentioned above. The mere fact that the court thinks his decision wrong

---

[59] *Dow* v. *MacKnight*, 1949 J.C. 38.

[60] *Graham* v. *McLennan*, 1911 S.C. (J.) 16.

[61] *Mackintosh* v. *Wooster*, 1919 J.C. 15, where, however, the witness objected to did not conduct the prosecution, though it was at his instance.

[62] *Muckarsie* v. *Wilson*, 1834, Bell's Notes, 99.

[63] *Stewart* v. *Fraser*, 1830, 5 Mur. 166; *Gibson* v. *Stevenson*, 1822, 3 Mur. 208; *Harper* v. *Robinsons and Forbes*, 1821, 2 Mur. 383.

[64] *Monaghan*, 1844, 2 Broun 131.

[65] e.g. *Davidson* v. *McFadyean*, 1942 J.C. 95.

[66] *Black* v. *John Williams & Co. (Wishaw) Ltd.*, 1923 S.C. 510, at p. 512 (where the arbiter's evidence is quoted); 1924 S.C. (H.L.) 22.

[67] *Glasgow City and District Railway Co.* v. *Macgeorge, Cowan & Galloway*, 1886, 13 R. 609 (where the arbiter was the only witness).

is not enough.[68] In *Glasgow City and District Railway*[67] the defenders owned an area of ground on part of which a building was erected. The railway company made a tunnel below this ground, and in terms of their private Act became liable for any "structural damage . . . to any building." A claim by the defenders was referred to arbitration, and the railway company sought to reduce the award on the ground that the arbiter took into account deterioration in the marketable value of the building and of the unbuilt-on ground. Proof before answer was allowed, but the pursuers failed. The arbiter's evidence was that he had taken into account only structural damage to the building, and he was never asked what he understood by structural damage. Accordingly the court could not say he had taken any irrelevant factor into account.

366. FOREIGNERS

A foreigner, even an enemy alien,[69] is a competent witness. If he does not speak English, his evidence ought to be interpreted by a sworn interpreter, who is *pro hac vice* an officer of the court. This was stated in a case where the accused was a foreigner,[70] but it seems equally applicable in the case of a witness.[71]

367. PRESENCE IN COURT

(a) **General.** At common law a witness who had been in court and heard the evidence of other witnesses was thereby rendered incompetent to testify.[72] The only exception was that skilled witnesses might be allowed to hear evidence of fact, but were required to withdraw during the evidence of other skilled witnesses.[73] It is no longer imperative in the Court of Session, High Court and sheriff court to reject any witness against whom it is objected that he has, without the permission of the court and without the consent of the party objecting, been present in court during the proceedings.[74] The court may, in its discretion, admit him where it appears to the court that his presence was not the consequence of culpable negligence or criminal intent and that the witness has not been unduly instructed or influenced by what took place in his presence, or that injustice will not be done by his examination.[74] The judge may raise the question himself, and need not wait for an objection. When the question is raised, it is for the party tendering the witness to satisfy the court (1) that the presence of the witness was not the consequence of culpable negligence or criminal intent and (2) either (a) that he has not been unduly instructed or influenced by what took place in his presence or (b) that injustice will not be done by his

[68] *Rogerson* v. *Rogerson*, 1885, 12 R. 583.
[69] *Patrick Macguire*, 1857, 2 Irv. 620.
[70] *Liszewski* v. *Thomson*, 1942 J.C. 55.
[71] Dickson, *Evidence* (3rd ed.) §1793.
[72] *Docherty and Graham* v. *McLennan*, 1912 S.C. (J.) 102.
[73] Dickson, *Evidence* (3rd ed.) §1761.
[74] Evidence (Scotland) Act, 1840 (3 & 4 Vict. c. 59), s. 3. As to skilled witnesses, see §413 sub-para. (d).

examination. These points were settled in a case[75] where no objection was taken, but the sheriff, on ascertaining that a defence witness had been present and that he was to speak to material facts, disallowed him without further enquiry. This disallowance was upheld since the burden was on the defence to satisfy the sheriff that he might properly admit the witness in his discretion, and no attempt had been made to discharge the burden. This appears to be the only reported decision, and there has been no judicial guidance as to whose culpable negligence or criminal intent is involved, or as to how the court is to be satisfied on the points mentioned. The Act applies only to the three courts mentioned, and not, for example, to a police court.[72]

(b) Parties to the Cause. So long as the parties themselves were not competent witnesses they no doubt attended at proofs and jury trials. This practice has continued, although they are now competent witnesses. They remain in court and, if they wish, give evidence. Indeed, it has been held that they cannot be excluded, though the fact that they have heard the earlier evidence may be taken into account in assessing the value of their own evidence.[76]

The question of a prosecutor giving evidence has already been considered,[77] and it has never been suggested that the presence of the accused in court lays him open to objection as a witness.

(c) Solicitor Conducting Case. It is no objection to a solicitor as a witness that he is engaged in or even actually conducting a civil cause, and has therefore been present in court.[78] The statute[79] which abolished agency and partial counsel as a ground of exclusion excepted a solicitor acting in the cause, but this exception was repealed.[80] The present rule necessarily follows, and there is no need to appeal to the Act which deals specifically with presence in court.[74]

Although in a police court a person who has heard the evidence is an incompetent witness,[72] a solicitor defending in that court is competent on the grounds just stated.[78]

368. BANKER'S IMMUNITY

A banker or officer of a bank is not compellable in any proceedings to which the bank is not a party, to prove matters which can be proved by a copy of an entry in the books, unless by order of the judge made for special

---

[75] *Macdonald* v. *Mackenzie*, 1947 J.C. 169.
[76] *Perman* v. *Binny's Trs.*, (O.H.) 1925 S.L.T. 123.
[77] See §364.
[78] *Campbell* v. *Cochrane*, 1928 J.C. 25.
[79] Evidence (Scotland) Act, 1852 (15 Vict. c. 27), s. 1.
[80] Evidence (Scotland) Act, 1853 (16 Vict. c. 20), s. 2. There is an exception in a declarator of marriage founded on promise *subsequente copula*: 1853 Act, s. 4; Evidence Further Amendment (Scotland) Act, 1874 (37 & 38 Vict. c. 64), ss. 1, 3.

cause.[81] But since the accuracy of the copy must be proved,[82] it is necessary, unless the proof is by affidavit, to call an officer of the bank to do so.

369. DIPLOMATIC IMMUNITY

(a) **Ambassadors.** The immunity of ambassadors, their wives and families[83] and their suites, from legal process rests on comity and is part of the common law.[84] As ambassadors since 1707 have been accredited to the Court of Saint James, it is not unnatural that all the authority is English, and the "common law" referred to in the decisions is the common law of England. In view, however, of the basis of the privilege, its wide acceptance and its great antiquity,[85] there is no reason to doubt that it is also part of the common law of Scotland. Sanctions for the enforcement of the privilege are provided by the Diplomatic Privileges Act, 1708,[86] which enacts that "all writs and processes sued forth or prosecuted whereby the person of any ambassador or other publick minister of any foreign prince or state . . . or the domestick or domestick servant of any such ambassador or other publick minister may be arrested . . . shall be . . . utterly null and void."[87] The Act further imposes penalties on any person who sues forth or prosecutes such writ or process and their solicitors and all officers executing any such writ or process.[88] It seems improbable that the framers of the Act had the question of witnesses in view, and it does not appear to have been raised in any reported case. But if the sections are translated into Scottish terms they would include application for, and execution of, letters of second diligence, which means that both by common law and statute an ambassador or a member of his suite cannot be compelled to attend as a witness.[89] The immunity may be waived by the ambassador *quoad* himself or a member of his suite.[90] A statement by a law officer on behalf of the Foreign Office as to the status of a person in this connection is conclusive.[91] It is then for the court to determine whether that status confers immunity.[92] The "suite" of an ambassador means his counsellors, secretaries and clerks and his servants, with the possible exception of servants who are nationals of the state to which he is accredited.[83] If this last case arose, it might be

---

81 Bankers Books Evidence Act, 1879 (42 & 43 Vict. c. 11), s. 6. For the Act generally, see §301.

82 *Ibid.*, s. 5.

83 *Engelke* v. *Musmann*, [1928] A.C. 433, L. Phillimore at p. 450.

84 *Ibid.*, L. Dunedin at p. 447, L. Warrington of Clyffe at p. 458.

85 See preamble to the Diplomatic Privileges Act, 1708 (7 Anne. c. 12).

86 7 Anne c. 12.

87 *Ibid.*, s. 3.

88 *Ibid.*, s. 4.

89 Special consent may be required to execute letters of second diligence in a consular office: Consular Conventions Act, 1949 (12 & 13 Geo. VI. c. 29), s. 4, and Orders made thereunder.

90 *R.* v. *A. B.*, [1941] 1 K.B. 454.

91 *Engelke* v. *Musmann* (*supra*). Section 6 of the Act, which provides for the registration of the names of ambassadors' servants, applies only to sec. 4. See *The Amazone*, [1940] P. 40, at p. 47.

92 *Ibid.*, at p. 436, para. 27 of the Attorney-General's case.

treated in the same way as the statutory limitations.[93] Her Majesty may restrict these immunities, except in respect of things done or omitted to be done in course of performance of official duties.[94] This power has been exercised in respect of a number of states.[95]

(b) Commonwealth Countries, Ireland and Cyprus. The chief representatives of Canada, Australia, New Zealand, India, Pakistan, Ceylon, Southern Rhodesia, and the Republics of Ireland and Cyprus have the immunities of ambassadors, and their families, and (subject to the limitation mentioned in sub-para. (e)) their official staff and their families, and their domestic staff, have a corresponding immunity.[96] The chief representative may waive the immunity of any person.[97] A certificate by the Secretary of State is conclusive evidence of any fact relevant to the question of immunity.[98]

(c) International Organisations. Her Majesty has power to confer by Order in Council certain immunities and privileges on the personnel of any organisation which has been declared by Order in Council to be an international organisation, and their families.[99] The personnel is divided into two classes, and the immunity of the lower class extends only to things done or omitted to be done in the course of the performance of official duties.[93] A considerable number of such Orders have been made.

(d) Miscellaneous. Immunities are, or by Order may be, conferred on members of other international bodies.[1]

(e) Limited Immunity. In each case where the immunity rests on statute it is conferred upon certain classes of individual only in respect of things done or omitted to be done in the course of the performance of his duties. It seems probable that the framers of the provisions did not have in mind the question of such person being cited as a witness. No doubt if he were a witness to an ordinary road accident he would be a compellable witness. But the position is not so clear if one of the cars involved was that

---

[93] See sub-para. (e).

[94] Diplomatic Immunities Restriction Act, 1955 (4 Eliz. II. c. 21). See sub-para. (e).

[95] See Guide to Government Orders.

[96] Diplomatic Immunities (Commonwealth Countries and Republic of Ireland) Act, 1952 (15 & 16 Geo. VI. and I Eliz. II. c. 18), s. 1 (1), (6), as amended by the Cyprus Act, 1960 (8 & 9 Eliz. II. c. 52) Sched., para. 8. Further amended to include Ghana (5 & 6 Eliz. II. c. 6), Malaya (5 & 6 Eliz. II. c. 60), Nigeria (8 & 9 Eliz. II. c. 55), Sierra Leone (9 & 10 Eliz. II. c. 16), Tanganyika (10 Eliz. II. c. 1), Uganda (10 & 11 Eliz. II. c. 57), Trinidad and Tobago (10 & 11 Eliz. II. c. 54), and Jamaica (10 & 11 Eliz. II. c. 40).

[97] *Ibid.,* s. 1 (5).

[98] *Ibid.,* s. 1 (3). A list is published from time to time in the Gazette of persons who appear to be entitled to immunity. See also Diplomatic Immunities (Conferences with Commonwealth Countries, &c.) Act, 1960 (10 & 11 Eliz. II. c. 35).

[99] International Organisations (Immunities and Privileges) Act, 1950 (14 Geo. VI. c. 14), s. 1.

[1] German Conventions Act, 1955 (4 Eliz. II. c. 2): European Coal and Steel Community Act, 1955 (4 Eliz. II. c. 4): International Finance Corporation Act, 1955 (4 Eliz. II. c. 5). See also International Development Association Act, 1960 (8 & 9 Eliz. II. c. 35), s. 3.

of the chief representative of Canada carrying the chief representative to Balmoral. The chauffeur would not be compellable, but a spare driver sitting beside him might be. The question is not likely to arise, since in a doubtful case the immunity would probably be waived.

CHAPTER XXIX

HEARSAY

370. SECONDARY AND PRIMARY HEARSAY

Hearsay evidence is evidence of what another person has said. So defined it includes both secondary hearsay, which may be admissible as indirect evidence of the facts alleged in the statement, and primary hearsay, which may be admissible as direct evidence that the statement was made, irrespective of its truth or falsehood. Although these two grounds for admitting hearsay are totally distinct,[1] they are easily confused.[2] The usual 'definition of "hearsay" includes secondary hearsay only,[3] but the main difficulties arise under primary hearsay and in the distinction between secondary and primary.

371. SECONDARY HEARSAY: MAKER OF STATEMENT

Hearsay is usually inadmissible as evidence of the facts alleged in the statement.[4] This is one of the applications of the best evidence rule, which excludes indirect evidence when direct evidence is, or ought to be, available.[5] The only recognised exceptions occur where the maker of the statement is dead or permanently insane or, at least in a civil cause, a prisoner of war.[6] The fact that he has disappeared is insufficient.[6] A suggestion that hearsay is admissible where the maker of the statement is permanently disabled by illness from giving evidence, which appears analogous to permanent insanity, has been left open.[7] There must be at least *prima facie* evidence

---

[1] *Jackson* v. *Glasgow Corporation*, 1956 S.C. 354, L.P. Clyde at p. 361, L. Russell at p. 363, L. Sorn at p. 365.

[2] See § **379**.

[3] Dickson, *Evidence* (3rd ed.) §244; Cross, *Evidence* (1958), 3.

[4] Dickson, *Evidence* (3rd ed.) §245. In *Grant* v. *H.M. Advocate*, 1938 J.C. 7, the conviction was quashed because a passage was read to the jury from a medical report narrating a statement made by a witness implicating the accused.

[5] The others are the exclusion of parole evidence of the terms of documents (§ **229**) and of description of things (§ **420**).

[6] *H.M. Advocate* v. *Manson*, 1897, 21 R. (J.) 5, at pp. 9, 10.

[7] *McKie* v. *Western S.M.T. Co.*, 1952 S.C. 206, at p. 215.

that the maker of the statement is dead, permanently insane or a prisoner of war.[8] Moreover, he must be a person who would have been a competent witness, so that a prosecutor cannot lead evidence of a statement made by the deceased wife of an accused unless the wife would have been in the circumstances a competent witness. Owing to the frequent extensions during the nineteenth century of the class of competent witnesses the question has arisen as to the date on which competency fell to be tested. There seem to be three possible dates, (1) the day when the statement is tendered in evidence, (2) the day the maker of the statement died, and (3) the day when the statement is alleged to have been made. The point can seldom arise now and seems to be unsettled.[9] Hearsay of hearsay is probably admissible,[10] provided that each statement fulfils the necessary conditions as to the makers and the nature of the statement.[11]

372. SECONDARY HEARSAY: NATURE OF STATEMENT

Although the maker of the statement is proved to be dead, permanently insane or a prisoner of war, and would have been a competent witness on the material date, evidence of the statement is inadmissible if the circumstances raise a presumption that it does not truly reflect what was in his mind.[12] Such a presumption arises if the statement was made on precognition, because it is not spontaneous or voluntary.[13] This includes a precognition taken for the purposes of another action.[14] But a precognition made part of a dying deposition[15] was admitted,[16] and so was oral evidence of what a deceased person said while being precognosced, given from recollection and without reference to the written precognition.[17] Statements made to a solicitor with a view to raising an action are excluded.[18] An averment does not become evidence on the death of the party making it.[19] An affidavit is not received as secondary evidence of the deponent, at least if it was drawn by a solicitor,[20] and certificates are rarely received.[21] A statement made as evidence in another cause is admissible, provided there is

8 Dickson, *Evidence* (3rd ed.) §269.
9 *Dean's Judicial Factor* v. *Deans*, 1912 S.C. 441, L.P. Dunedin at p. 448. See also *Lovat Peerage Case*, 1885, 10 App. Cas. 763; Dickson, *Evidence* (3rd ed.) §§266, 267.
10 *Smith* v. *Bank of Scotland*, 1826, 5 S. 98; *Deans's Judicial Factor* v. *Deans* (*supra*), where hearsay of hearsay was considered without comment. See also *Lovat Peerage Case*, 1885 (*supra*), at p. 774. But the last two were pedigree cases and possibly unsafe guides in other actions.
11 See §372.
12 *Geils* v. *Geils*, 1855, 17 D. 397, at p. 404.
13 *Young* v. *National Coal Board*, (O.H.) 1960 S.C. 6; *Macdonald* v. *Union Bank*, 1864, 2 M. 963; *Stevenson* v. *Stevenson*, 1893, 31 S.L.R. 129; *Ormond*, 1848, Ark. 483.
14 *Graham* v *Western Bank*, 1865, 3 M. 617.
15 See §410.
16 *Petersen*, 1874, 2 Coup. 557.
17 *Ward*, 1869, 1 Coup. 186; Dickson, *Evidence* (3rd ed.) §271. This is difficult to reconcile with the cases cited in note 13.
18 *Traynor's Executrix* v. *Bairds & Scottish Steel, Ltd.*, (O.H.) 1957 S.C. 311.
19 *Cullen's Trustee* v. *Johnston*, 1865, 3 M. 935.
20 *Tennent* v. *Tennent*, 1890, 17 R. 1205, at p. 1225. As to affidavits, see §407.
21 *Lauderdale Peerage Case*, 1885, 10 App. Cas. 692, at p. 707.

nothing to discredit it as a full record.[22] Letters written[23] and probably a diary kept[24] by a deceased person are admissible unless they appear to be prejudiced or tendentious.[25] The dying deposition of any person who might have been a competent witness is admissible.[26]

373. SECONDARY HEARSAY: PROOF AND WEIGHT

If the statement was oral it is proved by the evidence of those who heard it, and they are subject to cross-examination as to the circumstances in which it was made, e.g., whether it was elicited in answer to leading questions, whether the deceased had means of knowledge, whether he was actuated by some emotion.[27] While the fact that two or more witnesses speak to the statement does not add to its weight in law, for it still remains the evidence of one witness,[28] its reliability will be increased if several people can speak to it, since there is more opportunity to test their recollections.[29] If the statement is written, it must be proved by whom it was written, and similar questions of circumstances may arise as in the case of an oral statement. Since the reliability of the maker of the statement cannot be tested by cross-examination, such secondary evidence is received *cum nota*, and, if ambiguous, is read *contra proferentem*.[30]

374. SECONDARY HEARSAY: PEDIGREE CASES

These are in a class apart, though decisions in ordinary hearsay cases are from time to time discussed in the opinions or speeches, and points decided in them may apply to ordinary cases.[31] Family tradition as to propinquity may be proved by the deliberate statement of a deceased person, but only if he had special means of knowledge.[32]

375. PRIMARY HEARSAY: GENERAL

It is frequently necessary to prove that a statement has been made, e.g., in actions based on misrepresentation or for damages for slander or arising from a contract entered into orally, or in a trial for perjury or extortion. The party leading the evidence does so merely to establish that the statement was

---

[22] *Geils* v. *Geils (supra)*; *Coutts* v. *Wear*, (O.H.) 1914, 2 S.L.T. 86; *Gordon* v. *Grant*, 1850, 13 D. 1, at pp. 10, 27.
[23] *McAlister* v. *McAlister*, 1833, 12 S. 198; *Tennent* v. *Tennent (supra)*, at pp. 1223, 1224.
[24] Opinions, however, were reserved in *Hogg* v. *Campbell*, 1864, 2 M. 1158.
[25] *Madeleine Smith*, 1857, 2 Irv. 641.
[26] *Stewart*, 1855, 2 Irv. 166. See §371.
[27] *Gordon* v. *Grant*, 1850, 13 D. 1, at p. 11.
[28] *Deans's Judicial Factor* v. *Deans*, 1912 S.C. 441, at p. 447; *Wallace* v. *Ross*, 1891, 19 R. 233.
[29] *A.* v. *B.*, 1858, 20 D. 407, at p. 416.
[30] *Walker's Trs.* v. *McKinlay*, 1880, 7 R. (H.L.) 85, at p. 98.
[31] The principal more modern cases are *Alexander* v. *Officers of State*, 1868, 6 M. 54; *Macpherson* v. *Reid's Trs.*, 1877, 4 R. (H.L.) 87; *Deans's Judicial Factor* v. *Deans*, 1912 S.C. 441; *Dysart Peerage Case*, 1881, 6 App. Cas. 489; *Lauderdale Peerage Case*, 1885, 10 App. Cas. 692; and *Lovat Peerage Case*, 1885, 10 App. Cas. 763.
[32] *Macpherson* v. *Reid's Trs. (supra)*; *Alexander* v. *Officers of State (supra)*.

made. He is probably not concerned with its truth, and indeed his case may be that it was untrue. It may be proved that a witness has previously made a statement differing from his evidence,[33] or that a party has made an extra-judicial admission or confession.[34] Further, statements proved to have been made by a person, orally or in writing, may be evidence of his state of mind[35] or of his feelings towards another person.[36] Evidence of a statement by a third party to a witness is admissible to explain the witness's actions[37] and frequently to explain grounds on which a medical or other expert witness bases an opinion. Where the defence was that the accused acted under duress, evidence of threats used against him by persons who were not witnesses was held admissible.[38] Evidence of statements was held admissible on the ground that they had no material bearing, except that they rendered the case more intelligible.[39] It may be competent to prove that a conversation took place between people who were not witnesses, or at least were not asked about the conversation, merely to establish the subject of discussion,[40] or to prove the character of the premises where it took place.[41] Evidence of statements may be competent as part of proof of character or reputed ownership.[42] Evidence that a witness has at some earlier date identified the accused, or a production, may either support the identification by the witness at the trial, or if he cannot identify at the trial, may possibly take the place of such identification.[43] The main legal difficulty arises over *de recenti* statements and statements forming part of the *res gestæ*, and the confusion between them.[44]

376. DE RECENTI STATEMENT

Evidence may be led of a statement made by a witness shortly after the occurrence. Such evidence is not corroboration. Its only effect, if the statement tallies with the witness's evidence, is to enhance his credibility,

---

[33] See § 343.
[34] See §§ 29 *et seq.*
[35] *Mackintosh* v. *Fraser*, 1859, 21 D. 783, 792 (writings by pursuer alleged to be insane); *Cairns* v. *Marianski*, 1852, 1 Macq. 212 (deceased's books as evidence of facility); *Milne*, 1863, 4 Irv. 301, at p. 342 (accused's declaration as evidence of insanity); *Coles* v. *Homer and Tulloh*, 1895, 22 R. 716, at p. 737; *Watson* v. *Watson*, 1934 S.C. 374. Evidence of state of mind generally is mentioned at §§ 24 *et seq.*
[36] *Rose* v. *Junor*, 1846, 9 D. 12; *King* v. *King*, 1841, 4 D. 124 (expressions of enmity against a party).
[37] *Hunter* v. *Dodds*, 1832, 10 S. 833.
[38] *Subranamiam* v. *Public Prosecutor*, [1956] 1 W.L.R. 965.
[39] *McDonalds, Ltd.* v. *Adair*, 1944 J. C. 119. It is thought that this case is wrongly rubricked "*res gestæ.*" The *res* was the sale in the shop. Presumably there was corroboration of the purchaser's evidence that she bought the lace from the appellants, though the report does not disclose what it was.
[40] *Ryan* v. *Mill*, 1947 J.C. 28.
[41] *McLaren* v. *Macleod*, 1913 S.C. (J.) 61, 7 Adam 110 (brothel).
[42] Dickson, *Evidence* (3rd ed.) §248.
[43] Macdonald, *Criminal Law* (5th ed.) 325. The passage from Dickson, *Evidence* (3rd ed.) §1776, does not go so far, nor does §263. See § 383.
[44] See § 378.

by showing that his story has been the same from the beginning.[45] Although such evidence may be theoretically admissible in any case, it is tendered mainly in cases of physical injury. Probably for this reason it is sometimes said[46] that a *de recenti* statement by the injured party is admissible. But this is inaccurate. Unless the party is a witness, his credibility cannot be set up, and evidence of the statement is not admissible, at least as a *de recenti* statement. The period within which the statement must have been made depends on circumstances. It should be short, so as to reduce the chance of concoction, and it should have been made to the first natural confidant, e.g., a girl to her mother. Where a girl of thirteen only saw her mother three days after the alleged assault and told her then, the mother's evidence of the girl's statement was held admissible.[47] A boy of seven was a witness. Evidence was admitted from subsequent witnesses as to what the boy had said to them within forty-eight hours of the incident.[48] On the other hand such evidence was rejected in an action of damages for alleged assault where the girl's statement was made to the third person she met and even then not at the first opportunity.[49] In *A.* v. *B.*[50] evidence was admitted of a statement as to paternity made by a woman at the birth of her child. This was clearly wrong. As was pointed out in *Gilmour* v. *Hansen*,[51] the *de quo* was the intercourse months before the statement was made. Evidence is admissible of a *de recenti* statement by an accused person for the purpose of showing that his story has been consistent.[52] A *de recenti* letter written by a witness and sent to his employers describing events may help to set up his credibility.[53]

377. RES GESTÆ

"*Res gestæ* is the whole thing that happened,"[54] and this includes not only "exclamations uttered or things done at the time by those concerned,"[54] but also exclamations forced from an onlooker[55] by the events.[56] Such exclamations are facts, real evidence,[56] which may found inferences as to the nature of the acts which they accompany or which gave rise to them. Evidence that members of a crowd of which the accused formed part were shouting "à la Bastille" would (assuming French law to be the same as

45 *Morton* v. *H.M. Advocate*, 1938 J.C. 50; *Burgh* v. *H. M. Advocate*, 1944 J.C. 77; *Barr* v. *Barr*, 1939 S.C. 696; *Gilmour* v. *Hansen*, 1920 S.C. 598. In the last two cases the evidence was inadmissible because the statement was not *de recenti*.
46 Lewis, *Evidence*, 44, 325.
47 *Anderson* v. *McFarlane*, 1899, 1 F. (J.) 36.
48 *Stewart*, 1855, 2 Irv. 166, at p. 179.
49 *Hill* v. *Fletcher*, 1847, 10 D. 7. The girl, being pursuer, was not an admissible witness.
50 1858, 20 D. 407, at p. 417.
51 1920 S.C. 598, at p. 603.
52 *Pye*, 1838, 2 Swin. 187; *Forrest*, 1837, 1 Swin. 404.
53 *Gibson* v. *National Cash Register Co.*, 1925 S.C. 500.
54 *Greer* v. *Stirlingshire Road Trustees*, 1882, 9 R. 1069, L. Young at p. 1076. It is thought that the hearsay of the children's statements founded on by L. Craighill was inadmissible. L. Rutherfurd Clark had difficulty, L. J-Cl. Moncreiff preferred another ground, and L. Young dissented.
55 *Ewing* v. *Earl of Mar*, 1851, 14 D. 314.
56 *Lejzor Teper* v. *The Queen*, [1952] A.C. 480, L. Normand at p. 487; *O'Hara* v. *Central S.M.T. Co.*, 1941 S.C. 363, L. Moncrieff at p. 390. For the facts of the latter, see § 379.

Scots) yield an inference that the accused were guilty of mobbing and rioting.[57] Evidence of protests by the alleged victim of an assault would found an inference that the interference was uninvited. While such exclamations "may be spoken to by those who heard them, an account given by anyone . . . is an account only, and not *res gestæ*."[54] The distinction between *res gestæ* and a subsequent account was emphasised by Lord Normand, who explained that what he said applied to Scotland.[58] "It is essential that the words sought to be proved should be, if not absolutely contemporaneous with the action or event, at least so clearly associated with it, in time, place and circumstances, that they are part of the thing being done, and so an item or part of real evidence and not merely a reported statement."[59] His Lordship then described English decisions illustrating the narrow limits of the doctrine.[59] The last of these was a trial for assault by throwing a stone, in which evidence had been wrongly admitted that an unknown woman had pointed to the accused's door and said: "The person who threw the stone went in there." Lord Normand commented: "The words were closely associated in time and place with the event, the assault. But they were not directly connected with that event itself. They were not words spontaneously forced from the woman by the sight of the assault, but were prompted by the sight of a man quitting the scene of the assault, and they were spoken for the purpose of helping to bring him to justice."[60] The phrase "words spontaneously forced from the woman by the sight of the assault" and Lord Moncrieff's words, "an exclamation forced out of the witness[61] by the emotion generated by an event,"[56] bring out clearly the reason why such evidence is admissible. The exclamation is an involuntary reaction, real evidence, as both judges described it, and from this real evidence may be inferred the nature of the incident which gave rise to it. It is thus independent evidence.

The duration of the *res gestæ* varies according to circumstances. In a trial on a charge of conspiracy it was held to include all the acts of conspiracy.[62] The opinion was expressed by Lord Moncrieff that in the case of an accident it might include the victim's recovery of consciousness.[56] This principle was applied in a trial for ravishing an imbecile girl, who was considered unfit to take the oath and was rejected as a witness. Evidence was admitted from her mother as to "the first statement or exclamation she made" when she arrived home, this being likened to the cry of a child or even the scream of an animal.[63] This may also explain why in *O'Hara* v. *Central S.M.T. Co.*,[56] Lord Moncrieff founded on the fact that a little while after the accident the driver challenged a bystander with getting in the way. It was the first opportunity for the discharge of the driver's pent-up emotion.

In an action of separation by a wife, who was not then a competent witness, on the ground of cruelty, a witness found the wife in a distressed

---

57 Dickson, *Evidence* (3rd ed.) §256.
58 *Lejzor Teper* v. *The Queen (supra)*, at p. 486.
59 *Ibid.*, at p. 487.
60 *Ibid.*, at p. 488.
61 Not necessarily a witness. It may be a person unknown.
62 *Hunter*, 1838, 2 Swin. 1, at p. 12.
63 *Murray*, 1866, 5 Irv. 232.

state, and during the interview the wife said something. The witness was asked what it was, and the Lord Ordinary sustained an objection. This decision was reversed by a majority in the Inner House, but the difference of opinion arose, not as to whether the utterance formed part of the *res gestæ*, but as to what the *res gestæ* were. The majority thought they were the interview between the wife and the witness, of which the utterance clearly formed part. The dissenting judge thought that the *res gestæ* were some earlier interview between the wife and the husband, and no one suggested that the utterance could have formed part of that.[64] The decision is therefore no authority for the view that utterances subsequent to the event are admissible

378. CONTRAST BETWEEN DE RECENTI STATEMENT AND RES GESTÆ

In spite of Dickson's statement[65] that the two principles are akin, they are in fact totally different.[66] Proof of a *de recenti* statement is admitted for its bearing on the credibility of a witness, and is therefore confined to statements by witnesses.[67] It is not corroboration, and it may have been made after some interval. A statement forming part of the *res gestæ*, on the other hand, may have been made by some unknown person;[68] it must be part of the event; and it is independent, and possibly corroborative, evidence. Indeed, if a *de recenti* statement is one made shortly after the occurrence it cannot by definition be part of the occurrence. This seems to have been overlooked in *O'Hara* v. *Central S.M.T. Co.*,[69] where two of the judges in defining *res gestæ* said that the statement should be at least *de recenti* and not after an interval which would allow time for reflection and for concocting a story. These are almost the very words used in an earlier case to define a *de recenti* statement,[70] and they leave out of account that no "story" can be part of the *res gestæ*.

379. CONTRAST BETWEEN PRIMARY AND SECONDARY HEARSAY

A pleader who has successfully secured the admission of hearsay as primary may have the good fortune to see it treated by the jury, or even the judge, as secondary, and therefore as evidence of the facts stated in it. Once the evidence has been led, this may easily happen. In *O'Hara* v. *Central S.M.T. Co.*[71] a bus swerved suddenly, and the pursuer was thrown off and

[64] *A.B.* v. *C.D.*, 1848, 11 D. 289.
[65] *Evidence* (3rd ed.) §258.
[66] It is not very clear under which principle the judges treated a witness's remark in *Jordan* v. *Court Line*, 1947 S.C. 29, at pp. 35, 39, 41.
[67] *Greer* v. *Stirlingshire Road Trustees*, 1882, 9 R. 1069, seems to be the only exception, apart from old cases where the person was not a competent witness. For comments on this case, see §377, note 54.
[68] *Ewing* v. *Earl of Mar*, 1851, 14 D. 314.
[69] 1941 S.C. 363. For the facts of this case, see §379.
[70] *Gilmour* v. *Hansen*, 1920 S.C. 598, L.P. Clyde at p. 603.
[71] 1941 S.C. 363.

injured. The defence was that the driver had swerved to avoid knocking down a man who ran in front of the bus. The only direct evidence in support of the defence was that of the driver, but he was held to be corroborated by facts and circumstances. There was, however, evidence as to statements made by a man who was not a witness, and opinions were delivered *obiter* as to the admissibility and effect of this evidence. The conductress said that after the bus had stopped, which it did immediately, and she and the driver had attended to the pursuer and helped her into a shop, the driver brought a man to her, who admitted crossing in front of the bus and gave her a paper containing his name and address. About ten minutes after the accident the paper was handed to a police officer. He interviewed a man at once, and the man told him he did cross the road, but was not in the way of the bus. The view of the majority was that the statement to the conductress was part of the *res gestæ*, although it was not made until some time had elapsed. When the majority came to deal with the statement to the constable, they appear to have lost sight of the ground on which the first statement had been admitted and it became an "admission," while the second became a "qualification" of it. The Lord President referred to "the unsworn evidence of someone who is not adduced as a witness" and then considered the effect of the two statements together just as if they had been evidence. [72] Lord Fleming "preferred" the statement given to the conductress to the later statement given to the policeman. [73] All this was just to treat the statements as evidence of the facts in them. Lord Moncrieff dissented, taking the view that the "event" terminated on the man's arrival on the pavement. [74] In the circumstances of the case, evidence that as, or just before, the bus swerved some unknown spectator had shouted, "Watch the bus" or that the driver had shouted, "Look out, you fool," would clearly have been admissible as part of the *res gestæ*. Such evidence would have founded an inference that there was somebody in the way. *O'Hara* v. *Central S.M.T. Co.* [71] was referred to without comment in *Lejzor Teper* v. *The Queen*, [75] but it is difficult to see how either of the man's utterances was part of the thing done and not a reported statement. The opinions of the majority in *O'Hara* [71] appear irreconcileable with those in *Jackson* v. *Glasgow Corporation*. [76]

[72] at p. 383.
[73] at p. 386.
[74] at p. 390.
[75] [1952] A.C. 480. See §377.
[76] 1956 S.C. 354, at pp. 361, 363, 365.

CHAPTER XXX

SUFFICIENCY OF EVIDENCE

380. INTRODUCTORY

(a) **General.** "Sufficiency" means sufficiency in law. Evidence which satisfies the tribunal as to where the truth lies may not be sufficient in law to entitle the tribunal to give effect to its opinion.[1] On the other hand, evidence which is sufficient in law may not satisfy the tribunal.[2] When the evidence has all been led two questions arise. Is there sufficient evidence in law to entitle the tribunal, jury or judge, to decide in a particular way? That is a question of law for the decision of the judge, and it is only if it is answered in the affirmative that the second question, viz., whether the tribunal is satisfied with the evidence, arises. The first question is the main subject of this chapter, but the second is briefly discussed in the following sub-paragraph.

(b) **Weight of Evidence.** This has been said to depend on the rules of common sense.[3] In assessing the value of the testimony of a particular witness much may depend on his demeanour, his apparent intelligence, his means of knowledge, on the coherence of his testimony with facts otherwise established,[4] and also on the manner in which his testimony has been elicited.[5] The value of expert evidence depends on the authority, experience and qualification of the witness.[6] The weight to be attached to the evidence adduced for a party as a whole depends to some extent on its volume. Great weight attaches to the evidence of a body of witnesses agreeing with each other whose reliability is not suspect,[7] and, where all the witnesses appeared

---

1 A jury on being directed to acquit because the evidence was insufficient in law, has been known to enquire, "Must we?"
2 In *Sim* v. *Sim*, 1831, 12 S. 633, the evidence was sufficient in law, but the tribunal was not satisfied by it.
3 *Lord Advocate* v. *Lord Blantyre*, 1879, 6 R. (H.L.) 72, L. Blackburn at p. 85.
4 See §**342**, sub-para. (b). See also *Kay* v. *Rodger*, 1832, 10 S. 831.
5 *McKenzie* v. *McKenzie*, 1943 S.C. 108 (evidence elicited by leading questions).
6 *Davie* v. *Magistrates of Edinburgh*, 1953 S.C. 34, L.P. Cooper at p. 39, L. Russell at p. 42.
7 *Jordan* v. *Court Line*, 1947 S.C. 29 (reversing the Lord Ordinary), where, p. 36, failure to cross was founded on. See also *North British Rly.* v. *Wood*, 1891, 18 R. (H.L.) 27, at p. 34.

to be honest, the court proceeded on the testimony of the pursuer and one independent witness as against the uncorroborated testimony of the defender.[8] Again, a number of pieces of evidence all pointing to the same result have great weight.[3] While it is unnecessary for a party to call every possible witness, some importance may attach to failure to call what may be described as an obvious witness. In two cases[9] the court founded on such failure against the party who might have been expected to call the witness. An appeal court will consider the weight of evidence for itself in so far as it does not depend on factors available only to the judge who saw the witnesses.[10]

381. PROOF OF CASE OR PROOF OF FACTS

"No person can be convicted of a crime or a statutory offence, except where the Legislature otherwise directs, unless there is evidence of at least two witnesses implicating the person accused with the commission of the crime or offence with which he is charged."[11] "Our rule of law is that a case is not to be proved against a defender by the evidence of a single witness. . . . There must be independent corroboration found in admission[12] or in the testimony of some other witness."[13] While these general negative propositions are unchallengeable, they seldom provide a positive answer to the question whether the evidence is in the circumstances sufficient.

To justify a conviction on a criminal charge one or more facts must be proved. The old form of indictment brought this out clearly, since it specified the crime in the major premiss and narrated the facts to be proved in the minor. Whether the facts averred constituted the crime was a question of criminal law. Whether the evidence led was sufficient to establish each fact was a question of the law of evidence. Similarly, in a stated case, while the question whether the facts found entitled the lower court to convict or to acquit is a question of criminal law, the High Court may remit back for a statement of the evidence on which a fact or facts were found proved,[14] the purpose being to enable the High Court to decide whether that evidence was sufficient. In a civil cause several facts may have to be proved to justify the decision. A sheriff court interlocutor with its findings in fact illustrates this. Whether the facts proved justify the decision is a matter of the particular branch of substantive law. Whether the evidence is sufficient to prove a particular fact is a matter for the law of evidence.

Evidence is thus concerned with proof, not of cases, but of facts, and, from this point of view, facts fall into three classes, (1) crucial facts,[15] (2)

8 *Duncan* v. *Wilson*, 1940 S.C. 221 (reversing the Lord Ordinary).
9 *Jordan* v. *Court Line* (*supra*), at pp. 35, 41; *Coles* v. *Homer and Tulloh*, 1895, 22 R. 716, at pp. 732, 739. In both cases the Lord Ordinary was reversed.
10 *Thomas* v. *Thomas*, 1947 S.C. (H.L.) 45.
11 *Morton* v. *H.M. Advocate*, 1938 J.C. 50, L. J-Cl. Aitchison at p. 55.
12 As to judicial admissions, see §48.
13 *Maitland* v. *Glasgow Corporation*, 1947 S.C. 20, L.P. Normand at p. 25.
14 In *McArthur* v. *Stewart*, 1955 J.C. 71, the court remitted to the sheriff-substitute to state the evidence on which he had made a crucial finding, and on his report held that the evidence was sufficient. So also in *Dow* v. *MacKnight*, 1949 J.C. 38.
15 See §§382-385.

evidential facts[16] and (3) procedural facts.[17] The opinion evidence of an expert, which does not fall into any of these classes, does not require corroboration.[18]

382. CRUCIAL FACTS: GENERAL

These are the *facta probanda*,[19] the facts which in a criminal cause establish the accused's guilt of the crime charged[20] and must be libelled in an indictment or complaint, expressly or by statutory implication,[21] in order that the libel may be relevant. In a civil cause they are the facts which a party must, or ought to, aver in order to make a case relevant to be sent to proof.[22] Unless by statute a single witness is sufficient,[23] such facts require "legal proof"[24] or "full proof,"[25] which consists of either the direct evidence of two witnesses,[26] or two or more evidential facts spoken to by separate witnesses[27] from which the crucial fact may be inferred, or of a combination of the direct evidence of one witness and of one or more evidential facts spoken to by other witnesses[27] which support it.[28] Lord McLaren's dictum that any fact in the case may be proved by the testimony of one credible witness,[29] though cited by the court in subsequent cases,[30] is irreconcilable with the decisions cited below.[31] The direct evidence of a single witness does not become sufficient proof of a crucial fact because he is not cross-examined,[32]

[16] See §§ 386-389.

[17] See § 390.

[18] *Davie* v. *Magistrates of Edinburgh*, 1953 S.C. 34.

[19] Described as "crucial facts" in *Farrell* v. *Concannon*, 1957 J.C. 12, at p. 19; *Lockwood* v. *Walker*, 1910 S.C. (J.) 3, at p. 5; "essential facts" in *Bisset* v. *Anderson*, 1949 J.C. 106, at p. 110; *Stewart* v. *Glasgow Corporation*, 1958 S.C. 28, at p. 45; "essential matter" in *Gillespie* v. *Macmillan*, 1957 J.C. 31, at p. 39; "essential elements" in *McCourt*, 1913 S.C. (J.) 6, at p. 8; and "material facts" in *McArthur* v. *Stewart*, 1955 J.C. 71.

[20] Some procedural facts unconnected with the accused's guilt, are essential to a conviction, e.g., a private prosecutor's title, which must be libelled and proved: *Lees* v. *Macdonald*, 1893, 20 R. (J.) 55. See § 390.

[21] As to averments implied by statute, see §88.

[22] As to averments in civil causes, see §3.

[23] See § 384.

[24] In *O'Hara* v. *Central S.M.T. Co.*, 1941 S.C. 363, L.P. Normand several times used the phrases "full legal proof" and "legal proof" with the meaning stated in the text.

[25] Used by Dickson, *Evidence* (3rd ed.) §1807, and in *Moore* v. *Harland & Wolff*, 1937 S.C. 707, at pp. 715, 721.

[26] An accused, if he chooses to give evidence, may in effect be the necessary second witness for the prosecution: *McArthur* v. *Stewart* (*supra*).

[27] A witness cannot corroborate himself: *Morton* v. *H.M. Advocate*, 1938 J.C. 50, L. J-Cl. Aitchison at p. 54.

[28] *O'Hara* v. *Central S.M.T. Co.* (*supra*), at p. 379.

[29] *Lees* v. *Macdonald*, 1893, 20 R. (J.) 55, at p. 58.

[30] *Morton* v. *H.M. Advocate* (*ut supra*): *Gillespie* v. *Macmillan*, 1957 J.C. 31, at p. 37.

[31] See notes 49, 50, 52.

[32] *Criminal causes: Morton* v. *H.M. Advocate* (*supra*), disapproving expressly observations in *Strathearn* v. *Lambie*, 1934 J.C. 137, and impliedly those of L. J-Cl. Macdonald and L. Lee in *Lees* v. *Macdonald*, 1893, 20 R. (J.) 55; *Wilson* v. *Brown*, 1947 J.C. 81, L. Mackay at p. 94, L. Jamieson at p. 96; *McArthur* v. *Stewart*, 1955 J.C. 71, L. J-G. Clyde at p. 74. *Civil causes: Stewart* v. *Glasgow Corporation*, 1958 S.C. 28; *Moore* v. *Harland & Wolff*, 1937 S.C. 707.

nor is it sufficiently corroborated by a false denial by the accused[33] or, except in an action of affiliation and aliment,[34] a party in the witness box,[35] or by the silence of an accused when charged,[36] or by selections from the opposite party's unproved averments.[37] Nor is any fact proved merely because witnesses who deny it are not believed.[38]

383. CRUCIAL FACTS: CRIMINAL CAUSES

(a) **Identification of Accused.** In every criminal cause the fact that the accused was implicated in the commission of the crime or offence is crucial,[39] and therefore requires full legal proof.[40] It may sometimes be proved by the evidence of the same witnesses who speak to the commission of the crime or offence. On other occasions it may have to be proved by the evidence of witnesses who have no knowledge of the commission of the crime or offence. So, for example, in a prosecution for driving a motor vehicle recklessly,[41] the identification of the accused as the person who committed the offence may be proved by the witnesses who observed the reckless driving, and, at the same time, were able to recognise the driver. The witnesses to the reckless driving may, however, have been unable to recognise the driver. In this case it may be possible to prove that the accused was the driver at the relevant time by the evidence of a witness who saw him driving the vehicle immediately before, and of a witness who saw him driving it immediately after, the period of recklessness, in circumstances which prove beyond reasonable doubt that no other person could have occupied the driver's seat during the intervening period when the recklessness occurred. Where the offence arises from the presence of a vehicle or vessel, with which the accused has been associated in evidence, the identification of the vessel becomes a crucial fact. So when it was proved that a vessel was trawling illegally a conviction of the master was quashed because only one witness could identify the vessel.[42] The extent to which an accused may be sufficiently identified by his voice has not been fully explored, but such evidence is admissible.[43] When an accused was identified visually by one witness and aurally by another the conviction was quashed, not because the aural identification was inadmissible, but because the two witnesses contradicted each other.[44]

The proper practice is that the witnesses who purport to identify the accused as the person who committed the crime should point him out in court

---

[33] *Wilkie* v. *H.M. Advocate*, 1938 J.C. 128. The alleged lie was not told in the witness box, but the opinions cover the general point.
[34] See §**174.**
[35] *Davies* v. *Hunter*, 1934 S.C. 10.
[36] *Robertson* v. *Maxwell*, 1951 J.C. 11.
[37] *Stewart* v. *Glasgow Corporation*, 1958 S.C. 28; *Lee* v. *National Coal Board*, 1955 S.C. 151.
[38] *Cameron* v. *Yeats*, 1899, 1 F. 456.
[39] *Morton* v *H.M. Advocate*, 1938 J.C. 50; *Mitchell* v. *Macdonald*, 1959 S.L.T. (Notes) 74.
[40] See §382.
[41] Road Traffic Act, 1960 (8 & 9 Eliz. II. c. 16), s. 2.
[42] *Harrison* v. *Mackenzie*, 1923 J.C. 61.
[43] *McGiveran* v. *Auld*, 1894, 21 R. (J.) 69.
[44] *Burrows* v. *H.M. Advocate*, 1951 S.L.T. (Notes) 69-70.

as the person of whom they are speaking. It is probably not sufficient that they merely refer to him by name.[45] Merely to identify him as the person named in the indictment or complaint is valueless.[46] If a witness cannot identify the accused it may be sufficient to prove by other evidence that on an earlier occasion, for example at an identification parade, he did identify the accused as the person concerned.[47]

(b) Commission of the Crime. Some crimes consist of a single act, in which case the fact that the act was done is crucial and requires full legal proof.[40] Assaults frequently fall into this category, and another example was the offence of having commercial petrol in the tank of a private car.[48] But other crimes and offences are compound, that is to say they arise from the coincidence of two or more independent facts, none of which supports any other. Each of these independent facts is crucial and requires full legal proof.[40] The common law crime of using lewd and libidinous practices consists of two crucial facts, the use of the practices and the age (or other disability) of the victim,[49] and that of obtaining money by fraud of four crucial facts, the representation, its falsity, the payment induced by it and the accused's knowledge of its falsity.[50] The same applies in statutory charges. In proceedings under the Prevention of Crime Act, 1908,[51] two crucial facts must be established, the previous convictions of the accused and his age.[52] The convictions in these three cases were quashed because there was not full legal proof of one of the crucial facts. In a statutory charge of neglecting to maintain a child whereby assistance was granted under the National Assistance Act, 1948,[53] both failure to maintain and the granting of assistance are crucial.[54]

384. STATUTORY EXCEPTIONS

Some statutes contain a provision that an offence may be proved by the evidence of one credible witness.[55] If such evidence is led, the court is not

[45] *Wilson* v. *Brown*, 1947 J.C. 81, at p. 96; *Bruce* v. *H.M. Advocate*, 1936 J.C. 93, at p. 95.
[46] *Bruce* v. *H.M. Advocate (ut supra)*.
[47] Macdonald, *Criminal Law* (5th ed.) 325. There is no judicial authority. In *Wight*, 1836, 1 Swin. 47, the witness had already identified the accused from the witness box. Dickson, *Evidence* (3rd ed.) §263, treats the case as one of *de recenti* statement, and the passage at §1776 is not definite.
[48] *Bisset* v. *Anderson*, 1949 J.C. 106. See also *Callan* v. *MacFadyean*, 1950 J.C. 82.
[49] *Lockwood* v. *Walker*, 1910 S.C. (J.) 3, where the child's evidence as to her age was not corroborated.
[50] *Townsend* v. *Strathern*, 1923 J.C. 66, where only one witness spoke to the accused's knowledge of the falsity of her representation.
[51] 8 Edw. VII. c. 59.
[52] *McCourt*, 1913 S.C. (J.) 6, where the only evidence of age was that of one witness.
[53] 11 & 12 Geo. VI. c. 29, s. 51.
[54] *McArthur* v. *Stewart*, 1955 J.C. 71, where only one crown witness spoke to the granting of assistance, and but for the accused's admission in cross-examination, the conviction would have been quashed.
[55] Game (Scotland) Act, 1832 (2 & 3 William IV. c. 68), ss. 1, 2, 6; Salmon Fisheries (Scotland) Act, 1862 (25 & 26 Vict. c. 97), s. 28; Poaching Prevention Act, 1862 (25 & 26 Vict. c. 114), s. 3, as construed in *Anderson* v. *Macdonald*, 1910 S.C. (J.) 65; Trespass

entitled to reject it merely because other witnesses, apparently available, were not called.[56] If one witness would suffice, and the prosecution adduces two, who contradict each other, the court may disbelieve one and convict on the evidence of the other.[57] The one witness required may be a *socius criminis* if his evidence is accepted as credible.[58] Under the Food and Drugs (Scotland) Act, 1956,[59] the certificate of an analyst is sufficient evidence of the facts therein stated, unless the other party requires the analyst to be called as a witness. If the analyst is not so called, and there is no counter evidence, the certificate becomes conclusive,[60] but, if evidence is led for the other party, the whole evidence must be considered and the certificate may be rebutted.[61] If the analyst is required by the other party to be called as a witness, his oral evidence is sufficient.[59] These innovations on the law of evidence are limited to the precise words of the provision in question, and, when Regulations (now repealed) provided that a certificate by an analyst was to be evidence of the facts therein stated, it was held that this merely excused the personal attendance of the analyst, and that neither his certificate, nor his oral evidence, if given, could suffice for a conviction without corroboration.[62]

385. CRUCIAL FACTS: CIVIL CAUSES

The crucial facts in any civil cause ought to be discoverable from the written pleadings. They are the facts which ought to be averred in order that the averments may relevantly support the party's pleas-in-law. Each of such facts requires full legal proof.[63] So in a claim under the Workmen's Compensation Act, where the rules of evidence were held to be the same as in an ordinary civil action, it was a condition precedent to a relevant claim that the workman should have taken all reasonable steps to obtain employment. Only one witness, the workman himself, gave evidence about his efforts to obtain work, and this crucial fact was held not to be proved.[64] In a case where the burden of proof rested upon the defenders to prove that their driver was not negligent when his omnibus suddenly swerved, they

(Scotland) Act, 1865 (28 & 29 Vict. c. 56), s. 4; Salmon Fisheries (Scotland) Act, 1868 (31 & 32 Vict. c. 123), s. 30; Roads and Bridges (Scotland) Act, 1878 (41 & 42 Vict. c. 51), s. 124; Taxes Management Act, 1880 (43 & 44 Vict. c. 51), s. 21 (6); Licensing (Scotland) Act, 1959 (7 & 8 Eliz. II. c. 51), ss. 131, 133; Road Traffic Act, 1960 (8 & 9 Eliz. II. c. 16), s. 14 (4); Summary Jurisdiction (Scotland) Act, 1954 (2 & 3 Eliz. II. c. 48), s. 31 (2), as to which see *McDermott* v. *Stewart's Trs.*, 1918 J.C. 25.
[56] *Jopp* v. *Pirie*, 1869, 7 M. 755. *Cf. Macrorie* v. *Mackay*, 1909 S.C. (J.) 18.
[57] *Coventry* v. *Brown*, 1926 J.C. 20. (The section in the Excise Management Act, 1827, with which this case was concerned is now repealed).
[58] *Manson* v. *Macleod*, 1918 J.C. 60; *Dow* v. *MacKnight*, 1949 J.C. 38.
[59] 4 & 5 Eliz. II. c. 30, s. 42 (1). The terms of the sub-section seem to make the reasoning in *Callan* v. *MacFadyean*, 1950 J.C. 82, inapplicable. There is a similar provision in the Road Traffic Act, 1962 (10 & 11 Eliz. II. c. 59), s. 2 (3).
[60] *Chalmers* v. *McMeeking*, 1921 J.C. 54.
[61] *Bisset* v. *Anderson*, 1949 J.C. 106, at p. 113; *Todd* v. *Cochrane*, 1901, 3 Adam 357.
[62] *Bisset* v. *Anderson* (*supra*). As to statutory certificates more fully, see § 206.
[63] See § 382.
[64] *Moore* v. *Harland & Wolff*, 1937 S.C. 707.

averred that a pedestrian ran suddenly into the path of the vehicle. In proof of this crucial fact the evidence of the driver alone was held to be insufficient.[65] In order to prove negligence against a local authority who were in possession and control of a clothes pole in a back court it was essential for the pursuer to prove, not only that the pole was defective through rust at the time when it broke, but that it had been defective at an earlier time when the defenders had an opportunity of discovering the defect. It was held that the defective condition of the pole at the earlier period was not sufficiently proved by the evidence of one witness.[66] The specialties arising in consistorial causes[67] and in actions of affiliation and aliment[68] are mentioned elsewhere.

386. EVIDENTIAL FACTS: GENERAL

These are facts which individually establish nothing, but from which, in conjunction with other such facts, a crucial fact may be inferred. They are frequently described as circumstantial evidence, to which reference has been made in an earlier chapter.[69] The evidence of a single witness is sufficient proof of each fact which is used in this way. It has been explained that two witnesses are unnecessary to establish each of such facts "because the aptitude and coherence of the several circumstances often as fully confirm the truth of the story as if all the witnesses were deponing to the same facts."[70] An evidential fact may also be used in conjunction with, and as providing sufficient corroboration of, the direct evidence of a single witness, so that combined they provide sufficient evidence of the crucial fact. "If one man swear that he saw the pannel stab the deceased, and others confirm his testimony with circumstances, such as the pannel's flight from the spot, the blood on his clothes, the bloody instrument found in his possession, his confession[71] on being taken, or the like; certainly these are as good, nay better even, than a second witness to the act of stabbing."[70] In the example quoted, the flight, the blood on the clothes, the blood on the knife and the confession,[71] are evidential facts, each of which is sufficiently proved by the evidence of one

---

65 *O'Hara* v. *Central S.M.T. Co.*, 1941 S.C. 363. The driver's evidence was held to be corroborated by facts and circumstances.

66 *Stewart* v. *Glasgow Corporation*, 1958 S.C. 28. It is impossible to reconcile with these decisions the apparent assumption in *Dampskibsselskabet Svendborg* v. *Love & Stewart, Ltd.*, 1916 S.C. (H.L.) 187, that the number of logs loaded on a ship, which was the fact in issue, could be proved by one witness who tallied at the fore hatch and one who tallied at the after hatch.

67 See §§ 158 *et seq.*

68 See §§ 170 *et seq.*

69 See §§ 8 *et seq.*

70 Hume, II, 384. See also Dickson, *Evidence* (3rd ed.) §1811. What is required is a "concurrence of testimonies": Hume, II, 383.

71 An extrajudicial confession in a criminal cause may be proved by the evidence of one witness: *Mills* v. *H.M. Advocate*, 1935 J.C. 77; *Innes* v. *H.M. Advocate*, 1955 S.L.T. (Notes) 69 (although described as a link in the chain, the confession was truly a strand in the cable). Such a confession, however, is insufficient by itself to justify a conviction unless supported by other evidence. Similar rules apply to extrajudicial admissions in civil causes. As to the probative effect both of extrajudicial confessions and admissions, see § 30.

witness, if it is used to support, and receives support from, direct testimony or other evidential facts in order to establish the crucial fact that the deceased was stabbed by the accused. Although the example mentioned above has reference to a criminal cause, the same principles apply to evidential facts in civil causes.[72]

387. EVIDENTIAL FACTS: CRIMINAL CAUSES

(a) Cable Analogy. Examples of evidential facts which may constitute the strands in a cable of circumstantial evidence are given in an earlier chapter,[73] and also in the previous paragraph. The application of the same principle to evidence of similar criminal acts is mentioned in the next paragraph.

(b) Chain Analogy. The rule which allows each of a number of evidential facts, because of their "aptitude and coherence," and their "concurrence," to be proved by the evidence of a single witness, has now been extended to include independent facts, having no aptitude, coherence or concurrence, from which, if *all* of them are proved, the fact in issue inevitably follows by a process of, or akin to, mathematical calculation. Facts of this kind are like the links in a chain,[74] failure in any one of which makes the whole chain useless. These facts are also mentioned in an earlier chapter.[75] When a motor vehicle's speed, which was the fact in issue, had to be calculated from the distance between two points, the exact time when the vehicle passed the first point and the exact time when it passed the second point, it was held that each of these three essential facts could be proved by the evidence of a single witness.[76] When it is sought to establish a fact in issue by excluding all the other possibilities, it would seem to follow that each of the other possibilities may also be excluded by the evidence of a single witness.[75]

388. SIMILAR CRIMINAL ACTS

(a) Interrelation of Character, Circumstances and Time. Where an accused is charged with two or more crimes and only one witness implicates him in each, they afford mutual corroboration if the crimes are so inter-related by character, circumstances and time as to justify an inference that they are parts of a course of criminal conduct systematically pursued by the accused.[77] It is difficult, and not as a rule particularly helpful, to consider the character and the circumstances of the crimes separately, and in fact they seldom are

---

72 See § 389.
73 See §§ 8, 9.
74 In *Scott* v. *Jameson*, 1914 S.C. (J.) 187, L. Guthrie described them as facts which "require to be proved" and form a "consecutive chain." The Lord Justice-General (Strathclyde) described them as fundamental facts or important facts.
75 See § 9. sub-para. (b).
76 *Gillespie* v. *Macmillan*, 1957 J.C. 31; *Scott* v. *Jameson*, 1914 S.C. (J.) 187. For reasoned criticisms of these decisions, see *Corroboration of Evidence in Scottish Criminal Law*, 1958 S.L.T. (News) 137; W. A. Wilson, *The Logic of Corroboration*, 1960, 76 Scottish Law Review, 101.
77 *Ogg* v. *H.M. Advocate*, 1938 J.C. 152, at p. 157.

Q

so considered.[78] What is required to justify the inference is that the crimes should exhibit common features. The fact that indecent offences have been committed against young children establishes the necessary character.[79] General illustrations are given by Lord Sands,[80] by Lord Wark,[81] and by Dickson.[82] The question of time relationship depends to some extent on the nature of the crimes. "A man whose course of conduct is to buy houses, insure them, and burn them down, or to acquire ships, insure them, and scuttle them, or to purport to marry women, defraud and desert them, cannot repeat the offence every month, or even perhaps every six months."[83] The principle was applied in sustaining a conviction on nine charges of indecent assault (of which six rested on the evidence of a single witness) by an employer on his women employees, within his own premises, over a period of about three years. Moreover, but for a technical misdirection of the jury, the court would have sustained convictions on six charges of assault of an amatory nature by him on women employees over a period of four years.[84] The principle was also applied to two charges of attempting within three weeks to bribe professional football players to lose a match by the same method,[85] to six charges of assault (all but one spoken to by only one witness) committed with a razor in a small district in Glasgow within four months, on persons unknown to the accused, and apparently motiveless,[86] and to charges of incest with the accused's two daughters over a period of six years.[87] But the court refused to apply the principle to three charges of indecent conduct, each in different circumstances, at intervals of one year and eighteen months.[88]

(b) Common Purpose. A similar rule applies when the several crimes charged are all directed to the same end. The most obvious example is subornation of perjury.[89] Where there is subornation or attempted subornation of two or more witnesses at the same trial or proof, each incident spoken to by one witness is corroboration of similar evidence by another. The purpose is clear, to influence the result of the trial or proof. The same reasoning would have been applicable to the case of the professional footballers referred to above, if the bribes had been offered in respect of the same match.[85] It was applied where the charges were of attempts to induce two partners of a firm to render fraudulent accounts,[90] and the reset of goods

[78] They were distinguished in *Ogg* v. *H.M. Advocate* (*supra*), at p. 159.
[79] *Burgh* v. *H.M. Advocate*, 1944 J.C. 77, at p. 80; *Moorov* v. *H.M. Advocate*, 1930 J.C. 68, at pp. 74, 89.
[80] *Moorov* v. *H.M. Advocate* (*supra*), at p. 88.
[81] *Ogg* v. *H.M. Advocate* (*supra*), at p. 160.
[82] *Evidence* (3rd ed.) §§1809, 1810, quoted in *Moorov* v. *H.M. Advocate* (*supra*), at p. 80.
[83] *Moorov* v. *H.M. Advocate* (*supra*), at p. 89.
[84] *Moorov* v. *H.M. Advocate* (*supra*).
[85] *McCudden* v. *H.M. Advocate*, 1952 J.C. 86.
[86] *H.M. Advocate* v. *McQuade*, 1951 J.C. 143.
[87] *H.M. Advocate* v. *A.E.*, 1937 J.C. 97. See also *H.M. Advocate* v. *McDonald*, 1928 J.C. 42; *H.M. Advocate* v. *Bickerstaff*, 1926 J.C. 65.
[88] *Ogg* v. *H.M. Advocate* (*supra*).
[89] *Moorov* v. *H.M. Advocate* (*supra*), at p. 74.
[90] *H.M. Advocate* v. *Tannahill*, 1943 J.C. 150, at p. 154.

stolen by employees of the same warehouse on three occasions within a year.[91] How delicate the subject is appears from the fact that, as an illustration of circumstances in which the principle would not apply, Dickson[82] mentions uttering forged notes to different persons at different times. The plain object of these acts would appear to be the marketing of notes forged by the accused or his friends.

389. EVIDENTIAL FACTS: CIVIL

(a) General. As in criminal causes, each evidential fact which is a strand in a cable of circumstantial evidence may be proved by the evidence of one witness.[92] Where the fact in issue was that an omnibus commenced to move from a stopping place while the pursuer was in the act of boarding it, this was held to be sufficiently proved by the direct evidence of the pursuer, an evidential fact spoken to by one witness, viz., that the pursuer was standing at the stopping place before the omnibus reached it, and judicial admissions that the omnibus stopped at the stopping place and that the pursuer was injured while boarding it, at or near the stop.[93]

(b) Slander. "In an action of damages for uttering the same slander on two or more occasions, the case may go to the jury on the evidence of one witness to each instance, for the witnesses mutually corroborate each other."[94] But the rule is wider and has been held applicable where the slanders were not the same.[95] It applies even if it would have been possible to call other witnesses.[96] If, however, some of the slanders are not proved so that only one is left, it cannot stand on the evidence of one witness, there being no corroboration.[97]

(c) Adultery. The direct evidence of one witness to an act of adultery[98] is sufficiently corroborated by evidence of indecent conduct given by another witness,[99] and a fortiori by evidence of adultery given by another witness.[1]

390. PROCEDURAL FACTS

This phrase is used to mean what have been described as incidental facts[2] or matters of procedure[3] in a criminal trial. They are not crucial because

---

[91] Harris v. Clark, 1958 J.C. 3.
[92] Dickson, Evidence (3rd ed.) §§1808, 1811.
[93] Spindlow v. Glasgow Corporation, 1933 S.C. 580. Cf. Maitland v. Glasgow Corporation, 1947 S.C. 20.
[94] Dickson, Evidence (3rd ed.) §1808, quoted and applied by L.P. Dunedin in McVicar v. Barbour, 1916 S.C. 567, at p. 569.
[95] Wilson v. Weir and Strang, 1861, 24 D. 67; Cullen v. Ewing, 1832, 10 S. 497; both discussed in McVicar v. Barbour (supra).
[96] McVicar v. Barbour (supra), L. Mackenzie at p. 577.
[97] Wilson v. Weir and Strang (supra).
[98] See §167.
[99] Whyte v. Whyte, 1884, 11 R. 710.
[1] Sim v. Sim, 1834, 12 S. 633.
[2] Lees v. Macdonald, 1893, 20 R. (J.) 55.

they are neither the commission of the crime nor the accused's implication in it; nor are they evidential because they do not yield any inference in support of a crucial fact. Although proof of them may be essential, the evidence of a single witness is sufficient. They include the title of a private prosecutor[2] and the warning preceding medical examination given to a person charged with driving a motor car while under the influence of drink to such an extent as to be incapable of having proper control.[3] After some variation in judicial opinion an aggravation of a crime has been held to be within this class.[4] In a charge of theft, or of theft by housebreaking or by opening a lockfast place, the fact that the house or the place was properly locked[5] and the ownership of the stolen property[6] are also regarded as procedural or incidental facts.

[3] *Farrell* v. *Concannon*, 1957 J.C. 12.
[4] *Davidson*, 1841, 2 Swin. 630.
[5] *Davidson* (*supra*); *Cameron*, 1839, 2 Swin. 447.
[6] *Lees* v. *Macdonald* (*supra*), at p. 56.

CHAPTER XXXI

CONFIDENTIALITY

391. GENERAL

Evidence of communications, written or oral, may be excluded on the ground that they were confidential. With certain exceptions, communications between husband and wife[1] and between partners[2] and professional communications between solicitor and client[3] are confidential. Generally speaking, communications between other persons are not confidential, unless they have passed in connection with the preparation of the case, in other words have been made *post litem motam*,[4] or possibly during an attempt to reconcile the parties.[5] Where there is doubt whether communications between solicitor and client were professional or whether other communications were *ante* or *post litem motam* the court can decide by reading the documents[6], or, in the case of oral evidence, by allowing it under reservation.[7] An undespatched letter or a private diary is not a communication and is confidential, but confidentiality may be waived, e.g. by leaving it lying about.[7a]

392. THE DECISIONS

The question of confidentiality is most frequently raised on a motion for approval of a specification of documents.[8] But confidentiality is not the

---

[1] See § 355.
[2] *Tannett, Walker & Co.* v. *Hannay & Sons*, 1873, 11 M. 931; *Pearson* v. *Anderson Brothers*, 1897, (O.H.) 5 S.L.T. 177. There does not appear to be any reported exception, but fraud might be one, as in the case of solicitor and client.
[3] See § 393.
[4] See § 394.
[5] See § 398.
[6] *Clippens Oil Co., Ltd.*, v. *Edinburgh and District Water Trustees*, 1906, 8 F. 731, at p. 742; *Munro* v. *Fraser*, 1858, 21 D. 103; *Hay, Thomson and Blair* v. *Edinburgh and Glasgow Bank*, 1858, 20 D. 701.
[7] *MacNeill* v. *MacNeill*, (O.H.) 1929 S.L.T. 251.
[7a] *Watson* v. *Watson*, 1934 S.C. 374; *Creasey* v. *Creasey*, 1931 S.C. 9. An admission on record of its existence is not enough; *Duke of Argyll* v. *Duchess of Argyll*, 1962 S.C. (H.L.) 88. See also § 35.
See § 297.

only reason for refusing approval. The averments may not justify the call,[9] or, in the exercise of its discretion, the court may refuse the call as unreasonable.[10] Many of the decisions on recovery of documents are what the first Lord President Clyde once described as "waifs and strays from the Outer House," have the word "confidentiality" in the head note, are grouped in the Faculty Digest under confidentiality, general or particular, and appear to have been cited indiscriminately. A considerable number of them are dangerous guides. Some were decided on the ground that the averments did not justify the calls.[11] In several there is no opinion, and it is impossible to tell on which of the grounds argued, if these are stated, the Lord Ordinary proceeded.[12] In one case reports were held confidential after a certain date, but the significance of the date does not appear from the report.[13] In some confidentiality was reserved, and accordingly they decide nothing.[14] Others were decided on the ground that the documents could not be evidence and could only be used in cross.[15] Such decisions were influenced by the supposed effect of *Livingstone* v. *Dinwoodie*,[16] and have no bearing on confidentiality.

393. SOLICITOR AND CLIENT

As a general rule, a solicitor is neither entitled nor bound, without his client's consent, to disclose information communicated to him by his client for professional purposes, viz., for the purpose of either seeking advice or giving instructions, nor is he entitled or bound without such consent to disclose the advice he gave. After some variations in judicial opinion,[17] it may now be taken as settled that such communications "are privileged, although they may not relate to any suit depending or contemplated or apprehended."[18] This dictum was *obiter*, since the case was decided on averments of fraud, but it has never been disapproved or criticised, and obviously if the privilege were restricted to communications relating to an action pending or apprehended, a solicitor's position would be no different from that of any other person. The purpose of the rule is to enable a man to consult his solicitor freely,

9 See § **288**.
10 See § **287**.
11 *Earl of Morton* v. *Fleming*, (O.H.) 1921, 1 S.L.T. 205; *Northern Garage, Ltd.* v. *North British Motor Manufacturing Co., Ltd.*, (O.H.) 1908, 16 S.L.T. 573. See § **288**.
12 *William Whiteley, Ltd.* v. *Dobson, Molle & Co., Ltd.*, (O.H.) 1902, 10 S.L.T. 71; *Simcock* v. *Scottish Imperial Ins. Co.*, (O.H.) 1901, 9 S.L.T. 234.
13 *Sutherland* v. *John Ritchie & Co.*, (O.H.) 1900, 8 S.L.T. 100. The same is true of the report, *quoad* reports by servants, of *Tannett Walker & Co.* v. *Hannay & Sons*, 1873, 11 M. 931.
14 *Logan* v. *Miller*, (O.H.) 1920, 1 S.L.T. 211; *Thomson* v. *Thomson*, (O.H.) 1907, 14 S.L.T. 643; *Macbride* v. *Caledonian Railway Co.*, (O.H.) 1894, 2 S.L.T. 61.
15 *MacKinnon* v. *National S.S. Co.*, (O.H.) 1904, 12 S.L.T. 411.
16 1860, 22 D. 1333. It is now recognised that this decision had a much more limited effect. See § **289**.
17 See Dickson, *Evidence* (3rd ed.) §§1670-1674.
18 *McCowan* v. *Wright*, 1852, 15 D. 229, L. Wood at p. 237. L. J-Cl. Hope said the same at pp. 231, 232. In *Munro* v. *Fraser*, 1858, 21 D. 103, L.P. McNeill founded on L. Wood's dictum.

without the risk of everything that passed being revealed to some future opponent. A tenant made over the crop to his landlord and then sold the turnips to a third party. The landlord consulted his solicitor as to whether he should sue the purchaser for the price of the turnips, and did not do so. The tenant's estates having been sequestrated, it was held in an appeal by the landlord against a deliverance by the trustee that the communications about the turnips were confidential, although at the time they passed no one could have contemplated the appeal.[19] Where the issue depended on the intention with which the defender's predecessor expede a general service, correspondence between the predecessor and his solicitor was held confidential, although at that time the dispute could not have been foreseen.[20] The privilege extends only to information obtained in a professional capacity, [21] and it has been held that a statement made by an accused to a solicitor who declined to act was not confidential.[22] Statements made by a solicitor to his client are not confidential if the only purpose is to show that the statement was made. Where the defenders averred delay on the part of the pursuer in making his claim, confidentiality did not attach to correspondence between the defenders and their solicitors in so far as it tended to instruct an earlier claim.[23] There is no confidentiality when the existence of the relationship of solicitor and client or the extent of the solicitor's authority is in issue. In an action against a solicitor for payment of the expenses of a previous action in which the pursuers averred that the defender had been *dominus litis* and acted without instructions, they obtained a diligence to recover correspondence between the defender and the alleged client, a plea of confidentiality being repelled.[24] Where parties were in dispute as to the terms on which a previous action had been settled, the pursuer obtained a diligence to recover letters between the defender and his solicitor so far as tending to establish the solicitor's authority to settle and the defender's approval of the settlement.[25] There is no confidentiality if it is averred that the communications were made for the purpose of obtaining advice or assistance in committing crime or other illegal act.[26] In a declarator of marriage the plea of confidentiality was repelled in respect of communications between the alleged husband (deceased) and his solicitors.[27] The privilege extends to communications with the solicitor's clerks[28] and probably to those made to an intermediary for

---

19 *Munro* v. *Fraser* (*supra*).
20 *Lady Bath's Exrs.* v. *Johnston*, 12th Nov. 1811 F.C.
21 Dickson, *Evidence* (3rd ed.) §1668; Hume, II, 350.
22 *Davie*, 1881, 4 Coup. 450. A hard doctrine. The opposite was held in England; *Minter* v. *Priest*, [1930] A.C. 558.
23 *Anderson* v. *Lord Elgin's Trs.*, 1859, 21 D. 654. It is not clear from the report whether solicitors were involved, but the head note contains the words "agent and client," and Dickson treats it as a solicitor and client case; *Evidence* (3rd ed.) §1677.
24 *Fraser* v. *Malloch*, (O.H.) 1895, 3 S.L.T. 211.
25 *Kid* v. *Bunyan*, 1842, 5 D. 193. L. Fullerton referred to the Lord Ordinary's "guarded" interlocutor, to which the Inner House adhered.
26 *McCowan* v. *Wright* (*supra*); *Morrison* v. *Somerville*, 1860, 23 D. 232; *Millar* v. *Small*, 1856, 19 D. 142.
27 *Mackenzie* v. *Mackenzie's Trs.*, 1916, 1 S.L.T. 271, 53 S.L.R. 219, a very special case decided partly on the ground that status was in issue.
28 Dickson, *Evidence* (3rd ed.) §1665.

transmission to or from the solicitor.[29] The title to plead confidentiality is with the client and, if he waives it, the solicitor, if a witness, must answer, and, if a haver, must produce.[30] If the client is not a party or even if he is dead, a party has taken the plea without objection.[20] If the client calls his solicitor as a witness, there is no confidentiality.[31]

394. POST LITEM MOTAM: MEANING

Communications to or by a litigant in connection with his investigations into an accident, an alleged breach of contract, a consistorial dispute, or other event giving rise to the action, are, generally speaking, confidential. "The general rule is that no party can recover from another material which that other party has made in preparing his case."[32] This, it is thought, is the true meaning of the proposition that communications *post litem motam* are confidential. So stated, the proposition is too wide. The mere date of the communication is immaterial. Even the substitution of *propter* for *post* is not enough. An admission or confession is not necessarily confidential, still less a casual remark about the dispute. It must be something said or written with a view to preparation of the case. A report obtained after the action has begun is, in the ordinary case, confidential,[33] but the rule is much wider. It applies not "merely after the summons has been raised, but after it is apparent that there is going to be a litigious contention,"[34] or, more briefly, as soon as litigation is "threatened or mooted."[35] There is *lis mota* "after an accident, and even before any claim has been made,"[36] "once the parties are at arm's length, or are obviously going to be at arm's length."[37] These opinions are certainly in accord with modern conditions, when as soon as an accident occurs the victim or his representatives consult a solicitor and the person who may be responsible communicates, in terms of his policy, with his insurance company. A similar extension applies in breach of contract. A dispute under a mining lease arose in 1848, but the action was not raised till 1852. The Lord Ordinary repelled an objection to the confidentiality of engineers' reports obtained by the pursuer in 1848 and 1851, but the Lord Justice-Clerk clearly thought he ought not to have done so, presumably on the ground that there was *lis mota* in 1848.[38]

---

[29] *Ibid.*, §1666; *Stuart* v. *Millar*, 1836, 14 S. 837, L. J-Cl. Boyle and L. Medwyn: *contra* L. Glenlee.

[30] Bell, *Principles*, §2254; Dickson, *Evidence* (3rd ed.) §1682.

[31] Evidence (Scotland) Act, 1852 (15 Vict. c. 27), s. 1.

[32] *Anderson* v. *St. Andrews Ambulance Association*, 1942 S.C. 555, at p. 557.

[33] *Clippens Oil Co.* v. *Edinburgh and District Water Trustees*, 1906, 8 F. 731, at p. 740.

[34] *Admiralty* v. *Aberdeen Steam Trawling and Fishing Co.*, 1909 S.C. 335, at p. 340.

[35] *Whitehill* v. *Glasgow Corporation*, 1915 S.C. 1015.

[36] *Young* v. *National Coal Board*, 1957 S.C. 99, at pp. 101, 106, 108. In *Anderson* v. *St. Andrew's Ambulance Association* (*supra*), photographs of the locus of an accident taken the day after were held confidential. *Cf. Black* v. *Bairds & Dalmellington*, 1939 S.C. 472, where a report of a *post mortem* examination was held not confidential, *quoad* the facts stated.

[37] *Ibid.*, at p. 105.

[38] *Wark* v. *Bargeddie Coal Co.*, 1855, 17 D. 526, 1859, 3 Macq. 467, at p. 488.

395. POST LITEM MOTAM: APPLICATION

(a) **General.** The plea of confidentiality was sustained as regards communications between the head office and a branch after the dispute had arisen.[39] The Lord Ordinary repelled the plea *quoad* reports by engineers after the question had arisen, and the Lord Justice-Clerk plainly thought that he was wrong.[40] The exception that proves the rule occurred in an action of damages for wrongously obtaining and insisting in an interim interdict. An engineer's report was made to the defenders after the granting of the interim interdict, and this was held not to be confidential or, at least, not wholly confidential, on the special ground that the state of knowledge of the defenders when they continued to insist in the interim interdict was important.[41] Efforts have been made to assimilate the position of a layman assisting a litigant to that of a solicitor, and this attempt has led to some apparent difference of judicial opinion.[42] In *Gavin* v. *Montgomerie*,[43] Lord President Hope expressed the view that if a litigant employs a layman to advise him or collect evidence, communications between them are confidential. In *Stuart* v. *Miller*,[44] Lord Medwyn agreed with this dictum, but Lord Justice-Clerk Boyle, Lord Meadowbank and Lord Glenlee seem to have read it as meaning that the layman was in the same position as a solicitor, and disagreed. But all the Lord President said was that communications in preparing the case are confidential, and the ground of judgment in *Stuart* v. *Miller*[44] was that the correspondence did not relate to the case.

(b) **Reports by Servants.** By an arbitrary exception to the general rule[45] reports by a servant present at the time of an accident made to his employer at or about the time of the accident[46] are held not to be confidential,[47] and it makes no difference that the report has been passed to the employer's insurance company.[48] If the report contains a list of witnesses, even this is not con-

---

[39] *Hay, Thomson and Blair* v. *Edinburgh and Glasgow Bank*, 1858, 20 D. 701; *Rose* v. *Medical Invalid Ins. Co.*, 1847, 10 D. 156, where the defenders' local agent was called as a defender. Dickson (*Evidence* (3rd ed.) §1658) cites this case in a chapter headed "Communications between parties on the same side of the cause." This seems misleading. Communications between such parties *ante litem motam* are not necessarily confidential.

[40] *Wark* v. *Bargeddie Coal Co.*, 1855, 17 D. 526; 1859, 3 Macq. 467, at p. 488, where the details are more fully stated.

[41] *Clippens Oil Co.* v. *Edinburgh and District Water Trustees*, 1906, 8 F. 731, at p. 740; 1907 S.C. (H.L.) 9.

[42] Dickson, *Evidence* (3rd ed.) §1666.

[43] 1830, 9 S. 213, at p. 219.

[44] 1836, 14 S. 837.

[45] *Young* v. *National Coal Board*, 1957 S.C. 99, L. Mackintosh at p. 106, L. Blades at p. 108.

[46] These words were omitted from the specification in *Stuart* v. *Great North of Scotland Railway Co.*, 1896, 23 R. 1005, and *Muir* v. *Edinburgh and District Tramways Co.*, 1909 S.C. 244, in which the diligence was refused, so that technically they are distinguishable from the later cases.

[47] *Finlay* v. *Glasgow Corporation*, 1915 S.C. 615; *Macphee* v. *Glasgow Corporation*, 1915 S.C. 990; *Whitehill* v. *Glasgow Corporation*, 1915 S.C. 1015.

[48] *Russell* v. *Alexander & Sons, Ltd.*, (O.H.) 1960 S.L.T. (Notes) 92; *Brennan* v. *David Lawson, Ltd.*, (O.H.) 1947 S.L.T. (Notes) 47.

fidential, and a final effort to upset this part of the exception failed, in spite of doubts on the bench.[49] Doubts as to the soundness of the entire exception are still expressed,[50] and it is unlikely to be extended.[51] It appears to rest on a theory that the purpose of the report is to enable the employer to improve his methods, "presumably for no other purpose than to put the owners in possession of the true facts."[52] Whatever may have been the position in collisions at sea in 1900, a principal, if not the principal, purpose of the report to-day, after a traffic or industrial accident, is to enable the employer's insurance company to decide on their attitude to a claim of damages.[53] It remains to be seen whether the rule will be reconsidered on the principle *cessante ratione legis, cessat ipsa lex.*

396. ANTE LITEM MOTAM: APPLICATION

The plea of confidentiality was repelled as regards letters between a litigant and his agents (not law agents) before the action was contemplated;[54] *quoad* the evidence of an accountant who had examined the defender's books some time before the dispute with the pursuer arose;[55] *quoad* a factor's report made years before the action;[56] *quoad* reports by employees before the date when presumably the dispute arose;[57] and *quoad* letters from engineers and contractors written long before the dispute arose.[58] In the last case the Lord Justice-Clerk said: "The inquiry in connection with which the diligence is asked relates to transactions alleged to have taken place at a time when, it is said, no dispute existed, or . . . could have existed; and when, therefore, no occasion arose for confidential communications . . . between employer and employed, in regard to that matter." During the reconstruction of the *Scotsman* office blasting operations were alleged to have caused damage to a neighbouring house on 15th August, 1899. In an action against the proprietors, diligence was granted for recovery of reports by the contractors to the defenders from 1st March to 1st November, 1899, a plea of confidentiality being repelled. The significance of the latter date does not

[49] *McCulloch* v. *Glasgow Corporation*, 1918 S.C. 155.
[50] *Anderson* v. *St. Andrew's Ambulance Association*, 1942 S.C. 555, L. Moncrieff at p. 559.
[51] *Young* v. *National Coal Board* (*supra*), at pp. 101, 106, 108.
[52] *Scott* v. *Portsoy Harbour Co.*, (O.H.) 1900, 8 S.L.T. 38, quoted in *Whitehill* v. *Glasgow Corporation* (*supra*).
[53] See *Young* v. *National Coal Board* (*supra*), at p. 105.
[54] *Stuart* v. *Miller*, 1836, 14 S. 837. The rubric is misleading. It does not state the very limited recovery allowed, nor the grounds on which the plea was repelled.
[55] *Wright* v. *Arthur*, 1831, 10 S. 139.
[56] *Mitchell* v. *Berwick*, 1845, 7 D. 382. It is thought that Dickson (*Evidence* (3rd ed.) §§1665, 1666) founds too sweeping propositions on these three decisions by failing to notice that the communications were *ante litem motam*.
[57] *Tannett, Walker & Co.* v. *Hannay & Sons*, 1873, 11 M. 931; *Morrison & Mason Ltd.* v. *Clarkson Brothers*, (O.H.) 1896, 4 S.L.T. 157, where recovery was allowed to the date of raising action.
[58] *Caledonian Rly. Co.* v. *Symington*, 1913 S.C. 885. This case, in argument and to some extent in the opinion, seems to have been mixed up with solicitor and client. The rubric brings out the point accurately, except that it fails to state that ultimately the Lord Ordinary repelled the objections to confidentiality and that this was acquiesced in.

appear from the report, but it is difficult to believe that the dispute had not arisen before then.[59]

397. CONFIDENTIALITY IN THE POPULAR SENSE

(a) **General.** A person may make what is popularly called a confidential communication, only to find that in law it is not so. The particular cases dealt with in this paragraph have this in common that the recipient of the secret has an interest in maintaining it because the imparter is more likely to give a full and true account if he thinks that it can go no further, or, at any rate, that his name will not be disclosed. Accordingly, the objection is often taken by the recipient.

(b) **Banks, Insurance Companies, Etc.** Such institutions in the course of their business receive reports which expressly or impliedly are regarded as confidential. Reports to insurers *post litem motam* are confidential in law under the ordinary rule,[60] but, although judicial opinion is not uniform, it is thought that reports *ante litem motam* are not. In a petition for disentail proof was allowed to ascertain the value of the interests of the later substitute heirs. They averred that the first substitute heir had suffered from ill health and were granted a diligence to recover medical reports made to an insurance company to which he had applied for a policy on his life, the company's plea of confidentiality being repelled.[61] The same result followed in three other cases in the Outer House,[62] but not in a fourth,[63] where, although the only objection reported is confidentiality, there is no opinion, so that the reason for the decision is uncertain. The ground of decision in a fifth case[64] is unknown, but if it was confidentiality it seems difficult to justify. In a sixth case the plea, if taken, was repelled because misrepresentation was averred.[65] The plea was repelled when taken by a bank[62] and by a railway company.[62]

(c) **Doctors.** A doctor's position is peculiar in this that he obtains a great deal of information about his patient from observation, and there can be no doubt that, while such information is confidential in the sense that the doctor has a duty not to publish it, it is not confidential in the sense here relevant. He is bound to give it in evidence if called on.[66] The question of the confidentiality of an oral or written communication to a doctor does not

[59] *Sutherland* v. *John Ritchie & Co.*, (O.H.), 1900, 8 S.L.T. 100.
[60] *Wilson* v. *Keir & Cawdor*, (O.H.) 1947 S.N. 55.
[61] *McDonald* v. *McDonalds*, 1881, 8 R. 357.
[62] *Elder* v. *English and Scottish Law Life Ass. Co.*, 1881, 19 S.L.R. 195 (where the insurance company was defender); *Kinloch* v. *Irvine*, 1884, 21 S.L.R. 685 (where, in a reduction of a will, a railway company refused to produce medical reports obtained in connection with an accident to the testator years before); *Foster, Alcock & Co.* v. *Grangemouth Dockyard Co.*, 1886, 23 S.L.R. 713 (refusal by bank to produce correspondence).
[63] *Hope's Trs.* v. *Scottish Accident Ins. Co.*, (O.H.) 1895, 3 S.L.T. 164.
[64] *Simcock* v. *Scottish Imperial Ins. Co.*, (O.H.) 1901, 9 S.L.T. 234.
[65] *Macdonald* v. *New York Life Ins. Co.*, (O.H.) 1903, 11 S.L.T. 120.
[66] *A.B.* v. *C.D.*, 1851, 14 D. 177, at p. 180.

seem to have been raised, but the ordinary rule would seem to apply to it, the communication being confidential only if made in connection with the dispute. The evidence of Sir Patrick Heron Watson in *M'Ewan* v. *M'Ewan* was not objected to as confidential.[67]

(d) Clergymen. The mere fact that a statement is made to a clergyman does not render it confidential.[68] Nor according to Hume[69] is a voluntary confession. Other writers are doubtful.[70] Lord Moncrieff may not have had this particular point in mind, but he laid down clearly that confidentiality attaches only to communications to spouses or solicitors,[71] and there would be something unsatisfactory about a rule which encouraged a criminal to have the best of both worlds, easing his conscience and evading punishment at the same time. In any event, if the privilege exists, it is that of the party, not of the clergyman.[72]

(e) Journalists. A journalist must state the name of the person from whom he obtained information he has published, if such disclosure is relevant to the case and he is directed by the judge to do so.[72a]

398. CONCILIATORS

There is authority in England for the view that communications to persons who are trying to reconcile the parties to a dispute are confidential. This applies whether the interview was with the parties together or only with one. The rule has been applied to probation officers,[73] counsel[74] and a clergyman.[75] All these were consistorial causes, and the reason behind the rule is the interest of the state that reconciliation should be effected, and that reconciliation is more likely if people can speak freely knowing that what they say cannot be used against them. Either spouse has a title to insist in the plea of confidentiality, and they may waive it, which either does if he or she gives evidence as to what passed at the interview.[76] The question does not appear to have arisen in a reported case in Scotland, but the reason for the rule seems equally strong here.

399. PUBLIC POLICY

Evidence may be excluded on the ground that disclosure of the facts would be contrary to public policy. This question has arisen almost ex-

---

[67] *A.B.* v. *C.D.*, 1904, 7 F. 72, at p. 74, note, L. Young at p. 83; 1905, 7 F. (H.L.) 109.
[68] *McLaughlin* v. *Douglas and Kidston*, 1863, 4 Irv. 273.
[69] II, 335, 350.
[70] Alison, II, 471, 586; Macdonald, *Criminal Law* (5th ed.) 315.
[71] *H.M. Advocate* v. *Parker*, 1944 J.C. 49.
[72] Dickson, *Evidence* (3rd ed.) §1685, note (c).
[72a] *Att.-Gen.* v. *Mulholland*, [1963], 2 W.L.R. 658.
[73] *Mole* v. *Mole*, [1951] P. 21; *McTaggart* v. *McTaggart*, [1949] P. 94.
[74] *Pool* v. *Pool*. [1951] P. 470.
[75] *Henley* v. *Henley*, [1955] P. 202.
[76] *McTaggart* v. *McTaggart* (*supra*).

clusively in connection with the recovery of documents,[77] but similar principles apply to oral evidence. The Lord Advocate cannot refuse to disclose the name of his informant, unless he states that it would be contrary to public policy to do so.[78] A conviction was quashed where a police officer's refusal to disclose the name of his informant was sustained by the magistrate.[79]

[77] See § **295.** See also *Jennings* v. *Glasgow Corporation*, 1937 S.C. 180, as to disclosure of information by the Public Assistance Department of a local authority.
[78] *Henderson* v. *Robertson*, 1853, 15 D. 292.
[79] *Thomson* v. *Neilson*, 1900, 3 F. (J.) 3.

CHAPTER XXXII

EVIDENCE ON COMMISSION

400. GENERAL

It is incompetent to take evidence on commission in a criminal trial.[1] In civil causes the general rule is that evidence can competently be led only (1) on averments which have been remitted to probation and (2) in presence of the tribunal of fact. But there are two exceptions. First, where for some specific reason there is a danger of evidence being lost the court may appoint a commissioner to take the evidence and report, and this power may be exercised before any averments have been remitted to proof, or even before there are any averments. Evidence so taken is said to be taken to lie *in retentis*. Secondly, after proof has been allowed, or issues approved, and a diet fixed, the court may appoint a commissioner to take the evidence of a witness who will probably not be able to attend the diet. So described, these exceptions are not mutually exclusive, but the broad distinction is that the first case depends on an emergency and the second does not. Accordingly, the material differences[2] relate to the reasons for granting commission, the time at which application may be made and, in some cases, the procedure.[3]

401. EVIDENCE TO LIE IN RETENTIS

(a) **Reasons.** The reason is usually stated generally as risk of the loss of the evidence, but that is plainly too wide. Any prospective witness may die unexpectedly. The risk must be one peculiar to the witness, and the usual risks are that the witness is so old or infirm or unwell as to be in danger of early death, or that he is obliged to go abroad[4] permanently or for a prolonged period. Hitherto it has usually been assumed that a witness aged seventy or over is in danger of early death, and commission has been in practice allowed on proof of his age,[5] but the vital statistics and the frequent appearance in the witness box of witnesses over seventy years of age may

---

1 *H.M. Advocate* v. *Hunter*, 1905, 7 F. (J.) 73.
2 The distinction is clearly recognised in the Evidence (Scotland) Act, 1866 (29 & 30 Viet. c. 112), s. 2, and the Sheriff Courts (Scotland) Act, 1907 (7 Edw. VII. c. 51), Rule 70.
3 For the procedure in commissions to take evidence furth of Scotland, see § **406.**
4 Bankton, *Institute*, iv, 30, 27, quoted in *Boettcher* v: *Carron Co.*, 1861, 23 D. 322, at p. 325; Dickson, *Evidence* (3rd ed.) §1727; Rules of Court, 1948, Rule 125A.
5 Dickson, *Evidence* (3rd ed.) §1728; *Wilson* v. *Young*, (O.H.) 1896, 4 S.L.T. 73.

lead to reconsideration of this assumption. Age, if challenged, is proved by production of a birth certificate.[6] Nevertheless, it is a matter of discretion, and commission was refused to examine two aged witnesses when plenty of younger members of the congregation were available to prove a slander alleged to have been uttered from the pulpit.[7] Infirmity or sickness is proved by production of a medical certificate on soul and conscience, and, if it is challenged, a remit may be made to a doctor appointed by the court.[8] It used to be the practice to require production of such certificates, birth and medical, before the commissioner,[9] but the more logical and convenient modern practice, if there is a question, is to produce them when the commission is applied for. Since Bankton[4] wrote, greater facilities have been created for the taking of evidence on commission of a witness furth of Scotland.[10] The mere fact that the witness is going abroad does not therefore mean that his evidence is necessarily lost. But the existence of these facilities has not been regarded as an impediment to granting commission.[11] Indeed, the fact that the witness is examined in Scotland by counsel or solicitor in the case, rather than abroad on interrogatories,[12] may outweigh the disadvantage, if it exists, that the averments have not been remitted to probation.[13] The mere fact that the witness is going abroad is not enough. He must be obliged to go, e.g., on Government or other employment,[14] or, in the case of a party, by inability, owing perhaps to lack of means, to remain in Scotland till proof is allowed.[15] Where the witnesses were about to go abroad in course of their employment with the party asking for the commission, the court in one case refused the application[16] and in others granted it.[17] An application was refused where the witness was going abroad on holiday.[18] In one exceptional case commission was granted to take the evidence of the only two possible witnesses to the facts, a situation to which the phrase *penuria testium* was applied, presumably on the ground that one might die unexpectedly.[19]

(b) Time and Procedure. The emergency justifying the application may

---

6   *Watsons*, 1829, 8 S. 261; *Morison* v. *Cowan*, 1828, 6 S. 1082.

7   *Dudgeon* v. *Forbes*, 1832, 10 S. 810.

8   *Lunn* v. *Watt*, (O.H.) 1911, 2 S.L.T. 279. This was done of consent.

9   Dickson, *Evidence* (3rd ed.) §1738.

10 See §**406.**

11 In *Grant* v. *Countess of Seafield*, 1926 S.C. 274, a diet of proof had been fixed and the witness could have been examined on commission abroad. Yet the court would apparently have allowed her to be examined in Scotland if she had been obliged to go abroad.

12 See §**403,** sub-para. (c).

13 *Hay* v. *Binny*, 1859, 22 D. 183; *Grant* v. *Countess of Seafield (supra)*, at p. 280.

14 *Galloway Water Power Co.* v. *Carmichael*, 1937 S.C. 135; *Pringle*, 1905, 7 F. 525; *Neill*, 1911, 48, S.L.R. 830.

15 *Anderson*, 1912 S.C. 1144.

16 *Munn* v. *Macgregor*, 1854, 16 D. 385.

17 *Hansen* v. *Donaldson*, 1873, 1 R. 237; *Sutter* v. *Aberdeen Arctic Co.*, 1858, 30 Sc. Jur. 300.

18 *Grant* v. *Countess of Seafield (supra)*.

19 *Copland* v. *Bethune*, 1827, 5 S. 272. In *Malcolm* v. *Stewart*, 1829, 7 S. 715, commission was granted of consent. It was refused in *Maltman's Factor* v. *Cock*, 1867, 5 M. 1076, where the *penuria testium* was not admitted.

arise before the action has been raised, and in such circumstances the Court of Session has power under the *nobile officium* to grant commission.[20] The application is accordingly by petition to the Inner House,[20] or possibly in extreme urgency to the Vacation Judge.[21] Evidence so taken may be used in an arbitration[20] and, it is thought, *a fortiori*, in the sheriff court. After a summons has been signeted,[22] but before calling, the application is made by letter to the Deputy Principal Clerk of the General Department, with a note of the names and addresses of the witnesses, and, after notice to the other party, is disposed of by a Lord Ordinary.[23] After calling, the application is by motion.[24] In the sheriff court evidence in danger of being lost may be taken "at any time" by the sheriff or by a commissioner.[25] If the party applying for the commission is resident furth of Scotland he may be ordained to sist a mandatory before commission is granted.[26]

402. AFTER ENQUIRY ALLOWED

When the practice of taking proofs on commission was abolished in the Court of Session, power was expressly reserved to the court (*a*) on special cause shown, or with consent of both parties, to grant commission to take the evidence in any cause in which commission to take evidence might, according to the existing law and practice, be granted, and also (*b*) to grant commission to take the evidence of any witness resident beyond the jurisdiction or unable by reason of age, infirmity or sickness[27] to attend the diet of proof.[28] Although on a strict construction these are independent powers, it is not necessary to treat them as such, since the whole question is one for the discretion of the court. Accordingly, in granting a commission, the court relied on the pursuer's poverty as a special cause under (*a*) and the witnesses' residence in England under (*b*).[29] Since witnesses in England and Northern Ireland may be cited to attend the Court of Session,[30] that may be

---

[20] *Galloway Water Power Co.* v. *Carmichael* (*supra*).
[21] Rules of Court, 1948, Rule 2 (*a*) (i). There are no reported decisions on this point, but for illustrations of extreme urgency, where the Lord Ordinary on the Bills exercised the *nobile officium*, see *Edgar* v. *Fisher's Trustees*, 1893, 21 R. 59: *Logan*, 1890, 17 R. 757; *Glasgow International Exhibition* v. *Sosnowski*, 1901, 39 S.L.R. 28. *Cf. Buchanan*, 1910 S.C. 685, and *Aberdeen University Court*, 1901, 4 F. 122.
[22] Probably the effect of Rules of Court, 1948, Rule 120 (*a*), which requires production of a signeted summons.
[23] Rules of Court, 1948, Rules 124 (*a*), 120.
[24] *Ibid.*, Rule 124 (*b*). After service the Vacation Judge may act: Rules of Court, 1948, Rule 2 (*a*) (i); *Mathewson* v. *Mathewson*, 1931 S.L.T. 416.
[25] Sheriff Courts (Scotland) Act, 1907 (7 Edw. VII. c. 51), Rule 63. There must, it is thought, be in existence an initial writ on which the sheriff can write. Lewis (*Sheriff Court Practice* (8th ed.) 137, *Evidence*, 184) takes the view that the writ must have been served, but gives no reason. Contrast Rule 125A. of the Rules of Court, which deals with the same point and contains the words "after service of the summons."
[26] *Hansen* v. *Donaldson* (*supra*); *Sandilands* v. *Sandilands*, 1848, 10 D. 1091.
[27] See §401, sub-para. (*a*).
[28] Evidence (Scotland) Act, 1866 (29 & 30 Vict. c. 112), ss. 1, 2.
[29] *Lawson* v. *Lawson*, 1930 S.C. 18. Since the witnesses were resident in England, the decision does not go beyond s. 13 of the Conjugal Rights (Scotland) Act, 1861 (24 & 25 Vict. c. 86). See *Grant* v. *Countess of Seafield*, 1926 S.C. 274.

a reason for refusing a commission to examine such a witness.[31] Commission has also been refused where the evidence of the witness was likely to be very important.[32] Although, as a general rule, the court does not grant commission to take the evidence of a party, there may be exceptions where great hardship would be caused, and something depends on the nature of the evidence the party is expected to give.[33] A sheriff has power to grant commission to take the evidence of a witness resident beyond the jurisdiction, or at some place remote from the seat of the court, or who is by reason of illness, age or infirmity unable to attend the proof.[34]

403. THE COMMISSION

(a) **Names of Witnesses.** As a general rule the applicant must furnish the names of the witnesses he desires to examine so that they may be inserted in the commission.[35] In some older cases commission was granted to examine witnesses, the party undertaking to give the other side notice of their names.[36] Where a letter of request from a foreign court requested that evidence might be obtained from a limited company in Scotland, the court ordained the company to appoint representatives to be examined before the commissioner.[37]

(b) **The Commissioner.** In the Court of Session a practising advocate is usually appointed, if the commission is to be executed within a reasonable distance of Edinburgh.[38] If the distance is considerable a sheriff-substitute is often appointed. In the sheriff court a solicitor or the sheriff clerk may be appointed.

(c) **Interrogatories.** Until 1907 examination on interrogatories was compulsory. Now the Court of Session may, on the motion of any party, dispense with interrogatories in all cases where the commission falls to be executed within the United Kingdom, and may also dispense with interrogatories where the commission is to be executed abroad, on being satisfied that such a course is expedient in the interests of the parties to the cause and conducive to the administration of justice.[39] This reproduces the original provision of 1907, which has been described as peculiarly expressed and ambiguous.[40] Probably it means that special cause must be shown for

---

[30] See §334.
[31] *Mackintosh v. Fraser,* 1859, 1 D. 783, at p. 793.
[32] *Western Ranches Ltd. v. Nelson's Trustees,* 1898, 25 R. 527.
[33] *Anderson v. Morrison,* 1905, 7 F. 561; *Samson & Co. v. Haugh,* 1886, 13 R. 1154.
[34] Sheriff Courts (Scotland) Act, 1907 (7 Edw. VII. c. 51), Rule 70.
[35] Rules of Court, 1948, Rule 124 (a); *Western Ranches Ltd. v. Nelson's Trustees,* 1898, 25 R. 527; *Crawford & Law v. Allan S.S. Co.,* (O.H.) 1898, 16 S.L.T. 434.
[36] *Hunt v. Commissioners of Woods and Forests,* 1856, 18 D. 317.
[37] *Lord Advocate,* 1925 S.C. 568.
[38] The Lord President described this as proceeding "in the ordinary way"; *McCorquodale,* 1923 S.L.T. 520. Rule 122 (a) of the Rules of Court, 1948, is not applied to commissions to take evidence.
[39] Rules of Court, 1948, Rule, 124 (c).
[40] *Dexter & Carpenter v. Waugh & Robertson,* 1925 S.C. 28.

dispensing with interrogatories if the commission is to be executed abroad, whereas there will usually be dispensation if it is to be executed in the United Kingdom.[40] The suggested reason for the distinction is that counsel or solicitor in the case can probably attend the commission in the United Kingdom, but not abroad.[40] The matter is one of discretion. Reasons for dispensing with interrogatories are the time, expense and difficulty of framing them and the risk that they may turn out inadequate. The main reason for insisting on them is that a foreign commissioner may allow foreign practitioners to introduce a great deal of irrelevant evidence.[40] There is no statutory provision relating to the sheriff court, but the practice there is the same.

404. EXECUTION OF COMMISSION

A certified copy of the interlocutor granting the commission is the warrant for citing witnesses. Letters of second diligence may be granted. The witness is sworn, examined, cross-examined and re-examined as at a proof and the evidence recorded. Whether the examination is on interrogatories and cross-interrogatories, or not, the commissioner may put any questions he considers necessary. He must decide any question as to the admissibility of evidence. In the Court of Session, if his decision is not objected to, it is final. If objection is taken, the evidence should be noted on a separate paper and sealed for the decision of the court. In the sheriff court any objection is noted, if desired.[40a]

405. USE OF REPORT AT TRIAL OR PROOF

The deposition may be used if the judge is satisfied that the witness cannot attend.[41] If the witness is English[42] or a foreigner, that is sufficient.[43] Where evidence has been taken to lie *in retentis*, the opposite party may insist on a re-examination if the witness is available,[43] but this right is seldom, if ever, used. If the party who obtained the commission does not use it, his opponent is entitled to do so.[44] In any event, the deposition cannot be used unless it is expressly made part of the evidence at the trial or proof.[45] If the witness is examined at the proof, the evidence taken on commission cannot be used for any purpose, and in particular cannot be used to contradict evidence given in court.[46] Apparently a party who examines his opponent on commission is not barred from referring to his oath.[47]

406. COMMISSION FURTH OF SCOTLAND

(a) England and Northern Ireland.[48] There are alternative methods of

[40a] Maclaren, *Court of Session Practice*, 1047-1050; Sheriff Courts (Scotland) Act, 1907 (7 Edw. VII. c. 51), Rules 65, 71, 73, 74. See also §§ **349, 350.**
[41] *Willox* v. *Farrell*, 1848, 10 D. 807.
[42] *Ainslie* v. *Sutton*, 1851, 14 D. 184: 1852, 1 Macq. 299.
[43] *Boettcher* v. *Carron Co.*, 1861, 23 D. 322.
[44] A.S., 16th February, 1841, s. 17.
[45] *Cameron* v. *Woolfson*, 1918 S.C. 190.
[46] *Forrests* v. *Low's Trs.*, 1907 S.C. 1240.
[47] *Laing* v. *Nixon*, 1866, 4 M. 327. See § **316.**

enforcing attendance before the commissioner. Either the witness is cited to attend, and if he fails to do so, application is made to a superior court in England or Northern Ireland, as the case may be, for an order on him to attend;[49] or an application may be made direct to the superior court for an order.[50] If in either case he fails to obey the order, he is liable to punishment by the court. Where the commission is granted by an arbiter, the authority of the court must be interponed before it can be enforced.[51]

(b) H.M. Dominions.[52]   Attendance before the commissioner may be enforced by application to a court of the country where the commission is to be executed.[53]

(c) Foreign States.   The party wishing to examine the witness may apply to the Court of Session[54] or the sheriff[55] for a letter of request addressed to the appropriate court to examine the witness on interrogatories or to appoint some person to do so. The letter is delivered to the Foreign Office, which transmits it.

48 See Government of Ireland Act, 1920 (10 & 11 Geo. V. c. 67), s. 69 (*a*); General Adaptation of Enactments (Northern Ireland) Order, 1921 (S.R. & O. 1921, No. 1805), s. 5.
49 Evidence by Commission Act, 1843 (6 & 7 Vict. c. 82), ss. 5, 6, 7. This Act is printed in Lewis, *Evidence*, 348, but owing to the omission there of the preamble to section 5 the provisions are made to appear as if they applied only to commissions granted by English courts.
50 Evidence by Commission Act, 1859 (22 Vict. c. 20).
51 *John Nimmo & Son Ltd.*, 1905, 8 F. 173; *Blaikies Brothers* v. *Aberdeen Rly. Co.*, 1851, 13 D. 1307.
52 This includes the Irish Free State; Irish Free State (Consequential Provisions) Act, 1922 (13 Geo. V. c. 2), s. 6; Irish Free State (Consequential Adaptation of Enactments) Order, 1923 (S.R. & O. 1923, No. 405), s. 3; Ireland Act, 1949 (12 & 13 Geo. VI. c. 41), ss. 1-3.
53 Evidence by Commission Act, 1859 (22 Vict. c. 20); Evidence by Commission Act, 1885 (48 & 49 Vict. c. 74).
54 Rules of Court, 1948, Rule 126.
55 C.A.S.. L. II.

CHAPTER XXXIII

AFFIDAVITS: DYING DEPOSITIONS

407. AFFIDAVITS: GENERAL

An affidavit is a written *ex parte* statement made on oath or affirmation[1] before one having authority to administer oaths.[2] With one rare exception[3] affidavits are not evidence at common law.[4] The effect of an affidavit made in terms of a statute depends on the terms of the statute. Their main use is in commissary, bankruptcy and entail proceedings, in declarators that a testamentary writing is holograph,[5] and under the Rules of Court and the Bankers Books Evidence Act, 1879.[6]

408. BEFORE WHOM

Any affidavit may be made before a sheriff, magistrate or justice of the peace.[7] A sheriff, who is *ex officio* a justice of the peace, or a justice of the peace may act outside his jurisdiction, even in England,[8] and an English justice of the peace may act in Scotland.[9] If the magistrate or other person is entitled to act, a misdescription of his office does not nullify the affidavit,[10] nor does the fact that his wife is an interested party.[8] Any affidavit may be made abroad before a British diplomatic officer or consul.[11] Further, in commissary proceedings it may be made before a sheriff-clerk or his depute, before a notary public in the United Kingdom, before a commissioner of oaths in England or Northern Ireland,[12] and out of the United Kingdom

---

1 Oaths Act, 1888 (51 & 52 Vict. c. 46).
2 Dickson, *Evidence* (3rd ed.) §§1534, 1537.
3 In the *Lauderdale Peerage Case*, 1885, 10 App. Cas. 692, an affidavit by a deceased person was accepted as evidence. In *Shields* v. *North British Railway Co.*, 1874, 2 R. 126, affidavits were lodged, but no importance seems to have attached to their form, and no attempt was made to use them as evidence. See also *Tennent* v. *Tennent*, 1890, 1205, at pp. 1210, 1225.
4 *Glyn* v. *Johnston*, 1834, 13 S. 126.
5 Act of Sederunt, 19th July, 1935, par. 1 (2).
6 42 Vict. c. 11, ss. 4, 5. See §§**301, 368.**
7 Dickson, *Evidence* (3rd ed.) §§1534, 1537.
8 *Kerr* v. *Marquis of Ailsa*, 1854, 1 Macq. 736.
9 *Taylor* v. *Little*, 1822, 1 Sh. App. 254.
10 *Paterson* v. *Duncan*, 1846, 9 D. 950.
11 Commissioners for Oaths Act, 1889 (52 & 53 Vict. c. 10), s. 6.
12 Supreme Court of Judicature (Northern Ireland) Order, 1921 (S.I. 1921, No. 1802), s. 2.

before a local magistrate or notary public;[13] and in bankruptcy before a commissioner of oaths in England or Northern Ireland,[12] and abroad before a magistrate or justice of the peace or other person entitled to administer oaths in the country, certified to be such by a British minister or consul or a notary public.[14]

409. FORMALITIES

The deponent must appear in person before the magistrate or other person, and he must be put on oath,[15] or affirm. Each page of his deposition ought to be signed both by the deponent and by the magistrate.[16] If the deponent cannot write, it is sufficient that the affidavit so bears.[17] An alteration *in essentialibus* nullifies the affidavit,[18] unless it is initialled both by the deponent and the magistrate[19] or it is plain that it was made before signing.[20] An unauthenticated marginal addition was disregarded.[21] An illegible signature alleged to be that of the deponent has been held to be set up by the magistrate's signature.[22] What appear to be clerical errors have sometimes been disregarded[23] and sometimes not.[24]

410. DYING DEPOSITION

Where there is a risk of a material and competent witness in a criminal case, whether he be the injured party or not,[25] dying before the trial, his deposition may be taken so that it may be put in evidence at the trial if he dies before it.[26] In practice it is usually taken on behalf of the Crown, but the accused has the same right to secure evidence in his favour.[27] The deposition is taken on oath, usually by a sheriff-substitute, but it may be taken by a justice of the peace or other magistrate.[28] It is not necessary that the witness should believe himself to be dying.[29] The questions are put by the sheriff-substitute or the procurator-fiscal (or, if the witness is being examined for the defence, by the accused's solicitor) and the deposition is normally recorded by the sheriff-clerk or his depute.[30] It is then read over to the deponent and

---

[13] Executors (Scotland) Act, 1900 (63 & 64 Vict. c. 55), s. 8.
[14] Bankruptcy (Scotland) Act, 1913 (3 & 4 Geo. V. c. 20), ss. 21, 22.
[15] *Blair* v. *North British and Mercantile Ins. Co.*, 1889, 16 R. 325.
[16] Dickson, *Evidence* (3rd ed.) §1539.
[17] *Paul* v. *Gibson*, 1834, 7 W. and S., 462.
[18] *Jardine* v. *Harvey*, 1848, 10 D. 1501; *Miller* v. *Lambert*, 1848, 10 D. 1419.
[19] *Dow & Co.* v. *Union Bank*, 1875, 2 R. 459.
[20] *Dyce* v. *Paterson*, 1846, 9 D. 310, at p. 313.
[21] *Mackersy* v. *Guthrie*, 1829, 7 S. 556.
[22] *Perryman* v. *McClymont*, 1852, 14 D. 508.
[23] *Taylor* v. *Manford*, 1848, 10 D. 967; *Foulds* v. *Meldrum*, 1851, 13 D. 1357.
[24] *Anderson* v. *Monteith*, 1847, 9 D. 1432.
[25] *Stewart*, 1855, 2 Irv. 166.
[26] Macdonald, *Criminal Law* (5th ed.) 330; Dickson, *Evidence* (3rd ed.) §1754.
[27] Dickson, *Evidence* (3rd ed.) §1754.
[28] Dickson, *Evidence* (3rd ed.) §1755.
[29] *Brodie*, 1846, Ark. 45; *Stewart* (*supra*).
[30] Dickson, *Evidence* (3rd ed.) §1755; Renton & Brown, *Criminal Procedure* (3rd ed.) 85, 86.

signed by him on each page, if he is able to write. If not, this is recorded. It is also signed by the sheriff-substitute and two witnesses, usually the doctor and the sheriff-clerk.[30] At the trial the deposition is spoken to by two witnesses, one of whom should be the sheriff-substitute, and they should establish that the deponent realised what he was doing.[28] As evidence the deposition does not have the weight of evidence given by a witness who has been cross-examined.[31]

Where a deposition cannot be taken a dying declaration may be recorded by any responsible person.[32]

[31] *Brodie (supra).*
[32] Macdonald, *Criminal Law* (5th ed.) 330.

CHAPTER XXXIV

OPINION EVIDENCE

411. INTRODUCTORY

(a) **General.** Testimony, which at first sight appears to be of fact, may prove to be actually of belief or opinion. Identification of a person is one instance.[1] This may range from "That is my partner" to "That is the stranger I saw in the close that night." Each statement on analysis is one of belief founded on inferences, but, while the former would normally be accepted as equivalent to a statement of fact, the latter is obviously one of belief. Cross-examination on the former is unlikely to be effective, but may greatly reduce the weight of the latter. The question is thus in practice one of degree. This chapter is concerned with evidence which either bears to be of opinion or belief or at least is of that nature. Such evidence is in many cases admissible from any witness, but where the opinion depends on specialised knowledge it may be taken only from an expert in that sphere. Handwriting and foreign law, either of which may require opinion evidence, are dealt with below.[2]

(b) **Limitations.** A question is inadmissible if its purpose is to elicit an opinion on the actual issue before the court. In a trial on a charge of exhibiting obscene books it is incompetent to ask a witness whether in his opinion the books are obscene, for that is for the court to decide.[3] In an action for reduction of a will Lord Justice-Clerk Inglis directed the jury that the question whether the testator had the capacity to sign the will was a question for them, not for the medical witnesses, to whom it had been put, which seems to imply that he would have sustained an objection to the questions.[4] A witness may not be asked whether the driver of a vehicle was to blame, or whether he considered conduct malicious.[5] There was at one time doubt as to whether in an insurance case it was competent to ask a skilled witness whether a particular fact would have influenced a prudent underwriter and was therefore

1 Dickson, *Evidence* (3rd ed.) §392.
2 See §§ **414, 415,** where the subjects are dealt with fully. For fingerprint evidence, see §**12.**
3 *Gellatly* v. *Laird,* 1953 J.C. 16, at p. 27. See also *Campbell* v. *Tyson,* 1841, 4 D. 342. See also § **339,** sub-para. (c).
4 *Morrison* v. *Maclean's Trs.,* 1862, 24 D. 625, at p. 631. Dickson, *Evidence* (3rd ed.) §391.
6 *Baker and Adams* v. *Scottish Sea Insurance Co.,* 1856, 18 D. 691, at p. 699 (Fourth Exception).

material or whether this was not a matter for the court,[6] but such questions are competent.[7]

412. ORDINARY WITNESS

As already observed,[8] evidence which is accepted as fact may really be opinion. But what is obviously opinion evidence may be admissible from an ordinary witness. Identification of handwriting[9] or of property[10] are examples. In an action of divorce on the ground of adultery a witness who had described the position of the defender and the alleged paramour when she entered a room was allowed to be asked what immediate impression she formed.[11] While that decision was expressly rested on the ground that the impression was immediate, evidence was allowed of an opinion which to some extent must have rested on reflection and special knowledge. In a written slander the names had been left blank, and a witness was allowed to be asked to whom in his opinion the slander applied.[12] Opinions have been expressed, *obiter*, that a witness who has described a depression in a pavement may be asked whether he saw anything dangerous about it.[13]

413. SKILLED WITNESS

(a) General. A skilled witness is a person who, through practice or study or both, is specially qualified in a recognised branch of knowledge, whether it be art, science or craft.[14] If his opinion is not based on the principles of some recognised branch of knowledge, it is useless, and probably inadmissible, because it cannot be tested by cross-examination. Accordingly, his qualification and experience must first be established,[15] his own evidence being usually sufficient, though cross-examination has been known to reduce pretensions.

(b) Basis of Fact. Since the opinion is based on a certain state of facts, it is valueless unless the facts are proved. Where a pursuer sought to prove by skilled evidence that from the condition of a pole in October it must have been in a dangerously corroded state in the preceding May, she failed because she did not prove by sufficient evidence the condition of the pole in October.[16] In a criminal trial the connection of the panel with the crime depended, *inter*

---

7 *Dawsons, Ltd.* v. *Bonnin*, 1921 S.C. 511 at pp. 517, 519, 521; 1922 S.C. (H.L.) 156, at pp. 160, 166, 172. In *The Spathari*, 1924 S.C. 182; 1925 S.C. (H.L.) 6, the facts were so clear that, if opinion evidence as to materiality was led, it was not referred to in the opinions or speeches.
8 See §411.
9 See §414.
10 Dickson, *Evidence* (3rd ed.) §392.
11 *King* v. *King*, 1842, 4 D. 590, at p. 596. Similar evidence was led without objection in *Wilson* v. *Wilson*, 1898, 25 R. 788.
12 Dickson, *Evidence* (3rd ed.) §392: *Edwards* v. *McIntosh*, 1823, 3 Mur. 374.
13 *Hewat* v. *Edinburgh Corporation*, 1944 S.C. 30, at p. 35.
14 Dickson, *Evidence* (3rd ed.) §397.
15 *Ibid.*, §398.
16 *Stewart* v. *Glasgow Corporation*, 1958 S.C. 28. See also *A.B.*, v. *Northern Accident Ins. Co.*, 1896, 24 R. 258, decided on similar grounds.

alia, on a comparison by a skilled witness between material used for the crime and material said to have been found in the panel's pocket. The Crown, however, failed to establish by sufficient evidence that the material had been found in the panel's pocket, and accordingly the opinion evidence was useless.[17] Where in a collision case the court was asked to infer from the damage to one of the ships that the other must have been going at a high speed, the argument failed at the outset on the ground that the only evidence of the damage was that of the damaged ship's own master.[18] Again, the experts may have failed to take all the facts into account or have proceeded upon unjustifiable assumptions. In another collision case the experts, in drawing conclusions from marks on one of the ships, had left out of account the possibility of the ship rolling, or, to put it another way, had assumed that the sea was absolutely smooth.[19] Lastly, the alleged facts on which an opinion is based may be disproved or explained so as to deprive them of significance. Where medical opinions that a testator was insane depended partly on supposed delusions and peculiar conduct, it was established that one of the supposed delusions was a fact and another probably true, and that the conduct had been characteristic of the testator before insanity was suggested.[20] In these cases the facts on which the skilled witnesses proceeded were closely connected with the facts in issue, but where they are not, enquiry into them may be refused, not on the ground that they are irrelevant, but on the ground that limits must be set to the enquiry.[21] The question has arisen mainly where the sanity of a panel at the time of the occurrence, or of a testator, is in issue, and it is proposed to lead evidence of mental abnormalities in other members of his family. Here the practice of the High Court of Justiciary and the Court of Session diverges. In the High Court the point has arisen in two ways. In some of the cases the question was whether some of the panel's relations were insane, and with one exception,[22] this has always been disallowed.[23] So far as the reports show, it was not proposed in the last two of these cases to use this evidence as the basis of skilled evidence, but merely to leave it to the jury, so that the decisions are not surprising. But in *Dingwall*[24] skilled evidence had been led tending to show that insanity in relations increased the probability that the panel was insane. In other cases skilled evidence was excluded.[25] On the other hand, in an action for reduction of

---

[17] *Forrester* v. *H.M. Advocate*, 1952 J.C. 28. See also *Carraher* v. *H.M. Advocate*, 1946 J.C. 108, at p. 118.

[18] *The "Nerano"* v. *The "Dromedary,"* 1895, 22 R. 237, at p. 246.

[19] *S.S. "Rowan"* v. *S.S. "Clan Malcolm,"* 1923 S.C. 316, at p. 340. *Cf. Gardiner* v. *Motherwell Machinery and Scrap Co.*, 1961 S.C. (H.L.) 1, where the opinion evidence rested on an unproved assumption.

[20] *Morrison* v. *Maclean's Trs.*, 1862, 24 D. 625, at p. 645.

[21] *Swan* v. *Bowie*, 1948 S.C. 46, at p. 51. "Life is not long enough to allow an exhaustive inquiry into every side issue which has or may have a bearing upon the main issue": *Houston* v. *Aitken*, 1912 S.C. 1037, at p. 1038. See §14.

[22] *Galbraith*, 1897, 5 S.L.T. 65.

[23] *Edmonstone*, 1909, 2 S.L.T. 223; *Brown*, 1855, 2 Irv. 154; *Gibson*, 1844, 2 Broun 332.

[24] 1867, 5 Irv. 466.

[25] *McClinton*, 1902, 4 Adam 1, 13 (where the question was not very happily framed); *Paterson*, 1872, 2 Coup. 222 (where L. Cowan was clearly doubtful and rejected the

433

R

a will on the ground, *inter alia*, of the testator's insanity, the Lord Ordinary refused to admit to probation averments of mental abnormality of relations. But in the Inner House, where most of the High Court decisions were cited, the pursuers were allowed to add averments which showed that the excluded averments would be the basis of skilled evidence, and all the averments were admitted to probation.[26] In an action of damages for slander contained in letters, where the only issue was authorship, proof was allowed of averments that the defender had written other letters as a basis for skilled evidence.[21]

(c) Specialties. It is competent to take the witness's opinion, based on his special knowledge, on facts observed by himself (including the results of tests made by himself or in his presence)[26a] or spoken to by other witnesses. The opinion may be as to the probable cause of facts[18] or their probable result.[19] He may refer to books, and any passages adopted by him become part of his evidence.[27] Parts of a book not so adopted are not evidence, and the court may not rely on them.[27] In collision cases in the Court of Session, if a nautical assessor is sitting, no skilled evidence is competent on nautical matters,[28] and in other cases, if an assessor is sitting, only one skilled witness may be led on each side on a matter within the qualification of the assessor, unless leave is obtained.[29] A skilled witness does not require to be corroborated,[27] but even if he is uncontradicted the court is not bound to accept his evidence.[27]

(d) Presence in Court. Since the skilled witness is to give his opinion on the facts, it is usually helpful that he should be in court and hear the evidence of the witnesses to fact, and as a general rule this is allowed unless objection is taken, the witness being excluded while other skilled witnesses are giving evidence of opinion.[30] This course was followed, although the Crown demurred,[31] but not where counsel for the panel refused to consent,[32] and once it was not followed where there was apparently no objection.[33] If the witness is to speak to facts as well as opinion, he ought to be withdrawn while other witnesses are speaking to these facts. But even if he is not, the court may allow his evidence on fact to be taken.[34]

(e) Cross-examination. This may be on two lines. First, the cross-

Lord Justice-Clerk's view in *M'Que*); *McQue*, 1860, 3 Irv. 578 (where the Lord Justice-Clerk apparently thought that the judge should supply the expert knowledge).
[26] *Houston* v. *Aitken*, 1912 S.C. 1037.
[26a] Both parties may have to be present: *Irvine* v. *Powrie's Trustees*, 1915 S.C. 1006.
[27] *Davie* v. *Magistrates of Edinburgh*, 1953 S.C. 34. In *Williamson* v. *Cleland*, 1913 S.C. 678, the Lord President based his opinion partly on books never referred to. See § **52.**
[28] Rules of Court, 1948, Rule 162.
[29] *Ibid.*, Rule 51.
[30] *Laurie*, 1889, 2 White 326; *Pritchard*, 1865, 5 Irv. 88; *Milne*, 1863, 4 Irv. 301.
[31] *Murray*, 1858, 3 Irv. 262.
[32] *Dingwall*, 1867, 5 Irv. 466, at p. 471.
[33] *Granger*, 1878, 4 Coup. 86.
[34] Evidence (Scotland) Act, 1840 (3 & 4 Vict. c. 59), s. 3. The statement in Macdonald, *Criminal Law* (5th ed.) 295, that he cannot be examined on the facts, is wrong. See §367.

examiner may challenge the soundness of the conclusions drawn by the witness from the facts as the witness has assumed them. Second, the cross-examiner may ask the witness for his opinion on the facts as the cross-examiner hopes to establish them.[35] The witness's opinion may be the same as that of the cross-examiner's experts, which is thus reinforced, and if it is not, the cross-examiner is not open to the observation that he has failed to give the opposing experts an opportunity to state their opinions.

(f) **Necessity for Skilled Evidence.** If the court is to be asked to draw an inference of a technical nature, skilled evidence must be led.[36] Where the court was asked in a collision case to infer from the marks on one ship that the speed of the other must have been high, it held itself unable to do so in the absence of skilled evidence.[18] In another collision case, where it was sought to establish the position of the ships by means of photographs taken at the time of the collision, the Privy Council held that the lower court ought not to have used this evidence because no skilled evidence had been led to explain the effects of planes, perspectives, etc.[37]

414. HANDWRITING

(a) **Direct Evidence.** Where the genuineness of handwriting is in issue the best evidence, if it is available, is that of the purported writer. In a trial for uttering, where the Crown must prove that the document is forged, it has been held that opinion evidence is incompetent unless the purported writer is examined[38] or his absence satisfactorily explained.[39] This rule does not seem to have been departed from,[40] and it would probably apply in a civil case where it is averred that the party supporting the document forged it himself, or knows it to be forged, for that is to charge him with the crime of uttering.[41] Another class of direct evidence is that of witnesses who saw the writing carried out, such as an attesting witness.[42]

(b) **Opinion Evidence.** This may come either from witnesses who claim to be familiar with the handwriting of the purported writer or from skilled witnesses, who compare the questioned writing with specimens admitted or proved to be in his handwriting. There is old authority[43] for the view that the evidence of skilled witnesses is of little value, greatly inferior to that

35 Dickson, *Evidence* (3rd ed.) §401, thinks this should be done in chief, but if it is not, the cross-examiner should do it: *Wilson* v. *Thomas Usher & Son*, 1934 S.C. 332, 337 (evidence on facts).
36 But *cf.* the cases in note 25 where the High Court refused to admit skilled evidence on insanity.
37 *United States Shipping Board* v. *The St. Albans*, [1931] A.C. 632, where counsel supplied the expert evidence.
38 Dickson, *Evidence* (3rd ed.) §200; *Humphreys*, 1839, 2 Swin. 356, at p. 374.
39 *Wilson*, 1857, 2 Irv. 626, at p. 631.
40 In *Richardson* v. *Clark*, 1957 J.C. 7, Mrs. Shiells presumably denied the signatures at the trial.
41 *Arnott* v. *Burt*, 1872, 11 M. 62, at p. 74.
42 *Stirling Stuart* v. *Stirling Crawfurd's Trs.*, 1885, 12 R. 610.
43 e.g., *Forster* v. *Forster*, 1869, 7 M. 797, at p. 804.

of persons familiar with the genuine writing and to the opinions of the court, and certainly insufficient alone to establish the point. But the court has recently refused to affirm these statements in view of the advance in the scientific study of handwriting.[44] According to Dickson[45] where a party seeking to prove that a document is, or is not, in his handwriting, tenders a document as genuine for purposes of comparison, that document must be earlier in date than the document in question. The reason given is that otherwise the allegedly genuine document might be specially prepared for purposes of comparison. This dictum rests on two early cases[46] and may be a relic of the old rules which took such a low view of human nature that a witness with an interest was excluded.[47] No doubt such a document would be closely scrutinised, but it may be held that modern methods are a sufficient safeguard. It may be one which is inadmissible for any other purpose.[48]

(c) **Opinion of Jury and Judges.** Differing views have been expressed as to whether it is competent for the jury to make their own comparison and proceed upon that. In several civil cases[49] this practice was approved, and in a trial for uttering[50] Lord Deas, after refusing to allow a skilled witness to be examined for the Crown, remarked "So far as comparison went, the jury could look at the documents and judge for themselves." On the other hand, Lord President Boyle cautioned a jury that they were not to found their verdict on a comparison of handwriting, but on the evidence they had heard,[51] and in a criminal trial Lord Justice-Clerk Hope said that the court did not think it right to allow the jury to see the documents, so as to make a comparison in the box. The Crown was bound to prove the case against the prisoner by evidence on which his counsel could animadvert (and, it may be added, cross-examine). Whatever might be the rule in civil cases, the inspection of documents by fifteen gentlemen, none of whom could be examined as to the ground of his opinion, was not a satisfactory way of establishing guilt in a criminal court.[52] It is thought that the latter is the sounder view for the reasons given in the last mentioned case, which were recently repeated in relation to a somewhat different point.[53] But even if this be so, the opinions of the witnesses must depend on features of the writing, and the jury can hardly be expected to weigh these opinions, and the effect of cross-examination, unless they see the documents. From that it is but a short step to making an independent comparison. No doubt for that

[44] *Richardson* v. *Clark* (*supra*).
[45] *Evidence* (3rd ed.) §411.
[46] *Cameron* v. *Fraser & Co.*, 1830, 9 S. 141; *Ross* v. *Waddell*, 1837, 15 S. 1219.
[47] Dickson, *Evidence* (3rd ed.) §1542.
[48] *H.M. Advocate* v. *Walsh*, 1933 J.C. 82; *Davidson* v. *H.M. Advocate*, 1951 J.C. 33. This may not be so in a civil cause. See §**238**.
[49] e.g., *Paul* v. *Harper*, 1832, 10 S. 488; *Bryson* v. *Crawford*, 1834, 12 S. 937.
[50] *Beveridge*, 1866, 3 Irv. 625.
[51] *Gellatly* v. *Jones*, 1851, 13 D. 961.
[52] *Robertson*, 1849, J. Shaw 186, at p. 191, not cited in *Beveridge* (*supra*). It is perhaps indicative of the practice at the time that the Advocate Depute had told the jury that they would have an opportunity of comparing the documents.
[53] *McCann* v. *Adair*, 1951 J.C. 127.

reason, though it is competent for the jury to take the documents with them when they retire,[54] the judge frequently refuses to allow them to do so.[55] In principle it seems equally objectionable that judges should found their opinions on private examination of documents, but it has been done,[56] and there does not seem to be any reported disapproval.

415. FOREIGN LAW

(a) **General.** Foreign law[57] is a question of fact,[58] and if it is not admitted[59] or ascertained under statutory procedure or by remit to foreign counsel, it must be proved by the evidence of skilled witnesses. The court will not attempt to construe a foreign statute for itself without the aid of skilled witnesses.[60] The House of Lords, however, as the final court of appeal in civil matters from all parts of the United Kingdom, has judicial knowledge of Scots, English and Northern Irish law, and may take cognisance, without need of evidence, of matters of the law of one jurisdiction in an appeal originating in another, and that even though the foreign law has not been pleaded or argued.[61] Also, for income tax purposes only, the English law of charities must be regarded as part of the law of Scotland and not as foreign law, so that in this class of case the Scottish courts must themselves seek to interpret the English decisions as to what is or is not a "charity."[62] This exception is justifiable by the need for a common tax code and uniform interpretation thereof.

(b) **Statutory Ascertainment.** If any court, which includes a criminal court, a Lord Ordinary and, it would seem, a sheriff,[63] is of opinion that it is necessary or expedient to ascertain the law of any other part of Her Majesty's dominions,[64] applicable to the facts[65] of a case, it may remit to a superior

---

54 *Slater* v. *H.M. Advocate*, 1899, 2 F. (J.) 4.

55 *Gellatly* v. *Jones* (*supra*); *Robertson* (*supra*).

56 "I am inclined to place considerable reliance on the evidence of my own eyes"; *Stirling Stuart* v. *Stirling Crawfurd's Trs.* (*supra*), at p. 621; "What is conclusive to my mind is the real evidence afforded by the signature itself . . . compared with the admittedly genuine signature," "I believe that your lordships have come to the same conclusion on an examination of the documents": *National Bank of Scotland, Ltd.* v. *Campbell*, 1892, 19 R. 885, at pp. 887, 890.

57 This means any law other than Scots.

58 This hardly needs authority, but see, for example, *Campbell's Trs.* v. *Campbell*, 1903, 5 F. 366.

59 As in *Studd* v. *Studd*, 1880, 8 R. 249; 1883, 10 R. (H.L.) 53.

60 *Higgins* v. *Ewing's Trs.*, 1925 S.C. 440; *Kolbin & Sons* v. *Kinnear & Co.*, 1930 S.C. 724, at pp. 737, 748, 753; 1931 S.C. (H.L.) 128 (point not raised in H.L.); *R.* v. *Governor of Brixton Prison: ex parte Shuter*, [1960] 2 Q.B. 89. *Cf. Great Northern Railway Co.* v. *Laing*, 1848, 10 D. 1048.

61 *Elliot* v. *Joicey*, 1935 S.C. (H.L.) 57.

62 *Inland Revenue* v. *Glasgow Police Athletic Assocn.*, 1953 S.C. (H.L.) 13.

63 *Macomish's Exrs.* v. *Jones*, 1932 S.C. 108.

64 The Republic of Ireland is not part of Her Majesty's dominions, but it is not a foreign country for the purposes of any law in force in the United Kingdom: Ireland Act, 1949 (12 & 13 Geo. VI. c. 41), s. 2 (1).

65 As ascertained by a verdict or other mode competent (which would include findings by the court) or agreed.

court of that part for its opinion.[66] The court has a discretion and refused to exercise it where the court to which the remit was asked had concurrent jurisdiction.[67] A remit may be made although skilled evidence has been led.[68] The opinion obtained is conclusive,[69] except that the Judicial Committee and the House of Lords are not bound by the opinion of a court whose judgments they have power to review.[70] There are similar provisions for[71] the ascertainment of the law of a foreign state (which in this context must mean a state not part of Her Majesty's dominions) with which Her Majesty has entered into a convention.[72]

(c) **Remit to Foreign Counsel.** The court may make such a remit of consent, and the opinion is binding,[73] except that if the opinion is on English law the House of Lords may disregard it.[74] Where a remit was made to two counsel, and they differed, a remit was made to a third.[75] The remit ought to be carefully limited to questions of law. When a remit was so framed as to ask the opinion of counsel, *inter alia*, on the construction of a will which raised no question of foreign law, the court was narrowly divided as to whether they were bound by counsel's views on construction, and by seven to six decided in the negative.[76]

(d) **Skilled Witnesses.** Such evidence is usually given by members of the bar, but, in spite of an *obiter* dictum by Lord Young,[77] there seems to be no reason why it should not be given by solicitors, its weight varying with the standing of the witness. English counsel would be accepted to state the law of any country where English law prevailed. So the court remitted to English counsel for an opinion on the law of Newfoundland, which was English law.[78] Where the witnesses differ, the court is bound to weigh the evidence

---

[66] British Law Ascertainment Act, 1859 (22 & 23 Vict. c. 63), ss. 1, 5.
[67] *MacDougall* v. *Chitnavis*, 1937 S.C. 390. What must be necessary or expedient is not, as the Lord President said, the remit, but the ascertainment of the foreign law.
[68] *MacDougall* v. *Chitnavis* (*supra*); *De Thoren* v. *Wall*, 1876, 3 R. (H.L.) 28.
[69] 1859 Act, s. 3.
[70] *Ibid.*, s. 4. *De Thoren* v. *Wall* (*supra*).
[71] The only difference seems to be that under the 1861 Act only the Inner House or the High Court may remit. See *Macomish's Exrs.* v. *Jones* (*supra*). This distinction may render the precise status of the Republic of Ireland of some importance, if indeed either Act applies to it. See note 64.
[72] Foreign Law Ascertainment Act, 1861 (24 & 25 Vict. c. 11): no convention has been entered into: Phipson, *Evidence* (9th ed.) 407.
[73] *Duchess of Buckingham* v. *Winterbottom*, 1851, 13 D. 1129, at p. 1141; *Baird* v. *Mitchell*, 1854, 16 D. 1088, at p. 1092.
[74] *Macpherson* v. *Macpherson*, 1852, 1 Macq. 243.
[75] *Kerr* v. *Fyffe*, 1840, 2 D. 1001.
[76] *Thomson's Trs.* v. *Alexander*, 1851, 14 D. 217. The decision would have been the other way, if L. Dundrennan had not died before the judgment was signed and been succeeded by L. Cowan, who took the opposite view.
[77] *Dinwoodie's Executrix* v. *Carruthers' Exr.*, 1895, 23 R. 234, at p. 238. So far as the report discloses there was no dispute as to English law, but only as to whether it applied.
[78] *Thomson's Trs.* v. *Alexander* (*supra*).

as in any question of fact.[79] There seems to be no reason in principle why the court should not reject the opinion, even if it is uncontradicted, as it may do in the case of any other skilled witness.[80] There is, however, no reported instance.[81]

---

[79] *Kolbin & Sons* v. *Kinnear & Co. (ut supra)*; *Girvan, Roper & Co.* v. *Monteith*, 1895, 23 R. 129, where, at pp. 132, 135, there was discussion of the evidence.
[80] See §**413**, sub-para. (c).
[81] In *Ross* v. *H.H. Sir Bhagat Sinhjee*, 1891, 19 R. 31, uncontradicted evidence of English law was regarded as conclusive.

CHAPTER XXXV

REAL EVIDENCE

416. GENERAL

There is little profit in attempting to reach a logically impregnable definition. Such a definition either is departed from or unduly restricts the discussion of practical questions. Thus Dickson,[1] having defined real evidence as "evidence derived from things,"[1] immediately proceeds to treat the things as the evidence. Cross,[2] after a criticism of previous definitions, defines it as "anything . . . which is examined by the tribunal as a means of proof." This excludes things upon which witnesses base opinions and which the tribunal may never have any opportunity of inspecting at all because they cannot be moved or because they have perished. The term is therefore here used in a wide sense to include both a thing, which may be a human being, any features of the thing which are significant, and the inferences to be drawn from the existence of the thing or from its significant features. It may, for example, include broken glass and dried mud left on a road after a motor-car collision, their exact positions on the road, and the inferences which arise from their existence and positions, or the cut behind the right ear of the victim of an assault and the inference that he was attacked from behind by a right-handed person. Further, an exclamation which is part of the *res gestæ* is real evidence,[3] and so is the fact that the accused ran from the scene of the crime. The question of drawing inferences from things and their features is dealt with under opinion evidence,[4] and is mentioned only briefly at the end of this chapter,[5] which is mainly concerned with the recovery of the thing when it is not in the possession of the party desiring to use it,[6] the necessity for lodging it before the trial or proof,[7] and the necessity for its production at the trial or proof.[8]

---

[1] Dickson, *Evidence* (3rd ed.) §1815.
[2] *Evidence* (1958) 10.
[3] See §377.
[4] See §413, sub-para. (c).
[5] See §421.
[6] See §§417, 418.
[7] See §419.
[8] See §420.

417. RECOVERY: CRIMINAL

(a) **Person of Accused.** There is an important difference in the powers of recovery before arrest, when the police have not sufficient evidence to justify arrest, and after arrest, when they are trying to obtain further evidence, but a principle applicable to both cases is that a man is not bound to supply evidence against himself.[9] Before arrest the right is limited to such observation as is possible without interfering with the person. So it is not competent to search a person without his express consent[10] or to take his fingerprints[11] or scrapings from his fingernails.[12] Nevertheless, valuable evidence may be obtained without interference. It is usually the general appearance and behaviour of a driver which lead to his arrest on a charge under section 6 of the Road Traffic Act, 1960.[13] On the other hand, after arrest the accused may be stripped and searched,[14] and he may be required to exhibit his hand for observation of a cut,[15] and his fingerprints may be taken,[16] all without a warrant and without his consent. It has not been decided generally whether the evidence so obtained may be used if the accused is tried on a more serious charge than that under which he was at the time detained, but, in a trial for culpable homicide, evidence was admitted of the results of a medical examination of the accused made with his consent when he was in custody on a statutory charge of driving under the influence of drink.[17] Sometimes a witness, when asked if he can identify the accused, says that he could only be certain if he heard the accused speak. It may be that the accused, if asked to speak, should be warned that he need not do so, on the ground that by doing so he is supplying evidence against himself.[18] Where at the request of the police an accused gave a specimen of his handwriting, the specimen was held to be properly admitted for comparison with forged documents, but the accused had been told that he need not do so unless he wished, and that the specimen might be used in evidence.[19] In the same case it was held competent to use the accused's signature on a fingerprint form, adhibited without warning, on the ground that it was not taken for purposes of comparison and was in the same position as any casual writing by the accused.

(b) **Things.** In great emergency the police may search without a warrant.[20]

---

[9] *Adair* v. *McGarry*, 1933 J.C. 72, at p. 88.
[10] *Adair* v. *McGarry* (*supra*), at p. 90; *McGovern* v. *H.M. Advocate*, 1950 J.C. 33, at p. 36.
[11] *Adamson* v. *Martin*, 1916 S.C. 319; *Adair* v. *McGarry* (*supra*), at pp. 79, 90.
[12] *McGovern* v. *H.M. Advocate* (*supra*).
[13] 8 & 9 Eliz. II. c. 116.
[14] *McGovern* v. *H.M. Advocate* (*supra*), at p. 36; *Adair* v. *McGarry* (*supra*), at p. 80.
[15] *Forrester* v. *H.M. Advocate*, 1952 J.C. 28, at p. 34.
[16] *Adair* v. *McGarry* (*supra*). *Byrne* v. *H.M. Advocate* was heard along with this case and treated as identical. But there was a distinction. *McGarry's* fingerprints were taken before he was brought before a magistrate, *Byrne's* after he had been committed by the sheriff. In view of the observations in *Stark and Smith* v. *H.M. Advocate*, 1938 J.C. 170, as to the rights of the police after committal, this distinction may be important.
[17] *McKie* v. *H.M. Advocate*, 1958 J.C. 24.
[18] *Adair* v. *McGarry* (*supra*), at pp. 88, 89.
[19] *Davidson* v. *H.M. Advocate*, 1951 J.C. 33.
[20] *H.M. Advocate* v. *McGuigan*, 1936 J.C. 16.

The procurator-fiscal may also, by the hands of the police, take possession of an article without warrant if the custodier of it consents.[21] Apart from these two cases the police are not entitled without a warrant to take possession of an article from a third party, or from the accused if he is not in custody.[22] A warrant may be granted to search for stolen goods of a specified nature in the premises of a person who has not been apprehended or charged.[23] This decision (by a court of seven judges) does not go beyond that, the decision in *Bell* v. *Black and Morrison*[23] was distinguished and approved rather than disapproved, and the case shows that great care is necessary in framing a warrant in such circumstances. A warrant must be precise in the sense that it authorises search for and seizure of documents and other articles tending to establish guilt of the specified crime.[23] If the police in executing it come across an article clearly connecting the accused with another crime, they may probably seize it on the ground that, if they do not do so, the owner will dispose of it as soon as their backs are turned.[23a] They are not entitled, however, to carry off a mass of papers and rake through them to see if they can find evidence of another crime.[24] If the seizure has been illegal, the thing may not be admitted in evidence, but the court has a discretion.[25] It is the practice of the Crown to make available to the defence any document likely to assist the defence, and this presumably applies to any object, but if the Crown refuses, or the object is in the possession of third parties, a petition to the High Court, or to the sheriff, is probably competent.[26]

418. RECOVERY: CIVIL

(a) **Persons.** In an action of damages for personal injuries the court may, and, if asked, normally does, ordain the pursuer to submit himself for examination by a doctor selected by the defenders.[27] Frequently the pursuer attends at the doctor's consulting room, but in normal circumstances he will not be ordained to go far from home.[27] A pursuer has been ordained to submit to examination before the closing of the record.[28] In consistorial causes an order has been made for examination of a party,[29] but where proof had been allowed on the defender's plea that the action was incompetent because the pursuer was of unsound mind, it was held that no order for examination of the pursuer should be made until the defender had established

---

21 *Watson* v. *Muir*, 1938 J.C. 181. Much stolen property is recovered in this way.
22 *Lawrie* v. *Muir*, 1950 J.C. 19; *Fairley* v. *Fishmongers of London*, 1951 J.C. 14.
23 *Stewart* v. *Roach*, 1950 S.C. 318, where *Bell* v. *Black and Morrison*, 1865, 5 Irv. 57, was explained. See *H.M. Advocate* v. *McKay*, 1961 J.C. 47.
23a *H.M. Advocate* v. *Hepper*, 1958 J.C. 39.
24 *H.M. Advocate* v. *Turnbull*, 1951 J.C. 96.
25 See §2.
26 *Downie* v. *H.M. Advocate*, 1952 J.C. 37.
27 *McDonald* v. *Western S.M.T. Co.*, 1945 S.C. 47.
28 *Smyth* v. *Gow*, (O.H.) 1895, 2 S.L.T. 473.
29 *X.* v. *Y.*, (O.H.) 1922 S.L.T. 150 (an action of adherence and aliment where the defence was refusal to consummate and examination of the pursuer was ordered); *A.B. or D.* v. *C.D.*, (O.H.) 1908, 15 S.L.T. 911 (a declarator of nullity on the ground of impotency where examination of the defender was ordered).

a *prima facie* case.[30] In a nullity case refusal to submit to examination infers an admission of incapacity,[31] and in any other case would at least probably affect the burden of proof. No one can be compelled to give a sample of blood for testing,[32] and before a person consents to give a sample he ought to be made fully aware of the consequences.[33] The court has no power to order a witness, as distinct from a party, to submit to examination, and the result is that evidence founded on an examination for one side is inadmissible unless the witness is willing to submit to examination for the other.[34]

(b) **Things.** These, other than documents,[35] cannot be recovered by diligence under a specification.[36] The proper method is by motion for production[37] or inspection, e.g., of premises or machinery.[38] Where the order is for inspection, the names of the persons who are to inspect must be furnished. In unusual circumstances a chemical test of documents has been authorised, provided that both parties were present.[39] Where a thing has been recovered in some irregular way, e.g., by theft, it may nevertheless be admitted.[40]

419. LODGING OF ARTICLES BEFORE TRIAL OR PROOF

(a) **General.** Except in a summary criminal trial and in the Small Debt Court a party, as a general rule, must lodge beforehand in the hands of the clerk of court any article on which he intends to found at the trial or proof. The purpose is to give his opponent an opportunity to examine the article and, if he wishes, have it examined by experts. Stucco impressions of the accused's boots were excluded when they were not in the Crown list of productions and were only brought to court by the witness,[41] and a witness was not allowed to demonstrate that a key fitted a lock, when the key was lodged and included in the Crown list, but the lock was not.[42] Lodging may

[30] *A.B.* v. *C.B.*, 1937 S.C. 696.
[31] Fraser, *Husband and Wife* (2nd ed.) I, 104.
[32] *Whitehall* v. *Whitehall*, 1958 S.C. 252.
[33] *Irvine* v. *Mitchell*, 1958 S.C. 439.
[34] *Borthwick* v. *Borthwick*, (O.H.) 1929 S.L.T. 57, 596; *Davidson* v. *Davidson*, 1860, 22 D. 749.
[35] As to recovery of documents, see §§ **287** *et seq.*
[36] *Mactaggart* v. *Mackillop*, (O.H.) 1938 S.L.T. 559; *Lord Advocate* v. *Fleming*, 1864, 2 M. 1032, at p. 1061.
[37] *Mactaggart* v. *Mackillop (supra)*; *Bell* v. *Hamilton's Trs.*, 1889, 16 R. 1001; *Jardine's Trs.* v. *Carron Co.*, 1864, 2 M. 1372.
[38] *Bell* v. *Hamilton's Trs.*, 1889, 16 R. 1001; *Murray* v. *The Waterproofing Co.*, 1914, 1 S.L.T. 46; *Stevenson* v. *Gray & Sons*, 1902, 9 S.L.T. 489; *Clippens Oil Co.* v. *Edinburgh and District Water Trs.*, 1904, 12 S.L.T. 40; *Routledge* v. *Somerville & Son*, 1866, 4 M. 830; *Brown* v. *Brown & Somerville*, 1840, 2 D. 1356.
[39] *Irvine* v. *Powrie's Trs.*, 1915 S.C. 1006. The argument that the pursuer must first establish a *prima facie* case was rejected: see note 30.
[40] *Rattray* v. *Rattray*, 1897, 25 R. 315; *MacColl* v. *MacColl*, (O.H.) 1946 S.L.T. 312. See § **2**, sub-para. (b).
[41] *Milne*, 1866, 5 Irv. 229.
[42] *Goodwin*, 1837, 1 Swin. 431. *Smith*, 1837, 1 Swin. 505, is of doubtful authority. See Dickson, *Evidence* (3rd ed.) §1819.

be dispensed with if it is impracticable[43] or there is some good objection to it, provided that timeous notice of the intention to use the article is given to the opponent so as to enable him to examine it.[44]

(b) **Criminal.** In solemn procedure the notice is given by appending a list of the Crown productions to the indictment and to the service copy. The productions themselves must be lodged with the sheriff clerk of the district where the trial is to be held,[45] or, if the trial is before the High Court in Edinburgh, in the Justiciary Office.[45] No time by which this must be done is fixed by statute or otherwise. The test of whether the lodging is timeous is whether the accused has had a fair opportunity to examine the productions.[46] A century ago a remarkably short time was regarded as sufficient, and the onus was placed on the accused of proving prejudice.[46] If the accused is to object to the use of a production on the ground that he has not had a fair chance to examine it, he must give notice before the jury is sworn, so that if his objection is upheld the diet can be deserted *pro loco et tempore*.[47] It is competent for the prosecutor, with leave of the court, to put in evidence a production not in the list, provided he has given the accused two clear days' notice.[48] The accused must give three days' notice of a production, unless he can satisfy the court that he was unable to do so.[49] If a Crown production is sealed the court may give the accused authority to open it.[50] In summary procedure, although there is no obligation to give notice of or lodge productions before the trial, the practice of the Crown is to act fairly.[51]

(c) **Civil.** In the Court of Session productions to be used at a proof or jury trial must be lodged seven days beforehand.[52] In an ordinary or a

---

[43] See § **420**.

[44] *Baird* v. *Leechman*, (O.H.) 1903, 11 S.L.T. 200.

[45] Criminal Procedure (Scotland) Act, 1887 (50 & 51 Vict. c. 35), s. 24. Productions unsuitable to be kept in an office, such as livestock, may be lodged with a representative of the sheriff clerk or of the Clerk of Justiciary: *Stark and Smith* v. *H.M. Advocate*, 1938 J.C. 170.

[46] *Watt*, 1859, 3 Irv. 389 (bank's books available two days before trial): *Kerr*, 1857, 2 Irv. 608 (watch lodged at 9.30 on morning of trial): *Aymers*, 1857, 2 Irv. 725 (book lodged an hour before trial, but only required to compare extracts lodged ten days before). Under an Act of Adjournal of 17th March, 1827, it is enough, if the trial is in the sheriff court, to lodge the day before the trial, but this Act is little heard of, and insistence on its provisions might cause great injustice.

[47] *Watt* (*supra*); *Kerr* (*supra*).

[48] Criminal Procedure (Scotland) Act, 1921 (11 & 12 Geo. V. c. 50), s. 1.

[49] Criminal Procedure (Scotland) Act, 1887 (50 & 51 Vict. c. 35), s. 36.

[50] Hume, II, 388. Where the procurator-fiscal's letter-book was lodged to prove copies of three letters, and otherwise sealed up, the defence, before pleading, moved for an adjournment. The Crown objected on the ground that the rest of the book contained confidential letters and stated that the book contained no other letters connected with the case, and that would appear to be in general a sufficient answer. But the court refused the adjournment on the ground that the Crown proposed to use only the three letters, which, by implication, prevented the accused from using any letters favourable to the defence: *Wilson*, 1857, 2 Irv. 626.

[51] See *Smith* v. *H.M. Advocate*, 1952 J.C. 66. If there were serious prejudice to either side, the trial might be adjourned: *Maciver* v. *Mackenzie*, 1942 J.C. 51, at p. 54.

[52] Rules of Court, 1948, Rules 129, 141.

summary cause in the sheriff court productions must be lodged four days before the proof or trial.[53]

420. PRODUCTION AT TRIAL OR PROOF

The article itself is the best evidence of its appearance at the time of the trial or proof. Accordingly, an oral description of it in its absence is inadmissible, provided that it is practicable and convenient to produce it.[54] It would seem to follow that expert evidence based on such an article would also be inadmissible. Unless the thing were available, it might be impossible to cross-examine an expert, and further there might be a risk that the experts were speaking of different things. There appears to have been at one time some variation in the decisions,[55] but it is thought that the stricter rule would now be adhered to, if objection is taken. A description by a witness is competent where the article is perishable or the relevant feature evanescent. A dead body need not be produced,[56] and a description of a person's appearance and conduct at a particular time is evidence as to his state of sobriety then. Again the article may be an immoveable object away from the court.[57] Lastly, it is not thought necessary after a motor accident to leave a damaged vehicle unrepaired for months until the trial or proof. The question is "whether the production is practicable and convenient."[58] In a trial on indictment, when a witness gives evidence that he has examined a production lodged eight days before the second diet, it is not necessary to prove that he received it in the same condition as when it was taken possession of by the procurator-fiscal or the police and returned by him, unless the accused gives four days' written notice that he does not admit that it was so received or returned.[59]

421. USE AT TRIAL OR PROOF

The article itself is evidence only of its appearance at the time, and justifies simple inferences, e.g., that a box has been forced open, that a witness's

---

[53] Sheriff Courts (Scotland) Act, 1907 (7 Edw. VII. c. 51), Rules 68, 142.

[54] *Maciver* v. *Mackenzie*, 1942 J.C. 51, where no objection was taken to oral descriptions, and consequently no explanation offered for the failure to produce; *MacLeod* v. *Woodmuir Miners Welfare Society Social Club*, 1961 J.C. 5. *Cf. Paterson* v. *H.M. Advocate*, 1901, 4 F. (J.) 7, where adequate grounds of judgment would have been (1) that no objection was taken to the Crown evidence, and (2) that as the sheep were presumably on the Crown list of productions they could have been produced by the defence. *Cf.* also *Stewart* v. *Glasgow Corporation*, 1958 S.C. 28, where evidence was led without objection as to the condition of a pole not produced, a fact on which two of the judges remarked at pp. 30, 38.

[55] Dickson, *Evidence* (3rd ed.) §§1817 *et seq.*

[56] *Punton*, 1841, 2 Swin. 572.

[57] There is statutory provision for a "view" by jurors before the trial: Jury Trials (Scotland) Act, 1815 (55 Geo. III. c. 42), s. 29; Rules of Court, 1948, Rule 140. See *Redpath* v. *Central S.M.T. Co.*, (O.H.) 1947 S.N. 177, and § 52, note 60. But a private inspection by the tribunal is incompetent; *Hattie* v. *Leitch*, 1889, 16 R. 1128, at least if it influences the decision: *Sime* v. *Linton*, 1897, 24 R. (J.) 70; *Hope* v. *Gemmell*, 1898, 1 F. 74.

[58] *Maciver* v. *Mackenzie* (*supra*), at p. 55.

[59] Criminal Justice (Scotland) Act, 1949 (12, 13 & 14 Geo. VI. c. 94), s. 35.

arm has been injured,[60] that the accused is sufficiently powerful to have committed the crime,[61] and that jewellery has been "got up" to deceive.[62] A bottle proved to have been found at the scene of a crime, and bearing fingerprints, provides evidence of the accused's presence at the scene, if the jury is satisfied that the fingerprints are his.[63] But the tribunal may not be entitled to draw an inference from its own examination unless the party against whom the inference is drawn has an opportunity to challenge it.[64] Where the matter is technical, lay opinion is not admissible. A police officer can only say that marks on clothing look like blood. In such matters, where skilled knowledge is required, only expert evidence is admissible.[65]

[60] *Aitken* v. *Wood*, 1921 J.C. 84.
[61] *Withers* v. *H.M. Advocate*, 1947 J.C. 1091.
[62] *Patterson* v. *Landsberg*, 1905, 7 F. 675, at p. 681.
[63] *Hamilton* v. *H.M. Advocate*, 1934 J.C. 1, at p. 4.
[64] *McCann* v. *Adair*, 1951 J.C. 127. See §**414**, sub-para. (b).
[65] See §§**411** *et seq.*

CHAPTER XXXVI

INTERNATIONAL PRIVATE LAW

422. INTRODUCTORY

One branch of international private law determines by the law of which state a question is to be decided. The purpose of this chapter is more restricted. It is merely to consider in what circumstances it is necessary to go beyond Scots law at all, so that admission or proof of some foreign law is required.[1] This question appears to arise in two situations, (1) when a deed which, to put it broadly, has some foreign connection is tendered in evidence, and (2) when it is sought to prove an obligation which has some foreign connection. It has been said that a party who maintains that a foreign law applies must aver clearly what that law is and how it establishes some point in his favour,[2] but this cannot be a universal rule. The point may arise on the admissibility of evidence, and a party may not know, when the record is closed, how his opponent proposes to prove his averments.[3] The older decisions may not always be safe guides.[4]

423. FORMAL VALIDITY OF DEEDS

(a) General. The formal validity of a disposition of heritage depends on the law of the country where the heritage is situated,[5] and that law also determines whether the property is heritable or moveable.[6] Other deeds, including personal obligations relating to heritage,[5] may be formally valid on a direct application of Scots law in three ways. First, a deed executed abroad is valid if it is executed in accordance with the solemnities required

---

1 As to proof of foreign law, see § 415. Proof of foreign judgments and the taking of evidence for a foreign court are also dealt with.
2 *McElroy* v. *McAllister*, 1949 S.C. 110, at pp. 118, 123, 137; *Griffith's Judicial Factor* v. *Griffith's Exrs.*, 1905, 7 F. 470, at pp. 475, 477; *Valery* v. *Scott*, 1876, 3 R. 965, at p. 967. See also *Whitehead* v. *Thompson*, 1861, 23 D. 772.
3 *Bain* v. *Whitehaven Railway Co.*, 1850, 7 Bell's App. 79, where the House of Lords rejected an argument that evidence of English law as to the validity of a document should not have been admitted because it was not averred. Foreign law is assumed to be the same as Scots law if no difference is averred: *Rodden* v. *Whatlings, Ltd.*, (O.H.) 1961 S.C. 132.
4 *McElroy* v. *McAllister* (*supra*), L.P. Cooper at p. 135.
5 Erskine, iii, 2, 40.
6 *Macdonald* v. *Macdonald*, 1932 S.C. (H.L.) 79.

by the Scottish conveyancing statutes.[7] An arbiter in a Scottish submission executed his award in England. His attempt to follow the conveyancing statutes failed, but it is plain that if it had succeeded, the court would have held the award validly executed without reference to English law.[8] Secondly, a deed is valid if it is executed in Scotland in any mode sufficient by Scots law, the *lex actus*.[9] The point has not arisen for direct decision in Scotland, but the court applies the rule to deeds executed abroad. An award executed in England was sustained because it was sufficiently executed by English law,[8] and so was a mandate.[10] Thirdly, the deed is valid, no matter where it was executed, if Scots law is the proper law of the contract, which usually means the law of the place where the contract is to be performed, and it is validly executed by Scots law. While there does not seem to be any decision to this effect, the proposition is supported by an *obiter* dictum of Lord Justice-Clerk Inglis (as he then was),[11] by the strongly expressed opinions of modern writers,[12] and by the principle of *Purvis's Trs.* v. *Purvis.*[13] Should it not be possible to support the formal validity of a deed by any of these direct applications of Scots law recourse may be had to the foreign *lex actus*, the law of the place of execution,[8] or to the foreign law of the contract.[12] The assumption hitherto made, viz., that it is sufficient to support the deed on any one of these grounds, although not universally accepted, has the support of a dictum by Lord President Inglis,[14] the course followed by the court in *Earl of Hopetoun* v. *Scots Mines Co.*,[8] the opinions in *Purvis's Trs.* v. *Purvis*,[13] and the views of modern writers.[12] The question does not arise where the only law applicable is the *lex actus*.[15] Stamping is dealt with above.[16]

(b) Wills. At common law a will executed in conformity with the law either of the deceased's domicile or of the place of execution carries moveables.[17] The form of the question put to the consulted judges in *Purvis's Trs.* v. *Purvis*[13] suggests that these are mutually exclusive alternatives. The testamentary writings were executed in Sumatra by a domiciled Scotsman, and the pursuers contended that their validity must be decided by Scots law, under which the execution was insufficient. The question put was whether

---

[7] *Valery* v. *Scott*, 1876, 3 R. 965, L.P. Inglis at p. 967. But *cf. Shedlock* v. *Hannay*, 1891 18 R. 663, L. Kinnear at p. 669. As to the conveyancing statutes, see §§ **90, 176** *et seq.*

[8] *Earl of Hopetoun* v. *Scots Mines Co.*, 1856, 18 D. 739.

[9] *Valery* v. *Scott* (*ut supra*); *Shedlock* v. *Hannay* (*ut supra*).

[10] *Great Northern Railway Co.* v. *Laing*, 1848, 10 D. 1048. The court satisfied itself by an examination of the English statutes. For a comment on this method of ascertaining English law, see *Higgins* v. *Ewing's Trs.*, 1925 S.C. 440, at p. 449. See § **415**, sub-para. (a).

[11] *Stewart* v. *Gelot*, 1871, 9 M. 1057, at p. 1062.

[12] Dicey, *Conflict of Laws* (7th ed.) rule 152; Cheshire, *Private International Law* (6th ed.) 236.

[13] 1861, 23 D. 812. The case is described in sub-para. (b).

[14] *Valery* v. *Scott* (*ut supra*).

[15] *Shedlock* v. *Hannay* (*supra*); *Tayler* v. *Scott*, 1847, 9 D. 1504. As to the requirements of Scots law, see § **104**.

[16] See § **237**.

[17] *Macdonald* v. *Cuthbertson*, 1890, 18 R. 101, at p. 104; *Chisholm* v. *Chisholm*, (O.H.) 1949 S.C. 434. As to execution by Scots law, see § **104**.

Scots law or the law of Sumatra ruled, and the answer was in favour of the latter. But, as the opinions show, the answer ought to have been "both." The joint opinion of eight of the consulted judges contains this passage: "We agree . . . that a testator making his will in a foreign country has his option either to follow the formalities prevailing at the place of his domicile or those of the place of execution."[18] By statute a bequest of moveables made outside the United Kingdom by a British subject is well executed if made according to the forms required by the law either of the place where made, or of the testator's domicile when it was made, or of his domicile of origin.[19] Further, every bequest of moveables made within the United Kingdom by a British subject is well executed if executed in accordance with the forms required by the law at the time at the place where it was made.[20]

At common law heritage cannot be bequeathed and a deed conveying it *mortis causa*, if not holograph or adopted as holograph, requires authentication in terms of the statutes. It has, however, been held that as the combined result of the Wills Act[19] and the Titles to Land Act, 1868,[21] a will executed in England, sufficiently authenticated by English law to carry moveables, also carries heritage in Scotland.[22]

424. INTERPRETATION AND EFFECT OF DEEDS

The law governing these matters depends generally on the intention of the granter or the parties, as indicated in the deed.[23] Where the deed is to be interpreted by foreign law, and in particular where it contains foreign technical terms, expert evidence, or its equivalent, is usually required to explain these.[24] But if there is no relevant averment of any technical meaning attaching to any term, the court will construe the deed for itself.[25] Even where a deed falls to be interpreted by Scots law, but contains foreign technical terms, explanatory evidence may be required,[26] But whatever the intention of the parties, it may be frustrated by the *lex situs*,[27] or displaced by statute.[28]

---

[18] at p. 825. See also L. Kinloch at p. 827, L. Cowan at pp. 833, 834.
[19] Wills Act, 1861 (24 & 25 Vict. c. 114), s. 1.
[20] *Ibid.*, s. 2.
[21] 31 & 32 Vict. c. 101, s. 20.
[22] *Connel's Trs.* v. *Connel*, 1872, 10 M. 627. See also *Studd* v. *Cook*, 1883, 10 R. (H.L.) 53, at pp. 54, 59.
[23] *Hamlyn & Co.* v. *Talisker Distillery Co.*, 1894, 21 R. (H.L.) 21 (commercial contract); *Mackintosh* v. *May*, 1895, 22 R. 345 (lease); *Corbet* v. *Waddell*, 1879, 7 R. 200 (marriage contract); *Mitchell & Baxter* v. *Davies*, 1875, 3 R. 208 (will).
[24] *Higgins* v. *Ewing's Trs.*, 1925 S.C. 440, where proof before answer of English law was allowed; *Studd* v. *Cook* 1883. 10 R. (H.L.) 53, where there was a minute of admissions as to the meaning of English law terms, which became unnecessary when the case reached the House of Lords; *Cooper* v. *Cooper*, 1888, 15 R. (H.L.) 21.
[25] *Griffith's Judicial Factor* v. *Griffith's Exrs.*, 1905, 7 F. 470 (no relevant averment of any technical meaning attaching to the word "effects" under the foreign law); *Thomson's Trs.* v. *Alexander*, 1851, 14 D. 217 (opinion of English counsel that the terms had no technical meaning).
[26] *Mackintosh* v. *May* (*supra*).
[27] *Hewit's Trs.* v. *Lawson*, 1891, 18 R. 793.
[28] *English* v. *Donnelly*, 1958 S.C. 494.

425. PROOF OF OBLIGATIONS

(a) General. The validity and effect of an obligation is governed by the *lex contractus*, which may be the *lex actus*, the *lex situs*, the *lex solutionis* or the *lex domicilii*,[29] but questions of evidence are ruled by the *lex fori*, e.g., "whether a witness is competent or not, whether a certain matter requires to be proved by writing or not."[30] The problem is to distinguish the validity and effect of the obligation from proof of it.[31]

(b) Validity and Effect. If under the *lex contractus* the obligation can be constituted only by a particular method, e.g., by writing, and that method has not been adopted, no obligation exists.[32] On the other hand, a contract of service for a term of years entered into orally in England and valid by English law was sustained.[33] Further, the obligation may have come to an end because the *lex contractus* imposes upon it some restriction or limitation, e.g., "by affecting the contract itself with regard to endurance, which is one of its essentials."[34] This was held to be the effect of the Act, 1695, cap. 5, which provides that no cautioner "shall be bound . . . for longer than seven years." Accordingly, it was held that the Act did not apply to a cautionary obligation entered into in India.[35] Again, the *lex contractus* may provide that the obligation shall cease after a certain period. In an action to recover under a mortgage executed in England the court allowed proof before answer of an averment that by English law the right to recover had been extinguished by lapse of time.[36] But in an action against a Scottish firm for the value of goods illegally obtained by them in England more than six years before, the court repelled a plea founded on the English Statute of Limitations.[37] It was pointed out that the obligation arose *ex lege*, not *ex contractu*.[38]

(c) Limitations of Proof. In an action by an English company for payment of calls on shares, objection was taken to the admissibility of a witness on the ground of interest, but no one suggested that the question should be decided otherwise than by Scots law.[39] In the same case the pursuers, to

---

29 *Carse* v. *Coppen*, 1951 S.C. 233, at p. 240. L. Brougham's contrast between *lex actus* and *lex fori* is not nowadays exhaustive; *Bain* v. *Whitehaven Railway*, 1850, 7 Bell's App. 79, at p. 93; *Don* v. *Lippmann*, 1837, 2 Sh. & Macl., 682, at p. 723.
30 *Bain* v. *Whitehaven Railway* (*ut supra*).
31 *Yeats* (sometimes cited as *Yates*) v. *Thomson*, 1835, 1 Sh. & Macl., 795, where L. Brougham, at pp. 835 *et seq.*, elaborated the distinction with great emphasis; *Don* v. *Lippmann* (*ut supra*); *Hamlyn & Co.* v. *Talisker Distillery*, 1894, 21 R. (H.L.) 21, at p. 26.
32 Dickson, *Evidence* (3rd ed.) §§1007, 1009.
33 *Dale* v. *Dumbarton Glass Co.*, 1829, 7 S. 369.
34 *Alexander* v. *Badenach*, 1843, 6 D. 322, L. Fullerton at p. 329: see also L. Jeffrey at p. 329. In *McElroy* v. *McAllister*, 1949 S.C. 110, L. Russell, at p. 127, observed that Lord Campbell's Act gave a right of action, but limited the duration of the right.
35 *Alexander* v. *Badenach* (*supra*).
36 *Higgins* v. *Ewing's Trs*, 1925 S.C. 440.
37 *Farrar* v. *Leith Banking Co.*, 1839, 1 D. 936.
38 *Ibid.*, at pp. 949, 950.
39 *Bain* v. *Whitehaven Railway* (*supra*). See also *Stewart* v. *Gelot*, 1871, 9 M. 1057, L. Cowan at p. 1064.

prove that the calls had been made, produced call letters with a printed signature and were allowed to lead evidence that by English law these letters were sufficient. It was held in the House of Lords that the sufficiency of the letters was a matter of evidence to be decided by Scots law and that evidence of English law should not have been allowed. The effect of a bill of lading as evidence must be determined by Scots law, not by the law of the flag or of the place where the contract was made.[40] In the leading case on prescription it was held that the sexennial prescription applied to a bill drawn and accepted in France because it limited the mode of proof, not the endurance of the obligation.[41] Since the triennial prescription merely limits the mode of proof, it was held to apply to a solicitor's account incurred in London.[42]

426. PROOF OF FOREIGN JUDGMENTS

(a) **Statutory Provisions.** If the statutory provisions for the registration and enforcement of foreign judgments are followed, no special question of evidence arises. There are separate statutes relating to judgments pronounced respectively in (i) England, Northern Ireland and, possibly, Eire,[43] (ii) those of Her Majesty's Dominions, protectorates and mandated territories to which the Act has been applied,[44] and (iii) those other countries, described specifically as "foreign" countries, to which the Act has been applied.[45] Her Majesty may apply the 1933 Act[45] to any Dominion.[46] A common feature of these statutes is that they apply only to decrees for payment of money, and the fact that a judgment includes a decerniture for expenses does not *per se* render a judgment registrable.[47] It has not been decided whether it is competent to register part of a United Kingdom or Dominion judgment which decerns for payment.[48] In the case of a United Kingdom judgment the debtor need not be subject to the jurisdiction of the Scottish courts,[49] and there is nothing in the other Acts to prevent this rule from being followed in the case of Dominion and "foreign" judgments. Diligence on an extract of a registered United Kingdom judgment may be sisted or suspended.[50] The Acts and the Rules of Court provide for setting

---

[40] *Owners of the "Immanuel"* v. *Denholm & Co.*, 1887, 15 R. 152.
[41] *Don* v. *Lippmann (supra)*.
[42] *Campbell* v. *Stein*, 1818, 6 Dow 134.
[43] Judgments Extension Act, 1868 (31 & 32 Vict. c. 54); Inferior Courts Judgments Extension Act, 1882 (45 & 46 Vict. c. 31). As to Eire see *Doohan* v. *National Coal Board*, (O.H.) 1959 S.C. 310.
[44] Administration of Justice Act, 1920 (10 & 11 Geo. V. c. 81); Rules of Court, 1948, Rule 261.
[45] Foreign Judgments (Reciprocal Enforcement) Act, 1933 (23 Geo. V. c. 13); Rules of Court, 1948, Rule 262.
[46] Reciprocal Enforcement of Judgments (General Application to His Majesty's Dominions, etc.) Order, 1933 (S.R. & O. 1933, No. 1073). The Act applies to Belgium, France, Australia, India, Pakistan, Germany, Norway and Austria.
[47] *Platt* v. *Platt*, 1958 S.C. 95.
[48] *Platt* v. *Platt (supra)*. Parts of a "foreign" judgment are registrable: Foreign Judgments (Reciprocal Enforcement) Act, 1933 (23 Geo. V. c. 13), s. 2 (5).
[49] *English Coasting and Shipping Co.* v. *British Finance Co.*, 1886, 14 R. 220.
[50] *Wotherspoon* v. *Connolly*, 1871, 9 M. 510; *Cumming* v. *Parker, White & Co.*, (O.H.) 192 S.L.T. 455.

aside the registration of a Dominion or a "foreign" decree.[51] Entries of judgments in foreign registers to which the Act is applied may be proved by certificate, subject to the conditions in the order applying the Act.[52] Many orders have been made, but, so far as judgments are concerned, they apply only to judgments on status, e.g., divorce and adoption.

(b) Common Law. A foreign judgment may be proved by production of a copy proved by parole evidence to be accurate.[53] But, at least in the absence of any relevant attack on the judgment, a copy is sufficient if its correctness is certified, e.g., by the seal of the court, by a notary public, or by a British consul.[54]

427. EVIDENCE REQUIRED FOR FOREIGN COURT

When evidence is required for a foreign court[55] from a witness in Scotland, the Court of Session, or any judge thereof, may, if satisfied by a certificate by the ambassador or other diplomatic agent, or, if there is none, by a consul, that the cause is a civil one depending before a court having jurisdiction, order the witness to attend for examination before a named person.[56] Although the Act does not expressly so provide, the application is made, not by a party, but by the ambassador or diplomatic agent,[57] or the consul,[58] or by the Lord Advocate[59] or an agent[60] on behalf of the ambassador or consul. Where the evidence was required from a company, the court ordained the company to appoint representatives to be examined on its behalf.[61]

[51] See *Medinelli* v. *Malgras*, (O.H.) 1958 S.C. 489.
[52] Evidence (Foreign, Dominion and Colonial Documents) Act, 1933 (23 Geo. V. c. 4):
[53] *Stiven* v. *Myer*, 1868, 6 M. 885.
[54] *Whitehead* v. *Thompson*, 1861, 23 D. 772; *Frizell* v. *Thomson*, 1860, 22 D. 1176; *Disbrow* v. *Mackintosh*, 1852, 15 D. 123; *Sinclair* v. *Frazer*, 1768 M. 4542, 1771, 2, Pat. App. 253.
[55] Foreign Tribunals Evidence Act, 1856 (19 & 20 Vict. c. 113).
[56] It is obvious from the terms of the Act that this means a court outside the United Kingdom. Witnesses in other parts of the United Kingdom come under other legislation: Attendance of Witnesses Act, 1854 (17 & 18 Vict. c. 34). See §334.
[57] *Baron de Bildt*, 1905, 7 F. 899.
[58] *Reid*, 1890, 17 R. 790; *Robinow*, 1883, 10 R. 1246.
[59] *Lord Advocate*, 1925 S.C. 568; *Lord Advocate*, 1909 S.C. 199.
[60] *Blair*, 1883, 10 R. 1223.
[61] *Lord Advocate*, 1925 S.C. 568.

PAGE INDEX

453

PAGE INDEX

AUTHENTICATION STATUTES. *See also*
EXECUTION OF SOLEMN WRITING:
PROBATIVE WRITING: SOLEMN WRIT-
ING—
   applicability of, 84, 85, 109, 110, 111
   cautionary obligation, applicability to,
     109
   credit-sale agreement, applicability to,
     110
   description of, 85
   hire-purchase agreement, applicability to,
     110
   obligationes literis, applicability to, 84-99
   solemnities required by, 181-207
   writings in re mercatoria, applicability to,
     100
AVERMENT. *See* WRITTEN PLEADING
AWARD. *See* ARBITRATION

BANK: BANKER—
   acknowledgment by, in re mercatoria, 102
   books of, copy of entry in, as evidence, 330
   compellability of, 390
   confidentiality of communications to, 419
   docquet on account with customer, 103
   joint stock, sale of shares of, 112, note
BANKRUPT. *See also* SEQUESTRATION
   admission by, admissibility of, against
     creditors, 34
   conjunct and confident person, grant to,
     64
   deposition of—
     admissibility at trial, 32
     cross-examination on, 367
     recovery of, 322
   prescription, interruption of, by claim,
     136
   presumption—
     of existence of insolvency, 64
     that grant without value, 64
   reference to oath of, 353
BANKRUPTCY. *See* BANKRUPT: SEQUESTRA-
TION
BARTER—
   consensual contract, a, 152
   mode of proof of contract of, 152
BASTARDY. *See* LEGITIMACY
BEARER BOND—
   proof of trust in relation to transfer of,
     121
BEFORE ANSWER. *See* PROOF: REFERENCE
TO OATH
BEST EVIDENCE RULE—
   article not produced, 445
   hearsay, 394
   terms of document not produced, 243
BESTIALITY—
   conviction of, as evidence in divorce, 171
   standard of proof of, 80, 167
BILL OF EXCHANGE. *See also* CHEQUE—
   acceptor of—
     admission by one of several, 35
     delivery to, renunciation by, 131, note

mandate to, proof of, 154
relationship with—
   co-acceptor, proof of, 274
   drawer, proof of, 107, 281
authentication of, 104, 105
blank in, 197-198
burden of proof regarding, 67, 104
contract associated with, proof of, 107-108
contradiction, explanation, variation of,
   107, 108, 258, 259-260
date of, ante, post, wrong, 106
   presumed accuracy of, 55, 106
definition of, 104
delivery of, proof of, 108
destruction of, by creditor, 60, 248
discharge of, proof of, 107, 108
foreign, prescription of, 451
incomplete, proof of debt vouched by, 125
mandate to draw, accept or indorse, proof
   of, 154
oral agreement regarding, proof of, 107
parole evidence as to liability under, 106-
   108, 259-260
payment of, proof of, 107, 108, 125
prescribed—
   adminicle of evidence, as, 116-117, 141
   debt contained in, proof of, 141-143
   payment due under, proof of, 129
   writ of party, as, 116-117
promissory note, definition of, 104-106
sexennial prescription of, 139-143
signature—
   authentication of, not presumed, 55
   burden of proof of, 104
   executor, of, after drawer's death, 105
   modes of, 105
   per procuration, 106
   statutory rules for, 105
summary diligence on, 106
writing in re mercatoria, as, 101, 104-106
writ of party, as, 116
BISHOP. *See* CHURCH
BLANK IN WRITING—
assignee's name, 200
authority to holder to complete, 197, 198
bill of exchange, blank in, 197-198
cautionary obligation, blank in, 201
creditor's name, 197, 200
disponee's name, 200
extrinsic evidence inadmissible to complete, 302-303
history of use of, 197
material part, in, 200
partly printed deed, rule for, 199
personal bar in relation to, 198, 201
precept of sasine, blank in, 197
probative nature of deed, 198
trust disposition and settlement, blank in,
   201, 202
words inserted in, effect of, 201
BLIND PERSON—
execution of deed by, if able to write, 202,
   note
instrumentary witness, incompetent as,
   194

456

BLIND PERSON—*continued*
notarial execution of deed by, 202
BLOOD TEST, 443
BOND—
bearer. *See* BEARER BOND
contradiction, explanation, variation of, 259
creditor's name blank in, 197, 200
defective, evidence of antecedent obligation, 94, 95
disposition in security, and—
discharge by circumstantial evidence, 128
effect of destruction of, 60
how established, 88
oral agreement regarding, 267, 268
inaccurate record of transaction—
judicial admission that, 280-281
reference to oath that, 281, 282
in re mercatoria, 94, note
liquid document of debt, as, 94, 95
obligatio literis, as, 94, 95
personal, effect of destruction of, 60
sum inserted in blank—
due under, 201
for which redeemable, 201-202
BREACH OF CONTRACT—
acquiescence in, mode of proof of, 303
burden of proof of—
initial, 67
when breach admitted, 67
character of defender in damages for, 18
heritage, regarding, proof of, 87
safe custody, regarding, burden of proof in, 68
BREACH OF PROMISE OF MARRIAGE—
character of pursuer—
put in issue, 19
relevant to damages, 18
illegitimate child of pursuer, relevance of, 19
recovery of defender's books, 323
BUILDING—
contract—
mode of proof of—
payment due under, 129
performance of, 125
not superseded by disposition, 261, 275
variation of, 308
multiple contract for, and sale of heritage, 261, 275
mutual gable, cost of, 263
restrictions, presumption of conformity with, 54
BURDEN OF PROOF. *See also* STANDARD OF PROOF—
accused, on. *See* ACCUSED
affecting final judgment, 66
affiliation, in, 176
bill of exchange, as to, 67, 104
change of domicile of origin, of, 62
civil case, in, 65-75, 167
consistorial case, in, 167
criminal case, in, 76-78
defender, on—

circumstances placing, 69, 70, 71-75
what must be proved, 72
domicile, change of, 62
donation, of, 55, 56
fact within knowledge, of, 68, 77
general rules as to incidence of, 67-69
gratuitous nature of services, of, 56
initial and subsequent, 69
interest free loan, of, 56
meaning and effect of, 65
Minister of Pensions, on, 67
party alleging affirmative, on, 67
presumption affecting, 50, 51-64, 67, 69
prosecutor, on, 76, 371
pursuer, on, 67, 69
res ipsa loquitur, 72, 73
service pro hac vice, of, 62
shifting of—
civil case, in, 70-75
contract, in, 70, 71
criminal case, in, 61
general rule as to, 70, 71
meaning and effect of, 67
negligence, in, 70, 71-75
statute determining, 67
undischarged, circumstances in which, 79
unimportant when truth established, 66
who—
leads in proof, 65, 66
"makes it appear" to the court, 68
"satisfies" the court, 68
written pleadings as determining, 69
BURGH RECORDS—
as evidence, 234
BUSINESS BOOKS. *See also* MINUTE OF MEETING—
as evidence for the owner, 241
company, of, in action against company, 119
docquet written and subscribed in, 102-104
partnership, of, in action against partners, 119, 120
prescription of holograph, 139
presumed accuracy of, 55
proof, as—
debt in prescribed bill, of, 142
loan, of, 118, 119
trust, of, 120
recovery of, by diligence, 322
solicitor of party, of, 119, 332
unsigned, 120, 235
writ of party, as, 118-119, 120, 142, 332
BYE-LAW—
proof of, 222, 228

CALENDAR—
judicial knowledge of, 49
CARRIAGE BY LAND—
burden of proof when goods damaged in, 68
offer for, as writing in re mercatoria, 101
CARRIAGE BY SEA—
burden of proof—

CONFESSION. *See* EXTRAJUDICIAL CONFESSION: JUDICIAL ADMISSION
CONFIDENTIALITY—
  ante litem motam, 413, 418
  bank, 419
  clergyman, 420
  conciliator, 420
  diary, 413
  doctor, 419
  husband and wife, communications between, 379
  insurance company, 419
  journalist, 420
  letter undespatched, 413
  lis mota as test, 413, 416
  partners, communications between, 413
  post litem motam, 416
  probation officer, 420
  public policy, 325, 420
  servant, report by, 323, 417
  solicitor and client, 414
CONFIRMATION—
  will deemed probative on grant of, 214
CONSENSUAL CONTRACT. *See* CONTRACT
CONSISTORIAL CASE—
  adherence, 166, 167
  adultery in. *See* ADULTERY
  bestiality in. *See* BESTIALITY
  collusion—
    divorce, in, 168
    effect on sufficiency, 168, 169
    nullity, in, 168
  cruelty in. *See* CRUELTY
  declarator of marriage, 163, 166
  decree in absence after proof, 46, note
  dissolution of marriage, 62
  divorce. *See* DIVORCE
  English decree as bar to divorce, 46, note
  extrajudicial admission in—
    against whom admissible, 169
    averment of, 169
    conviction as, 170, 171
    decree as, 170, 171
    general, 169
    implied, 170
    sufficiency of, 169
  identification of defender in, 172
  judicial admission in—
    against whom admissible, 168
    implied, 168
    sufficiency of, 167, 168
    meaning of, 166
  nullity of marriage, 162, 166, 168
  oath, reference to, 343
  parties as witnesses in. *See* WITNESS
  proof in—
    burden of, 167
    commission, on, 167
    general, 166-175
    need for, 166
    sheriff court, in, 167
    standard of, 167
  reference to oath in, 343
  separation, action of, 166, 167, 170, 171
  similar act, evidence of, in, 16, 17, 172, 173, 411
  sodomy in. *See* SODOMY
  status, action concerning, 31, 46, 47, 166
  undefended—
    need for evidence in, 166
    proof of marriage in, 161
    sufficiency of evidence in, 169
CONSTRUCTION. *See* EXPLANATION OF WRITING
CONSUL—
  letters of second diligence, execution of, 391, note
  notary public, power of, to act as, 239
CONTRACT. *See also* OBLIGATION: INTERNATIONAL LAW.—
  breach of. *See* BREACH OF CONTRACT
  burden of proof in, 69, 70
  collusion as to form of written, 271
  consensual—
    examples of, 152, 153, 154
    matters requiring writ compared, 113
    meaning of, 152
    quinquennial prescription of, 143, 144
  corporeal moveables, as to, proof of, 152
  deceit as to form of written, 271
  executory, variation of, 308
  foreign—
    proof of, 450
    stamping of, 251
  fraud, proof of, in relation to, 160
  holograph of both parties, 212
  incomplete, followed by rei interventus, 311
  innominate and unusual, 132-134
  intention of parties as to—
    form of, 92, 93
    meaning of, 282, 286, 287, 288
  judicial knowledge of recognised classes of, 49
  knowledge of parties at time of, 292
  multiple, including heritage, 261, 275
  oral—
    incorporating writing, 256
    invoice as affecting, 257
    partly written and partly, 256, 275
    sale note recording terms of, 257
  pupil incapable of consent to, 51
  real, meaning and proof of, 152
  rei interventus following incomplete, 311
  relief obligation as part of, 124
  requiring writing—
    constitution, for, 84, 85, 86, 87-99, 108, 111
    proof, for, 84, 85, 86, 114, 123, 132, 134
  rules of association incorporated in, 264
  shifting of burden of proof in, 70, 71
  schedule incorporated in, 264
  specification incorporated in, 264
  stamping, 251
  true nature of—
    extrinsic evidence of, 270-273, 280-282
    reference to oath as to, 281, 290
  unilateral promise as part of, 134
  written—
    acquiescence in breach of, 303

S

Jury Trial (Civil)—
admission in, minute recording, 43
issue including unnecessary matter, 82
objection to evidence, procedure on, 2, 362
Jury Trial (Criminal)—
direction to jury assumed to be followed, 2
intimidation of witness, relevance of, 21, 365
objection to evidence, procedure on, 2, 4, 21, 363
plea of guilty—
not accepted, 44, 45
withdrawn, 44, note, 45
prejudicial statement in—
co-accused's confession, 36
expert's report, 21, note, 394, note
written evidence, 21
verdict—
evidence in civil action, as, 31, 170, 171
res judicata in civil action, as, 47
Justice of the Peace—
notarial execution by, 202

Kirk Session. See Church: Minute of Meeting
Knowledge—
dangerous characteristics, of, 22
earlier accident or injury, evidence of, 22
fact within—
burden of proof—
accused, on, 77
party, on, 68
implied admission of, 44
falsity of averment, of, judicial slander in, 23
guilty. See Guilty Knowledge
judicial. See Judicial Knowledge
vicious disposition of dog, of, 22
Known or Reputed Thief—
previous convictions in support of charge, 22, 406

Landlord. See Lease: Rent
Latitude—
time, place, quantity, of, in criminal charge, 82
written pleading, in, 81
Law—
fiction of, 51
foreign, proof of, 437
judicial knowledge of, 48
Lease—
actings of parties as interpreting, 297
agreement collateral to—
admissibility of, 275
inadmissibility of, 276
agricultural—
arbitration in, 95
implied term of, 263
ancient, actings of parties under, 296

"as tenanted by," evidence of meaning of, 300
constitution and proof of, 88
contradiction, explanation, variation of, 257, 258, 261, 267-268
co-tenants, proof of relationship between, 274
custom as interpreting, 299
date of—
entry, admissibility of proof of, 277
termination, admissibility of proof of, 277
defective, contradiction of, 258
delivery of produce by tenant, proof of, 125
draft, variation of, 258-259
estate rules incorporated in, 264
homologation, constitution and proof by, 314, 315
implied term of—
contradiction of, 263
custom of trade as to, 299-300
incomplete agreement for, actings on, 311
meaning of word in—
admissibility of evidence of, 284
reference to oath of, 290
missing term in, proof of, 277, 299
missives—
operative after date of, 262
superseded by formal, 261
notice—
to remove, evidence as to, 260, 273
of intention to remove, evidence as to, 260, 273
oral agreement—
affecting, not proveable, 267, 268, 269, 276
exception as to, 281
quinquennial prescription as to, 143, 144
rei interventus, constitution and proof by, 310-312
rent under. See Rent
renunciation of, mode of proof of, 131
triennial prescription as to—
urban, 147
written, 145
variation of, by oral agreement, 305
Legacy. See Testamentary Writing
Legal Diligence. See Diligence
Legal Fiction—
irrebuttable presumption, and, compared, 51
Legitimacy—
bastardy, declarator of, a consistorial case, 166
declarator of, a consistorial case, 166
husband's knowledge of pregnancy, presumption from, 63
illegitimacy, standard of proof of, 80
pater est quem nuptiae demonstrant, 63
presumption of, 63
recognition of, during lifetime, 63
standard of proof—
of period of gestation in, 47, note
to rebut presumption of, 80

PAGE INDEX

LETTER—
anonymous, to press, recovery of, 324
covering holograph, enclosing offer, 213
contract constituted by, contradiction etc. of, 259
failure to reply to, implied admission, as, 32
prisoner, of, sent from prison, 37
proof of dispatch of, 55
recoverable, when, 321
stolen, whether admissible, 2, 169, 443
torn up draft, as evidence in divorce, 34, 169
undispatched, admission contained in, 33
writ of party, as, 333

LETTERS PATENT—
proof of, 225

LIBEL—
amendment of, 82
differences between, and proof, 82, 83
latitude of time, place, quantity in, 82
superfluous statement in, 83

LICENCE HOLDER—
special capacity as, held admitted, 78

LIFE, DURATION OF. *See* HUMAN BEING

LIMITED COMPANY. *See* COMPANY, LIMITED

LOAN OF MONEY—
debtor's books as proof of, 118, 119, 332
docquet on list of loans, authentication of, 103
effect on—
later bill of exchange, of, 140-141
later bond, of, 94, 95
endorsement on cheque as proof of, 115, 118
interest on. *See* INTEREST
judicial admission of—
disproof of qualification of, 114, note
makes proof unnecessary, 114
qualified, 114-115
proof of—
exceptions to general rule, 115
general rule, 114
receipt of money, effect of, 57
reference to oath of—
admission on, 114, 115
deposition of repayment on, 340, 348
qualified admission on, 114, 115, 340, 348
repayment of—
burden of proof of, 115, 340
mode of proof of, 129, 340, 348
restriction of proof of, effect of failure to plead, 114
series of loans, proof of, 115
solicitor's account including, 115
writ of debtor—
bill of exchange as, 116
business books as, 118, 119, 332
creditor's writ as, 333
express acknowledgment of loan, 116
from which loan inferred, 115-118
from which *not* inferred, 118
I O U as, 117

letter as, 116, 117, 118, 333
prescribed bill as, 116-117, 140-141
written acknowledgment—
in re mercatoria, 102
loan, of, 114, 116, 117, 119
on debtor's behalf, 116
qualified, 114-115
receipt of money, of, 56, 57, 116

LOAN OF MOVEABLES—
borrower, burden of proof on, 68
mode of proof of contract of, 152
real contract, a, 152

LOCAL AUTHORITY—
authentication of deed by, 184
minute of, evidential value of, 236

LOCATIO CUSTODIAE. *See* SAFE CUSTODY

LOCATION. *See* HIRE OF MOVEABLES: LEASE: SAFE CUSTODY

LOCUS POENITENTIAE—
contract committed to writing, in, 90, 91, note, 92, 93
homologation, exclusion by, 309, 314
rei interventus, exclusion by, 309, 310

LUNATIC—
witness, as, 375

MAGISTRATE—
threat or inducement by, 38

MALICE—
collateral fact in proof of, 23
judicial slander, proof of, in, 23
murder, notice of antecedent, in, 24
slander—
proof of, in, 23
recovery of documents to establish, in, 324

MANDATE—
accounting with mandatory, prescription in, 149-150
acknowledgment of loan by solicitor, for 154
advocate, of, presumed in litigation, 155
circumstances from which inferred, 154
consensual contract, a, 154
contradiction, explanation, variation of, 260
debts, for payment of, 154
destruction of mandant's will, for, 154
drawing, accepting bill of exchange, for, 154
general, presumption of continuance of, 62
gift, for payment by way of, 154
implied term of, proof of variation of, 260
investment of money, for, 154
mode of proof of—
rule regarding, 154
exceptions to rule, 155
payment by mandant, proof of, 129
proxy, form of, to vote at meeting, 155-156
purchase of shares in ship, for, 154
safe custody, for, burden of proof in, 68

475

ROAD VEHICLE—*continued*
public service, injury to passenger in, 69, 70, 75
road authority, liability for skidding, 22
unfitness to drive, 37, note
ROBBERY—
conviction of—
reset on charge of, 82
theft—
on charge of, 82
on proof of, 83
ROUP. *See* AUCTION
ROYAL PROCLAMATION—
judicial knowledge of, 221

SAFE CUSTODY—
burden of proof in contract including, 68, 71
delivery of writing for, 59
deposit for, contract of, 68, 152
destruction by fire of vehicle in, 71
quinquennial prescription relating to, 144
SALE OF GOODS. *See also* MOVEABLES—
bill of exchange, effect of, 140-141
burden of proof in, 69, 70
cash, for, proof of payment in, 129
consensual contract, 152
credit, on, proof of payment in, 128
custom affecting implied term of, 299
delivery in, 158, 272
fitness for particular purpose in, 293
mode of proof of, 152
multiple contract as to heritage and, 261, 275
offer for, in re mercatoria, 101
oral, prescription of, 143, 144
pro forma, evidence of true contract, 271, 272
renunciation of rights under, 131
trustee in sequestration in relation to, 280
SALE OF HERITAGE. *See* HERITAGE
SANITY. *See also* INSANITY—
general presumption of, 53, 54, 70
SCOTTISH PRIVY COUNCIL—
acts of, 221
SEARCH WARRANT, 441, 442
SEAWORTHINESS. *See* SHIP
SEDUCTION—
character in action for, 18, 19
SELF DEFENCE—
burden of proof of, 76, 77
collateral evidence to rebut, 25
implied admission in, 45
special defence of, 76, 77
standard of proof of, 76
uncorroborated evidence of, 76
SEMIPLENA PROBATIO—
affiliation, in, 176, note
delivery, in proof of, 241
edict, in action on the, 241, note
SEPARATION. *See* JUDICIAL SEPARATION
SEQUESTRATION. *See also* BANKRUPT—

conjunct and confident person, grant to, 64
deposition in—
cross-examination based on, 367
recovery of, 322
trial, admissibility of, at, 32
mandate to vote in, form of, 155
minute of meeting in, as evidence, 237
prescription interrupted by claim in, 136
presumption—
of insolvency, 64
that grant without value, 64
reference to oath in, 353
sederunt book in, as evidence, 237
trustee—
admission by, binding on creditors, 34
declarator of trust by, proof in, 280
reduction by, proof in, 280
sederunt book as evidence against, 237
SERVANT. *See also* SERVICE—
admission of negligence by, 35
report by, recovery of, 323, 417
SERVICE—
accounting by servant, proof of, 130
admission by servant—
negligence, of, 35
part of duty, as, 35
contract of—
actings of parties interpreting, 297
conditional execution of, 279
duration of, 89
informal, 89
in re mercatoria, 86
judicial admission of, 89
oral, 89
performance of, proof of, 125
reference to oath of, 89, 348
rei interventus as to, 89
salary and commission, on, 89
variation of, 257, 260, 305
general employment presumed to continue, 62
presumed to be for payment, 56, 348
pro hac vice, onus of proof of, 62
relative, payment for services to, 56
report by servant, recovery of, 323, 417
right to payment for work done, 89
triennial prescription as to, 145, 148
wages—
domestic servant, of, 129
judicial knowledge of, 49
proof of payment of, 129
triennial prescription of, 145, 147, 148
written contract of—
oral agreement as to, 260, 267, 268-269
variation of, 257, 260, 305
SERVITUDE—
modes of constituting, 88
prescriptive, presumption underlying, 60
SETTLEMENT OF DISPUTE—
abortive negotiation for, admission during, 28, 420
agreement not to sue, proof of, 160
confidentiality, 28, 420
extrajudicial admission during, 28

WITNESS—*continued*
interpreter, 36, 389
intimidation of, 21, 365
lunatic, 375
medical examination of, 443
memory of, refreshing, 363
mental defective, 375
party as—
  compellability of, 171,
  consistorial action, in, 171,
  need not admit adultery, 171, 370
  other party, for, 172, 180
  sufficiency of evidence of, 171, 172, 176
police photographs shewn to, 22
previous conviction, reference to, by, 22
privilege of, 369
recall of, 359, 360, 367
refreshing memory of, 363

WORD, MEANING OF. *See* EXPLANATION OF WRITING

WRIT. *See* PROOF BY WRIT: WRITING

WRITING—
alteration of. *See* ALTERATION OF WRITING
ancient date, of, 295-296
attestation of. *See* EXECUTION OF SOLEMN WRITING
authentication statutes. *See* AUTHENTICATION STATUTES
business books. *See* BUSINESS BOOKS
circumstances surrounding, 290-294
collateral agreement as to. *See* COLLATERAL AGREEMENT
conditional—
  delivery of, 278
  execution of, 278
contract in. *See* CONTRACT
contradiction of. *See* CONTRADICTION OF WRITING
copy. *See* COPY OF WRITING
criminal trial—
  expert's report in, 21, note
  irregularly obtained in, 3, 4
  letter from prison in, 37
  written evidence in, 21, 228
custom in relation to, 298-300
defective. *See* SOLEMN WRITING
destruction of—
  evidence of, 7
  presumptions from, 59, 60
discharge of. *See* DISCHARGE
drafting error in, 270, 290
execution of. *See* EXECUTION OF SOLEMN WRITING: HOLOGRAPH WRITING: MERCANTILE WRITING: PROOF BY WRIT
explanation of. *See* EXPLANATION OF WRITING
extrajudicial admission in, 27, 33
extrinsic facts referred to in, 300
fraud in relation to, 160
holograph. *See* HOLOGRAPH WRITING
implied term of. *See* IMPLIED
incorporation of other, 264, 265

informal. *See* HOLOGRAPH WRITING: MERCANTILE WRITING: PROOF BY WRIT
in re mercatoria. *See* MERCANTILE WRITING
irregularly obtained, 2, 3, 4
liquid document of debt, as, 90, note, 92, 94, 95
meaning of, 183, note, 196, 209, 264
missing term in, 276-278, 299
mutilated, 59, 248
notatial execution of. *See* NOTARIAL EXECUTION OF WRITING
obligatory, as basis of action, 90-91, 92
official, in criminal proceedings, 228
partly—
  printed, 199
  pencil, 183, note, 209,216
pencil, in, 183, note, 209, 216
performance of. *See* PERFORMANCE
possession of, presumptions from, 59
probative. *See* PROBATIVE WRITING
record of earlier agreement, 92, 93
recovery of. *See* RECOVERY OF DOCUMENT
rejected clause in, 294
revoked clause in, 294
solemn. *See* SOLEMN WRITING
stamping. *See* STAMPING OF DEED
subsequent actings of parties to, 295-298
tenor, proof of. *See* TERMS OF DOCUMENT, PROOF OF
testamentary. *See* TESTAMENTARY WRITING
undelivered—
  admission in, 33
  alteration of, 191, 215, 216
  burden of proof that, 68
unilateral, 94, 95, 259
untrue record of transaction—
  admitted, 280-282
  proof that, 270-273
  reference to oath that, 281, 290
variation of. *See* VARIATION OF WRITING
writ, proof by. *See* PROOF BY WRIT
written pleading. *See* WRITTEN PLEADING

WRIT OR OATH. *See* PROOF BY WRIT: REFERENCE TO OATH

WRITTEN EVIDENCE. *See* PROOF BY WRIT: WRITING

WRITTEN PLEADING—
amendment of, 81
averments—
  admission distinguished from, 43
  alternative, 43, 44, 137
  failure to deny, 44, 137
  "not admitted," 44
  proof different from, 80-82
  relevance of, 4, 5
burden of proof determined by, 69
difference between—
  averment and proof, 80-82
  libel and proof, 82, 83
judicial admission—